Managing Global Innovation

"The lessons learned are invaluable. The book is a real tour de force, probably destined to become a standard in this field for some time to come."
Jeff Huang, Professor, Harvard University

"Anyone in positions responsible for global innovation should read this valuable book."
Li Gong, Chairman and CEO, Mozilla Online Ltd.

"Important reading for senior management and a must for R&D leaders."
Karl Weinberger, Senior Vice President, Schindler

"A feast of delights... deserves a very wide readership."
Phil Galen, ICI Technology

"Globalization of innovation is ongoing and will create winners and losers. This outstanding book shows you the way to join the winners."
Armin Meyer, Chairman & CEO, Ciba Specialty Chemicals

"Deep and useful insights for innovation leaders in industry, with the why's and how's for managing R&D operations in foreign countries."
Charles F. Larson, President Emeritus, Industrial Research Institute

"In the inevitable trend towards global R&D, China is becoming a world technology actor and a defacto choice for R&D. This book will surely become a reference work for those who want to understand all aspects of the China question and innovation."
Hervé Cayla, CEO France Telecom Beijing Orange Lab

"Based on a wealth of up-to-date information, the authors provide unique insights into the implications for both R&D managers and governments of the globalization of innovation."
Torbjörn Fredriksson, Senior Economist, UNCTAD

"This book has the most in-depth and extensive coverage of global R&D management as I have ever seen. The insight of multinational company R&D in China as well as China's joining globalization R&D value chain is timely."
John Chiang, former President, Motorola (China) Technologies Ltd

"If the 21st century is truly to be the knowledge-era, then the global deployment of R&D activities will become the front-lines of economic competition. This work summarizes the latest in what we know about how we can do this better."
William A. Fischer, Professor, IMD

Roman Boutellier
Oliver Gassmann
Maximilian von Zedtwitz

Managing Global Innovation

Uncovering the Secrets
of Future Competitiveness

Third edition

 Springer

Prof. Dr. Roman Boutellier

- Professor of Innovation and Technology Management, ETH Zürich, Switzerland
- Former CEO and Managing Director of SIG, Schaffhausen, Switzerland
- rboutellier@ethz.ch

Prof. Dr. Oliver Gassmann

- Professor of Technology Management and Director of the Institute of Technology Management, University of St. Gallen, Switzerland
- Former Head of R&D Technology Management, Schindler Elevators, Switzerland
- oliver.gassmann@unisg.ch

Prof. Dr. Maximilian von Zedtwitz

- Professor of Technology and Innovation Management, Tsinghua University, Beijing, P.R. China
- President, AsiaCompete Int'l Ltd., Hong Kong SAR, P.R. China
- Senior Advisor, Arthur D. Little (China) Ltd.
- max@post.harvard.edu

ISBN 978-3-540-25441-6   e-ISBN 978-3-540-68952-2

DOI 10.1007/978-3-540-68952-2

Library of Congress Control Number: 2008921152

© 2008, 2000, 1999 Springer-Verlag Berlin Heidelberg

Production: le-tex Jelonek, Schmidt & Vöckler GbR, Leipzig
Cover design: WMX Design GmbH, Heidelberg

Printed on acid-free paper

9 8 7 6 5 4 3 2 1

springer.com

Preface to the Third Edition

If R&D and innovation in the 1990s were about more internationalization, more corporate entrepreneurship, and more information-integration, then the 2000s have been about consolidating and expanding these trends further: more globalization including the technology mavericks of China and India, more open and inbound innovation integrating external technology providers, and more web- and Internet-enabling of innovation processes by involving R&D contributors regardless of their location. The corporate R&D powerhouses of the 1980s are now mostly history. Even where they survived, they had to yield to corporate efficiency efforts and business-wide integration programs. Still, it would be unfair to belittle them in retrospect as they have found new roles in corporate R&D and innovation networks. In fact, the very successes of centralized R&D organizations of the 1970s and 1980s made possible the revolution of globalized innovation that we have been witnessing since the 1990s.

The first two editions of *Managing Global Innovation*, published in 1999 and 2000, were testimonials of an increasingly internationalizing world of innovation and R&D. In this third edition of *Managing Global Innovation*, we have retained the basic structure of two conceptual parts (I and II) and three case study parts (III, IV, V). However, we have greatly revised all chapters, including the final "Implications" chapter (part VI), and incorporated new chapters and cases that illuminate and describe the recent trends in the context of the beginnings of global innovation in the 1980s and 1990s. In particular, we expanded on the notion of external drivers of R&D internationalization, and we added chapters and cases on R&D in China and India. We've also added more on the management and organization of global R&D, such as technology listening posts and leading R&D units.

In the three case study parts we added several new cases written specifically for this book: Siemens, BMW, Fujitsu, Huawei, SAP, and Swiss Re. BMW and Fujitsu are classical examples of global R&D organizations. Siemens and Huawei are illustrations of innovation in China, with Huawei being a true example of a company from an emerging country (China). Swiss Re illustrates global innovation in services, another up-and-coming field of the 2000s. SwissRe and SAP also address the increasingly important field of intellectual property management in R&D. The present SAP case replaces our earlier SAP case on project and program management. All other cases were slightly updated but retained mostly intact as per their date of writing. They remain interesting cases in their own right and their appropriate setting within global R&D. Only one case study – Nestlé – had to be eliminated as the company had moved forward.

This revised third edition is based on several hundred more research interviews with R&D managers and directors around the globe. It incorporates our own combined experiences of more than sixty years as R&D managers, chief executives of technology companies, or directors of international researchers and scientists. But, first of all, this book lives off the wealth of knowledge presented by the case study authors, all of them accomplished innovation leaders with their respective companies. Our sincere gratitude and professional acknowledgement goes out to them. Secondly, we are indebted to our colleagues and research associates who have assisted in putting everything together and making sure it has become this presentable whole that it is now. In addition to those already acknowledged in the first two editions, we would like to extend special thanks to Sharmila Egger, Marcus Keupp, Markus Skriver, and Moritz Vischer, and last but not least Andreas Biedermann, who was crucial in putting all the pieces together.

We hope you will find reading this book as much a source of inspiration and fun as it has been to us while writing it.

November 2007

Zurich, Switzerland   *Roman Boutellier, ETH Zurich*
St. Gallen, Switzerland   *Oliver Gassmann, HSG St. Gallen*
Beijing, P.R. China   *Maximilian von Zedtwitz, Tsinghua University*

Preface to the Second Edition

Globalization has changed the face of R&D. Local knowledge clusters are not only tapped by multinationals but increasingly by small and medium-sized companies as well. Global R&D networks speed up the evolution of technology and ask for new management concepts. Modern communication technologies create the global village, but customers become more fastidious and request their own specific products, well localized, well tuned into their present business. Integrated technology is required to cope with these needs. The danger of over-engineering has never been as great as today. The question is frequently not whether some new features are technically feasible but whether customers are willing to accept and pay for it.

The first edition of *Managing Global Innovation* was sold out after few months, clearly indicating the search for solutions to these challenges. This second edition has been revised for clarity and actuality. We have taken care to work in recent research findings as well as updating the case studies where appropriate.

This book is based on the growing importance of industrial global innovation and the lack of concepts to manage it. For this book we conducted 320 interviews in 40 technology-based, highly internationalized companies, including additional interviews in 1998 and 1999 for the second edition. Our interview partners were R&D managers and research directors from companies in Europe, USA and Japan. They spent a lot of time with us to discuss their viewpoints on this topic. We complemented this valuable body of insight with the latest findings in academic research and management science.

Managing Global Innovation is divided into six parts: In part I we analyze the international dispersion and drivers of R&D locations, as well as concepts and trends of global R&D organization. Using a top-down approach, we break down the challenges of global innovation to requirements of transnational R&D project organization. In part II we focus on five cross-functional fields in global innovation: Increased awareness of external customers, interfaces between research and development, multi-stakeholder perspectives in transnational R&D processes, modern information and communication technologies as enablers of such processes, and human resource management.

In parts III, IV, and V we present 18 in-depth case studies of successful practice companies in the three different types of industries: Science-driven (pharmaceuticals/chemicals/food), high-tech-driven (electronics/software), and dominant-design-driven (electrical/machinery). In alphabetical order, these companies are

ABB, Canon, Ciba, Daimler, DuPont, Hewlett-Packard, Hitachi, F.Hoffmann-La Roche, IBM, Kao, Leica Microscopy, MTU, Nestlé, SAP, Schering, Schindler, Unisys, and Xerox.

We have chosen a case-study approach since the complexity of global R&D management is great and experience so limited. In our research, the case study companies have been identified as leading their industries in global R&D management. Most of these case studies were written by senior corporate R&D officers, based on a uniform concept we provided and their determination to share.

The case studies represent a wealth of knowledge and experience: They show a vast range of organizational forms, from completely centralized to globally dispersed, from technology-driven to fully customer-oriented. We have tried to show some patterns and some consistencies, well aware of the need to keep the balance with a contingency approach. Some basic rules should help managers in their strategic and day-to-day decisions, others are aimed at the broad range of organizational forms and management of R&D on a global scale.

Many people participated in making this book. We are grateful to our colleagues who have given us invaluable assistance in preparing this book. Particularly helpful in reviewing and proof-reading have been Sabine Böttcher, Gregory Huber, Carmen Kobe, Ursula Koners, Sara Leu, and Stefan Schweickardt. But most of all we would like to thank the case study authors who spent valuable time to share their experiences with our international R&D community. They have given us the cases needed to sort out a few dilemmas and, as we hope, a few general rules and hints that may be of some help to all R&D managers trying to cope with globalization in the 21st century.

January 2000

St. Gallen, Switzerland   *Roman Boutellier*
St. Gallen, Switzerland   *Oliver Gassmann*
Cambridge, Massachusetts   *Maximilian von Zedtwitz*

Contents

Part I
Challenges and Trends

I.1 Challenges of Organizing International Research & Development

> *„Technology is the major source of economic growth."*
> *Graham Mitchell, 1998*

1 Changes in the Global Innovation Environment

Global R&D and innovation is mostly a matter of multinational companies (MNCs). With the exception of a few highly international SMEs (small and medium-sized enterprises) and so-called "born-global" start-ups, MNCs define the landscape of global innovation. Multinational companies determine the international division of labor with their production, R&D, marketing, and sourcing strategies; they transfer technologies and management skills, and they influence regional growth through foreign direct investments. Specifically:

- In 2002, the 700 largest R&D spending firms of the world accounted for 46% of the worldwide total R&D expenditure, and 69% of worldwide business R&D expenditure (UNCTAD, 2005).
- Some MNCs such as Ford, Toyota, DaimlerChrysler, Siemens, General Motors, or Pfizer spent more than US$ 5 billion on R&D in 2002 alone – each of them more than Brazil, Spain, Russia, or India. In fact, Ford (with US$ 6.8 billion in 2002) would be the tenth largest business R&D investor in a list including countries, ranked just behind Sweden (US$ 7.3 billion) but ahead of Italy (US$ 6.6 billion).
- MNCs increased their foreign R&D from an average of 15% in 1995 to 18% in 1998 (Roberts, 2001); an UNCTAD survey found that in 2003, firms spent an average of 28% of their R&D budget abroad (UNCTAD, 2005).
- At the country-level, foreign R&D is also growing: For instance, in the 1990s, German firms set up more overseas R&D sites than in the previous fifty years combines (Ambos, 2005), and Japanese overseas R&D increased more than tenfold from 0.3% of total Japanese R&D spending in 1986 to 4% in 2002 (UNCTAD, based on METI data).

These investments in R&D are significant, and the share of overseas R&D is impressive. Given that worldwide business R&D investment is estimated at about US$ 550 billion in 2006 (extrapolating data from 2002 as reported by UNCTAD,

2005), and using conservative interpretations of Roberts and the UNCTAD shares of business R&D internationalization, worldwide investment in international R&D is about US$ 100 billion. That is similar to the country GDP of Algeria, the Philippines, or Romania (Worldbank, 2007).

High-tech firms are not only heavy R&D investors but also grow faster (UNCTAD, 2002). As a comparison of annual global growth rates by industry between 1985 and 2000 shows, high-tech firms (>5% R&D/sales, e.g., electronics, IT, pharmaceuticals) grew the fastest at an average of 16% per year, and medium-tech (e.g., chemicals, auto) still about 11% per year. A recent report by TEKES (Hirshfeld and Schmid, 2005) demonstrated that technology intensity is valued by investors, and market capitalizations were highest for industries with high R&D intensities (see Table I.1.).

Global R&D and innovation are thus not only a result of global business, they are also important contributors and drivers to this phenomenon.

1.1   The Origin of Global Innovation and R&D

Historically, the internationalization of companies started with the opportunistic development of international sales. Later, foreign markets were developed more systematically, first through exports and later with the establishment of local production and utilization of inexpensive labor. Existing products needed to be localized to new markets, and unless these adaptations were done from the R&D headquarters, local R&D units were set up to form the seeds of what would later be transformed into global R&D networks. Mergers and acquisitions played a significant part in this development, particularly the more recent cross-border M&A cases of ABB, AstraZeneca, Sanofi-Aventis, or DaimlerChrysler. Small countries with small home markets and limited resources facilitated this phenomenon: Switzerland and the Netherlands, for example, were always forced to export and build resources abroad. This has led to the specific management challenges in R&D that were going to discuss in this book.

Traditionally among the most centralized functions of the firm, R&D is adjusting to world-wide dispersion of talent and technology creation. Two thirds of the UNCTAD 2005 survey responded that the share of foreign R&D is set to increase, while only 2% indicated the opposite (UNCTAD, 2005). While US companies

Table I.1.1. The market values of R&D intensive industries.

| | Medium-tech | | High-tech | | |
	Automobiles	Chemicals	Pharma	Software	Biotech
R&D Spending	$41 bn	$10 bn	$34 bn	$10 bn	$9 bn
Revenue	$1,021 bn	$176 bn	$267 bn	$78 bn	$16 bn
R&D/Sales	4.0%	5.6%	12.8%	12.7%	56.0%
Market Cap	$376 bn	$175 bn	$1,061 bn	$498 bn	$196 bn
Market Cap/Sales	0.4	1.0	4.0	6.3	12.2

Source: Hirshfeld and Schmid (2005). US$ values.

have accumulated a large stock of foreign investment over the past decade, they also have become net recipients not only in foreign investments but also in R&D. Foreign companies carry out more R&D in the United States than US companies do abroad. Many companies today face the challenge of building up an international network of R&D laboratories to tap global human resources.

The growing involvement in foreign-based R&D is one of the most significant developments in the operations of multinational companies. According to the National Science Foundation (NSF, 2001), total US foreign R&D expenditures have increased from US$ 2.2 billion in 1978 to more than US$ 6 billion in 1988 and to US$ 18 billion in 2001. Some industry groups were allocating particularly large percentages of their R&D budgets to foreign-based R&D. According to data from the Bureau of Economic Analysis of the US Department of Commerce, foreign R&D expenditures in the US increased from US$ 15.5 billion in 1994 to US$ 29.9 billion in 2002. By 1995, 676 R&D facilities in the US had been acquired or established by over 350 foreign companies from 24 countries (Serapio and Dalton, 1997). Currently, the US is the most dominant R&D country in the world.

But the dominant position of the US in global R&D is not uncontested. Research done by the OECD (2006), the United Nations (UNCTAD 2004 - 2006) and others show that Europe and Japan have their unique strengths in R&D, and that China and India in particular are catching up with respect to R&D capacity. The WIR 2005 report (UNCTAD, 2005; see Fig. I.1.1) devotes several chapters to R&D internationalization and development and concludes:

- Technology is advancing faster than ever before;
- R&D is among the least internationalized function of MNCs;
- The degree of R&D internationalization is rising;
- It is growing fastest in some developing countries, notably Asia;

Source: UNCTAD World Investment Report (2005: 128)

Fig. I.1.1. Worldwide location of majority-owned foreign affiliates engaged in R&D, 2004.

Table I.1.2. Ten Principles for Globalizing R&D.

	Principle
1.	Don't be fooled by the cost chimera.
2.	Globalization is flammable – proceed with caution.
3.	Start with product and process research.
4.	Standardize before you go abroad.
5.	Communicate clearly on goals, procedures and expectations.
6.	Don't underestimate cultural differences.
7.	Cross-pollinate to ease cultural barriers.
8.	Always have a lead team.
9.	Focus on the long term.
10.	Get moving.

Source: The Economist Intelligence Unit (2004).

- MNCs relocate segments of R&D so as to access foreign pools of research talents;
- Firms from developing countries are setting up R&D units abroad.

Many of these studies were conducted by international organizations, and much of the literature on R&D internationalization well into the 1990s has focused on the economic and political perspective. Most research on this topic has taken place on a macro-economic or industrial level (Fig. I.1.2).[1] Earlier research on international R&D, dating back to the 1970s[2], was either based on economic analysis or was based on a few companies only. Management research has long neglected international R&D.[3] While an economic analysis of supply and demand factors explains *why* a particular R&D laboratory was established in a particular country, it offers little insight into *how* to manage foreign laboratories (De Meyer, 1993).

More recent work, however, does aim to provide concepts and tools for dealing with international R&D. The experience that has been made by MNCs over the last decades has been summarized into easy-to-remember lists of Do's and Don'ts (see Table I.1. for a recent example). Unfortunately, this well-meant advice is usually too general to be practicable. R&D internationalization depends on too many factors, many of them unpredictable and not rooted in sound R&D and innovation thinking.

Rubenstein (1989) was among the first to describe the management problems in decentralized R&D, but systematic treatments of global R&D management operations are scarce. Research and development activities require intensive communication and close, informal collaboration. These work requirements pose serious problems for managers of cross-border R&D. Despite the difficulties, international

---

[1]   See Patel (1996), Papanastassiou and Pearce (1994), Beise and Belitz (1996), NIW et al. (1995), Amstad et al. (1996), Håkanson (1981).

[2]   Hanson and Van Rumker (1971), Papo (1971), Terpstra (1977), Ronstadt (1977 and 1978), Mansfield et al. (1979), Lall (1979), Behrmann and Fischer (1979 and 1980), Hewitt (1980), Malecki (1980), Hirschey and Caves (1981), Håkanson (1981).

[3]   See Cheng and Bolon (1993), Granstrand et al. (1993), Cantwell (1992).

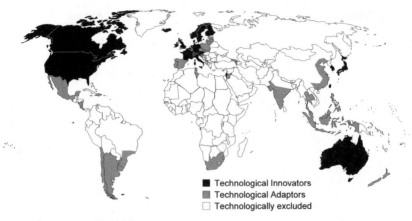

Technological Innovators
Technological Adaptors
Technologically excluded

Source: The Economist (June 22nd 2000).

Fig. I.1.2. Technology is innovated only in a small part of the world.

R&D is expanding apace. Local foreign-market customers demand higher levels of technical service and customized products. Developing regional markets, such as the European Union, offer greater rewards for modified products to meet local market requirements. Larger regional markets also encourage more new product development. On the other hand, leading-edge technologies and customers are located throughout North America, Japan, and Europe. To gain access to these cutting-edge technologies, companies send their own scientists to participate at on-site laboratories and increase their own absorptive capabilities. For a growing number of companies, the benefits of international R&D outweigh the costs (Gates, 1995).

The worldwide dispersion of R&D, an increasing competitive pressure for new and innovative products, and the fusion of formerly unrelated technologies to form new industries has led to a decline in central R&D. Resources are being directed toward shorter-term projects for new product development and technical service. Since the majority of overseas R&D units are serving the parent company's operating businesses, they benefit from this trend towards customer-oriented product development.

Although corporate R&D groups may have fewer resources, they retain an influential position in directing their global R&D network to align technical activities with business strategy. Managers of global R&D networks have the responsibility of setting clear missions to overseas laboratories whose effectiveness depends on their credibility. The corporate R&D group can help in building this credibility by developing centers of specialization in overseas laboratories, defining their role in the company's overall technical network (Gates, 1995). But building up centers abroad requires money, i.e., foreign direct investment (FDI), and FDI has gone up and down with the economic cycles over the last few years.

1.2   *Foreign Direct Investment and Transnational Firms*

The total amount of foreign direct investments (FDI) grew fivefold from US$ 200 billion to US$ 1,100 billion per year between 1991 and 2001. The average annual increase accelerated from about 1% in the first half of the 1980s to 34% in the second half. This foreign direct investment is mostly due to MNCs and shows their growing influence. The share of MNCs in worldwide added value increased from 2% to 6% between 1982 and 1994. The number of MNCs has increased significantly. More than half of the worldwide MNCs are headquartered in France, Germany, Japan, UK and the USA. By the early 1990s there were an estimated 37,000 MNCs in the world with at least 170,000 foreign affiliates. By 2004 the number of MNCs had risen to some 70,000 with at least 690,000 foreign affiliates, almost half of which are now located in developing countries (UNCTAD, 2005). The foreign direct investment shows the effect of MNCs to recover R&D investments on a global scale.

R&D plays a critical role in building a multinational company's global competitive advantage. It generates revenues and employment on a global scale if it is well synchronized with social changes, markets, competitors, suppliers and new technologies, and is accompanied by direct investment. Foreign direct investment involves not only a transfer of resources, but also the acquisition of control. This seems to be the essential purpose behind the increase in foreign direct investment (Krugman and Obstfeld, 1994).

The inflow of FDI may indicate special location advantages while the source of FDI represents the particular strength of individual companies. FDI flows are concentrated to a small number of OECD countries. US, Japan, Germany, France, and UK account for 61% of all FDI outflow of US$ 424 billion in 1997. In 2005, the global total of FDI outflows amounted to US$ 778.7 billion (UNCTAD 1999, 2005) The major recipients are the same, only Japan is replaced by China.

Even within MNCs, the economic power is concentrated on a small group of companies. In 1995, the 100 largest MNCs (i.e. 0.4% of all MNCs) controlled about US$ 3,500 billion, of which US$ 1,400 billion was located outside their home countries. They accounted for one third of all FDI, one fourth of overall sales, and 16% of the work force (5 million employees). In 2005 the top 100 MNCs accounted for 12% of foreign assets, 18% of total sales and 14% of em-

Table I.1.3. Outflow of FDI from five major countries (billion US$).

	1991	1993	1995	1997	1999	2001	2003	2005
USA	33.5	69.0	95.5	114.5	209.4	124.9	151.9	n/a
Japan	30.7	13.7	21.3	26.0	22.7	38.3	28.8	45.8
Germany	22.8	17.4	35.3	34.3	10.9	36.9	25.6	45.6
France	23.9	20.6	17.5	24.6	26.9	86.8	57.3	115.7
UK	16.0	25.7	37.8	58.2	20.1	58.8	55.0	101.1
Total	126.9	146.4	207.4	257.6	290.0	345.7	318.6	n/a
Global Total	199.3	240.9	352.5	423.7	1092.6	721.5	612.2	778.7

Source: UNCTAD Reports (1991-2006).

ployment of all MNCs in the world (UNCTAD, 2005). Thus the relevance of the biggest companies is slowly but steadily decreasing.

The amount of foreign assets of MNCs does not reflect the full significance of their international activities: In order to better understand internationalization, UNCTAD developed a transnationality index as a measurement compound of foreign assets, foreign sales, and foreign employment (see Table I.1.3). This list better reflects the economic activities of companies outside their home country. It is interesting to note that none of the ten largest companies by sales is among the ten most transnational companies. More than 75% of the value-added activity is still carried out at their parent locations (Hirst and Thompson, 1996; Table I.1.4).

Now as before, the investments of these companies are concentrated on major industrial countries, although some developing countries, particularly dynamic Asian economies, are likely to attract higher foreign investments. European companies tend to invest in North-America, and conversely, North-American companies give preference to European countries. Asian countries remain the preferred investment countries for Japanese companies, although Western companies are increasing their investments in this region as well. As a general pattern, MNCs tend to invest according to market-potential and market volume.

The increase of foreign investment is dominated by large MNCs in preferred geographical regions. With improved communication and logistics systems, the costs of information and transportation decreased dramatically. Therefore, MNCs

Table I.1.4. The top 20 transnational companies ranked by foreign assets.

	2004	2002	2000	1998	1996	1994	1992
1	GE	GE	Vodafone	GE	GE	Shell	Shell
2	Vodafone	Vodafone	GE	GM	Shell	Ford	Exxon
3	Ford	Ford	Exxon	Shell	Ford	Exxon	IBM
4	GM	BP	Vivendi Univ	Ford	Exxon	GM	GM
5	BP	GM	GM	Exxon	GM	IBM	Hitachi
6	Exxonmob.	Shell	Shell	Toyota	IBM	VW	Matsushita
7	Shell	Toyota	BP	IBM	Toyota	GE	Nestlé
8	Toyota	Total	Toyota	BP	VW	Toyota	Ford
9	Total	France Tel	Telefonica	DaimlerChr.	Mitsubishi	Daimler Benz	AlcatelAlstom
10	France Tel	Exxon	Fiat	Nestlé	Mobil	Elf Aquitaine	GE
11	VW	VW	IBM	VW	Nestlé	Mobil	Philips
12	Sanofi-Av.	EON	VW	Unilever	ABB	Mitsubishi	Mobil
13	Deutsche Tel	REW	Chevron T.	Suez	Elf Aquitaine	Nestlé	ABB
14	RWE	Vivendi Uni	Hutchison	Wal-Mart	Bayer	Nissan	Elf Aquitaine
15	Suez	Chevron T.	Suez	ABB	Hoechst	ABB	VW
16	EON	Hutchison	DaimlerChr.	Mobil	Nissan	Matsushita	Toyota
17	Hutchison	Siemens	News Corp.	Diageo	Fiat	Roche	Siemens
18	Siemens	Electricite	Nestlé	Honda	Unilever	AlcatelAlstom	Daimler Benz
19	Nestlé	Fiat	Total	Siemens	Daimler Benz	Sony	BP
20	Electricite	Honda	Repsol	Sony	Philips	Fiat	Unilever

Source: World Investment Report (2006, 2004, 2002, 2000, 1998, 1996, 1994).

Table I.1.5. The top 20 transnational companies ranked by a compound index (calculated as the average of ratios of foreign assets to total assets, foreign sales to total sales and foreign employment to total employment).

	2004	2002	2000	1998	1996	1994	1992
1	Thomson	NTL	Rio Tinto	Seagram	Seagram	Thomson	Thomson
2	CRH	Thomson	Thomson	Thomson	ABB	Solvay	Matsushita
3	Nestlé	Holcim	ABB	Nestlé	Nestlé	RTZ	Nestlé
4	Vodafone	CRH	Nestlé	Electrolux	Thomson	Roche	Holderbank
5	Alcan	ABB	BAT	BAT	Solvay	Sandoz	Thomson
6	R. Ahold	Roche	Electrolux	Holderbank	Holderbank	ABB	ABB
7	Philips	Interbrew	Interbrew	Unilever	Electrolux	Electrolux	Electrolux
8	Nortel	Publicis	Anglo Am.	ABB	Unilever	Nestlé	Philips
9	Unilever	News Corp.	AstraZeneca	Smithkline-B	Roche	Philips	Sandoz
10	BP	Philips	Philips	SCA	Michelin	Unilever	Seagram
11	AstraZeneca	Vodafone	News Corp.	Rio Tinto	Philips	Glaxo-W.	Unilever
12	Lafarge	Nortel	Akzo Nobel	News Corp.	Kvaemer	Akzo	Smithkline-B
13	Hutchison	AstraZeneca	Cadbury S.	Roche	Nortel	Seagram	Mitsubishi
14	Roche	BP	R. Ahold	Philips	Bayer	Bayer	Michelin
15	L'Air Liq	Reed El.	Vodafone	L'Air Liq	C&W	Alcan	Alcan
16	Sanofi-Av.	Alcan	Michelin	Akzo Nobel	Glaxo-W.	Michelin	Glaxo-W.
17	Diageo	Suez	Danone	Diageo	Eridania	Total	Roche
18	Mittal Steel	Danone	Roche	Michelin	Grand Metr.	BP	Lonrho
19	Suez	R. Ahold	Diageo	Exxon	Total	News Corp.	Ericsson
20	Total	Total	L'Air Liq	Glaxo	Novartis	BAT	Petrofina

Source: World Investment Report (2006, 2004, 2002, 2000, 1998, 1996, 1994).

were able to establish most activities of the value chain in important markets. This includes product and technology creation.

MNCs control over 80% of the privately owned technological resources (Dunning, 1993). Some of them – Ford, Toyota, DaimlerChrysler, Microsoft, General Motors, or Pfizer – are expected to spend more than US$ 7 billion in 2007 on R&D, with Pfizer exceeding US$ 10 billion (Duga and Studt, 2006). Corporate R&D budgets grow faster than national R&D spending, which means that more and more MNCs will be ranked as top investors in science and technology, ahead of countries such as Canada and Sweden.

Cantwell (1995: 171) neatly summarized the importance of technology leadership in R&D and manufacturing internationalization: „International dispersion of activity is led by technology leaders." We too have focused on large companies that have proven records for R&D prowess and internationalization. International R&D is an increasingly important phenomenon in the economic activity of firms.

1.3   Rise in Technological Competence in Developing Countries

A study by the US Government on the most important markets of the future in the coming two decades outlines the importance of the 'big emerging markets' that will change the face of the global economy (Garten, 1996). These future markets include above all China and India, but also Hong Kong and Taiwan, South Korea, Indonesia, Republic of South Africa, Poland, Turkey, Argentine, Brazil, and Mexico. Some of these economies grow fast; some of them belong to the most populated countries in the world (e.g., China and India alone account for 40% of the global population). Their share of the net world social product will double from 10% to 20% between 1995 and 2015.

The US Government estimates that more than US$ 1 trillion will be invested in these countries in infrastructure projects over the next decade (telecommunication, energy systems, and airports). This offers big opportunities for export and direct investment.

With respect to knowledge, changes will be even more dramatic: The former Soviet Union possessed one fourth of the trained scientists in the world (Sherman and Tymon, 1994). India produces every year more university graduates than the US, 40% of which have degrees in science and engineering (Naisbitt, 1996). 34% of all students in China focus on engineering, another 16% on natural and life sciences, as compared to a total 14% of science and engineering graduates in the United States (MOST, 2003; NSF, 2004). Improvements in international information technology and telecommunications capabilities have made it possible for scientists and engineers to collaborate from nearly anywhere in the world. Many Asian countries such as India, Singapore and China have made substantial investments in telecommunications, education and customs concessions to promote local R&D investments by foreign multinationals. Since 1989, Indian software exports have grown 40% per year, reaching US$ 325 million in 1993, and exceeding US$ 1 billion in 1996 (Naisbitt, 1996). The government of Karnataka, host state to Bangalore and India's Silicon Valley, estimated total Indian software exports in 2004 at more than US$ 16 billion (Economist, April 21st, 2005; see Fig. I.1.3). It

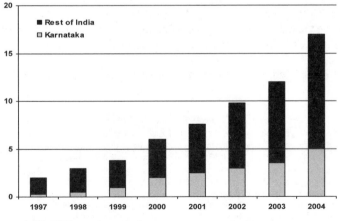

Source: Government of Karnataka

Fig. I.1.3. Indian software exports 1997-2004: Growth of 35% per year mainly in clusters.

Table I.1.6. Split of R&D resources of top 10 nations (in billion US$ PPP).[5]

	Total R&D 2004 [US$ bn]	Industry [%]	Government [%]	Academia, Others [%]	Funds from abroad [%]
USA	302	61	31	8	-
Japan	120	74	18	8	-
PR China	109	58	33	6	3
Germany	52	65	32	0	2
India	46	23	75	2	-
France	44	52	38	2	8
UK	36	47	27	6	21
S. Korea	27	74	24	2	-
Brazil	24	38	60	2	-
Russia	17	31	60	1	9

Source: Global R&D Report, R&D Magazine – September 2005 p G3.

seems that these engineers do not want to leave their home countries; they prefer to set up well-developed „green islands" in their home countries. Globalization of R&D will therefore be felt the earliest in areas where no large capital investment is needed, no production site, i.e. in the brain power and knowledge industry.

In these emerging markets, the legal conditions for technology development are less restrictive than in some developed Western countries. According to a study by NIW et al. (1995), the main disadvantages for establishing R&D sites and production in Germany are due to legal and institutional conditions. German chemical companies cite unfavorable German laws for relocating R&D to the US.[4] For instance, BASF established a research center in Boston for circumventing legal constraints in biotechnology and genetics research.

Political instability may suffice to move R&D abroad. „Vetocraties" create significant uncertainty about political issues, such as the role of animal testing in Switzerland. Such push regulation leads to an increased relocation of R&D and manufacturing to emerging knowledge centers and markets. Some developing countries are characterized by less constraining laws which regulate health policy and environmental issues while foreign investment accelerates their economic development.[6]

On the other hand, many emerging markets have become quite self-confident

---

4   Von Boehmer, Brockhoff and Pearson (1992), Gerpott (1990 and 1991).

5   Some studies use purchasing-power-party (PPP) adjusted values instead of foreign exchange rate equivalents. We cannot resolve the inconsistency of these data in this book, but we have marked all PPP numbers as such. Using PPP for R&D is questionable because R&D salaries (which account for about half of all R&D expenditures) do not follow the general goods basket (varying significantly against national average price levels). Also, many non-salary-related expenses, such as rent, infrastructure, and PCs, are often at Western rather than local prices, hence invalidating R&D PPP further. While PPP has good use in some areas of international comparison, we advise to be careful in interpreting R&D expenditures in the context of PPP.

6   Significant differences in legal requirements need to be overcome in order to achieve a triad-compatible product.

Table I.1.7. The top 10 R&D spending nations in 2004 (US$ in PPP).

Country	R&D as % of GDP 2004	Total R&D 2004 [$ bn]	Total R&D 2005E [$ bn]	Total R&D 2006E [$ bn]	Rank 2006E
USA	2.7	302	312	321	1
Japan	3.2	120	123	126	3
PR China	1.5	109	125	140	2
Germany	2.2	52	53	54	5
India	1.4	46	53	58	4
France	2.2	44	44	45	6
UK	2.0	36	37	38	7
S. Korea	2.9	27	28	30	9
Brazil	1.6	24	28	33	8
Russia	1.2	17	19	20	10

Source: Global R&D Report, R&D Magazine – September 2005, p G3.

(the development of domestic S&T by means of foreign inward technology transfer has been dubbed "New-Techno-Nationalism"). By imposing import and export quota, market entry barriers, tolls, and standards, they attract foreign companies to invest in local R&D infrastructure and R&D sites. Besides manufacturing, local content regulations frequently include R&D as well. Singapore, for instance, approves the foundation of new companies only of certain capital intensity or a minimum amount of intellectual assets, and it has ceased to subsidize manufacturing altogether. However, Singapore matches every research investment made in the city state with an equivalent subsidy support of its own.

Such pull regulations have an impact in the pharmaceutical industry. Through regulations for clinical trials of new products, host countries force the establishment of local adaptation R&D units.[7] In some countries, medicine prices are determined by the government, and companies gain a higher premium on their sales if they have carried out local product R&D (Roussel et al., 1991).

From a resource point of view, many countries in emerging markets are still unattractive for R&D internationalization, but this is changing: For instance, the University of Kuala Lumpur switched from using Malaysian textbooks only to English-language engineering education. Since these countries are aware of their high market potential, they are self-confident enough to require more local R&D activities by foreign companies. Nevertheless, technology creation will be centered around the existing clusters for many years to come. New centers will emerge gradually.

---

[7]   In the 1980s and 1990s, Canada, Brazil, France, India and Japan tried to induce foreign companies to establish local R&D units (see Granstrand, Håkanson, and Sjölander, 1993). China is perhaps the best known example of the 2000s. Behrmann and Fischer (1980) report that almost half of the investigated American MNCs (14 out of 35) and about one quarter of European MNCs (4 out of 18) experienced strong pressure from the host country government regarding their R&D location decision.

1.4   Decreasing Technology Acceptance in Western Countries

Legal regulations are strongly related to a society's position towards technology. In highly-developed industrial countries a decline in public acceptance of untested technologies, and the low regard of society for engineering in general, can lead to the transfer of R&D to other countries. Low acceptance of technology can result in restrictive legislation in relation to R&D activities or, indirectly, in conditions which do not stimulate innovation. The risks of R&D as perceived by society lead to high costs within the company. Genetic engineering, biotechnology and experiments on animals are currently at the center of public debate in Europe.

In the last years, increasing skepticism concerning technological advances could be noted in industrialized countries especially among younger generations. In Germany, the number of university entrants for instance in mechanical engineering has dropped by a factor of four within few years and has recovered only after some years. In the US, about 415,000 master's and bachelor's degrees were awarded in science and engineering in 2002, or about 17% of all degrees. The share of US recipients has been steadily declining: Half of the graduate and post-graduate degrees were given to students from China, Taiwan, India, and South Korea (NSF, 2007). No European country made the top-10. In China, 50% of all degrees are in science and engineering, and the enrollment of graduate students has grown fivefold between 1998 and 2005.

Reservations about the value of technology differ widely in their political-economic context; we assume perception of the role of technology plays a more dominant role than the technology itself. They may lead to restrictive laws about R&D or, more indirectly, to little stimulating factors for innovation. The status that technology and R&D enjoy in society has a direct impact on overall operating costs (see also von Boehmer et al., 1992).

However, when discussing where to locate R&D it is often forgotten that a critical public attitude to technology can actually encourage innovation. China has

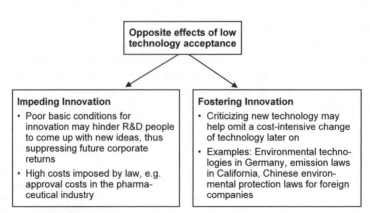

Source: Gassmann (1997a: 83)

Fig. I.1.4. Technology acceptance and innovative environment.

the most stringent environmental regulations for foreigners, which can lead to rapid nationwide convergence on these standards. This encourages the development of dominant designs which become a *de facto* standard. Germany's strict environmental regulations are one of the reasons for its leading position in the field of environmental technology. Californian exhaust gas regulations have worldwide acceptance as the target standard for exhaust gas emission in the automobile industry.

California's strict safety and environmental regulations have turned the US into ABB's key market for the development of transformers. Safety aspects concerning earthquakes and freedom-from-oil attracted ABB to base their development of a transformer suitable for the „triadic" American, European, and Japanese markets in California. A high level of technological awareness, and timely criticism of a specific technology, can prevent a subsequent cost-intensive changeover to a different technology. The lack of technological acceptance appears to put highly-developed industrial countries at a disadvantage to emerging countries in relation to the location of R&D. In the long run, sound critique is not necessarily an impediment for innovation. However, if speed and time-to-market is important and qualified personnel and technical resources are available, companies will chose to relocate their R&D activities. A typical example is provided by genetic engineering in Germany and Switzerland, where leading companies concentrated their efforts in countries more conducive to genetic research such as the US or the UK.

1.5   Establishing Global Standards and Dominant Designs

Television is certainly one of the driving forces for more and more global products: Nike shoes, BMW designs, McDonald's restaurants and Boeing planes have become world wide standards. The "hunt for the global product" is greatly supported by international R&D networks. The early and accurate realization of a dominant design, i.e. a de-facto standard of a product, is essential for recovering R&D expenses, production and distribution processes. Examples of dominant designs in today's market include DVDs, QWERTY-keyboard, MP3 compilation, and USB memory sticks. Customers and suppliers also benefit from worldwide standardization of specifications. By participating in relevant committees and consortia such as the International Standards Organization (ISO) or national equivalents through local R&D representatives, new product structures and technologies are proposed in optimal accordance with the particular strengths of the participating companies. Companies that cannot participate in the decision process are forced to incur costly adaptations to their production processes and their products in order to meet the standards imposed by their rivals.

The dominant design model was formulated by Abernathy and Utterback (1978) and Utterback (1994). Market structures are strongly influenced by technology life cycles and the accumulated product and process know-how of firms. In the beginning of a new cycle, product-related innovation prevails over process innovation. The market contenders are a growing number of small as well as large companies pursuing competing product concepts (fluid phase).

Typically, the market will prefer one of the product concepts which establishes itself as a dominant design. The greater the utility of the technology standardization for the market, the faster the dominant design will prevail, and the more dynamic the market will grow (markets with increasing marginal return).

During the emergence of a dominant design, competition between companies shifts from product to process innovation (transition phase). Those companies unable to make this transition will disappear: Companies are acquired by competitors or retreat from the market. Only a few companies will remain in the market. The technology has reached a mature stage (rigid phase), and the market is characterized by standardized and interchangeable problem solution concepts. Process innovation is carried out by the few dominant market players; the focus lies on cost reduction and rationalization. Competition is fought over price, not product performance.

Based upon the consideration of dominant designs, companies pursue four innovation strategies:

1. Invention leader;
2. Innovation leader;
3. Early follower;
4. Late follower.

The *invention leader* is often an R&D-intensive small company (e.g. biotechnology or computer start-ups). Its access to capital is restricted, and it usually has little know-how in implementing and sustaining the business development of its ideas.

The *innovation leader* succeeds in bringing the invention to the market by considering technological as well as market requirements. A dominant design may be established by erecting technology barriers (patents, tacit knowledge building) and market-entry barriers (distribution channels, marketing data). Intel's microprocessor chips are a typical example.

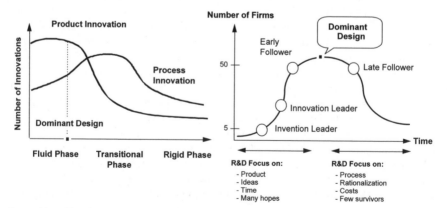

Source: Adapted from Utterback (1994).

Fig. I.1.5. The model of the dominant design.

The *early follower* imitates recently introduced products or technology once a dominant design is apparent. He differentiates himself from the innovator with superior marketing concepts, technology modifications, refined after-sales service, or simply drastic cost savings based on scale-effects.

The *late follower* enters a market characterized by mature technologies and established players. Cost leadership is the main alternative to achieve market share. This approach has been successful for insulation and plastic products in the sanitary installation equipment business, but it is prone to fail in dynamic markets such as telecommunication.

The key to choose the appropriate competition strategy is the ability to recognize the emergence and inherent potential of a dominant design in all important markets on a global scale (e.g. IBM PC). A dominant design is characterized by:

- Decreasing market dynamics;
- Decreasing number of competing firms;
- Falling prices;
- Convergence of the alternative product concepts towards a standard;
- Reorientation away from technology towards consumer utility.

It is strategically important to recognize these developments early. Appropriate tools are technology monitoring, patent research, competitor and technology analysis as well as market analysis, and all this on a global scale. Companies have to be present with market-oriented R&D employees in the most important markets word-wide.

1.6   Towards More Market Segmentation and Customer Focus

Internal and external customers of R&D become more and more demanding. A key paradigm is market-orientation by which R&D managers try to overcome the push/pull concept which has characterized R&D after the Second World War.

Market orientation can take place early in the R&D process, especially when research and development are distinct organizations and effective means of knowledge transfer are required. Typically though, R&D market-orientation applies to the integration of internal and external customers of R&D, such as service units, manufacturing, and product users.

In many markets, lead users can be identified and integrated in the product development process because they represent the market needs of the future and may provide new product concepts and design data as well. They need not be in the usual customer base, and they need not to illuminate the entire novel product, process or service that one wishes to develop (von Hippel, 1986). Many R&D-intensive companies have embraced the underlying principles of the lead user concept. IBM knows the 'first-of-a-kind' customer, or lead customer, who is involved in the innovation process as early as in the pre-project activities to an eventual R&D project.

The lead user concept exploits the profound know-how of technologically outstanding customers. In some markets, such as the electronic consumer goods markets, buyers have become increasingly knowledgeable about products. At the same time, their expectations and demands about new products rise. Standardization and product differentiation issues must be resolved, which necessitate product localization efforts by subsidiary R&D units in coordination with the parent R&D organization. Customer companies are trying to make inroads in the domain of the original company, putting R&D under additional pressure.

Market segmentation, customizing and individualization of products and services do not always do the trick, and the company is caught in the complexity-cost trap. The management of technology platforms and product variants, as well as product replacement strategies becomes increasingly important: Global R&D has to manage the dilemma between central, top-down economy of scale and the decentralized demand for individual products and this with ever shorter product cycle times, at least in some markets.

1.7   Reduction of Product Cycle Times

Fast fish catches slow fish: Some technologies become obsolete quickly. The reduction of the innovation cycle time period has been a major motivation for entering strategic technology partnerships, which can be witnessed primarily among high-tech firms in information technologies, biotechnology, and new materials.

New products are developed at an advancing pace in order to stay competitive. The increase in technology development also reduces innovation cycle times in many industries. This trend could be intensified by shortening product life cycle times. However, as has been shown in a number of research studies, product life cycles of many products stay constant. Vacuum cleaners, cars and other typical goods of daily use are being used for about the same length of time as was the case ten or twenty years ago. Warranty duration of these products has even been extended, and spare parts are provided up to ten years for coffee machines, lawn mowers, and similar equipment. Even amortization periods for industrial plants have not changed much. The situation is different for products in the information technology industry (e.g. PCs, mobile phones), since they consist of electronics and software modules with much higher improvements per time period than conventional mechanical parts. Thus, we see more and more products in the market at the same time.

The deliberate reduction of the time between the conception of a product until its market introduction (time-to-market) is a central management issue. The time-to-market problem is not a problem of R&D alone - time savings during the pre-production and production start and guaranteed high quality during market introduction are crucial in high-speed competition.

The break-down of international trade barriers with WTO and the recognition that science and technology are important contributing factors in gaining and maintaining competitive advantage have led many companies to globalize R&D and thus optimize input factors such as people, ideas and technology, and output such as innovative products and processes. Each company must first of all comply with down-to-earth requirements by the critical customer who does not care if the product was conceived on a world-wide or local basis. The competitive environment in the automotive industry forced Volkswagen to increase the required functionality of their VW-Passat by 50% between 1990 and 1996, and in the same period reduce delivery times by more than 60% (Eversheim, 1997). At the same time, other competitive product criteria like quality, safety, environmental compatibility, technology, design, price, and performance must be at least maintained or improved.

The management of product platforms thus becomes a crucial capability for technology-based companies. R&D is expected to cope with increasing product complexity and variant numbers, and decreasing lot sizes, product life times, and innovation cycles. For the VW-Passat, the number of variants has risen from 20 in 1970 to 38 in 1980 and 104 in 1988 to over one million in 2005 due to mass customization via an Internet tool that enables car configuration. During approximately the same time, innovation cycles had to be reduced from eight years in 1970 to five years in 1980 and two years in 1990 (Eversheim, 1997). These market-induced challenges call for superior management concepts, the concentration on the core business of the company, and the integration of R&D done by suppliers on a global scale.

1.8   Concentration on Core Competencies: Benefits through Knowledge Management

Data for the US indicate that companies spent more than US$ 5 billion for R&D conducted outside their firms, including contracts to other companies, universities, and non-profit-organizations. This amounts to 4.7% of the companies' funds for total in-house R&D in 1995, a substantial increase from 3.6% in 1990, and under 2% in the early 1980s (Jankowski, 1998). The pharmaceutical industry estimates that it will make 50% of its sales from inlicensed products by 2010 at the earliest.

According to the Federal Agency CRADA database of the Technology Publishing Group, the total number of new Cooperative Research and Development Agreements (CRADA) in 1994 and 1995 (2,100) was 50% higher than the number executed during the previous two years (1,400). Thus R&D is being outsourced more and more.

In the early 1990s, the „resource-based view" has become a strong movement in strategic planning. Not the exploitation of short-term opportunities but rather the resources (i.e. the core competencies) are the source of corporate success. The identification, cultivation and exploitation of these competencies allows the company to differentiate itself from competition and to prevail in global competition.

As a result, core competence thinking has become a widely promoted approach to focus and develop organizational resources. In the domain of R&D, the competencies can be characterized as bundles of technologies and skills. Technologies are mainly explicit, formalized knowledge about the application of scientific and technical know-how in products and production processes. Therefore, most technologies can be acquired rather quickly and cost-efficiently: Imitation time has become much shorter. Relevant skills to build certain competencies are created and enhanced through long-term and often painful organizational learning processes in research and development. Since they are difficult to formalize and transfer, the acquisition of such skills is considered time consuming, costly and always involves a strategic approach.

The knowledge management perspective on core competencies shows three main points (Fig. I.1.6):

1. The identification of the technical competencies which are key to success (i.e. the technical core competencies)
2. The ability to communicate the technical core competencies throughout the management of the whole company (R&D marketing)
3. The identification of the technical core competencies provides the opportunity to focus on the issues of the protection, exploitation and enhancement of these competencies.

Management of intellectual resources produces a leverage effect on R&D investments (Hasler and Hess, 1996). Conventional methods of knowledge and technology creation exploit the potential of intellectual resources in a limited way. Technologically advanced products of little added-value and not saleable on the market are the result. Successful innovations are characterized by a correct anticipation of customer needs, detailed knowledge of supply channels, and intelligent application of external technology: All intellectual resources of a company, internal and external, have to be integrated.

1.9 *Early Integration of Suppliers*

Some of the most important trends in supply management as outlined by Arnold (1990) are based on innovative capability. Since dynamics in general has increased in many industries, product development times must be reduced as well.

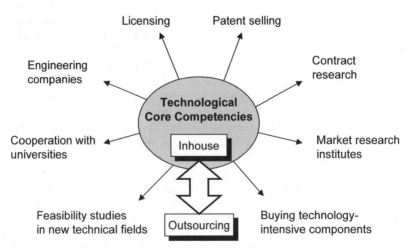

Fig. I.1.6. Outsourcing of intellectual resources to external technology suppliers.

Interorganizational division of labor is increasingly international, posing higher challenges for collaboration between development units and suppliers. At the same time, information is transferred more easily and readily, which improves market and transaction transparency. These factors press for a strategic change from traditional purchasing to supply management, giving rise to integrated global sourcing. In most markets the integration of the supplier's technical know-how becomes a key issue. A timely and sustained integration of upstream technology providers helps to win suppliers for long-term cooperation. Supply management thus becomes the turntable for know-how and innovation. Development tasks previously carried out by the R&D organization are increasingly outsourced to supply partners. Global sourcing not only reduces purchasing costs but also improves overall quality of products, as the world-wide best suppliers can be accessed (Grove, 1997). High-tech is moving from vertically integrated, large companies to horizontal competition: Competition takes place among suppliers at the same stage of the value chain.

Early supplier involvement (ESI) plays a crucial role for leveraging supplier capabilities in the joint product realization effort. ESI is aimed at time-to-market and innovation gains. As a cross-functional and interorganizational product development initiative, ESI extends the concept of concurrent engineering to the integration of external contributors in the R&D process. Early means not that suppliers are involved as early as possible, but rather as early as needed. ESI is typically suitable for the development of those innovative and complex items functioning as the key product differentiators. Frequent benefits are the reduction of product and process failures, overall product life cycle costs, and the big opportunity to merge more technologies than MNCs master in-house.

1.10 Merging Technologies

Since 1990 we observed a strong trend towards the emergence of complex technologies. Kodama (1995) calls this „technology fusion". Examples are the conver-

Table I.1.8. Different approaches to intellectual resources: conventional and intelligent companies.

Intellectual Resource	Conventional Company	Intelligent Company
Knowledge	Power	Added-value potential
Patents	Result of R&D activity	Starting point for technology- based innovation
Market research	Justification for new product development	Starting point for innovation brainstorming
Databases	Individual support tool, controlling mechanism	Organizational and distributed knowledge of high quality
Workshops	Exchange of information and experience	Product and service development
Library, archives	(Physical) collection of books, journals, and documents	(Virtual) location for inspiration, information and exchange

Source: Hasler and Hess (1996: 159).

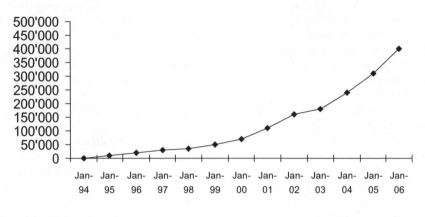

Source: Internet Software Consortium.

Fig. I.1.7. Number of Internet domain hosts worldwide.

gence of electronics with mechanics („mechatronics"), with optics („optronics"), with biology („bionics"). Products become more and more complex. But the complexity is hidden from the customer: Today's Windows is much simpler to handle than the first version, but is far more complex. A further example for such complex technologies is multi-media which has evolved from melting three former independent industries: computers, telecommunications and entertainment. For example, video game consoles have been common to be in combination with DVD players, and the Internet has become a regular entertainment system. MP3 players and mobile phones, which integrate music and video recording features have become a trend. The integration of electronics in textiles will be an upcoming research topic. Computing becomes ubiquitous. The growing importance of gene technology in the 1990s shows dramatically how the whole pharmaceutical industry can be changed. In the 21st century many companies will be forced to compete within these complex technology fields. This requires the capability to integrate diverse knowledge which is dispersed all over the world among different organizations. Managing technology fusion will be the key competence to survive this competition.

In order to bring together technologies from merging industries, R&D collaboration is to be carried out often on a global scale. R&D collaboration not only results in the necessary synergy but also allows a specification to share its risks and resources with other companies, academia, and governments across cultures and nations. Technology is too expensive to be developed alone. Competitors are foes as well as partners. The challenge lies in finding common grounds to form strategic alliances in order to exploit a potential which neither partner could do by himself.

1.11 New Information Technologies Make the Knowledge-Based Society Possible

As the information revolution continues quietly after the dot-com bubble, new possibilities for storing, retrieving and communicating information are created. World-wide access to information is facilitated by the Internet and its standardized protocols. Often, information is made available on the Internet before it is published via traditional channels. New information technologies break down the walls both inside the company and to the outside world.

Integrated media systems have exploded in the last years. The number of Internet hosts has grown from 14.7 million in 1995 to about 90 million in 2000 and to nearly 330 million in 2005.

Investment in emerging technologies is becoming the second-biggest corporate expense, after salaries and benefits (Nikias, 1998).

One of the most striking characteristics of the trends in R&D is the substantial shift of R&D activity from the manufacturing into the non-manufacturing or service sector. In 1995, firms in the service and non-manufacturing industries accounted for 24% of total R&D performance in the US, compared with 19% in 1990, and an estimated 8% in 1985 (Jankowski, 1998). Whereas "before 1983 service industries spent less than 5% of total industrial R&D in the U.S.; by 2002, their share reached 43%. The total value of R&D by services was US$ 82 billion compared to US$ 109 billion for manufacturing in 2002" (UNCTAD, 2005b: 110). Also within traditional manufacturing industries, R&D resources are geared towards services and information technology: General Electric sees E-commerce and electronic trading a key market of the future, Nokia has launched an E-business initiative, and IBM pumps half of its US$ 5 billion R&D budget into Internet-related areas.

We also see a change in firms' R&D expenditure rankings. Companies like Microsoft, Sanofi, or Nokia were not among the top 100 in 1986 but were ranked among the top 20 in 2005. Intel was ranked 46th in 1986, 9th in 1996 and 14th in 2003 (UNCTAD, 2005). Computer software and biotechnology firms are increasingly prominent R&D performers. The biggest in R&D is still Ford who spent nearly US$ 7 billion in 2005.

The dramatic fall of international telephone costs together with the Internet give the many well educated engineers direct access to some of the world's most desired information. Nowadays, video conference has become one of the valuable tools which enables communication and international teamwork on a much cheaper and faster basis. Today, knowledge and skills are the most important sources of comparative advantage and many third world countries are now making substantial investments in training. R&D labor in developing countries will compete with expensive engineers in developed countries. In 1999, US companies spent US$ 145,000 per R&D employee overseas and US$ 188,000 back home (UNCTAD, 2005). The sources of technology will shift from developed countries into low-labor cost countries. The need for international technology transfer is growing.

1.12 Knowledge Gets More and More Important

Knowledge acquisition and know-how are of central importance in R&D. In this century the amount of knowledge has tremendously increased. The number of scientific journals was 100 at the beginning of the 19th century, 1,000 around 1850, over 10,000 around 1900 and in 1995 there were about 100,000 journals worldwide. In 2005 we have approximately 16,000 periodical journals and over 2,000 publishers that produce some 1.2 million articles a year (Economist, Aug 5th, 2004). It is estimated that every 10 to 15 years the amount of published scientific literature doubles. These numbers have a human equivalent: There are over 5 million people working in the area of knowledge production in R&D departments - this is approximately 90% of all scientists who have ever lived (Nefiodow, 1990; Pfiffner and Stadelmann, 1995). „The information revolution is transforming the nature of competition" (Porter, 1985) and R&D is the most important element in industrial technology intensive organizations to source, filter, generate and diffuse knowledge. „Science does not advance by piling up information – it organizes information and compresses it" (Simon, 1997: 226). The organization of R&D must therefore be designed to selectively retain information, process knowledge, and apply know-how.

Global knowledge creation processes in research have become more and more routine. The worldwide S&E publications output captured in Science Citation Index and Social Sciences Citation Index grew from approximately 466,000 articles in 1988 to nearly 700,000 in 2003, an increase of 50%, and international co-

Table I.1.9. R&D intensity: company and other (non-federal) R&D funds as % of net sales in R&D-performing firms.

Industry	2001	2002
Manufacturing	3.6	3.2
Non-manufacturing	4.0	4.1
Scientific R&D services	36.5	17.6
Software	19.3	21.4
Computer systems design, related services	16.5	14.3
Management of companies	7.8	7.6
Trade	6.2	5.0
Architectural, engineering, related services	5.2	5.3
Health-care services	4.1	15.1
Newspapers, periodicals, books, databases	2.7	2.8
Transporting and warehousing	2.4	0.5
Construction	1.4	0.6
Mining, extraction and support	1.3	3.2
Finance, insurance and real estate	0.7	0.6
Broadcasting and telecommunications	0.5	0.7
Information	4.4	4.0
All Industries	3.8	3.6

Source: World Investment Report (2005: 110).

authorship in scientific publications doubled between 1980 and 1995 (NSF, 2007). The number of US scientific publications remain flat during this period, causing it to fall from 38% to 30% of worldwide publications. China, Singapore, Korea and Taiwan's share grew sevenfold during this period, albeit from a low base of around 1.6% (China) or 0.5% (Korea) of worldwide publications (Zhou and Leydesdorff, 2006). In 2003, 20% of all articles had at least one foreign author, up from 8% in 1988 (NSF, 2007). Overall, international collaborations in academic R&D are on the rise.

Knowledge knows no boundaries. On the one hand, multinational companies must rely on information tools to coordinate and concentrate knowledge flows across geographical distances. This adds management complexity to everyday R&D management. On the other hand, geographical dispersion of R&D sites is a formidable institution to tap knowledge clusters and absorb know-how.

Most companies are not using their intellectual resources up to their full potential, due to conventional barriers to innovation, information overflow and suboptimal use of information and communication technologies. Although there is a continuous demand for increases in productivity and innovation output, a metric for knowledge management is nonexistent. There is some optimization in terms of IT-infrastructure and library services, but the strategic approach is missing. Such an intelligent approach has to differentiate among types of knowledge, using instruments like technology intelligence, selective knowledge bases, systematic knowledge engineering, patent offices, competitor analysis, knowledge diffusion and last but not least intrinsic motivation of R&D people.

1.13 Payback Thinking in R&D

Today's time horizons are fairly short in the typical operating division. There is little time for peripheral explorations of potentially applicable science or technology. The tendency is to go with off-the-shelf items that suppliers can provide or that divisional people can „polish up" for a specific application (Rubenstein, 1989). Even pharmaceutical firms spend today 34% on marketing and only 18% on R&D (Angell, 2004). Every project should pay back in a short time, e.g., less than two years in most European companies.

In view of the size, time horizon, and scope constraints common for most product divisions, it is unlikely that the divisional technology group will be allowed or encouraged to venture into potentially new areas as spin-offs from mainline divisional products and markets. There are exceptions when they fit into the divisional managers plans or hopes for a broadening or deepening of his product line and market segments. He may send the message to look for "new applications of our manufacturing technology or capacity" or "new variations of our products to keep our customers happy" or "loss leaders that will help us get a toe into the market." In the highly fragmented market such thrusts have the potential for getting those toes stepped on. Many good ideas for diversification by one division are squashed at corporate or group level because „that's another division's territory." Ideas are seldom donated to other divisions and, with no place to go, generally die at the point of origination (Rubenstein, 1989).

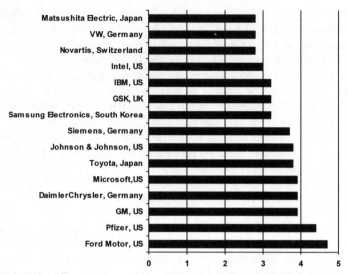

Source: Data adapted from DTI.

Fig. I.1.8. R&D Spending: By company, 2005-06*, in British £m (* Financial year ending in 2005 or 2006).

For „far out" researchers, projects, ideas, and approaches, there are only limited role models in the decentralized company. The younger and more adventuresome members of a divisional lab do not have senior colleagues immediately at hand whose path they can follow into new areas. On the contrary, the informal pressures are typically in the direction of „sticking to your knitting" and „let's get the job done that we're getting paid for. Leave the far out stuff to the corporate research lab or people in larger divisions" (Rubenstein, 1989). Too many projects with proven short pay-back times in well-known fields are on a waiting list and are fighting for resources against more adventurous projects.

Given the narrow focus and modest size of the typical division lab, as well as the time and other pressures, there is little slack for technical renewal: there is a tendency towards technical over-engineering in well-known fields. Most engineers do not read much beyond their current technical field of interest, unless they are enrolled in an advanced degree program or are freed to engage in job rotation as in many Japanese companies. Divisional technologists generally get rewarded for a high degree of specialization, a higher level of competence and reputation for what they know. They are thereby encouraged to stick to what they know and not to venture into new fields or the cutting edge of their own field, which may entail high individual risks. There are exceptions: 3M asks its engineers to venture into new fields for 10 to 20% of their total working time. Companies undertake much effort to coordinate their R&D activities more tightly. Many major breakthrough innovations have been highly centralized projects (Fig. I.1.9).

Table I.1.10. R&D spending by non-manufacturing activities in the United States, 2002 (billions US$. Some numbers are approximate estimations).

Industry	R&D spending
Mining, extraction and support activities	0.700
Utilities	0.100
Construction	0.164
Trade (also includes industrial conglomerates and high marketing spenders)	25.000
Information	17.870
Transportation and warehousing	0.300
Newspapers, periodicals, books, databases	0.614
Software	12.927
Broadcasting and telecommunications	1.600
Other information services	2.600
Finance, insurance and real estate	1.903
Architecture, engineering, related services	4.159
Computer systems design, related services	11.983
Scientific R&D services	13.034
Other professional and scientific services	1.182
Management of companies and enterprises	0.148
Health-care services	4.200
Other	0.900
Total non-manufacturing	81.824

Source: World Investment Report (2005: 110).

The challenge for management is to allocate its scarce R&D resources on a global scale at three major levels:

1. Corporate R&D projects;
2. Divisional R&D projects;
3. Regional projects.

The case studies in this book show three general tendencies:

1. The more risky the new project, the tighter corporate control and the more corporate money is allocated. Risky means not only from the technical or market perspective, but also from the point of view of internal acceptance and reputation. If the new technology or project is competence-destroying, acceptance within the company will be low (Tushman and Rosenkopf, 1992).
2. High R&D expenses can be recovered only through global markets. But many products require localization, which can be carried out only by insiders: Either employees from the regions or, even better, within the region itself. The higher the localization, the more money is going to be allocated to regional R&D. This is how many overseas R&D locations started in the early 1990s.

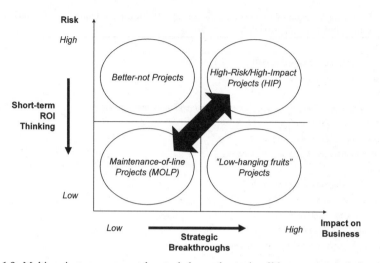

Fig. I.1.9. Multi-project-management has to balance the trade-off between tactical short-term maintenance of line projects and strategic long-term high-risk/high-impact (HIP) projects.

3. The more risk-averse the company, the more high-risk small projects are pursued for years and years. The risk is spread out over a large number of small projects, risk is managed following an insurer's attitude: The law of great numbers prevents great turmoil.

Thus, there will be projects with emphasis on long-term corporate view-points as well as regional ones, but most will take place within the divisions and are directed towards improving existing products or creating products for the next generation. Even in R&D we have to manage the well known dilemma between motivation and coordination.

1.14 More Emphasis on Corporate Culture

Depending on shared markets and common technology interests, some groups of divisions (especially when they are under the same group executive) may help each other technically in networking for scientific and technical information, technology transfer, and technical assistance. Groups and divisions may even share the support of a technical information center or library. They may cooperate in accessing new technology and share their skills and experiences. In the general case of autonomous, specialized, and highly differentiated divisions, this is not common and each division is on its own technically. Exceptions may occur for assistance they can buy from outside or from the corporation, through a corporate research laboratory. Networking among divisions is not the typical operating mode for most firms, with exceptions such as a given division being a supplier to another division in the firm (Rubenstein, 1989).

Strong team spirit within one division often builds a barrier against cooperation with „outsiders," especially other divisions that may be competing for the same funds and top management attention. Perceived self-sufficiency and unwillingness to admit deficiencies or weaknesses further inhibit cooperation (Rubenstein, 1989); an issue often met in South-East Asia, where face-saving is a strong cultural factor. The Not-invented-here (NIH) syndrome, rivalry and mistrust also emerge from profit-center thinking. Only few firms with a strong corporate culture towards openness and communication (e.g. IBM or General Electric) succeed in overcoming the negative effects of profit-center thinking. The often noticed immobility of top researchers further hinders the establishment of networks across divisional, geographical and functional boundaries. Many companies still struggle with job rotation concepts. Divisions tend to retain their experienced personnel because they value divisional progress above carrier development of their top specialists. Such specialists are more likely to have established a personal network which they do not want to give up for a job reassignment.

1.15 New Generations of Project Management

The working environment of development at a business unit is not conducive to contemplative, leisurely, exploratory activities connected with research. The pressures are toward highly focused technical activities that will directly and quickly support operations – development, production, procurement, sales, and services. It sounds like there is not a very good case for decentralized R&D having their interest in spending time working with other units on „their" problems or problems of possible future interest to the corporation as a whole. Instead, a tight and sophisticated project management is sought after. However, at the same time, management must not forget to build up a learning organization and prepare for the future. Mechanisms of advanced R&D project management have to combine today's efficiency with tomorrow's competitiveness (see Fig. I.1.10).

2   Key Topics in Global R&D Management

The outlined changes in the global environment of technology-intensive multinationals have led to complex topics in organizing global R&D. In the following section we summarize the key issues which have emerged from our empirical research and the case studies in this book.

2.1   Trends and Drivers in R&D Location

One major challenge for R&D is the heritage of corporate decisions inflicted upon R&D without consulting R&D about its long-term consequences. Mergers and acquisitions are challenges for R&D, because they usually require dramatic changes in the way R&D is used to do its business. Typically, synergy between newly acquired R&D units and corporate R&D labs are hardly realized without major reorganizations affecting all R&D units. Elimination of acquired R&D labs due to cost-cutting imperatives may destroy the motivation and knowledge-based

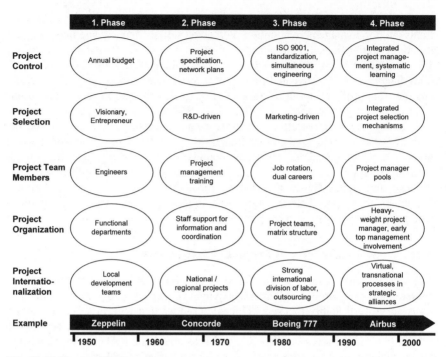

	1. Phase	2. Phase	3. Phase	4. Phase
Project Control	Annual budget	Project specification, network plans	ISO 9001, standardization, simultaneous engineering	Integrated project management, systematic learning
Project Selection	Visionary, Entrepreneur	R&D-driven	Marketing-driven	Integrated project selection mechanisms
Project Team Members	Engineers	Project management training	Job rotation, dual careers	Project manager pools
Project Organization	Functional departments	Staff support for information and coordination	Project teams, matrix structure	Heavy-weight project manager, early top management involvement
Project Internatio-nalization	Local development teams	National / regional projects	Strong international division of labor, outsourcing	Virtual, transnational processes in strategic alliances
Example	Zeppelin	Concorde	Boeing 777	Airbus
	1950 1960	1970	1980	1990 2000

Fig. I.1.10. Phases of R&D project management.

resources of those labs because the top-qualified scientists tend to leave a company in transitional periods when job security is low (Gerpott, 1995). Should the acquired R&D organization be left intact, NIH-syndromes occur and competition between R&D labs impedes the exploitation of potential synergy.

Closely related to the failure of not exploiting non-mainline developments is the question of how large an idea pool can be generated in a small- or medium-size divisional lab. The hit ratio for new ideas is very small and depends on how radical they are, and how far away they are from the company's or the industry's narrow scope. In the pharmaceutical industry, one in ten thousand makes it to commercialization. On average, Stevens and Burley (1997) estimate that it takes 3,000 raw ideas to produce one substantially new commercially industrial product. In dominant design industries, a medium size division may have a sufficiently large idea pool to beat the odds. Although science-driven industries like specialty chemicals or small high-tech companies may have enough ideas, they may not have the stamina to overcome the unavoidable flops which may end up costing a few hundred million US$ each. Specialized R&D locations need networking, the funding network being the minimum.

2.2   Towards the Integrated R&D Network

While the trends in overall organizational evolution of companies appear to increasingly match global stimuli and local responsiveness, the company needs to build internal complexity and flexibility in order to cope with the external world. The second half of the last century has witnessed the emergence of large-scale projects and their management. R&D projects are a formidable tool not only to intensify and concentrate the workload in a particular area of interest, but also to integrate and leverage external resources and thus achieving superior productivity and goals. Open innovation helps to integrate external knowledge.

In most MNCs, R&D locations have evolved historically through mergers and acquisitions. Since most companies started in a home base, grew up and exported from that ethnocentric and more or less homogeneous center, there is a strong tendency to stick to the parent. Only few companies like IBM, ABB or Novartis have become truly international through building up a global integrated R&D network that is being managed as a whole. The internationalization of R&D is driven in part by the external pull forces of access to markets and new technologies, and in part by internal push forces of cooperation and competition, and global integration and local autonomy.

2.3   Establishing Overlaying Structures

Although many companies still struggle with implementing a situation-driven, contingent approach to project management, the competitive arena of the 21st century also includes the management of informal networks across corporate boundaries and geographic borders. Coordinating such a network from one center alone is practically impossible; most companies pursue at least a mixed centralized/decentralized approach. Successful concepts for positively supporting and exploiting networks in and across companies include the technology gatekeeper, job-rotation through R&D, business units and external research institutes, project manager pools and professional clubs. These overlaying structures are particularly relevant when international innovation activities are concerned.

The case studies show that at least four structures are relevant, combining informal, process, functional, and regional structures. All these structures overlay each other on a global scale and should be managed simultaneously.

2.4   Global Innovation Project Teams

Supported by modern information and communication technology, time and cost pressures force the increased interconnection of decentralized R&D activity to transnational R&D processes. „Virtual project teams" are formed. Such project teams are spread out over several locations, their boundaries expand and shrink according to their responsibilities and they are strongly supported by modern information technologies.

If know-how, competencies, and resources for a specific R&D project are geographically distributed, management has the choice to either collocate all required resources or to adapt the project organization to accommodate the transnational needs. Since resources and individuals may not be relocated easily, virtual R&D teams are frequently the only choice. The international division of project work is possible only if certain conditions regarding the type of innovation, the availability of resources, the type of information exchange and the systemic nature of the project are met. The one extreme is complete self-coordination with no central project authority or control, and the other extreme is complete centralization of the project team and all required resources with closely controlled integration of external R&D partners.

2.5   *Market Orientation in R&D*

Customer-oriented R&D is defined as research activities that are consequently adjusted to the needs of internal and external customers. The success of this customer focused approach depends on the degree that modern research centers understand themselves as goal-oriented solution providers. Corporate R&D acts as a genuine partner for all corporate functions instead of a budget-maximizing antagonist. A major obstacle to customer orientation is the often dominant technology-push thinking. Internationalized R&D activities impede efficient communication between R&D and their customers. Nevertheless, new tools and organizational forms are required to meet customer requirements (Fig. I.1.11).

R&D is often measured in terms of time-to-market. While time-to-market considerations gain more and more importance in industries with slow or standard cycle products (such as specialty chemicals, operating system software, automobiles), fast cycle product industries make their living with the speed at which they fulfill customer needs. Fast cycle products are characterized by unique product features that change frequently, have many derivative products, and low barriers to entry. Their life cycles are low, often less than a year. In these industries (e.g.

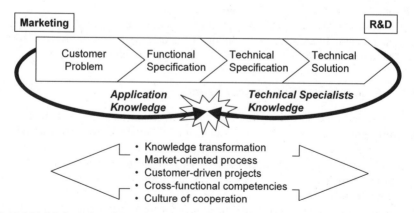

Fig. I.1.11. Market-oriented R&D requires an adequate combination of technical and application knowledge.

telecommunication, microprocessors, personal computers), prices fall rapidly as new models are launched. What organizational form should be chosen for basic research, product R&D, or process R&D? How would they interact given the different surrounding pressures on R&D?

2.6   Listening Posts

DaimlerChrysler with its more centralized technology has an international technology review with highly renowned researchers. A dilemma arises: Breakthrough innovation is very rarely initiated by existing customers, customer orientation is not enough; R&D has sometimes to anticipate future needs, along with all the risks in this approach. On an international scale, this poses special problems: Who knows best what Japanese customers appreciate and are willing to pay ten years from now? Is it the corporate headquarters at Stuttgart or the listening post in Tokyo? The case studies show that a problem-oriented approach seems to work rather well. In some companies, advanced development and research are thinking in terms of problems and less in solutions. In any case, listening posts are becoming increasingly popular means to tap into local centers of excellence, not just for industrial companies but also for national governments (e.g., Finland's TEKES or the Swiss Science Consulates).

2.7   Managing the R-to-D Interface

In order to ensure future cash-flow, companies engage in innovative activity. According to the degree of progress, such innovations are usually distinguished between research or development, technology or product development, and long-term or short-term R&D. Moving innovation from research to development requires a consideration on a global scale:

- Cultural gap: Free-wheeling researchers versus tightly lead-product development with cost and time pressures;
- Knowledge background: Scientists versus engineers;
- Controlling: Strategic research planning with loose control versus milestone planning with sophisticated controlling and performance measurement;
- Differences in reporting structure: Central research versus operating business units;
- Time horizons: Long-term knowledge creation versus short-term knowledge transformation in products;
- Geographical distance: Central research labs and decentralized business unit development.

In spite of such formal distinctions, companies pursue a pragmatic approach to organizing around these tasks. Specific problems arise because development often follows mostly decentralized production, and research is retained at the central headquarters for better protection and strategic control. Differences are also observed in deliberate placing of R&D: Development is often located near production or the market, and research in internationally reputed „brain-clusters." Innovation processes are often characterized by personnel discontinuity. The overall workload is divided between scientists and engineers, and there is no core team which is responsible for the complete project from beginning to end. Geographical distances must be bridged, which incurs problems of communication frequency and interaction costs.

Development is often integrated in business units, while research is under central corporate authority. Differing funding schemes, salaries, and cultures introduce interpersonal and interorganization problems to be solved. Development employs engineers and research depends on scientists. The transfer of knowledge between research and development in MNCs is thus almost automatically a transorganizational and international phenomenon which must be addressed with new forms of organization and management.

2.8   *Transnational R&D Processes*

The differentiation of the R&D process into the well-known three phases of pre-project, project execution and market introduction improves considerably process transparency and reduces the cost-intensive development phase significantly (Fig. I.1.12). Although the characteristics of the three phases are different, few companies approach them with differing management methods.

The creative phase requires soft management approaches, ensuring freedom and flexibility of scientists and engineers. In this phase, tacit knowledge is transformed into explicit knowledge, or communicated to other members of the team. In order to keep up intrinsic motivation, it is important to create a team spirit, a common project culture, and a shared understanding of project goals as well as the underlying system architecture.

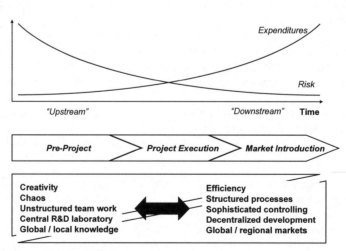

Fig. I.1.12. Every phase has different requirements.

In the execution phase of the project, the focus shifts to efficient implementation of these goals. Costs and milestones are used in determining the progress of the project. Compared to the pre-project phase, different coordination and control mechanisms are used to successfully complete the project.

The third phase, market introduction, is in most cases a truly global project and needs completely different approaches: Sales people have to be convinced and motivated with just a small number of direct contacts over large distances.

All R&D project phases allow a different degree of integration of international contributors and participants in the innovation process. It is important to find the right form of organization for each phase and each project. Critical success factors must be considered well in advance to ensure that upcoming problems are taken care of as they occur.

2.9   ICT as Enablers for Dispersed R&D Projects

In 1997, 90% of the information and communication technology (ICT) market was in the US, Europe, and Japan (Glenn and Gordon, 1997). Several initiatives and companies accelerate Internet access in developing countries. A recent study shows that this 90% market share has decreased to 76% (Europe: 32%; USA: 29%; Japan: 15%) in 2005. The "rest of the world" has revealed increased growth (European Information Technology Observatory, 2005). In 2000, there were 93 millions Internet hosts worldwide, the number has grown to 318 million by the end of 2004 (Internet System Consortium). The number of Internet users has reached close to 1 billion in 2005 (Internet Usage Statistic). There is more Internet traffic than voice telephony.

Information technology is creating a „planetary nervous system" (Fig. I.1.13). This is only the beginning: In 1999, a special Internet study was launched to study the extension of the internet into interplanetary space.

In this rapidly interconnected environment, not only new businesses but also new forms of R&D emerge. Work can be done almost anywhere and anytime. Global teamwork will replace old hierarchical patterns of work organization. Integrated media concepts will do away with compartments and artificial boundaries; productivity becomes more important than privacy of work. Laptops, mobile communication, and computing power will facilitate mobility of workers, making the static manager obsolete.

Communication patterns change and the hierarchical organization gives way to modern, network-like work arrangements. International R&D projects characterized by high division of labor rely heavily on the effective use of such ICT. Virtual R&D communities and the deliberate and well-coordinated utilization of ICT increase R&D effectiveness in international R&D projects. Open source software is developed in communities whose members work more and more like peer-reviewed scientists and take their motivation not from personal monetary gains but from achieving reputation and merits in a global engineering community. Apache and Linux are products that represent challenges not only to Microsoft but as well to our understanding of copyright and patents.

Top-performing companies use different ICT tools in different phases of the

R&D process. Traditional project management techniques remain important. E-mail and video-conferencing cannot replace face-to-face contact urgently needed to build soft factors for efficient team work. The work breakdown structure and the competitive environment (maximal cycle time, target specificity) determine whether a virtual form of organization can be used in R&D. Companies placing emphasis on distributed competencies and cooperative forms of organization can expect to benefit most from ICT in R&D.

2.10 Leading R&D Units

Succeeding in international R&D is, ultimately, not just a matter of smart decisions taken at the headquarters. Besides the many engineers and R&D teams in the various locations, it is the R&D unit heads – R&D directors and senior R&D managers – who translate the strategic goals into actionable directives and examples in the context of local language, culture, and expectations.

The establishment of a new R&D site somewhere in Thailand, Brazil or Norway is not a copy-paste of an existing, steady-state R&D labs back home. The initial R&D director will have to act like a start-up entrepreneur and hire the first handful of employees from a hotel room, setting up shop perhaps in a local service office. This is not the most conducive environment to conduct R&D, obviously, but the focus in those early stages is the development of an organization, not the development of scientific breakthroughs or new products. What is expected from

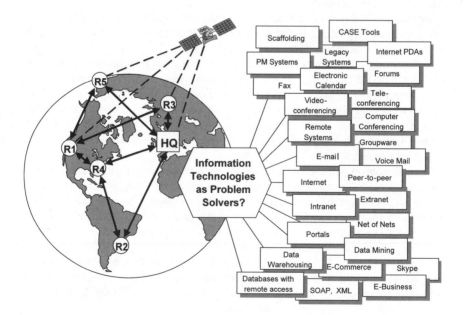

Fig. I.1.13. Use of information technology is essential, but not sufficient to ensure success.

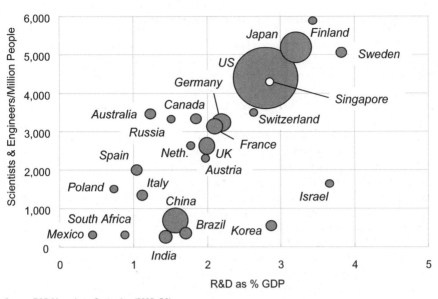

Source: R&D Magazine – September (2005: G2).

Fig. I.1.14. Engineers and R&D expenditures change the global picture.

these initial R&D directors, however, is not something that is usually cultivated or trained in mature R&D organizations, and this is one of the reasons why so many new R&D sites struggle to impress their sponsors.

When making the decision about the new leader of an R&D unit, top management is always torn between two alternatives: The expatriate director who knows the company well and in whom the top management has trust and confidence, or the locally hired director who is in touch with the culture, the local staff, and the local scientific community. Unfortunately, in international settings, the local-expatriate manager doesn't really exist: Anyone who has spent enough time to become a trusted corporate man has lost substantial familiarity with the local community and the trust of the locals, and the expatriate who has spent sufficient time in a target country to understand local culture and customs and people enough to feel confident to lead an R&D effort will face reservations and suspicions from headquarter management of his global/national allegiance.

As so often, R&D management will be forced to make a suboptimal decision, complaining about the lack of good local management or internal candidates, and question the usefulness of the original decision altogether. What few of them realize is that their plight is to a great degree self-imposed and predetermined by their own organizational culture and behavior that has led to the given international R&D configuration and culture. In more mature and seasoned international R&D organizations, senior and middle R&D managers are far more accepting of local-global tensions and more skilled and managing flexibly the often contrasting expectations of headquarters and local country organizations.

2.11 *Managing Knowledge and Human Resources*

As a knowledge-creation and uncertainty reduction process, R&D depends heavily on the quality and sustainability of communication among R&D staff. Overcoming the many barriers to effective communication is difficult enough in one R&D location, and they seem insurmountable when geographical distances separate scientists, engineers, R&D teams, R&D managers, top management, lead users, and customers.

In order to retain innovative capability, R&D people must be motivated and trained. Good projects and exceptional people attract and hold the best scientists and engineers to work for a particular company. They stay if they realize that the company allows them to fulfill their intrinsic goals as well. A company must provide them with the opportunity to develop themselves according to their personal interests and create career paths with mutual benefits for the employee and the company. Because job security today is less and less given, this is a non-trivial challenge. Creative and innovative personalities are sometimes not the most self easy-to-deal-with people, some need a stable environment others want to work as freelancers rather than wheels in a well functioning hierarchy.

If the company fails to hold its best people, knowledge-creation and dissemination will deteriorate. Idea generation and effective transfer of know-how is predominantly face-to-face. Science is global, technology is local. In transnational R&D teams, face-to-face contact is not always possible, and special instruments and organizational means must be introduced. Managing knowledge thus becomes a world-wide exercise, involving global coordination and local implementation.

Knowledge, in particular tacit knowledge, is hard to communicate if the people who own it do not move. Increasing the mobility of the R&D staff is an important

Table I.1.11. The top 10 research employers in 2004.

Country	Researchers	Technicians	Total
USA	1,300,000	NA	NA
PR China	821,000	NA	NA
Japan	650,000	NA	NA
Russia	490,000	330,000	820,000
Germany	266,000	119,000	385,000
France	190,000	NA	NA
UK	160,000	NA	NA
South Korea	143,000	NA	NA
India	129,000	110,000	239,000
Canada	114,000	36,000	150,000
Spain	84,000	31,000	115,000
Total	4,347,000	626,000	1,709,000

Source: R&D Magazine – September 2005, p G14.

challenge to lay the basis for exploiting the know-how available in all the corners of the company. Since it becomes clear now that „knowledge travels with heads," multinational companies reinforce their efforts in creating personal and corporate networks in which people can move and exchange ideas and experiences.

Some companies choose a "progressive" approach by hiring substantial numbers of young graduates just to see them leave after they have been trained. This is a "flight forward" approach that is very cost intensive. Even though some countries are abundant with engineering and technical talent (see Table I.1.11), the damage done to the firms in question should not be neglected. At the same time, from an individual's point of view, it is during the first years of one's career that multiple experience help build a greater horizon, and perhaps the economy as a whole benefits from this opportunistic behavior in the long run.

These challenges must be addressed by the modern technology-intensive multinational. The best companies distinguish themselves by making a concerted effort in approaching the many different and often diverging issues of managing global R&D processes. The second best may not fail but they will miss out on opportunities in global business which the more competent and proficient ones will be able to exploit.

I.2 Extent of R&D Internationalization

> *"The question on what is foreign R&D is undefined*
> *for a multinational company with truly global R&D."*
> *Frans Greidanus, SVP Research, Philips*

1 International R&D and Countries

The top R&D spenders worldwide account for a high share of total R&D input in each of the triad nations, thus indicating the importance of (international) R&D activities carried out by multinational companies (illustrated in Table I.2.1). The significance of international R&D activities is even larger when indirect influence of these companies on small- and medium-sized enterprises is taken into account.

The US alone spent about US$ 329 billion on R&D in 2006 (Duga and Studt, 2006), up from US$ 206 billion in 1997 (NSF, 1999), or approximately 2.6% of the US's GDP (Jankowski, 1998). In the US, R&D grew particularly strong in the early 1980s (average of 7%) and the mid-1990s (6% p.a.), but declined (-2.2%) between 1992 and 1994.

Between 1985 and 1993, overseas investment in R&D by US firms increased three times as fast as domestic R&D. In 2000, US companies spent on average US$ 17 billions in R&D abroad. This accounted roughly for 10% of overall industrial R&D investments (Science and Engineering Indicator 2004) compared to 6% in 1985 (National Science Board, 1996). In the same period, the amount of US$ 29 billions was spent for R&D in the US by foreign companies. This contributed to 16.1% of the total US$ 181 billions spending for industrial R&D in the US according to the Bureau of Economic Analysis. The share of majority-owned foreign affiliates R&D in the US rose from 9% to over 15% (National Science Board, 1996).

Thus, around 2000, investment in international R&D by US companies used to be roughly equivalent to R&D expenditures by majority-owned US affiliates of foreign companies. However, since then more industrial R&D has been flowing into the US than US firms were investing overseas. Europe has been both the main source and destination of US-foreign industrial investment. European companies invested US$ 11.6 billion of R&D in the US in 1995, and only US$ 1.7 billion in the Asian and Pacific region. For comparison, in 2001, US companies spent

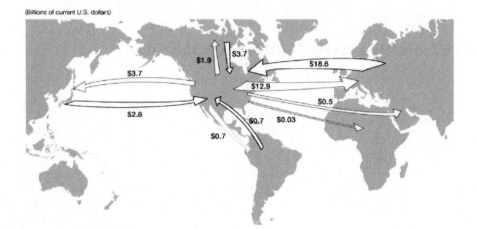

Source: National Science Board, Science and Engineering Indicator (2005).

Fig. I.2.1. Foreign-owned R&D in the US and US-owned R&D overseas (units in billions of US$).

US$ 11.6 billion in R&D in EU countries (UNCTAD, 2005) and US$ 2.4 billion in Asian and Pacific R&D. Fig. I.2.1 shows the latest R&D in- and outflows available from the National Science Board.

In contrast, Japan is less involved in foreign R&D, both as a source and as a recipient. Although Japan is the second largest R&D investor as a country (or third-largest if the European Union is counted as a country), only 3.4% of its R&D is done by foreign companies (UNCTAD, 2005). Still, it is the fifth most attractive region to host foreign R&D, having attracted hundreds of international R&D centers. It was estimated that Japanese multinational companies performed less than 5% of their R&D abroad (Buderi et al., 1991). The recent establishment of Japanese laboratories in Europe, the US and China may have increased the significance of Japanese-based global R&D (see e.g. Dalton and Serapio, 1995).

South Korea has mirrored Japan's technological development to some extent. In Samsung, LG, and a few others, Korea has some very strong domestic high-tech firms. It is the eighth strongest investor in R&D worldwide (UNCTAD,

Table I.2.1. Global R&D spending 2004.

Country	Billion US$ (PPP)	% Share of Total Global R&D
US	302	33
Europe	226	25
Japan	120	13
China	109	12

Source: R&D Magazine, September (2005 : G1).

Table I.2.2. How much of a country's R&D is done by foreign affiliates of MNCs?

Country	Expenditures (US$ million)	Share of Total Country Business R&D
Argentina	24	23.2%
Brazil	898	47.9%
Canada	3,070	34.8%
China	2,748	23.7%
Czech Republic	325	46.6%
France	3,986	19.4%
Germany	7,170	22.1%
India (1999)	103	3.4%
Italy	1,964	33.0%
Israel	726	20.7%
Japan	3,197	3.4%
South Korea	167	1.6%
The Netherlands	1,042	24.7%
Singapore	715	59.8%
Sweden	4,032	45.3%
Turkey (2000)	45	10.6%
UK	10,049	45.0%
USA	27,508	14.1%
Estimated World Total	66,933	15.9%

Source: UNCTAD (2005), based on latest figures (2001-2003) provided by national sources and OECD AFA database.

2005), but ranks only 26th as a host of foreign R&D, and only 1.6% of its R&D is done by foreign companies. This may change soon, as at least 15 new R&D centers were established by foreign companies in 2004 alone, and another 12 in 2005, among them Microsoft, Siemens, and Sun.

According to our own data (von Zedtwitz and Gassmann, 2002), European companies performed about one third of their R&D outside their home countries, US firms about 15%, and Japanese firms about 5%. Half of the European R&D internationalization is internal, i.e. to other European countries. No reliable data is available for India and China, but their R&D internationalization is estimated to be below 1%.

The pioneers of R&D internationalization are high-tech companies operating in small markets and with little R&D resources in their home country. ABB, Novartis and Roche (Switzerland), Philips (Netherlands), Nokia (Finland) or Ericsson (Sweden) had to conduct R&D in foreign research laboratories abroad, as key skills and people were increasingly in short supply at home. Swiss, Dutch and Belgian companies had more than 50% of their R&D carried out outside their home country by the early 1990s.[8] Companies such as General Electric and General Motors in the USA, Toyota and Fujitsu in Japan, and DaimlerChrysler in Germany with large home markets and a substantial domestic R&D base were less forced to internationalize their R&D activities. Only in recent years did increased competition from within and outside their industries force these companies to source technological knowledge on a global scale.

---

[8]   Pearce and Singh (1992), Vorort (1994), Granstrand et al (1993).

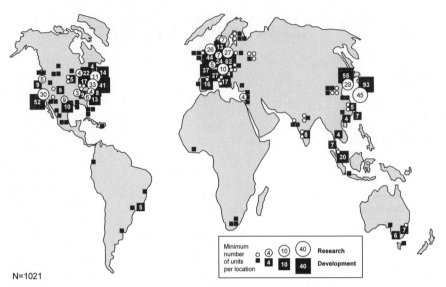

N=1021

Source: Annual reports, company documents, interviews (1994-1999).

Fig. I.2.2. Spatial dispersion of 1021 R&D sites (of 81 companies) around the world: R&D concentration in centers of innovation based on our own database (see also Table I.2.6).

International R&D often makes up a significant amount of a host country's own R&D effort. Based on data presented in Table I.2.2 we find that some countries (like Brazil, the Czech Republic, Singapore) see about half of their business R&D conducted by foreign companies. Developing countries (like India, Turkey) still have comparatively low rates of R&D internationalization. Countries from Eastern Europe have a relatively high share of foreign R&D, probably due to the long tradition in basic research and sciences and the absence of a significant domestic industry that would be in the position to make use of it. The global amount of foreign R&D is estimated at nearly US$ 67 billion; given that this figure is based on data published in 2001-2003 and probably collected in the two or three years prior, it is probably underreporting the actual amount of foreign R&D investment. Assuming the same percentage (15.9%) and an estimated global business R&D expenditure of US$ 550 billion (see UNCTAD, 2005; the OECD, Duga and Studt, 2006), we again arrive at a total volume of US$ 100 billion for 2006/2007.

Roberts (1995) prediction of a continuing rise of international R&D was accurate: Most of the surveyed companies enlarged their share of foreign R&D since then. Our research suggests that many companies plan to further increase their number of international R&D sites in the next 5 to 10 years. While most R&D laboratories are concentrated in the triad countries, new R&D sites are now created in the newly industrialized economies of South-East Asia (see Fig. I.2.2). A survey by INSEAD and consulting firm Booz, Allen & Hamilton of 186 companies in 19 countries and 17 industrial sectors accounting for approximately 20% of total global R&D spending showed that more than three quarters of all R&D sites planned through 2007 will be set up in China and India. The survey also revealed that about 31% of all R&D employees will work in India and China by the end of 2007 (Doz et al., 2006).

The answer to what is international R&D is sometimes a different one for companies in small countries. Consider the R&D center of Novartis in Basel, which sits right on the border to France. R&D employees regularly have lunch in restaurants across the border. Some Novartis R&D facilities are within 5 minutes walking distance but technically abroad. Is this international? Or consider Sun Microsystem's R&D units in Boston and San Diego. Both centers are located in the US, but they are separated by more than 4,000 kilometers and three time zones. The only way to cooperate between those two sites is by deploying means and processes used in international R&D.

As can be seen, international R&D has risen from a side effect to a quite important and far-reaching phenomenon. Management of such activities is characterized by a significantly higher degree of complexity than is the case for local R&D. The extra costs of international coordination must be balanced by synergy effects such as decreased time-to-market, improved effectiveness, enhanced learning capabilities, or localization of products. Corporate top management is left with the decision on how to design their R&D organization.

2   International R&D and Multinational Companies

Although SMEs do engage in international R&D, the bulk of global R&D is done by MNCs. Our own research and data sources are focused on technology-based MNCs with a international R&D experience. These companies are attracted to locate their R&D activities at centers of technological excellence, i.e. regions characterized by a high rate of new technology output, or where local markets are large enough to support product adaptations. R&D and innovation abroad is also intensified by the scarcity of resources at home. The location patterns indicate that knowledge, technology and product creating processes are asymmetrically distributed worldwide.

Based on more than 400 interviews conducted in nearly 100 technology intensive companies from most OECD countries – and including India and China – between 1994 and 2006, we analyzed how leading companies adapt their global R&D organizations.[9] Most of these companies perform a significant amount of R&D abroad. The data gathered for Fig. I.2.3 is based on corporate annual reports and interviews with R&D directors and managers in 1996/7 and 2005/2006.

The left graph in Fig. I.2.3 depicts the 1997 situation among 34 MNCs.[10, 11] For

---

[9]   For a detailed description of our research methodology, see Gassmann (1997a), Gassmann and von Zedtwitz (1998, 1999), von Zedtwitz (1999), von Zedtwitz and Gassmann (2002a, 2003), von Zedtwitz et al. (2004), Boutellier, et al. (2007).

[10]   There is no significant interdependence between R&D intensity and R&D internationalization (see Gassmann and von Zedtwitz, 1999).

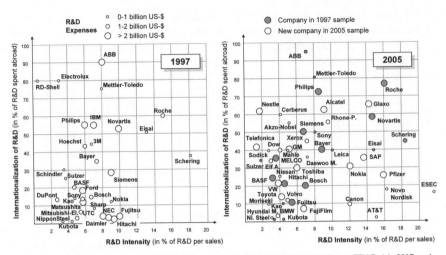

Source: Based on Gassmann and von Zedtwitz (1998), extended by Boutellier, Chen and Löffler, at ETH Zurich, 2007, and von Zedtwitz at Tsinghua, 2007.

Fig. I.2.3. Expanding and increasing R&D internationalization: 1997 - 2005.

example, Hitachi spent more than US$ 4 billion on R&D in 1996, which translated to an R&D ratio of 9% to overall sales. Despite substantial R&D engagements in US and Europe, only 3% of all R&D expenses were invested abroad. Hitachi's R&D internationalization profile was thus similar to companies such as NEC, Daimler-Benz and Fujitsu. The 1997 situation also reveals the following:

- Some companies are highly internationalized in R&D (ABB, Mettler-Toledo, Royal Dutch/Shell, etc.), these are typically the results of intensive merger and acquisition activity.
- Confirming our results at the country-level, companies from Europe tend to be the most international, and companies from Japan the least international in R&D. There are too few US companies in the sample to allow reliable interpretation.
- Among the 34 companies of the 1997 graph, the average R&D internationalization was about 25%, weighed to the total R&D investment. This resulted in an international R&D total of about US$ 10 billion per year represented in this graph.

Although most companies had a higher degree of internationalization in terms of sales and production sites, the share of R&D carried out away from headquarters

---

[11] Our chart represents data on a corporate level. It neglects differences in R&D ratio and internationalization on individual business units but captures the shared use of R&D resources available to several business units. Consequently, some business units may have ratios different from their parent company. As our intent was to demonstrate the overall significance of R&D internationalization and R&D intensity, we anticipated a certain variance per company and accepted the company's average figures as satisfactory indicators.

and home countries continued to rise. Roche invested nearly 80% in international R&D in 2004, as compared to 60% in 1998. At Siemens, the number of foreign R&D employees rose by 60% between 1989 and 1993, as compared to a 6%-rise of German R&D employees. Overall, the 2005 situation reveals that:

- There are more large R&D investors, reflecting an increase in overall R&D spending, as the reclassification of individual companies present in both samples indicate.
- The extended sample of 51 MNCs is far more international than the 1997 sample, reaching an average of 35-40%. This results in a total R&D volume of about US$ 30 billion spent internationally per year.
- Many companies increased their R&D internationalization (e.g., Roche, Siemens, Hitachi, Philips), although some remained at their levels or even reduced overseas R&D (e.g., Kubota, Eisai, Nippon Steel, Kao).
- Despite most of the companies without much change in the ratio of R&D internationalization are Japanese, quite a few Japanese companies made substantial strides with R&D abroad (e.g., Hitachi, Nissan, Fujitsu, Toyota, Mitsubishi Electric).
- Except for the M&A and the pharma companies in the sample, no other industrial classification suggests itself.

International R&D is thus advancing. Despite this trend the present international distribution of R&D in many companies is not the result of rational location planning but rather a side effect of not directly R&D-related decisions, most notably mergers and acquisitions. About 70% of all acquisitions are based on a market-driven rationale (see e.g. Granstrand, et al. (1993), Håkanson and Nobel (1993)). Personal motives of top managers and the overall business climate also play a decisive role. Mergers and acquisitions come in waves. The peak was reached in 2000 and went sharply down afterwards. Between 1992 and 1995 alone, worldwide M&A doubled from US$ 369 billion to about US$ 740 billion, and surpassed US$ 1 trillion in 2003. Cross-border M&A alone reached US$ 716 billion in 2004 (UNCTAD, 2006).

Since the acquisition of innovative firms has become a strategy for gaining quick access to new technologies (e.g. Granstrand and Sjölander, 1992), the acquirer faces the challenge of rearranging the R&D activities of both firms in order to ensure some form of synergy exploitation. Gerpott's findings (1995) suggest that post-acquisition strategy decisions should be centrally made, as the advantages of a quick and clear provision of R&D strategy and implementation of organizational changes outweigh the motivation costs that might be incurred within the acquired R&D units. He stresses the importance of installing additional integration programs to improve R&D integration success.

The management of cross-border R&D is thus significantly more complex than local R&D management. The extra costs of international coordination must be balanced by synergy effects such as decreased time-to-market, improved effectiveness, understanding the needs of local markets and enhanced learning capabilities. While the theme of globalization is an old one, there is still not enough experience in the internationalization of R&D. De Meyer and Mizushima (1989:

139) statement if the late 1980s, „globalization of R&D is typically accepted more with resignation than with pleasure," is basically still true today.

Corporate top managers are confronted with finding the optimal R&D organization based on the type of R&D activities, the present geographical configuration of other value-adding activities such as production and marketing, and the degree of coordination between contributors to R&D processes. In our analysis we have found that the design of international innovation processes is determined by the dispersion of R&D sites, their specialization, and the necessary as well as possible degree of cooperation between R&D activities. R&D organizations differing in their behavioral orientation and their competitive environment are thus likely to assume different organizational configurations.

3   Factors Driving R&D Internationalization

Besides mergers and acquisitions, shorter product development cycles, global competition, increased customer expectations and technological risks have been major reasons to internationalize R&D. While the traditional motivation for internationalizing corporate activities can be found in improving cash-flow and turnover quickly (international exporting and marketing) or reducing operating costs (e.g. setting up production in low-wage countries), short-term ROI objectives are difficult to achieve when internationalizing R&D.

3.1   Enablers of R&D Internationalization

In our collection of factors that support R&D internationalization (see Table I.2.3), we follow a classification scheme used by Beckmann and Fischer (1994). Local markets, resources and synergy potentials, political circumstances and fiscal considerations are among the most cited drivers for R&D internationalization. Synergies will become even more important over the next years because of the growth in mergers, acquisitions and cooperations (Fig. I.2.4).

Input-oriented factors encompass drivers related to personnel, know-how and infrastructure. Proximity to markets, customers, and image are output- or product-oriented factors. Political and socio-cultural factors such as local content rules, technology acceptance and public approval times, play an important role for locating R&D abroad. Direct cost advantages (such as the often publicly discussed labor costs) rarely influence the internationalization of R&D, but other efficiency-oriented factors such as costs of coordination and transfer, and critical laboratory size do have an even bigger impact on international R&D organization. Direct costs may become more important in the coming years as the other factors improve in low labor cost countries (Thurow, 1996). The Leica case shows as well that costs may at least be one of the triggers for internationalization.

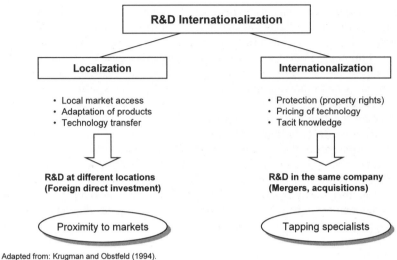

Adapted from: Krugman and Obstfeld (1994).

Fig. I.2.4. Internationalization and localization of R&D activities.

The development of local products requires the early involvement of market and customer application know-how, which is more likely to be found in regional business units. Companies with local R&D exhibit an inclination towards over-emphasizing different local market specification in order to support local auton-omy and independence from the parent company. Host country restrictions, such as local content requirements, tolls, import quota, and fulfillment of standards, can attract R&D into key market countries (*pull regulations*), but have been harmo-nized through WTO over the last 10 years. On the other hand, home country re-strictions may induce companies to move R&D abroad (*push regulations*): Euro-pean regulations caused biotechnology R&D to be transferred to the US and to South Korea.

The 1990s have seen an effort of many large companies to consolidate their ac-tivities in order to realize synergy and coordination potential in international R&D. Transnational R&D projects are managed more easily if the R&D network consists of competence centers such as is the case for Roche or Schindler, given that complementary competencies are provided locally. With increasing comple-mentarity of resources, competencies, and knowledge bases, as well as the divi-sion of labor and specialization of work, synergy potential in R&D projects can be exploited.

Thus, when establishing a new R&D site, rational criteria such as running costs, potential synergy with local production facilities, or a favorable research environ-ment may play a decisive role. Ford chose Aachen in Germany as its new Euro-pean R&D location not only because of its proximity to one of the most indus-trialized regions in Europe. Aachen is also the home of one of the most prestigious technical universities in Europe (RWTH Aachen), thus enabling Ford to easily acquire highly qualified scientists and engineers. Technical cooperation with local universities and institutes facilitates the acquisition of new technologies and supports strategic technology monitoring. Aachen, which is located close to the Netherlands, Belgium and France, serves as an ideal listening post for the notoriously varied European tastes and expectations. Ford finds it easier to design and develop product variants or to monitor European Community politics (affecting automobile manufactures in terms of environmental laws, for instance) from Aachen than other attractive locations such as Cambridge, UK.

Multiplication effects in know-how transfer occur when people from different locations become part of the same team: Informal know-how transfer by means of sharing experience is often more efficient than formal distribution of knowledge by means of blueprints, internal memos or licenses. Specialists are attracted to places where other specialists are. The underlying motive is less a perceived kinship between members of the same profession than striving for job security, since the propensity to find a related job is higher in a cluster area of industry concentra-

Table I.2.3. Enablers of R&D internationalization may be differentiated between input and output related factors, and between efficiency and political or socio-cultural factors. Frequently, R&D internationalization is a by-product of decisions or developments outside the traditional scope of R&D.

Input-oriented	• Information and communication networks • Center-of-innovation • Infrastructure • Qualified human resources	• Adaptation to local production processes • Scientific community • Tapping informal networks • Country-specific cost advantages
Output-oriented	• Improving local image • Customer-specific development	• Closeness to lead users • Local values • Market and customer proximity
External	• History • Peer pressure • Tax optimization	• Acquisition of parent company • Merger
Efficiency-oriented	• Improving flexibility through new organization • Critical mass • Reduced project failure risk through parallel development • Making use of many time zones • Proximity to production, marketing, distribution	• Learning curve • Reduction of development cycle time • Overcoming logistic barriers • Lower R&D personnel costs
Political / socio-cultural	• National and legal conditions • Patenting laws • Protectionist barriers • Predictable labor relations • Local content	• Legal restrictions • Acceptance • Subsidies • Taxes

Source: Beckmann and Fischer (1994); De Meyer and Mizushima (1989); Gassmann and von Zedtwitz (1996b); Håkanson and Zander (1988); Carnegie Bosch Institute (1994); Krubasik and Schrader (1990); von Boehmer, Brockhoff, and Pearson (1992); direct investigation.

Table I.2.4. 10 hot spots in the US for technology development.

Location	Technology	Major companies
Albuquerque, NM	Microchips	Intel, Motorola, Philips, Honeywell
Austin, TX	Computers, software, biotechnology	IBM, Samsung, Motorola, TI, 3M
Boston, MA	Computer, telecommunications, biotechnology	Lycos, hundreds of start-ups
Boulder, CA	Computer, aerospace	300 high-tech startups
Huntsville, AL	Aerospace	Cummings Research Park, Honeywell, Hughes, Lockheed, UTC
Portland, OR	Electronics	Intel, Tektronix, US West
Provo/Orem, UT	Software	Novell
Research Triangle Park, NC	Pharmaceuticals, microelectronics, computer, telecommunications, biotechnology	98 research companies
San Francisco Bay, CA	Software, computers, electronics	HP, Intel, Xerox, Oracle, Sun, Silicon Graphics
Seattle, WA	Aerospace, communications, biotechnology, software	Boeing, Microsoft

Source: Adapted from Cornello (1998).

tion (e.g. Boutellier et al., 1995). Other specialists mean other companies and other suitable jobs: The specialist gets some degree of social security as well as the information needed to stay an expert in his field. For example, Singapore is a worldwide center for logistics, Salt Lake City for software programmers, Silicon Valley for information technology and microelectronics (Table I.2.4).

Scientists of the same area enjoy exchanging their ideas with people from inside and outside the company. The most intense links are the ties with the alma mater, the university where graduates spent several years of their lives (Harhoff and Licht, 1996). The establishment of a corporate-wide network rests heavily on those side-effects of informal contacts between members of different R&D sites. It is a management challenge not only to exploit informal networks for international R&D activities, but also to foster the creation of new personal bonds between geographically separated R&D units. Once a year, the world leader in cement production, Holcim, arranges a one-week seminar at the site of the world-economic forum in Davos, Switzerland. Approximately 200 engineers exchange best practices. Nevertheless, the company is completely decentralized: No unit can be forced to accept any of the best practices. Holcim heavily relies on informal transfer.

Scanning offices or small listening posts, set up to monitor local research and maintain scientific networks, tend to increase in scope and responsibility. An independent research center is the logical consequence. The driving factors in research evolution are:

- Full exploitation of local talent;
- Augmenting home-base knowledge;
- Ensuring critical mass;
- Prestige of individual researchers;
- Fiscal considerations.

3.2   *Barriers to R&D Internationalization*

The case for R&D internationalization is not unchallenged. Using patent data from 1969 to 1986, Patel and Pavitt (1992) show that research and development of core technologies were still highly domesticated in 1986. Reasons against internationalization are plenty (see Table I.2.5). We divide our determinants against international R&D into a set of reasons explicitly opposing R&D internationalization versus a set of reasons favoring centralization of R&D. The individual items in this list are not necessarily mutually exclusive: A reason against internationalization may at the same time be a strong cause for centralization. Again, as in Table I.2.3, some factors may be more prevalent in some industries than in others.

As stated before, many companies internationalized their R&D in the context of mergers and acquisitions. But merger and acquisitions may also lead to a reduction of R&D locations. For example, a redirection of strategy following a merger has led Novartis to actually reduce the number of central research laboratories by abandoning its former Ciba R&D site in Takarazuka, Japan. During the integration phase, i.e. when the two parent companies are being joined together, R&D units are being evaluated for future fit and performance, and many of them are either merged (if in the same general vicinity), sold off, closed down, or spun off.

Yet, more R&D sites are established each year than existing R&D sites are dissolved (e.g. Howells, 1990; Dalton and Serapio, 1995). Divesting of acquired R&D units is usually associated with high costs (e.g., pension funds payments, social plans) and has a very negative impact on the morale of the remaining employees. Valuable technological competence with possibly high strategic potential may be lost (Pearson et al., 1993) or even turned over to competition. Given a range of technical specialties and a generally modest size, divisional labs are seldom able to assemble a „critical mass" of people to blitz a complex or big problem that requires different facets of a given specialty or a broad range of skills and knowledge. This means that divisional technology people are frequently out of their strong areas of competence even in their own fields when they attack other than familiar problems or try to sally into new areas (Rubenstein, 1989).

3.3   *Closing R&D locations*

Centralizing R&D activities in centers of innovation (see Fig. I.2.2) is mainly triggered by efficiency-thinking. We do not imply that the pendulum swings back completely to centralized concepts. Rather, we identified a trend of concentrating R&D in worldwide leading areas of excellence. This is particularly true for basic R&D activities. It requires the painful decision of closing down R&D sites. The principal criteria for such closures are:

- Size;
- Significance of local market;
- Availability of human resources;
- Critical know-how;
- Productivity.

Productivity measurements of production or sales centers are difficult, but for R&D sites adequate monetary figures indicating management results can be implemented only indirectly and with much imperfection. Schindler chose a credit-point-based solution for bringing profit center thinking into R&D: For each project which is ordered by field operations, a contract is made. After R&D delivers the new product, the field operations assign credit points for R&D performance. At the end of the year, corporate R&D management results are measured by how much the sum of all credit points exceeds the previously agreed R&D budget. This introduces pressure to reduce cycle-times and increase first-pass-yield. Nevertheless, this scheme has been found inappropriate as a factor in the decision to close down entire R&D units.

The output of an R&D unit can be measured by its ability to fulfill the requirements of 1) research, 2) market and 3) manufacturing (Fig. I.2.5).

Research

Short time-to-market and breakthroughs require a sound foundation in basic knowledge. This is especially true for science-driven industries as shown in the cases of DuPont and Roche. Technology development should be completed before engaging in a new product development project. The number of patents is an indicator for an R&D unit's ability to conduct research. Publications are another measure in research. For instance, with its five international and eight domestic R&D centers in 1997, NEC overseas laboratories contributed 24% of all papers presented by all NEC staff at major international conferences and academic journals (Goto, 1997). NEC's figure of 24% is comparable to IBM's 27%. Despite geographical limitations, foreign R&D laboratories may be surprisingly more productive in terms of research output.

Table I.2.5. R&D internationalization is balanced by factors disfavoring international R&D activities and factors favoring R&D centralization.

Factors in support of central R&D	Obstacles to international R&D
• Economies of scale (critical size)	• Immobility of top class personnel
• Synergy effects	• Critical mass (for startups)
• Higher career potential	• Redundant development
• Minimal R&D costs and development time	• Language and cultural differences
• Better control over research results	• Much of scientific and technical information worldwide available by Internet
• Communication intensity	• Specific know-how easily lost when support not present
• Legal protection	• Political risks
• Common R&D culture	• No wage advantages in triad nations
	• Coordination and information costs

Source: Behrmann and Fischer (1980); De Meyer and Mizushima (1989); Coombs and Richards (1993); Carnegie Bosch Institute (1994), von Boehmer, Brockhoff, and Pearson (1992); Beckmann and Fischer (1994); Gassmann and von Zedtwitz (1996b); Allen (1977); direct investigation.

Market

Many strategically placed R&D units need to demonstrated their maturing R&D capability by successfully replacing their corporate funding with projects contracted from business divisions. Market requirements are best considered by an R&D unit when it sells a high percentage of its projects to business units. Getting an order from a business unit or field operation means going with the market pull. At ABB, most projects are funded according to the „two-source principle": At least one business unit has to pay part of the project - even in the research stage.

Manufacturing

Operations and manufacturing requirements are best considered when the R&D unit is proficient in *concurrent engineering*. The less technological groundwork is needed after the start of a development project, the better is the quality of advanced development.

A rough indication of the productivity of an R&D unit is given by the number of patents, projects sold to business units and degree of concurrent engineering measured in terms of manufacturing costs and time-to-market. But measuring R&D productivity remains a difficult and perhaps questionable task: Even Davenport (1993), one of the prominent proponents of business process redesign and rationalization, has proposed that hard productivity numbers should be replaced with direct evaluation of R&D employees by their experienced managers. Patterson (1993), the former HP head of R&D, shows that 'negative' results achieved in a start phase can be a sign of high productivity. If the R&D unit is able to show early that the project cannot be carried out for technical reasons, management can reallocate the resources to new projects.

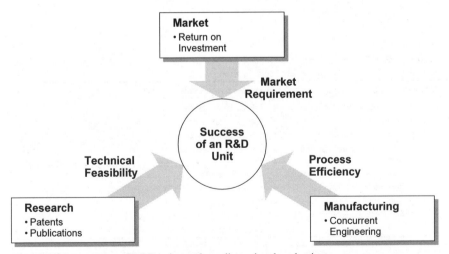

Fig. I.2.5. Measurement of R&D units - a three-dimensional evaluation.

4   Conclusion

While the internationalization of industrial R&D of the 1980s and 1990s has reached a remarkable level, it has been predominantly limited to large MNCs. In our study of some of the largest R&D spenders and the most global industrial innovators, we have seen that internationalization is mostly triggered by historical mergers and acquisitions, localization needs, and the need for skills. These are still the driving forces in 2007.

The search for R&D competencies has favored R&D internationalization in recent years, particularly since technical knowledge is increasingly concentrated in know-how clusters around the world. The "hunt for the best heads" leads to the establishment of local research and development, mainly in order to absorb critical competencies and to support organizational learning. Taxation and research subsidies (NIH in the US) have as well become attractive parameters in listed companies. Customer proximity facilitates the efficient cooperation with local development in business units or with lead customers. Market requirements are met more effectively and more rapidly. Costs and control considerations slow down or even reverse the internationalization process: Critical mass is still important.

Hence, international R&D involves increased complexity and new challenges to management. The extra costs must be balanced by synergy effects like decreased time-to-market, improved effectiveness, enhanced learning capabilities, or localization of products. Geographical distances and different time zones impose limits on communication and inflict additional costs. Interacting with new customers from unfamiliar cultures poses high personal challenges. Dealing with these challenges affects the underlying R&D organization. There is no one best approach. The development and establishment of international R&D activities is an evolutionary process involving organizational learning. Such processes take years. Hence, international R&D organization is based on the design of international innovation processes which in turn are determined by the complexity of the product, by the dispersion of R&D competencies and the necessary degree of cooperation between R&D units.

Table I.2.6. Major R&D sites of surveyed companies indicating size and research areas (listed according to industry, with number of people (p.) where data was available).

Electronics and Software Industry	
AT&T	• In 2000: 15 to 20 R&D sites world-wide (Bell Labs in the USA), research laboratory in the Netherlands • Design Centers in Japan, Taiwan, Singapore and in several European countries
Bosch	• Research and advanced development in Germany only • Development in Switzerland, the USA, Brazil, Mexico, Rep. of South Africa, Australia, Spain, China, Japan
Canon	• Interactive systems in Surrey (UK), Computer networks and software in California, Imaging Technology in Sydney (Australia), Telecommunications in Rennes (France), Systems Management in Berkshire (UK) • 22 R&D locations in Japan: Shimomaruko, Canon Research Center, Fuji Susono. Total of 7,300 R&D researchers • Together with Toshiba Corporation, launching joint research of integrated circuits (ICS) in 2004
Fujitsu	• 4 major R&D Sites in Japan, several divisional R&D sites abroad • Cooperation with Siemens in PC in 2005 and R&D collaboration with leading academic and independent research institutes • Today, 1,500 research scientists at Fujitsu labs in Japan (Kawasaki), China (Beijing, Shanghai), UK (London), and the US (California, Texas, Maryland) • 11,000 development engineers around the world in 2006
Hewlett-Packard	• Basic and Applied Research (total of 1,400 p.): Palo Alto (US), Bristol (UK), Tokyo (Japan), Haifa (Israel), Beijing (China), St. Petersburg (Russia), Bangalore (India) • U.S. locations: Cupertino, Folsom, Mountain View, Newark, Palo Alto, Rohnert Park, Roseville, San Diego, San Jose, Santa Clara, Santa Rosa, Sunnyvale, and Westlake Village, California; Colorado Springs, Fort Collins, Greeley, and Loveland, Colorado; Wilmington, Delaware; Boise, Idaho; Andover and Chelmsford, Massachusetts; Exeter, New Hampshire; Rockaway, New Jersey; Corvallis, Oregon; Aguadilla, Puerto Rico; Richardson, Texas; Everett, Spokane and Vancouver, Washington • Asia-Pacific: Melbourne, Australia; Beijing, Qingdao, and Shanghai, China; Hachioji, Kobe, and Musashino, Japan; Seoul, Korea; Penang, Malaysia; Bangalore, India; Singapore • Europe: Grenoble, Isle d'Abeau, and Lyon, France; Böblingen and Waldbronn, Germany; Dublin, Ireland; Bergamo, Italy; Amersfoort, The Netherlands; Barcelona, Spain; Bristol, Ipswich, Pinewood, and South Queensferry, UK • The Americas: Campinas, Brazil; Calgary, Edmonton, Montreal, Richmond, Vancouver, and Waterloo, Canada; Guadalajara, Mexico
IBM	• Corporate research centers: USA: Hawthorne and Yorktown Heights, Almaden, Austin, Switzerland: Zürich, China: Beijing, Japan: Tokyo, India: Delhi, and Israel: Haifa. • R&D laboratories in USA and Canada: Toronto, Rochester, Boulder, San Jose, Tucson, Austin, Boca Raton, Charlotte, Raleigh, Eastfishkill, Poughkeepsie, Endicott, Burlington • R&D laboratories in Asia-Pacific: Tokyo, Yasu, Beijing, Shanghai • R&D laboratories in Europe: Hursley, Böblingen, La Gaude, Rome • Sold its personal computer segment, along with several R&D units, to China-based company Lenovo in 2004.
Matsushita Electric Industrial	• R&D sites in the USA (since 1980) • Software development in Taiwan (since 1981); development in Singapore (since 1990) and Great Britain (since 1984) • R&D site in Germany (since 1991) • Established a software site in Dalian, China in 2004

Table I.2.6. Major R&D sites of surveyed companies indicating size and research areas (listed according to industry, with number of people (p.) where data was available). (continued)

Electronics and Software Industry

Mitsubishi Electric
- Research center in Great Britain (Cambridge) and in the USA (Sunnyvale)
- Decentralized development at some manufacturing sites
- R&D centers: Information Technology R&D Center, Industrial Design Center (Japan), Mitsubishi Electric Research Lab Inc. (US), Mitsubishi Electric Information Technology Center Europe B.V. Mitsubishi Electric Information Technology research centers in Rennes (FR) and Guildford (UK)"

NEC
- 2006: R&D laboratories based in Japan, employing approx. 1,800 people. 6 overseas R&D laboratories in Princeton and San Jose (US), in Bonn (since 1994) and Heidelberg (Germany) in Acton (UK) and Beijing

Nokia
- Corporate Research in Helsinki, Tampere, Dallas and Boston, Bochum
- 2004: 20,722 people employed in R&D centers in 12 countries representing 37% of total workforce.
- R&D centers adjacent to leading technical universities in 12 countries

Philips
- Seven corporate research labs in Europe, USA and Asia: Eindhoven (Netherlands), Aachen and Hamburg (Germany), Redhill (United Kingdom); Briarcliff Manor (USA); Bangalore (India) and Shanghai (PR China).
- In 2000, research center in Shanghai established employing approx. 80 research scientists in 2007

SAP
- Central R&D in Walldorf, Germany
- SAP labs in Japan (since 1992, 1317p in 2005), Palo Alto, USA (since 1996, approx. 1500p in 2005), France (since 1998 as complete subsidiary of SAP AG Germany), India (since 1998, approx. 3000 in 2005), Shanghai, China (since 2003, approx. 400 in 2005), Montreal, Canada (R&D center focuses on cutting-edge software products), Budapest, Hungary (since 2005), Bulgaria (since 2000, approx. 280 software developers in 2007), and Israel (approx. 600p)

Sharp
- R&D bases in Japan, Oxford (UK, since 1990), US, Taiwan, and India
- 2005: total number of employees 55,000 (31,200 in Japan and 23,800 overseas)

Sony
- Development in Belgium, Germany, and Great Britain (since 1987)
- A total of 7 R&D labs in the USA (e.g., since 1987 in San Jose)
- Technical center in Singapore (1994)

Unisys
- USA: San Jose CA, Salt Lake City UT, Mission Viejo CA, Roseville MN, Tredyffrin PA
- Tokyo, North Ryde (Australia, France, Milan (Italy), Amsterdam (Netherlands)

Xerox
- Corporate research centers in Webster (US), Palo Alto (US, Mississauga (Canada, Grenoble (France), Cambridge (UK)
- Technology centers in El Segundo CA, Webster NY, Palo Alto CA

Electrical and Machinery Industries

ABB
- Corporate research in Switzerland (Baden), Sweden (Västeras), Germany (Heidelberg), Italy (Milan), Norway (Oslo), Poland (Cracow), Beijing (PR China), Finland (Vaasa)
- Regional laboratories in Windsor CT and Raleigh NC

BMW
- Central R&D in Munich, Germany
- Main R&D centers in Gaydon, UK and Steyr (Austria)
- Design studios in California, test sites in France and Germany

Table I.2.6. Major R&D sites of surveyed companies indicating size and research areas (listed according to industry, with number of people (p.) where data was available). (continued)

Electrical and Machinery Industries

Daimler-Chrysler	• Research centers and listening posts in Palo Alto, USA, Portland, Shanghai, Bangalore, Japan, Moscow • Central Research in Germany (6 locations), India, China, Japan, Russia and the US • Detroit/Dearborn (former Chrysler R&D center)
Hitachi	• Fundamental research in Great Britain (since 1989, Cambridge, Micro-electronics), Ireland (since 1989, Dublin, Information Science), France (Sophia Antipolis, Mobile communication), Germany (Munich, Automotive systems). • Centers for industrial design in Germany (Munich) and Italy (Milan) • Development in the USA (San Francisco, Detroit, Princeton) since 1989 • Technical center in Singapore since 1995 • 3,000 researchers in central research laboratories, 9,000 engineers in development centers as of year 2000 • R&D division in US (Bisbance, Santa Clara & California) • R&D centers in Beijing, Shanghai, Singapore • As of 31st March, 2005, 2,800 employees in R&D group
Mettler-Toledo	• R&D in Switzerland (Uster-Greifensee), Germany, Asia-Pacific (Shanghai and Shangtsou), and USA. 75% of R&D is performed outside home country
Otis	• Engineering Centers in Farmington (USA), Kawasaki (Japan), Gien (France), Madrid (Spain), Berlin (Germany), Stathagen (Germany) • Engineering facilities in China, Czech Republic, France, Germany, Japan, Korea, Spain and the United States
Schindler	• Advanced development, technology scanning & monitoring and development of software, cars, drives, safeties and system concepts, and corporate R&D in Ebikon (CH), Morristown (New Jersey, USA), Shanghai (P. R. China), and Sao Paulo (Brazil) • Module development and market-driven development take place at the decentralized sites: landing doors in Melun (F), sheet metal components in Mulhouse (F), electronics in Locarno (CH), hydraulic systems in Stockholm (Sweden) and Morristown (USA), gears in Zaragoza (Spain) • As of 2005, approx. 500 engineers in the R&D centers throughout the world
Siemens	• Research laboratory in the USA (Princeton). More than 2,600 people in the USA (of which 1,000 in software development) in year 2000 • Several development sites through high-tech company acquisition; significant increase of foreign R&D personnel. • Centers of European R&D in Austria, Switzerland, Italy, Belgium, France, Great Britain, Sweden • In Western Europe more than 5,500 people for software development alone in year 2000. R&D in Japan only with joint venture companies • As of September, 2004, approx. 45,000 researchers and developers at over 150 development centers in more than 40 countries around the world. The majority of the researchers and developers based in Germany (51.1%), USA (15.2%), Austria (6.8%), China (3.7%), France (2.8%), UK (2.8%), Italy (2.7%), Switzerland, India, Romania, Croatia and other (8.1%)

Table I.2.6. Major R&D sites of surveyed companies indicating size and research areas (listed according to industry, with number of people (p.) where data was available). (continued)

Electrical and Machinery Industries

Sulzer	• Research only in Switzerland (Winterthur); central research incorporated as an independent company (Innotech) • Divisional development in 45 sites in 12 countries; Centers in Switzerland, Germany, the UK, France, and the USA • As of 2005, employs approx. 120 p in R&D
United Techno-logies	• Central R&D in the USA (East Hartford) • Development in Spain (Madrid, since 1992), Germany (Aachen, since 1994) and Japan (To-kyo, since 1992) • In 2005, approx. 450 engineers worked in the R&D centers

Pharmaceutical and Chemical Industry

BASF	• Biotechnology research in Boston (USA) • Development in New Jersey (USA) • Materials development in the Netherlands and in Japan • In 2006, approx. 7,000p employed in the R&D worldwide.
Bayer	• R&D center in Germany (Wuppertal), Belgium: Merger of Bayer subsidiary Agfa Inc. with Gevaert (since 1964) • R&D sites in the USA: since 1954 (Mobay in Pittsburgh); Acquisition of Cutter Laboratories (1974), Miles Laboratories (1978) and Cooper Technicon (1989). Several R&D related involvements in the USA in the eighties. Biotechnology research in West Haven (since 198. 20% of total R&D budget and ca. 2,000 employees in the USA • Acquisition of Canadian Polysar's Rubber Division in 1990. Continuation of R&D after government intervention for foreign investment • R&D sites in Japan: Yuki Research Center; pharmaceutical research in Osaka (1990); Kyoto (since 1995)
Novartis	• Central research Basel (Switzerland), Vienna (Austria), Tokyo (Japan), Cambridge (UK), Emeryville, Palo Alto, Maryland, and Summit (US) • R&D units in Buenos Aires (Argentine), Kundl (Austria), North Ryde and Wentworthville (Australia), Sao Paulo (Brazil), 10 locations in Switzerland, Montreal (Canada), Barcelona (Spain), 4 locations in France, 5 locations in Germany, Mumbai (India), Bologna and Origgio (Italy), Shah Alam (Malaysia), Mexico City (Mexico), Enkhuizen (NL), Johannesburg (South Africa), Bromma and Filipstad (Sweden), Docking and King's Langley (UK), 7 locations in the US. • R&D centers in New Jersey (Oncology, Arthritis), Cambridge, Boston (Diabetes, Oncology), Horsham, London (Chronic Pain), Basel (FMI, Nervous system), Transplantation, Oncology), La Jolla (GNF), Vienna (Dermantology) and Singapore (NITD) • Since De. 2006, R&D center in Shanghai
Du Pont	• 1,350 p. at central facility, 2,780 p. in the US, 425 p. abroad. Total of 35 international sites, up from 25 in 1993. • Around 40 R&D and customer service labs in the US, around 35 labs in 11 other countries employing 1,500 people at the Experimental R&D center in Wilmington, DE.

Table I.2.6. Major R&D sites of surveyed companies indicating size and research areas (listed according to industry, with number of people (p.) where data was available). (continued)

Pharmaceutical and Chemical Industry

Eisai	• Research in the USA (Boston) and in the UK (London)
	• Clinical development mainly outside Japan
	• Research facilities in the US including Eisai Research Institute in Andover, MA. Eisai Medical Research Inc. in Ridgefield Park, new Jersey; Eisai Research Triangle Park facility in North Carolina.
Hoechst	• As for year 2000, R&D in 16 countries: in Western Europe (19% of R&D expenditures; in particular in France, but also in Austria, Italy, Great Britain and Spain), in the USA (20%) and in Japan (2%). Other foreign R&D through M&A in the USA and Western Europe
	• Capital holding in pharmaceutical company Roussel Uclaf (since 1974) and acquisition of US chemical company Celanese (1987) intensified R&D internationalization
	• Hoechst became subsidiary of Sanofi-Aventis group on 31 Dec. 2004.
Kao	• European central R&D in Germany (Darmstadt), Barcelona
	• R&D labs in the USA (Pittsburgh), Cincinnati, France, Spain, Taiwan, Germany, Indonesia, and Thailand.
	• Small R&D sites in Sweden, France, and Great Britain
	• Four research centers in Japan (Tokyo, Wakayama, Tochigi, Kashima), and 11 R&D laboratories in year 2000
	• Total of 300 researchers abroad in 14 locations as for year 2000
Roche	• Basic research in Switzerland (Basel) and in the USA (New Jersey)
	• Industrial R&D in the USA: Alameda, Nutley, Research Triangle Park, Palo Alto
	• In Europe: Great Britain (Welsyn Garden City, Belgium (Gent), France (Strassburg; Village-Neuf), Italy (Milan);
	• In Japan: Kamakura
	• Small R&D centers with special tasks and divisional development in all important markets
	• R&D centers in Graz (Austria), Mannheim, Penzberg (Germany), Basel, Rotkreuz (Switzerland), Alameda, Genentech, Indianapolis, Nutley, Palo Alto, Pleasanton (US), Chugai (Japan).
	• Approx. 5,829 researchers and developers in 2005
Royal Dutch / Shell	• In 2000: Westhollow, Texas (1,350 p.), Bellaire (550 p.), Amsterdam (about 1,390 p.), Oakville (150 p.), Calgary (130 p.), Hamburg (140 p.), Arnhem (250 p.), Louvain-La-Neuve (210 p.), Schwabenheim (190 p.), Grand-Couronne (270 p.), Berre (120 p.), Atsugi (190 p.), Sittingbourne (600 p.), Rijswijk (650 p.), Thornton (590 p.)
	• Total of 6,900 researchers
Schering	• HQ R&D in Berlin, Germany
	• R&D in the USA: Biotechnology in Richmond since 1991; acquisition of two biotechnology companies and a Shell site in Richmond; Wayne
	• Diagnostics research and development in Japan (Osaka)
	• Research centers at 9 sites throughout Europe, the US and Japan
	• As of year 2005, Collaboration partners – Research (8 partners), development (10 partners), marketing (3 partners), and production (1 partner)
	• Company was taken over by Bayer in Dec. 2006 and renamed to Bayer Schering Pharma AG

Source: Annual reports, company documents, interviews (1994 - 2007).

I.3 Foreign R&D in China

1 The Rise of China as a Destination of Foreign R&D

1.1 China's Innovation Potential

China has become a major destination for R&D related foreign direct investment. Since the second half of the 1990s, technology-intensive multinational companies (MNCs) have explored China as a location for their R&D activities. As a market of potentially 1.3 billion customers, market-related drivers used to be very strong.

Recent trends indicate, however, that foreign R&D laboratories in China are not only important vehicles for local market development but also increasingly important sources of locally developed technology. China has also build up an impressive record with respect to science and technology, and has become the third most R&D intensive country in the world, at least in purchasing power parity (PPP) terms (OECD, 2003).[12] Already in 2001, total R&D spending in China reached nearly US$ 60 billion PPP, third behind the United States and Japan only which had expenditures of US$ 282 billion and US$ 104 billion respectively, and ahead of Germany's US$ 54 billion. China had the second highest number of researchers in the world with 821,000, behind the 1.3 million in the US but ahead of Japan and Russia, with 650,000 and 490,000 respectively (Table I.1.11).

Since the opening of China in the 1980s Western companies transferred technologies to China for implementation in local manufacturing joint ventures. Only recently did they start to explore China as a platform for new product development. Structural and economic reforms, as well as a growing body of experience in managing intercultural R&D sites, have furthered this trend. In one of the earliest surveys, Xue and Wang (2001) identified 34 R&D units in China established by foreign MNCs by early 2000. In an aggregation of three different lists, the Chinese S&T Statistical Office identified 82 different foreign R&D labs in China in August 2002 (STS, 2003). This may still be underestimated: Motorola alone

---

[12] As mentioned earlier, PPP is an appropriate means to assess R&D expenditures and investments: R&D is best measured in output, not input. PPP in China is particularly questionable because a) R&D salaries do not follow the average goods basket (about 10 times the national average) and, b) half of R&D expenses are non-salary-related, and rent infrastructure, PCs, etc., are Western prices. Using PPP for R&D in China is thus not very meaningful. We therefore prefer the more traditional foreign exchange rate conversion.

# of R&D labs / year

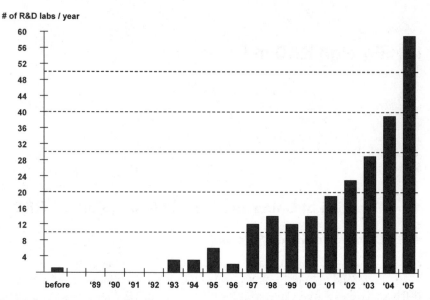

Fig. I.3.1. Number of new R&D labs in China set up by MNCs until 2005 (own data covering 463 R&D sites established up to 2005, some dates of set-up not reported).

lists 18 R&D units in China on its website in 2003, and had plans to open up 7 more (People's Daily, 2003). Ten more multinationals publicly announced new R&D centers in 2002 alone and more than a dozen in 2003 (with BEA Systems establishing its first and LG its largest foreign R&D site), while many other and smaller companies usually do not even advertise their Chinese R&D investments. Own research tracked the development of the growth of R&D in China, covering 507 foreign R&D centers in China (von Zedtwitz, 2004; von Zedtwitz et al., 2007). The latest Chinese Government figures are about 750 foreign R&D units. China has thus reached a number of foreign R&D laboratories that is second only to the US in a remarkably short period of time (Fig. I.3.1 summarizes the years of establishment for foreign R&D labs in China). Once labor, education and innovation conditions in China improve, we can expect foreign-based R&D to become even more significant.

2   How Important is Foreign R&D in China?

Despite the impressive growth figures of China in general and foreign R&D in particular, the realized amount of foreign R&D in China is still relatively limited. A quick calculation will give us an idea of the magnitude of the investment.

In 2004, China invested CNY 197 billion, or 1.23% of its GDP, in R&D. Of the expenditure, 66.8% was spent by enterprises, with three-quarters at large and medium sized companies. 23.1% of this amount was invested by foreign companies, including those from Hong Kong, Macau, Taiwan (together 8.1%) and other countries (15.0%). In other words, R&D spending by large and medium-sized foreign companies contributed about 11.5% of the total enterprise R&D spending in China. This is approximately comparable to what foreign companies spend on R&D in the US (15%). However, 11.5% of CNY 197 billion is CNY 22.6 billion, or about US$ 2.7 billion: hardly impressive given that Microsoft, Ford or Pfizer alone spend more than US$ 5 billion every year.

To cross-check this calculation, let us take the official number of 750 R&D labs, multiply this number with an estimated 50 researchers per lab (most labs are actually much smaller and only a few number into the hundreds), multiply the result with an average annual salary of US$ 40,000 per researcher (about one third of US levels) and multiply this by two (as salaries, on average over most industries, account for about 50% of R&D costs), we also arrive at about US$ 2.8 billion estimated annual R&D investments in China.

Foreign R&D spending in China is thus still small, but rising with the influx of more FDI (about one billion US$ per week), the national 10% annual GDP growth rate, and the individual expansion of foreign R&D centers in China in size and numbers. Thus, from a macro-perspective, foreign R&D in China is still in an early stage of its development.

3   Research on R&D in China

International R&D has been investigated more thoroughly in (and by) some countries than others (see table I.3.1). R&D management in China has gone largely unnoticed, partly due to difficulties in doing adequate research in China but also because China-based R&D had been limited in size and impact to the outside world (Fischer, 1983; De Boer et al., 1998; Li and Atuahene-Gima, 2001; Liu and White, 2001). There is very little systematic research on foreign R&D in China as this is a relatively new phenomenon. More recent research has been published by Greatwall (2002) and Walsh (2003). While the Greatwall report is written and published in Chinese for a Chinese audience, the report by Walsh reflects a strong US American perspective on international R&D in China. An earlier survey by Wu (2000) was published in Chinese only and did not focus on adding to our conceptual understanding of foreign R&D in China. Xue and Wang's (2001) report is an unpublished research memorandum based on a survey of 34 foreign R&D centers in China.

Building on this research, this chapter focuses on why China is so attractive R&D, and whether there is a particular domestic location predisposition. Also, how are foreign R&D established and managed? For this purpose, the research concentrated on extensive literature analysis focuses, a survey of 507 R&D centers of foreign multinationals in China, and almost one hundred semi-structured research interviews with R&D directors of wholly-owned multinational's R&D centers in China or those with a foreign majority ownership stake. The China-based R&D centers were identified through an exhaustive search using press re-

Table I.3.1. Literature on international R&D by geographic focus.

Focus	Key literature
General	Cordell (1973), Ronstadt (1977), Behrman and Fischer (1979), Hewitt (1980), Hirshey and Caves (1981)
Europe	Sweden: Hakanson and Zander (1988), Hakanson and Nobel (1993a and 1993b); Germany: Wortmann (1990); UK: Papanastassiou and Pearce (1996)
Japan	Westney (1993), Kenney and Florida (1994), Papanastassiou and Pearce (1994), Asakawa (1996), Odagiri and Yasuda (1996)
USA & Canada	Ronstadt (1977), Mansfield et al. (1979), Dalton and Serapio (1995), Dunning and Narula (1995), Niosi (1997)
P.R. China	Wu (2000), Xue and Wang (2001), Greatwall (2002), Walsh (2003), von Zedtwitz (2004), Gassmann and Han (2004)

leases, company websites, local industry associations, and professional publications. The data collected about these centers included at the very minimum R&D focus, location of the center, and ownership – to allow an overview of R&D activities in China – but often included more detailed information such as date of establishment, directorship history, program management, case studies etc. The origin of the 285 companies accounting for the 507 R&D centers represented in this chapter varied, both in terms of industry and geography, including 39 from Japan, 99 from Europe, 105 from the US, 23 from Taiwan, and 19 from other countries (mostly Canada, Korea, Hong Kong, India; see Table I.3.2). The principal research questions pertained to 1) Strategic mission; 2) Location reasons; 3) Lab establishment; 4) R&D director selection; 5) HQ-subsidiary relations; and 6) General management insights in China. All answers were captured in writing and written feedback was sought from the research interview partners; secondary and tertiary data sources were included as well. All in all, the intention was to fulfill Yin's (1988) requirements of data triangulation in case study research. The structure of this paper follows largely the outline of the questions presented above.

3.1   Mission and Mandate of Foreign R&D in China

Individual R&D units rarely have an absolute focus on either research ("R") or development ("D"): it is the nature of innovation to blend science, technology and market related efforts into a single direction. Nevertheless, R&D sites are usually established with a specific R&D mission and mandate to complement a perceived need in the parent organization—determining the R&D mandate is thus one of the first steps in establishing a foreign R&D laboratory.

After nearly two decades of technology transfer into local joint ventures, it has become more popular to establish wholly foreign-owned firms in China. Foreign firms now enter China for R&D with one of these three entry modes: 1) wholly owned independent R&D labs, 2) R&D departments or R&D activities conducted under a branch of a Chinese operation or within its joint venture with the Chinese partners, and 3) cooperative R&D with Chinese research universities and R&D institutes. Their principal missions include 1) to act as a linkage between China's specific market demand and technology of their parent company; 2) to act as an

Table I.3.2. National origin of some well-known companies with R&D in China.

Europe (99)	USA (105)	Japan (39)	Other (42)
Nokia, Ericsson, Bayer, Hoffmann-La Roche, Volkswagen, Firmenich, SAP, Schindler, Tetrapak, Electrolux, Unilever, Nestle, Alcatel, Novo Nordisk, Siemens, Philips	Microsoft, Motorola, Lucent, DuPont, Proctor & Gamble, IBM, Honeywell, Intel, UTC, Oracle, Dell, Hewlett-Packard, Sun, GM, Kodak, Agilent, Qualcomm, GE	Ajinomoto, Hitachi, Toshiba, Yamaha, Matsushita Electric, Canon, Toyota, Sharp, Sony, Fujitsu, Honda, NEC, NTT DoCoMo	Acer, Infosys, BenQ, Tata, Nortel, Merry Electronics, LG, Samsung

important part of corporate R&D; 3) to demonstrate their commitment towards the Chinese government. While these missions typically overlap in larger R&D labs, most units have clearly delineated missions, often in connection to specific goals stipulated by their corporate sponsors.

Although the mandates of most of these labs are clearly development focused, indicating support of local business and customers (China is among the top three markets in optical networks, mobile handsets, and elevators), not all development carried out in China is targeted at the Chinese market only. Several companies emphasized that their China R&D labs have worldwide mandates for some of their products and technologies. The rationale for moving world product mandates to China is also found in cost efficiency (e.g., salaries of Chinese engineers are still about one forth of US or European comparables). Inexpensive labor can also lead to R&D results faster, particularly if R&D work can be executed independently and concurrently. The dynamics in some industries in China (e.g., telecommunications) also speeds up time-critical feedback and prototyping cycles in the product development process.

Generally speaking, in China the best engineering graduates will seek work (or graduate studies) overseas, the second best will go after foreign companies or government careers. These second-best engineers are still of impressive technical competence and education. Furthermore, once trained by one foreign company (i.e., familiar with Western management methods and good command of English) they are very attractive recruits for other foreign companies with nearby operations. As a consequence, engineering expertise has reached high standards, particularly within foreign R&D units in China (and salary levels have risen as well).

"To become a well-respected R&D unit in China" is another frequent R&D mission. Image is important, and a good reputation helps recruiting local scientists and engineers. The local laboratory must therefore develop a clear technical competence that contributes to both the local community and the parent's international R&D network. Me-too product development is not the focus of such labs.

Local and global standards are also on the agenda. The Chinese culture and language are best explored and incorporated locally. Since China is a sizeable and fast developing market in many product categories, a technical standard established in China may have a good chance of becoming a world standard. For this reason, telecommunications firms work closely with technology standardization bodies both inside and outside China.

Thus, market proximity and technology competence are strong reasons for foreign companies to set up research and development in China, although intellectual property issues remain a concern particularly for non-public-domain R&D. Several R&D centers do not conduct indigenous technology R&D but rather focus on technology monitoring and corporate R&D representation. While these R&D units would not qualify as fully-fledged R&D labs by most interpretations, they are nevertheless part of the parent company's international R&D network and form a nucleus of future R&D investment.

3.2   Motivations to Set Up R&D in China

Most international R&D investments follow local market and customers, i.e. the need to develop more localized products. M&A is a major means to assimilate overseas R&D units. In an interesting contrast to common practices among developed countries, very few of the five hundred studied Chinese R&D centers were acquired by a foreign multinational: most of them are Greenfield investments.

Greenfield investments presuppose rational decision criteria. What are some of the main reasons to locate R&D in China? For R&D entry into a particular target country, five principal classes of drivers are considered: input, output, efficiency, political/socio-cultural factors, and R&D-external factors. Among the major input drivers are certainly the availability of scientists and engineers in China: 2.5 million students graduated from China's 3,000 universities and colleges including 14,000 Ph.D. holders in 2002 alone (Ministry of Education P.R.C., 2003). High-tech zones and science parks (such as Zhongguancun in Beijing) offer excellent and modern research conditions. Furthermore, many of them offer favorable tax and investment incentives. The major output drivers include image boosting of the parent's business in China: a Chinese R&D center improves the company's recognition both within the Chinese administration and the Chinese population. Product localization is also more effectively done directly in China particularly when the required know-how is only available in tacit form. Efficiency drivers are mostly related to costs savings in terms of salaries, although those must be counterbalanced with additional investments necessary to start and maintain an R&D site in China. Also, as more and more of the business is located in China, coordination of new product development with the distant headquarters would reduce R&D efficiency. Government policies, *guanxi* (the Chinese art of establishing and cultivating personal connections), subsidies, and the eagerness of Chinese engineers to put in long hours contribute to attractive social and political factors. Furthermore, the political stability of China is probably often underappreciated by the popular press but certainly a decision factor in strategic management of MNCs. Lastly, MNCs set up R&D in China because they believe China will constitute a major part of their business soon, if not yet already. Several well-know companies such as Volkswagen, ABB and Schindler already generate more profits and more sales from China than in their respective home countries.

3.3   Locations of Foreign R&D Units in China

Once a decision to set up R&D in China has been made, strategic management still has several options for locating R&D within China. For instance, the Greatwall (2002) report claimed (based on a total of 25 R&D labs) that Beijing was a preferred R&D site for IT companies and Shanghai for automotive and chemical companies. Our data shows that Beijing is also a place for telecommunications and electronics companies, while Shanghai attracts more food, pharmaceutical, and engineering companies (see Fig. I.3.2). In industries where central government involvement is still critical (telecoms, for example), or in industries where a concentration of engineering schools is critical (computers, for example), then Beijing is a natural choice. In other industries where style or fashion or taste is critical, Shanghai may be preferred.

Research prefers access to local scientific communities while development must be close to internal or external customers. These considerations play also a role in various regions of China, although several other factors influence the location decision. The two primary locations in China are obviously Beijing and Shanghai, with Tianjin (near Beijing), Suzhou (near Shanghai) and the Southern cities of Guangdong, Shenzhen and Hong Kong as second-tier R&D attractors. It is interesting to note that 82% of all foreign R&D sites are located along a relatively short (given China's geographic dimension) strip between Beijing and Shanghai, and 67% in Beijing and Shanghai alone.

Although China still attracts more development than research overall, it appears that R&D units with a research mission tend to locate themselves in Beijing whereas development laboratories choose a location in or in the vicinity of Shanghai. Although Shanghai has some excellent infrastructure and institutes for basic research, this city has a longer history of hosting foreign companies, and it is natu-

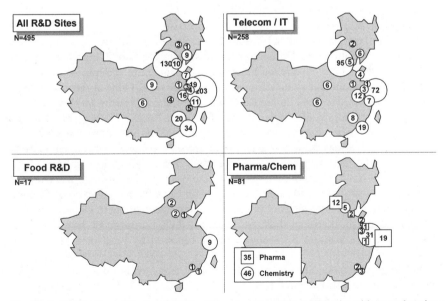

Fig. I.3.2. Distribution of foreign R&D in China, based on 495 R&D units with exact location data, separated for telecom/IT/software, food, pharmaceutical/chemistry industries.

rally that foreign companies established development units close to their first regional headquarters and production facilities. Expats and many educated Chinese also prefer to live in Shanghai, often cited as the most modern city in China. Crowding-out effects may be appearing in some industries, and salary costs are increasing as a consequence of Shanghai's attractiveness.

Beijing, on the other hand, offers location advantages for research-intensive R&D units. Beijing is home to almost 100 universities, the Chinese Academy of Sciences, and the Zhongguancun district, a high-tech zone with many R&D laboratories and start-up companies. Also, China is governed from Beijing, and thus a center of most standard-setting and decision-shaping bodies. Beijing also offers an attractive option for a second R&D site besides Shanghai, and then often the new research lab is to be removed somewhat from the faster-paced Shanghai labs.

3.4   Who Runs Foreign R&D Units in China?

If managing an international R&D unit is difficult, managing one in a culture and environment as distinct as China must be particularly difficult. This, incidentally, applies even to American-Born-Chinese who return to China as *haiguis* (Chinese abbreviation for "overseas returnees"). A director of a new R&D lab must possess certain skills that go beyond the leadership of an established lab, and these skills must work in the local culture. In addition to scientific or technological qualifications, this individual is also responsible for ramping up the local R&D organization and meet R&D performance targets in the context of China's fast-growth economy. 'Copy-Paste' approaches of existing Western R&D departments into a new business and science environment are not possible.

What people are selected to start up the Chinese R&D operations? This decision depends most importantly on the R&D mission and the intended degree of coordination between China and headquarters. Somewhat surprisingly, more than two thirds of the initial R&D directors in the sample were non-Chinese, and many had no or little China experience before being assigned to the job. Most of Chinese R&D directors had significant overseas experience. Only in rare cases local Chinese were hired to head up the R&D lab; often, these persons are then part of a local group promoting the initial proposal to start R&D in China. Most of the Chinese directors had significant overseas experience, or were born abroad.

Returning overseas Chinese are an important source of R&D managers particularly among US companies, and has increased in general for foreign R&D labs. Since the US has a large population of Chinese origin, either through work-related immigration over the past decades or the pursuit of study and education, US companies can draw on a larger pool of engineers and managers with Chinese linguistic and cultural background than, for instance, their European or Japanese competitors. Initial expatriate R&D directors are replaced by local or overseas Chinese.

While development sites were predominantly managed by expatriate directors, the picture is not so clear for research. Microsoft's research lab in Beijing was headed up by a Chinese director who had significant work and management experience in the US. Hitachi's research unit, however, is run by a Japanese, and one of Nokia's research labs, which had a dual mission of research and some development, was ramped up by a Finnish manager with marginal China experience.

What were the criteria for top technology management to select R&D directors? Whether in research or development, familiarity with the company's lines of business and strong internal networks were a clear advantage. Interest and dedication to an overseas appointment helped, as indicated for instance by previous work experience in the company's international R&D organization. Familiarity with Chinese culture and language was only a secondary criterion in most appointments. This may be explained by the larger share of development sites in the sample (development usually puts more emphasis on internal networks versus external scientific contacts), the lack of suitable bilingual/bicultural candidates, and the hesitation to assign directorship of critical technical and intellectual property to a local in a country that has a notorious reputation of uncontrolled knowledge diffusion.

Expatriates also assumed key roles as department heads or group managers. One of the interviewed directors said that "no-one should be hired outside the company without the group manager's input." Expatriate managers bring in their network to other business units, thus strengthening the project portfolio of the new R&D lab, particularly if it has a development or process focus. Locals hired too early may not be compatible with the group manager's expectations.

The managing director or COO of a lab, however, was generally a local Chinese. It would be nearly impossible for a non-Chinese to handle relations with local authorities and partners with the necessary cultural and interpersonal etiquette. After the initial buildup of a core group consisting of expatriate and local engineers, some labs aim to sustain further growth through on-site partnerships with local technology suppliers and collaborators. The foreign R&D labs thus created a virtual organization of technical partners around the core R&D unit. Managing such a network is preferably assisted again by the local Chinese manager and COO (for a more managerial discussion, see von Zedtwitz et al, 2007).

3.5   Coordination with Central R&D and Headquarters

There are several ways how the parent organization can coordinate and influence the R&D lab's management, and a rich literature exists on this topic. This contribution already mentioned the role of expatriate managers and experts who transfer company processes, routines and culture. What are other typical forms of coordination between the local R&D lab in China and the parent organization? What are some of the concerns and expectations at both ends of the organization?

Many R&D directors felt that there was too little support from headquarters during the startup of the R&D lab. Initial operations were started quite autonomously, except in cases where R&D was started from within existing offices. Some R&D directors reported difficulties from having to coordinate headquarter as well as local country head expectations. Technical support was usually provided by headquarters, and managerial support—if any—from the local country organization. Given that R&D centers are usually either corporate or divisional funded, there is room for disagreement over resources in the initial set-up phase, and potentially competition between country management and the corporate R&D headquarters. Initial R&D directors were thus ideally self-starters, "people who create something out of nothing." This is similar to the situation encountered by many startup entrepreneurs, except for a stronger financial support from headquarters.

At the operational level, it was critical for many labs to start out with projects that would attract good people and would also be completed relatively quickly. Building a reputation of success validated risky decisions made by top managers who had sponsored the local R&D lab. This meant that technology was not only transferred to China successfully, but also that new products or processes developed locally was to be used by internal customers and business units.

The amount of internal coordination and integration seems to be a matter of leadership style, culture, and previous experience. Good internal coordination, however, sometimes informal networking, seemed to be crucial to help an R&D lab off the ground. Other R&D units had formalized program and project management for HQ coordination. Coordination meetings with platform and program managers, sometimes as often as every two weeks, made sure that the new Chinese R&D unit was recognized as a new node in the international R&D network. Information and communication technologies such as computer-supported group work and intranets were of great help.

Performance measures tended to be focused on process phases or increasing result orientation. Project-based criteria such as meeting predetermined milestones (e.g., target headcounts and number of projects) and stage-gate were used to asses some of the R&D ramp-up accomplishments, and the relative unfamiliarity with the target country as well as the still emergent structures of newly started R&D labs led to many R&D units being evaluated differently. In the extreme case, headquarters had stipulated no other expectations than the complete transfer of a particular technical competence by a given year. R&D lab performance was evaluated in personal meetings between the R&D director and technology top management at headquarters, with the vice-president of R&D using his judgment and experience to asses the progress of the Chinese R&D unit. Patents, patent applications, papers and other output-related indicators of R&D performance were rarely used in these recently established R&D sites due to the expected time lag. A more frequently used criterion was the number of projects in relation to employees and their distribution over the expected technological expertise to be developed. In some cases, particularly in development units, team-based and project-specific measures were used to assess the quality of individual projects. Overall, however, the evaluation of initial R&D units was carried out with sensitivity to the particular early-stage nature of the R&D unit and the general unfamiliarity of the company in establishing R&D in China.

4 Differences in Management Styles

The Chinese have a very positive perception of innovation and technological advancement. Given the amount of technology transferred through foreign direct investment and local training programs, China is clearly interested to learn from the West. But is the West interested to learn from China? The answer is 'yes', if we understand research as a home-base augmenting function (in the Kuemmerle (1997) terminology). It is not clear how many of the foreign R&D units in China are dedicated to research only, but our data indicates that probably a quarter of them have a research and technology listening mandate to fulfill in addition to product development. In an earlier data set, 26 of 80 foreign R&D units had a focus on research, collecting local scientific information and developing technology locally, and passing these results on to other corporate R&D labs outside China (von Zedtwitz, 2004). The answer is 'no', however, if we assess prevailing attitudes and perceptions of Western managers towards Chinese science and technology. Currently, Western companies seem to be trapped in short-term profit maximization and bottom-line thinking. The key to succeeding in China is always based on a long-term strategy.

The emerging management literature on China is filled with examples on how to deal with the Chinese (e.g., Chen, 2001). Much of this work is relevant to the discipline of R&D as well. However, R&D is a particularly touchy subject for Chinese and Westerners alike, as until recently (a few hundred years ago) the Chinese have been of thousands of years one of the most technologically advanced civilization in the world, whereas the Westerner is proud of the technological achievements made over the past 300 to 400 years (e.g., Huff, 2003). The findings in this chapter underscore the sensitive nature between the technological self-understanding of the Chinese and the Western managers. As one Western expatriate R&D manager mentioned during this research, it is important to refrain from a colonial attitude when dealing with Chinese business partners. *Guanxi*, saving face and cultural sensibility are still important in China, but questions arise whether expatriate managers fall into two categories: those who insist on their own culture in China, and those who become overly adapted to Chinese thinking. There was some evidence in the research that Chinese managers were expected to adhere to Western style management and also got away with behaving relatively un-Chinese, while Western expatriates compromised perhaps too much on their Western values devoted much effort to pursuing China-style management. *Guanxi*—strategically understood—is not just helping day-to-day networking but also facilitates a company's long-term prospects by building good relations with local governments ('local citizen' role). The directors of Chinese R&D labs have to play important intermediary roles between the local Chinese culture and the prevalent culture in their parent companies.

Western managers also often expect assurances (as, for instance, in the case of intellectual property protection) which they are unlikely to obtain from their Chinese counterparts. There are two principal reasons: 1) China changes too fast to be reasonably predictable even for the Chinese, and 2) the Chinese culture tries to avoid sources of future conflict (when, for instance, a forced promise cannot be kept). Good honest personal relationships and networks help over difficult times: this favor is also extended to the genuinely interested Westerner. But this approach premises a long-term commitment by the foreign company.

5 Interaction with the Local Innovation System

The Chinese Government promulgated a policy that attracts foreign R&D investment to China. Interestingly, the presence of foreign R&D labs is not unanimously welcomed. Foreign R&D labs lure some of the best Chinese scientists to work for foreign companies with agendas benefiting primarily their own international business objectives rather than goals of possibly Chinese national importance. Also, Chinese high-tech companies disapprove of the foreign R&D labs greater attraction among highly educated young university graduates. Hence, foreign R&D is regarded very much as competition by the domestic high-tech industry.

But the migration of scientists is bidirectional: While the Chinese government may be worried that intelligent manpower is lost to foreign private industry, non-Chinese R&D firms are concerned about the uncontrolled dissipation of know-how to local competitors. However, the more foreign companies establish R&D sites with the mission to develop technology and do research locally (i.e., to learn and transfer knowledge from China to abroad), the less they are concerned with unwanted local spill-over, as in the worst case locally generated knowledge is lost back into the local scientific community. This argument, however, only holds for early-stage R&D where patents are not yet of concern. Stronger intellectual property rights and their consistent enforcement will certainly have positive effects on the interaction of foreign R&D centers with the Chinese scientific and engineering community.

Generally, there is a perception on both sides that the interaction between foreign and domestic R&D is not as strong as it could be (Wang, 2004; Yuan and Lu, 2005). To begin with, the dominance of foreign R&D in China is not as impressive in the international context as one would assume: R&D spending by large and medium-sized foreign-invested companies contributed only about 11-12% of the total enterprise R&D spending in China, despite the huge FDI inflow (this figure is close to the share of foreign R&D in the US). But the impact on domestic S&T seems to be less predictable than in the US. In China, foreign companies give significant attention to training (project management, creativity and innovation techniques, etc.), and the know-how passed on in training dissipates in often untraceable ways once R&D employees change jobs. However, when they seek other employers, many thus trained Chinese find work with other foreign companies, as they already possess much needed skills now. Hence, they may not go back into the domestic R&D community.

The general state of cooperation between foreign R&D labs and Chinese universities is still in its infancy, too. Only few universities have technology transfer or cooperation offices that facilitate cooperative projects through support of contractual agreements, licensing schemes, faculty specializations, etc. A widespread problem in university–R&D lab interaction is the difference between academic and industrial culture, although many Western R&D director found that Chinese universities had a stronger focus on applied sciences than Western universities. However, there are also linguistic difficulties as well as problems related to project management, at least in the view of the interviewed R&D managers.

Proximity to high-tech start-ups in China was an often cited reason to locate

R&D in Beijing, Shanghai, or one of the other technology-zones in China. Many high-tech start-ups have settled in High-Tech Development Zones (HTDZ), where they benefit from tax breaks (see also Chen and Shih, 2005). According to own estimates, there are between 6,000 to 8,000 start-ups in the telecommunications sector in Beijing alone (in HTDZs, university parks, incubators, and strewn across various parts of Beijing). However, it is not always clear what constitutes high-tech, and whether the scope of the R&D work is truly innovative or just an exploitation of a business model copied form elsewhere. Access to these start-ups is difficult as no consolidated listings exist, and certainly not with the necessary technological and business-relevant details included. Engaging with truly innovative high-tech start-ups is one of the reasons of presence of foreign R&D labs in China, but there is little evidence that this option is supported and exploited widely.

6 Managing Chinese R&D Staff

What can be learned from our other findings for the management of foreign R&D sites in China? Many of these insights tend to be general and not specific to R&D management. For instance, "face-saving" requires Western managers to be more sensitive towards their Chinese employees than they would be with most Westerners. Therefore management must respect certain ways of communication in order to win the respect, and eventually trust, of their mostly Chinese workforce. For instance, direct criticism, even constructive one, will not lead to better performance. Praise of accomplishments of peers will indirectly but more successfully change the behavior of underperformers.

Many R&D directors stated that they had shifted from a relatively open management style to more control and direction, partly because choice and responsibility for own action was not part of recent Chinese education and culture, partly because the recruited engineers tended to be young and at junior levels. This is in no disagreement with the observation that Chinese employees were more individualistic than expected and behaved more like e.g. their US counterparts than their Japanese colleagues, who value group achievement over individual performance. It could be argued that with China's rapid internationalization and adoption of more capitalist values individual expectations and cultural behaviors have changed. In this case, Hofstede's (1980) findings concerning China will have to be considered now with more caution.

As mentioned, foreign R&D units tended to be staffed mostly with young Chinese employees. For instance, the average age of the workforce at Ericsson's R&D lab was 27 years, and another R&D director was the oldest employee in his company at age 36. Perhaps these are indications of a new profile of expatriate management, which has so far suggested that seniority be preferred over youth in China. Although most expatriates were non-Chinese, there was a clear indication that most companies with a long-term strategy in China spend much effort to develop their local R&D directors. Additionally, some companies had started to build a pool of international R&D managers who have acquired important on-the-job lessons about starting overseas R&D operations previously and are now redeployed to start up laboratories in China.

Chinese engineers are very attracted to working in a foreign R&D lab because this experience serves them as a springboard into top positions in other companies in China, and offers them a possibility to obtain training or education in the US (for example), usually coupled with a US visa. These elements of intrinsic motivation must not be ignored by R&D directors; they are excellent leverage points for developing future leaders and highly skilled scientists. Lucent, for instance, has sent most of their newly hired engineers abroad for training. As a result, they now have a highly dedicated workforce that is competing to become Lucent's worldwide center in their chosen technological competence.

Employee turnover is of great concern to most companies investing in China, as it is often responsible for unwanted knowledge transfer and technology spillover to competing firms. Firms who exhibited low attrition rates (as low as 8% per year) reasoned that in addition to the reputation of working for a well-respected Western company they also offered very competitive salaries, exciting projects and good training opportunities. Good projects were important not only to maintain efficient R&D operations but also to get the new R&D site off the ground: this would attract the right people and also build the new R&D centers international reputation. The challenge is of course to have a new R&D organization going at full speed quickly. Experienced expatriates and visionary R&D directors are crucial in this process.

7 Conclusions and Outlook

This contribution focused on management issues of R&D sites of foreign technology-intensive companies in China. Most of these foreign R&D sites have been established in the late 1990s and early 2000s. Assuming that China continues its economic and societal transformation, and considering present trends in R&D internationalization in the US and Europe, we predict China will establish itself as the second-most populous country in terms of foreign R&D labs within a few years. More investments in R&D in China can be expected from the pharmaceutical/biotech industry, from mid-tech companies whose markets have moved to China (e.g., in the mining, construction and exploration businesses, and from suppliers whose main customers have set manufacturing operations in China and demand adequate technical and R&D support locally (e.g., automotive suppliers).

Few of the existing R&D laboratories in China have exploited their full potential yet, and most are still in the process of establishing themselves within the Chinese scientific and technical communities as well as within the company-internal R&D network. A quite large number of foreign R&D sites are engaged in research and technology development, indicating that it is time to revise the decade-old perception of China being merely a recipient of technology, and to consider her as an increasingly important source and provider of global technology. One of the great attractions of China, the presence of indigenous innovative high-tech start-ups and research labs, is still fairly underexploited by foreign R&D

units, partly because accessing them is difficult, partly because the level of inno-vativeness is unknown, and partly because of problems of interaction. The state of intellectual property rights and possible knowledge leakage are of great concern to corporate strategist, but taking from the rich is less frowned upon than taking from the poor. However, with China developing strong technological competencies and indigenous R&D reputation over time, Western and Japanese companies are well advised to take China into the international R&D equation.

I.4 Internal Drivers

„Globalization of R&D is typically accepted
more with resignation than with pleasure."
Arnoud De Meyer and Atsuo Mizushima, 1989

1 Five Organizational Concepts of International R&D Organization

The amount of R&D units outside the parent country has grown considerably during the last two decades. Local know-how and technology access, as well as proximity to customers and local markets have been the major drivers. Internationalization has taken place mainly by establishing greenfield R&D sites, expansion of R&D capabilities in local subsidiaries, or acquisitions of local companies or companies with local R&D sites.

Deliberate internationalization of R&D has often been neglected in favor of international expansion of sales and production. As long as international R&D in a company was a minor phenomenon, top management had to deal with more urgent problems. With many companies now spending a considerable share of their R&D budget overseas, they are more concerned with the efficient allocation of their international R&D resources. But their R&D managers still find little conceptual guidance in organizing international R&D. Only few procedures for managing cross-border R&D processes have become widely accepted, and their application is often problem-centered and industry-specific.

To begin with a framework for international R&D, what is missing is a clear typology of organizational concepts of international R&D. International R&D offers the opportunity to exploit competitive advantages, but their optimal utilization depends on the appropriate organizational setting. The multinational companies that we investigated in our research (some of which are described in detail in this book) provide proven as well as novel answers and solutions on how to realize this potential.

Our literature analysis shows that the examination of organizational trends in R&D has focused to international R&D taxonomies,[13] but a truly comprehensive

---

[13] See e.g. Cordell (1973), Ramstad (1977), Behrmann and Fischer (1980), Pearce (1989).

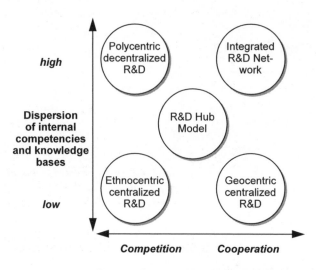

Degree of cooperation between R&D sites

Source: Gassmann (1997a: 49).

Fig. I.4.1. Five concepts of organizational design can be distinguished by analyzing the degree of cooperation between R&D sites and the dispersion of internal competencies and knowledge bases.

model for organizational change in R&D organization has not been achieved.[14] In order to consider both stabilizing and progressive forces in international R&D, we looked at different structural and behavioral approaches to organizing R&D on a global scale. Combining the work of Bartlett (1986) regarding MNCs and the work of Perlmutter (1969) concerning basic behavioral patterns of MNCs we classify international R&D organization into five organizational concepts (Gassmann and von Zedtwitz, 1999):

- Ethnocentric centralized R&D,
- Geocentric centralized R&D,
- Polycentric decentralized R&D,
- R&D hub model,
- Integrated R&D network.

These concepts differ in the distribution of internal competencies and knowledge bases and the degree of cooperation between R&D sites (see Fig. I.4.1 and Table I.4.1).

We identified a general trend towards more cooperation and more decentraliza-

---

[14]   Recent research in this area includes De Meyer (1993a, b), Grandstand et al. (1993), and Pearson et al. (1993), which have been further refined by e.g. Chiesa (1996a), Kuemmerle (1997a), and Medcof (1997).

Table I.4.1. Five ideal forms of international R&D organization.

Configuration	Organizational structure	Behavioral orientation
Ethnocentric centralized R&D	Centralized R&D	National inward orientation
Geocentric centralized R&D	Centralized R&D	International external orientation
Polycentric decentralized R&D	Highly dispersed R&D, weak center	Competition among independent R&D units
R&D hub model	Dispersed R&D, strong center	Supportive role of foreign R&D units
Integrated R&D network	Highly dispersed R&D, several competence centers	Synergetic integration of international R&D units

tion of R&D. Although the pace and intensity of this trend differs between companies in each industry as well as between industries, effectiveness and costs considerations apply to most R&D-intensive MNCs. They are forced to continuously align their international R&D activities with their overall integrated network concept. In the following sections we describe each concept in more detail and illustrate it with examples from our research sample. Also, we explain what organizational trends we observed in the investigated companies. Finally, we attempt a cost-based explanation for what drives international organizational R&D evolution.

2 Ethnocentric Centralized R&D

In the *ethnocentric centralized* R&D organization, all R&D activities are concentrated in one home country. It is assumed that the home country is technologically superior to its subsidiaries and affiliated companies in other countries, a notion which also defines the asymmetrical information and decision structures between home base and peripheral sites. Central R&D is the protected „think tank" of the company, creating new products which subsequently are manufactured in other locations and distributed worldwide (e.g. Toyota in UK, Volkswagen in China). The core technologies, which ensure long-term competitiveness of the company, are guarded as a „national treasure" in the home country base.

Besides effectively protecting against uncontrolled technology transfer, this concept demonstrates high efficiency due to scale and specialization effects. It is a rebirth of Schumpeter's assumption of increasing returns to scale in R&D, which results in low R&D costs and short overall development times. An efficient R&D unit therefore requires a certain critical mass of capital and personnel. Physical collocation of R&D employees, standardized management systems and a common understanding of R&D vision and values promote the flow of information between scientists at the R&D center and facilitate the control of R&D activities (Fig. I.4.2).

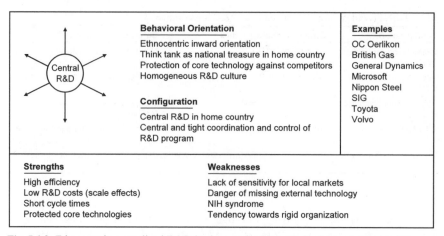

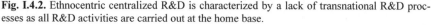

Fig. I.4.2. Ethnocentric centralized R&D is characterized by a lack of transnational R&D processes as all R&D activities are carried out at the home base.

The main drawbacks of ethnocentric centralized R&D are:

- Lack of sensitivity for signals from foreign markets and foreign technology trends;
- Insufficient consideration of local market demands;
- Not-Invented-Here syndrome for results from R&D in other companies; and
- Tendency towards a rigid organizational structure (Quinn, 1985).

An MNC should choose this organization only if it goes for global products and does not consider differentiating between regional markets. The success of Microsoft shows that centralized R&D can be highly competitive and successful both at home and abroad when competencies and resources are abundant in the home country and a truly global product is accepted by the customers. If the company manages to establish a dominant design (Utterback, 1994) on a worldwide basis, then an explicit international orientation of R&D appears unnecessary.

If the market (global or domestic) has traditionally been served from a central location, the company must have extraordinary motives to locate R&D outside the immediate range of operations. As a company in the heavy industry, Nippon Steel came under enormous competitive pressure from low-labor-cost economies. The company has four corporate research laboratories near Tokyo (about 1,000 researchers) and R&D units at seven steelworks (about 150 researchers) supporting the factories and performing customer-related tasks. Local development units serve as interfaces between the steelworks and the central R&D laboratories (see Fig. I.4.3). Corporate R&D was centralized in order to improve communication and to share the use of costly facilities. Plant engineers and researchers communicate easily about plant layouts and achieve cost reductions (the plant engineer's interest) as well as new products (the researcher's interest). New processes, materials and chemicals are introduced at the group level.

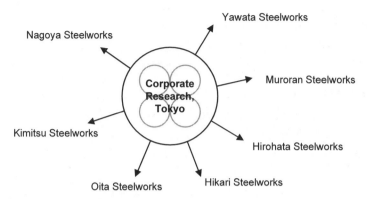

Fig. I.4.3. Ethnocentric centralized R&D at Nippon Steel in 1999.

Steel making is a highly complex procedure requiring the continuous improvement of process and handling know-how. It is very difficult to establish a new plant abroad due to the large plant investments and the difficulties in technology transfer on the one hand, and due to working conditions on the other hand. Steel production is less attractive for highly industrialized countries, where technological knowledge is abundant. Unfortunately, protectionism is high in developing countries because the first steps into industrialization usually start with the heavy industries. Thus, even though Nippon Steel engaged in business partnerships through technical and financial cooperation, it continued to conduct all R&D centrally in Japan (see also Herbert, 1990, Kimura and Tezuka, 1993). The company also diversified into other domains of research, such as information technology, life sciences, and chemicals. For instance, in 1994, only 55% of all R&D expenses were invested in the traditional steelmaking research, and 45% were assigned to R&D for 'new businesses'. In the 2000s, Nippon Steel also conducts R&D in materials, energy, and the environment.

3   Geocentric Centralized R&D

The ethnocentric configuration becomes inappropriate when a company becomes more dependent on foreign markets and local competencies. The *geocentric centralized* model overcomes the home base orientation of the ethnocentric approach through a multicultural and multinational work force while retaining the efficiency advantage of centralization. This requires appropriate investments in training and recruiting R&D personnel to increase their international awareness. At the central R&D site, knowledge of worldwide external technologies is accumulated and the sensitivity of R&D employees for international markets is increased. It helps to send R&D employees abroad to collaborate and engage with local manufacturing, suppliers and lead customers. International awareness can be further improved by recruiting foreign engineers with work experience in foreign cultures (Fig. I.4.4).

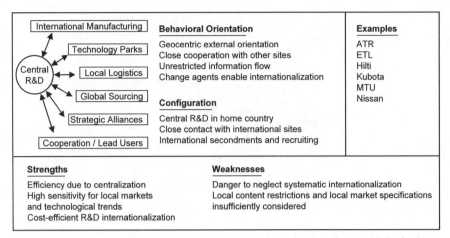

Fig. I.4.4. A geocentric R&D organization overcomes the lack of market sensitivity by interacting closely with international partners.

Nissan has successfully implemented the geocentric model in the early nineties. In the development of the Primera automobile, targeted for the European market, Nissan formed a core project team in Western Europe. Back in Japan, this team was supported by some hundred engineers who all had experienced European culture during numerous visits. Primera was the first major market success for Nissan in Western Europe (Fig. I.4.5).

Kubota, a Japanese company with four central R&D laboratories, established a technology development headquarters to ensure company-wide coherence of all R&D carried out in five divisions. As R&D activities differ from division to division, formalized coordination between all R&D units can be quite complex. Kubota therefore relies on indirect means of coordinating R&D: The exchange of R&D personnel, also at the manager's level, fosters cross-functional collaboration. Kubota has no international R&D locations, as its main business takes place in the

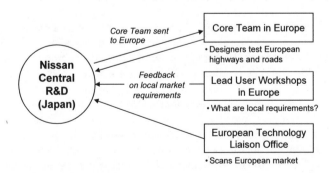

Fig. I.4.5. Nissan's Primera development.

domestic market. Strong linkage is emphasized between the home-based R&D organization and global production sites, which develop new markets. A computerized information network covering the entire corporation rationalizes corporate processes and accelerates the innovation process, integrating researchers worldwide.

Geocentric centralized R&D offers a simple way to somehow internationalize R&D without giving up the advantage of physically centralized R&D. The implementation requires a reorientation of values and behavior of home-based R&D personnel. Change agents within top management having intercultural experience and interests are needed to push for international orientation of all employees.

4   Polycentric Decentralized R&D

Ethnocentric and even geocentric organizations often fail to recognize crucial local requirements such as local codes and market requirements. This deficit is overcome by the *polycentric decentralized* R&D model which is prevalent in companies with strong orientation towards regional markets (typical for many European MNCs in the 1970s and 1980s). Their foreign R&D laboratories have evolved from local distribution and manufacturing units, mainly in order to respond to customer product localization requests (Fig. I.4.6). The organizational structure is characterized by a decentralized federation of R&D sites with no corporate R&D center supervising the internationalization effort. Information flow between foreign sites and the home base is limited, reports on current R&D activities are often late.

The R&D director of a subsidiary in a polycentric decentralized R&D organization reports to local management. This organization is characterized by high autonomy and little incentive to share information in early project stages with central R&D. Efforts to preserve autonomy and national identity impede cross-border coordination, and therefore lead to inefficiency on a corporate level and duplicate R&D activities. The company runs into the difficulty of losing focus on given technologies. It is even more difficult to achieve technology convergence.

Many foreign R&D units of multinational firms were rather inadvertently acquired as a by-product of international M&A activity (Cantwell and Mudambi, 2005), so that in many multinational firms, cooperation between different R&D units that do not share a history of collaboration is difficult (Criscuolo and Narula, 2006). While a successful innovation network configuration theoretically involves recognizing where the innovation value resides in the network and developing capabilities and mechanisms to understand and access such value, practically, this is problematic for firms embedded in their own base of knowledge and patterns of relationships (Perks and Jeffery, 2006).

In 2000, Royal Dutch/Shell spent almost US$ 700 million on R&D carried out by 12 research establishments all over the world. At that time, the four elements to Shell Research were the research coordination in London and The Hague, the Shell Group Laboratories, the Shell Oil Research Organization, and operating company laboratories. All group laboratories reported directly to the Shell Group

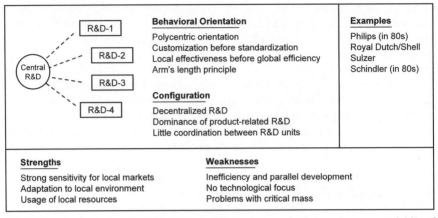

	Behavioral Orientation	Examples

Fig. I.4.6. Polycentric decentralized R&D organizations are created through merger activities of the parent company. The major challenge is to overcome the isolation of formerly independent R&D units and to integrate them into a wider R&D network.

research coordinator, whose tasks were comprised of coordination and planning of research activities (Fig. I.4.7).

Both threats and opportunities of Shell's R&D organization can be exemplified in the development case of Carilon, a multiple-application polymer discovered in the Amsterdam R&D center, then transferred to a Belgium R&D laboratory and eventually to the Westhollow Research Center in Houston between 1984 and 1997. Duplicate R&D and Not-Invented-Here syndromes had to be overcome to reach the decision of moving Carilon R&D to Houston, as USA was the eventual target market. What was characterized as „the most poorly managed project" in the company's history, became eventually known as the first multinational product development at Shell. The decision to give one R&D center the lead and the introduction of a market development unit turned the polymer into a success story for Shell Chemical Company. In retrospect the multi-site configuration was more an asset than a problem, especially in the commercialization phase. Carilon succeeded because entrepreneurial business spirit eventually overcame technology orientation, secrecy problems and difficulties in process technology development.

The polycentric decentralized R&D configuration is the „dying model" among the five forms of international R&D organization. Although the benefits of extreme market orientation are clear, most MNCs feel the pressure to reduce R&D costs. The emergence of distinct capabilities at each site, corporate-wide technology strategies, and the elimination of redundant development activities requires the proactive coordination of R&D units; hence the polycentric decentralized configuration gives way to hub or network-like structures of organization. However, most companies find themselves in polycentric R&D configurations after mergers of near-equals, or during transformations from a holding-structure to more integrated corporate management.

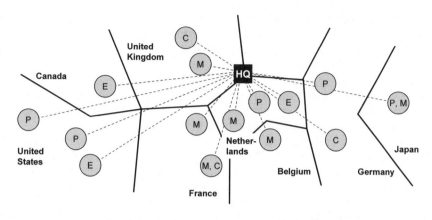

P: Oil and chemicals products and processes   M: Materials, fuels and plastics
E: Oil and gas exploration and production   C: Crop protection and environmental studies

Fig. I.4.7. Shell's international network of R&D units.

5   R&D Hub Model

The R&D *hub model* with its tight central control reduces the risk of suboptimal resource allocation and R&D duplication. Former Ciba-Geigy's Head of R&D François L'Eplattenier maintained that „only those who know how to control R&D from their home base know how to manage an international company strategically." The R&D center in the home location is the main laboratory for all research and advanced development activities, establishing a worldwide lead in most technological fields. Foreign R&D sites are confined to designated technological areas; they usually start as technology listening posts. The R&D center tightly coordinates decentralized R&D activities by means of an R&D framework program and resource allocation. This model guarantees an efficient technology transfer and permanent technical assistance. A central R&D unit may be formed as a legal entity to own all the technological knowledge and intellectual property (Fig. I.4.8).

The Research and Technology Department of Daimler-Benz (which later merged with Chrysler), one of the largest industrial groups in automobiles and transportation, had its corporate research center in Stuttgart, Germany. Five other locations in Germany were integrated into corporate research through acquisition of the parent company or internal reorganization. Starting in 1995, Daimler-Benz established local R&D presence outside Germany. R&D internationalization was driven by two factors: search for centers of innovation and market proximity. The Research and Technology Center in Palo Alto was located near major information technology companies near Stanford University in Silicon Valley. Thus, as early as 1997, Daimler-Benz introduced a prototype car dubbed 'internet multimedia on wheels', integrating latest communication technologies to operate an automobile as a node in the internet network. The car was linked with the Internet and was able to transmit as well as receive information from the Internet. The Research Center India was established in Bangalore in order to be present in this region of high software productivity, when India's software industry grew by 40% annually. Daimler-Benz not only expected substantial input for its multimedia, telematics and manufacturing solutions, but also considered Bangalore as a bridgehead for gaining access to local subsidiaries and the Indian industry (Fig. I.4.9).

The second internationalization factor was to locate R&D close to the market. In Shanghai, a joint research laboratory was established to support the microelectronics subsidiary Temic in electronic packaging. These R&D activities were tightly coordinated with microelectronics research in Germany, and scientists were exchanged between China and Germany on a regular basis. Already in 1996, the Vehicle Systems Technology Center in Portland supported the US-American Freightliner subsidiary. The aim was to introduce local market specifics early in the product development process particularly in automotive system technology. Another research focus was on human factors engineering. The Portland center was coordinated with automobile research in the German headquarters and other international R&D sites.

The four foreign R&D centers were also responsible for local technology monitoring. In Russia and Japan, where Daimler-Benz was not present with research centers of its own, this task was assigned to designated listening posts. Their agenda also included technology scanning, initiation and coordination of research cooperation, and the establishment and maintenance of scientific networks.

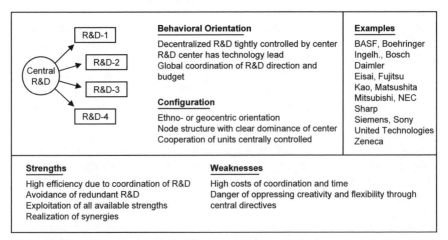

Fig. I.4.8. The R&D hub model is usually a reaction by centralized companies to the internationalization of resources. As the decentralized R&D units evolve and gain proficient know-how in their respective technology area, the hub model is superseded by a network organization.

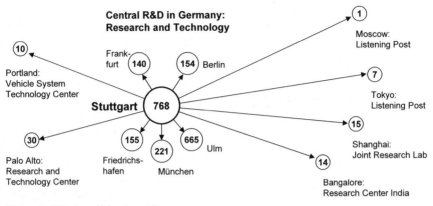

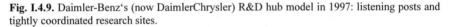

Fig. I.4.9. Daimler-Benz's (now DaimlerChrysler) R&D hub model in 1997: listening posts and tightly coordinated research sites.

Another example with an R&D hub organization is the United Technologies Corporation, a high technology company in the aerospace, building systems and automotive industries. The corporate research center UTRC (United Technologies Research Center) is located in East Hartford, Conn., from where the international R&D activities are coordinated. Development is decentralized in competence centers, most of them in the US, as well as some in Japan and Europe. UTRC operated small outposts in Germany, Spain and Japan, to facilitate access to local talent and resources. Another rationale for local presence was proximity to the market and to local universities and other research institutes. Since access to technological knowledge external to the company is crucial for sustaining continuous innovation, UTRC encouraged intensive networking, conferencing and bilateral research contacts. Foreign UTRC units served as bases for local UTRC researchers to convey technological information back to central research in East Hartford. One of the main tasks of UTRC was to realize synergy effects from a multitude of technological competencies for further exploitation in product development at UTC's business units (e.g. Pratt&Whitney, Otis, Sikorski).

The advantages of the hub model rest in the quick recognition of local demands and the sustaining integration of global R&D input. The innovativeness of the company is reinforced by the exploitation of the dispersed competencies and the variety of inputs. The main drawbacks are found in the rising costs of coordination and time as well as the increased danger of suppressing creativity, initiative and flexibility in decentralized R&D sites by central directives.

A critical success factor of the hub model is the size of the foreign R&D units: On the one hand, each unit must be large enough to ensure a critical mass of operation, on the other hand, it must not exceed an upper limit at which the risk of redundant activities is too large (see Kuemmerle, 1997b for an analysis of laboratory size and its determinants). The management systems of all R&D sites should be compatible, as intensive information flow between the center and the decentralized R&D units must be ensured. The center has to maintain sufficient competence to be accepted as the technology leader and to coordinate all worldwide activities effectively.

6   The Integrated R&D Network

The full exploitation of competencies in locations dispersed all over the world is hardly possible in an MNC through a set of bilateral treaties between a dominant center and peripheral units. The classical dyadic center-subsidiary relation is re-interpreted in the *integrated R&D network* model. Domestic R&D is no longer the center of control for all R&D activities, but rather one among many interdependent R&D units which are closely interconnected by means of flexible and varied coordination mechanisms (Fig. I.4.10).

Each unit in the network specializes in a particular product, component or technology area, perhaps a set of core capabilities. Sometimes this unit takes over a lead role as a competence center. This unit is then responsible for the entire value generation process, not just for product-related R&D. A unit is assigned a 'world product mandate' (Pearce, 1989) if it holds exclusive rights to manufacture and market a product, and if it agrees to carry out all the necessary R&D activities. This company knows best about potential markets and application areas for this product, being responsible for the coordination of product generation and worldwide market introduction.

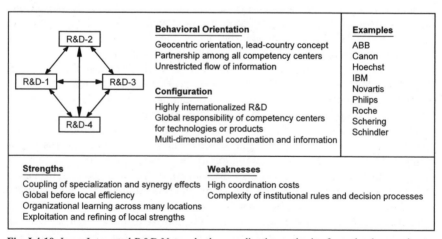

Fig. I.4.10. In an Integrated R&D Network, the coordination authority for technology and component development is allocated based on individual strengths and capabilities of R&D units. Transnational projects are a significant component in this organization; high standards of collaboration and coordination are required.

When products are created in one location but exploited in another (e.g. in a distribution or manufacturing site), the company faces a taxation problem. Technology creation activities induce costs at the R&D location, while the technology exploiter makes a profit. According to the arm's length principle, affiliated companies and subsidiaries are to be treated as legally independent companies. They have to purchase know-how and technology for a justified transfer price. If these transactions do not follow open market conditions or do not reflect actual costs, they can be subject to a tax correction. The decision on an R&D location is thus often influenced by a controller's taxation considerations and less by technology or environmental advantages (Braun, 1994).

This situation gets even worse if R&D is heavily subsidized through state-funded programs or large national programs. After the home country paid for the creation of new technologies and knowledge, the MNC is in position to transfer the knowledge into low-tax countries where technology can be exploited without paying no or very low taxes.

A third difficulty arises from the time lag between expenditures and revenues in all R&D activities: this is one of the reasons why in many companies very much R&D is still coupled with big manufacturing units. The returns from products sold by local companies who at the same time pay for manufacturing offset the expenses for R&D. Since R&D expenditures are only a small fraction of overall production costs, the rationale for the eventual location follows manufacturing rather than innovation reasons, which leads to sub-optimal location conditions for R&D. The whole legal unit nevertheless achieves a financial break-even point and keeps tax payments at a minimum. Tax and property rights issues thus have a strong impact on the R&D organization.

The network organization is able to overcome the tax problem which appears e.g. in the polycentric configuration. All R&D units sell their technology to a central technology company which gets its revenues through technical assistance fees, royalties and lump sums from the manufacturing units. Nestlé perfected this model: In 1997, Nestlé's R&D network consisted of 15 research centers and 21 R&D units in 10 countries, running an annual R&D budget of over half a billion Swiss Francs. Most of the R&D locations were acquired during the market-oriented expansion of the company. Each of the research centers specialized in a particular technology area. In 2000, the coordination of worldwide activities and the identification and exploitation of synergies was managed by less than 20 people who resided in the legally independent R&D company called Nestec. Besides R&D coordination, Nestec also took care of technology and know-how transfer and looked after technical service for the globally dispersed production sites. Each of the about 300 production sites entered a license contract with Nestec for services and the usage of the Nestlé trademarks, with Nestec being the legal owner of all Nestlé technologies (Fig. I.4.11).

Nestec shared its know-how with group companies through a technical assistance agreement. When entering into such an agreement, Nestec's partners had access to R&D results, norms and quality standards, and a considerable stack of industrial know-how, including the assistance of qualified specialists and R&D support for market introduction. Nestec also offered professional development and

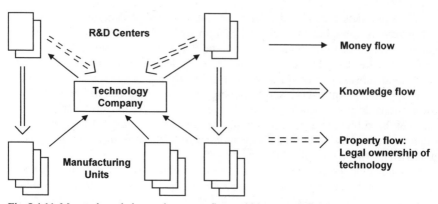

Fig. I.4.11. Money, knowledge, and property flows within a tax-optimizing technology-intensive company such as Nestlé.

management training. This ensured a common corporate culture integrating the traditions, mentalities and cultural differences of more than 3,000 employees from 60 countries around the world.

Schindler Lifts (the worldwide leader in escalators and second in elevators) started to establish a competence-based R&D network in 1996. Schindler's rapid expansion was based mainly on acquisitions. Its R&D was therefore dispersed over several units in Switzerland, France, Spain, Sweden, Brazil and USA. In order to avoid duplication and to realize synergy, its management identified and analyzed core competencies in R&D. These core competencies and the change from a functional organization (i.e. software, mechanics, electronics) to a module-oriented organization (i.e. drive, control, hoistway, car) were the basis for a major reorganization of R&D in 1998. In the new organization, R&D activities were conducted in three areas: corporate R&D, manufacturing R&D and field operations engineering. Each R&D area had its own mission; the efficient cooperation of these areas in a highly interdependent network was a prerequisite for the low cycle-time development of advanced product systems (Fig. I.4.12).

In contrast to the hub model, foreign R&D units in the integrated R&D network assume strategic roles for the entire company: A competence center should not only act as a sensor for possible change in its area, but should also engage in defining strategies and business development. Although polycentric decentralized R&D units may also establish local competencies, the R&D network makes sure that their skills and knowledge are best leveraged for the benefit of all R&D units. Various companies, among them Nestlé and Philips, moved from a polycentric decentralized organization towards an integrated R&D network, thus increasing global efficiency of their R&D. The pharmaceutical industry is also characterized by a consequent development towards the competence-based organization. Pharmaceutical giants such as Bayer, Hoffmann-La Roche, Novartis, Hoechst and Schering assign their R&D centers clear missions.

The integrated R&D network requires a change from simple control structures

Corporate R&D

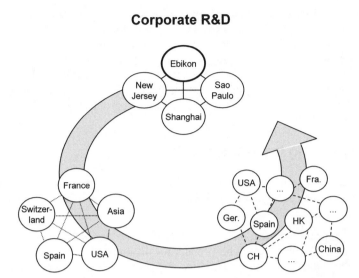

Manufacturing R&D   **Field Operations Engineering**

Fig. I.4.12. Schindler develops its competence-based R&D network in order to overcome a polycentric decentralized organization of R&D locations.

to a set of complex coordination structures. In particular, the role of the central R&D site changes from a control center to an R&D unit with equal duties and some coordination lead. Flexible connections and relations between network partners allow better usage of available competencies, realize specialization as well as scale effects, and reduce the risk of parallel development. Multi-site projects pose an ideal forum for task-oriented resources, while their temporary character reassures their flexibility. Although the coordination of R&D projects and the management of information flow requires tight control, this control is not exercised by a central R&D unit for the sum of all projects, but for each project by one of the (decentralized) competence centers.

Two principles are vital for the R&D network: Subsidiarity and moving centers of gravity. Subsidiarity is the principle that defines the relationship between one R&D center and the other centers: Whatever can be managed by the decentral units is not taken care of in the center. The center of gravity is allowed to move for projects and core capabilities: Whoever knows best, takes over the lead.

In the integrated R&D network, the role of the R&D sites and the involved individuals should be defined anew for each project. The scope of perspective and interorganizational flexibility is supported by career paths that offer not only vertical but also cross-functional and horizontal assignments. Learning processes are initiated by institutionalized as well as sporadic exchange of information and experience. These learning processes are facilitated by special coordination, especially if these processes are spanning several locations. The coordinators promote intensive flow of communication between all nodes of the network. A central staff department (e.g. central project management at Bayer) must ensure that project management tools (manuals, design guides, ICT support, PM systems, etc.) are in all R&D departments, as this ensures efficiency through standardization and routinization. The role of such standard operating procedures is significant for the success of international R&D activities („standardized problem solving").

7   Organizing International R&D

The organizational form of R&D is not rigid but subject to continuous change. Five principal trends of organizational change have been identified in our research (Fig. I.4.13).

Trend 1:   **External orientation**: Many companies with centralized R&D start internationalization with product localization. They have realized that their R&D processes have to be aligned better with international (sales or procurement) market needs. In order to incorporate expertise from foreign centers-of-innovation, the R&D center is opened to external information and feedback. This trend of cultivating foreign sensitivity is particularly strong in the automobile industry.

Trend 2:   **Establishing listening posts**: Companies establish listening posts in areas of technological expertise around the world. Tapping of foreign technology and knowledge bases becomes an important source of know-how. The effort of many large Japanese companies in building up basic research laboratories in Europe is a part of establishing a network of tightly controlled R&D units. An example of this trend is Hitachi with its research centers for information science in Dublin and for microelectronics in Cambridge. The exploitation of synergies between coordinated R&D sites becomes more important.

Trend 3:   **Empowerment of foreign R&D**: Due to increasing competencies and technological strengths of decentralized R&D units, companies that up to recently exerted rather tight central control over their R&D sites grant more autonomy and empowerment. The competencies and technological strengths of the R&D units increase, as they are assigned a strategic role in the R&D network This improves flexibility and generally fosters creativity in local units. Information flows freely, and each site follows a defined R&D mission.

Trend 4:   **Integration of decentralized R&D sites**: Company growth based on mergers and acquisitions and strong local R&D capabilities often result in relatively autonomous R&D units. If they recognize the benefits of integration and interconnection of their R&D activities, centers of expertise are created and mechanisms for international R&D coordination are introduced. For example, General Motors created competence centers for each component group such as its engine development in Rüsselsheim. As a result, duplicate R&D occurs less often, and a clear technological focus can be set.

Trend 5:   **Re-centralization**: Integrated R&D networks are implemented in some truly global companies. Pressures of focus and costs reduction force companies with an integrated R&D network to concentrate on a small number of leading research centers and a re-centralization of decision in few competence centers. The goal of this consolidation is to better exploit scale effects and to improve the coordination of worldwide dispersed R&D activities by reducing the amount of parallel R&D and intensifying network-internal cross-border technology transfer.

How do we explain the trends towards the integrated R&D network which we have observed in the international R&D organization in the examined companies? The search for an optimal organization has been discussed in several theories of the new institutional economics: Property rights (Coase, 1937), principal agency (Ross, 1973), transaction costs (Williamson, 1987), as well as new combined approaches such as the consideration of different knowledge types and their organizational costs (Jensen and Meckling, 1996). These approaches could serve to explain the trends towards the integrated R&D network. For our discussion we focus on those organizational concepts with dispersed R&D and decreasing degrees of central coordination: the R&D hub model, the integrated R&D network, and polycentric decentralized R&D.

For simplicity we assume a given number of R&D sites. In Fig. I.4.14 we have depicted and aggregated the major cost drivers for organizing decentralized R&D

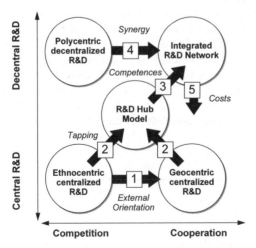

Source: Gassmann (1997a: 61).

Fig. I.4.13. Five major trends drive the evolution of R&D organizations.

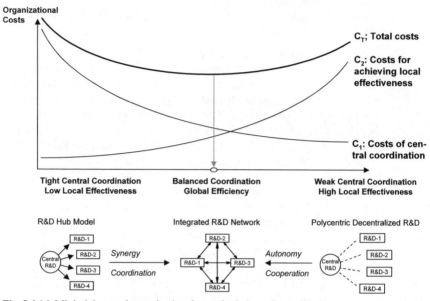

Fig. I.4.14. Minimizing total organizational costs by balanced coordination.

activities in two cost curves: One for costs of central coordination (C_1), the other for costs of achieving local effectiveness (C_2). The relative height and shape of the curves are only a rough estimate because they also depend on a number of secondary cost drivers as well as company-specific characteristics. The shape of the two costs curves is concave because of increasing marginal costs of central coordination, and increasing marginal costs of effectiveness and duplication.

Tight coordination leads to costs of central coordination C_1. The principal factors are transactions costs in the widest sense, costs of maintaining a sophisticated information system, and opportunity costs of ignoring local market requirements and not exploiting local resources. Strong local market orientation leads to costs of achieving local effectiveness C_2 which consist of duplication costs due to „reinventing-the-wheel" and unintended parallel development, costs due to subcritical mass such as fixed costs for infrastructure and administration, agency costs resulting from conflicts of interest in cooperative behavior, and opportunity costs for the lack of know-how spill-over and synergy between the R&D sites (see Fig. I.4.15).

It is important not to confuse the combination of the two main cost aggregates. These costs are, after all, total economic costs, not direct monetary costs. Clearly, the costs of coordinating an integrated network is much higher than the costs of coordinating a number of essentially dyadic relationships between the center and foreign R&D units, as it is in the hub model. The compilation of the typical cost drivers in the two cost curves results in average cost intensities for central coordination and achieving local effectiveness.

Transaction costs

\+ Costs for maintaining a sophisticated information system

\+ Opportunity costs for ignoring local market requirements

\+ Opportunity costs for ignoring local resources

\= **Costs of central coordination (C_1)**

Duplication costs due to parallel development

\+ Costs due to sub critical mass

\+ Agency costs resulting from conflicts

\+ Opportunity costs for the lack of know-how spill-over

\= **Costs for achieving local effectiveness (C_2)**

Total Costs = $C_1 + C_2$

Fig. I.4.15. Costs of central coordination and costs for achieving local effectiveness.

The total costs of organizing decentralized R&D is minimal where the sum of the two cost aggregates C_1 and C_2 is minimal. It appears that the total costs C_T are lowest in the integrated R&D network which is characterized by balanced coordination and effectiveness with leveraged competencies.

Management has to be aware that the strategic shift from one organizational concept to another, i.e. from the polycentric decentralized or the hub model to the integrated network, is influenced by different factors. It is

- determined more by careful consideration of opportunities and risks than by the output of a mathematical formula which gives hints about cost-optimization;
- rather driven by external decision parameters such as the organization of the entire corporation, the development of the information technology infrastructure, or by political interests;
- more of an evolutionary character than a discrete quantum leap.

The trend towards more centralization within the integrated R&D network can also be explained if we drop our initial assumption of a fixed number of R&D sites. The costs of coordination are correlated to the number of sites in the R&D organization. The more the R&D sites need to be coordinated, the higher are costs of central coordination (e.g. due to maintaining organizational coherence), and the higher are costs of achieving local effectiveness (e.g. due to less economies of scale). The reduction of R&D sites naturally necessitates a recentralization of control within the international R&D organization.

8   Conclusions

From the investigated companies we derived the following five concepts which differ in organizational structure and behavioral orientation:

- Ethnocentric centralized R&D;
- Geocentric centralized R&D;
- Polycentric decentralized R&D;
- R&D hub model; and
- Integrated R&D network.

Within these concepts we observed five major trends:

- Orientation of R&D processes towards international markets and knowledge centers;
- Establishment of tightly coordinated technology listening posts;
- Enlargement of autonomy and authority of foreign R&D sites;
- Increased integration of decentralized R&D units;
- Increased coordination and re-centralization of R&D activities into fewer leading research centers in order to improve global efficiency.

The trends towards the integrated R&D network can partly be explained by the minimization of total organizational costs. In the entire sample we identified a clear trend towards the presence in a few but leading geographical areas. These regions stand out because of excellence in technological innovation or because of their role as lead markets. Simultaneously, a large number of companies strive for an enhanced exploitation of synergy between decentralized R&D locations. Global efficiency prevails at the costs of local effectiveness.

The search for optimal balance between coordination and control is reflected in hybrid structures and intermediary configurations detected in some of the investigated companies. Since changes in behavioral orientation are a lengthy process, successful quantum leaps in multinational R&D organization are next to impossible.

These trends further increase the significance of transnational R&D projects. They represent an invaluable tool to handle multi-site coordination, the reduction of duplicate R&D efforts, and the realization of synergy effects. With the rapid development of new information and communication technologies it is expected that the costs of coordinating decentralized R&D will further decrease. The importance of R&D internationalization and global knowledge creation processes for competitive advantage will therefore further increase for technology intensive multinationals.

I.5 External Drivers

„ The key to good R&D management is the linkage between R and D.''
Jim McGroddy, VP IMB Research, 1997

1 Four Archetypes of Externally Driven R&D Internationalization

In the previous chapter we have outlined trends and evolutionary patterns for international R&D organization based on internal distribution and allocation of R&D resources. As we will describe in Part II, the contracted term "R&D" beguiles us into disregarding the inherent differences between research and development. The necessities of science, compared with the needs of engineering and development, entail different managerial problems (see e.g. Leifer and Triscari, 1987). Differences between research and development in terms of location rationales and work culture effectuate different geographical distribution and concentration in different regional centers. In this chapter, we present a model of R&D internationalization that focuses on external sources of knowledge as well as the exploitation of home-based-generated but locally implemented forms of knowledge.

Research and development sites of the same company are not necessarily collocated. For instance, AstraZeneca operates research as well as development units in the United States. One of their research units in Waltham, Massachusetts focuses on Infectious Diseases. Since there is no complementary development in the US, their research findings are transferred to a development laboratory in Sweden. Of IBM's ten principal international R&D locations, only the Tokyo site maintains both research and development in the same building. Similar separation of research and development can be observed at ABB, Hewlett-Packard, Canon and others.

This separation of R and D has important consequences for the quality and extent of collaboration within R&D. Furthermore, it flies in the face of efficiency and streamlining programs. So, why do we see this separation of research and development, even though the prevailing view R&D processes should be as integrated as possible? What are the factors that influence the differences in internationalization between research and development, and what managerial difficulties emerge from this phenomenon?

The decision where to establish new R&D units is made by senior technology management, usually in consultation with representatives from the central R&D, strategy and business departments. This decision considers R&D-specific factors such as the quality of input at the new site (through tapping local talent, engaging in local scientific cooperation, etc.), the quality of expected output (cooperation with local customers and local development, market proximity, etc.), and the general operating efficiency (critical mass, project hand-over, costs issues, etc.) of this R&D unit (as outlined in Part II). The decision is also affected by R&D-external factors, such as tax optimization, reliability and stability of the local political and social system, and image enhancement.

The literature on the global differences between research and development is still somewhat patchy. Mergers and acquisitions distort the picture of R&D expansion based on internal growth. Ronstadt (1978) noted that about a quarter of all R&D investments that he had studied were incidental through M&A activity of the parent company, and none of these acquisitions had pursued with the intent to gain access to the organization's R&D resources (see also e.g. Pausenberger and Volkmann, 1981; Håkanson and Nobel, 1993). Most contributions that distinguish between research and development management neglect the international dimension (e.g. Eldred and McGrath, 1997a,b; Iansiti 1998). Knowledge transfer and diffusion have been identified as a major management challenge in international R&D contexts. Kuemmerle (1997) and Chiesa (1996) suggested models of R&D organization that center around the knowledge creating and transferring capabilities of R&D laboratories.

Based on our own research on 81 companies representing 1021 R&D sites, we first identified two principal drivers that were responsible for natural R&D internationalization: the quest for external science and technology and the quest for new markets and new products. These gave rise to four archetypical forms of international R&D organization (von Zedtwitz and Gassmann, 2002a; Fig. I.5.1):

- *National Treasure* R&D: Domestic research and domestic development;
- *Technology-Driven* R&D: Dispersed research and domestic development;
- *Market-Driven* R&D: Domestic research and dispersed development;
- *Global* R&D: Dispersed research and dispersed development.

Most of the 81 R&D organizations that we studied fall clearly into one of these four categories: 'National Treasure' R&D accounts for 10 companies, 'Technology-Drive' for 7, 'Market-Drive' for 42, and 'global' for 19. As noted above, special circumstances in the process of R&D internationalization give rise to inconsistencies and hence a less-than-100% fit with the proposed categories. In total, three R&D organizations were hard to assign to one of the four archetypical forms. In these ambiguous or unclear cases, international R&D was either not determined by either science or market access, or the drivers for internationalization were too mixed to warrant a discernible classification. Wherever we observed strong substantiation for either market or science access, we categorized accordingly. The following four case studies illustrate the effects of these drivers on the management of R&D internationalization.

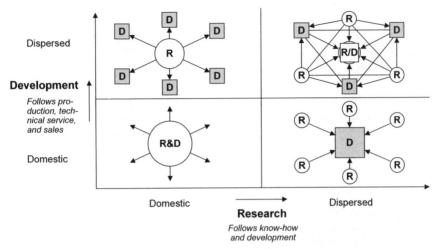

Source: von Zedtwitz (1999: 251).

Fig. I.5.1. Four archetypes of R&D internationalization on the basis of external drivers.

2 National-Treasure R&D: Domestic Research and Domestic Development

The R&D organization with both research and development at the home base is called the 'National-Treasure' model. R&D is kept at home because core technologies are easier to control or critical minimum mass is important (see e.g. Patel and Pavitt, 1992). There is little R&D at the international level, although important technological advances may be monitored from home via local representative offices and international patent scanning. Companies with a National-Treasure R&D organization are either in a strong dominant design position in its main technologies or their principal market is domestic. Neither requires much adaptation for foreign markets. R&D management is ethno- or geocentric, with foreign experts usually limited to advisory or consulting roles. The home-based management style is viable as long as technological dominance can be maintained.

The Japanese machinery company Kubota owned a strongly centralized R&D organization (see Fig. I.5.2). Kubota established a technology development headquarters to ensure company-wide coherence of all R&D carried out in four central R&D laboratories and 49 R&D units in five divisions. All central R&D laboratories and most of the R&D units were located in the Osaka-Kyoto area (central Japan). Kubota invested about 4.5% of its sales in R&D, and 15% of this amount was reserved for technology development. About 430 researchers were employed in the central R&D laboratories, and some 1,600 R&D engineers worked in plant and factory-based R&D units.

Kubota:
- US$ 8.0bn of sales in 1998
- Work force of 15'000
- 17% international sales
- 4.5% R&D/Sales
- no international R&D
- R&D staff about 2'000

49 R&D units in 23 plants/factories in the five divisions of:
1. Housing Materials & Materials
2. Environmental Control
3. Farms & Industrial Machinery
4. Materials
5. Pipe & Fluid Systems

Four central R&D labs:
1. Advanced Technology Laboratory
2. Technology Development Laboratory
3. Computational Research Center
4. Electro-Technology Center

Source: von Zedtwitz and Gassmann (2002: 576).

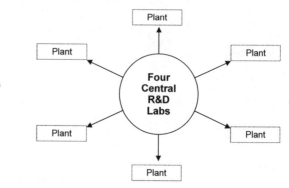

Fig. I.5.2. Kubota's National-Treasure R&D organization.

Kubota had no international R&D locations since the domestic market was still dominant. However, strong linkages existed between global production sites and the home-based R&D organization, since the production sites were a principal provider of new market needs and customer feedback. A computerized information network connected the entire corporation, rationalizing corporate functions and accelerating the innovation process by giving employees worldwide access to Kubota researchers and their work. Kubota thus engaged in a variety of international research and development projects while retaining the efficiency advantage of centralization.

3   Technology-Driven R&D: Dispersed Research and Domestic Development

In 'Technology-Driven' companies, research is more internationalized than development. Access to local centers-of-scientific-excellence and the relative scarcity of scientific personnel at home drives a substantial share of the technology identification and creation process abroad. Development remains centralized because of a number of factors, including scale effects in the development process (e.g. establishment of technology platforms, access to specialized testing equipment), proximity to central control and decision making, protection of commercial results, synergy effects (e.g. improved communication in during the innovation process, technical cross-fertilization), or the high information and coordination costs associated with international R&D projects. These centralization factors are less important in research as long as the scientific results are easy to communicate to the R&D center and the mission of each research lab is sufficiently focused.

Xerox is a good example of a company with a strong focus on technology (see Fig. I.5.3). Over the past decades, the document processing industry has been substantially affected by electronic and information technologies. As a result, Xerox Research – which was originally modeled along the lines of earlier centralized research organizations – was gradually decentralized (see our Xerox case in this book). There were five research sites worldwide: Webster, New York; Palo Alto, California; Mississauga, Canada and two locations in Europe: Grenoble, France, and Cambridge, United Kingdom. Each site had a specific research focus and was strategically located to leverage area industry and academic competencies relevant to that region and research focus. Research and Technology Development at Xerox was centrally managed under the Corporate Research and Technology group with direct line-of-site to the CEO. Corporate Research and Technology had an average annual headcount of 1,320; about 80 of which are in Europe.

Technology centers developed and delivered new technology to business groups. Although management of the technology centers was centralized, resources were located as to align with the development groups and manufacturing sites they delivered to. The three primary technology centers had offices in El Segundo, California; Webster, New York; and Palo Alto, California. Engineering was found mainly in the same locations: Product development teams were geographically collocated with the primary manufacturing sites serving their respective product markets. The largest manufacturing site was in Webster, New York

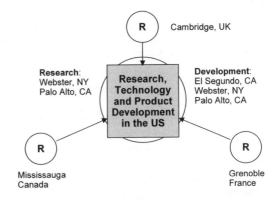

Xerox:
- US$ 18.2bn of sales in 1997
- Work force of 92'000
- 65% international sales
- 5.8% R&D/Sales
- Research staff about 1'320

R&D Organization:
- Research:
  Centrally managed but strategically located to leverage area industry and academic competencies.
- Technology Development:
  Centrally managed but collocated with manufacturing sites they deliver to.
- Engineering/Product Development:
  Management is decentralized and teams are collocated with primary manufacturing sites.

Source: von Zedtwitz and Gassmann (2002: 577).

Fig. I.5.3. Xerox's Technology-Driven R&D organization.

responsible for approximately 65% of Xerox manufactured end products. The second largest manufacturing site in the United States was El Segundo, California. Although there were no manufacturing facilities in Palo Alto, California, this site was the third largest development center in the United States. Development in Palo Alto focused primarily on software product development.

4   Market-Driven R&D: Domestic Research and Dispersed Development

Companies with highly dispersed development and little internationalized research have typically followed the call of the market; therefore they constitute the 'Market-Driven' model. Business development is dominated by customer demands and not by scientific exploration. Research is of low significance in the overall R&D effort and is kept at home to retain critical mass. Technology monitoring is carried out from home or in association with local development groups. The benefit of conducting research internally is often questioned, and research is under pressure to provide added value to product development and new business creation.

R&D at Schindler, a worldwide leader in elevators and escalators with a turnover of over 8 billion Swiss Francs, was characterized by the market-driven paradigm (see Fig. I.5.4). Schindler's core mission was to be a global service company with strong customer orientation. In this industry, it was considered crucial to respond to regional customer requirements such as codes, standards and passenger behavior. Many of the company's 45,000 employees worked in technical service or in direct customer contact. On the other hand, Schindler had to realize global synergies in product innovation.

In order to combine global efficiency with local effectiveness, Schindler organized R&D around three levels:

- Corporate R&D was responsible for system engineering, development of key components and breakthrough innovations. This R&D took place mainly in Ebikon (Switzerland), Morristown (New Jersey), Shanghai (China) and Sao Paulo (Brazil). A special department of Corporate R&D, 'Technology Management' was responsible for advanced development, technology monitoring, competitor analysis and strategic technology management, with the principal location in Ebikon and minor outposts in Morristown and Shanghai.
- Manufacturing R&D was collocated with the component factories. Being responsible for incremental product improvements, these activities were located in Spain (Zaragoza), France (Mulhouse, Melun), Switzerland (Locarno), USA (Gettisburgh, Sydney), Malaysia (Ipoh) and China (Shanghai).
- Field Engineering was responsible for customized solutions, including local adaptation of the elevator to specific customer requirements. These engineering activities were conducted at every large field organization distributed over the 100 countries in which Schindler is represented.

These three levels enabled the organization to make best possible use of its com-

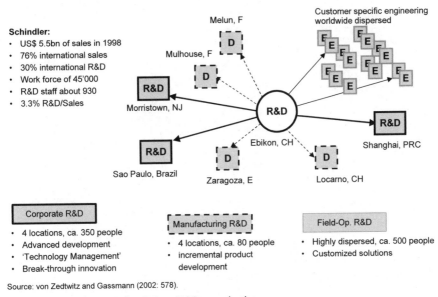

Source: von Zedtwitz and Gassmann (2002: 578).

Fig. I.5.4. Schindler's Market-Driven R&D organization.

petencies. Synergies and platform concepts are brought in through Corporate R&D, while local solutions were found locally near downstream activities. Recently, Schindler also showed signs of more and more technology-driven internationalization. The systematic internationalization of Corporate R&D and the establishment of innovation outposts for technology management indicated that Schindler was heading towards a global R&D organization.

5   Global R&D: Dispersed Research and Dispersed Development

Finally, 'global' companies have distributed research as well as development worldwide. These companies aim for global coordination of their R&D activities; most of them feature integrated R&D networks. Centrifugal forces have become stronger then centralizing forces. Research is located where there is high-quality scientific input expected from centers-of-excellence. Development labs conform to local demands and standards. The additional costs of maintaining transnational R&D are offset by the creation of business and market advantages. In global R&D networks, local science can be quickly absorbed and adapted for utilization elsewhere; and single development centers can take the lead to prepare products for global market launch. Managing R&D in this environment is significantly more complex and more costly than in the traditional R&D organization.

Global R&D organizations have been established, for instance, in the highly

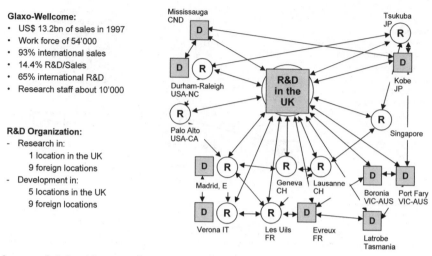

Glaxo-Wellcome:
- US$ 13.2bn of sales in 1997
- Work force of 54'000
- 93% international sales
- 14.4% R&D/Sales
- 65% international R&D
- Research staff about 10'000

R&D Organization:
- Research in:
    1 location in the UK
    9 foreign locations
- Development in:
    5 locations in the UK
    9 foreign locations

Source: von Zedtwitz and Gassmann (2002: 579).

Fig. I.5.5. Glaxo-Wellcome's global R&D organization.

competitive pharmaceutical industry. Headquartered in the UK, Glaxo-Wellcome had a 4.72% share of the US$ 275 billion global pharmaceutical market in 1998. It was the second largest pharmaceutical company both in Europe and the US, with market shares of approximately 5% and 6% respectively. In 1998, 7 of its products were in the world top 50. As a pharmaceutical company, Glaxo-Wellcome identified disease areas of unmet medical need and determined mechanisms by which they might be addressed, mainly through developing and registering new medicines. Created in 1995 by the merger of two major companies, Glaxo-Wellcome's R&D was distributed around the world (see Fig. I.5.5). Principal sites for R&D were Stevenage, Greenford and Ware in the United Kingdom; Research Triangle Park and Palo Alto in the USA; Tsukuba Science City, Japan; Verona, Italy; Les Ulis, France; Madrid, Spain; and Mississauga, Canada. Research locations focused on special areas. The two major research centers in Stevenage, Hertfordshire UK and in the Research Triangle Park in North Carolina covered the widest range of research areas. They were supported by smaller locations focusing on e.g. antimicrobial and anti-fungal research (Madrid), bioinformatics (Geneva), or disease models (Lausanne) and the Affymax Research Institute in Palo Alto, California, which was engaged technology development in screening and combinatorial chemistry.

6   External Forces and Trends

Operating with constrained resource availabilities in R&D (budget, manpower, etc.), management will prioritize its efforts as to how and when to internationalize

R&D. Two principal *external* location drivers are dominant:

- *Access to local markets and customers*: If forces of local markets and customer compliance prevail, the company will develop a decentralized development structure.
- *Access to local science and technology*: If critical scientific knowledge is globally dispersed, international research outposts will be established to feed back technological information to development.

Because of resource and capacity constraints, this R&D internationalization will follow either trend 1 or trend 2 (see Fig. I.5.6). Once the R&D organization has reached - driven by either of the two principal internationalization factors of access to science or access to market - a satisfactory mode of operation, the respective other factor may prevail in extending R&D internationalization further. This leads to four principal trends of internationalization in research and development:

Trend 1:   **Internationalization of Research**: If the company has no or limited access to science from its home base, it may have to establish local research units which directly tap into scientific communities, centers-of-innovation, and local talent pools. This is often the case when the company's R&D center is located in a country with strong engineering but relative scarce scientific research capabilities (e.g., Daimler between 1988 and 1996, Canon between 1988 and 1992, and Eisai).

Trend 2:   **Internationalization of Development**: If the company's business requires local product adaptation and intensive customer cooperation, it is likely that local development units are established that deploy and implement technology created at the R&D center. Foreign markets

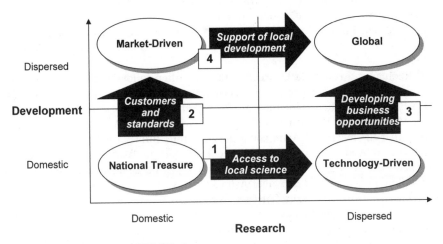

Source: von Zedtwitz and Gassmann (2002: 581).

Fig. I.5.6. Principal determinants and trends in internationalization of research and development.

have become more important than the domestic market. However, the main technological inputs originate at the home base (e.g., Leica in the 1980s and 1990s, SAP and Unisys in the 1990s).

Trend 3:   **Development follows Research**: In science and technology-driven industries, development units may bring prospective new business opportunities from research to the market. These development units are often located close to the local research site and characterized by high personnel and infrastructure integration. However, their organizational structure and their reporting lines are different (e.g., Canon between 1993 and 1998, and Xerox in France recently).

Trend 4:   **Research follows Development**: The evolution of local development sites and the necessity to provide more substantial research support locally may result in the on-site establishment of research units. In the strive to establish competence-based R&D networks, local development units become exclusively responsible for a particular technology and hence must acquire the necessary research capability to support subsequent development and maintenance of this technology (e.g., Schindler between 1997 and 1999).

Only corporations with large resources to spend on R&D, or companies in which strategic imperatives override a more reasonably timed and staged expansion, will internationalize both research and development simultaneously. They often do so in separate research and development organizations. For instance, IBM internationalized research around the same time as development, establishing a fairly independent research organization (IBM Research) and retaining development in the IBM business units. IBM Research has followed trend 1, while development at IBM followed trend 2. In the 1980s and 90s, IBM developed an integrated R&D network by aligning worldwide R&D activities and guiding both R&D organizations towards the 'global' model. A similar development took place at Hewlett-Packard and Philips. In general, however, resource constraints and industry requirements will tip the balance towards one of the two major internationalization trends.

Reorganizations of R&D structure (as they often follow mergers and acquisitions of the parent companies) may seemingly lead to a reversal of above trends. Cost saving and the exploitation of synergy effects being a principal motivation for M&A activity, redundant R&D units are closed down or collocated. For example, after the merger of Astra and Zeneca, Astra's former Rochester, New York, lab was moved to a newly established R&D site in Waltham, Massachusetts, which also integrated R&D activities from Zeneca's development unit in Wilmington, Delaware, and two other Astra sites in Worchester and Cambridge, Massachusetts. However, AstraZeneca's overall investment in R&D in the United States was maintained or even expanded, since other R&D units in Sweden and the U.K. were being cut in staff simultaneously.

Similarly, a strategic initiative to strengthen corporate research and development at Schindler has led to a reduction of research sites. These sites, however, were not eliminated but—except in one case—moved to the supervision of business units as their work has become increasingly product-oriented. Hence the significance of international development has been improved, giving corporate research the flexibility to concentrate on strategic investments in technology development in China.

Such events can be seen as corrections to 'jungle-growth' internationalization in R&D. They are aimed at reducing the costs of conducting R&D both domestically and abroad, improving local effectiveness of development (e.g., project management constraints and synergy-building) and global utility of research (e.g., economies of scale and platform/competence management).

7   Differentiating the Four Archetypes

7.1   *International R&D Models Revisited*

In the previous chapters, we described an internally-driven model of R&D internationalization. Other management researchers have come up with similar structures. Kuemmerle (1997), for instance, looked at the role of individual R&D sites and distinguished home-base-augmenting laboratories (with the objective to create knowledge and then transfer it back to a central R&D site) and home-base-exploiting laboratories (commercialize knowledge by transferring it from the company's home base to the laboratory site abroad). Chiesa (1996) discerned between experimentation and exploitation structures within the same R&D organization.

The four archetypes are a concept based on external factors driving R&D internationalization. Comparing it with the internally-driven model, the 'National-Treasure' companies appear to fall within the geo- and ethnocentric paradigm, the 'Technology-driven' companies relate best to the hub-model, 'Market-driven' companies follow typically polycentric R&D internationalization, and the companies denoted here as 'global' companies are found to be either striving for integrated R&D networks or retain a polycentric decentralized R&D configuration.

What is different in our two models is that they describe not only static R&D organization but also how and why they evolve over time. While many models deepened our understanding of a multitude of different location factors for individual units, we have summarized these factors and concentrated on two principal external drivers that affect the development of the R&D organization as a whole.

How can we explain the emergence of the four archetypes? Let's look at the most promising candidates: ethnic/cultural background of their decision makers, geographical-cultural origin of the companies, differences on science/engineering focus with R&D.

7.2   *Differences by Geographical-Cultural Origin*

It was as far back as the 1980s that Perrino and Tipping (1989) noted that European companies were more aggressive in establishing foreign R&D outposts, often through the acquisition of entire firms, than their American counterparts. Japanese companies relied on home–based development, licensing and listening posts to acquire technology rather than overseas R&D.

European companies are characterized by the 'Market-Driven' model mostly because of their need to seek outside markets to attain scale economies, and relative ease of establishing development units within the European continent. Intra-European internationalization of accounts about for half of the total R&D internationalization in our R&D location database of more than a thousand sites. Of 352 R&D locations in Europe, 133 R&D were owned by companies form other European countries. If they were not considered as international R&D sites, Europe would be left with 30 research sites from extra-European companies, and 95 development sites, or just about half of their previous rate of internationalization.

Due to their large home markets and their strength in domestic research, many American companies have been found to adhere to the 'National-Treasure' paradigm. Japanese companies too focused on the 'National-Treasure', partly because of the domestic market but also because their liability of foreignness – coupled with preference to keep outposts under close control – has made it more difficult for them to "feel at home abroad" (Matsuo, 2000). Only fairly recently did many American companies engage in the 'Market-Driven' approach, due to the rising relative importance of foreign markets. Japanese companies are internationalizing as well, but rather due to their relative weakness in domestic research. Instead of R&D following manufacturing, many Japanese companies have chosen to internationalize research first in order to prepare the ground for local development and manufacturing. This constitutes the 'Technology-Driven' paradigm. With the relatively strong emphasis on technology implementation in Japanese companies, cultural and social factors like tight personal networks and narrowly meshed company interdependencies have made it difficult for them to establish productive development centers outside Japan.

Similar regional attributions for 'global' companies are difficult to make. Only few Japanese companies so far have established significant overseas presence in both research and development. A number of European and US companies have spread research and development evenly in dominant regions around the globe. 'global' R&D is thus less likely determined by geographic provenience but rather by maturity of an internationally dispersed R&D organization.

7.3   *Differences by Industry*

The 'Market-driven' paradigm is the most prevalent and obvious way of R&D internationalization. It is pursued in almost all industries, and is particularly strong in electrical, machinery and chemical companies. In these cases, technology platforms developed at home are the bases for local product development. There appears to be little need for elaborate international research networks.

Internationalization of development occurs more naturally as a consequence of internationalization of sales and local market support. Therefore, there are relatively few examples where research is more decentralized than development. It appears that some pharmaceutical and electrical companies internationalize research before development, following trend 1. The pharmaceutical industry appears to be the most internationalized in research: it operates about one foreign research site for every foreign development unit. In fact, most of the 'global' R&D organizations are in the pharmaceutical and IT/electrical industries. Companies of more traditional business such as automobiles, heavy industry and oil exploration concentrate their R&D resources in the home country. Even the information technology and electrical industries have a moderate emphasis towards more domestic research, perhaps due to the high share of US companies in the IT industry and the strength of US IT research. Only the pharmaceutical industry spends as much on R&D abroad as it does at home.

7.4   Different Drivers for Sciences and Engineering

Geographical/cultural analysis indicates that in the mid- to long-term, differences between geographic origin for the majority of R&D organizations seems to level off. The industrial analysis points to different rates and trends of internationalization between industries, but we have found too many counter-examples to warrant possible hypotheses like "pharmaceutical companies tend to establish 'global' R&D organizations."

More than geographic origin or industry, the relative importance of science and engineering appear to influence the direction of R&D internationalization. Let's characterize those two professions briefly. Scientists aspire to find new phenomena and create new knowledge. Their time horizon is usually long: Some scientists devote their entire career to the advancement of a very specialized subject. Scientists identify themselves stronger with their field than with the company they work for. Their main contacts are other scientists, although there is a strong tendency to work and obtain credit as an individual. Commercial objectives are often absent and their success uncertain and it is a difficult task for the director of a research department to match thematic freedom with budgetary constraints.

Engineers develop new technology and products mostly by utilizing existing knowledge in a novel way. There is often a strong time pressure to meet technical, performance and market targets. Almost exclusively, these goals require the close cooperation with other engineers as well as frequent contacts with suppliers and lead customers. Technical specifications and commercial objectives are defined or negotiated with production, marketing, or customers. Executing a development project is thus more a matter of process management than of people administration.

These R&D-internal demands help to explain the two principle motivations to establish R&D sites abroad:

- Proximity to other corporate activities (e.g. manufacturing) and proximity to local customers, which favor the operation and productivity of engineering and local product development;
- The quest for technical know-how and expertise available in only a few centers-of-excellence around the world, which favor the productivity of research and technology monitoring.

Since productivity requirements in science are different from engineering, the

Table I.5.1. Location drivers for research and development.

Reasons to locate 'Research' in a particular location:	Reasons to establish 'Development' in a particular location:
• Proximity to local universities and research parks	• Local market requirements
• Tapping informal networks	• Global customers request local support
• Proximity to centers-of-innovation	• Customer proximity and lead-users
• Limited domestic science base	• Cooperation with local partners
• Access to local specialists / recruiting	• Market access
• Dissipating risks among several research units	• Local citizen image
• Support of local development projects	• Simultaneous product launching
• Adhering local regulations	• Use of different time zones
• Local patenting issues	• Country-specific cost advantages
• Subsidies	• Facilitating scale-up in manufacturing
• Low acceptance of research in home country (e.g., genetics)	• Process innovation and adaptation to local production
	• National protection
Science & Technology Drivers	**Engineering & Market Drivers**

Source: Adapted from von Zedtwitz and Gassmann (2002: 584).

internationalization of research follows a different rationale from the one in development. The internationalization of research is driven by access to local science and absorption of know-how of global value (see Table I.5.1). In international development, understanding and reacting to the local market and the efficient cooperation with local customers (manufacturing, development partners) are important drivers.

New R&D units are rarely set up as fully-fledged R&D centers. Most of them are established as rather small units that have to prove their viability first. Because of different science and engineering orientation, their internal evolution towards more mature R&D sites may be quite different. In many cases we saw how development units evolved from local market support units, while research units evolved from scanning and listening posts. For instance, Leica's product development unit in Singapore is based on their previous technical service expertise and local manufacturing cooperation, and Daimler's research center in Palo Alto was originally conceived as a listening post.

The drivers of R&D internationalization lead to an evolution of R&D labs. (Fig. I.5.7). Typically, technical offices, established to serve local customers, tend to build up their own development centers. Driving factors are:

- Gaining autonomy from headquarters;
- Ensuring that equipment and talent is used to full capacity;
- Serving increasing local market needs;
- Increasing prestige.

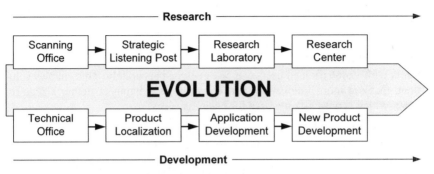

Source: Gassmann and von Zedtwitz (1996b: 9).

Fig. I.5.7. Internal forces drive the evolution of research and development.

8   Conclusions

In this chapter we have underlined the importance of external drivers for the location of R&D. Access and support of local markets as well as access to local science and technology give rise to four archetypical forms of R&D organization in which research and development are not necessarily collocated. Four generic trends describe the evolution of R&D organizations from one archetype into another.

At the same time, there is a strong movement in favor of a re-integration of the two disciplines that claims to improve overall innovation efficiency. Detz (1996: 31) states that "the isolation of this (research) function in separate units, often physically separated from a company's other technology activities, and remote geographically and strategically from the needs of the company's businesses ... made technology transfer exceedingly difficult." 'Seamless integration' of R&D processes would, so their protagonists claim, lead to shorter development times, improved technology transfer and project hand-over, higher customer orientation, and reduced overall costs.

We are therefore confronted with a fundamental tension between centrifugal forces that try to establish distance between research and development for greater R&D effectiveness, and centripetal forces that try to integrate research and development for stronger customer-orientation and higher economic efficiency.

The current trend towards shorter time-to-market certainly favors the quality and intensity of communication and collaboration, which are achieved by frequent face-to-face contact, physical collocation (see especially Allen, 1977), and modern information and communication technology. However, we believe that physical and organizational separation between research and development has also advantages:

- Research and advanced development teams can better evaluate radical new technologies 'offline';
- Mid and long term platform teams are not just extended capacity resources for time critical projects;
- Pilots with visionary lead users can be developed separately. This enables solutions that are more innovative than the average existing customer's requirement, which is normally the base for business cases.

Thus, at the possibly high costs from inefficient communication and long-distance collaboration processes, research needs to be conducted in places where scientific input can be maximized and where the environment is more conducive to carry out research. A calm environment is needed to cultivate 'new buds', including separate performance evaluation criteria and a more focused and specialized research infrastructure. Removed from distracting short-term concerns of development managers and corporate administration, these teams are more likely to pursue radical ideas, possibly leading to break-through innovations. The installation of research teams in scientific hot-spots like Silicon Valley, science clusters such as Route 128 near Boston, Massachusetts, and research parks allows the emergence of such a creative dynamic.

'Seamless integration' must not lead to tearing down all walls between research and development. Research must be organized according to the task at hand, not the function. This may well mean that the entire innovation process must bridge geographical distances, synchronize different technologies, and overcome organizational reservations. Two fundamentally different attitudes in R&D must be aligned or even merged. Thus, the dilemma between well-separated research and development and an efficient knowledge transfer needs specific managerial attention. Management of dispersed research must address technology and knowledge transfer between remote locations, the ivory-tower syndrome, and the guidance of colorful and individualistic personalities in basic research.

I.6 Establishing Overlaying Structures

„There's absolutely no reason why an organization that you created two years ago has any relevance to the organization that you need two years from now."
Les Vadasz, Senior Vice President, Intel Corp.

1 Perspectives of R&D Organization

1.1 Four Structures for Managing International R&D Organization

Many managers struggle with obsolete R&D organizations when they establish global R&D processes. Traditional R&D organization have been designed with a ethnocentric paradigm in mind that proves to be insufficient for many new challenges: R&D managers must learn to manage an additional organizational level in order to ensure global R&D efficiency.

For our purpose of describing global R&D management and organization we suggest four perception structures or layers of R&D organization (Fig. I.6.1). The *geographical distribution* of R&D (Structure I) obviously exerts a significant influence on the company's overlaying organization structures. *Functions and hierarchies*, i.e. organizational charts, reporting structures and specialized research departments (Structure II), are important to maintain a status quo and improve highly routinized tasks, but they are inappropriate for mastering the dynamics of global innovation. The regional and hierarchical structures are the bases for transnational organizations and, at the same time, responsible for many barriers in global R&D management (Fig. I.6.2).

In our research sample we have found promising approaches to organizing industrial R&D in technology-intensive companies on a global scale. These approaches were not restricted to R&D offices or new management functions. The companies which we studied were found to address global R&D management in an exceptional way and were more concerned with the way projects are carried out, processes are designed, personal networks are established and informal links are maintained. We discerned their approaches along the two principal objectives of *increasing R&D effectiveness* and *improving R&D communication*. They constitute Structures III and IV. These two overlaying structures can help to overcome the barriers introduced by geography and rigid functional organization (Structures I and II).

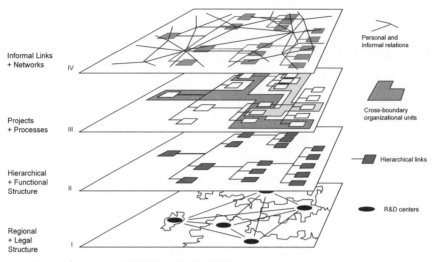

Informal Links
+ Networks   IV

Projects
+ Processes   III

Hierarchical
+ Functional
Structure   II

Regional
+ Legal
Structure   I

Personal and
informal relations

Cross-boundary
organizational units

Hierarchical links

R&D centers

Source: Gassmann and von Zedtwitz (1998b), von Zedtwitz (1999).

Fig. I.6.1. Four levels of structure in international R&D organization.

1.2   The Project / Process and Informal Links / Network Structures

The project / process structure is defined as the sum of all corporate mechanisms and procedures that do not fit into the general hierarchical line structure. In international R&D, elements of this structure address the increasing demands on flexibility and dynamics in corporate innovation. This structure also affects the creation and sustainability of an informal network structure encompassing relations both within and outside the company. Since this informal network structure powerfully transcends the entire organization, we expect great potential to be exploited by managing this network structure more deliberately. Constituents of overlaying structures as described in more detail in this chapter all affect informal structures.

The idea of viewing an organization as a set of interlinked structures is not new. Our model is related to the hypertext organization of Nonaka and Takeuchi (1995). They point out that there are two types of knowledge, explicit and tacit. Knowledge creation demands a new organizational structure called 'hypertext organization'. This organization consists of a project-team layer, a business-system layer, and a knowledge-base layer. The key characteristic of the hypertext organization is the ability of its members to shift contexts.

Schoonhoven and Jelinek (1990) distinguish between formal, quasi-formal, and informal structures. Formal structure is captured in the organization charts as sub-units, positions, and reporting relationships; and informal structure consists of the unsanctioned patterns of interaction devised around social and task requirements that the formal organization has failed to take into account. Quasi-formal structural elements are committees, task forces, teams, and dotted-line relationships;

they are functionally sanctioned by the organization but not designated in form, not specified in a formally defined charter, nor delimited rigidly in membership.

Hagström and Hedlund (1994) decompose the internal organization of a firm into three structural dimensions: position, knowledge, and action. The positional structure denotes the formal status, location and authority and, in many cases, reflects the prerequisites of exploitation. The knowledge structure aims at combining different elements laterally rather than deriving one from the other. The action structure consists of multi-skilled, multi-knowledgeable, and temporary project teams.

Our 4-structure-model puts additional emphasis on the informal structure as a major determinant for international R&D organization. Informal linkages and personal networks play a fundamental role for making things happen in multinational companies. Computer information networks link people together but restrict information flow to codable data. Especially in R&D, where frequent and often complex communication is crucial, globally dispersed R&D teams face seemingly insurmountable challenges to ensure robust information exchange and effective coordination.

Functional, hierarchical, and project-based forms of organization channel internal information and delimit external information exchange. Allowing for informal means of communication reaching outside the individual's organization unit helps to overcome information and comprehension problems. By definition, informal communication cannot be commanded but only provided for. In international projects and R&D processes, communication assumes a pivotal role for success. Since team members or colleagues are not necessarily located next door and cannot be asked during the coffee break or by walking across the hallway, all the communication, information exchange and coordination of project activities must be arranged for in advance. Therefore, depending on the complexity of the project, the organizational form of R&D ranges from highly decentralized (little central coordination needed) to strongly centralized (bilateral self-coordination is not possible).

If communication is to take place between dispersed teams or project members, information is more likely to be misinterpreted, lost, or simply not available. These principal communication problems have traditionally been addressed by up-front coordination or designated communication platforms. However, this approach is inherently insufficient because only what is explicitly known in advance can be made explicitly available for dispersed R&D teams during the project. Once an organizational unit (e.g. a large multi-year project or a new R&D location) has been established, subsequent communication and coordination changes drive up costs and tend to be handled less efficiently than information requests for which the organization has been originally designed for.

Organization in technology-intensive companies are in constant flux. Routine activities tend to become obsolete quickly. In the following we exemplify some typical constituents of overlaying structures that serve the purpose of information exchange and efficient project execution on a long-term horizon. These include technology offices, technology management competence centers, virtual project management pools, and central project management in the project and process

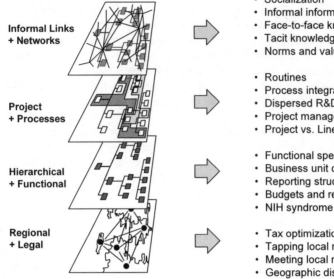

Informal Links + Networks
- Socialization
- Informal information-flow
- Face-to-face knowledge transfer
- Tacit knowledge
- Norms and values

Project + Processes
- Routines
- Process integration
- Dispersed R&D teams
- Project management
- Project vs. Line

Hierarchical + Functional
- Functional specialization
- Business unit optimization
- Reporting structure
- Budgets and resource allocation
- NIH syndrome

Regional + Legal
- Tax optimization
- Tapping local resources
- Meeting local market requirements
- Geographic distances
- Constrained communication

Fig. I.6.2. Issues in international R&D organization.

structure, and extended visiting programs, professional clubs, professional networks, and virtual faculties in the informal links and network structure.

2   Constituents of the Project and Processes Structure

2.1   *Schering: Office of Technology*

The purpose of Schering's office of technology was to seek relevant information, prepare it for internal use, and to look for its acceptance within the company (Schering was, at the time of writing, concluding a merger with Bayer). The technology head office of Schering was located in Berlin (ten people), with an additional six people in Richmond and four more in Osaka (as of 1997). The office stayed in close contact with the scientific community, organized seminars and conferences, and looked after the diffusion of critical information to Schering's researchers. There was a very important informal element to this task, which often is forgotten when operating network-like structures. If R&D must be outsourced due to time constraints or insufficient internal know-how, the technology office initiated contracts with external R&D partners. In this case, the respective units or departments would contact the office and state the internal deficit and its request for outsourcing. The office then initiated a search process in order to find the required knowledge.

2.2   IBM and Bayer: Central Project Management

Projects carried out by members from different R&D locations provide the basis for a corporate-wide learning process. This learning process can be expedited by organized double-loop learning (Argyris and Schön, 1978): A central project management office takes care of all evolving routines, improves them continuously, and propagates all documentation and training needed by the project teams in the company. It acts as a coach and trainer for new organizational routines (Nelson and Winter, 1982). Best practices are multiplied across the entire company as fast as possible.

At Bayer, a corporate office called Central Project Management maintains this role. It provides the R&D units with standardized project management tools such as project manuals, development guides, IS support, and project management systems. „Standardized operating procedures" provide efficiency needed at Bayer for the development activities carried out routinely.

At IBM, decentralized VSE (Virtual Storage Extended) system development, involving more than 20 system components, is managed by four specialists from a central office (Fig. I.6.3). Each member of the office is responsible for a new release of the system. The number of members fluctuates in accordance with the number of projects assigned to the office. Among the tasks that they deal with are the collection of requirements and specifications for a VSE release, the technical evaluation of project ideas, technical systems design, project controlling and coordination, project documentation, and VSE product planning.

Project supervision and coordination requires a worldwide integration of all VSE development projects with respect to deadlines, milestones and project targets. Experienced senior advisory programmers screen, evaluate and refurbish

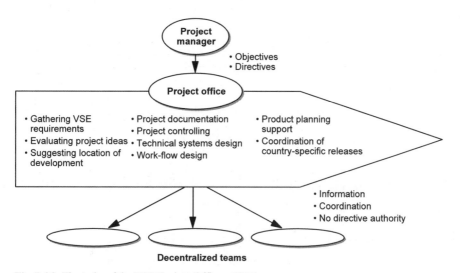

Fig. I.6.3. The tasks of the VSE-Project-Office at IBM.

new project ideas and proposals, turning them into formal project proposals. All requirements are listed and prioritized. If a completely new project idea comes up, the office finds out which parts may be developed by the original proponent and which parts may be contracted to other R&D sites.

Every project member has access to the project status document. This document is regularly updated by the office and serves as an information tool for identifying if a milestone has been reached and when the project may move into another phase. The project office also coordinates the development of national language versions of the VSE operating system. The English original is transferred to local R&D sites in other countries and translated into local languages. Operative management of project schedules and technical interfaces in highly standardized development processes is the main task of IBM's project office. The double-loop activities are not as distinct as at Bayer.

2.3   Schindler: Institutionalizing Technology Management

In order to concentrate and promote technology management throughout its worldwide R&D network, Schindler institutionalized fundamental R&D activities as a competence center. Schindler's technology management is responsible not only for advanced development but also for monitoring external technology development, industries and competitors, knowledge building and mapping, internal R&D liaison, core competence maintenance, benchmarking, as well as external promotion (Fig. I.6.4).

Due to the diversity of responsibilities and activities, technology management

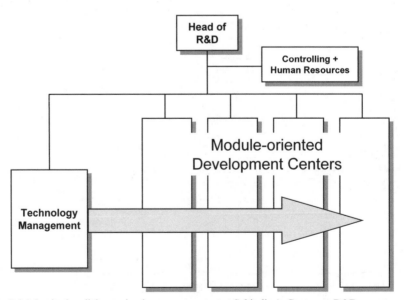

Fig. I.6.4. Institutionalizing technology management at Schindler's Corporate R&D.

was established at a corporate level independent from individual R&D units. Task forces are deployed across development disciplines and modules irrespective of geographical location or functional specialization. The technology management team also coaches high-risk/high-impact projects and supports corporate-wide technology planning. With a little over a dozen qualified and experienced experts, this team strives for cross-fertilization and technology integration across the entire company. With this institutionalized technology management, Schindler updates and develops its technical core competencies and promotes organizational learning through modern knowledge management tools.

2.4 Roche: Virtual Project Management Pools

The systematic nurturing of project leaders may be backed up by a specialized project management department (Fig. I.6.5). Hoffmann-La Roche's Pharma Division established a department called „International Project Management" which coordinates a resource pool of about 50 project managers for all R&D projects worldwide.

Every project manager is fully assigned to this geographically decentralized department. The director of this „virtual" resource pool assigns his people as manag-

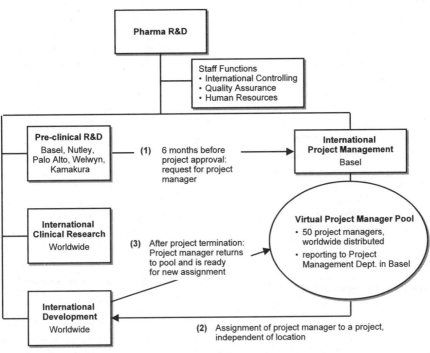

Source: Gassmann (1997a: 214).

Fig. I.6.5. Project management department as a virtual project management pool.

ers to projects as part of a global program to ensure standards in quality and project procedures. Upon completion of the project, a project manager is returned to the resource pool. As there are more projects in the pipeline as potential projects managers available, he is immediately reassigned to a new project.

Since this department reports directly to the board, the internal position of R&D project managers has been improved. The establishment of a project manager pool is a clear signal for empowering one of the scarcest competitive resources. Roche manages to retain much of the valuable procedural know-how of how to conduct and lead international projects not only on a project level, but also in a position where it can be reapplied when needed. Project offices are especially valuable when projects are very long, sometimes up to 15 years as in the pharmaceutical industry. No individual is able to carry out more than 2 or 3 projects. In a project office he may learn from dozens of projects.

3   Constituents of the Informal Links and Network Structure

3.1   ATR, Nippon Steel, Hitachi: Let Knowledge Travel with Heads!

Some companies are particularly good at internalizing external know how through hosting visiting researchers. This is especially important for companies without overseas R&D sites: hosting foreign researchers and engineers in the parent company can be a major source of intercultural exchange. Visiting researchers are often assigned to collaboration projects that are funded by several business units.

The Advanced Telecommunication Research Laboratories (ATR) - a Japanese basic research company – has recognized the importance of foreign input and established intensive relations with overseas research communities. Research projects are defined based on the competence and interest of new researchers, as long as the projects fit in the overall research program. A large number of foreign researchers work in mixed teams with Japanese scientists, but all of R&D management remains in Japanese hands. ATR employs 50-60 invited foreign researchers for periods from one month up to several years, while some of the foreign researchers hold long-term jobs. In 2006, ATR employed 202 domestic and 56 foreign researchers. The majority of the Japanese researchers come from over 40 supporting companies and generally stay for three years before they return to their home companies. This resulted in a turnover of about more than 1,500 Japanese researchers and nearly one thousand foreign researchers since the late 1980s. ATR researchers produce a high amount of internationally co-authored articles. Collaboration goes on after the foreign researcher has gone back to his home country. Thus, ATR, although entirely domestically organized, is a company with many international inputs and a global network.

This is in stark contrast to the general Japanese corporate research workforce, which is mainly Japanese, and can not be compared in diversity with its American or European counterparts. Two thirds employ no foreign researchers, and of those who do, almost 90% employed less than 10 (Hicks et al., 1994). Hence, Japanese companies engage in visiting programs such as Nippon Steel's „Visiting Researcher Program" Hitachi's HIVIPS (Hitachi Research Visit Programs) The latter was considered a major step towards internal R&D globalization at Hitachi. Hundreds of foreign researchers from industrial laboratories, institutes, and universities have been invited to stay at Hitachi laboratories for one year on average. Almost 40% of the visiting scientists come from Europe, and 35% from the US, but the share of researchers from Asia rises as Hitachi is placing more emphasis of R&D in Asia.

The main objective to exchange researchers is to support the establishment of a professional network, to foster creativity, and to integrate the very best people on a global scale.

3.2 DuPont and Dow-Corning: R&D Communication in Professional Networks

People networks are becoming an important factor in information and knowledge flow within and between organizations. Functional and hierarchical structures have been built and established to meet business needs, customer requirements and geographical constraints. They encapsulate people in their immediate organizational units. Networks can overcome self-imposed barriers between parts of the organization.

Over 240 technology-related networks, and more than 180 other non-technical networks helped DuPont to reduce costs, find new suppliers, develop standards, conduct training and development workshops, and transfer technology (Norling, 1996). DuPont distinguishes between

- „Content" networks: Subject-, knowledge-, or competency-based networks of people with a common interest or focus;
- „Situational" networks: Common-role or common-condition networks of people sharing a common situation;
- „Work-Flow" networks: Functional or capability-based networks of people with the responsibility to run a work process, frequently across organizational boundaries.

New ways of communicating, most notably e-mail, have made networking easier and more prevalent. Still, networking remains a „contact sport." The rapid transformation of an invention into a commercially successful innovation is often hindered by the preoccupation with short-term, and imminent problems, the „not-invented-here" syndrome and a „re-invention of the wheel," as well as less-than-critical mass and insufficient time constraints of the R&D personnel.

Dow Corning Europe has thus decided to create a totally new communication system: the „Club" concept (see Easton and Parbhoo, 1998; Fig. I.6.6). The idea is to get together those people from different groups, industries, and functions who are involved in a specific field of science or technology. People step out from their rigid company structure for a day or two to gather at an informal science forum. The objectives are essentially communicating, sharing, and coaching. Senior employees can share their experience and wealth of knowledge, and newer employees are given an environment in which they can find alternative appreciation and support of their activities outside their immediate organizational unit. Objectives include:

- Improve understanding of fundamental concepts;
- Raise awareness of techniques available in the company;
- Share experiences, problems, failures, and successes;
- Provide a forum for peer review of ideas, theories, and data interpretation;
- Get to know colleagues.

Participation in any meeting is voluntary. The time for preparation and follow-up is kept minimal. The intention is not to impose yet another activity, but rather to provide means to gain time.

The club is an ideal forum for specific training in key areas of science and technology. Such specialized training is further enhanced by invited experts from within and outside Dow Corning. By establishing links with experts from universities, clubs can act as catalysts for new research projects and forms of research sponsoring. Some clubs bring in representatives from key suppliers to update the participants on new technology developments. Technology transfer both within and from outside the company is thus another valuable aspect of club activity.

Despite the success of clubs and other network-based activities, there are barriers to effective networking (see also Norling, 1996; Easton and Parbhoo, 1998) such as

- *Geography*: Face-to-face communication is essential and cannot be replaced by e-mail or telephone;

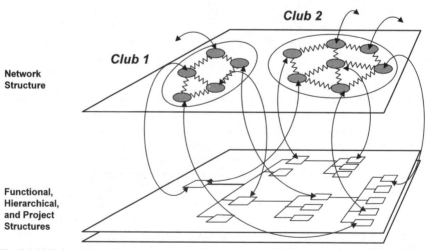

Fig. I.6.6. Clubs serve as loose networks to draw people with common interests and problems out of the hierarchical, functional and project structure to communicate across departmental boundaries.

- *Time*: Time which is often not available must be invested;
- *Behaviors and networking competencies*: Individual skills and abilities, and personal relationship building are a prerequisite for effective networking;
- *Lack of value*: It must be clear what the benefits are for each member;
- *Costs and resources*: Besides investment in time, networking will either induce direct costs or will use other limited resources;
- *Awareness of network*: Often, networks are known only to a small number of people. The more people that have the opportunity to participate in club activities, the more effective the network;
- *Critical mass*: If interest in a particular topic or club is limited, or if the potential base of a network is too small, it is difficult to build and maintain a network.

A network or club exists only as long as there is a common interest and effective pay-back to each participant. Any form of a network is best established and maintained, by ensuring the following success factors:

- *Maintain an informal structure*: Soft factors such as group culture, team spirit, and informality are often more important than rational and technical motives.
- *No exclusivity*: Clubs may become an elite circle rejecting new members who would have much to contribute.
- *Find management support*: Support from above nurtures and encourages cross-organizational activity.
- *Maintain specificity of topic*: The club or network addresses the need for a prompt access to expertise. A long-term mission should be created and adhered to. Clarity and focus of the network must be ensured.
- *Reposition the club*: If the theme has lost its attractiveness or has phased into a new topic, the focus should be reformulated and new members invited in.

The success of science and technology clubs at Dow Corning and the positive experience with professional societies at DuPont and other companies suggest that such networks may indeed effectively integrate different functions and organizational units. By increasing the sensitivity of individuals for information sharing, further improving interpersonal communication tools and skills, and designing networks for reduced information complexity, network structures are a formidable tool to overcome many of the shortcomings found in traditional organizations.

3.3 Daimler-Benz: Scientific Networks and Virtual Faculties

The capability to leverage external know-how and competence becomes a core competency in itself. Increasing technological complexity and a cut-back in R&D budgets force R&D departments to look outside their own walls for sourcing the technologies of the future on which to build successful products.

Even before its merger with Chrysler, Daimler-Benz established an international network of leading experts who acted as consultants and visionaries for research and technology (R&T). This network, the 'Circle Member Group' (CMG), consisted of about 20 renowned professors and academics in microelectronics, material sciences, information technology, automotive systems, production, traffic systems, engines, and environment from leading universities in Europe, the US, Japan, and China (Fig. I.6.7).

Each of the CMG members was tutored by a scientific representative of one of the research and technology units of Daimler-Benz. Representative proposed new members to the Circle and acts as a personal and scientific liaison to the research and technology units. Besides having access to Daimler-Benz R&T resources and contacts, CMG members were also remunerated for their duties.

At an annual CMG conference, all CMG members and senior representatives of Daimler-Benz research met to learn about new trends both in academia and industry, and to establish new personal and professional contacts between each other. Much of the formal coordination of the CMG is provided by the Strategy & Audit department (FTS) of Daimler-Benz R&T. This department also supported member selection and qualification, and administrative service for the Circle. Membership in the CMG is sponsored by Daimler-Benz R&T.

Besides keeping Daimler-Benz abreast of new technological developments, CMG members collaborated in research projects and help Daimler in recruiting high-potentials from leading universities. The CMG was a platform to maintain long-term relationships between academia and industry; its members typically served three years in the CMG and may extend their partnership.

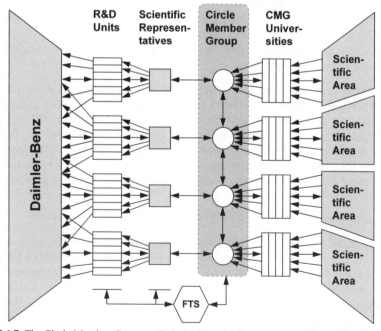

Fig. I.6.7. The Circle Member Group set Daimler-Benz in direct contact with world-wide leading experts in science and technology.

Daimler-Benz benefited from this virtual faculty not only as a technology fore-casting group, but also more concretely through cooperative projects and recruit-ment of top-notch scientists. By providing an appropriate organizational frame-work, university scientists and R&D experts shared and collaborated in an often informal setting. Not confined by organizational boundaries and fiefdoms, CMG members brought in advice and experience in relevant and crucial technology fields.

4   Conclusions

It is easy to alter lines on an organizational chart. It is much more difficult to change behavior, culture, or strategy. Managing the internationalization of R&D remains a key challenge for the coming years. Technology-intensive companies continue to disperse their R&D activities around the world.

Since conventional R&D organization is already constrained by hierarchical and regional barriers, it is often inadequate for the necessities of modern global R&D management. The most important requirements are managing cultural diver-sity, coordination of decentralized processes, global R&D project management, and integration of dispersed know-how.

Overlaying structures address these requirements directly. We have outlined some organizational forms that successfully respond to these issues in global R&D. For instance, we have seen that central project offices are called for in highly routinized, incremental innovation projects, characterized by clearly de-fined responsibilities (IBM and Bayer cases). A similar central department, "Vir-tual project management departments" like at Roche and project manager career ladders, ensure professionalism and quality of project execution. Highly trained and motivated project managers are an incredible asset for a company relying on the success of its R&D projects. It is the project manager and not the R&D scien-tists who should control the innovation process. Access to external know-how as well as the dissemination of internal knowledge is handled by a technology office serving as „the eyes and ears" of the company.

Exchange and visiting programs bring new ideas, new methods and new con-tacts into the company (ATR, Nippon Steel, Hitachi), even if the company has no foreign R&D sites at all. Some of the best innovations emerge from a network of different cultural and technical backgrounds. Networks like the Circle Member Group at Daimler-Benz establish a firm link to the scientific community and dis-tant research issues of long-term relevance to a particular company. Pay-offs are often hard to quantify but missed opportunities are guaranteed to occur if one fails to capture early technology signals from outside. In turn, professional clubs dis-seminate and diffuse know-how and experience within the company (DuPont, Dow Corning). Effective communication between different functions takes place outside the established internal information links. Yet, effective communication can never be dictated: it is all voluntary.

No company in a knowledge or technology-intensive industry can do without overlaying structures. At the center of overlaying structures are R&D individuals,

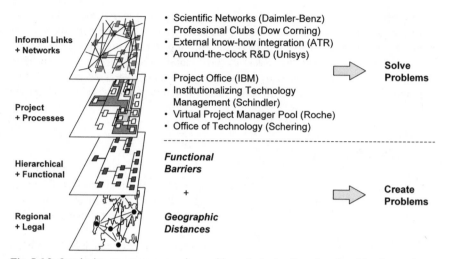

Informal Links
+ Networks

- Scientific Networks (Daimler-Benz)
- Professional Clubs (Dow Corning)
- External know-how integration (ATR)
- Around-the-clock R&D (Unisys)

Project
+ Processes

- Project Office (IBM)
- Institutionalizing Technology Management (Schindler)
- Virtual Project Manager Pool (Roche)
- Office of Technology (Schering)

Solve Problems

Hierarchical
+ Functional

Functional Barriers

Regional
+ Legal

+

Geographic Distances

Create Problems

Fig. I.6.8. Overlaying structures can solve problems that arise from functional barriers and geographic dispersion.

processes, and communication. The best possible use of R&D is to make the best possible use of the R&D staff, which includes providing them with the right means and tools and capabilities to exchange and test ideas, communicate, and work efficiently. Scientists and engineers are particularly eager to learn, as their chosen profession is nothing other than learning about new things and adapting it to another situation or context. Once they feel caged up, intellectually speaking, they are likely to divert their energy elsewhere or leave the company altogether.

At the center of communication in the R&D organization is the individual. Only through him will good R&D outcome be effectively transferred to the customer. Free information flow is the fundamental for working in a competence-based R&D network. Those who are afraid to loose people, be reminded: You are measured by what you share with others, not with what you retain for yourself. Close cooperation improves innovative capabilities and speeds up R&D cycles. Therefore, communication is essential for ensuring knowledge and technology transfer across the entire company.

I.7 Organizing Virtual R&D Teams

„Transnational R&D projects – key to competitiveness,
impossible or mismanaged?"
Gunnar Hedlund

1 Organization of Virtual R&D Teams

The strong decentralization of R&D and the dispersion of centers-of-excellence in the 1980s and 1990s have led to increased transnational R&D processes. A central dilemma in the organization of dispersed projects is project efficiency versus the effective use of specialized knowledge in dispersed knowledge centers.

To cope with these challenges, virtual project teams are formed. Such teams are spread over several locations; their boundaries expand and shrink according to their tasks and they are heavily supported by modern information technologies. Modern information and communication technologies can reduce the necessity to collocate project activities, but they cannot solve problems related to trust building, team spirit, and the transfer of tacit knowledge. An appropriate organization form needs to be found.

Virtual organization and virtual teams are hailed as the solution to these problems.[15] Goldman, Nagel and Preiss (1994) define the virtual organization as an opportunistic alliance of core competencies distributed among a number of distinct operating entities within a single large company or group of companies. Alternative definitions perceive the virtual organization as a temporary network linked by information to share skills, costs and access to one another's resources. In the extreme case, it has no central project office, no supervising organization, no hierarchy, and no vertical integration.

If virtual R&D teams have been described in literature, concrete concepts how to organize virtual R&D teams under which circumstances are generally missing. Our contingency approach to the organization of such teams attempts to close the research gap at least partially. In-depth case studies from technology-intensive multinational companies concerning several international R&D projects illustrate our findings with projects found at Hitachi, MTU, BMW, and ABB.

---

[15] See for example O'Hara-Devereaux and Johansen (1994), Howells (1995), Gassmann and Boutellier (1997).

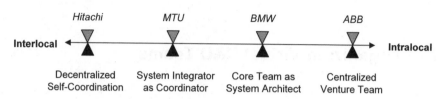

Fig. I.7.1. Four case studies exemplify virtual project organization in technology-intensive companies.

We identify four forms of virtual team organization by which R&D projects involving multiple locations are carried out. Ordered by decreasing degree of autonomy, these four team concepts are: (1) decentralized self-organization, (2) system integrator as coordinator, (3) as system architect, and (4) centralized venture team.

In our analysis we examined which model is optimal for which type of project. Our contingency approach for organizing an international R&D project is based on the following four determinants: (1) type of innovation (radical-incremental), (2) systemic nature of the project (systemic-autonomous), (3) the mode of knowledge involved (tacit-explicit), and (4) the degree of resource bundling (complementary-redundant).

2   Decentralized Self-Coordination

Decentralized self-coordinating teams are suitable if standards for interfaces between locally developed modules are available and clearly defined. Such modules are relatively autonomous product modules with low specificity that can be produced and sold independently from the entire product system. Decentralized self-coordination is well-suited to independent profit centers or business units participating in the project that have a high self-interest in the development of the module.

The only control instrument is the project budget approved by supervisory committees and assigned to involved R&D sites to carry out their share of the development project. Such an independent and multilateral coordination of teams succeeds only if the generic basic product architecture remains unchanged as for example in the computer industry. In addition, this product architecture must be explicitly known and understood in all participating R&D sites, supported by available standards and norms.

Due to the lack of central coordination and of personal contacts, it is often difficult to identify the appropriate contact in a decentralized team for a given issue. „Mirror organizations" in the involved R&D site help find the required specialists in complex project organizations. Such a symmetrical organization of teams greatly supports direct communication between corresponding specialists at the operative project level without involving project leaders (Galbraith, 1993). For instance, mirror organizations have been established to facilitate direct communi-

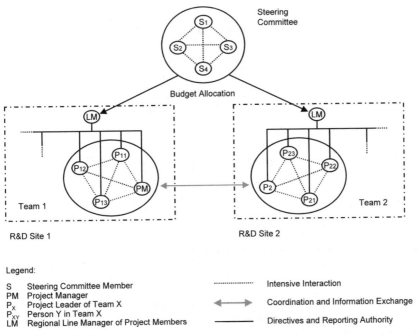

Legend:

S	Steering Committee Member	··········	Intensive Interaction
PM	Project Manager		
P_x	Project Leader of Team X	←——→	Coordination and Information Exchange
P_{xy}	Person Y in Team X		
LM	Regional Line Manager of Project Members	———	Directives and Reporting Authority

Source: Gassmann (1997a).

Fig. I.7.2. Decentralized self-coordination between remote project teams.

cation between teams in the US and Germany working in the strategic alliance between MTU in Germany and Pratt&Whitney in the US in the field of jet-engines.

If interfaces or project objectives are not clearly defined at the start of the project, the innovative success of the decentralized project team is highly jeopardized. Due to little interaction between remote teams, no integrated problem solutions will be found. There is no central project coordination with strong authority and decision power in case that critical project situations arise and priorities are to be set. Overall project goals may be disregarded because they are in conflict with the interests of regional line managers. Unless the steering committee has been endowed with directive power over line managers in decentralized R&D locations, a „heavy-weight project manager" (Wheelwright and Clark, 1992) is missing.

Hitachi's European Virtual Research Laboratory

In Europe, Hitachi started R&D operations differently from those in the US or Japan. Because there were no significant local manufacturing operations at that time, Hitachi aimed to pursue research with universities and research institutes. This concept neatly coincides with the global research collaboration observed in the academic world. Starting with research centers at the Universities of Cam-

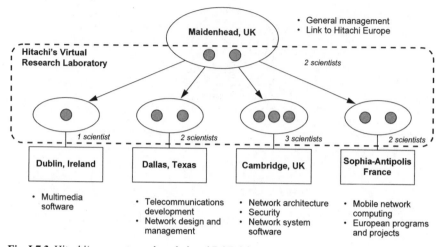

Fig. I.7.3. Hitachi's competence-based virtual R&D laboratory.

bridge and Dublin, Hitachi expanded in Munich and Milan to employ now more than 80 research staff. The administrative headquarters are at the European research headquarters in Maidenhead, UK.

In 1997, Hitachi formed a virtual research laboratory called Hitachi European Telecommunications Lab. The goal was to pursue research in telecommunications systems and the development of network system software. Research was designated to four of the most suitable locations: Cambridge, UK, Dublin, Ireland, Sophia-Antipolis, France, and Dallas, US. These locations dynamically group and operate collaboration projects that can change in location and partners (Fig. I.7.3). The network includes Dublin because of its competence in multimedia related contents software, and the Center of Communications Systems Research at Cambridge University, which was engaged in security issues and future network architectures. The Dallas Laboratory provided network design and network management competence. Research administration remained in Maidenhead.

Access to standardization consortia was also important. At Sophia-Antipolis, a science city in the south of France, Hitachi found not only competence in mobile computing and communications, but also local partners engaged in European framework programs and committees such as EURECOM, ESPRIT, and ETCI.

Research was distributed among ten scientists in those five places. Individual scientists were given a lead by holonic management which yielded a maximum of power and freedom to the individual while making sure that the researcher understood and pursued the overall goals of the research laboratory and how his work affected his own research and that of his colleagues.[16]

---

[16]   See also the Hitachi case study in this book.

Summary

If product modules can be developed relatively independently from each other, self-coordinating teams only need to achieve multilateral integration of module interfaces. Regional line managers of the teams assume the control over module development. The overall project is supervised by a steering committee that approves and assigns the project budget.

3   System Integrator as R&D Coordinator

Interface problems that occur in self-organizing teams can be reduced if a system integrator assumes a coordination role. A system integrator harmonizes interfaces between modules, coordinates decentralized R&D activities, defines work packages, and supervises overall system integration (technical interface management). At Micro-Compact Car, the former joint venture between Daimler-Benz and SMH, the Swiss watchmakers, this approach is called „parallel development."

The system integrator is responsible that the work packages in a project are completed on time (temporal interface management), and that each contribution and service of the participating cost and profit centers is kept track of (administrative interface management). Moreover, he should take care to integrate the different functional and regional units in the project team (social interface management).

During the system test of highly complex product architectures, a system integrator should make sure that the different component variants are tested with all the interfaces in the product architecture. Sometimes it is impossible to check all variant combinations. For instance, an X-ray apparatus consists of approx. 100 sub system variants from which more than one million different system can be realized (Erens and Verhulst, 1996). Testing all of these variants is next to impossible.

The system integrator is required to travel extensively to manage technical and social interfaces. If conflicts still cannot be handled this way, he summons the entire team or at least parts of it to meet face-to-face in order to settle the dispute or problem.

As a 'global knowledge engineer', the system integrator is responsible for managing knowledge transformation processes and the aggregation of the decentralized created knowledge. He must translate between the project manager and his teams, as well as between the teams themselves. Sometimes it can be necessary to have several system integrators in a decentralized project.

Because teams are separated by geographic distances, team spirit is difficult to achieve. Differing interests of project teams can endanger project success, as the system integrator has no directive authority over the decentralized teams. Informal relations and frequent communication between the system integrator and project members prove to be more effective, as well as his strong personal commitment. At Micro-Compact Car, the most important criterion in the SMART-project for the choice of partners was the partner's motivation to participate and learn in such a virtual organization.

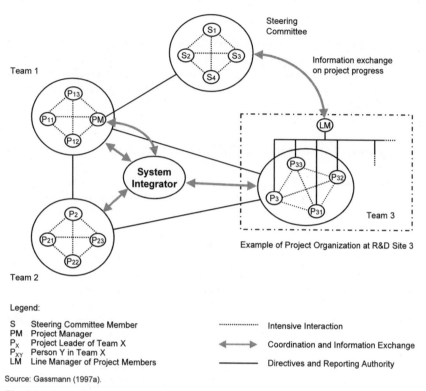

Legend:

S	Steering Committee Member
PM	Project Manager
P_x	Project Leader of Team X
P_{xy}	Person Y in Team X
LM	Line Manager of Project Members

················   Intensive Interaction

◄─────►   Coordination and Information Exchange

─────   Directives and Reporting Authority

Source: Gassmann (1997a).

Fig. I.7.4. System integrator as coordinator of decentralized R&D teams.

MTU's Example of International High-Tech Cooperation

Motoren- und Turbinenunion Munich (MTU) builds jet engines for military and civil aircraft and is a member of the Daimler-Benz group. In order to share development and financial risks, the Advanced Propulsion System development has been carried out in a partnership with Pratt&Whitney (USA), MTU (Germany) and Fiat Aviazione (Italy). These core companies were involved with a national network of suppliers, universities, and research institutes. The program was partly funded by each company's national technology program.[17]

Windtunnel tests of different engine models and component tests have been performed at Fluidyne (USA), Calspan (USA), ARA and BAE (Great Britain), DNW (The Netherlands) and DLR and ILA (Germany). The reason for these widely spread activities was primarily the large number of possible engine configurations which had to be investigated in parallel.

---

[17]   See also the MTU case study in this book.

Depending on their core competencies, the different partners chose their preferred components. Correspondingly they took over the responsibility for the technology development of this specific component. This procedure has proved to work quite satisfactorily. A new evaluation is only necessary if the engine configuration changes considerably (system innovation). In case a partner wished to terminate the contracts unilaterally, all the technology developed thus far by this partner would have to be given to the other partners disposal.

It was recognized early in the project that a real team approach was crucial to the success of the program. A top-management review meeting took place twice a year in the partner companies in an alternating sequence. Participants had been the board members, the program managers and members of engineering. The presentations had mainly done by specialists and not by management. By this procedure a close coupling between the decision level and the engineering level was guaranteed. This mutual appreciation of each other's work was crucial for continuous motivation in this extreme complex international environment.

Integrated product management teams were responsible for the technical progress within budget and time. They reported to the board members in a three month time interval.

A project manager was appointed at each of the three main participants to coordinate the integrated product management teams and different local teams („R&D Coordinator"). These local teams were involved in improving engine performance, designing a test bed for a special component, or developing fiber reinforced mate-

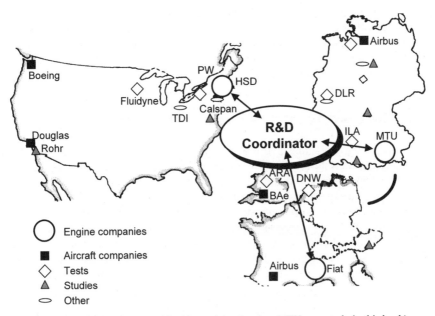

Fig. I.7.5. Ducted Technology, world-wide participation (see MTU case study in this book).

rials. Generally the members of these teams had been chosen from different disciplines: designers, aerodynamic and mechanical engineering staff, test engineers and so on. Thus it was ensured that the final product and not a special technology was the focus.

Depending on problem specifics, specialists came together in one location to find a solution. An example for specialist teams were „C-teams" for turbine development at MTU. C-teams designed binding standards of turbine components for module development (blades, compressor, fan) in „B-teams." These standards defined construction guidelines for modules and processual norms and work practices. During project execution, C-teams were expected to bring in their functional and specialists knowledge in product design, construction practice, and evaluation and clarification of rule deviations. C-teams had been established for important components of turbines as well as special manufacturing processes (e.g. project external experts for blade casting).

International phone conferences together with fax and datanet exchange became routine. These multifunctional teams met every week in each company. International video conferences were arranged if necessary. The progress of the work in the different teams was presented every three or four months to the integral product management teams. This procedure guaranteed that the different technology paths at the end would lead to the engine. This procedure was accompanied on the international platform by regular internal reviews within the partner companies themselves.

Summary

The system integrator is responsible for harmonization of interfaces between modules, temporal and technical coordination, work package definition and system integration. Module development is carried out by decentralized teams. Generally, the system integrator has little power over decentralized project activities as the directive authority resides with local line managers.

4   The Core Team as a System Architect

According to the protagonists of the "rugby-approach", companies that have their teams working closely together control their product development processes better. [18] Their approaches to team management emphasize a physical collocation of R&D in one place, preferably in a room with no separating walls. The requirement for intralocation is in sharp contrast to any endeavors of international and translocal execution of R&D projects (Lullies, et al., 1993).

Due to limited human resources and project size it is impossible to have all members involved in a project integrated tightly in a team and sharing the same intensity of communication among each other; many of them are engaged in line

---

[18]   See Takeuchi and Nonaka (1986), Nonaka and Takeuchi (1995) for more on the rugby approach; Katzenbach and Smith (1993) for team management.

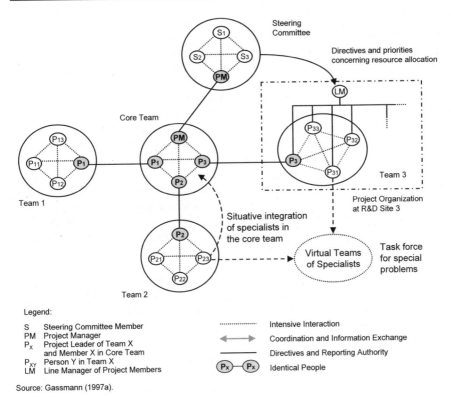

Legend:

S   Steering Committee Member
PM   Project Manager
P_X Project Leader of Team X
      and Member X in Core Team
P_{XY} Person Y in Team X
LM   Line Manager of Project Members

.... Intensive Interaction

◄──────► Coordination and Information Exchange

─────── Directives and Reporting Authority

$\text{(P}_x\text{)}$─$\text{(P}_x\text{)}$ Identical People

Source: Gassmann (1997a).

Fig. I.7.6. Core team as a system architect.

or additional project responsibilities at their parent location. If in a highly complex R&D project intralocal project execution is not possible because of the immobility of its project members or the complexity of the project, the second-best solution to bringing together all project members in one place is the introduction of a collocated core team. In comparison to the concepts of self-coordination and system integration, this approach is characterized by the highest degree of translocal coordination, intensity of communication, and most integrated problem solution.

Each team is focused to develop a properly delineated module as a part of the entire system. The leaders of the decentralized teams are members of the core team. According to our interviews, these teams usually consist of less than 10 to 15 people and establish themselves at the location of overall project management.

The core team develops and maintains the system architecture of the new product during the entire project process. It also defines specification lists and the interfaces between modules. If problems of technical interfaces occur during the execution of the project, they will be solved by the core team as a whole as the core team must guarantee the integration of the individually developed modules to a working system.

Similar to the system integrator, the core team is responsible for temporal and administrative interface management. It is in a much better position to integrate diverging interests of functional and local organizational units and to translate between differing cognitive contexts (cognitive bridging, Ridderstråle (1992: 14)).

Good linkages between the core team and the project supervising steering committee are guaranteed by the participation of the project manager as a member in the steering committee. He also ensures direct information flow between project teams into the steering committee. The team members technically report to their team leader who, in turn, report to the project manager. By this means, the technical control over the predefined work packages is ensured.

Since team members often have other line duties to fulfill (matrix organization), competence and responsibility conflicts occur. As personnel evaluation and hence career development of the project member is carried out by the line manager at the decentralized R&D unit, the individual is tempted to neglect unrelated project interests. In strategic projects the steering committee should therefore have direct influence on the line manager concerning the prioritization of projects and resource allocation.

The joint occupation with problems in a core team results in completely new solutions outside predefined concepts and frameworks (architectural or radical innovation (Henderson and Clark, 1990)), and differs substantially from organization by self-coordinating teams or a system integrator. Core teams are required if new products with a high degree of novelty are to be developed and intralocal project execution is not possible because of restricted resources.

If the core team is unable to solve a specific problem because it lacks expert knowledge, specialists from decentralized team are temporarily included until the problem is resolved. The boundary of the teams expands and shrinks according to the project tasks. It is important not to expand the core team above a critical size in order to guarantee its efficient operation. If explicit expert knowledge is needed from several teams, tele- or video-conferences may suffice to bring together the input from specialists of the participating R&D units. Limited and clearly defined problems may be addressed by the core team by directly contacting specialists and jointly solving the problems. Specialists teams are created if the problem is highly complex and involves several modules. Due to their geographic separation, these specialists form a virtual team.

Car Development at BMW

BMW is a car manufacturer with headquarter in Munich, Germany. Other companies belonging to the BMW group are Mini Cooper and Rover. R&D at BMW is organized in a matrix of functional competencies (car body, chassis, automobile electronics, and engines) on the one axis, and the car series (3xx, 5xx, 7xx, special cars) on the other axis. R&D is mainly carried out in Munich (Germany), Gaydon (UK), and Steyr (Austria). Design studios are located in California, Aschheim (Germany) and Miramas (France). Approximately more than 12,000 engineers and specialists work on the development of products and production processes.

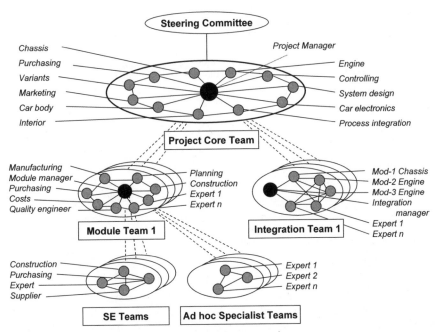

Fig. I.7.7. Team organization at BMW's car development project.

The project organization for developing a new car is assumed by a supervisory project team coordinating module and integration teams (Fig. I.7.7). Due to the matrix organization, each part of the car is represented in the project by a module team (e.g. chassis for a new BMW 318) which is thematically equivalent but individually staffed in each series, type, and occasionally variant derivative (e.g. convertible). R&D employees are members of several teams, thus ensuring know-how transfer on a functional and personal level.

A development project consists of approximately 40 modules, not including modules for derivative cars (convertible, extra door, etc.). Altogether, BMW works on about 200 modules at any given time. A car development project is divided into the four phases of definition, concept development, series development, and line maintenance. In each series there is at least one car under development. Together with special car projects (e.g. Roadster), about 10 products are under development at any time. Modules are created during the final phase of concept development and last until the completion of the development phase. Quality-related modules continue to exist even after market introduction (Fig. I.7.8).

No module is engaged in two different car series development projects at the same time; overlapping activities only take place within the same car series project. Since series development projects usually are in different phases of the overall project, problems and issues differ, hence no synergies are gained. Also, working in two separate projects has detrimental effects on individual work efficiency.

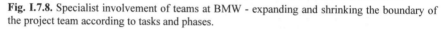

	Definition Phase	Concept Development	Series Development	Maintenance of Line
Definition Team				
Concept Team				
Core Project Team				
Integration Teams				
Module Teams				
Maintenance Teams				
SE-Teams				
Ad hoc Specialist Teams				

Fig. I.7.8. Specialist involvement of teams at BMW - expanding and shrinking the boundary of the project team according to tasks and phases.

Modules are highly flexible and continuously change in size and members. Design engineers participate up to the development stage, during which other people, such as prototype developers, join the team. During series development, manufacturing engineers are integrated in the project. Every employee at BMW participates in at least one module. The module and project managers should not change during the entire development phase, but the participation of module and other project members fluctuates as required.

Each core project team coordinates as many modules to a given function (e.g. engine) as deemed necessary considering the different requirements from product variants. Module teams supervise so-called „simultaneous engineering teams" (SE teams) when external partners are integrated in the development project. SE teams consist of internal experts and key component or technology suppliers. For instance, BMW has simultaneous engineering teams for car locks or window levers. There is a continuous effort to use the Internet for the intense communication between BMW and its suppliers. The amount and quality of the exchanged information depends on the autonomy and development competence of the supplier.

Summary

A core team is a geographically collocated steering team acting as a system architect and constituting itself as a central node which is responsible for conceiving product architecture, defining specifications and interfaces, coordination and control of decentralized activities, as well as system integration.

Module development is still carried out by local teams whose team leaders are part of the core team. Specialists solve functional problems in virtual teams and are situatively integrated in the core team. A steering committee directly supervises local line managers and ensures their compliance with project interests.

5   Centralized Venture Team

A geographically centralized venture team is responsible for planning and development of a product starting with idea generation and ending with the product's market introduction. Removed from the company's line organization, a venture team allows the uninhibited cooperation of specialists from several functional areas. In order to effectively implement its decisions, it is fully empowered: Full technical and business responsibility is given. The team is free to pursue new and original solutions without perpetually asking for approval. This is likely to lead to radical new product and process concepts.

In order to achieve the ambitious objectives in venture teams, face-to-face communication and informal connections between team members are strongly supported. This is greatly facilitated by physical collocation which is considered a the principal factor for effective and short-time development. Cross-functional collocation overcomes compartmentalized thinking. By physical proximity and intensive communication, the centralized venture team promotes integrated solution strategies as advanced by the rugby approach and thus radical innovation.[19]

This organization form is chosen for strategic R&D projects such as the GT24/26 at ABB, „Top projects" at Bosch, or „Golden badge projects" at Sharp. Staying within project budgets has a lesser priority than technical goals and time-to-market. Frequently, such projects are central in developing an attractive business opportunity by achieving a substantial advantage in the market, or to close gaps to fast-moving competitors.

The centralized venture team involves the greatest cost burden. Direct costs are less important compared to opportunity costs for collocating the team. The project members are exempted from other line or project duties in their R&D locations and are dispatched to the central project location. Since specialists are often intensively engaged in such activities, their removal from their parent location imposes great opportunity costs for venture teams. Usually, this organization leads to overcapacity in R&D since a reintegration of the team members after the project is finished is not easy at all. Hence, centralized venture teams can only be justified for strategic projects of extreme importance.

ABB's GT24/26 Think-Tank Gas Turbine Development

Although several international R&D units were involved, the GT24/26 gas turbine development at ABB is an example for a strongly centralized R&D project. The GT24/26 project represented a breakthrough innovation in gas turbine development - as a consequence, for instance, more than a hundred patents were filed. Due to shrinking markets for high-power turbines in the 1980s, ABB drastically reduced R&D in this field, until a 1991 market analysis showed that turbines generating more than 130 Megawatts („high end turbines") would become a multi-billion-dollar market. Lagging three to five years behind their main competitors

---

[19]   See studies by Brockhoff (1990), Picot, Reichwald, and Nippa (1988), Lullies, Bollinger, and Weltz (1993).

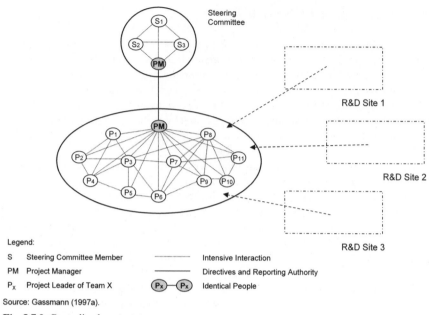

Source: Gassmann (1997a).

Fig. I.7.9. Centralized venture team.

(General Electric, Siemens and Westinghouse), ABB initiated a very ambitious R&D project called GT24/26 to excel over its competitors in terms of quality, time, and costs. The short development time in particular seemed unattainable, since technological foundations had still to be developed. Because market entry timing was paramount, this project called for new management methods to ensure fast-cycle development time, competitive advantage and customer orientation.

In order to achieve these aims, an R&D project team of several hundred people from 20 nations was created. Specialists from basic technologies, such as material and environmental sciences, but also from different functional departments, such as production, assembly, and service formed a highly interdisciplinary team; the know-how gathered was highly complementary.

The project structure was characterized by high international division of labor. The ABB research center in Baden, Switzerland, provided the new combustion technologies, and Baden researchers were subsequently engaged in integrating these technologies in the new turbine. The main share of the turbine development took place in Baden, including the development and production of the combustion chamber and turbine blades as well as final assembly of the turbine. ABB Mannheim was responsible for R&D and production of rotors, requiring profound technological know-how. Less technology-intensive components were developed in locations with cost advantages. In addition to ABB R&D units, external companies participated in the turbine development through contract R&D, development cooperation, and integration as a lead user.

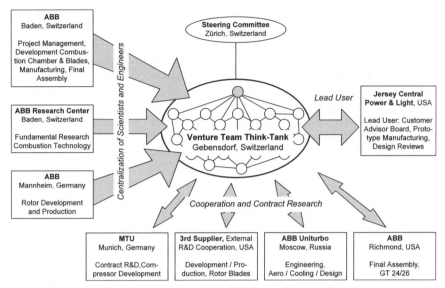

Fig. I.7.10. Centralized venture team at ABB GT 24/26 gas turbine development.

All project members were concentrated in a single open-space office in a two-story building in Gebensdorf, a village near Baden, Switzerland. This „think-tank" facilitated not only easy cross-functional communication, but also helped to keep critical know-how inside the project. ABB took care not to accidentally release any information to competitors: All project members were sworn to secrecy, and even the Gebensdorf building retained an innocent living apartment exterior. Since ABB had enlisted many people outside ABB for integrating external know-how, the central project location also helped to create a common project and innovation culture. The strategic importance, the high-flying objectives, and the seal of confidentiality supported the creation of a common project spirit.

The GT24/26 development project enjoyed high priority within ABB Power Generation. The project leader reported directly to the head of development and the general manager. The steering committee met once a month. In critical phases of the project, even the Board of Management was involved. Most of the project members were completely assigned to the project and reported only to the project manager. The project manager was responsible for all activities between research, development and production, including the completion of the first two gas turbines and their installation at the customer sites. The strong position of the project manager facilitated his access to critical and limited resources, such as functional specialists in particular technical areas.

The design of production tools was started before the product development phase was concluded. Contrary to sequential development projects, the parallel development of the turbine development in combination with the spatial distances between product and production tool development units created coordination problems. Since rotor development was located in Mannheim, its manufacturing personnel was relocated to Baden in order to ensure the necessary intensity of communication.

Due to high R&D costs and time pressures, ABB deployed the concept of innovation marketing: the close interaction of R&D, marketing, and innovative product users. Innovation marketing aims at aligning internal and external technological constraints by coordination among the main innovation participants, improving technology transfer, cross-functional communication, and market introduction times. The principal management approach combines heavy-weight project management, design-for-manufacturability, benchmarking, and simultaneous engineering.

GT24/26 was the first simultaneous engineering project at ABB. Since vital technological know-how was lacking and the pressure to reduce development time was enormous, ABB engaged in this project before the necessary materials research were completed. In order to simultaneously develop end-product components while fundamental research was still under way, research and development was collocated in one building in Gebensdorf, Switzerland.

The main success factors of the GT24/26 development are the centralization of the project team in one location (i.e. think-tank), the coordinated parallelization of activities and cross-functional cooperation, strong top-management commitment, and the integration of potential and lead customers. ABB's top management fully supported the project, yielding considerable authority and decision power to the GT24/26 project manager. Cross-functional teams, lead users, researchers, and development engineers collaborated during the entire project. The GT24/26 generation was a technological breakthrough and moved ABB from a late follower into a technical leader in the field of high-end turbines within a short time frame. Compared to previous projects, the time-to-market could be reduced by 60% and the number of modules cut nearly to half.

Summary

As the case studies showed: every project type requires its own organization and management forms (Fig. I.7.11). In order to form a centralized venture team, participating R&D sites dispatch specialists to the team for the entire project duration. The heavy-weight project manager has full access to his assigned resources. The venture team is collocated, preferably in the same building or even room. Due to the high costs involved, companies choose a centralized venture team approach only for strategic projects under extreme time pressures.

6   Contingency Approach to Virtual R&D Teams

Every project manager would prefer a physical collocation of team members in the sense of Takeuchi's and Nonaka (1986) rugby approach. Communication, the core of R&D activities, functions just better. Already Allen (1977) demonstrated that physical collocation is favorable. However, organizing innovation processes in a

Virtual Project Organization	*Decentralized Self-Coordination*	*System Integrator as Coordinator*	*Core Team as System Architect*	*Centralized Venture Team*
Case	**Hitachi**	**MTU**	**BMW**	**ABB**
Managed by	• R&D Director	• R&D Coordinator	• Project manager	• Strong project manager
Work load	• Distributed	• Separable	• Integrative	• Interdependent
Started by	• Regional center	• Lead partner	• Regularly	• Top Management
Goal	• Telecommunications	• New technology	• New car	• Top-class turbine
No. Locations	• 4 locations	• 25 locations	• 1 center + suppliers	• 1 center + 8 key suppl.
No. members	• 10 members	• Several dozens	• hundreds of engineers	• about 200 engineers
Leadership	• Holonic Management	• Strategic alliance	• Coordination	• Autocratic + clear goals
Product-Character	• Software and research modules	• Engine components	• Module-oriented highly complex product	• Modular system
Organization	• Decentralized scientists	• Decentralized project teams	• Module teams	• Matrix-organization, centralized team
Routinization	• Medium, Coupled: Small research projects	• Medium: Established industry	• High Same for each car	• Low First SE project
Duration	• Ongoing	• Ongoing	• 6-8 Years	• 3 Years

Management	Bilateral communication Common corp. culture	Multiple interface mgmt Knowledge engineering	Translocal coordination Integr. problem solution	Tight coordination Intensive communication

Fig. I.7.11. Case studies in comparison: Every project type requires a different form of organization and management.

multinational company with several geographically dispersed R&D competence centers and even more production facilities naturally leads to decentralized project teams. Bringing teams together is often very costly, also in terms of opportunity costs. Some specialists cannot be moved to a central project location.

Therefore, if a project requires the integration of dispersed know-how, the project organization is decided case by case (contingency approach): Some projects can be conducted decentralized, some projects are only successful if the teams are working at one location. There is no single solution for every project type. Our previous studies have shown that physical collocation of R&D teams is indicated by four principal factors (Gassmann, 1997a):

- Type of innovation: incremental versus radical;
- Systemic nature of the project: systemic versus autonomous;
- Mode of knowledge: explicit versus tacit;
- Degree of resource bundling: complementary versus redundant.

According to these studies, interlocal execution of projects is possible if:

- The innovation is incremental;
- Project tasks are relatively autonomous;
- Explicit knowledge prevails;
- Redundant resources are available.

The collocation of the project team in one place is required if:

- A radical innovation is pursued;

- Project tasks are systemic;
- Tacit knowledge plays a central role;
- Complementary resources are deployed.

Based on these organizational forms of virtual project teams it is possible to arrange them according to spatial decentralization. In the centralized venture team, all project members are collocated in one place. If a core team acts as a system architect, all relevant team leaders and project managers meet in one centralized location. The system integrator moves between geographically dispersed R&D teams trying to coordinate them. There is little physical contact between self-coordinating teams. Fig. I.7.12 summarizes the suitability of each organizational form depending on the situational conditions of a project.

7   Conclusions

In academia as well as in industry, virtual teams are praised as the future form of project organization because of ever-more powerful information technologies and increasing project complexity. Virtual teams are a mirror of our multioptional society that dislikes hierarchies and fixed bindings. Amazingly, we were unable to find any recommendations under what conditions and circumstances such teams should be engaged and in what way. We attempt to close this gap by presenting four forms of project organization:

- Decentralized self-coordinating teams;
- System integrator as coordinator;
- Core team as system architect;
- Centralized venture team.

The organizational form of virtual teams must be specifically tailored to the project tasks. Depending on the type of innovation, the systemic nature of the project, the mode of knowledge involved, and the degree of resource bundling, different concepts of organizing virtual teams are required. The degree of virtuality depends on those determinants. Breakthroughs continue to need face-to-face teams - though new information and communication technologies have started to have an impact.

New ICTs are the main drivers and enablers for virtual R&D teams, but real communication is based on trust and understanding. ICT cannot act as a substitute for traditional project management in virtual teams. Replacing travel and face-to-face communication in transnational R&D projects by ICT-based communication places particularly high demands on the project leader. Cultural tolerance and empathy between the project leader and the team prove to be a basic condition for the communicative openness required.

This has led Hitachi to its on-site policy when dealing with scientists at different locations. Contrary to requesting researchers to see their supervisor or project manager at his (potentially far away) office or to exclusively report electronically, managers visit R&D sites and deal with their subordinates face-to-face. This

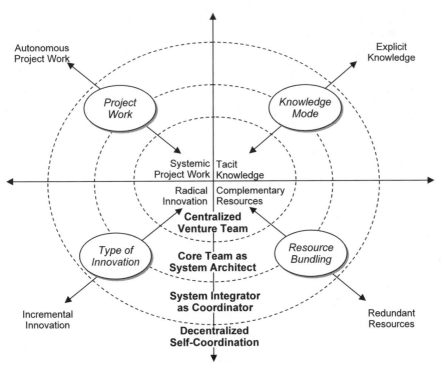

Source: Gassmann (1997a: 161).

Fig. I.7.12. Suitability of organizational forms for transnational R&D teams.

shows their respect for the work of individual scientists. Hierarchical barriers are pulled down. Manager and project members enjoy an open and friendly working atmosphere.

In general, especially after a company has moved up the learning curve, we see a reduction of time-to-market and of R&D costs. Since the virtual integration of dispersed teams can take place from anywhere, ICT-based R&D offers great opportunities for customer-oriented R&D. If one is capable of retaining not only core competencies in-house but also the skills to manage an ever-changing network of suppliers and external partners, then a great flexibility can be achieved in all stages of R&D. Furthermore, the most competent companies can be integrated in the R&D process to optimize the use of resources. Internal complexities can be reduced and overall coordination costs will fall.

Especially in emerging technologies or large and costly projects like the new Airbus A380, virtual R&D can help to spread the risk, distribute costs among a network of companies, and make use of the best specialists worldwide. It is crucial to identify and maintain a strategic competitive position through some core capability. Nevertheless, traditional coordination methods and tools are required. Not every project or undertaking is suited to virtual execution. The decision whether a project should be carried out in a virtual configuration must be made case by case and is mostly dependent on time, resources, and experience with virtual work.

**Part II
Emerging Patterns**

II.1 The Market as a Challenge for R&D

> *,,Make your business competitive by making*
> *the business of your customers more competitive. "*
> *Mack Hanan - Business Growth Consultant*

1 Push versus Pull Orientation

Market orientation is the single most important reason for increasing R&D effectiveness. On the other hand, aligning R&D activities completely with existing customer demands may have negative effects on the role R&D has to fulfill on a corporate level. In particular, there is rising concern about sustained long-term innovativeness when R&D is focused to early on customer demands.

Market-oriented R&D management implies two things at the same time: To

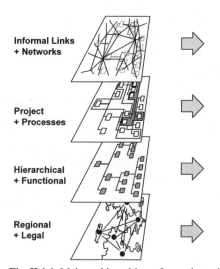

**Main Problem Drivers
for Market-Orientation in R&D**

**Informal Links
+ Networks**

- Unable to make use of external networks
- Incompatible communication networks
- Language differences between
  R&D and customer

**Project
+ Processes**

- Obsolete R&D tools
- Discover customer needs
- Funding
- Mismatch between organization and
  dynamic markets

**Hierarchical
+ Functional**

- Short-term need vs. long-term innovation
- Technology-Push thinking
- Bureaucratic structures
- Compartmentalization

**Regional
+ Legal**

- Distance between customer and R&D
- Neglect of new markets

Fig. II.1.1. Main problem drivers for market-orientation in R&D.

face the needs of the existing market and to secure long-term innovativeness including not yet existing markets. Research institutes of all disciplines are subject to this fundamental conflict. The problem of meeting short-term customer demands and securing long-term innovativeness is equally present in central research laboratories of large multinational companies as in independent research laboratories.

Customer-oriented R&D management is driven by the needs of internal and external customers. Customer-orientation is different from market-orientation because, simply put, customer-orientation focuses on known customers while market-orientation includes the unarticulated needs of potential or future customers as well. The success of this customer-focused approach, therefore, depends on the degree to which R&D centers understand themselves as goal-oriented solution providers. Too many corporate research centers still act as budget-maximizing antagonists. Technology-push thinking is still widespread. Dispersing R&D activities impedes direct communication between research and its customers, i.e. the development groups located elsewhere (Fig. II.1.1). New tools and organizational forms are required to meet customer requirements.

While basic research laboratories understand themselves as scientific institutions largely removed from direct market tribulations, many engineering companies have realized that they are service providers operating with increasingly fickle customers. Due to the decrease of funds for basic research and the growing understanding of downstream corporate operations as internal customers (e.g. advanced development), research must be designed as a customer-oriented and market-oriented service.

Companies operating in quick-paced commodity markets with short development cycles have adapted a market-oriented management. Technology-oriented companies with rather complex processes for service and product creation are confronted with the principles of market orientation when profound market changes in competition or customer demand endanger the survival of the firm. Many of them do not know how to cope with the extremely difficult task of customer orientation in long-term R&D. Inward oriented companies with a strong R&D emphasis tend to treat the customer as a means toward the financial goal rather than as a market partner whose needs have to be discovered, sometimes even created, and satisfied.

R&D units will have to solve practical problems for customers unless they have customer-neutral public or corporate funding. Our studies show that research centers of technology-intensive multinationals are increasingly financed by those business units for which they conduct projects as negotiated contract research (Fig. II.1.2). Business unit financing does secure 'money-sponsor orientation' but not customer orientation, although it is a step in the right direction. Frequently, R&D is indifferent about who actually pays for their research projects. Real customer-orientation therefore calls for more effective management methods.

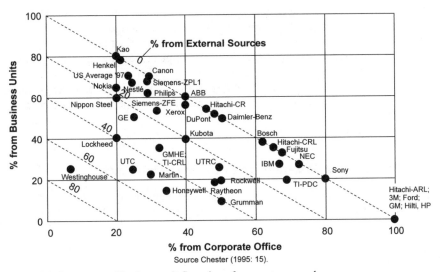

Fig. II.1.2. Percentage of business unit financing of corporate research.

2   Focusing R&D on Market Needs

2.1   *Technology Push versus Market Pull*

Before the 1960s, technology and R&D management was built on Vannevar Bush's philosophy of „Technology Push" which meant that scientific progress would by itself produce results of commercial potential if the people and technology involved were sufficiently capable and qualified. This concept dates back as far as the 16th century, to Francis Bacon (Kealey, 1996: 4). In the US it was quite successful in some areas as long as the scientific base and impulse was strong due to highly qualified immigrants from Europe after World War II, and the pressures from the Cold War during which the big nations were afraid of being outsmarted by the enemy through new weapons based on basic research. However, with the radical changes of the global economic regime from 1960 on, new 'pull' factors for technology emerged (see Archibugi and Iammarino, 2002, for an extensive discussion of these factors).

Mostly as a reaction to the many failures of new product introduction, a new model emerged which stated that innovations should be driven by market forces and customer demands. R&D would then create the necessary products to satisfy those demands. This „Market Pull" has profound implications for the management, funding, and organization of R&D.

The market pull model led to the divestiture of many central research laboratories, and this trend is getting stronger as many of the large nations meet financial bottlenecks due to social spending on their aging population. As a negative side effect this created serious problems for companies that relied on radical technology breakthroughs or long-term innovativeness. Diversification into new industries, cost reduction programs, focus on core competencies, and a change of pace in the emergence of new technologies have greatly added to the loss of direction in the organization of R&D. Today, the major challenge is to create an understanding between business people and technologists such that a corporate technology strategy can be formulated and implemented and implemented respecting both market demands and technological capabilities.

2.2   Instruments of Market- and Customer-Orientation

Theory and practice have produced a number of methods to combine technology seeds with market needs. We briefly introduce particular helpful instruments:

- Lead user concept
- Concept testing
- Conjoint analysis
- Quality Function Deployment (QFD)
- Technology strategy - product/market strategy integration
- Two-channel funding

Von Hippel's lead user concept (von Hippel, 1986) identifies potential customers who present strong needs that will become commonplace in the market in the near future. Today's lead user requirements are future needs of an important market segment, so the supplying company can optimally tailor its product with the help of carefully selected market partners. Because lead users have a strong interest in having their demands fulfilled first, they can support and enhance the quality of product design and reduce overall time-to-market; they are problem providers.

A major challenge is the generic inability to predict consumer reaction to completely new products and services, as Moore (1982) outlines. Concept testing is a tool which can be applied by R&D to find out early about potential market success of promising ideas before committing substantial funds to it. It is also a valuable tool to determine potential target markets and how the concept might be improved. As concept testing is fairly well established the greatest gain for R&D could come from improving its application. Moore (1982), amongst others, emphasizes that a sufficient amount of money should be invested on idea generation, and that the early communication of ideas should be ensured. Formal boundaries such as the proper methodology for carrying out the tests are crucial for gaining interpretable results, as well as sampling a sufficiently large number of participants from the market. The crucial problem remains the same: All concept testing addresses only the questions asked by the model used.

Conjoint analysis is a method to evaluate consumer preferences of existing designs. As Page and Rosenbaum (1987) explain, „the purpose of conjoint analysis is to enable the researcher to take a respondent's overall evaluation of a set of objectives or concepts and decompose those evaluations into separate scores, called utility values, for the various attributes of the objects that led to the respondent evaluating them the way he did." The decision maker has an implicit set of utility functions for each product attribute, which he is not necessarily able to articulate or may even not be aware of. The objective of conjoint analysis is to uncover these utility functions that determine his preference for the different alternatives among a set of multi-attributive alternatives. The researcher may thus derive not only which of the attributes are adding value to the new product, but also what these attributes must fulfill in terms of performance.

Another tool for the translation of market requirements („what") into product specifications („how") is Quality Function Deployment (QFD). This leads to a better communication between the customer on the one side and R&D project staff on the other. The roots of modern QFD are found in the Japan in the 1960s. Yoji Akao and Masao Kogure developed a systematic methodology to transpose customer requirements of a to-be-developed product into technical product specifications. The „voice of the customer" was to be translated into the „language of the engineer". At the core of the QFD concept is the „house of quality", which combines technical specifications and customer requirements. QFD proved extremely successful. Toyota reported cost reductions of up to 60% for some products in the late 1970s. By 1997, QFD had still not been introduced in many places in the world.

On the strategic level, technology evaluation and planning as well as market forecasting are often done by rules-of-thumb. What is often missing is the integration of technology strategy and product/market strategy. Project evaluation and execution is based on both and must eventually fulfill both of the required roles. If a combined strategy is missing, a number of typical deficiencies occur such as insufficient definition of a project, insufficient planning, resource bottlenecks, and unclear targets (Wheelwright and Clark, 1992). This can be fixed by developing a well-defined R&D strategy (Fig. II.1.3). Its four main goals are:

- Prioritization of R&D projects;
- Integration and coordination of functional, organizational and technical tasks;
- Directing R&D activities towards the business target;
- Improvement of R&D capabilities in order to secure long-term innovation.

The most important tool seems to be the new widespread 'two-channel-funding'. Corporate culture nowadays is driven by financial factors. Commitment by all players in an R&D-project is, therefore, obtained through financial contribution only. Therefore, many successful companies fund their R&D jointly through business units and corporate money; e.g. at ABB, no project exists that is not funded by both parties. Simply showing interest is not enough. Involvement is proved through direct financial participation.

Tools are only enablers - they are not sufficient for success. Every R&D-practitioner knows that his knowledge is based on science, operational rules, and tacit knowledge; knowledge which he has acquired through many years of trial-and-error and that is not easily transferred to other employees. The team and the organization play a decisive role. Questions such as what formal and informal relationships exist between which members have to be addressed.

2.3   *Organizational Forms for R&D Market-Orientation*

Market-orientation must be supported by an appropriate R&D culture and R&D organization. For instance, Schindler's Corporate R&D established an Innovation Marketing department, and ABB performs innovation marketing for improving market introduction times in very large projects.

Schindler's Innovation Marketing department explicitly drives the product planning process between R&D and its internal customers ("field operations"). On the one hand, it represents the voice of the customer within R&D. Thereby, the manager responsible for innovation marketing, who has abundant field and technology experience, coaches the R&D project managers - especially in establishing contact with worldwide dispersed field operations and during the subsequent market introduction phase. On the other hand, Schindler's Innovation Marketing sells R&D output to field operations. This can be very helpful in industries where the customers are more conservative and innovations are less triggered by market pull (Fig. II.1.4).

In the following, four examples of customer-oriented research are presented and discussed in greater detail. Hoffmann-La Roche Ltd. and Siemens Inc. are two large and research-intensive companies in the pharmaceutical and electronics/telecommunication industry, respectively. General Electric (GE) is a major electrical-technical company, and EGU is a Czech research institute specializing in energy production engineering.

An important R&D method for customer-oriented technology development is road mapping. Siemens uses road-mapping and technology planning as instruments for market-orientation in its central research laboratories (Weyrich, 1995 and 1996). Long-term innovativeness and short-term customer-orientation are

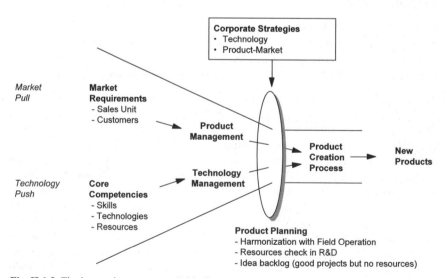

Fig. II.1.3. The innovation process at Schindler.

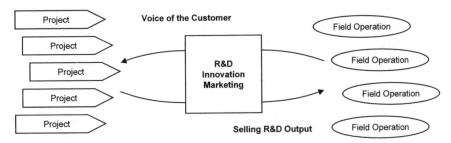

Fig. II.1.4. R&D Innovation marketing improves relations between R&D, manufacturing and sales relations.

difficult to combine in the same organization. GE has introduced a new funding system as well as cross-functional teams for more market-orientation (Edelheit, 1998). Research processes conducted in a competence based matrix organization helps to ensure a balance between market and technological knowledge. EGU undertook a reorganization in order to be better prepared for the changes in eastern European politics and opening markets (Haedrich, 1996). Spinning off research teams into independent R&D companies improves entrepreneurship as well as organizational flexibility. Roche secured market success from one of its R&D projects by spinning off its LCD research group into an independent company called Rolic Ltd. (von Zedtwitz, Schadt, and Brauchli, 1996). Last but not least, a key issue of organizing research in a globalizing environment is the geographical dispersion of research teams. Centralizing research activities improves communication and creativity, although the introduction of advanced information and communication technologies increasingly facilitates decentralization of subsequent development.

3   Siemens - Positioning Central Research

Siemens is one of the world's largest providers of electrical and electronic products, systems, and devices, with more than €75.5 billion in sales in 2005. The company's business areas are clustered in six large core businesses (information and communication, automation and control, power, transportation, medical, and lighting). 47,000 employees are engaged in R&D, spending €5.2 billion on R&D in 2005, Siemens is one of the most technology-intensive companies in the world.

More than half of the researchers and engineers at Siemens work outside Germany. R&D has been spread to over 38 countries with centers in the US, Austria, and the UK. For instance, American and European customer expectations for telephone systems differ in functionality and performance. Standards and regulations in the two markets are significantly different as well. In addition, customer orientation implies a local presence in the country in which a company is operating. Siemens considers itself a 'good citizen' in any country and not just a large multinational trading and manufacturing company. Given this policy it is necessary to design and implement value chains in each country in which Siemens operates, integrating R&D, production, distribution, and marketing. This results in close cooperation among R&D, technical service, and marketing, and helps in focusing R&D on market requirements.

R&D internationalization is not only driven by customer and market orientation, but also by the availability of resources. For example, software development accounts for half of all development costs at Siemens. As software can be produced everywhere, and in particular more cheaply outside Germany, Siemens runs large software centers in Spain and India. It also cooperates with leading research institutions to reduce in-house development costs, amounting to more than 1,000 cooperative research projects.

The main node of Siemens' international R&D network is its research and development technology unit, comprising all central R&D activities. The core R&D locations include Munich-Perlach, Erlangen, Berlin (all three in Germany), Princeton, New Jersey, Roke Manor, UK and Beijing, China. The main task of Central Research is securing long-term innovation power by generating potential breakthrough innovations.

Central Research has to deal with the full range of possible innovations. This means that it has to support market-oriented, incremental innovations as well as long-term, radical innovations. Therefore, Central Research has to design and develop technology synergies and concentrate R&D operations in projects with clear goals as well as defined time horizons and cost margins (see Fig. II.1.5). Each of the Central Research sections covers one cluster of strategic importance to Siemens' core technologies.

The R&D program is optimized in a complex selection process within Central Research based on intensive communication with the operating units. The most important instrument is technology planning based on 'roadmaps', by which forecasted technology developments are compared and correlated with the technology requirements that are expected for future product generations (see e.g. Groenveld, 1997). Technology planning supports the optimization of a short- and medium-term close-to-the-market R&D program. Technology requirements derived from future product generations are compared with anticipated technology evolution with a planning horizon of about five years longer than in the business units.

Innovation fields constitute the basis for Siemens' long-term R&D. Future R&D areas and potential innovation drivers are monitored and ground-breaking basic research is carried out. In contrast to technology planning, innovation fields are conceived in a top-down and holistic approach. They are subject to a long time-horizon and aim at anticipating technological or market discontinuities, and generating new business opportunities. Scientists involved in innovation fields do research with a time horizon of up to 20 years, sometimes making their work quite detached from direct market needs.

The most important tools for optimizing medium-term technology planning are Multiple Generation Product Planning (MGPP) in Siemens business operations and Core Technology Roadmaps at Central Research. The two-stage MGPP integrates product and technology planning at a business level. In the first stage, busi-

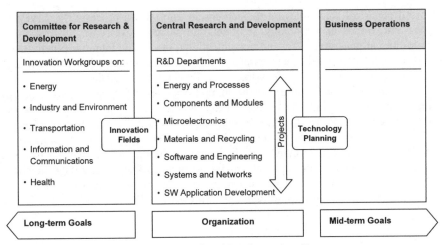

Fig. II.1.5. Organization of Central Research and Development at Siemens.

ness area roadmaps according to product groups or systems are drafted. Fig. II.1.6 shows an example of the Automotive Systems Group. In the second stage, a three-step process is implemented to determine key systems and processes, along with the necessary key components, core processes, and technologies.

Apart from the systematic definition of technology needs for the business areas, this tool can be used for make-or-buy decisions. Useful synergies are highlighted along the referential links. The technologies which have thus been recognized as necessary are compared to the actual stock of technologies available at Central Research. The evolutionary development of these technologies is depicted in so-called technology roadmaps.

Each core technology roadmap consists of 'streets' defined in the language of the customer, i.e. the language of the business operations. Core technology topics for which Central Research believes they are able to secure competitive advantages for business operations are clearly separated from technologies in which Central Research is not (yet) present. A technology roadmap leads to an all-encompassing technology vision. These visions are also communicated as long-term goals to non-industrial, external research institutes.

It is the aim of this broadly-based technology planning to visualize central R&D activities not only in core technologies, but also in the design of large projects. Central R&D and decentralized development units in business areas are encouraged to develop a common point of view on supply and demand, which should eventually result in clearly defined project agreements. Because of the dynamics in technology and the business environment, technology planning is a revolving process that is to be applied and updated at least once a year.

Customer-oriented R&D is supported by research in the above-mentioned innovation fields. In cooperation with work groups of the committee for research and development, Central Research systematically defines the general requirements for all electrical areas relevant to Siemens in a top-down process. By surveying long-term trends in technology, markets, and society, researchers in innovation fields aim at generating new and unconventional ideas. The interdisciplinary Central Research department that carries out this research is relatively small, but may call on scientists from other departments or divisions when needed.

Siemens was able to improve the market-orientation through a two-stage approach combined with intense internal discussion: The business units follow the market very closely, try to achieve high responsiveness towards customer needs. The central research units are uncoupled from the customers, pursue longer-term goals and try to achieve their market-orientation through responsiveness towards business unit needs. This approach has the advantage of separating the efficiency-driven business units with their daily business problems from the more long time, technology and effectiveness-driven units of research.

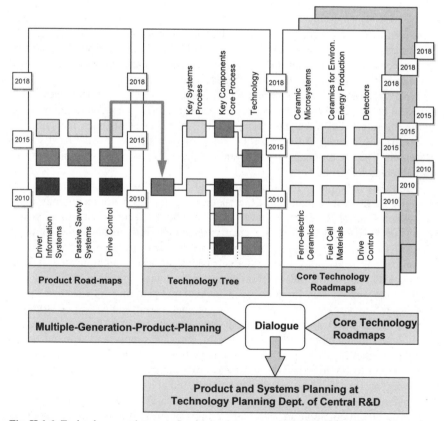

Fig. II.1.6. Technology requirements fine-tuning by means of Multiple Generation Product Planning and Core Technology Roadmaps.

4   General Electric - Staying Vital through Business-Orientation and Cooperation

General Electric (GE) has been famous for being No. 1 or No. 2 in every market it operates. Recognizing that this placement depends very much on how narrow the markets were defined, GE redefined many of its markets such that their market share dropped below the 10% or even 1% level. This shifted thinking at GE from established businesses to new opportunities. Today even more emphasis has been put on innovation and new ventures.

GE reacted to the challenges of speed, costs, and quality by making fundamental changes to corporate R&D in the 1980s. The main changes were made in:

- The funding system;
- Creating the boundary-less company.

With the old system, two thirds of the funds for corporate R&D were 'assessed funds', i.e. granted by the CEO's office. This was changed to a system in which 50% of the funds had to come from contracts with GE business units, 25% from external contracts, and only 25% from these assessed funds. Business units are free to buy research services from anywhere. They can do it themselves, get it from universities, national labs, or even competitors. The only constraint is that they are not allowed to cut their funding for corporate R&D by more than 20% in a year.

This market mechanism of funding ensures that GE's Corporate R&D Center works on those projects that are vital to its business units. The actual allocation of the funding is done in close cooperation with key customers in the business units. Some 100 key objectives are identified at the beginning of the year, and their progress is monitored and reviewed regularly. At the end of the year, the customers decide how well the R&D Center has achieved the objectives.

This system achieves a higher customer-orientation than an elaborate project portfolio which is sold to the business units. The R&D Center is measured not in terms of technological or scientific achievements but in how well it served the businesses. This is done mainly by voting dollars in terms of the amount the business units are willing to pay for research the next year. At the same time, 25% of the funding from corporate headquarters enables the R&D Center to work on high-risk, exploratory, or unpopular research for which no single business unit is willing to pay alone.

The GE Corporate R&D Center today serves all of the 6 GE business areas. It employs some 1,900 scientists from disciplines such as chemistry, electronics, software and management science. The overall R&D expenditure at GE of US$ 3.4 billion in 2005 is distributed among the Center and the laboratories around the world, having a total staff of 2,500 researchers (see Fig. II.1.7).

The removal of boundaries at GE rests on intensive cooperation with the business units. This helps to share similar values and a common language for the company as a whole. In carrying out R&D projects, researchers team up with engineers from development and manufacturing, as well as experts from marketing and service from the business units. Unlike before, when research, engineering, manufacturing, and marketing were carried out sequentially, this team works together from the beginning to the end. The term 'one-coffee-pot' teams has been coined to describe this approach, because the team members are gathered at the same table, around the same coffee pot, throughout the project.

Working in cross-functional teams often means that researchers work on the factory floor. As part of the Center's technical support, researchers are directly involved in working with external customers, going into the field to utility plants, as well as becoming part of business teams.

The role of corporate R&D during much of this century was to improve the performance of products and occasionally creating new ones. In the past ten years, the rules of the game have changed: Speed, low costs, and high quality have to be achieved without sacrificing performance and innovation. The globalization of markets and technology introduced new customers, new opportunities, and new competitors. Higher speed from laboratory to markets was needed, at lower costs, and with products of higher quality.

Especially large companies, like GE, with established rules of how R&D was to be run, were challenged. In the 1980s, GE was focused on research for technology's sake, irrespective whether that technology would contribute to GE businesses or not. This mind-set has changed. Today, every GE researcher must work in a vital project, i.e. a project with an identified impact on future products and services, or a high-risk program with the potential to create an entirely new business. This was achieved by changing the funding system, and by requiring all research to be done work in cross-functional teams.

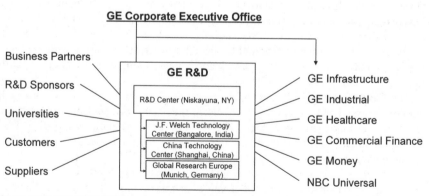

Source: Adapted from Edelheit (1998).

Fig. II.1.7. General Electric's Corporate R&D Center serves all of its business units as well as external customers.

5   EGU - Matrix Organization in a Research Environment

In the former eastern European block, most research institutes enjoyed a centrally-planned environment in which needs were given by administrators and yearly forecasts were taken as fixed. The basic question was not „Whom can I offer what solution to what conditions?" but rather „How can I meet the plan with the given resources; maybe slightly exceed it and thereby distinguish myself as a successful enterprise?" The danger to be evaluated on the basis of services or products was rather small. After the collapse of the Soviet Union, the Czech research institute EGU set out to radically reorganize in order to focus on market and customer demands.

EGU's main research strengths encompassed power plant engineering, IT design and system control engineering. Various consulting services were offered in accordance with its R&D strengths. The former organizational structure of EGU is depicted in Fig. II.1.8. Due to the functional hierarchy and concentration of defined technologies, there was little freedom for creating new technologies. This organization was to change after the political reorganization because it faced the following three problems:

- Differences that emerged between corporate and market structure prevented an effective transformation of in-house competencies into marketable services and products. EGU's activities were focused in the wrong market segments.
- Synergies between technology competencies and potential success factors were not exploited and prevented a clear differentiation from EGU's competitors.
- As the development of services related to EGU's core businesses was not supported, potentially profitable market-segments were not discovered and consequently expanding EGU's business fields were restricted.

The mere introduction of a marketing department did not solve the problems and discrepancies that had evolved between company organization and its environment. It was therefore decided to engage a German consulting company to develop a modern organizational lay-out which would be appropriate with the requirements of today and solve long-grown problems.

A suitable structure which was to combine technology and market driven innovation was found in a matrix organization. The implemented organization concentrates internal resources in „technology centers" (TC) and directs target-group specific services into „strategic business unit centers" (SBUC).

In order to promote technology integration of radical innovations into everyday business operations, it was necessary to include temporary project teams. Combining the matrix with an interlacing project structure secured efficient resource pooling and resulted in a multi-dimensional matrix organization. A well-organized multi-project management now allows efficient know-how transfer and customer orientation.

Each SBUC consists of a set of functional managers, project managers, and administrative and sales staff. All SBUCs are independent and self-responsible

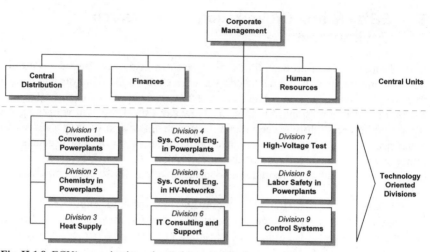

Fig. II.1.8. EGU's organization prior to the reorganization.

profit centers converting self-developed strategies. They serve as contact offices for customers and coordinate customer service directly. SBUCs are characterized by their own distribution departments and autonomous new project acquisition. Order management and coordination of corporate resources for execution of a complex project reside within these units. The projects are led by members of the SBUC to ensure customer focus.

In consultation with project leaders from SBUCs, TCs provide them with manpower and other resources. TCs are responsible for the operational execution of projects and ensure technology leadership of the company by continuous improvement of the methods and systems employed. They guarantee the competence of the corporation in relation to the customer, the competition, and the international, technical-scientific community.

Before a TC is created, it must be verified that it is required by market demand. The concentration of competencies in a TC is evaluated on the basis of minimum customer requirements and comparable competitor performance potential. This also allows EGU to determine the investment share of the participating business areas. If a TC is not used any more, two alternatives are considered. First, the technological resources may be refocused. If this is not possible, then, secondly, the individual technologies must be given up or removed from that TC in order to restore overall competitiveness. The TC evaluation follows a formal three-step procedure:

- Identification of quality and quantity of the available resources under consideration of machinery equipment on the one hand and know-how of the employees on the other.

- Evaluation of the resources by measuring them in terms of the minimal technology requirements which potential customers in the respective business areas might have.
- Comparison of own performance potentials with those of the main competitors.

The technologies employed for service and product generation play a minor role in SBUC formation, since a SBUC will have to be defined with the customer and not the technology in mind. It has to be identified which customers demand what services in the individual market segments, and which customer problems are solved with the services offered by the SBUC. Last but not least, the concentration of individual activities in SBUCs improves transparency for customers who want to identify the appropriate contact quickly for their specific problems and expect optimal service throughout the entire project life time.

Especially in externally-oriented SBUCs, extroverted people with salesman characteristics are called for. People in the pure research environment usually exhibit other qualities. Technically-trained and business-oriented people will identify customer problems quickly and serve as interpreters between customers and internal TCs. In case a company fails to fill the SBUC positions with qualified management personnel, the danger of impeding entrepreneurial progress is large. The step from technology to customer orientation has not yet taken place in the minds of many employees. Appropriate training and education must support changes in management and organization.

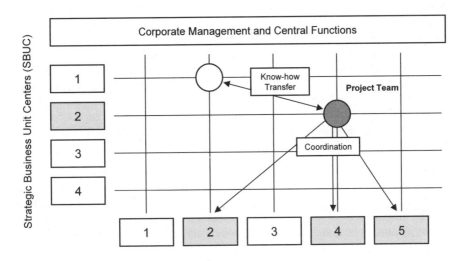

Fig. II.1.9. A matrix organization that integrates research and services.

6   Rolic - Selling Liquid Crystal Research to Customers and Markets

Spin-off companies are commonly regarded as small ventures, freed from the constraints of their parent organization, to commercialize a new technology or particular know-how (Roberts and Malone, 1996). Rolic, a research-based company engaged in liquid crystal (LC) substance development and LC engineering, gained more operational freedom when the original inventor and his research team left Hoffmann-La Roche to create their own enterprise (Fig. II.1.10).

The origins of modern LCDs date back to the 1970s, when two large Swiss companies, Hoffmann-La Roche and Brown Boveri & Cie. (now ABB) joined forces to investigate the applicability of electro-optical field-effects in medical devices (von Zedtwitz, Schadt, and Brauchli, 1996). Schadt and Helfrich of Roche discovered the electro-optical twisted nematic (TN) effect, which is fundamental to every modern LCD device today. Schadt also played a central role in developing and providing much of the LC substances now needed in LCD devices.

Despite the apparent superiority of liquid crystals over comparable display technologies, they initially failed to attract the interest of the market. Roche subsequently reduced research in liquid crystals. When the Japanese industry began to fill the shelves with pocket computers and watches equipped with LCDs, BBC and Roche realized the full market potential of their original discovery too late. Although Roche established itself as an important LC substance supplier to Japanese LCD producers, research in this field was internally never fully accepted. At the beginning of the 1990s, Roche decided it would abandon R&D on LC substances.

Since the innovative capability of the Roche LC team was sufficiently proven, it was declared unwise to tear apart this successful research team. It was agreed to further support the team with venture capital and to establish Rolic Ltd. as a research company with the designated goal to carry on LC-related research under the leadership of the original inventor, Martin Schadt. With this spin-off, Rolic gained strategic and operational freedom unknown to the LC research group before. The task of its approximately 30 scientists and engineers is to discover and transform new electro-optical effects of today's and future LCD technologies. Rolic also designs and develops liquid crystals and functional organic materials.

The main products of Rolic are patents and know-how. They form the basis for future technologies in the areas of electro-optics and LC materials. Rolic specializes in:

- The conception, optimization, and adaptation of new electro-optical devices;
- The synthesis of new application specific organic materials up to the prototype stage;
- The management of world-wide R&D relationships between Rolic, the chemical/pharmaceutical and the electronics industry, as well as the research institutions located around the world.

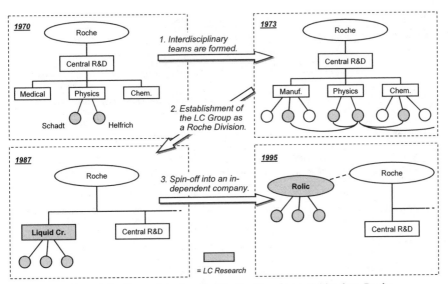

Fig. II.1.10. The path leading to the spin-off of the liquid crystal activities from Roche.

This know-how is vital for chemical and electronics companies in their battle for optimal positioning in emergent technologies and for reducing the time-to-market. It is Rolic's explicit strategic intent to develop their research products in close contractual collaboration with a few selected high-tech device manufacturers from the early prototype stage to the innovative, manufacturable product. For this reason, intensive R&D personnel exchange is just one instrument to ensure efficient joint development. Rolic also provides consulting and technology transfer until the industrial realization of the LCD device is secured. By licensing out its LC patents, Rolic is able to supply the proper and appropriate liquid crystals already at the beginning of the production process for new devices. Based on its device and chemical patents, Rolic earns a considerable portion of its total income in royalties. Rolic therefore focuses on R&D of new electro-optical devices, device-specific organic substances, and the application engineering in cooperation with electronics and chemical companies. Mass production of devices and device-specific substance are not carried out by Rolic, but by its licensees.

Apart from its primary research focus on nematic liquid crystals, Rolic pursues medium and long-term research goals to ensure the development of future technologies based on other scientific principles, resulting in developments such as cholesteric LCD projection systems and ferro-electric LCDs.

The spin-off into an independent research company was an important step towards customer-oriented research. The LC activities at Roche, which were born out of the diversification strategies popular in the 1970s, were put into a new organizational framework without the organizational confinements necessary for hosting all the other activities at Roche involving a wide range of pharmaceutical and chemical research. The establishment of Rolic as a mission-guided research

Table II.1.1. The four cases and their drive for market-orientation in comparison.

Characteristics	Siemens	General Electric	EGU	Rolic
Initial motivation	Range and complexity of technology	Declining competitiveness	Wrong markets, poor transformation of technological strengths	Creating own business on base of existing research and focus
Research philosophy	Sustain long-term innovation	Be No. 1 or No. 2 in every market GE operates	High-quality technology services	Technology leadership, consulting and services
Desired solution	Aligning research and business plans	Transfer speed, costs, quality	Combine technology and market-driven innovation	Spin-off
Main tool of customer-orientation	Innovation fields; road-mapping	Funding scheme, collaboration	Matrix organization, multi-project management	Direct interaction between scientist and customer
Key challenge	Correct identification of trends	Balance short- vs. long-term	Shift of mind-set, elimination of old technology centers	Maintain personal network
Decentralization of company	High	High	Low	Low
Decentralization of R&D	11 research centers, 150 R&D labs	1 global research center, 3 technology and research centers	Low	Low

company was a logical consequence of the growing autonomy of the LC group at Roche: From individual research, i.e. from a small team of researchers working in separate laboratories, to a separate LC research group. Schadt's personal dedication and interdisciplinary vision bridged the traditional gap between the chemistry and physics laboratories at Roche, which taken alone were fundamentally inappropriate for any serious LC research. Unfortunately, a necessary and consequent business champion in top management was missing from early on.

The Rolic example also demonstrates the extremely interlaced networking in the chemical industry. Both national and foreign resources are tapped in LC research and development. The researchers at Rolic are internationally leading scientists who have made major contributions to the establishment and advancement of LCDs and LC material technologies. These scientists have been exposed to international research at an early stage in their career, either by spending extensive time periods abroad or by collecting wide-spread experience through international contacts. Adequate management of information and mutual trust are indispensable in R&D cooperation or strategic alliances. The technological competence and the innovation potential of each alliance partner in his respective special field is also of central importance.

By reorganizing its LC activities, Rolic concentrated on the value chain in downstream industries. Long-term success was achieved by customer-orientation in research management. A research-driven invention without an envisaged target market or even a vague conception of product design had thus found its logical conclusion after long years of uncertainty and battles for in-house acceptance in a new organizational and strategic framework of an independent research company.

7   Conclusions

The presented examples demonstrate the diversity of approaches towards customer-oriented research. Customer-oriented R&D means to concentrating on customer-relevant problems, on specific technological competitive advantages, and raise the scientists' awareness for market demand. It is not enough to include business unit managers in steering committees of research projects: Long-term innovation is given too little attention. Customer orientation works best when fully integrated with all corporate functions, explicitly supported by corporate strategy, and backed-up by customer-driven funding. Unfortunately, consequent customer focus in research is restricted by bureaucratic structures and therefore calls for seemingly unconventional forms of project organizations.

Technology development is a team sport; key players include not only the researcher, but also development engineers, product and manufacturing engineers, suppliers, and marketing and sales staff. It is very important to contact potential R&D customers early in the research process. This is beneficial to gain the customers' acceptance, to raise the scientists' credibility, to obtain an understanding of the customers' needs and problems, and to establish a continuous interchange of ideas as research proceeds. Thus, everyone involved will feel ownership and assume responsibility for the project. Contributions from a team that engages a diverse range of stakeholders significantly enriches the quality of research.

Extreme customer-orientation comes, of course, not without inherent disadvantages. Exclusive business-unit funding, for instance, endangers the long-term perspective of corporate research. The four cases also describe how to counteract the sometimes detrimental side effects. Table II.1.1 lists key characteristics, advantages, and dangers of customer-orientation in research in each of the five cases.

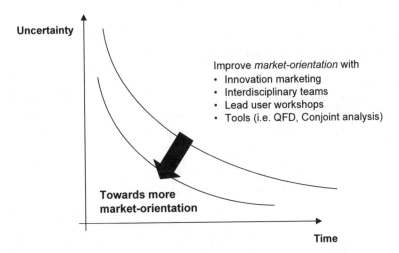

Improve *market-orientation* with
- Innovation marketing
- Interdisciplinary teams
- Lead user workshops
- Tools (i.e. QFD, Conjoint analysis)

Fig. II.1.11. Increased R&D productivity through increased market-orientation.

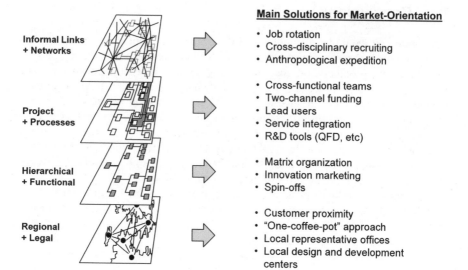

Main Solutions for Market-Orientation

Informal Links + Networks
- Job rotation
- Cross-disciplinary recruiting
- Anthropological expedition

Project + Processes
- Cross-functional teams
- Two-channel funding
- Lead users
- Service integration
- R&D tools (QFD, etc)

Hierarchical + Functional
- Matrix organization
- Innovation marketing
- Spin-offs

Regional + Legal
- Customer proximity
- "One-coffee-pot" approach
- Local representative offices
- Local design and development centers

Fig. II.1.12. Main solutions in R&D market-orientation.

The customer of technology is frequently wrong about the requirements (Frosch, 1996). His statement of the problem to be solved is either too shallow or short-term, or it is a formulation of what the customer thinks is the problem. The technologists, on the other hand, are wrong, too, but in complementary ways. Here, research customer-orientation comes into full play. What happens in successful problem-solving, i.e. the successful definition of a technology, product concept or process, is the joint redefinition of the problem along with the redefinition and creation of the solution. In this dialogue, the very specific technological knowledge and the implicit customer application knowledge are merged.

Experience clearly shows that technical success of a project is not sufficient for commercial success of the product. Even if technical problems get solved there remains the uncertainty of commercialization. Doing things right is not enough - doing the right things is even more important. This also includes the focus of the right goals. The closer a project is oriented towards the market, the higher is the certainty of market success later. Usually, market orientation increases during the execution of a project. But a strong customer focus at the beginning can shift this curve and, thereby, increase R&D productivity, by using instruments such as QFD, lead user workshops, and matrix organizations (Fig. II.1.12).

Problems arise from the different time horizons for research and for business operations: The time horizon required in industrial R&D is not on the time scale of the immediate business needs. The research results implemented in development units now stem from people who worked in research laboratories 15 to 20 years ago. Research must therefore anticipate future customer needs just as much as it must satisfy current demands.

A matrix organization with technology centers and strategic business unit centers proves to be a successful organizational form in order to focus internal resources on specific services for relevant customer needs. Superimposing this structure with a project organization introduces the required flexibility and ensures cross-functional learning. Function-centered and business-centered strengths of R&D organization can be combined. Cross-functional teams help transform function-centered R&D operations towards more customer-orientation. However, given that many R&D organizations have to overcome M&A of outside R&D centers, and a disposition to understand internal know-how better than external knowledge, the required degree of cooperation is sometimes difficult to achieve.

Customer-oriented research does not imply that all R&D is carried out by the business units. Research must remain a distinct functional force in its own right. Market-orientation is achieved by approaching the customer and inviting his early involvement in the innovation processes. In order to accomplish these two principal objectives, fulfilling the needs of the market and ensuring long-term innovativeness, a balance must be maintained which is based on the high quality of the research work force and the respect for the market partner.

II.2 Technology Listening Posts

1 Listening Posts in R&D

Knowledge brokerage, from external sources to internal users, has always been a core activity of R&D organizations. However, as technologies become increasingly complex, and new technologies combine to form new markets, individual companies are restructuring R&D to improve their knowledge and technology transfer capability (see Table II.2.1 for a list of recent industry-transforming phenomena). In part, this is done through focusing on certain stages of the R&D process. Thus, knowledge creation and basic research is being partially re-legated to academic institutions and to highly specialized agents (e.g. university science parks and incubators). External knowledge sourcing and the attraction of bringing in outside-in innovations instead of reinventing the wheel are becoming the guiding principles. In part, this is done by assigning technology gathering and listening roles to designated research units, the so-called technology listening posts.

Technological listening posts are particularly often seen in centers of technological excellence and innovation clusters. Following Porter's (1990, 2001) definition, clusters are regional concentrations and networks of companies, specialized suppliers, service providers, firms in related industries, and associated institutions

Table II.2.1. Principal phenomena in innovation and their effects on R&D.

# Phenomenon	Effect on R&D
1 Technology fusion	Interrelated product architectures and product development processes
2 Tighter margins due to competition, industry maturity	Tighter R&D budgets
3 Shorter time-to-market	Reduced product development cycles
4 New technologies, especially in ICT	Dispersed concurrent R&D, more virtual R&D
5 Globalization and worldwide competition	Developing global local products
6 More technological uncertainty	Uncertain value of scientific knowledge
7 Only few star researchers responsible for new technologies	More cooperation with leading universities and research institutes
8 Emergence of new centers of innovation	Need to extend R&D into yet another new locale

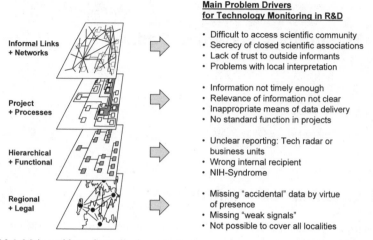

Fig. II.2.1. Main problems for technology monitoring.

(i.e., universities, standards agencies, and trade associations) that compete partially at the marketplace but also cooperate in pre-competitive fields. Silicon Valley in the United States is perhaps the best known example of a cluster, but there are many other examples, such as wireless technologies in Finland, chemical technologies in Basel, biotechnology in Boston and materials sciences in central Germany.

The local character of tacit knowledge makes the presence in and access to these innovation clusters so important for leading companies since only ideas, knowledge and technology that are not widely available via Internet and other modern information technologies can provide sustainable competitive advantage. In the 1990s, many companies started to establish listening posts in order to tap into otherwise inaccessible embedded (tacit) technical knowledge that was presumed to have significant impact on their businesses. For instance, BMW established several listening posts in the United States and in Japan. They successfully gained momentum in several new innovations that are currently differentiating this car manufacturer and are originally derived from its listening post activities.

The establishment of listening posts and the management of an efficient flow of knowledge from innovation clusters towards R&D units can thus open new and promising opportunities for companies. We define a listening post (LP) as a peripheral element of a decentralized R&D configuration with a specific strategic mission and sophisticated mechanisms for knowledge sourcing. Nevertheless, all organizational units, even purchasing and local sales offices, have the potential to be "the eyes and ears" of a company; the listening function is not necessary restricted to LP R&D units.

2   Towards Organizational Concepts for Listening Posts

The notion of a technology listening posts has two antecedents in management research. The first is based in international R&D management and thus has been discussed at length earlier in this book. The second focuses on knowledge as the most important strategic resource of the firm.

Many companies understand that the basis for their competitive advantage is their knowledge base, while innovation is crucial to sustain these advantages (Johannessen et al., 1999). Nonaka and Takeuchi (1995) and Leonard-Barton (1995) argued that knowledge is a productive source for innovation and economic growth. Technology knowledge creation processes are increasingly sophisticated, broad and expensive and the "ability of a firm to recognize the value of new, external information, assimilate it, and apply it to commercial ends is critical to its innovative capabilities" (Cohen and Levinthal 1990: 128), since many organizations lack the ability to listen to their external world and efficiently process the signals received (Allen, 1977).

Recent literature shows strong evidence of technology sourcing as a motive for foreign direct investments. Kuemmerle's 1997 and 1999 concepts explicitly distinguished between 'home-base exploiting' and 'home-base-augmenting', and other research showed that small designated technology listening posts demand lower R&D investments that fully-fledged R&D units.[20]

The Japanese were the first to establish listening posts at a large scale. In the 1980s the Japanese Ministry of Economy, Trade and Industry (METI) needed to overcome a poor incentive system for fundamental research. METI nurtured a national push of fast-follower and imitation strategies which were accompanied by efficient product development methodologies such as systems engineering, kaizen, quality circles and rapid prototyping. In addition, they tried to tap and source knowledge about basic and applied research offshore. Several Japanese companies launched technological listening posts in centers of excellence first in the United States and England and later on in other countries. But Almeida's (1996) research suggested that Korean and European multinationals also sourced knowledge early from US firms in order to upgrade their technological abilities in areas in which they were weak. US firms have set up listening posts in Japan and China to stay breast of new technology trends there. Technological listening is certainly not confined to firms from underdeveloped or technologically limited countries.

Although we have a number of typologies of international R&D and considerable research on the topic of knowledge sourcing, our understanding of the various roles, types, missions, and classifications of listening posts has been relatively limited. Based on our own research we propose the existence of three types of listening posts (Gassmann and Gaso, 2004):

- Trend Scouts,
- Technology Outposts, and

---

[20]   E.g., Patel and Vega (1999), Weil (2000), von Zedtwitz and Gassmann (2002a).

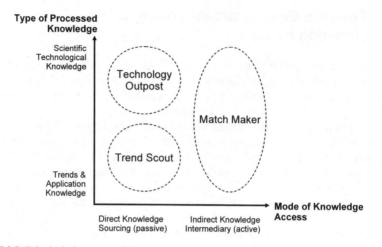

Fig. II.2.2. Principal phenomena in innovation and their effects on R&D.

- Match Makers.

We have classified these three different types according based on the type of processed knowledge and the alignment of the listening post (Fig. II.2.2).

The alignment of the listening post describes either the access to 'Direct Knowledge Sources' or the use of 'Indirect Knowledge Intermediaries'. The access to direct knowledge sources refers to the firsthand, personal process of gaining information on and knowledge of changes in the technical environment.[21] This occurs on a daily basis through scouts reading newspapers and journals, attending conferences, fairs, seminars, venture capital events or talking with peers, suppliers, customers and competitors.

Indirect Knowledge Intermediaries intend to source unique knowledge assets through either the exchange of information on a market basis, or the establishment of relationships with specific partner firms or specialized agents, i.e. the listening post acts as a broker between experts from his own (often central) R&D and specific partner firms. The establishment of such relationships can include consortia of competitors[22], partnerships with suppliers and/or customers[23], university and government collaborations[24], and co-developments, joint ventures and alliances[25]. These partnerships are usually characterized by an intensive period of interaction over time and a high degree of mutual learning (Hamel 1991).

The type of processed knowledge can be distinguished in trend and application knowledge as well as technological knowledge. On the one hand, trend knowledge

---

[21]   E.g., Aguilar (1967), Ghoshal and Westney (1991), Hambrick (1982), Sheen (1992).
[22]   E.g., Hagedorn (1993), Chiesa and Manzini (1998).
[23]   E.g., von Hippel (1988), Hakanson and Johanson (1992).
[24]   E.g., Etzkowitz and Leydesdorff (2000), TEece (1986), Bailetti and Callahan (1992).
[25]   E.g., Kogut (1988), Hamel (1991), Leonard-Barton (1995), Mowery et al. (1996).

refers to both macro- and micro trends. Macro trends are significant, marketplace-shaping trends, that take time to evolve and have the potential to dramatically affect the way consumers live and work, as well as their relationships and decisions. Micro trends are specific trends which range from what's "hot" and what's "not" in lifestyle, culture, and attitudes, to shopping habits, brand and media preferences, and online and offline activities. On the other hand, application knowledge entails information about future products, i.e. applications which are deployable through the migration and/or recombination of existing technologies.

Technological knowledge in this context enfolds certain classes of complex and sophisticated tacit knowledge. This knowledge is usually unique and therefore hard to imitate; it is often embedded within Centers of Excellence.

Each of these listening posts has a specific mission and a sophisticated mechanism for knowledge sourcing and therefore needs a different set of capabilities, as we will see in the siubsequent chapters.

3   Trend Scout

Trend Scouts focus on technological mega trends, new application areas and future potential, triggered by a changing society. Trend Scouts are located in trendy locations, lead markets or innovation clusters mostly. They often take over remote business development functions. Their mission is to gather and transfer trend and application knowledge from centers of excellence, lead users or other stakeholders to the company homebase R&D. Trend Scouts exhibit a small degree of regional embeddedness; resource allocation and coordination takes place centrally and job rotation programs with the homebase R&D are often used to transfer tacit knowledge efficiently. While the advantage of this configuration is the low investment for a steady presence and the high sensitivity to local markets, barriers to integration in local communities and NIH-syndromes at the homebase R&D constitute major weaknesses.

A good example of a trend scout is BMW's Palo Alto Technology Office

Table II.2.2. Profile of a Trend Scout.

Mission	To gather and transfer trends and tacit knowledge from Centers of Excellence, lead users or other stakeholders to the company homebase R&D center.
Configuration	Small degree of regional embeddedness
	Central coordination and control over resource allocation
	Job rotation programs
Strengths	Low investment for a steady presence in the target area
	High sensitivity to local markets and trends
Weaknesses	Hard to integrate in local communities if not regionally embedded
	NIH-syndrome, Home R&D center is reluctant to accept "new" ideas from outside, even though they themselves set up the listening post
Examples	BMW's Palo Alto Technology Office, BMW's Designworks in Los Angeles
	Daimler-Chrysler's listening posts in Tokyo and Daimler-Chrysler's research and technology center in Palo Alto

(PAYTO) in Silicon Valley.[26] Founded in 1998, it is staffed with 16 employees. Its mission is to be permanently on the look-out for new trends, highly specialized and unique technical knowledge and technologies and to seek and establish contacts with potential external partners. The combination of advanced technologies with product visions, market research, prototypes and customer responses often yields in breakthrough innovations.

At PAYTO, teams of three people have 90 days to identify, explore and develop new projects. The teams are often cross-functional, so that every project has the perspective of a marketer, an engineer and a scientist. If the team determines that the technology has a chance, the engineers begin to create a component and later on a prototype and test it in the interior of a production car. If the technology survives the rigorous testing procedure it goes to Munich and is showed to BMW's senior management.

As a recent innovative example, the new BMW car control mechanism in their 7-series – iDrive – marks BMW's entry into the era of intelligent cockpits by combining the overall control of more than seven hundred functions within one system with brilliant simplicity. When visionary customers began complaining that the dashboard was taking away their attention from the road, marketers, engineers and designers started thinking about a possible redesign and reduction of all the numerous knobs on the dashboard. BMW's Innovation Strategy Board relied on PAYTO, which delivered after 90 days a first draft of iDrive. In addition to suggesting a new technology, PAYTO found a small software company (Immersion) that could provide the technology, evaluated it, and showed it to BMW's senior management. Munich engineers continued to work with Immersion staffers on the iDrive device and after all, the new iDrive hit the street in a Z9 study vehicle at the 1999 Frankfurt Motor Show. BMW licensed the technology from Immersion and partnered Immersion with Japanese electronics component supplier Alps Electric to develop iDrive. Finally, iDrive showed up in the newly launched 7-series sedan.

4   Technology Outposts

Technology Outposts focus on specialized technological knowledge. Typically, their location is determined by technological excellence of an academic institution (e.g., MIT, Boston) or accumulation of academic and company high-tech players in innovative regions. In some cases excellent infrastructure has been the industrial attractor of such players (e.g., CERN, Geneva). A technology outpost's mission is to gather sophisticated technological knowledge and transfer technologies from centers of technological excellence to the homebase R&D. Outposts usually exhibit both a high degree of regional embeddedness in the particular scientific community and a high degree of independence and autonomy towards the central R&D. While they usually have top management commitment, they can often become "engineer playgrounds".

---

[26]   See also the BMW case in this book.

Table II.2.3. Profile of a Trend Outpost.

Mission	To gather sophisticated technological knowledge and transfer technologies from "Centers of Excellence" to the homebase R&D center.
Configuration	High degree of regional embeddedness in the scientific community High degree of independence
Strengths	High top management commitment Adaptation to local markets Exploitation of local resources
Weaknesses	Can often become "engineer playgrounds" Central directives from the homebase R&D center can suppress creativity and flexibility NIH-syndrome
Examples	Hitachi in Dublin and Cambridge Daimler-Chrysler's joint research lab in Shanghai and research center India in Bangalore BMW's Car IT in Munich BASF's biotech outposts close to Boston Schering's outpost in Tokyo.

For instance, Hitachi installed technology outposts in Dublin (Ireland) and Cambridge (UK) in 1988 to participate in the fundamental (and to some extent applied) research of leading universities. The Hitachi Cambridge Laboratory (HCL) focused on research in future 'revolutionary' innovative semiconductor devices which could open and lead the main world industry into the 21st century. Research on quantum devices is vigorously pursued, especially involving challenges such as use of the quantum „particle" nature of electrons, as well as ultra-high speed transmission of signals by using the probabilistic transmission of „quantum wave function". Hitachi's Dublin Laboratory (HDL) was established within the campus of Trinity College Dublin, in the building of Innovation Center – TCD-industry collaborative incubation center – researching advanced computing, especially ultra-parallel computing, and advanced recognition, including opto-neural networking. Both laboratories put great importance on the collaboration with universities, especially with on-site ones. HCL has been collaborating with the Microelectronics Research Center of the Cavendish Laboratory, Cambridge University, while HDL has been extending partnerships with Trinity College Dublin, Imperial College London and Oxford University.[27]

A good example of the synergy between Hitachi's Cambridge Laboratory (HCL) and Cambridge University was the discovery of the "Femto-Second Ultra-Fast Quantum Device" in 1995. Femto-second ultra-fast quantum device is the challenge of using the „wave" nature of an electron, to achieve future ultra fast switching devices for both high-end telecommunication and ultra-fast computing in the 21st century – an integrated information network age. This challenge requires extremely demanding and disciplined patience in accumulation of repetitive experimentation using extremely accurately controlled laser systems. In August of 1995, Hitachi HCL team, however, succeeded in creating and demonstrating the coherent „Femto-second" pulses, by the innovative scheme named „Coherent Destruction" and „Coherent Construction".

---

[27] See also the Hitachi case in this book.

After this success, the European government, invited the HCL team to participate in the ESPRIT network named "Phantoms" for future mutual research communication.

5   Match Maker

Match makers have pure diplomatic functions and act as ambassadors of a company. Their processes and skills are similar to external political institutions (e.g., the Swiss Federal Science Consulates called SwissNex, or a smiliar organization run by Finland's TEKES). Core competences of these match makers are the initiation, leverage and establishment of contracts and cooperations. They exhibit a high degree of regional embeddedness, are often organized autonomously and posses anextensive informal network.

DaimlerChrysler's listening post in Moscow is such a match maker. Its mission is the establishment of links between the central research center of the company, with 90% of the researchers located mainly in Germany, and Russian scientists (especially in the field of algorithms and material sciences).

In collaboration with the German Chamber of Industry and Commerce (DIHK), the Fraunhofer-Gesellschaft (FhG) and the German Federation of Industrial Cooperative Research Associations (AiF), the German Ministry of Economics and Labor set up 18 match makers in 18 different innovation clusters. These offshore contact offices offer German SMEs important support in international activities. Match makers introduce cooperation partners for research and development, advise on cooperations with foreign research institutes, organize seminars and exchanges as well as meetings of entrepreneurs, R&D directors and applied research scientists. Match makers analyze the research landscape in the host country, especially seeking new technological developments. The match makers of the Ger-

Table II.2.4. Profile of a Match-Maker.

Mission	To act as a mediator towards leading regional technology suppliers, research institutions and future relevant partners through the establishment of multidimensional relationships within the regional scientific community.
Configuration	High degree of regional embeddedness Often autonomously organized Huge informal network
Strengths	Access to new and/or complementary areas of knowledge Enables sharing of costs and risk Often breakthrough and radical innovations
Weaknesses	Often no ownership and control over the knowledge asset in question Knowledge losses through externalization NIH-syndrome
Examples	Technology Scouts of the German ministry of economics Daimler-Chrysler's listening post in Moscow BMW's Technology Office in Tokyo Siemens in Beijing.

many Ministry are mainly citizens of the host country with a deep technological understanding and huge informal network, and aim opening up foreign innovation sources and matching foreign R&D-partners with home-based SMEs.

6   Hybrid Listening Post Configurations

Typically, a company does not have only one type of listening post. A combination of the three types is usually more conducive to brokering knowledge from around the world back into the company. A good example for such a listening post network is BMW, which has a rather large centralized R&D organization in Munich. Central FIZ ("Forschungs- und Innovationszentrum", i.e., Research and Innovation Center) has become well-known because of its open and process oriented architecture allowing external suppliers to work directly with R&D. In order to overcome ethnocentric centralization and enrich external input, BMW has started to establish all three types of listening posts (Fig. II.2.3).

Specifically, BMW launched the following listening post activities:

- BMW's Technology Office in Tokyo, which operates as a match maker, was founded in 1981 and comprises of 30 employees in the mid-2000s. Beneath the gathering of trends and application knowledge, mainly Japanese employees act as door openers towards the Japanese scientific community and competing as well as non-competing companies with the aim to tap tacit and embedded knowledge.
- BMW's Designworks in Los Angeles was founded in 1972 and acquired in 1995. By 2005, 70 employees were working in this trend scout, gathering future trends and development of new car designs.
- BMW's Palo Alto Technology Office, another trend scout in the Californian Innovation Triangle, was found in 1998 and employed 16 staff members that were primarily concentrating on six strategic topics: 'Human-Machine Interfaces' for handling technology more simply; 'Mechatronics', for integrating sensor, actuator technology, and electronics; 'Information, Communication, and Entertainment' issues in automobiles; 'Driver assistance', through Telematics, for example 'B2X' for new portals and new opportunities for business communication; 'Materials and Production', e.g. form-memory alloys.
- BMW's Car IT, a technology outpost in Munich itself, was founded in 2002 and had 15 employees working in close relationships with suppliers and local universities and research centers on the definition and implementation of software systems and applications for the automotive industry.

Additionally, the innovation management department at BMW started an internet interface for the attraction of outside-in innovations called Virtual Innovation Agency (VIA). This can be understood as a non-institutionalized e-listening post aiming to source technological knowledge from outside the company. Thereby VIA had both a passive and active strategic alignment. The passive alignment refers to attracting outside-in innovations, whereas the active characteristic supported the external search for suitable innovation suppliers.

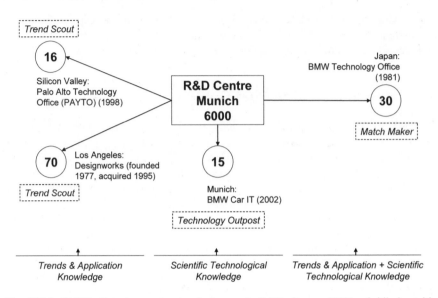

Fig. II.2.3. BMW's listening post network (corporate R&D sites or 100% subsidiaries with headcounts).

Through this Internet portal BMW was seeking development of new relationships with any potential external innovators: individuals, small companies, and large companies from other business centers and research centers. Those who developed an idea that could increase BMW's competitive advantage could use a website set up by the company to offer support while maintaining confidentiality of their idea (http://zulieferer.bmw.de/en/via/). If BMW decided in implementing the idea, it provided personal contacts in the appropriate special departments and reimburses the innovator for his idea.

BMW institutionalized filters and self-assessment procedures to help select innovative solutions which were best suited to go through the VIA. This way, the novelty, technical feasibility, and economic viability of the idea could be assessed effectively and quickly. VIA associates, acting as the first filter, assessed the survivors ideas, registered them, and reported their findings to the appropriate center of competence, which then analyzed the idea and the associates' reports. If the center of competence thought the idea had merit, a contract was signed to allow a market assessment.

7   Managerial Implications and Conclusions

This chapter presents three different types of listening posts: trend scout, technology outpost, and match maker. Each of these archetypes has a specific mission and a highly sophisticated mechanism for knowledge sourcing and therefore needs

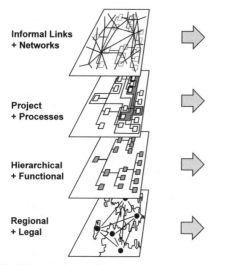

Main Solutions for Listening Posts

Category	Solutions
Informal Links + Networks	• Job rotation • Anthropological expedition • Able to read inbetween the lines • Reads "weak signals"
Project + Processes	• Project-based match-making • Own projects / products for HQ • Clear involvement in global innovation processes
Hierarchical + Functional	• Local representative office • Flat hierarchy • Charismatic / senior leader • Attached to local R&D unit
Regional + Legal	• Multi-lingual scouts • Local showcase R&D • Small local listening posts

Fig. II.2.4. Main solutions in technology listening posts.

a different set of capabilities. External knowledge sourcing so far neglected the development of a comprehensive understanding of the problem in the context of listening posts. A better understanding of the underlying mechanisms is needed as listening posts become new and promising opportunities for companies.

Much of the success of a listening post depends on a clearly designed mandate for such a center, the appropriate managerial culture "back home" to optimally use such an listening post, and be responsive to the signals emanating from it. Headquarter management must be clear on what is required from such an listening post, and personnel at the home center must also appreciate the importance of supporting and 'listening to' such an outpost.

It is not by chance that the Not-Invented-Here-syndrome is mentioned as a potential weakness of listening posts. It may be controlled to some extent depending upon which of the different listening post types is adopted, though our interviews indicate that the intensity of NIH and the prevailing reluctance to act upon the results of listening posts is strongly influenced by their operational involvement in R&D activities.

The following managerial implications summarize some of the impact the listening post have on the home base and the rest of the organization:

• Much depends on the knowledge-sharing culture of the home base organization. The headquarter management team must prepared to be open (on an ongoing basis) and share information with their listening post staff. Mutual understanding is crucial.

- The company should be clear on what technologies it is seeking (focus). All too often there is no clear policy on these questions, and the company addresses them at the last minute in response to an initiative raised from the listening post. Reasons are often indicated by too reactive, short-term management.
- Job rotation programs between the listening post and operational units increase mutual understanding and help building up redundant knowledge. Allen's (1977) early statement that 'the best way to transfer technical information is to move a human carrier' is more valid than ever. An assignment of maximum three years seems to be practical in several firms.
- Involvement in direct development projects enlarges the acceptance of a listening post since the value of the contribution is recognized. Especially in the ramp-up phase a part-time direct involvement in important projects increases internal recognition.
- It is important to consider who the listening post reports to and what communication channels it uses. The best medium seems to be face-to-face briefings and not fire-and-forget written newsletters.
- One must try to avoid the situation to provide information already known to the management, as it will be regarded as unnecessary and merely confirming what management instinctively already knew; and sensitize senior management to material that is completely new to them and help them accept it more readily, without risking their rejection or even responsibility of inconvenient disclosure. Îintelligence professionals often mention the 'shooting the messenger' paradox.
- Other issues deal with the integration of listening post with the parent organization into ongoing primary operations. There will typically be a number of different sources of information that need to be integrated carefully. For instance, a listening post can make use of the company's marketing people – those who are 'out there' making 'primary' contact with customers etc. or direct the mother company's business development personnel to act, or merely recommend action, or report on possible courses of action.

Another perspective is that of the technology involved, for example, is the company seeking more immediate and tactical inputs for development or longer term inputs at the research level. Note that R&D is not a homogeneous activity – just as research has a different dynamic from development – depending on the company, industry, technology, stage in product life cycles.

Listening posts need to be managed dynamically: what is appropriate when setting up an listening post is not applicable once the listening post personnel are an integral part of their surroundings. It is necessary and wise to rotate people, while retaining a core of those who develop relational and social expertise in particular geographical locations and markets. If the work of an listening post becomes routine, staff may no longer notice the signals they are supposed to be looking out for.

More work on listening posts and knowledge brokering is needed to develop these models and typologies, including the efficient and effective management of strategic listening posts, especially regarding their flow of knowledge, performance measurement and relationships with regional institutions and local knowledge pools (regional embeddedness).

II.3 Managing the International R-to-D Interface

„Brains are becoming the core of organizations
– other activities can be contracted out."
Charles Handy

1 The Three Roles of the R-to-D Interface

In technology-intensive firms, the two most prominent factors determining the business environment are technology and customers. For the role of R&D, the balance between the two can be tricky.

The purpose of a strategy is to gain a sustainable source of competitive advantage. Optimally, strategy aligns the needs of the customer with the organization's competencies. A principal alignment issue is whether the firm relies on a technology-driven strategy or a strategy-driven technology. In companies with a technology-driven strategy, technology determines the firms overall strategy. This mindset occurs in many research-based firms, where technological breakthroughs give rise to new commercial possibilities (e.g. technology start-ups). Technology shapes strategy (Werther, 1998).

Companies with strategy-driven technology strive to identify market and societal needs and then create technology competencies that enable them to fulfill those needs. They use technology as a source for competitive advantage (e.g. established firms). The market defines the optimal strategy and the required competencies to execute this strategy. Such companies are strongly development-oriented. Strategy shapes technology.

Yet, successful strategies are not judged by their approaches but by their results. If the customer favors a product over competing alternatives, the strategy is successful, regardless of the underlying approach. Technology-driven strategies, however, are opportunistic, which can lead to a lack of focus and deprive the firm of economies of scale required in production and distribution that normally follow from strategic plans. Lack of focus means that the firm is unlikely to create and sustain any core competencies which are essential in mature stages of an industry's life cycle. Strategy-driven companies are more likely to achieve multiple competencies as the basis for core competencies and technologies because strategic efforts have the customer as the common focus.

In research, the problem is not the lack of creative ideas but rather the lack of focus in an environment of abundance of ideas. Research management is about selecting the right ideas and having them prepared and refined for implementation. The goal of industrial research is to provide solutions that can be turned into salable products by development. It is not significant whether these ideas have been created by the firm's own research staff or if they have been acquired externally. The transfer of ideas, knowledge, and technology into successful development projects is the paramount task of research and technology development laboratories. The transfer of new knowledge to development and other downstream corporate functions is the only raison d'être for industrial research.

Hence, the management of this interface between research and development deserves our attention. This interface must fulfill three functions:

- Ensuring the right questions are asked (project creation);
- Ensuring the right ideas are selected (filter mechanism);
- Ensuring the ideas are properly implemented (transfer).

The creation of projects is the most challenging task for R&D. Is it right to pour hundreds of millions of dollars into the joint R&D projects of Daimler-Benz, Ford, and Ballard, with the uncertain outcome of obtaining a fuel-cell based engine in a few years from now? Or would it rather improve profits in the future if the money would be spent on improving existing engine technology? Asking the right questions fundamentally depends on the continuous and bi-directional information flow between R and D. Only if researchers with their insight into technical feasi-

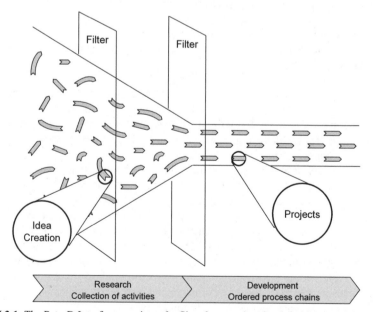

Fig. II.3.1. The R-to-D Interface consists of a filter for ensuring the right ideas are selected, and a transfer process ensuring the ideas get correctly implemented.

bility match their work with the developers' ideas about market acceptance, profitable products will find their way to the customer.

Filtering ideas is a profit-oriented evaluation of project proposals. Technology strategy and market strategy are balanced (see e.g. Wheelwright and Clark, 1991). Only high-potential ideas may be selected to ensure the quality of development projects in terms of technological maturity and customer perception.

Research should take an active stance in facilitating and supporting technology transfer between research and development. A research department that considers itself a free-service institution will not actively promote technology transfer to development and runs the risk of failing to meet important customer needs (ivory tower). Research results gather dust in their shelves because development has no use for them (a project creation and filtering problem), or because they are difficult to assess, access, and apply (a transfer problem). Cooperation at a strategic and project level has been proven to secure the alignment between research and development activities.

The transfer of knowledge between research and development in MNCs is often a transorganizational, cross-border phenomenon. Development mostly follows decentralized production, while research is retained at the central headquarters for better protection and strategic control or most often simply historical reasons. Hence, development is often located near production or the market, and research in centers-of-innovation and near large scientific communities such as leading universities. Geographic distances must be bridged, incurring problems of communication frequency and interaction costs.

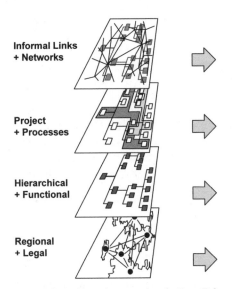

Main Problems for Managing the International R-to-D Interface

Informal Links + Networks
- Tacit knowledge
- Different working cultures
- Different communication patterns
- Geographical immobility of researchers

Project + Processes
- Different project/work cycle-times
- Technology hand-over
- Insufficient idea filtering and project creation

Hierarchical + Functional
- Different funding time horizons
- Compartmentalization
- Profit vs. cost center thinking
- NIH-syndrome

Regional + Legal
- Physical separation between R and D
- Unique R and D locations
- Communication frequency

Fig. II.3.2. Problems in managing the R-to-D interface.

2   Why is Research Different from Development?

In academic research, R&D is often treated as an entity. Surprisingly, most available taxonomies and classifications of different R&D configurations (e.g., Medcof, 2001) do not separate the 'R' from the 'D'. Getting over this simplification is necessary to understand the bottlenecks in technology transfer between R and D. Data are more readily available on R&D as a whole than on R or D alone. Moreover, the boundaries between R and D are blurred in reality as well, being subject to individual interpretation of the early value-adding activities in a firm. The absence of a unanimously agreed distinction between R and D makes it difficult to compare individual companies in the same industry, let alone between different industries.

2.1   What is „Research"?

Industrial R&D is predominantly development. Whereas development spending accounts for 62% of all US R&D activities, it accounts for 75% of industry's spending. Basic research, which accounts for 15% of US R&D spending, accounts for just 4% of industry's activities (Jankowski, 1998: 16).

'Basic research' is defined as experimental or theoretical work undertaken primarily to acquire new knowledge of the underlying foundations of phenomena and observable facts, without any particular application or use in view. 'Applied research' is investigation undertaken in order to acquire new knowledge. It is, however, directed primarily towards a specific aim or objective (OECD, 1992a). Medcof (1997: 303) summarizes research as „the process of discovering new scientific knowledge which has the potential to act as a platform for the subsequent development of commercially viable products and manufacturing processes."

Research is thus different from 'experimental development' which is defined by OECD (1993) as systematic work, drawing on existing knowledge gained from research and practical experience, that is directed to producing new materials, products and devices: to installing new processes, systems and services: or to improving substantially those already produced or installed. 'Development' is not intended to advance fundamental science.

Industrial R&D is divided into research or development, technology or product development, long-term or short-term R&D, or just R and D. Others distinguish between basic research, applied research, product development, process development, and technical service. In spite of such formal distinctions, companies pursue a pragmatic approach to organizing around these tasks. Reasons for engaging in research are manifold:

- Reduce costs of manufacture;
- Set up new businesses;
- Maintain leadership in core technologies;
- Attract excellent people.

Large multinationals or designated research companies engage the strongest in research. Industry-specific and even company-specific working definitions exist what is 'research' and what is 'development'. Because a commonly adhered to framework is missing, it is hard to make conclusive comparison between R and D across companies or even industries. Private enterprises do not use the term basic research itself on the basis of its strict definition. They prefer the term 'fundamental research' for describing the ground-laying work of their most advanced R&D activities.

The term basic, applied research and development are rather misleading and are not very useful for managerial decisions. A pragmatic approach is used by ABB which makes the distinction between R and D that goes into:

- Existing products;
- Next generation products;
- Later generation of products.

ABB thus makes the distinction according to the closeness to the market. It seems that this classification allows every employee to explain more or less instantaneously what he is working for. Due to the widespread use of the term „R&D", we will hold on to it in this context as well.

Even those companies which put emphasis on basic research never proceed to perform such research that has little connection to future business, i.e. basic research purely for science (genuine basic research). They consider the promotion of such basic research more and more a responsibility of the Government (especially the small companies that have a smaller research-intensity than large MNCs). However, private industry sponsors a considerable share of basic research at universities and similar institutes.

Chiesa (1996a) distinguishes between support labs, exploitation labs, and experimentation labs. He claims that experimentation and exploitation labs are part of different R&D structures. Experimentation labs are concerned with particular technologies while exploitation labs concentrate on a particular set of products. Hence, experimentation activities are managed at the corporate level, while exploitation activities are managed at the business unit level.

The pharmaceutical industry is making the clearest difference between R and D. Research consists of synthesis, biological tests, and pharmaceutical screening, lasting several years on average. At the end of this phase, R has produced a new substance, knowing its basic chemical and histological characteristics, and has some ideas about its therapeutic usefulness. The research process requires highly specialized know-how and resources; research is thus carried out in dedicated research labs established in major centers around the world. More and more research is being outsourced to universities and specialized small enterprises which have the best databases at their disposal. The development following research starts with clinical trials, involving tests with animals and human beings to find out about all the effects, risks, and applications of the new drug. Approval by governmental authorities and market introduction conclude the development process (Drews, 1998). This second part in drug-innovation is truly international since approval-procedures are still different from country to country.

In a study carried out by Leifer and Triscari (1987), the following propositions

Table II.3.1. Task environment characteristics of the main categories of R&D.

Type of Research	Degree of orienttation	Presence of common objectives	Payback criterion	Operational time horizon	Degree of uncertainty	Barriers to entry
Basic research	Minimal	Low	Long term	Long run	High	High
Applied research	Medium/high	High	Medium term	Medium run	Moderate	Medium
Development	Medium/high	Medium/high	Short term	Short run	Low	Low

Source: Howells (1984: 31).

about research and development were supported:

- The technology of research units are rated more non-routine than the technology of development units.
- There is a greater extent of interunit dependence for development units than for research units.
- Development units coordinate more with other organizational units than do research units.
- Members in development units place greater importance on other organizational units as sources of information than do members in research units.
- Members of development units process more information to and from people outside their own unit than do members of research units.

They also found that development units perceive the environment as uncertain as do research units, and that research units are relatively more tightly controlled than development units. Their study is inconsistent with results from other research, such as Tushman (1979a,b) who found that research units were less hierarchical than development projects. Allen et al. (1980) found that development projects perform better if the manager is more control-minded and structures internal technical communication.

Howells (1990) notes that the degree of centralization depends on the type of research work being considered. Basic research depends on good information links, and therefore proximity, with the head office. Applied research is more likely to be associated with individual product divisions to warrant specialized research for a certain product technology and good communication with the divisional headquarters is important. Most development activity is oriented towards plants and manufacturing work in terms of pilot plants, testing and prototype work (Table II.3.1).

Our own research suggests that a tighter supervision and control through top management is needed for break-through innovation or projects of strategic importance. If the innovation is concerned rather with ongoing improvement work, like in many dominant-design industries, loose control seems adequate.

2.2 Organizational Differences Between Research and Development

R&D is torn between the pressures for scientific and commercial results. Control and coordination needed for the sake of internal consistency seems to apply little to research-based organization. Bureaucratic and hierarchical control as well as social control does not work as much as scientists feel more affiliated with their profession than to their employers (Asakawa, 1996: 24; Drews, 1989). In international R&D, the difficulties of autonomy versus control become even more prominent: R&D experiences institutional differences at the functional level (research / corporate) as well as at the geographical level (host country / home country).

The actual dispersion of research sites and development sites reveals that in many cases, research and development are not collocated. Moreover, a separate research organization exists which is subject to its own organizational evolution. The internal configuration of firms plays a great role in this location decision, and 'obstacles' in these internal configurations can lead to the decision to not internationalize R, D, or both to a particular host country despite its attractiveness (Baldwin and Lin, 2002; Galia and Legros, 2004).

Among the reasons why R is not collocated with D are:

- D follows manufacturing, R remains at the central headquarters or follows external knowledge-clusters;
- D evolves from local market support, R evolves from scanning and listening posts, and university spin-offs;
- D is attracted to potential market output, R is attracted to the quality of scientific input.

Given that research consumes only a fraction of the overall R&D effort, and that the optimal size of research sites is not significantly smaller than the size of development units (see Kuemmerle, 1997b), it follows that not every development unit can be collocated with a research unit.

Since their location drivers differ, their geographical dispersion is different. Based on our research sample we could confirm that research sites and development sites are differently dispersed globally. Research sites are concentrated in California, Michigan and the Upper East Coast in the United States, in the United Kingdom, France and in Germany in Europe, and in the Kanto and Kansai regions in Japan. Development is more widely spread over all three Triad countries, as well as China, India, South-East Asia, South-Africa, and parts of South America. Israel has attracted research from computer-related and pharma companies, and Bangalore in India is a hot spot for Software research and programming. Other important R&D sites are Toronto, Beijing, Shanghai, Seoul, and Singapore.

Many firms attempt to foster good research by separating research from marketing and manufacturing (Medcof, 1997). It is also not unusual for research to be funded at the corporate level and development at the business level. This separation helps to prevent research from being consumed by the manufacturing and marketing imperatives of the firm, so that the research function can pursue its true mission.

Hirano and Nishigata (1990) identified a special organization for research separated from the other R&D organization. 7 of 12 studied Japanese companies had particular organizations titled basic research institutes or similar names, the remaining 5 performed research in other divisions of development. The reasons for the separate research establishment were:

- A calm and comfortable environment is more likely to cultivate new buds of business seeds for the next century.
- Make researchers and research managers aware that research is evaluated with a measure different from that of short-term development.
- Distunguish research management from development in terms of time and costs.

Hence, private companies seem to consider it necessary for the effective promotion of research to separate the organization from its traditional R&D function. However, it has been noted that this separation should better be with a low fence, indicating the transfer efforts being made as well as the recurrent determination of the extent of the separation.

R&D is thus mainly separated along the time horizon and the cycle times of the individual R&D activities. According to the type of work, e.g. for existing products, for next generation products, or for future technology, the R and D are distributed over the R&D organization. Typically, business units fund little long-term R&D which remains a domain of corporate R&D labs. Business units deal with product platform development, design and engineering services, while corporate R&D is concerned with fundamental research and technology development.

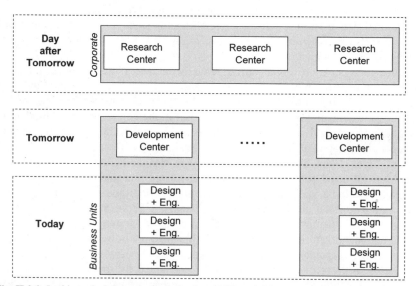

Fig. II.3.3. In this typical three-tier organization, R&D activities are separated according to time horizon and cycle times.

A three-tier organization is realized in very large companies (e.g. NEC, Hitachi, 3M and Xerox). R&D is organized, and separated, according to time horizons and specific competencies (Fig. II.3.3). At NEC, basic and fundamental research is carried out in the R&D Group. Three development laboratories are concerned with medium-term R&D, and system & product engineering units perform application engineering. For instance, while the engineering labs are working on the 64 Mbit DRAM, development labs work on the 128/256 Mbit DRAM, and R&D Group conducts research that prepares for the 1 Gbit version. With this deliberately introduced separation, technology transfer and communication mechanisms rise in importance.

Despite the relative research intensity in national institutes and universities, research in private companies enjoy some distinct advantages (see e.g. Hirano and Nishigata, 1990):

- Interdisciplinary research: Close cooperation between related specialties and disciplines.
- Easy maintenance of quality level of researchers: Researchers who are unsuited to research because of age or other reasons are more easily transferred into other functions.
- Flexible and dynamic management: Based on the general managers responsibility and flexibility, the individual scientists engage more flexibly in their projects (including accounting and personnel affairs).
- Concentration on research: Unhindered by other chores (such as lecturing or administration) scientists in private companies give priority to their exertion of their research abilities.

The main advantages of geographical research concentration revolve around the benefits of scale economies and research efficiencies in association with improved internal communication (Howells, 1990). This counteracts the trend of market-orientation in research which tries to improve information flows with other corporate functions, in particular development and production. Thus there appears to be an optimum size for research centers in terms of general efficiency.

Kuemmerle (1997a) investigated 129 R&D sites and discovered that development sites tend to have a larger optimal size (260 employees) than research sites (182 employees), probably, he suggests, because product development requires a more structured pattern of interaction among a larger number of working groups than research. Hence, research groups are more productive when their interaction with other researchers is less constrained, which is possible when the site is smaller.

In Carnegie Bosch Institute (1994) a group of senior R&D representatives concludes that for each core technology, research should be centralized although the central location does not have to be the world headquarters or the home location. This concept is fully acknowledged by companies organizing their R&D according to the integrated R&D network. This approach has been followed by Nestlé for many years. Today Nestle has two Research Centers in Lausanne (CH) and Tours (FR) in addition to eight Product Technology Centers and seven R&D centers distributed globally.

The main reason for centralizing research are costs (economies of scale), synergy and critical mass with specialists in one place, control, joint use of resources, and intense and quick interaction for consultation and collaboration in an uncertain, complex, and intangible research environment (see also Odagiri and Yasuda, 1996).

Design and development localization depends mostly on the product structure: Low-cost design has to involve manufacturing and suppliers as early as possible, and interaction has to be very close to arrive at the best possible ideas for manufacturing cost reduction. Design is therefore either closely coordinated with or handed over completely to suppliers. Integral design that tries to achieve maximum performance such as satellites or high-speed racing cars is usually carried out in one place (Fig. II.3.4).

The third approach, lowest time-to-market, is the most interesting one from the internationalization perspective: Modular design is still the best approach to achieve short time-to-market. Design and development can be spread over the whole globe, but system integration and coordination of all development activities may be better done in one central place. This approach is increasingly being chosen by the automobile industry: Anti-lock systems are designed at Continental near Frankfurt, and integrated in BMW cars in Munich.

2.3   *Management Differences Between Research and Development*

R&D practitioners have emphasized that crossing the interorganizational boundaries between R and D are at least as challenging as coping with geographical distances.

For instance:

- A different profile of people (thus having a different mind-set and communication culture) is typically employed (scientists versus engineers): Scientists look

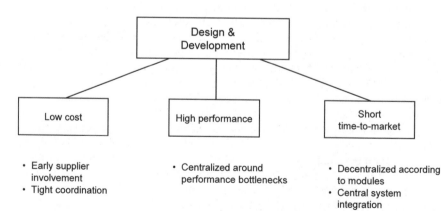

Fig. II.3.4. Three major considerations influence the decentralization of development and design work.

for a basic understanding and theories to explain facts, while engineers usually look for technical solutions good enough to eliminate the problem;

- R is often under central guidance while D is directed by business units;
- People in R are more likely to think and manage for longer term activities and projects than people in D.

The biggest difference between R and D are the results: The end result of product development is information: a plan (Juran, 1988). The plan consists of drawings, bits of metrics, process prescriptions, training lessons, etc., and allows for the market introduction of a product in the market with a clear idea about the probability of its success.

The end results of research is know-how which is hoped to be useful for developing a product, or know-how, that improves supporting mechanisms in development like finite elements, computer-aided-design, or management methods.

Research is frequently kept under direct central authority because the company wants to protect and control critical technology. The main reason is simply that there is no other way to control a complex field like research except by direct involvement of top management. The alignment of vital research can be done only face-to-face and a lot of management attention. This is one of the main reasons why in science-driven companies headquarters are usually close to research centers. Because directives based on strategic considerations are received directly from the top, research enjoys less freedom than development.

As development is usually carried out in business units, it is strongly dependent on the general manager of its business unit. As long as the business unit is making profit, nobody will dig too deep into its development department or projects. In this case, development is rather free in setting its own goals, choosing its own working methods, and taking its decisions in general.

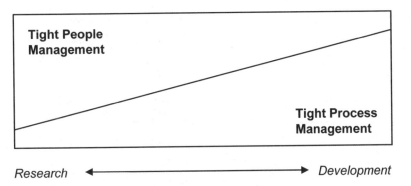

Fig. II.3.5. Research is managing people, while development is more concerned with getting the processes right.

These differences store potential conflicts when interaction (such as technology transfer) between R and D occurs. The management of research thus differs from the management of development. This is reflected in a unique set of critical issues for the research function.

Before we look at examples on how transfer is supported and executed, we look at the role of R&D funding as a means to align R&D activity with the needs of the customer (i.e. business units).

3   Ensuring Vertical Transfer of Knowledge through R&D Funding

Resource allocation and funding provides a major filter for research activities. A strong involvement of business units in project work and funding indicates a market-orientation of the R&D work and, generally, higher technology transfer success rates. The question how to fund research and who pays for it is therefore crucial for determining the success of providing guidelines and transfer support from research to development.

The relationship between how companies structure their R&D organizations and how they fund R&D operations is given in Table II.3.4 (Whiteley et al., 1998: 12-13). This data is based on US surveys for 1995. The data for 'Firms' origin from the IRI Annual R&D Survey while the data for 'Labs' were taken from the

Table II.3.2. The virtual organization and management of collaborative research and development activities in the pharmaceutical industry.

	Research	Development
Aim	Access external information	Acquire complementary resources
Potential Partners	Research centers, universities, personal network-based	Other firms and R&D centers
Scope	Broadly defined	Well defined
Timing	Not well defined	Well defined
People	Individuals highly important	Individuals vary according to task
Resources	Mainly 'human brains'	Resources vary according to task
Formal collaboration criteria	None, generic definition of scientific area	A few clear and explicit objectives
Selection of partners	On a personal basis, often centers-of-excellence	Following a rational and formal process
Cooperation Rules	None, as they would undermine collaboration	'Game rules' such as results, commercialization, time frames, contributions, coordination mechanisms, evaluation schemes
Managerial Approach	Maximize integration, communication, learning	Ensuring the defined criteria are respected
Result Measurement	Very difficult	Immediately
Overall Evaluation	Left with the scientists	Formal and corrective can be decided and implemented collectively by all partners

Source: Chiesa and Manzini (1997).

Table II.3.3. Advantages and disadvantages of sponsored research.

Advantages	Disadvantages
• Strategic business unit sponsorship facilitates interest and makes it easier to disseminate research	• If the business unit loses interest in the project or is under cost pressure, the research project is abandoned
• Double accountability for resources used in R&D	• Less likely to generate unanticipated discoveries
• An appropriate model for market-driven research, as specific products need to be generated	

Management Practices Survey. Combined, data for 68 firms and 168 laboratories are shown. None of the US industries is funding R&D centrally by more than 60%. The more business units are involved, the more they want useful results from the labs they pay.

Theory has advanced models of innovation, such as the linear feed forward model, the linear backtrack model, or the chain-linked model. The principal question a company must ask itself is whether it considers its research in a push or pull position, i.e., whether research is merely a knowledge warehouse as an 'all-you-can-need' service function for development, or whether research may actively sell its ideas to downstream functions, such as development, or even to external parties.

Without vertical transfer, R&D, and basic research in particular, has little justification for existence. However, the intra-firm transfer of knowledge is everything but easy. Analyzing an in-depth case study from the pharmaceutical industry, Currie and Kerrin (2004) showed that international R&D processes were not feasible despite a generous resource and ICT infrastructure that enabled intrafirm knowledge exchange. In fact, academic research knows little about the firm-level factors that facilitate or impede the integration of knowledge in firms with global technology strategies (Frost and Zhou, 2005). Therefore, practice has developed structural models and procedures to link funding and knowledge transfer.

In most companies, vertical transfer of knowledge is ensured primarily by one

Table II.3.4. Percentage of funding, all industries, US data.

Type	Number	Corporate Funds	Business Unit Funds
Corporate Labs of Centralized Firms	32	52.1%	38.5%
Corporate Labs of Hybrid Firms	68	58.6%	36.5%
Segment Labs of Hybrid Firms	37	4.7%	93.7%
Segment Labs of Decentralized Firms	31	6.1%	81.2%
Centralized R&D Firms	17	43.8%	50.8%
Hybrid R&D Firms	35	15.1%	77.3%
Decentralized R&D Firms	9	2.1%	87.1%
All Firms	86	26.8%	68.0%

Source: Whiteley et al. (1998: 12-13), IRI/CIMS R&D Database.

of two funding models, „sponsored research" or „R&D-driven research." With a sponsored research model, the business units or divisions request that specific research projects be carried out for them by R&D. In the R&D-driven research model, R&D generates ideas that it must then sell to business units or divisions. Both models exist in reality and both may be successful. For instance, SIKA, one of the world's most prosperous cement-add-on producers, has followed the R&D-drive for many years, making most of its R&D-money from licenses sold to SIKA's business units. On the other hand, ABB conducts almost no projects without the sponsorship and funding of its business units.

Inherent in the discussion and debate between these two fundamentally different models are the four following questions:

- What are the advantages and disadvantages of these two models?
- What organizational characteristics work better with one or the other model?
- What structures of control and accountability are needed for each model to work well?
- What is the role of each in facilitating transfer?

The answers to all these questions may depend on specific situations (contingency approach). The following section is based on a working report by the Carnegie Bosch Institute (1994).

3.1   *Sponsored Research Model*

In the „sponsored research" model, research is done only when a sponsor or champion in a business unit or division supports it; R&D does not start projects autono-

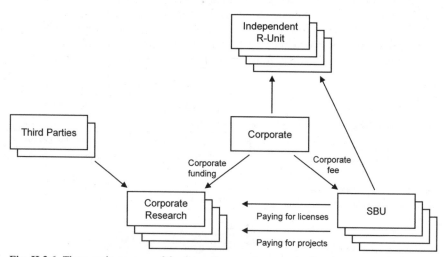

Fig. II.3.6. Three main sources of funding of corporate research: Corporate, strategic business units (SBU), and third parties.

Table II.3.5. Advantages and disadvantages of R&D-driven research.

Advantages	Disadvantages
• Allows a company to develop technologies and competencies that might not be immediately needed, but which could have strategic importance in the future. • Favors basic research.	• May result in considerable waste because none of the business units uses the results (particularly basic research). • May be not close enough to the needs of the customers.

mously. The identity and location of the sponsor may vary from company to company, so that sponsors may be the business unit itself, or they may be outside the business unit. Most often an business unit or division comes to the research group and tries to convince it that the business units proposed research has economic or strategic value. The business unit is lobbying for research resources. This procedure is used because corporate, not business unit, money usually pays for such research. Thus, accountability in this system rests with both the business unit or sponsor, which must convince research of the project's value, and with Corporate Headquarters, which pays for the work.

This model's strong emphasis on accountability may explain why resource-constrained companies prefer it. In some companies, the business unit may provide the majority of the funds, which tends to result in focus on solutions for short-term but highly valued market value. With this model, only ideas migrate from the business unit to R&D; the people stay put. In other companies, however, the business unit rotates people to R&D and then later regains these people. In this situation, the transferred individuals are more likely to take a project back with them from R&D because they have become „owners" of that project. They have most likely formed a group that will sustain itself outside R&D, allowing their idea to take root in the organization. If their project is successful, the individuals involved are more likely to be promoted, further increasing the chances that the idea will be used in the organization. This is an effective means of transferring ideas through people, but the practice is not a universal solution because its continual use can weaken the core research group.

Dilemmas arise if a sponsoring division loses interest in a project or runs out of money and cannot convince Corporate Headquarters to fund the project any longer. One option is to have Corporate Headquarters continue funding the project if it seems sufficiently interesting for the company overall. That is, sometimes R&D sustains an abandoned project because it and Corporate Headquarters believe the project is applicable in ways that the sponsor either did not see, need, or have the funding for. Indeed, some R&D managers believe that the R&D organization can be „smarter" than the business units involved because R&D's expertise with the technology may give it a better perspective on the research's ultimate utility. Thus, R&D may continue projects for which business units do not see the value. Nevertheless, this is always a difficult decision and finishing the project with corporate money eventually has to be defended before management. A project's contribution to core competencies can be a reason for continuation.

3.2   R&D-driven Research Model

In the other model of vertical transfer, R&D-driven research, the key is that ideas and research are generated independently by R&D without specific input or sponsorship of the business units or divisions. Once these ideas develop or research results are available, these ideas must then be sold to business units. In some firms, top management must endorse ideas before work can begin on them, but R&D clearly generates these ideas. Under this model, Corporate Research takes responsibility for disseminating potentially useful results to the business units. In one company this is done by talks, papers, reports, videos, and workshops. The regular participants at these workshops are researchers from both the company's other research labs and from development groups in the business units. In addition, this company schedules yearly exhibitions and research conferences where the labs display yet-to-be-applied findings that could potentially be used throughout the organization.

Sponsorship is one decision that must be made regarding R&D; another is who pays for the research. In some organizations, the sponsor and paying customer are the same unit, while in others these roles are divided. In many companies, corporate research is „free" for all business units. While this encourages the business units to take advantage of R&D resources, not surprisingly, there are always long lines of business units waiting for Corporate R&D to do their research. Given this backlog of requested work, how does Corporate R&D choose its projects? The company's overall corporate strategy is the main guideline. In addition, projects whose results are more likely to benefit several business units are more likely to be chosen. In most organizations, results generated by Corporate research for one research project are freely available to other business units. For example, in one firm, the International Group regularly adapts and improves on products developed for the US market, which are often perceived as the standard formulations.

3.3   Contingency Model for R&D Drive

The appropriateness of using sponsored or non-sponsored models may depend on whether the work is basic research or applied development. Basic research may be more successfully funded using an R&D-driven model in which corporate research is the sponsor. Applied development, for which specific goals exist, may be better sponsored by the strategic business unit that is responsible for the project. The appropriate sponsorship model also depends on the risk preferences of the organization, the methods of accountability and control, and the nature of the industry and projects. Other factors that may determine how much research should be sponsored and paid for by corporate headquarters include the size of the company and type of technology.

In most companies, a combination of approaches is used with the corporate share varying considerably depending on the specific situation. Most companies are looking for a consistent approach, a fair process that keeps intrinsic motivation of R&D specialists intact. If the company is going for close cooperation among business units and the incentives are high for all business units involved, it makes

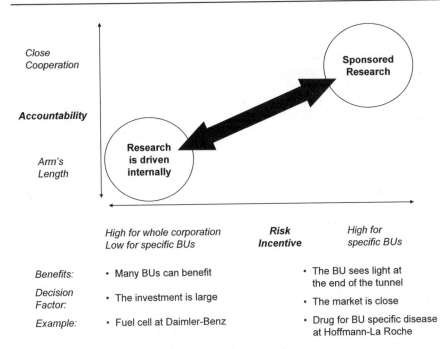

Fig. II.3.7. The tension between sponsored R and corporate R.

sense to sponsor research. On the other hand, if the company goes for a market approach, favors competition between different business units, and the incentives for all business units involved are low, internally-driven research is more appropriate, and eventually research has to sell its results to the business units.

4 How to Get Technology Across

Corporate research that fails to show new product basics to the company's business units will be pruned in cost-cutting programs. Research has little value to a company unless the results are implemented in a business unit. A major obstacle in the linkage between corporate research and business unit development has been the isolation of research in separate units, often physically separated from development, and remote geographically and strategically from the needs of the company's businesses. This isolation made technology transfer extremely difficult.

The most often cited problems in the area of global R&D include

- Intra-organizational NIH-syndrome;
- Effective use of knowledge and technology created elsewhere;
- Conflicting responsibilities and competencies between R and D;
- Insufficient downstream (D) orientation of upstream (R) activities.

Many companies underutilize their international research and development (R&D) structure of foreign subsidiaries despite legally possessing them and physically owning the necessary resources. In about 52% of firms investigated, despite possessing and controlling international R&D sites and resources, most innovations still come from headquarters. An intrafirm flow of knowledge does not seem to take place, neither is a systematic network of exchange relationships implemented (Doz et al., 2006). The global dispersion of R&D activities does not necessarily lead to improvements in innovative capabilities, and very little research has been undertaken to show how the various R&D structures adopted by MNCs affect their abilities to generate and deploy innovations globally (Persaud, 2005). Moreover, the lack of learning incentives and absorptive capacities on part of the recipient often lead to the failure of intrafirm technology transfer (Martin and Salomon, 2003).

Even among the top performers in global R&D, the transfer of technology and knowledge between research and development was dubbed 'ineffective', 'inappropriate', or even 'nonexistent'. Among the most important issues for improving the current state of R&D organization they mention integrated management of R&D, streamlining R&D processes, and an emphasis on the individual in the overall technology creation effort.

The 'average' research project spends about 17% of its time in skunk works, 56% in research prior to transfer, and 27% in the transfer process (Bosomworth and Burton, 1995). Souder, Nashar, and Padmanabhan (1990) defined technology transfer as „the managed process of conveying a technology from one party to its adoption by another party, e.g., from a developer to a user, a seller to a buyer, one department to another, etc. Conveying implies a systematic interpersonal process of passing the control of a technology from one party to another. Adoption implies strong emotional and financial commitments to routine use. Thus, transfer efforts that do not achieve adoption are failures." Schreckengast (1995) expanded the definition: „Technology transfer is the systematic transmission of new knowledge, skills, or tools from a developer to an adopter, which, if successful, results in the adopter making sustained use of the technology." Either definition is applicable for technology transfer between research and development.

In order to make positive use of these barriers, the R&D organization must be designed in a way that separates the creative research from the disciplined development but allows an early exchange of concepts and knowledge between the two domains.

Depending mostly on the size of the company and projects carried out, the research individual may work full-time in research: at ABB for up to five years, at Daimler-Benz (currently Daimler-Chrysler) until the late 1990s, for all his life. In smaller companies (like Leica Microsystems), the projects are much smaller, and a small number of individuals will do research and development more or less simultaneously, or they do research in a special lab for some months before coming back to a development project, completing full cycles between research and development.

At ABB, the research center near Baden, Switzerland, had been dramatically cut in size but was then expanded again. Today, young engineers from university

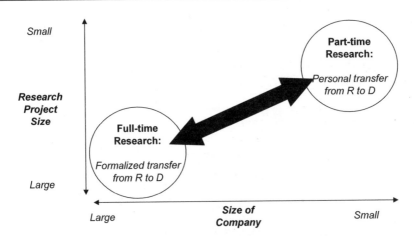

Fig. II.3.8. Different types of technology and know-how transfer between R and D.

enter research at ABB, stay for two or three projects before continuing their careers at an ABB business unit. Serving as a recruiting pool, the research center is very attractive for bright young researchers and allows an easy development from university style research to industrial research. ABB relies to a great extent on job rotation.

In the pharmaceutical industry, processes are far more formalized. Research usually hands over new and well documented substances. The security-sensitive pharmaceutical industry relies on well-defined processes and good laboratory practices to transfer results to development. The division between R and D is far more permanent for R&D employees in a pharmaceutical company than electrical engineering companies like ABB.

4.1 Model for Technology Transfer

A simple, symmetrical model based on Herzberg's two-factor theory (1966) shows the most important dimensions to be managed. In international transfers, language and distance play a dominant role, but general cultural differences may be as important (Fig. II.3.9).

Research should take an active stance in facilitating and supporting technology transfer between research and development. „Seamless innovation processes" are requested by several authors and practitioners. But „seamless" means no walls whatsoever between research and development. At the same time, the same practitioners are acting for different attitudes towards profit, short-term thinking etc. Thus, the dilemma between well-separated research and development and an efficient knowledge transfer has to be managed. Such a „seamless transfer" is best accomplished by a collaborative effort between R and D - in a variety of forms. Such collaboration takes place on all three levels of our structural model of R&D organization (see Fig. II.3.13):

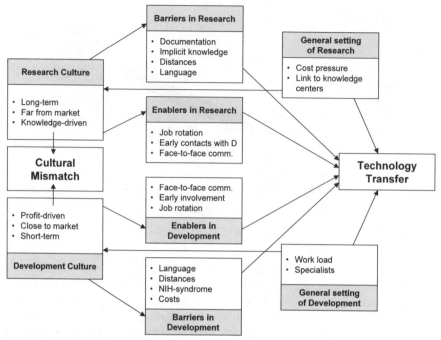

Adapted from Kloth (1996: 145).

Fig. II.3.9. A symmetrical model for technology transfer between R and D.

- Formal organization and strategy;
- Projects and processes;
- Networks and human transfer.

In the following, we briefly outline three successful approaches to transferring knowledge and technology within R&D. More examples can be found in the case studies in this book and in part I.

4.2   *Cross-functional Teams as Transfer Task Forces*

„Maximize opportunities for cross-functional relationships and organize teams around the horizontal process, not the function" (Dimanescu and Dwenger, 1996: 66). The increasing complexity of projects, the trend to outsource development activities, and the cooperative work in strategic alliances intensify the challenges for knowledge and technology transfer during the execution of a project. Dedicated core team members that are engaged full time from project start to end bring in continuity and coherence. This core team tries to achieve the right balance of skills and competencies, typically consisting of members from R&D, manufacturing, distribution, and marketing.

The emphasis on competencies is one of the most important breakthroughs in moving away from functional chimneys. Process teaming diminishes the power of old-style functional chimneys by transferring the power to project delivery teams that become the „buyers" of competencies. The important teaming feature of concurrent product development, the term used for such a non-sequential integrated approach, is the early involvement in the process by downstream players. Thus, manufacturing or distribution specialists, who may traditionally come into the picture only much later, become integral members of the core or extended team from the start.

Improved communication is a vital adjunct of concurrently managed R&D activity. Facilitating communication is the reason why much effort is aimed at achieving seamless electronic transfer of documents and files between members of development teams. But formal information exchange only captures explicitly formulated knowledge, neglecting the need to convey tacit knowledge which is notoriously hard to transfer.

Collocation is seen as the key to engage team members into face-to-face communication and problem solving. Face-to-face communication is often the only means to share context-rich information such as experience, know-how, and manual skills. Creating collocated teams, especially on an international scale, is not always easy because it requires the dislocation of project members away from their families. Ford Motor Company collocated a world-wide design team by electronically linking groups in several countries together when designing the Mondeo, its first true „world car." Such success stories for decentralized R&D project teams are rare and usually require a number of enabling preconditions.

Facilitation and improvement of communication was the reason why BMW centralized all R&D and engineering activity in the Research and Engineering Center in Munich. Prior to this centralization, R&D was distributed around the city of Munich. Although traveling between the R&D locations meant only one hour on average, it often inhibited face-to-face communication.

Unlike BMW, IBM has R&D units all over the world in order to get close to its customers and to engage local talent. Nevertheless, IBM aims at collocating research centers with development units. For instance, in 1993 the Tokyo research laboratory (TRL) moved from downtown Tokyo to the suburbs to share a building with the IBM Yamato development unit.

As a rule, projects teams are formed of both research and development. The amount of people participating in the project fluctuates with the type of work in the project stage. In the beginning of a project, when the goal is not yet clearly defined and uncertainty is high, two to five researchers from TRL push the project. Once the project matures and development skills are needed, up to ten engineers take over the project, replacing some of the researchers. Eventually, a number of manufacturing and marketing people are assigned to the project, working out manufacturability and ensuring marketability. Since members of research, development, and manufacturing are on the team at any time of the project, communication, and therefore knowledge and technology transfer is facilitated across these functions.

During the entire process, a small core team consisting of members from research, development, and manufacturing will provide technical and management guidance. The project manager typically comes from development. This core team, consisting of senior IBM employees, makes sure that experiences and insights obtained during the early phases of the project are handed down and observed in the later phases. They ensure inter-temporal knowledge transfer (Fig. II.3.10).

Other means to ensure knowledge transfer and meeting downstream needs are relationship managers, who represent IBM's worldwide Industry Solutions Units. These relationship managers form a bridge between research and marketing in each industry on both a global (IBM Research) and a local scale (Tokyo Research Laboratory).

Technology transfer does not work in a purely linear, sequential process. Project phases usually overlap and provide the opportunity to communicate and share information. Cross-functional teams and indigenous team staffing like at IBM Research in Tokyo support innovation through knowledge transfer while focusing on downstream requirements of manufacturing, distribution, and marketing.

4.3   Elaborate Job Rotation Schemes

The Japanese chemical company Kao conducted an 18-month-development project of hair cosmetics treatment. While such projects had been predominantly

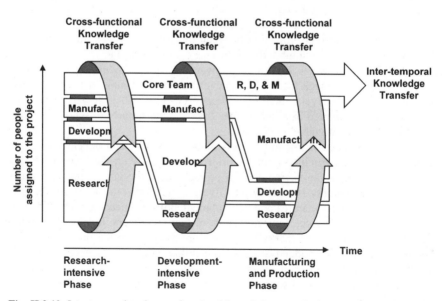

Fig. II.3.10. Intertemporal and cross-functional knowledge transfer between R and D through IBM's Transfer Task Forces.

carried out in Japan, local adaptation for culture, different treatment styles, and physiological differences required the integration of R&D in local markets. Concept development and advanced research still took place in Tokyo, but much of the actual product development had been carried out in regional R&D centers. Fig. II.3.11 depicts this concept in an example of hair treatment development in Tokyo and Darmstadt.

Know-how between Japanese advanced development and German development was transferred by mutual personnel exchange. First, a German scientist was sent to Tokyo for three months to take part in the concept creation with the local project team. During the development in Darmstadt, the Japanese project manager supported the German team for two months. In this case, personnel continuity ensured technology transfer.

4.4   Special Research and Strategic Business Projects

Corporate research assumes the two roles of far-out research and providing technology for business units. This is achieved by a certain independence from the business units in terms of funding and evaluation. In order to transfer high-potential technologies to business units quickly, many MNCs prioritize between projects, and evaluate and control them differently.

The Hitachi Central Research is one of the best research institutions in Japan. The duration of corporate research projects is generally around five years but may last up to ten years. Some of the technology exploited by business units today (e.g. tantal oxide technology) was invented more than 15 years ago at Hitachi Central Research. Now it helps Hitachi manufacture some of the smallest chips world-

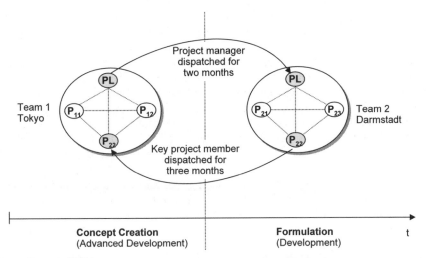

Source: Gassmann (1997a).

Fig. II.3.11. Personnel exchange at Kao: Hair cosmetic treatment.

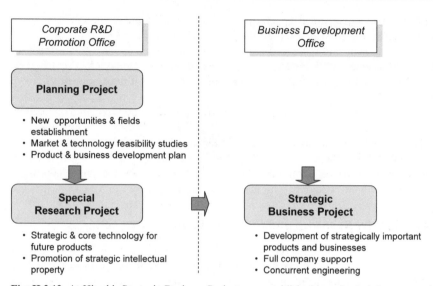

Fig. II.3.12. At Hitachi, Strategic Business Projects are established in order to bring new technology to commercialization quickly.

wide. If the company maintains a stable strategy for research, corporate research is able to foster and cultivate technologies and new competencies. The business units not only expect the research center to continuously develop technologies, they also expect breakthroughs (e.g., in the chip technology). Without such breakthroughs, the business units would soon run out of competitive technologies.

The Corporate R&D Promotion Office and the Business Development Office are the two guiding bodies through inter-laboratory R&D projects. Three types of projects are possible: Special Research Projects, Strategic Business Projects, and Planning Projects (Fig. II.3.12).

Planning Projects are small (3 months) and are sponsored by corporate R&D Promotion Office and the Business Development Office. The goals of the planning projects are to establish new opportunities and fields, conducting market and technology feasibility studies, and planning product and business development.

A Special Research Project is started by the Promotion Office through a Planning Project to evaluate opportunities, market & technology feasibility studies, and the product & business development planning. Its management is then handed over to Hitachi Central Research and turned into a Special Research Project with the aim to design strategic and core technology for future products and the promotion of strategic intellectual property. The output of this project is technology, and no product.

Strategic Business Projects were established around 1988 in order to ensure that the technology created in a special research project or by other R&D teams is transferred and utilized appropriately in one of the business unit. Originally, only Special Research Projects existed, but these projects were highly technology-oriented and often failed to create new businesses. After Strategic Business Projects pass a similar examination stage as a planning project, these projects are managed by the Business Unit and division heads. Approximately one fifth of overall R&D expenses is allocated to about 50 Strategic Business Projects. A highly inter-disciplinary approach is pursued. Often, concurrent engineering methods are applied, involving key people from manufacturing, design, marketing, sales, and corporate planning. Each project lasts between six months to two years and involves up to 150 researchers and engineers. Strategic Business Projects always enjoy the full support of the entire company, including high-priority in funding and staffing.

Strategic business and research projects were designed to carry out both strategically important product development and assessment of emerging new technology which will give major impact on business in the future. They ensure that the created technology is transferred and utilized appropriately in one of the business units. This mechanism is very important to transfer the technology from one research group to strategic commercialization.

5   Conclusions

The transfer of new knowledge to development and other downstream corporate functions is the only raison d'être for industrial research. The classification of the presented concepts for technology transfer justifies and validates the applicability of the four-structure model. While the problems of technology transfer are mainly derived from geography and functional separation (the bottom two levels), they are resolved by exploiting the potentials in the top levels of human relations, project and process management, and organizational support (in that order). It is hard to classify each of the presented solutions for international technology transfer to exactly one level of perspective. Each concept actually has an influence on all three top levels, although the creative focus resides in either organization, processes, or relations.

The transfer of ideas, knowledge, and technology into successful development projects is the prime task of upstream technology development and research laboratories. Three conclusions concerning technology transfer are drawn:

- Knowledge is best transferred by human beings directly involved;
- Some personal continuity between R and D phases ensure the required knowledge transfer;
- A clear separation of research sites from development sites together with managed face-to-face contacts greatly improves technology transfer and keeps the distance needed between R and D.

Many R&D collaboration forms designed for the swift execution of development projects (e.g. Simultaneous Engineering) appear to be inappropriate for managing the joint effort of R and D. Goals, mind sets, external pressure, and the nature of the tasks, are too different to make true simultaneity possible.

Close interaction warrants efficient hand-over processes between research and development. If research and development are geographically separated, as is often the case in multinational companies, ensuring this transfer efficiency becomes a complex issue.

The challenge is to filter those interactions that justify the resources and time spent for exchanging knowledge and technology. As excess communication leads to massive increase in information costs (Hansen and Nohria, 2004), the frequency of knowledge transfer is not necessarily correlated to the meaningfulness of transferred knowledge. Even when transaction costs associated with internal transfers of knowledge may be low, the value of this knowledge abroad may also be very limited (Rugman and Verbeke, 2003). Thus, firms should be concerned less with facilitators of knowledge transfer, but rather ask themselves if such transfer makes sense at all and with how they use what they know (Haas and Hansen, 2005).

By focusing on a people-centered approach, and by designing the right processes and structures to support them, knowledge and technology transfer between dispersed R&D locations can be improved dramatically. At the same time, research should retain independence from development to escape short-term focus and limited applicability of its work. Research has the responsibility to create new businesses as well, not just satisfying existing ones. Hence, the critical balance between research and development is continuously contested.

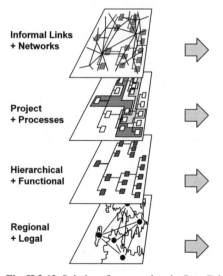

**Solutions for Managing
the International R-to-D Interface**

Informal Links
+ Networks

- Move people with projects
- Job rotation
- Long-term assignments
- Face-to-face knowledge transfer

Project
+ Processes

- Strategic Business/Research Projects
- Cross-functional teams
- Joint agreement on detailed project plan
- Cross-cultural teams

Hierarchical
+ Functional

- Two-channel funding
- Technology liaison officers
- Advanced technology labs
- Interdisciplinary programs

Regional
+ Legal

- Conditional collocation
- Mixing local and global recruiting
- Strategic separation

Fig. II.3.13. Solutions for managing the R-to-D interface.

II.4 Transnational R&D Processes

„Time waste differs from material waste
in that there can be no salvage.”
Henry Ford

1 Distinguishing R&D Phases

The separation of the innovation process into a pre-project and a development phase increases transparency significantly and reduces costs in the main development phase. What can be planned is to be distinguished from what cannot be planned. A third and often insufficiently considered phase of the innovation process is the introduction of the product in the market. The old Schumpeterian three-way classification is still of good use in international R&D processes.

Despite their different management requirements, many companies do not distinguish between these three phases in R&D projects (Table II.4.1). Compaq has made this distinction since 1987. It took a cross-functional team two years to define the specifications for a new personal computer during the pre-project phase. But this extended preparatory work allowed it to slash down the cost-intensive development phase to nine months.

Highly differentiated phase concepts are commonly accepted and applied in R&D practice, but they suffer from the strictly sequential execution of project phases and are, therefore, often impractical. On the other hand, if projects are carried out without reviews or milestones, there is the danger of achieving little effectiveness (doing the wrong things) and low efficiency (doing things wrongly). The pre-project phase is the domain of creative idea generation, advanced devel-

Table II.4.1. Differences between pre-project, development, and market introduction phase.

Criteria	Pre-project phase	Development	Market Introduction
Budget	Often none / low	Planned / high	Planned / high
Goals	Vague	Detailed	Detailed
Costs	Low	High	High
Processes	Not structured	Structured	Structured
Results	Unclear	Defined	Negotiated
Financial risks	Small	Medium	High

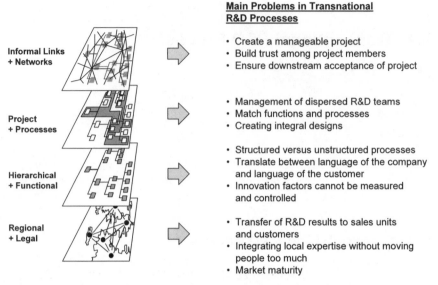

Fig. II.4.1. Main problems for creating and managing transnational R&D processes.

opment and, increasingly, a contingent preparation of the labor phases from a managerial point of view. Freedom of thought and an open playing field for engineers should be ensured. Only when the project proposal is finally approved, the cost-intensive development phase sets in with structured engineering methods.

After the spectacular success of the Manhattan and Apollo projects, most companies have concentrated their R&D management efforts on project management. Today we know, at least in principle, how projects work. But we still do not know how to get from the useful many ideas to the vital few projects which the R&D lab is capable of executing. Even more difficulties arise when the new product is to be introduced to the market. It is therefore suitable to distinguish three phases in the R&D process:

- Pre-project phase: How to create a good product concept and a manageable project;
- Development phase: How to manage a project;
- Market-introduction: How to transfer R&D results efficiently to operations and the customer.

The three phases are completely different. At every interface, a translation needs to be provided. Between the pre-project and the development phase we must translate from the language of the customer or scientists to the language of the company (market or technology driven). Between the project and the market-introduction phases, we need to translate from the company's technical language to the emotional language of the sales force and the customer. The main formal tool is quality function deployment, but this tool is not widely accepted in the R&D community.

The three phases differ from the international viewpoint as well. The pre-project phase is usually low-key, simmering for years without well-defined structures and strongly dependent on individuals communicating face-to-face to stimulate creativity. Thus, traveling on a global scale is a must in order to overcome the many challenges in transnational R&D projects (Fig. II.4.1).

The development phase focuses on efficient project execution. The plans and schedules developed in the pre-project phase are carried out. Work packages are

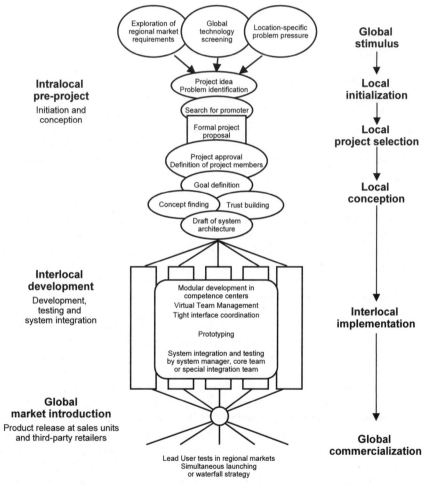

Source: Gassmann (1997a: 181).

Fig. II.4.2. Separating the innovation process into three phases increases R&D productivity.

allocated as modules to the best suited teams wherever they are located in the world. There is tight networking within the group and efficient coordination at the higher level of project management, and at the inter-group level. Discipline is most important.

The third phase of market-introduction is the truly international one: Teams are dispersed all over the world. They belong to different entities, perhaps meeting once a year and having different goals. Negotiating is the name of the game. Tight project management is recommended, but only few companies apply it (Fig. II.4.2).

In terms of costs, the incubation phase up to the specification list is usually very cheap, while development and market-introduction may well cost several hundred million of US dollars each.

2   Stage-Gate-Processes to Support Project Management

In R&D management practice, it is very rare to find clearly distinguishable and predetermined project phases executed exactly according to a predefined schedule. Although systems engineering offers some help in structuring the R&D process into well-sequenced project phases, R&D managers are generally not very successful in implementing these system engineering methods. ISO certification leads many companies to the illusion that all critical innovation factors can be measured and structured, although especially the early phases of R&D projects are highly non-linear.

Short cycle times in R&D projects require a consequent integration of project processes and line structures. A flexible segmentation of the process and the firm establishment of its segments in the line organization overcome the artificial separation between process and hierarchical organization. In the development process of the Smart, the former 'Swatch-Mobile', a compact car jointly initiated by Daimler-Benz and the Swatch watch company, there was congruence between project module, product module, supplier, manufacturing unit, and assembly unit. The individual modules were developed and are manufactured almost exclusively by suppliers, and eventually installed directly by the suppliers. Micro Compact Car, the former joint venture between Daimler-Benz and Swatch, focused on interfaces between suppliers and the system as a whole.

A combination of classical phase segmentation and process orientation (as in modern management theory) is found in the concept of the „stage-gate process" (O'Connor, 1994; Cooper and Kleinschmidt, 1991). Every step or „stage" necessary to complete a particular project task is linked to the next by a „gate" at which decisions for the continuation of the project are made. Contrary to milestones, gates are more flexible in terms of time, date and content. Gates allow a deliberate parallelization of phases as well as their recombination or adaptation to new requirements. At each gate the R&D project is analyzed and reviewed in its entirety, often including the presentation of competitor activities, market and technology developments. The number of stages and gates is project and industry dependent.

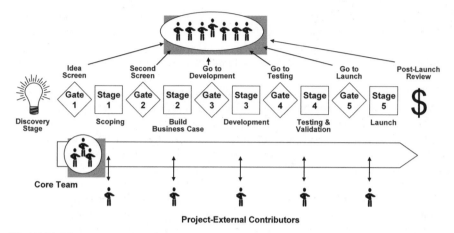

Fig. II.4.3. The stage-gate process.

Ex-ante agreements serve as guidelines for the collaboration of project participants (Fig. II.4.3).

The practitioner uses a variety of different taxonomies with slightly different meaning for this flexible approach to project management. European automobile manufacturers like Volvo and BMW have implemented this concept under the name of 'Gates and stages', or 'Gateway process'. Eastman Kodak calls it 'Phases and gates'.

In contrast to the milestone technique, which employs a purely formal set of planning instruments in product development, the stage-gate paradigm requires top management to be personally engaged in the development process. The fundamental idea behind this is: „You can get around a milestone, but you must go through a gate." Detouring around gates is not allowed. The decision about continuing or terminating a strategically important project is reached by the team with top management present in person. Traditional decision finding by collecting signatures on a formal approval document is pointless if high risk is involved and only little time is available.

Frequently, R&D decisions are reached in a peer pressure situation. If all other participants have already signed the decision, it is considered 'safe.' However, sequential activities and insufficient flow of information lead to delays and incorrect decisions. interfunctional integration and cross-functional teams in stage-gate processes not only ensure the integration of lower levels of the hierarchy, but also the clear involvement and position of top management. Thus stage-gate processes apply similar methods to R&D projects as have been followed in strategy formulation in the last few years: Strategy nowadays is being developed with participation of all hierarchical levels.

Stage-gate processes are not contradictory to the parallel execution of product and process development (Simultaneous Engineering), which rose to fame in the late 1980s. Yet, an intelligent combination of stage-gates and simultaneous engineering is required. An all-encompassing parallelization leads to coordination problems and lack of transparency; there is the tendency to delay the termination of unsuccessful projects and thus releasing important capacity. A minimal and in-advance defined parallelization, focusing on the time-critical path, remains enough of a challenge to management.

Thus, the differentiation between pre-project phase and main development phase is of utmost significance for the quick and efficient execution of R&D projects. While the first phase is constructed around soft factors conducive for creativity and concept creation, the second phase concentrates on effective and time-critical project management (execution phase). This distinction shows the best results. BASF underscores this distinction further by speaking of „activities" and not projects in the early phase of an R&D project. Only the formal approval by the steering committee of a business unit can transfer activities in a project. One of the first gates is thus equivalent to the conclusion of the pre-project activities. Management re-examines, together with the project team, market and technological foundations for product development and adapts the development process to project-specific peculiarities. Development becomes the required flexibility: A project characterized by incremental innovation in general requires less stages and gates than a project which is targeted at radical innovation.

The stage-gate exhibits a further advantage should customer specifications change or competitors introduce rivaling products, i.e. if high complexity and dynamics alter the competitive environment. At certain gates the project manager can allow to re-enter the idea funnel, review the system design and, if needed, update the entire product concept. Changing the system concept usually reduces motivation and necessitates the involvement of the entire development team. Managing the human resource is thus of utmost importance.

Besides the stage-gate process, the „loose-tight concept" also plays a central role in the design of R&D processes,[28] according to which the success of the project is dependent on the degree of organization during the R&D process. In the early stage of a project, the organization should be designed 'loosely,' becoming more and more rigid and tight towards the conclusion of the project. The varying degree of R&D project organization is imposed by constraints in time: While creativity and idea generation are highly important in the early stage, the management concern shifts to efficiency and project implementation on schedule in the later expensive stage.

Generally, there is only a vague idea about the eventual product design at the start of a development project. Participants differ greatly in their understanding of goals and contents. By communicating their ideas during the conception of the project, project members create a commonly shared knowledge and understanding of the subject. In the early phase of the project, tacit or implicit knowledge is transformed into explicit knowledge. Designing and generating product design drafts and specification lists must be done and decided on as a team. The top-management for technology at ABB is convinced that 'project creation' is one of the biggest challenges of the near future.

---

[28]   Wilson (1966), Albers and Eggers (1991) confirmed this hypothesis in their empirical studies.

3   Pre-project Phase: Fostering Creativity

The pre-project phase is relatively fuzzy while the development phase is clearly structured and defined. The pre-project requires strong management support since it relies heavily on experience, knowledge and know-how. Soft management factors are important, people management replaces process management: The best people are assigned to the most difficult tasks. The three central tasks during the pre-project are:

- The identification of the market segments (Who is the customer?);
- The work statement (What does the customer want?);
- The product requirement specifications (How can we fulfill the customer's needs?).

On a global scale, these three questions have to be asked for different regions. Depending on local differences, the company chooses a platform only or a global product at the other extreme (Fig. II.4.4).

3.1   The Product Concept Team

Without precise and detailed market segments even the best R&D team cannot guarantee product success. Geographic and cultural issues play a central role in the identification of the customer and of his needs. These needs are documented in the language of the customer: the work statement.

If the pre-project is well separated from the main development phase and managed by experienced people, it is possible to ensure that only well-tested technologies and market know-how will enter into the project phase. This project phase can then be designed as a task-specific process of high efficiency and structurability on stable know-how. Parallelization of activities during the pre-project is possible, but the separation between pre-project and project should always be

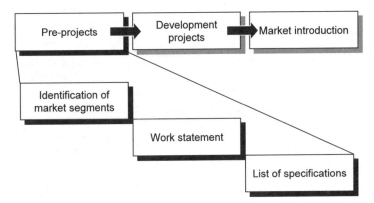

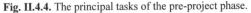

Fig. II.4.4. The principal tasks of the pre-project phase.

maintained, particularly during capital-intensive projects. R&D employees are unaccustomed to this approach, as they often try to integrate the latest ideas in the new product. It is often forgotten that new and insufficiently tested technology is a frequent cause for delays and extra project work.

Product conception is difficult to plan especially in break-through or platform projects. The number of alternatives and the technological uncertainty is too large. Nevertheless, a certain principal approach is suggested: The first step is to collect and review as many ideas as possible. Only if the ideas are original and novel, will the new product have the edge over rivaling products. In the next step the ideas must be transformed into concepts. Prototypes and precise documentation facilitate the communication with 'outsiders' such as customers, suppliers, and experts of the company not directly participating in product conception or the steering committee.

Product ideas need to be translated into technical parameters and their causal interdependencies. Useful tools are the House of Quality and Quality Function Deployment. A cross-functional team then reviews and evaluates the resulting concepts. The lack of technical feasibility, required resources, and market potential are main obstacles for successful innovations. Nevertheless, some product profitability calculation can be done already at this early point. In the automobile industry, as well as in architecture, this phase is called concept competition: A number of designers have proposed concepts (specifications lists) to a set of given conditions.

The idea-concept-evaluation cycle needs to be repeated until a useful and convincing product concept is created. Such a concept may be the basis for the specification list. The number of cycles and the length of each cycle depend mainly on time-to-market pressures. A cycle is not a well-defined phase but rather a form of

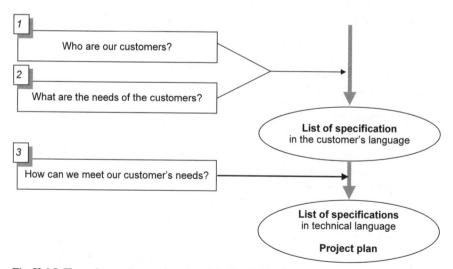

Fig. II.4.5. The main questions and results of the first R&D phase.

organization itself. In collaboration with external advisors the concept team quickly closes in on the innovative concept. The following principles help to get robust concepts in due time:

- React quickly: Customer, suppliers, and managers should evaluate immediately;
- Maintain an open communication culture and links between project team and line management;
- Do not suppress ideas: All ideas are considered good until proven otherwise. Consider potential risk factors early!
- Do not focus on certain ideas too early. Be always ready to reject ideas. Changing the perspective is important. The team should evaluate their ideas also from the standpoint of the customer, the suppliers, the shareholders, as well as the stakeholders.
- Play golf: Frequent change of scenery prevents the occurrence of the 'not-invented-here' syndrome.

The concept team should be formed of members from different functional departments such as development, marketing, production, or support. In the case of global products, different regions have to be included. At ABB Switzerland, more than 60% of the employees are non-Swiss. Ideally, the manager of the concept team is the eventual manager of the development project. Thus many companies ensure knowledge transfer between research and development.

The activities of the product concept team conclude with the specification list. This document is, in principal, a translation of the customer requirements into technical specifications. The customer requirements have been recorded in the work statement.

Besides the technical specifications the specifications list may also contain project plans and schedules, the time-critical path, technical alternatives, as well as technical and market risks. Larger projects should also include the most important concepts about procurement, production, sales, and market introduction.

This approach is standard and has a proven record, especially in international projects where geographic distances put a heavy burden on project management. It is very well suited for short development cycles and modular approaches. But there are other situations: If the MNC is looking for the highest performance or lowest costs, it then may have to go for an integral design with a very flexibly freezing point. The specification list for a formula-one racing car is constantly updated, several freezing points exist! Integral designs carried out on a global scale are the most demanding projects. Most companies try to circumvent such projects by collocating the most important project drivers, as ABB has done with its GT24/26 task force.

3.2   Idea Generation

During the definition and conception stage of the pre-project phase, the market and technology background is to be explored.

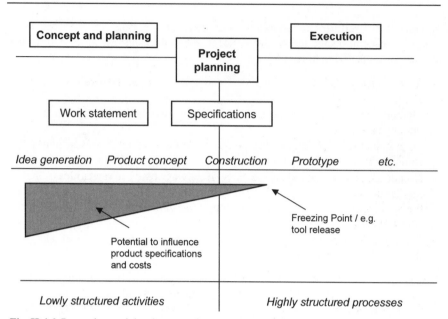

Fig. II.4.6. Pre-project and development phases in R&D: merging lowly structured activities and highly structured processes.

Exploration is needed based on traditional marketing research tools such as panel research, focus group interviews, sales and distribution questionnaires, scenario techniques, lead market analysis, and others. More recently developed tools include cooperative forms of R&D with lead users and „anthropological expeditions", during which the implicit user knowledge is activated in joint workshops (Leonard-Barton, 1995: 200). Technology screening may take place in a variety of forms, for instance by absorbing technological knowledge in leading-edge innovation centers, conferences, technology forecasts, expert interviews, patent database research, as well as reverse engineering of competitor products. Exploration is often conducted on a global scale, as market and technology stimuli converge in many industries.

Needs exploration and technology-potential screening are the two primary sources for good project ideas. On the one hand, the dominance of technology-focused engineers usually leads to over-engineered products which are not accepted by the market. On the other hand, short-term turn-over considerations by sales and marketing people with no technological vision reduce the long-term innovativeness of the company. Besides technology and market determinants, the generation of project ideas can be highly affected by location specific problems and pressures such as low capacity utilization, financial difficulties, and fashion trends. Ideally, project ideas result from a balance between market pull and technology push.

Low capacity utilization in a particular site (e.g. due to relocation of manufacturing to another site), fosters the active search for new businesses. Units with negative financial results and low cash-flows are under higher pressure for change than units with profitable products. At R&D units that were in danger of being rationalized due to global efficiency enhancement measures, we observed more than average creativity and propensity to initiate projects. However, if management does not succeed to define a clear framework and to induce a common vision, the imminent crisis is worsened by the growing paralyzation of the work force. For instance, the radical reduction of the work force at DASA (Daimler Aerospace)[29] in 1995 was linked to high uncertainty about the goals and changes in the leadership of MTU (DASA's subsidiary)[30]. Contrary to 'creative crisis' - as was experienced by ABB and IBM - MTU was characterized by paralyzation resulting in reduced idea generation and innovation.

Fashion trends often lead to the wish to enlarge one's product spectrum with the latest and most refined products in the market. Many R&D projects are thus not initiated because a market need was identified or a technological potential was to be exploited, but because one's image can be enhanced. A major driver of new project ideas is therefore, besides company-external market pull and technology push, a company-internal problem push. The two external drivers often work in a global environment, while the latter is local.

The innovation process in the chemical and pharmaceutical industry is also three-phased. BASF underscores the distinction between the pre-project and development phase by speaking of R&D 'activities' in the early R&D stages, and R&D 'projects' in later stages. Bayer defines milestones and project review meetings to take place not before entering the pre-clinical phase when the project is formally started (Fig. II.4.7).

3.3   Intensive Idea Flow and Workflow Systems

The idea generation for a single project can take place on a global scale, as demonstrated in ABB's workflow system PIPE (Project Idea, Planning & Execution). PIPE is a Lotus Notes based workflow system which transmits and distributes ideas, problems commentaries and solutions by means of modern information and communication technologies. The generator of an idea also selects the group of persons who may access his contributions. His initial idea, along with his evaluation of commercial potential and supplementary comments, are then refined and complemented with the ideas and suggestions of other participants of PIPE.

If the idea receives sufficient support, a formal project is proposed, for which detailed information about goals, risk, possible problems and available resources is required. Upon approval of the project proposal the program manager transfers this information into the PIPE Planning Application. The project idea is then integrated into the overall project plan. A project manager and the work packages of participating sites are determined. Local group managers propose local project

---

[29]   Merger between DASA, Aérospatiale-Matra, and CASA in 2000 resulted in the new group EADS.

[30]   DaimlerChrysler sold its share in MTU to Kohlberg Kravis Roberts in 2003. Since 2006 MTU is a widely held firm without dominant shareholders.

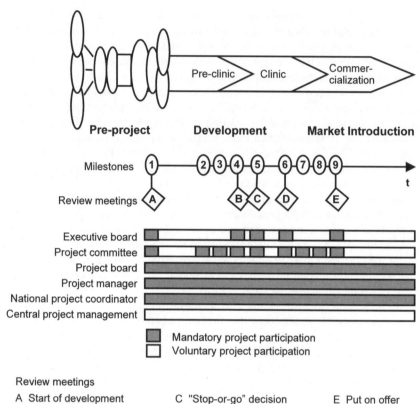

Fig. II.4.7. The R&D process at Bayer – the first milestones do not occur before the pre-clinical development phase.

schedules defining sub-goals, costs and means of funding. The consolidated project plan is then evaluated by the program manager, local corporate research managers, and business unit representatives, who announce their priorities by electronic mail.

PIPE also supports project execution. Simple and formalized project reports concerning costs, schedules and results serve as easy-to-distribute project information. A report archive logs the project history, thus facilitating exchange of experiences across several projects.

3.4   *Good Ideas Require Good Promotion*

Although stimulated by global determinants, the problem identification usually occurs by a single person or a collocated group of people. Looking for support for their thoughts they try to convince influential people in the company about the

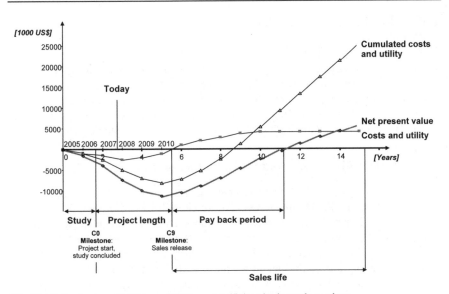

Fig. II.4.8. Product profitability and ROI - not sufficient in dynamic markets.

significance of their idea. The influence of such people is based on their hierarchical position (power promoters), their knowledge (functional promoters), or their communication abilities (process promoters).

Using groupware such as ABB's PIPE, the search for appropriate promoters may take place in many countries. Experience shows, though, that personal relations are most important for winning decision-makers for new ideas. Decision-makers are influenced by project opponents who bring in technological and economical arguments against a new project idea. Political arguments play an important role as opponents fear that new projects mean a reduction of resources for their own activities.

The better the idea generator communicates his intentions and visions, the more likely will he succeed in finding top-management support. Commercialization potential and project visions are often more important than technical decision criteria. As it is difficult to inspire people for an idea just by means of electronic mail and databases, we assume that despite the emergence and development of modern ICT the quest for promoters will remain a matter of face-to-face contact.

3.5 Product Profitability Calculation

If a project idea finds sufficient support and passes preliminary evaluations, in most companies a formal project proposal is made demonstrating technical realization and commercialization potential. Product profitability calculations are widely used as they are robust, but they are not always an appropriate tool for project evaluation. For instance, if a market has not yet developed a dominant design of product architecture, financial project evaluation can lead to unrealistic market forecasts.

Profitability calculation is based on forecasted market returns discounted to net present value (Fig. II.4.8). Before the emergence of a dominant design (e.g. mobile communication) a market is characterized by intense market dynamics, making sales forecasts highly unreliable. Figures with many decimal places provide only hypocritical precision: Project proposals should be complemented with qualitative data and evaluated in light of the firm's strategy and technological vision.

3.6   Project Approval - Rational Criteria and Politics

The project proposal is presented to a steering committee which is not necessarily located in the same R&D units where the project will be carried out. The „Investment Review Board" for the IBM S/390 system architecture meets in New York to decide about major project activities at the IBM Germany site at Böblingen. Transnational R&D projects usually require large budgets, which must be approved by the highest authorities of business areas. Project selection always takes place mostly at the location of the decision-maker. In most western companies, R&D employees still have to travel to their top management centers to get approval for their projects. At Hitachi, managers meet R&D employees in their actual working areas to emphasize the importance of human communication and relationship on research management (On Site Policy). Decisions about projects are thus made on a rather informal basis.

Project approval also includes a decision about project members and participating locations. In this stage it is determined if an R&D project is carried out transnationally or in only one place. This decision is rarely based on a structured top-down mode of evaluation, during which project requirements are systematically combined with competencies, know-how bases, and available capacities of potential R&D units. As the IBM Virtual Storage Extended (VSE)-development example demonstrates, project participation is determined in a political agreement finding process (Fig. II.4.9). Often enough, political considerations outweigh rational criteria.

During the early stages of a project, product profitability calculation should be seen as scenarios rather than forecasts. Resource and competency-based decision criteria are often neglected because of profit-center thinking, although they were economically rational from a corporate perspective. Each site strives for full capacity utilization. Projects financed by headquarters or central R&D are attractive as they bring additional funds and prestige into participating units. Examples for such centrally financed, strategic projects are „Top Projects" at Bosch, „Golden Badge Special Projects" at Sharp, „Core R&D" and „Strategic Business Projects" at Hitachi, and „Core Projects" at Siemens and NEC.

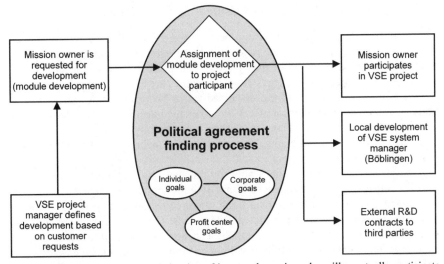

Fig. II.4.9. Rational criteria and balancing of interest determine who will eventually participate in a project (IBM, VSE-project).

4   Development Phase: Focusing on Efficiency

Once the participants are determined and the teams are formed in each location, the goal finding process sets in. In transnational projects this process is characterized by high complexity, as differing ideas about goals are not easily resolved due to geographical distances and cultural differences. Goal conflicts may occur between R&D (technologically advanced products), production (manufacturable products), marketing (customer-oriented products), and logistics (storable and transportable products).

In addition to these classical goal conflicts, regional perspectives complicate the situation. Representatives of operations favor global standardization, while country representatives request country-specific product variants. Each location tries to support the significance of his respective variant with forecasts about how much his variant will contribute to overall product turn over.

Most locations strive for larger development and manufacturing share, in order to utilize their R&D and production capacity and to develop new competencies in interesting technology areas. The various expectations of the participating interest groups may lead to minimal consent in the goal definition, and the participants eventually agreeing only on a rudimentary core concept (concept peeling). The project manager must have high moderation skills to prevent this minimal solution and to motivate and inspire the various participants for a commonly shared goal.

4.1   Product Architecture as a Critical Success Factor

The goal finding process is partly superimposed by concept definition, which determines the architecture of the product to be developed. Especially in interlocal development, the conception of the system architecture is a critical success factor for the entire project. If interfaces between modules are clearly defined, the definition of work packages for all the dispersed teams becomes much easier. Alterations in one module should not affect the other modules. Robustness reduces the amount of design changes in later stages and consequently the intensity of interaction between decentralized teams. This stability also makes standardized reporting possible within the same project.

The system architecture defines not only the success of the current product but also has far-reaching consequences. Only if interfaces are designed clearly and with a wide range of applications in mind, the architecture can serve as a product platform in future modular product developments. On a strategic level, product architecture decides whether the company can become a network-leader (Morris and Ferguson, 1993). A reduction of variant complexity (which is an essential part in cost reduction programs in all industries) is supported by a clear conception and designed stability in system architectures during the development phase.

4.2   Know-how Redundancy and Generalists

A stable system architecture is made possible if architectural knowledge is shared among the members of the core team. Much of corporate knowledge is tacit or implicit, i.e. resides within the heads of project members and is not easily accessible. During the project conception, socialization processes are therefore highly important to exchange crucial but otherwise unattainable knowledge. The construction of a common knowledge base goes in parallel with establishing redundant knowledge within project teams. As breadth (and not only depth) is supported, project-internal communication is also improved.

The turbine manufacturer MTU in Munich introduced ABC teams and thus separated team-adverse experts from project drivers. The A-team which is organized at the management level, defines the strategic framework for project teams (program decisions and reviews of critical milestones) and coordinates all teams involved in the project or on a global scale. A-teams coordinate e.g. the module development at Munich with overall engine design at Pratt&Whitney in the USA. B-teams carry out much of the component and parts development at usually one single location, while C-teams consist of highly qualified technical specialists (e.g. for rotor blade materials); they set design guidelines and are consulted by B-teams when specific problems occur.

The definition process of technical interfaces is also characterized by a psycho-sociological effect. Each team manager tries to ensure high tolerances in the interfaces of his module, as this increases the likelihood of successful development of his respective module. High tolerances imply higher costs at lower effectiveness. The project manager has thus to ensure that security thinking and risk aversion do not lead to too much slack.

The project manager should be a competent system architect in order to successfully implement a modular approach. He groups the functional elements of the system into components, defines clear interface standards and protocols, and assigns development tasks to specialist teams. When the system is decomposed, risky work elements should not be distributed among various modules but concentrated in one component. This critical module is then assigned to a highly qualified R&D unit which is also characterized by superior management skills. Risk concentration is not easy to achieve, as risk distribution is an integral part of portfolio thinking and team managers try to shift risk to other locations as well.

This structuring of the product architecture is one of the most decisive points in international R&D management. In large projects it may take 10 to 20 man years to obtain a robust architecture. In non-assembled products, product architecture may be compared to process architecture: If chosen with well defined interfaces, it can be developed and upgraded more easily.

4.3   Structured Engineering in the Development Phase

The activities in the development phase are more detailed, structured and in modular designs less interdependent as activities in the pre-project phase. While in the pre-project phase the emphasis is on goal-adequate concept generation, the focus shifts to efficient concept realization in the development phase. Since the cost-intensive later phase consumes most of the project resources, it requires a resource- and time-conscious project management. Capacity planning and multi-project management gain in importance.

In order to ensure access to critical resources during the development phase it is necessary that the project manager has direct access to the firm's power center. In some cases he reports to a steering committee directly below the executive board. Typical members of this committee are directors of business areas, R&D, marketing, manufacturing or regional areas. Such a heavy-weight steering committee increases the likelihood of successful commercialization of the project outcome.

At ABB, the strategically important „Common Technology" projects are managed directly by the business area director for power transmission. Only if the project has a good start and is well established will he hand the project management down to a lower-ranked manager. Since the steering committee is not capable of controlling the entire project due to lack of required special knowledge, component-specific sub-committees are formed for evaluation of the project activities. Expert knowledge serves as a foundation for sound decisions in steering committees as well as project management.

4.4   Prototyping

The complexity in innovation projects can be reduced by introducing tangible support tools and media. Not everyone knows how to read and understand blueprints and CAD print-outs. Until only a few years ago, prototypes were used to clarify open technical questions that could not be resolved by simulation and computations alone. Today, prototypes serve a wider role:

- To reduce risk (especially risks of scale);
- To learn from experiments (bundling of risk);
- To determine customer preferences (touch-and-feel);
- To communicate across functional interfaces (object as the message).

A prototype is a physical realization of the product or its components in various stages of product development. Prototyping includes not only the construction of the prototype, but also up- and downstream activities such as prototype design and testing.

Prototyping is a crucial instrument to steer and control development projects with respect to deadlines, technical improvements, parallelization, and resource concentration on critical problems. Prototyping and the product development process are highly interrelated, particularly for products with short life cycles (e.g. work stations). In later stages of development, prototyping responsibility is assumed by production.

The relative importance of prototyping varies between companies and industries. In the early 1990s, the Japanese automobile industry was twice as fast in prototyping as their competitors in Europe and the US were. Many European firms are still characterized by full-utilization and capacity thinking in workshops and laboratories, thus increasing the time-to-market. Prototyping becomes a bottleneck in the development phase.

During the development phase, four different functions of prototypes are distinguished:

- Principal development (function);
- Concept (system and function);
- Design (components, modules, system, and function);
- Production (components, modules, system).

Some companies distinguish between feasibility models, prototypes and the first series. Feasibility models serve to determine if a function is physically feasible. Production prototypes are constructed from materials and compounds actually used in the final product. First series are built by means of the production machinery in order to test the production process.

Prototyping must be tailored to the needs of the development project. Technology development has a different set of requirements for prototyping than product or variant development does. Three models of prototyping make the development phase more effective:

- Quick feed-back to construction (new technology);
- Integrated system solution (new product);
- Early production prototypes (variants and product maintenance).

Integrated system solutions require the prototypes to be built according to a predefined schedule. The schedule must be fulfilled regardless of the conclusion of work tasks necessary for that deadline. For instance, large software companies build a prototype every day to ensure product integration, i.e. to ensure coordination between the many dispersed teams.

Every prototype is the start to a new problem solving cycle. Based on the know-how and data available, the engineer formulates questions which he tries to answer by means of simulation and computation. Whatever remains undecided is tested by building a prototype. Hence the specifications of requirements for a prototype are of central importance. A prototype must be:

- Representative for the problem to be solved;
- Easy to test and these results easy to analyze.

Therefore, prototyping must be planned carefully (Design of experiments)! On the one hand, the focus on competencies and key technologies helps reduce the number of prototypes a company is going to build, on the other hand it requires a close collaboration with its suppliers. The prototype serves a communication tool across functional and company boundaries. The actual supplier of the prototypes assumes a significant role in the development process and must be selected according to:

- Know-how building (internal-external)
- Interface management (internal-external)
- Cycle times (as opposed to capacity utilization)

In recent years, experience gained in software development was transferred to R&D related to machinery and other equipment.

Rapid prototyping is often employed in order to determine customer acceptance and requirements. New technologies such as stereo-lithography make it possible to build a prototype within hours from CAD data files. Rapid prototyping is thus particularly useful in close-collaboration R&D with customers or suppliers. Combined with digital photography and the Internet, it is possible to transfer pictures of the product or test-series to distant R&D locations in very short time. Rapid prototyping bridges geographic distances.

Virtual prototyping is going one step further: The lift manufacturer Schindler initiated such rapid prototypes with virtual reality in 1998. Within advanced development radically new cabin designs have been developed. In order to save costly realizations those prototypes will be produced and tested in terms of psychology and perceived ride comfort within virtual reality. Virtual reality is no longer restricted to computer geeks in the entertainment business, but has found its way to traditional machinery industry.

5 Market Introduction: Focus on Time-to-Money

The final phase, market introduction, offers three important challenges to the company:

- Market introduction is a global project, often involving large distances between its participants;
- Not all the participants work for the same company, and much integrative and convincing work needs to be done;
- The costs often exceed the total costs of the two previous phases.

The key to success rests in professional project management. The different tasks of R&D, marketing, production, sales, and maintenance must be coordinated and integrated. Market and sales data are often not sufficiently considered in the R&D process. Distribution is rarely an issue when developing a product. Daily chores absorb too well the attention of the project members, and who do not sufficiently identify themselves with the project.

In order to carry out market introduction of a new product outside the daily activities it is necessary to assign a project manager with far-reaching competencies. He is responsible for the entire introduction phase from conception to controlling. Typically, product managers or R&D project managers do not have the necessary competencies and skills for this job.

The market introduction has to be orchestrated on all four levels of our model (see also Fig. II.4.12):

- New models will be successful only if the project manager masters all the informal contacts needed to convince a critical mass of the sales force.
- At the project and process level, systematic use of ICT provides the data needed for market segmentation.
- The hierarchical and functional level has a significant influence on what can be pushed through top-down by relying on organizational routines and what has to be negotiated in time-consuming travels.
- The regional structure of the company itself gives some clues about market maturity and the need for lead-user markets.

Frequently, conflicts arise with autonomous subsidiaries and independent sales and service partners. Sales representatives ignore central directives because they believe they know best about their market and thus individually introduce adaptations to market requirements. The project manager for market introduction should therefore have direct access to top management. He must decide about local adaptations in market introduction; he coordinates decentralized activities and he is eventually responsible for system integration.

Research findings suggest that an early market introduction is positively correlated with the competitive position. Counter examples such as the IBM personal computer and Glaxo's Zantac demonstrate that late market introduction can lead to success if the company is capable of learning from mistakes of the early introducers. The Gillette Sensor example shows that a long development cycle time is not necessarily detrimental if the product is innovative and flawless. Yet, the general time frame of market introduction does play a significant role. In principal, the introduction process can be synchronous (big-bang) or sequential (lead concept) (Fig. II.4.10).

Presenting the product to all target markets at the same time is called a big-bang market introduction. It requires tight project management. The introduction of Windows 95 with world-wide TV coverage and 2,500 invited guests is an example of a big-bang. Prior to that, Microsoft had tested beta versions with 400,000 selected users, trained 1,500 specialists to answer upcoming questions, and spent almost US$ 200 million on commercials and marketing alone. The market expected a new standard, and its introduction time was critical. The product was not

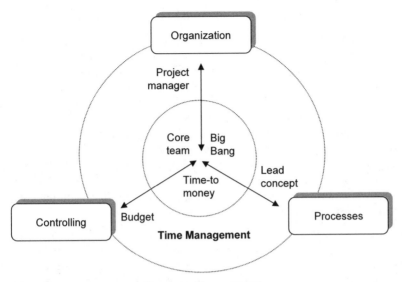

Source: Boutellier, Corsten, Lach (1997).

Fig. II.4.10. Principal alternatives in market introduction: resource management versus time management.

permitted to have any flaws in order to allow world-wide distribution. A big-bang is appropriate in intense competition, i.e. if the introduction is under high time-pressure and product quality is mastered by the company.

In the lead concept, the product is tested with lead customers or in lead markets, prior to world-wide introduction (Fig. II.4.11). Markets and customers often differ in how well they accept new products. Lead customers and lead countries assume a role as opinion leaders. For example, the Japanese market is more willing to accept innovative consumer electronics than the American or European market. Thus, Sony as well as Philips introduced the CD-player first in Japan, as did Canon with its new PC copier. Since the markets were not prepared for these products, learning was the underlying motivation. Since no time-pressure was involved, Sony, Philips, and Canon were able to improve the product based on the experience gained in the lead countries, and customers were given time to get used to the new product.

Besides the product, complementary services must reach the market as well. Although industrial services become increasingly important, they are still not systematically developed and introduced. If the product needs to be customized or localized to different markets and customers due to the development of individual services, the lead concept is the appropriate alternative. National or regional standards and laws often prevent a synchronous introduction in many markets and thus make a lead-concept introduction necessary.

Market introduction can thus be improved by the following conclusions:

- The market introduction should be carried out as a project with quantifiable goals, detailed schedules, defined work packages, and clear responsibilities for R&D, product management, sales, and local subsidiaries.
- The transition from the development phase to the introduction phase requires detailed and precise spade-work. Overlap in phases and temporary assignments in joint teams enhance knowledge transfer.
- If sales, customer service, and local subsidiaries are integrated into the R&D phase early, it increases product acceptance during the introduction phase. Most importantly, the headquarters should not decide entirely on its own terms.
- The controlling of product introduction presupposes clear goals and defined measures. In order to ensure costs transparency, all costs of introduction, including those in local subsidiaries, must be considered.

These suggestions and solutions must be adapted to the specific circumstances. If the company feels safe and the time-to-market is the issue, a combination of heavy-weight project manager, parallel introduction and emphasis on time-to-market is appropriate. If there are open questions and limited resources available, a mixture of core teams, lead concept, and overall budget is suggested.

6   Conclusions

By dividing the innovation process into three parts the innovation rate can be improved.

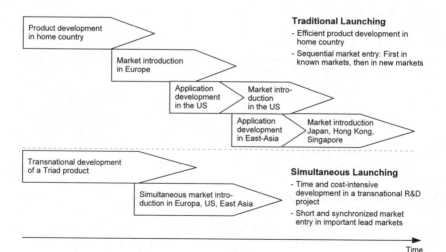

Fig. II.4.11. Simultaneous and traditional market introduction.

- Globalization does not change the basic aspects of the three generic innovation phases: pre-project, project, and market-introduction.
- The architecture of the product defines the project structure. The better the modularity, the easier the work in dispersed teams, and the easier globalization of R&D.
- The successful execution of interlocal innovation must place more emphasis on the creative pre-project phase, as the basis for the following cost-intensive development phase is defined here. Only in the project execution phase should the focus shift to measurable efficiency.
- Idea generation in early stages can be supported by modern computer technologies.
- Good ideas must be promoted. Potential promoters must be introduced to new ideas in early R&D stages.
- In order to transfer a project from the pre-project phase into the project phase, traditional product profitability calculation must be complemented with qualitative criteria such as competence establishment, learning opportunities, and product visions.
- A strong steering committee clears the way for project managers.
- The actual agents in a project are sometimes team-averse specialists, although their input is absolutely necessary for project success. A separation of project members into different teams (ABC-teams) can neutralize this conflict.

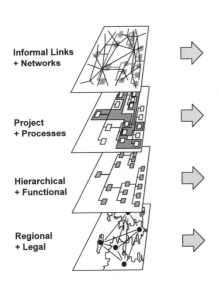

Solutions for Transnational R&D Processes

Informal Links + Networks
- Create informal network
- Create team identity
- 'Warm start-up'

Project + Processes
- Clear interfaces and work packages
- Distinguish clearly between R&D phases
- Systematic use of ICT
- Stage-gate processes
- Cross-functional teams

Hierarchical + Functional
- Find a product champion
- Multi-functional prototyping
- Loose-tight distinction
- Quality function deployment

Regional + Legal
- Use lead-markets
- Intralocal pre-project
- Interlocal project execution
- Global market introduction

Fig. II.4.12. Principal approaches to solve main problems in carrying out transnational R&D processes.

- During the development phase, highly structured engineering is required. Measurement criteria such as on-time delivery or first-pass yields used in manufacturing are applicable.

By large, internationalization does not change R&D processes completely but puts far more stress on project management. If integrated design gets close to being unmanageable, modular product architectures show their real strengths. The company usually needs far more time to prepare and plan the global project than in interlocal designs. The choice between collocating travel-averse engineers and heavy-weight project management is a delicate balance!

II.5 Information & Communication Technologies

„IT makes transactions transparent so that behavior is no longer hidden."
Chris Argyris

1 ICT Changes How R&D is Done

ICT (information and communication technology)-enhanced R&D is more different from regular R&D than most people realize. Granted, R&D as we understand it already makes heavy use of telephone communication, email, videoconferencing, etc. But the deployment of ICT into R&D project and process management fundamentally changes how R&D engineers go about their work: what they do, how they do it, and with whom. The changes that the use of ICT has brought about have come slowly, but their impact has been significant.

While the abundant presence of ICT has produced many benefits for R&D, it has also marginalized some established R&D methods based on collocation. For instance, many project management methodologies, creativity techniques, and product development concepts were expressively built around face-to-face contact of participating engineers. Now that many (if not most) R&D projects are international, involving two or more R&D sites providing staff and resources, questions arise such as, for instance, how to exploit all benefits of prototyping (a fair amount of which is based on the possibility of engineers testing handling and usability of a product, i.e. touch-and-feel properties), how to conduct effective brainstorming sessions (whose participants use often vague formulations for new, initial ideas, sketches or analogies, all of which are difficult and sometimes impossible to relay in a multi-cultural remote-site electronically-facilitated workshop), or how to best integrate lead users and their machines who are physically bound to be on the site of the installment of the product, e.g. a power plant or magnetic elevated train? Is travel perhaps the only solution to overcome these difficulties, despite all the advances in ICT?

2 The Need for ICT in Transnational R&D Projects

Intuitively, ICT appears to be very cost-intensive. For example, in 1993 a video conference lasting one hour (2x65kbit/s) via ISDN between Zurich and New York

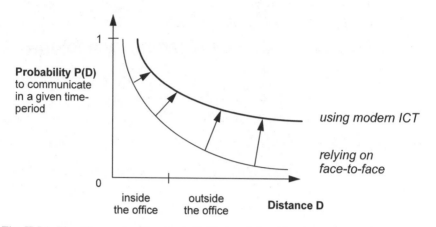

Fig. II.5.1. The Allen curve gives the logarithmic relationship of communication probability between physically separated R&D employees.

at the company's own premises cost CHF324 (Lautz, 1995: vi). For a reserved line between MTU in Munich, Germany and Pratt&Whitney in East Hartford, Connecticut, over €60,000 was spent per year. Decreases in telecommunication costs and the development of reliable online conferencing applications have brought down these costs to marginal levels. Still, the total cost of ICT in most companies constitutes about 10% of the total R&D budget (in some companies, expenses for ICT infrastructure can amount to as much as 20% of total R&D expenses). ICT may not be the highest expense in R&D (this is still reserved for salaries), but it is not a negligible cost item.

In our experience, the costs of not using ICT exceed those for using ICT by far. These indirect costs are the opportunity costs of sustained traditional face-to-face communication. If a decentralized team meets in person, considerable travel costs and travel times are incurred. The productive time lost during the nonproductive travel time represents a considerable cost factor. Moreover, the specialists are often indispensable in their home locations. Their absence is usually very costly, although it is not easy to quantify. In order to achieve the same effectiveness, traditional communication is far more expensive than the usage of a combined mix of face-to-face meetings and modern ICT.

In addition, the social costs of traveling are generally ignored. Extensive traveling often induces personal stress upon the travelers, their spouses and children, their colleagues and friends. It is thus very often a person's family which directly or indirectly determines the conditions for long-term personnel dispatches during large-scale transnational projects. As personal stress reduces the creative power and motivation of the individual, the resulting social costs influence the productivity in the project work. If these indirect, barely quantifiable costs were included in decision making, the use of ICT would definitely be supported from the point of view of overall costs.

Whatever the degree of internationalization, and whatever the cost of travel, the socialization phase at the start of a project has not lost its significance. Traveling to project partners remains a necessity in transnational R&D projects. These early project phases are crucial to build trust among project partners and provide the basis for further collaboration between dispersed project members. Later deployment ICT allows one to prolong the times between face-to-face contacts, but it cannot ultimately replace them.

The seminal empirical study by Allen (1977) shows that the probability of communication between two R&D employees decreases exponentially with increasing physical distance. This relationship was demonstrated both in the micro- (inside the same building) and in the macro-range (miles, kilometer distances) (Allen, 1977). However, due to the intensified utilization of ICT in R&D and the increasing experience with transnational R&D projects, this logarithmic relationship is expected to change (Fig. II.5.1).

In the 1960s and 1970s, information technology was seen more as an element improving overall efficiency and productivity than as a long-term competitive weapon (Howells, 1995: 173). It was used mainly to increase mathematical calculating speed. In lens design, for example, a zoom calculation required 10 to 20 man years before the advent of computers. In the 1960s, 6 months of number crunching often yielded much better designs (Fig. II.5.2).

In the 1980s, scientists refusing overseas placements led to the acceptance of ICT as a generic tool to change the way researchers work and communicate. While in the late 1980s the fax was considered the next "big thing" (in Japan, for instance, the predecessors to modern cell phones could be connected to specially designed, portable mini-faxes), the advent of the WorldWideWeb and the Internet in the 1990s has made most paper-based forms of communication obsolete. For instance, Telex services, the main means of long distance communication before the telephone, have been discontinued because email offered a cheaper and faster solution to text-based messages from home to home. By the mid-2000s, the next-

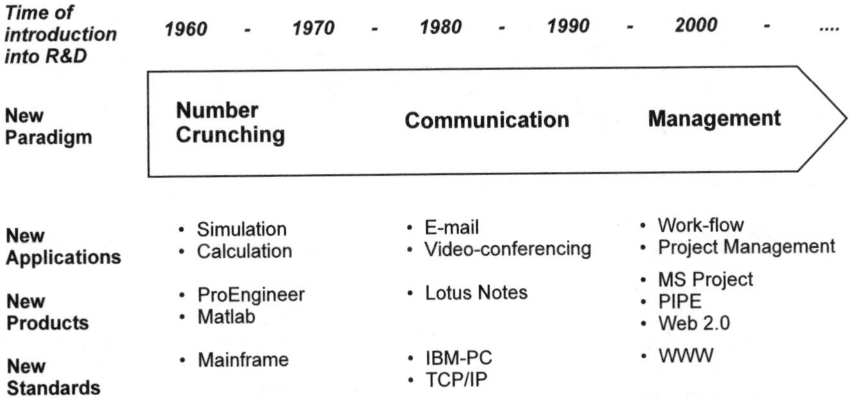

Time of introduction into R&D	1960	-	1970	-	1980	-	1990	-	2000	-	....
New Paradigm	**Number Crunching**				**Communication**				**Management**		
New Applications	• Simulation • Calculation				• E-mail • Video-conferencing				• Work-flow • Project Management		
New Products	• ProEngineer • Matlab				• Lotus Notes				• MS Project • PIPE • Web 2.0		
New Standards	• Mainframe				• IBM-PC • TCP/IP				• WWW		

Fig. II.5.2. Three phases of new ICT application in R&D.

generation Internet (Internet-2) is under development, and features used in the gaming industry are being introduced to virtual reality applications in professional solutions. The engineers of 2015 won't even remember (or know) what the world looked like without the Internet and omnipresent telecommunication.

Thus, if not only a powerful support tool in order to make existing processes more efficient, ICT has the potential to tremendously enhance the performance of R&D. This applies especially to R&D organizations that make use of ICT as a strategic instrument in order to achieve fundamental changes in the traditional R&D process.

3   Use of ICT in Decentralized Projects

The application and usage of ICT in everyday business life has become so common that its applicability is rarely questioned. Even project teams located in the same office utilize computer networks, e-mail and shared databases to simplify and improve their work.

However, there are many problems despite – or perhaps because of – this widespread use (Fig. II.5.3). For instance, the increase in communication opportunity leads to a concentration of electronically storable and transferable information. Much of the crucial information in R&D is tacit, however, and is either corrupted in the codification attempt or simply not communicated at all, e.g. due to a lack of the necessary organizational support.

Hence, the application of ICT in decentralized R&D projects is rather delicate

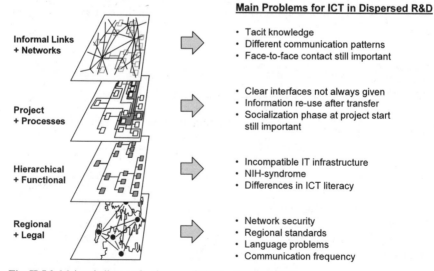

Main Problems for ICT in Dispersed R&D

Informal Links + Networks
- Tacit knowledge
- Different communication patterns
- Face-to-face contact still important

Project + Processes
- Clear interfaces not always given
- Information re-use after transfer
- Socialization phase at project start still important

Hierarchical + Functional
- Incompatible IT infrastructure
- NIH-syndrome
- Differences in ICT literacy

Regional + Legal
- Network security
- Regional standards
- Language problems
- Communication frequency

Fig. II.5.3. Major challenges for the use of ICT in dispersed R&D.

and possible shortcomings are abundant. If the project is carried out in several locations requiring the interaction of its members, the following preconditions favorably support cross-border teamwork (Howells, 1995: 176):

- The majority of the team members know each other via direct personal contact.
- The team is distributed to no more than three sites.
- Clearly identified objectives and a demarcated project organization are established at the outset.
- Access and utilization of ICT tools is guaranteed.
- Face-to-face contact and frequent mutual visits of key individuals still take place.

In such transnational R&D projects, ICT offer a great opportunity for improving the way in which R&D is operated and managed within companies. Benefits that have previously been restricted to centralized R&D organizations are now being exploited by distributed team structures as well (Howells, 1995; Gassmann, 1997a):

- Benefits of having access to specialist equipment as well as staff and reduction of isolation;
- Time-based benefits, exploitation of interaction potential and different time zones;
- Spatial flexibility of R&D, allowing one to contact customers, suppliers, labor, external experts through modern media;
- Promotion of creativity and quality;
- Formation of a personal network and trust building.

To illustrate how time-based benefits and access to specialists can be put to good use through ICT-based R&D processes, let's consider the example of a large US developer of system software and provider IT services (see von Zedtwitz, 1999, for the extensive case study). They have instituted an approach referred to as "Follow-the-Sun" or "Around-the-Clock" R&D (Espinosa and Carmel, 2003). In this case, towards the end of the working day on the US Pacific Coast the project work (design) is handed off to a Japanese team (for implementation) that in turn will hand off the project work to a French team (for testing) when its working day ends. Overlapping time windows or liaisons following the respective work hours of the other location facilitate coordination and allow for the necessary interaction. Thus, the project can be advanced continuously, without impediments of local labor restrictions or availability of local staff or contractors.

This example also helps illustrate two problems of international R&D: trust among decentralized team members. As it happens, each R&D site is mainly staffed with American, Japanese, or French engineers, and instructions they receive from the preceding shift is formulated in English, mostly, but certainly not in Japanese or French. Miscommunication and misinterpretations are frequent, leading to costly and time-consuming discussions both internally and, eventually, with the originating site. Over time, the confidence in the team delivering the preceding shift diminishes, and a soft version of the NIH (not-invented-here) syn-

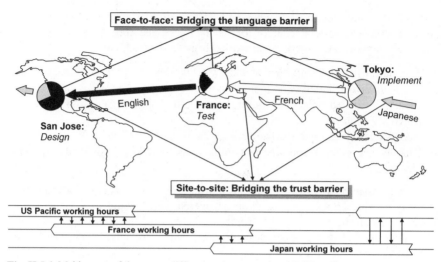

Fig. II.5.4. Making use of time zone differences in transnational R&D projects.

drome emerges: What comes in from the Americans, the French, or the Japanese team doesn't generally work, it can't work, they didn't follow our specifications.

Ingeniously, this company decided to take a few of the local recipient site team members and send them to the preceding shift team to act as interpreters of the information to be made sense of in the recipient's language and communicated effectively (Fig. II.5.4). This took care of the language barrier of multi-site R&D. It also aided with the trust problem, as now instructions, modules and preliminary results were handed down by their own team members, and not from the outside "enemy" team. After all, it was now a good colleague with whom one had shared offices for some time, who sat at the other end. Immediately, efficiency of this 24h-R&D process improved.

Trust as a factor affecting international R&D process quality is not a new revelation, but it is still not one that has been tackled satisfactorily. De Meyer, (1991) coined the term *half-life of trust*, i.e., the half-life of sufficient trust between two people using electronic communications. Periodic face-to-face contact is necessary to maintain a level of trust and mutual confidence high enough for effective team work. Such a process is illustrated in Fig. II.5.5.

Incidentally, the company in this example also realized that these international interpreters – all of them, of course, fully capable engineers in their own right – adapted to the local culture after some time, and thus lost some of the implicit trust imparted by the joint work with their colleagues at their home bases. Thus, they were replaced periodically every three months to allow resocialization with their roots.

While it is obvious that ICT is itself a set of technologies still under development, hence R&D-intensive, it is somewhat unfortunate that the support of ICT within R&D departments is often suboptimal for the following reasons.

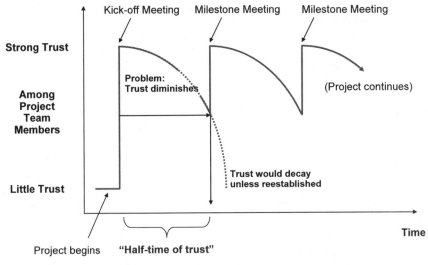

Source: Adapted from De Meyer (1991).

Fig. II.5.5. The half-life of trust in decentralized R&D projects.

R&D is rooted in the scientific and technical world including computer systems with strong number-crunching performance such as VAX or UNIX-based systems. The usage of the IBM PC-compatible business standard has been disdained until recently and is being only slowly overcome. Macintosh computers have been widely used in the academic environment and are especially known for their strengths in desktop publishing. Linux-based systems are becoming more popular since the early 2000s. Data exchange between different systems has remained cumbersome until today despite major efforts to bridge between all the different computer systems. In many R&D-intensive companies, R&D has relied on a VAX-world whereas logistics and administration took advantage of the input-output strengths of IBM-related systems. The ICT environment of R&D and the rest of the company have thus often taken separate paths.

Network security is a significant aspect of ICT in R&D. This includes not only the authorization to access project data but also the backing-up and safekeeping of data in the event of a network failure or system break-down. Technical people and scientists are often computer-savvy and use ICT in a way incomprehensible for people outside R&D or other members of the company. The Internet and the use of e-mail has its roots in a US defense-related computer network (ARPANET) which was transformed into a US-wide and eventually worldwide technical communication infrastructure, initially for academic research centers, and later for the general public.

Contrary to the routine and standardized data flow in many other corporate functions, R&D communication is highly intermittent in nature and ranges from video-conferencing to large-scale data transfer where speed and bandwidth are highly important. In addition to this is the recent decentralization of R&D itself which has introduced additional demands on ICT in order to be used as a management tool in international R&D (Howells, 1995). Consequently, R&D has been treated differently in terms of information systems and technology. R&D organizations in large companies often have their own ICT department, thus further segregating the information world of R&D and the rest of the company.

Private computer-communication networks have facilitated general networking between researchers. This trend supports the creation of inter-site research teams, the communication between researchers of the same company located in different countries, remote access to equipment and facilities, as well as unforeseen and spontaneous informal communication. Increasingly, R&D management utilizes ICT for coordination and control purposes, although the introduction of management information systems and decision support systems in R&D seems to have taken place surprisingly late compared to other corporate functions (Case and Pickett, 1989).

Project coordination and the exchange of technical information require media which are characterized by information richness (Trevino et al., 1987). The location-neutral availability of scheduling and technical information without having to incur significant time delays is important. The factual content of communication dominates. Daily communication can usually take place via e-mail. CAD systems, remote file systems, and on-line links to common databases are very important for the exchange of technical information.

Media which can convey a high degree of social presence appear to be more advantageous for promoting creativity and the development of a network. Creativity requires extensive ad hoc communication in which the need to communicate often arises unplanned. In the same way, activities aimed at building trust and developing informal ties cannot be fully schedule-driven.

The emotional aspect of communication plays an important role. Media which allow a broad spectrum of non-verbal communication (such as body language and gesturing) and are dialog-oriented (mutual exchange of information) can simulate face-to-face communication. Video conferences, teleconferences, and the telephone come closest to meeting this demand as long as the quality is comparable to what we are used in natural settings. In order to evaluate the overall advantages of ICT in R&D projects, the suitability of various ICT methods with regard to the above tasks and economic efficiency is illustrated in Figure II.5.6.

4   Selected ICT Instruments

4.1   *Electronic Conferencing for Day-to-Day Project Communication*

E-mail facilitates the communication via computers in computer networks. The users of the various computers are able to transfer messages and digital attachments to each other, which are stored in an „electronic mailbox." Information can be transferred to a single addressee or to several participants simultaneously. The largest and today most important network world-wide is the Internet; other computer networks include FidoNet, which is more and more replaced by the Internet, and a number of company-internal nets and single-machine systems (see Fig. II.5.7 for an example).

By e-mail, the project leader can transmit information affecting all project members in a time-and cost-saving manner. Managing a decentralized distributed project team is greatly simplified. E-mail systems also support the application of a series of workflow-related programs in transnational R&D projects. Resource

Technology	Developing an informal network	Promotion of creativity	Information exchange	Coordination support	Efficiency	Examples from software development
Videoconferencing	●	●	◑	◑	○	Project control, meetings, concept
Teleconferencing	●	◕	◔	●	◕	Project control, definition of interfaces, escalations
Telephone, voicemail	●	◑	●	●	◑	Definition of interfaces, project progress, escalations
Groupware	◕	●	◑	●	●	Electronic Brainstorming, process documentation
Fora	◕	◕	●	◑	●	Exchange of information, questions & answers
Intranet	◕	◕	●	●	●	E-Mail, communication
Client/Server environment	◕	◕	◑	○	◑	Development environment, shared databases
E-mail, memos	◕	◑	●	●	●	Mails, revisable documentation
LAN/WAN/GAN	◑	◕	●	◕	◑	Development library, development environment
File Transfer	◑	◕	◑	●	●	Presentations, spreadsheets, messages, FTP
CAD	◔	◕	◕	◑	◕	Hardware-display
CASE Tools	◔	◔	◕	◑	◕	Design concept, code generation
Electronic Calendar	◔	○	◔	●	◕	Organizing meetings
Project management systems	◔	○	◔	●	●	Project planning and control
Software library (database)	○	◔	●	●	◕	Progress of testing, source code
Remote systems	○	◔	◔	○	◕	Compiling, driver development, tests, telnet

Not suitable ○ ◔ ◑ ◕ ● Highly suitable

Source: Boutellier, Gassmann, Macho, Roux (1998).

Fig. II.5.6. Evaluation of information technologies in virtual R&D teams by experts at IBM.

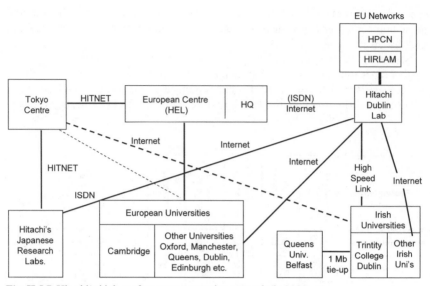

Fig. II.5.7. Hitachi's high-performance computing network (in 2000).

management programs give the project members access to a central schedule database which lets them check for meetings, conferences or employee absences. Programs even automate the usually laborious task of finding common dates for meetings (O'Hara and Devereaux, 1994). Compared with fax, the additional advantage of e-mail is that graphics can be sent better and faster. With increasingly higher performing computers and networks, audiovisual data (audio and video recordings etc.) and files in standard data types can be efficiently transmitted. Together with the paperless handling, this accounts for the attractiveness of e-mail over traditional information media.

Besides e-mail, personal messaging software (such as e.g. Skype, AOL Messenger, Microsoft Messenger, Lotus Sametime or Google Talk) facilitates electronic conferencing, allowing the exchange of information as text messages, entire documents and audiovisual form. Another functionality that is offered by modern conferencing and messaging tools is the shared whiteboard, where the communicating parties can see and work together on a common whiteboard.

Finally, online virtual offices with scheduling tools, project management tools, file sharing, shared whiteboards, intelligent document editors, etc. have the potential to completely digitize the workplace making it almost location independent. One such example is Microsoft Office Groove (www.groove.net).

Overall, the growing ubiquity of computing and communication equipment (e.g. in-flight Internet access, Tablet PCs, PDA, Blackberries, or Internet-enabled mobile phones) facilitates global team work through ICT. Other technologies that may facilitate global R&D in the future include 3D printers, data gloves, head mounted displays and eye tracking.

4.2   R&D Databases for Common Access to Project Data

R&D databases can store important, but not all the R&D results of a company. If all R&D units have access to common databases, unintentionally duplicated development of the same components is reduced. At IBM, for example, all central activities of the IBM Research Division are available in one database. Every IBM researcher can access this information. If a new problem emerges during a project, checking the database enables project members to first gain an overview of whether something similar is or has already been worked on at another location within the research division.

Schindler's Product Data Management (PDM) is such a sophisticated R&D database, facilitating extremely technical document management. It is currently extended to include all worldwide locations, providing full change management capability and version control functionality. PDM at Schindler is based on distributed databases and the latest web technologies.

The broad range of this shared information tool also intensifies communication between employees in different locations. A prerequisite is the integration and alignment of the information systems in the worldwide participating R&D units. The lack of standardization of information systems represents a significant problem in large companies. At Ciba-Geigy (now Novartis), for example, almost every regional company had its own information system right up to the mid-1990s. These were then to a great extent mutually incompatible. In 1995, a very costly project was launched in order to standardize and integrate these information systems.

The standardization of tools is a major problem for companies that grew through mergers and acquisitions or those with only loosely coordinated R&D sites (i.e. polycentric decentralized configuration). If data and communication is to be effectively and efficiently exchanged between dispersed sites, the company must make a decision which tools and data formats to use.

Schindler's R&D at Ebikon, Switzerland, used „Solid Designer" while the US sites - which were acquired from Westinghouse in the 1980s - were accustomed to „Pro-Engineer". The preference for a particular tool is influenced by the local environment (i.e. production methods, infrastructure, training of R&D staff). Often, the selection of a tool is a very political process.

It is also possible to introduce central CAD (Computer Aided Design) and other R&D-related computer systems to which all peripheral R&D units have on-line access. By these means, R&D projects can be conducted centrally up to the implementation phase and then transferred to the peripheral R&D units. Here the detailed design and the implementation are conducted in accordance with the requirements of the local market (Håkanson, 1990). In our research it was emphasized that access rights to international databases still represent an unsolved problem.

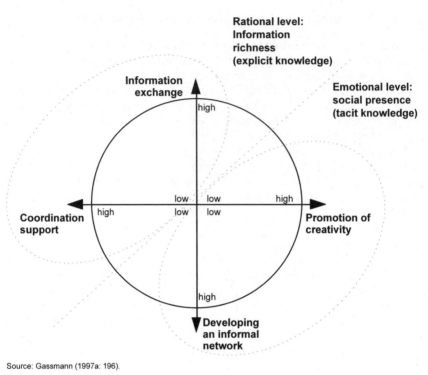

Source: Gassmann (1997a: 196).

Fig. II.5.8. Tasks of ICT.

4.3   Groupware for Electronic Brainstorming

Groupware is the ICT-based support for decentralized project meetings and is thus the group equivalent of bilateral e-mail communication. Every participant possesses a workstation via which he or she can communicate with the other participants in a computer network. Groupware provides comprehensive methods of supporting virtual R&D teams by means of special group-oriented, computer-based methods, such as electronic brainstorming, the common drawing up of agendas, various coordination methods or automatic protocol generation.

It appears that electronic brainstorming will gain importance in the future. Traditionally, group-dynamic creativity requires physical proximity. However, the latest developments in groupware also support electronically controlled virtual team sessions in the creative project phases (e.g. Group Systems or Lotus Notes). This enables an internationally distributed team to conduct brainstorming sessions to generate product ideas and alternative solutions during early phases of a project.

Brainstorming sessions follow a similar pattern in most groupware systems: the participants have parallel access to the system and enter their ideas simultaneously into their local PCs. By pressing the corresponding function key a team member can broadcast his or her ideas and in turn receive a random selection or the complete collection of other people's ideas. The combination of other ideas with one's own induces coming up with completely new and creative solutions. After the idea generation phase, the ideas can be examined and jointly structured according to keywords and then evaluated anonymously.

Groupware-based electronic brainstorming allows multi-location idea generation and has a number of other advantages over traditional forms of brainstorming. The social pressure of group conformance and the position of the team members in the hierarchy are greatly reduced by the anonymity of the contributors. An alternative to electronic brainstorming is "brainwriting" which follows a structured redistribution of other people's ideas and comments until every participant has had the chance to contribute at least once to every idea. For instance, in the „653 method" six participants propose three solutions or comments to a given problem or question. Each participant then transmits his comments to another participant, and receives the comments from some other participant. This is repeated five times, creating quickly a great number of comments or ideas. The main difference to electronic brainstorming is the structured approach to the exchange and accumulation of ideas.

Compared to sequential face-to-face communication processes, the asynchronous communication mode inherent to computer conferencing can be an advantage in solving complex problems. The inhibition of creative diversity associated with sequential problem-solving processes in face-to-face sessions in real time can be overcome in asynchronous communication, since the participants are encouraged to solve the problem from their own perspective. The parallel access to the system enables several suggestions to be generated at the same time. Particularly where groups are heterogeneous and contexts diverse, this can result in very innovative suggestions for solutions (O'Hara and Devereaux, 1994). The asynchronous mode also simplifies intercultural communication, since people who have to communicate in a foreign language have more time to read or to prepare a message than in face-to-face communication (Ishii, 1994).

Our own studies show that despite the advantages mentioned, groupware systems for brainstorming have hardly been used yet in transnational R&D projects. Leading companies such as IBM utilize groupware almost exclusively for coordination purposes. For example, all products under development are published in the RFA tool to eliminate redundant development („formal approval cycle"). IBM TERM lists all IBM terms to achieve uniform use. With the OfficeVision/VM tool, documents such as the on-line telephone book, IBM organizational information, time, location and meeting plans are managed via e-mail world-wide. Time planning within project groups is conducted with the TIME & PLACE application tool.

The creative phases up to now almost always have been conducted in one place. Our interviews with a large number of people show that besides purely communicative support, the systems available to date provide too little content support. The consequence of this is an unstructured flood of information. The complete lack of face-to-face contact also makes information exchange and processing hard to manage. However, great improvements in this area can be expected from hardware and software development. This trend to ICT is gaining acceptance and greater potential for creativity can be expected.

4.4   Tele- and Video Conferences for Crisis Meetings

For an overwhelming majority of large companies, teleconferences - due to simplicity, low cost, and the widely available infrastructure - are very popular instruments to support communication in transnational R&D projects. Teleconferences are frequently backed up by a simultaneous exchange of graphics or pictures ("upgraded teleconferencing"). Audiographic systems of this kind are particularly useful for design-based team work in which intensive real-time communication is required.

International teams make it necessary for some members to speak a foreign language. These participants are strongly inhibited in their communication because, to a large extent, teleconferences do not convey important elements of non-verbal communication: Body language in a narrow sense such as facial expression, eye contact, gesturing, posture and physical movement. In addition it is often difficult to identify who is speaking at the moment. Since teleconferences are difficult to control, experienced moderators, pre-defined agendas, and well-established group processes are critical success factors.

In transnational R&D projects, holding a video conference has many advantages over traditional project meetings: Participants of a video conference can always be contacted, since absence due to travel time is avoided. The ad hoc participation of additional experts and immediate access to information sources at the participating locations are possible. Since time-consuming preparations for travel are not necessary, the frequency of meetings can be increased and coordination procedures shortened. This means that the time required for development can be reduced. In comparison with other telecommunication services the additional exchange of visual information leads to greater information density and helps to improve the project members' understanding of the issues. The average human being can memorize almost 15% of audio information, but almost two thirds of the information if audio and visual impact is combined.

One disadvantage of this medium lies in the necessity of reserving times for the conference and the amount of time needed to set up the communication links. Yet, with the growing ubiquity of the Internet the communication link aspect is greatly simplified. Modern Internet access devices provide even home workers with ample communication bandwidth for videoconferencing. The most popular example is Skype, where anyone with a reasonable high-speed Internet access can communicate at no additional cost with anyone else who has Internet access anywhere in the world.

5   Dynamics in the Course of a Project

The development of personal networks and the establishment of an atmosphere of trust play an important role in the early phases of projects (see Fig. II.5.9). Champions for the project idea have to be found. Project members first have to get to know each other and then build up mutual trust. In this early phase it is important to create an atmosphere of acceptance among the locations involved and thus overcome the „not invented here" syndrome. Informal ties must be created so that the participants are familiar with their contacts in the various locations and the official channels of escalation can be reserved for real crisis. As far as possible, the use of face-to-face meetings in conjunction with informal e-mail should be promoted.

Idea generation and recombination, and the design of the system architecture demand a high degree of creativity. In this phase, the application of groupware is important. If applied properly, electronic brainstorming can foster and boost creativity to a great effect.

During the development phase itself, the structure of the informal network has already become robust and the funnel of ideas has been narrowed down significantly, so that the demand for creativity lessens (Wheelwright and Clark, 1992). The local development in the decentralized teams, which mainly exchange selective technical information via established interfaces is gaining importance.

During the implementation phase decentralized development activities are coordinated vigorously. The coordination intensity increases sharply just before the system integration phase. The coordinated effort to complete the development of individual modules is most important at this point.

It must be emphasized, however, that in this scheme innovation processes pro-

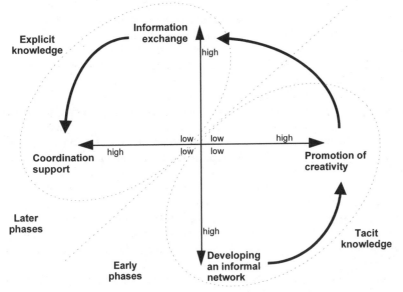

Source: Gassmann (1997a); Boutellier, Gassmann, Macho, Roux (1998).

Fig. II.5.9. Changing ICT demands in the course of a project.

gress by no means in a linear fashion. On the contrary, Van de Ven (1989) in particular, based on his event-based cross-sectional analyses, points out the non-linear progress rate of innovation processes. The present model only intends to indicate that during different innovation phases certain respective characteristics are more dominant. For instance, it cannot be ruled out that creativity is not required in later phases as well, although creativity is usually required more in the early phases than in later ones. The exclusivity of earlier deterministic phase concepts (e.g. Saynisch, 1979, 1989a,b) is replaced here by the dominance of certain phases.

6   Means to Measure and Lead Dispersed R&D Teams

One of the best introductions to managing dispersed teams is perhaps still Carmel's (1998) guide to managing global software teams, although more and more books are published on this topic. Many of the lessons cited there apply to the ICT-based management of international R&D projects in general.

Besides the best practices already cited in this and other chapters on virtual R&D teams, crucial to all ICT-supported R&D teams is the utilization of the proper infrastructure, one that is shared by all team members (to avoid compatibility problems), the selection and motivation of team members capable to work in virtual teams, and the establishment of accepted routines and processes of decentralized collaboration. Once those are in place, it is now up to the project manager to consider appropriate means to measure the performance of the virtual team.

One of the obvious measurement categories is costs. This includes specifically the costs of telecommunications, i.e. the purchase, rent or lease of the infrastructure, as well as ongoing costs of its usage. Travel costs should also be considered, including actual travel expenses as well as more difficult to obtain cost factors such as lost working days due to travel absence, travel related illnesses or sickdays, or stress-induced productivity reduction. Last but not least, there are costs of labor in each site, and some sites offer comparative advantages to high-salary countries such as the US, Japan, or Western Europe.

The next measurement category is the actual usage of collaborative technologies. How much time (per person) is being spent on making telephone calls, emails, video-conferences, Skype etc.? Differentiate this information further by the actual number of sessions or messages made on the phone or in discussion lists, by the nature of the technologies used (e.g., synchronous such as telephone calls or asynchronous such as email), and by intra- and inter-site components.

Issue management is a great category to measure how the team deals with problems. Many groupware tools offer simple ways to keep track of the number of issues raised and issues closed. The number of open issues should rise over the early development cycle . The issue closure index is a ratio of how many days it takes, on average, to close an issue.

Measures of efficiency are important, too. Delays are a count of the number of times one site's work was delayed because of wait for dependent tasks from other sites. Count the number of times activities resulted in overnight gain (this is a

Follow-the-Sun measure). Also, track blocking counts: A block occurs when one site or individual compensates for time loss on one task by working on another one. Ideally, count these with duration.

Additional measures include the time per person spent in formal face-to-face meetings. This is often called the Dilbert index, after the well-known cartoon character. The total time is divided by total person-time on the project. The team-building index is the number of days that individuals (managers and other team members) of one site spend at other sites (net travel days) divided by total of all person-days on the project (below %1 is usually too low). Count travel days as a separate measure. While raising the team-building index, minimize travel days.

Two points of advice are given for applying these measures:

1. The actual indices and ratios only make sense in the context of what one considers minimum or maximum values. It will take time and experience to find these out, as they differ depending on the nature of the project. Execution-style development projects will have a lower incidence of inter-site calls than the creativity-intensive stages of an R&D project. Only once appropriate benchmarks have been determined, one can actively make use of the measure to manage ICT-based R&D teams.

2. As always, people – and teams – will adapt to what is being measured. As a project manager, one must always retain a direct and non-ICT based rapport with the team to get a fair impression of the team's performance. For instance, the issue closure index can be easily manipulated by closing issues before they are resolved and opening up a new one with an identical issue title to continue the discussion. It is usually not very useful to impose checks and controls for every single loophole in the measures applied, as this reduced the respect and trust that the team has for the leader. Sometimes, less is more.

7   Limitations of ICT in Virtual R&D Teams

Industrial R&D processes are increasingly supported by ICT. Although communication has traditionally been one of the main productivity problems in R&D (De Meyer, 1991),[31] the communicative and managerial aspect of ICT in R&D has only been considered in depth in recent times. Supporting virtual R&D teams in transnational projects places the greatest demands on ICT, as Howells (1995: 176) stated: „....the establishment of a scientific and technical team located at several different sites but working on the same project represents the most far-reaching aspect of the use of ICT in R&D."

The introduction of ICT is frequently associated with a pronounced reduction in travel by researchers. For example, traveling costs at IBM have decreased drastically since video conferences have been introduced widely. The greatest challenges to the application of ICT in virtual R&D teams lie in the broad substitution

---

[31]   The positive correlation between communication intensity and the success of R&D projects has been confirmed by the empirical study of Ebadi and Utterback (1984).

of face-to-face communication among team members by ICT-based communication. It is precisely with respect to this point, however, that the limitations of ICT occur. Employing ICT in virtual teams means that sensory information, feelings, intuition and context are largely neglected due to a lack of person-to-person contact (De Meyer, 1991).

Much of communication is conducted non-verbally, i.e. body language, gesturing. This non-verbal communication is largely neglected in electronic information transmission. Especially in transnational R&D projects in which communication problems already arise from the differences in the languages and cultures involved, non-verbal communicational elements are highly significant. This problem is additionally intensified if the project participants come from context-rich cultures (e.g. Japanese and Chinese).

Substituting traditional face-to-face communication with ICT-based communication therefore has clear limitations. Although virtual R&D teams have a lot of potential, the realization of this depends on the extent to which suitable project management is conducted.

8   Conclusions

"Global organization cannot function without information technology. But the technology itself is not the answer to the myriad problems of working across geographical and cultural boundaries. The ultimate answers to these problems remain in the realm of human ... relations," argue O'Hara and Devereaux (1994: 74) about the application of ICT in global corporations. As shown clearly in a number of case studies in this book, the application of ICT is absolutely vital in large-scale international projects typically characterized by a high degree of division of labor. At the same time the case studies show that although the application of ICT is a necessary condition for virtual R&D teams, it is not by itself sufficient to guarantee project success. Rather, the technical tools must be complemented by adequate organizational and people's management (Fig. II.5.10).

For the application of ICT in virtual R&D teams, the following recommendations are made:

- A large part of the team should know one another before the start of the project. If this is not the case, intensive measures for developing team spirit are necessary at the start. For this purpose the team must be assembled in one place. Once an atmosphere of trust has been built up among the team members this must be continually revived, as it drops off in the course of decentralized cooperation („half-life of trust").
- The use of electronic conferencing, e-mail, common databases, and remote log-in (e.g. through intranets) is usually crucial if the virtual team is to work efficiently. Video conferences can be a useful complement to face-to-face meetings.

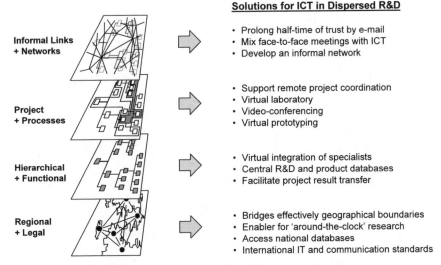

Solutions for ICT in Dispersed R&D

**Informal Links
+ Networks**

- Prolong half-time of trust by e-mail
- Mix face-to-face meetings with ICT
- Develop an informal network

**Project
+ Processes**

- Support remote project coordination
- Virtual laboratory
- Video-conferencing
- Virtual prototyping

**Hierarchical
+ Functional**

- Virtual integration of specialists
- Central R&D and product databases
- Facilitate project result transfer

**Regional
+ Legal**

- Bridges effectively geographical boundaries
- Enabler for 'around-the-clock' research
- Access national databases
- International IT and communication standards

Fig. II.5.10. Multiple uses for ICT in dispersed R&D.

- It is important that ICT are applied according to the situation; Information exchange, coordination support, creativity promotion and development of informal networks can represent a sensible framework for the application of ICT. ICT instruments should be selected according to the dominant task during each R&D phase.
- Despite the enormous progress made in ICT, face-to-face contact is still essential in transnational R&D projects. The degree of virtuality of R&D teams is influenced by the degree of trust required, the proportion of implicit knowledge and the complexity of the project. Integrated problem-solving strategies often still require interpersonal communication within traditional teams. The longer the duration of an R&D project and the greater the continuity of the team, the easier it is for face-to-face communication to be replaced by ICT-based communication.

II.6 Directors of International R&D Labs

"It is the personality and leadership of the initial director
who defines the culture and future of the R&D lab."
Li Gong, former Director of Sun R&D

1 R&D Directors: An Easy Choice?

1.1 Greenfield Investments as a Major Entry Mode for Global R&D

When new R&D labs are being set up, one of the key decisions is the choice of the first R&D director. This first director will have to be able to start a new R&D organization from scratch, establish himself – and itself – in a potentially very alien environment, and ensure the proper integration of the new lab into the global R&D organization.

From the perspective of R&D internationalization, not all 'new' R&D labs are actually new: many have been acquired through purchase of their parent companies, and some are sold directly, as for instance in the case of Ericsson's R&D centers in India bought by Wipro in 2003. In general, between 25% and 60% of all 'new' R&D labs are acquired[32], although there are differences between countries with respect to acquisition preferences: Japanese companies acquired less than 2% of their overseas R&D units (Yoshihara and Iwata, 1997). Since about 70% of all M&A's are motivated by market access[33], many acquired R&D units are discontinued or merged with the acquirers' local R&D centers during the consolidation period after an acquisition.

Given the recent rise of R&D in less developed countries, a substantial if not a majority percentage of overseas R&D units are created anew. This appears to be the dominant strategy particularly for laboratories with a research mission. Greenfield investments are the preferred mode of entry for R&D sites established abroad. Overseas R&D activity also emerges from internal evolution of local technical service and product adaptation units.[34]

---

[32] Ronstadt (1978), Behrmann and Fischer (1980), von Boehmer (1995), Hakanson and Nobel (1993a), Beckmann (1997), Cantwell and Mudambi (2005).
[33] Granstrand, Hakanson and Sjölander (1993), Hakanson and Nobel (1993b).
[34] See Brockhoff (1998) and Beckmann and Fischer (1994) for R&D sites with a research mission, Kuemmerle (1999), Caves (1996) and Mansfield (1984) for greenfield establishments, and Gassmann and von Zedtwitz (1996c) for internal evolution.

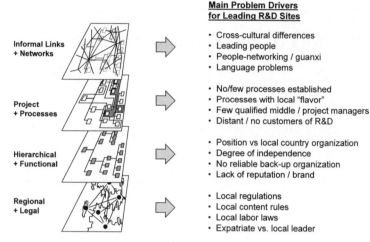

Fig. II.6.1. Main problems for leading R&D sites.

It is thus obvious how important it is to choose the 'right' new laboratory director. In addition to scientific or technological qualifications, this individual is also responsible for ramping up the local R&D organization and meet R&D performance targets. 'Copy-Paste' approaches of existing R&D departments into a new business and science environment are not possible.

To illustrate this point, consider Kuemmerle's (1997) account of a US electronics company that decided to staff its newly established UK research lab with an excellent researcher, albeit inexperienced manager. In addition, 11 of the 14 initial researchers had been hired locally and lacked deep ties with the parent company. Consequently, the lab had difficulties in expanding as expected, and senior employees left the R&D unit. All efforts to improve the situation failed until the initial laboratory leader was replaced by two experienced managers with good track records as researchers. Under this new leadership, the laboratory grew to its project size of 225 employees and met the targets of headquarters.

1.2 *Expatriates versus Local Managers*

The selection of the R&D director appears to be of a more practical concern and finds occasional mentioning in articles authored for R&D practitioners (see, e.g., von Krogh, 1994). Most studies draw little distinction between R&D and other functions. However, there is an extensive amount of literature on human resource deployment in multinational companies. Robock and Simmonds (1989: 570-575) summarized and outlined three principal types of international managers:

- *International executive cadre (geocentric style):* The company assigns the best person for the job. However, such people are rather expensive to sustain, they require strong central coordination, they have difficulties complying with local identification, and they block the career development of local managers.

- *National executives within each unit (polycentric style):* No training program is needed as they understand local languages and customs, and they guarantee continuity. Difficulties may arise from a gap between the parent's organization system and local operations, internal cross-cultural problems, and a certain inherent immobility.
- *Parent company's executives (expatriate):* The most frequent choice for transplanting successful practices and corporate knowledge. However, it blocks local promotion and is usually quite expensive.

There are two principal alternatives for overseas laboratory management: expatriates and local managers. Particularly during the start-up phase of an R&D facility, managers and employees were transferred from the parent company to the R&D laboratory. In most cases, technical qualifications were reported to be the prime determinants for the selection of the new lab leader. Many companies feel a certain need for home-country presence in the host country (usually the general manager or the local chief financial officer). Expatriates appear to be particularly attractive for R&D internationalization, since technology-intensive companies seek an efficient process to transfer knowledge and technical know-how embedded in key individuals. Additionally, expatriate managers are often home-grown, and they are trusted to retain the core missions, interest and secrets of the company even if posted in a distant country. Unfortunately, expatriate managers have a high failure rate, particularly in countries culturally different from the expatriate's home country (Zeria and Banai, 1985), and their presence in host countries is subject to enabling visa and work permit regulations. The use of expatriates is therefore a possible but not always preferred strategy.

This chapter focuses on the selection of initial R&D directors by suggesting:

- A model describing typical R&D director roles and their responsibilities;
- A guideline for making the R&D director selection decision.

2   Profiles of Initial R&D Directors

The selection or appointment of a new R&D director is always made based on a combination of factors. First of all, the candidate must be available and willing to accept the assignment. A special case of this is when the candidate is one of the main champions for the new R&D site. Second, the candidate must be sufficiently qualified for the job. There are different opinions as to what these qualifications should consist of, but usually include managerial as well as technical credentials. Some of the companies that we surveyed acknowledged that this was one of the decisions in which they had often—in retrospect—made too many concessions. For many companies, these are the only two formal considerations.

Companies with more experience with international R&D networks know that there are more factors to be considered. Some of them relate to the candidate and his or her ability to demonstrate entrepreneurial qualities, interact with superiors at a distance, or assimilate in a foreign culture. Other factors bring up strategic questions for the company, such as the mandate of an R&D site, its role in the international R&D network, and future directions it is expected to take. These considerations are difficult to quantify and may not yet have been completed by the time of the appointment.

Empirically, we have found the following eight styles among initial R&D directors (see Fig. II.6.2, von Zedtwitz, 2003):

- The expatriate director who is not familiar with local customs but nevertheless dispatched from the parent's R&D unit to run the new site;
- The expatriate director who is already familiar with local customs is dispatched from the parent's R&D to the new lab;
- The expatriate director who is promoted from the local country organization and familiar with local customs;
- The expatriate director who is recruited from outside the company but brings in a substantial local network and familiarity with customs;
- The national director who is recruited internally and assigned from the parent's R&D unit to return to his home country;
- The national director who is hired abroad from outside the company to return to his home country;
- The national director who is hired externally in the host country;
- The national director who is hired internally from the host country organization.

These initial R&D directors styles differ in the cultural background of each director, their familiarity with organizational procedures and customs, the linkage be-

Table II.6.1. Profiles of eight typical appointments of initial directors of foreign R&D units.

Style	Profile of Initial R&D Director	Examples
1	Expat, not locally familiar with the culture, international transfer	Leica in Singapore (1993), Nokia in Beijing (1998), Ajinomoto in Shanghai (2002)
2	Expat, locally familiar, international transfer	Daimler-Benz in Tokyo (1989), NEC in Princeton (1988), Acer in Shanghai (1997)
3	Expat, locally familiar and promoted from local country organization	Ciba in Takarazuka (1986), Proctor & Gamble in Beijing (1999), Ajinomoto in Portland (1998)
4	Expat, locally familiar and hired but from outside the company	Eisai in Boston (1989), Roche in Shanghai (2002)
5	National, internally recruited, international transfer	Daimler-Benz in Bangalore (1997), IBM in Haifa (1972) and Tokyo (1982)
6	National, externally recruited, international transfer	Microsoft in Beijing (1999)
7	National, externally but locally recruited	IBM in Zurich (1955), Xerox in Grenoble (1993), Lucent in Bangalore (1997), Novartis in Boston (2001)
8	National, recruited internally in local organization	Lucent in Shanghai (1999), Novartis in San Diego (1998)

Source: von Zedtwitz (2003).

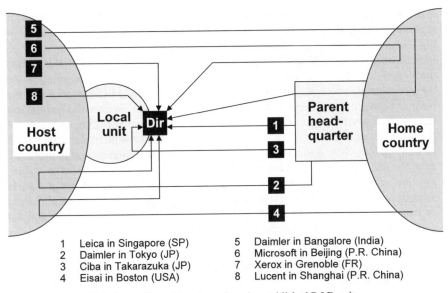

1 Leica in Singapore (SP)	5 Daimler in Bangalore (India)
2 Daimler in Tokyo (JP)	6 Microsoft in Beijing (P.R. China)
3 Ciba in Takarazuka (JP)	7 Xerox in Grenoble (FR)
4 Eisai in Boston (USA)	8 Lucent in Shanghai (P.R. China)

Fig. II.6.2. Eight different profiles of directors of newly established R&D units.

tween host and home country, and the mission assigned to the new lab. Other possible relevant factors are also described, such as lab size and managerial support from the parent headquarter. Individual examples of assignments have been selected to exemplify these styles (see Table II.6.1) in the following chapters.

2.1 Profile 1: Leica Microscopy in Singapore – Transfer of Corporate Know-how

With the introduction of a new product line in the early 1990's Leica Microscopy decided to manufacture in Singapore from the very beginning and support local operations with a new R&D site. Leica already operated seven R&D units in five countries. Since the expertise of design and development of stereomicroscopes was not available in Singapore, an expatriate manager was chosen to develop the required capability. It was assumed that an expatriate would implement the transfer much faster and with less risk than a locally hired director.

In 1993, an R&D laboratory of eight to ten engineers was to be built up from scratch. Corporate R&D management was looking for an experienced development manager who would be able to recruit and train local R&D staff, able to evaluate local suppliers and engage them in collaborations, and adept in cooperating with local production in order to meet high quality targets and production deadlines. As such, he had to be a good team-worker and communicator. He had to understand and implement technical as well as organizational requirements, such as interfacing CAD systems, docu-management, and ISO 9001 certification requirements. Although the effects on his career were initially unclear, a development manager from corporate R&D accepted the position. After a line-of-reporting change from the head of the business unit in Switzerland to the managing director in Singapore, the role of the expatriate manager was expanded to include other Leica products as well. As a consequence, the Singapore R&D team developed new R&D capabilities and hired additional engineers. According to the Swiss expatriate manager, the challenge of establishing R&D in Singapore was the balance between the expectations from the headquarters in Switzerland (on-the job training and coaching of microscopy projects) versus the challenging ambitions of the local management team. In summary, if efficient organizational routines must be built up quickly and the information as well as coordination stream is primarily from the headquarter to the host country, then companies usually resort to assigning one of their own to implement local R&D operations. Local integration is secondary: sometimes these expatriates have little experience about local culture or language. It is important that they understand the strategic imperative and act quickly (see also the Leica case study in this book).

2.2 Profile 2: Daimler-Benz in Japan – Research and Information Gathering

Japan was an important market for Daimler-Benz because of strong local competitors, a large domestic market, and cutting edge automobile technology development. Daimler-Benz realized how difficult the integration of a research center in the local scientific community would be in Japan due to the particular cultural and social environment. Thus, in 1989, Daimler-Benz started out with a technology liaison office in Tokyo. This small office was responsible for technology monitoring, i.e. the observation of key technology areas and identification of new trends, establishing research cooperation and maintaining expert networks, technology and market intelligence service.

A Daimler-Benz internal candidate with substantial Japan experience was selected to run the office. Three Germans and seven Japanese were employed for basic monitoring and project work. In order to cover a large number of technology fields and organizations each of them specialized in a specific technology field and worked on building a specific network in academia and industry. Profound understanding of the Japanese culture was a pre-requisite for the job as not only fluent Japanese but rather the ability to read 'between the lines' brought vital information. At the same time, the director had to understand what his Daimler-Benz internal customers expected. A German report newsletter was sent to the Daimler-Benz headquarters in Stuttgart and forwarded to selected decision makers, including the Daimler-Benz management board. The Tokyo listening posts was eventually expanded to perform corporate research activities for Daimler-Benz divisions such as research liaising and research cooperation support. This resulted in a more complex scheme of financing the technology liaison office by central research as well as business unit R&D.

Often, the initial mission of the new R&D site is to complement the headquarters activities with small-scale and highly focused research and information from host country. Linkages with the local scientific community are unidirectional or limited. However, the director must understand the local culture. Because the director has to fulfill an important interface role between host country and head-quarters, this individual is usually a senior expatriate with strong technological foundation, good knowledge of the local environment, and an established personal network within the organization.

2.3 Profile 3: Ciba in Takarazuka – Coupling Local Expertise with Organizational Integration

In the 1980's, Ciba—one of the predecessors of Novartis—recognized the grow-ing importance of Japan as a pharmaceutical market as well as its great scientific potential.[35] Access to Japanese basic research was difficult, since most scientific papers were published in Japanese and thus difficult to access by foreign readers. In Japan, personal exchange of information through old-boy and intra-company networks was at least as important as traditional information gathering.

In 1986, a steering committee was established to formulate and collect project ideas, nominate project leaders, and overview the start-up process. Ciba's Interna-tional Research Laboratories (IRL) were established at Takarazuka. A project leader was put in charge to centrally coordinate the divisional projects in Japan, and an expatriate already working in Japan was nominated as head of the new unit. Initially the costs were to be paid by the corporation, while it was stipulated that the research costs would later be allocated to the divisions and functions. The priority research themes included enzyme research and new materials. The lab was expected to grow to 120 scientists by 1992.

Ciba relied on expatriates to direct its Japanese R&D laboratory. In addition to the research director, three to five expatriate senior scientists provided linkages to corporate research and divisional laboratories. Besides introducing project man-agement processes, they also helped to establish English as the standard of internal communication. Since Ciba had anticipated the establishment of the Japanese lab with the establishment of a generous research foundation, it enjoyed a good repu-tation among local scientists and leading academics. Ciba had no difficulties in hiring young high caliber scientists: of the first 90 employees 40 came from the top three universities. Top scientists were hired right from the beginning to prop-erly man the key positions. Special attention was given to Japanese scientists who had lived abroad for some time as post-doctoral fellows. The recruitment was carried out by the head of IRL, which grew to more than 140 scientists by 1996.

IRL was later merged with a Sandoz R&D unit during the Novartis merger. It was found that if the new site was to interact closely with the local environment and scientific community, the company cannot rely on an inexperienced expatriate manager. Only expatriates with strong local roots or a local manager are good candidates. If the unit is also to be linked tightly into the international R&D net-work, the decision often is cast in favor of an internally promoted expatriate man-ager. But if first-class researchers are to be attracted, the director must demon-strate a credible long-term investment in the local scientific community.

---

[35] See the Ciba case in this book.

2.4   Profile 4: Eisai in Boston – A Locally Hired Expatriate Director

If access to a local scientific community or familiarity with local culture is dominant but no internal candidate available, a qualified expatriate may be hired locally in the host country to head the new site. For instance, Eisai had engaged in research collaborations with universities in the Boston area. As the cooperation was to be intensified, the R&D headquarters explored the possibility of collaborating professors or one of their senior associates to assume the director role. Eventually, a Japanese professor of Harvard Medical School was appointed as first director of the new research laboratory in Andover, not far from Boston, and inaugurated in 1987.

Directors without previous affiliation with the hiring organization must compensate this shortcoming with an ability to establish a good rapport with central R&D quickly. This can be done more efficiently if the new director and R&D headquarters managers share the same cultural preferences. Coordination and communication between local and central R&D is strongly facilitated. Hence, local expatriates have an advantage over local domestic candidates. At the same time, the local expatriate already possesses a strong local network, which will help him or her build the new R&D site. Another example is the Roche's research department in Shanghai, which was located on the premises of the local clinical development coordination unit. A Swiss expatriate PhD pharmacist was hired from a Chinese university to explore further expansion of local research efforts. This Swiss had no previous experience with Roche but had well-established scientific linkages and knew the local variations on medial research.

2.5   Profile 5: Daimler-Benz in India – Blend Local Roots with Corporate Experience

A large number of young scientists left their countries to pursue advanced studies and training abroad. After they succeeded and earned senior managerial or technical positions, some companies have sent them back to their country of origin as nuclei for new R&D laboratories.

In 1997, Daimler-Benz established a research center in Bangalore, India in order to tap into in a crucial region for information technology, software development, and communications research. The main objectives of the Bangalore center were:

- To be part of the global Daimler-Benz Research and Technology network;
- To act as a bridgehead for the Indian scientific community, comprising the nation's reputed universities, software industry and research establishments;
- To benefit from the cost advantages of doing research in India;
- To serve the needs of the business units and sister companies of Daimler-Benz in the Asian region.

An Indian scientist with a long career with Daimler-Benz was appointed as first director. His principal responsibility was to integrate Indian scientists from leading institutes such as the Indian Institute of Science in Daimler-Benz's research projects. This included sponsoring Ph.D. dissertations and Master theses of Indian students. Entire projects were contracted out to Indian institutes and other research companies. Another key activity was reverse engineering, an area in which Daimler-Benz expected to shorten development cycles significantly. The research center was to employ 50 scientists by 1998.

The research center's board of directors was filled with representatives from Mercedes Germany, Mercedes India, DASA, Debis, and Daimler Research & Technology to establish effective linkage to customers in local subsidiaries. The director's Daimler-Benz internal network helped to initiate the first project in a step-by-step procedure in January 1997. Later, projects commissioned by the DASA and Dornier divisions of Daimler-Benz followed. Internal networks were expanded by Bangalore scientists visiting the customer's headquarter in Germany for about 4-6 weeks in order to familiarize themselves with the particular problems. They returned to Bangalore with a very detailed „job description" and profound knowledge about the customer's expectations.

This is a common strategy for established multinationals. For instance, IBM had pursued this approach already with their Haifa research site in Israel and the Tokyo R&D unit in Japan. Armed with profound knowledge and experience of their parent company and its cultural background, these local but quasi-expatriate directors can readily reintegrate into their original ethnic environment. Often, they have sustained a scientific and social network at home, which they can draw on in order to link up the new R&D site into the right universities and institutions. Unlike many foreign newcomers, they do not experience a culture shock. They speak the local language and are familiar with local customs.

2.6   Profile 6: Microsoft in Beijing – Create Local Centers of Knowledge for Global Utilization

A less frequent approach is the recruitment of an international scientist with local roots but no corporate experience to head up a new research unit in the host country. This individual may bring in additional qualities such as strong managerial and entrepreneurial skills, and certainly familiarity with culture and customs in both home and host countries.

Microsoft chose this approach to start its research lab in Beijing, China. Although Microsoft employs some 13,000 employees in R&D, there are only two research sites outside the main Seattle lab: in Cambridge, UK, and San Francisco, California. Microsoft Research in Beijing (MSR China) was founded in late 1998 to establish a presence in the world's most populous country with one of the fastest-growing economies. With mathematical and scientific talent abundant in China, the Beijing lab hired more than fifty researchers in a short period. Its declared mission is to become one of the best computer science laboratories in Asia.

As initial director, Microsoft hired Kai-Fu Lee, a well-known expert in speech recognition, multimedia, and Internet technologies, in July 1998. Originally from China, Lee served as president of Silicon Graphics' multimedia software and as vice-president of Apple Computer's interactive media group. Lee convinced more than ten other Chinese scientists from R&D labs of Silicon Graphics, Hewlett-

Packard, RCA and DEC to follow him to Beijing. At the same time, he contacted local universities and institutes to identify and recruit ideal candidates. In the first eight months of its existence, the Beijing lab had more than 1,200 job applications.

Although China has been catching up quickly with leading countries in computer science research, the different lifestyle has reduced the average tenure for many overseas researchers to temporary or short-term visits at best. This adaptation is easier for Lee and his American-Chinese co-workers, as they are familiar with local customs, culture and language.

2.7   Profile 7: Xerox in France – Tap Local Excellence with a Strong Local Player

Xerox started a lab in Grenoble, France as part of its Xerox Research Center Europe with another location in Cambridge, UK. It was created with the objective of tapping new knowledge from the local scientific community and engage in scientific collaborations. Only a renowned local scientist would be able to understand the local scientific community, attract high-potential scientists, and establish lasting connections with local universities and scholars. Charged with the responsibility of expanding Xerox' research activities in human-computer interaction, on-line translation and multi-lingual theory, a highly regarded French scientist was hired as the first laboratory leader (see also Myers and Smith, 1999; Kuemmerle, 1997). Xerox designed the facility for 40 researchers. In order to connect new laboratory scientists into the Xerox R&D network, senior R&D management at Xerox in Palo Alto started a program for temporary transfer of Grenoble researchers to other Xerox sites. Since then, the lab has grown to 80 scientists and a development group was added (see the Xerox case study in this book).

The principal rationale for establishing overseas research sites are usually related to either access to local science or support of local development. They thus differ from the motivations of overseas development units. In greenfield research operations, access to local science is usually the prevalent motivation, as exemplified by the cases of Xerox' Research Center in Grenoble, as well as Yamanouchi's pharmaceutical and Sharp's basic research lab in Oxford, UK. In these cases, the new research director previously held senior academic positions or continued to be connected with a local university. For instance, Yamanouchi's R&D director Dr. Lackie was a former professor of Glasgow University. Furthermore, these research sites enjoyed substantial autonomy from the R&D headquarters. When Sharp Laboratory Europe was established in 1990, the then top R&D director Dr. Kataoka intentionally refrained from giving instructions to the lab in order to allow the development of its specific research practice (Asakawa, 1996).

2.8   Profile 8: Lucent in China – The National Director Directly Promoted from within a Country Unit

One of the main reasons to establish local operations is the recruitment and development of young high-potentials. It seems logical that young talented researchers are prime candidates to take over a leadership role if a local R&D unit is to be created. These people are connected into local scientific networks, and they are familiar with the routines and procedures of the parent organization.

The first director of Lucent's R&D site in Shanghai had been a member of the group that drafted the investment proposal. A Chinese national, she had been employed with Lucent's sales and marketing division in China. The R&D site was founded in early 2000 with ambitious plans of expansions into the rich telecommunications market in China. Due to global restructuring, the R&D site's staff had to be leveled off at 80 by 2002. The R&D lab is associated with Lucent's optical network group, doing some product localization but also new product development. Some product development competence was fully transferred to Shanghai. Although the R&D director is Chinese, a handful of expatriates assumed managerial and engineering positions. In the initial months of the new site, more than 150 Chinese engineers were hired, with about a third of them sent overseas for further training. As R&D director, she not only manages the lab but also oversees product management internationally.

Hiring locals into local R&D directorships is not very common as their company-internal network may be missing. Furthermore, multinational companies have generally developed internal talent identification systems. High-potentials are thus rotated abroad early into other corporate units where they stay for extended periods of time. The parent headquarters is always a station in their career. If they would then return to their origin, they would classify as directors of style 5.

Internal recruitment without prior rotation to the parent organization may take place in localized development units specializing in product adaptation, where the need for international organizational integration at the technology level may not be as great or takes place at the level of business unit – headquarter linkage. Local candidates may also be selected internally for research sites with a strong regional focus, when absorption and transfer of knowledge takes place within the country organization and is passed on to the global R&D network by more formal means.

3   Determinants of Director Selection

3.1   What Factors Determine the Choice of the Local R&D Director?

At least two rational factors appear to be crucial to corporate top-management in selecting the first lab director:

- The initial mission of the new R&D lab;
- The desired degree of central coordination.

The first factor is determined by the desired mission of the new R&D lab. Kuemmerle's (1997) categorization of home-base exploiting and home-base augmenting units describes principal missions of R&D sites in terms of information transfer. In many cases, this is equivalent to the crude differentiation between 'research' and 'development'. Home-base exploiting units include local product development sites, product adaptation units and R&D units supporting local production and manufacturing processes. Home-base augmenting units include research centers, local research laboratories, and technology listening posts, but also designated technology development centers with a 'world mandate'. Home-base exploiting units are here defined as units with a strong objective on implementation and market development, while home-base augmenting units are characterized by their focus on discovery, technology development, scanning, and monitoring. Home-base augmenting labs tend to be run by local national directors while home-base exploiting labs are more likely directed by managers recruited from within the company.

Related to the mission decision is the location of the new lab. Geographical locations involve different national cultures, and national culture affects not only the propensity for innovation (Shane, 1993) but also the management of R&D employees (Hoppe, 1993). Hence, the decisions for a particular cultural profile may become crucial in identifying R&D director candidates (Jones and Davis, 2000).

Cultural familiarity is related to the second determinant, the desired degree of central coordination, as it affects both intraorganizational and intraregional integration of the new lab. One the one hand, the director of the local lab plays a crucial role in integrating the new site into the existing R&D network. If he has a strong internal network, he will be able link his group into the overall R&D organization and potentially appease internal competition. He may be supported by senior employees dispatched from elsewhere in the company. However, their role is ambivalent: These expatriates not only support the new lab with both managerial and technological expertise, they may also limit the lab director's freedom in experimenting with new –and possibly locally more adept- forms of management, work routines, and research.

On the other hand, some directors are explicitly responsible for establishing good connections to the local community. In one case the new director had never visited the host country before he was assigned to his new position. It was more important that corporate R&D knew it had a director in the new lab who understood all of the in- and output mechanisms, who had an internal network to draw on, and who knew how to implement the strategic imperatives.

Home-base augmenting sites seem to be more likely to be set up by natives or expatriates with strong local roots. Their responsibility is to utilize local talent and return know-how for further implementation elsewhere in the company. The national director is in charge of integrating the lab into the local scientific community and improving its technological competencies. Since the transfer of research results takes place via selected individuals (visiting scientists and researchers in exchange programs) and managers (liaison officers), the director's network with the parent company and his comprehension of organizational particularities. Thus we can differentiate the bipolar distinction between expatriate and national manager to include two more pre-appointment qualities: ability to bridge between the parent company's national and the local host country's culture, and the background and familiarity of the candidate with the parent organization. Large differences among directorship candidates exist.

3.2 *Alternative Factors of Influence*

Besides rational determinants for the choice of a lab director, many more or less justifiable factors may play a role. We shall briefly consider behavioral aspects in organizational culture as well as the scale of R&D operations. They have important consequences for the evolution of the entire R&D organization and the evolution of individual R&D units.

The evolution of the international R&D organization is dependent on the cooperative behavior of its R&D units, most notably the R&D headquarter. The fundamental question here is, when is the R&D organization ready to accept a strong national R&D director? Before a national is given the job to direct a full-blown research center which is to develop its own technological core competencies, severe ethnocentric hurdles have to be overcome. These concern the development of international personnel policies, equivalent performance measures and reward structures, a global mindset, and a transnational workforce. The R&D headquarter must concede some of its power to allow for local freedom. This implies the de-marginalization of regional R&D units, and hence the ascendancy of national managers to directorship posts. In R&D organizations with a strong global perspective, national managers are more likely to become directors of new R&D units.

Differences in the intended eventual scale of R&D operations entail a different set of job responsibilities and hence a different profile of the ideal director candidate. With increasing degree of investment, companies may be more reluctant to impart control of the new unit to an outsider of the company. We would therefore expect that R&D units which are foreseen to grow are assigned to expatriate directors or at least nationals with an established track record with that company.

In multinational R&D practice, the picture is inconclusive. Ciba's large expatriate-directed R&D unit support the assumption, while the rather small R&D operations of Leica in Singapore and DaimlerBenz in Tokyo suggest that the scale of investment is not the only consideration. On the other hand, the fast growing Microsoft research center in Beijing is headed by a newcomer to Microsoft, and for its first international research laboratory in Zurich, IBM selected Prof. Dr. Ambros Speiser, a local professor at ETH Zurich. Size of investment and scale of operations appear to offer no valid conclusions about the ideal profile of directorship.

To summarize this discussion on the source of initial R&D directors we can formulate the following tentative conclusions:

- R&D sites founded with a home-base-augmenting mission are headed initially by a locally recruited R&D director; R&D sites with a home-base exploiting mission are headed by an expatriate director.
- Home-base augmenting R&D sites are run by R&D directors that have a good understanding of both the host and the parent culture; only home-base exploiting sites have expatriate directors unfamiliar with the local cultural environment.
- Home-base exploiting R&D sites are headed by internally recruited directors.

3.3   Initial R&D Director Succession

At this point it is useful to examine who should succeed the initial R&D director. The tendency may be to retain control close to headquarters. For instance, the initial director of Ciba's Japanese lab was succeeded by another expatriate, who in turn was followed by another expatriate. In most cases, however, the strategy is to build up local management. Thus, Leica's expatriate manager was succeeded by a Singapore national, and Canon's research head at Cambridge was promoted to CEO of Canon Research Europe. In Japan and in Israel, IBM preferred to assign local scientist with extensive headquarter experiences to lab directorships.

The efforts to balance between local and expatriate management is based on two counteracting tendencies:

- The more local integration is needed, the more likely a national director is chosen;
- The more organizational integration is needed, the more likely an expatriate director is chosen.

In the ideal case, local as well as organizational integration will be achieved. However, corporate top management often bypasses local integration benefits (and hence local R&D effectiveness) for protection their control over the remote R&D site. Thus expatriates from the headquarters are assigned to act and react as the prolonged arm of the parent.

We distinguish two major cost drivers. The argument is related to localization costs of R&D presented in the previous chapters One major set of cost drivers are related to local integration and effectiveness, including agency costs resulting from conflict between the local director and central headquarters and costs of 'cultural mismatch' between local and parent culture. The other et of cost drivers include costs of ensuring organizational integration and scale effects, including costs of central coordination, travel costs, as well as costs of not fully exploiting local talent and resources. Costs tend to grow exponentially at the extremes, and hence we are safe to assume that a minimum exists somewhere in-between.

For instance, expatriates drive up local integration costs through additional living subsidy expenses (e.g., "COLA": cost of living adjustments) and overseas salary compensation, while national R&D directors tend to incur organizational integration costs because of they are more likely to prefer local over global operations and because of missed product transfer opportunities due to their lack of a wide intra-organizational network. After the principal rationales for the initial director selection have been satisfied (e.g., rapid transfer of headquarter knowhow, or effective access of local science), the high organizational costs can no longer be justified. Corporate top management will aim at reducing overall organizational costs by assigning directors of the second generation. Locally trained expatriate managers and national managers with extensive headquarter exposure will take over. This would explain the conversion of management styles in greenfield and acquired establishments observed by Harzing (2002).

However, two issues arise:

- Shifting from one directorship style to another is associated with switching costs. If these switching costs (e.g., new project portfolio or management style) exceed the expected cost reduction, the short-term incentives for the switch are neutralized. In the extreme case, the resulting total curve (sum of costs of organizational integration, local integration, and switching costs) becomes convex, i.e. R&D units are stuck with a once given director style.
- Since the assignment and succession of directors is a series of discrete events, we cannot expect that a continuous fit with minimal cost structures can be achieved. Therefore, transnational coordination instruments and management routines are in place to support the local R&D director.

It must be stated that – in practice – decisions are sometimes taken against cost considerations. Sometimes, the reasoning is not objectively comprehensible.

4   Managerial Recommendations

The director of a newly established R&D unit must meet a diverse list of qualifications in order to be prepared for his various responsibilities. The new R&D director's qualifications typically include:

- Managerial and supervisory skills;
- Research and technical excellence;
- Interpersonal skills.

Much emphasis is given on technical qualifications, partly because it is easy to assess (e.g., publications and number of patents) but also because R&D productivity would suffer if scientists had little respect for the professional credibility of their supervisor. Managerial qualifications are also important but 'negotiable'. Too little attention is given to interpersonal skills such as leadership and motivation; unfortunately, it is a repeated source of failure of R&D directors. The following are some typical considerations for these general directorship qualifications for the three most frequent new directorship types: research, product development, and technology listening posts.

4.1   Three Qualifications of a Research Director

Managerial and supervisory skills: The initial director must be competent for administrative and day-to-day operations of his lab. Without this entrepreneurial business competence, the lab is doomed to fail soon. He must pioneer new business development in order to justify the lab's existence in the R&D organization. With good development candidates in his project portfolio, he will be able to generate funding from divisions and business units, and attract talented local scientists. He must be able to engage collaborative projects with local development, local business units and external partners. He must also be a leader and facilitator: He must be able to stimulate and develop his researchers, and provide them with the necessary resources and equipment to pursue their ideas.

Knowledge of the parent organization, its culture and its management systems, are crucial for establishing the lab as a part of the entire R&D network. If the local lab organization is similar to the parent's organization, scientists and project managers are more easily transferred abroad. Recognition can be given for comparable job tracks, and no one will consider an overseas appointment as a career hazard. However, understanding local regulations and business standards is equally important. The director must be capable of integrating different aspects of tax law, labor law, and safety issues.

Research and technical excellence: The new director must have an excellent scientific and technical reputation. Only a senior researcher is likely to provide external as well as internal credibility. External credibility is important in attracting talented local scientists – good people want to work with good people. Internal credibility comes into play when research themes are defined on a corporate-wide basis, or when project portfolio decisions have to be taken.

This technical competency may not be limited to a small science domain. The director must have achieved excellence in a variety of fields in order to be able to work with all of his researchers and to define appropriate technical programs. Insight in other domains of science and technology supports his anticipative skills, and he is in a better position to identify prospective areas of research and guide his scientists.

Interpersonal skills: The director must be able to blend the various challenges and responsibilities of establishing, leading and integrating a new research unit. He is expected to acquire or have acquired a strong background about the cultural and ethnic environment. He speaks the local language not only because facilitates technical communication with his local subordinates, but also because it demonstrates his devotion to his responsibility for the team and its success. Optimally, he has worked and lived in the region before and is familiar with local customs in a variety of aspects. He is curious enough to learn more about local culture without loosing the roots and principles of the parent culture.

He must be mobile. While many may be attracted to temporary visits at overseas R&D labs, a permanent position abroad means to leave friends and family behind. This applies even more to his immediate family: the spouse may not be as prepared to leave, and children are taken from their schools and friends.

As his job is to connect with local science and other company units, he must be an excellent communicator. He must be able to rely on his networking skills in order to establish the important connections to local universities and scientists, other R&D labs, and the parent headquarters. He also must be a good technical communicator, as the success of his lab will be evaluated on the results he is able to deliver. As such, he must retain a global perspective for science and technology both inside as well as outside the company.

4.2   *The Job Profile of a Local Product Development Director*

In general, the desired characteristics of a research director are also sought after in managers of development-oriented R&D units. However, as the emphasis of development tasks is more on commercialization, the director is required to be better linked into the parent organization in terms of culture, management systems, and networks. He does not only understand the business implications, he creates them. He is central in directing and sustaining external contacts with suppliers and lead customers, as well as internal contacts with local business units and research groups. He is therefore likely to be an expatriate manager with a good background in the relevant technology.

His paramount task is to bring the lab up to speed quickly. He must be able to draw on resources from within the company and transfer necessary technologies and key engineers. As such, his role is more a coordinator than a facilitator: Timely provision of information and resources is important. He must introduce structured development and management processes. Such a person must have a strong personality, be flexible in order to react to time pressures, and must understand the strategic issues and directions of the parent company.

4.3 The Job Profile of a Technology Listening Post Director

Scanning and technology listening units are rarely larger than a dozen of research specialists. The scope of actual research is limited and focused on information gathering and networking. Managerial and technical excellence is therefore not central. Nevertheless, running and coordinating scanning units and technology liaison offices successfully involves a special talent. The typical personal characteristics in technology scouts are:

- Generalists in terms of scientific/technical background;
- Diverse fields of interest;
- Broad engineering background;
- Colorful personalities;
- Not shy and not afraid of high-ranking counterparts;
- Seasoned rather than junior managers.

Directors of scanning units are typically expatriates. Their knowledge of the parent organization helps to identify relevant emerging technologies in the host country. Their company-internal network is important to relay this information to the appropriate nodes. Experiences with formal forms of feedback (such as emailed newsletters) have been mostly disappointing. Small scanning units do not enjoy the same status as other R&D units in the R&D organization, as they do not contribute unique competence to the R&D network and credibility is difficult to achieve. If a listening post is to achieve strategic importance, then the posts activities – and hence the director's responsibilities – must include bi-directional dissemination of information and managerial support for global R&D collaboration.

4.4 How to Support the Initial R&D Director

Regardless of the fact whether the R&D head is an expatriate or a national director, the parent company will support him with a number of corporate mechanisms. They focus on improving projects, people, and processes.

Reasonable definition of the R&D field: The new lab should conduct research in a field that complements existing R&D activities in the parent company. This must be respected in the technical qualifications of the new lab leader. Research in a new field will be met with relatively little internal resistance and can expect to require only low initial resources. The project portfolio must be designed with a customer in sight. Research projects should be characterized by reasonable targets with visible output for business units. Projects should be clustered such that technological competencies are created through cross-fertilization.

Investment in human resources: New sites should be allowed additional travel budgets. The newly hired scientists must travel to build a company-internal network. The new lab must be included in visitor exchange programs for effective technology transfer at the personal and project level. Personnel policies should be conform the parent's policies to the extent local laws and customs allow. Uniformity of titles for both technical as well as managerial positions facilitates the establishment of contacts with other units. Reward and recognition programs must be uniform in order to allow more than just temporary assignments of more ambitious employees. Promotion must not be hindered by antiquated or ethnic preferences, hence deterring talented native employees.

Institutional and process support: The new director must have the backing of corporate top management. Only if the new site will be considered as an important investment for both the company as well as the host country, the director will be able to attract the best people. Credibility is difficult to achieve if the new center has no unique competence within the company. A board of influential local scientists can help to tap local human and program resources. This may be backed up by additional investments in special foundations to create goodwill among local politicians and the scientific community.

5   Conclusions

In this chapter we presented eight typical profiles of initial R&D directors. The decision is more complex than making a choice between expatriate and local management. Based on two principal preconditions of the new lab (the mission of the new R&D site and the desired degree of central coordination), there are additional criteria for new R&D directors, such as their ability to network internally as well as externally, their professional and cultural background, and their personal predisposition to head up a new R&D site. Certain directorship profiles are also preferred given the initial mission of the R&D site, which may evolve according to an organizational cost argument. We also outlined some practical advice for profiling the initial R&D director, as well as some implications for supporting the lab from afar during the ramp-up phase.

We would like to close with the following concluding remarks: Location and mission are first, directors come second: The decision or approval of a new site usually ignores the directorship question until the lab's mission and location have been strategically determined. Selection details pertaining to the person of the director are often secondary operational considerations. Organically grown R&D

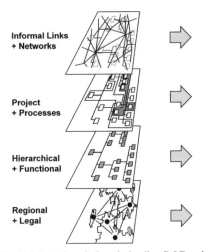

Main Solutions for Leading R&D Units

- Outbound job rotation of local engineers
- Short-term expatriate experts
- Invest in people-networking
- Transfer or define internal culture

- Start with successful project
- "Sexy" projects
- Clear transfer processes
- Switch from project to strategic growth

- Local COO
- Internal promotion of local talent
- Attractive overall compensation package
- Success planning

- Good infrastructure
- Attractive location in cluster
- Attractive work conditions

Informal Links + Networks

Project + Processes

Hierarchical + Functional

Regional + Legal

Fig. II.6.3. Main solutions in leading R&D units.

sites, however, make more opportunistic directorship decisions. Selection criteria for R&D directors should be made more transparent and explicit at least within the R&D organization.

Hiring: Across the board, the initial director's first operational responsibility is to recruit people. This will have to be well synchronized with the development of the project portfolio and the integration with other R&D and business units. Initial R&D directors who do not possess a flair for picking the right people will not do well.

Succession planning: R&D directors are not only involved in selecting their successors but also developing the original R&D mission. This should be well coordinated and requires long-term preparation by the incumbent director. Typically, subsequent directors are more rooted in the local community or possess managerial rather than entrepreneurial skills. Nevertheless, R&D units that develop internal incubation responsibilities or engage themselves in open-source innovation networks may require new qualifications from succeeding lab directors.

R&D start-up expert pools: It is not uncommon that a parting initial director takes over as R&D director in another newly established lab. For instance, the head of Ajinomoto's R&D in Shanghai had previously started a technology scanning office in the US. Some multinational companies have established pools of experts experienced in leading international projects, and while the new labs are started less frequently than new R&D projects, it would be wise to manage and invest in this particular talent pool.

II.7 Managing Knowledge and Human Resources

„We can know more than we can tell."
Polanyi, 1966

1 Building Bridges between Islands of Knowledge

Knowledge and people are irrevocably intertwined. The generation of knowledge, its communication to other people, and the cooperative effort to pull different pieces of knowledge together to create new products, are fundamental issues for organizing and managing global R&D.

Functional specialization and hierarchies separate operational know-how and labor control. Functional and hierarchical barriers create islands of knowledge and communication (Fig. II.7.1), especially if there are great geographical distances between different units. Each island, i.e. organizational unit develops its own rules and standards to share information, standards which are often incompatible with other units. Interdisciplinary teams and cross-functional projects solve some of these problems but they also create new ones, such as power struggles between project and line management, specificity of resources, reintegration of project members into the functional organization, and dissemination of project specific knowledge and capabilities (organizational learning).

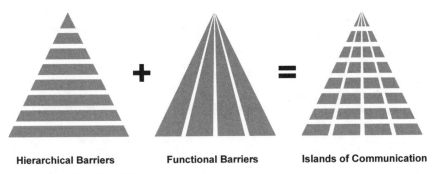

Hierarchical Barriers   **Functional Barriers**   **Islands of Communication**

Source: Hasler and Hess (1996: 161).

Fig. II.7.1. Functional and hierarchical barriers create islands of knowledge and communication.

Diverse customer demands, stakeholder perspectives, environmental issues, multi-site and multi-partner collaboration have driven project complexity to new heights. Informal linkages and networks have thus gained strategic importance in managing and organizing R&D. Delegation of decision power and reliance on individual capabilities have helped to overcome issues too complex to handle by centralized coordination. In such an environment, R&D needs flexible guidelines and real empowered knowledge workers. Hence, the management of people and knowledge is a fundamental issue to every innovative company (see Fig. II.7.2).

2   Knowledge Creation and Project Management: A Matter of Managing People

2.1   Dual Career Ladders: Project versus Line Management

Although personnel development in line management is highly developed in many companies, it appears problematic to identify and systematically develop a pool of highly skilled R&D project managers. Well-qualified project leaders often want to move into a line management function as this carries higher status. This is in contrast to the increasing need for project managers. Typically, qualified potential project managers are not recognized as such and miss a chance for their own career development (Domsch, 1993).

The consequences are inefficient allocation of employees, and frustration for

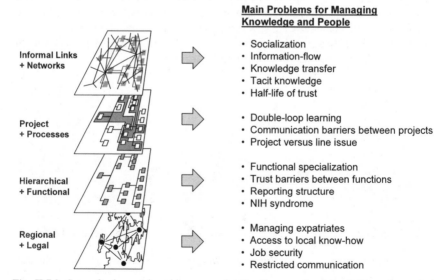

Fig. II.7.2. Some fundamental problems associated with managing knowledge and people in R&D organization.

the individuals concerned. In view of this, one of the most important aspects of knowledge management in R&D is to facilitate special project manager careers parallel to classical line management career paths, the so-called Y-model. Financial incentives, formal increases in the status of project leaders, and guidance towards appropriate career springboards for the individual are appropriate methods. Bosch, an automobile component supplier, has a motivating dual-career structure which enables successful project managers to achieve promotion systematically by managing increasingly significant projects. Such project managers begin by leading small projects for component development with limited budget. If they do this successfully, they are given responsibility for strategic system projects with a greater degree of complexity, large budgets and international teams.

Project leaders are especially suited to initiate team-learning, the key learning unit in organizations (Senge, 1990). Most decisions nowadays are made in teams, either directly or through the need for teams to translate individual decisions into action. Thus the project leader is at the heart of organizational learning, and the production of new knowledge. In global projects, this role becomes even more important, since the project leader is often the only team member who knows all the other participants through frequent traveling.

If it is necessary to communicate knowledge from one project location to another, and if the knowledge is of a type which cannot easily be coded („tacit knowledge"), communication can be achieved most effectively by moving people. Intensive job rotation from location to location is the basis for worldwide R&D networks and international projects. It provides the best means of building up a common knowledge base for everybody involved in a project. Sharing of partially redundant, overlapping knowledge between team members encourages efficient communication and coordination: „Sharing redundant information promotes the sharing of tacit knowledge, because individuals can sense what others are trying to articulate" (Nonaka and Takeuchi, 1995).

Within creative processes transfer of knowledge is ensured if employees make project-related moves between research, development, and production. At Philips value is placed on job rotation that includes both a change of function and a change of location, as this stimulates individual learning and the transfer of knowledge. The average length of stay at the Philips Research Laboratory is between five and seven years. Following this, most researchers transfer to a product development function. At Schering there is also relatively high fluctuation between the central research locations in Richmond (USA) and Berlin, although it is not related to projects.

Technology agents from development areas are frequently sent to production locations to support the transfer of technology. At Nestlé, transfer of technology from the R&D locations to production locations takes place within the legally independent technology company Nestec. This company owns the patents and trademarks. Know-how transfer is legally handled by means of long-term technical assistance contracts. This multilateral learning is of central significance in international R&D projects (Fig. II.7.3). Development of international project leaders becomes a major priority.

Companies such as ABB, IBM and AT&T use staff transfers systematically as a means of developing the employees' intercultural competence. There is an increasing requirement for „global managers". Internationalization of R&D processes pose additional challenges for human resource management. International recruiting, administration and development of R&D managers and scientists is not restricted to one location any more but must be coordinated on a global scale. Specifically, project manager careers have to be addressed differently.

2.2 Managing the Knowledge Pyramid

Knowledge management becomes more and more important. The creation and diffusion of knowledge is at the core of R&D and technology management. A fundamental distinction for organizing intellectual resources is between explicit and tacit knowledge.

Explicit knowledge is easy to articulate, document and describe by formal methods. It can be specified verbally, in print or graphically. It is quickly coded and transferred. Problems in association with such knowledge are found in uncertainty, ambiguity and low degree of detail. Highly codable information consists of quantitative data describing e.g. physical properties, geometrical forms, performance or manufacturing specifications. Such data are represented in tables, graphs or computer programs and are easily carried from one location to another.

Explicit knowledge when put into solid forms as in prototypes and products, or into documents (e.g. blueprints, construction drafts) is also relatively easily relocatable. As it is easy to code, the diffusion of knowledge is accelerated by the use of modern information and communication technologies. Interviews have shown

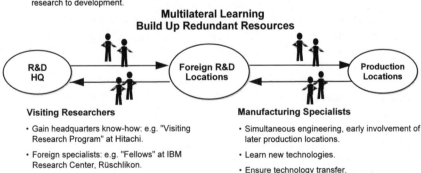

Expatriates
- Improve individual social competence ("cultural experience").
- Diffusion of HQ knowledge (especially in "technology-intensive" companies such as Bosch).
- Knowledge transfer with handover of project from research to development.

Technology Agent
- Support when handing over to production; knowledge transfer throughout project from development to production.
- Introduction of new technologies, support with scaling up, technology transfer.

**Multilateral Learning
Build Up Redundant Resources**

R&D HQ → Foreign R&D Locations → Production Locations

Visiting Researchers
- Gain headquarters know-how: e.g. "Visiting Research Program" at Hitachi.
- Foreign specialists: e.g. "Fellows" at IBM Research Center, Rüschlikon.

Manufacturing Specialists
- Simultaneous engineering, early involvement of later production locations.
- Learn new technologies.
- Ensure technology transfer.

Source: Gassmann (1997a: 211).

Fig. II.7.3. Multilateral learning increases the long-term rate of innovation.

that knowledge transfer rarely succeeds when sending machines, manuals or project books, but rather through direct personal contacts: „If the people themselves do not move, it is difficult to transfer the tacit knowledge they carry in their heads" (Leonard-Barton, 1995: 165).

Knowledge embodied in words and numbers represents only a small fraction of our total knowledge: The sentence „If Schindler only knew what Schindler knows" can be transferred to any company. Engineers in particular often think in non-verbal and non-articulatable concepts. They envisage an object, a picture or some other visual form that conveys their ideas. Much of the knowledge that is required to carry out an R&D project is not directly accessible. As Hedlund and Nonaka (1993) and Vincenti (1990) noted, it is hidden under the obvious surface and consists of components that are intuitive and not easily formulated. Such tacit or implicit knowledge includes experience and social knowledge. Experience consists of personal observation, practical knowledge, procedures, techniques, heuristics, and informal coordination. Social knowledge, on the other hand, is constituted by the understanding of founding standards and rules of a project team as well as the project culture (Fig. II.7.4).

The difference between explicit and tacit knowledge is deepened in an examination of syntax and semantics. Syntax of explicit knowledge generally builds on some kind of hierarchical classification scheme, which is often completed by a number of cause-and-effect relationships. Tacit knowledge in turn encompasses rich syntactical principles, which present the reason why it is hard to articulate. The syntax of tacit knowledge is dependent on the situational context and can therefore be interpreted only in specific situations. Furthermore, this syntax is characterized by a deep holistic and holographic meaning: „Tacit knowledge is structured more like an opera or great novel than like a house or a computer program. That is why stories, myths, great personalities, ceremonies are so important in communicating tacit knowledge" (Hedlund and Nonaka, 1993: 122).

Creating icons, glorification of individuals, and the formation of stereotypes are of great importance for the syntactical structuring of tacit knowledge: Sharp labels its strategically important projects „Gold Badge Special Projects". The name „Gold Badge" is derived from a badge worn by all Sharp employees; their president wears a golden one. To emphasize the importance of strategic projects, and to recognize their efforts, all team members of such a project are allowed to wear gold badges as well. „Gold Badge Special-Project" Teams were established in order to bring strategic products into marketplace as fast as possible. Such projects are to generate new products and to introduce them to the market within less than two years. These „Gold Badge Special Projects" resulted in successful products such as the ViewCam 8-mm the Camcorder the 4-inch-Color LCD, the Color-TFT-Liquid Crystal Display, the Electronic Organizer, the Magnet-Optical-Disc Memory, the Hologram Laser Pick-up, the EL Display and the Mini-Disc.

In semantics, tacit knowledge is crucial as it assigns meaning to data and facts. As the deeper meaning of a message is often coded in complex symbols and rituals (but is not completed reducible on them), that meaning can only be coded in tacit knowledge. All the ISO-handbooks are not sufficient to make the routines needed for efficient R&D happen: Organizational routines are learned on the job,

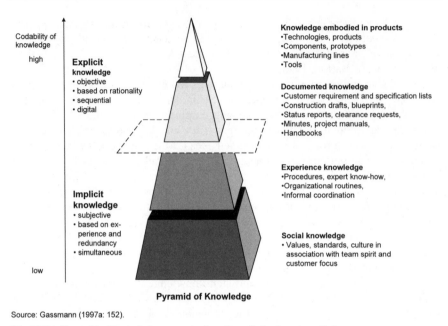

Codability of knowledge

high

low

Explicit knowledge
• objective
• based on rationality
• sequential
• digital

Implicit knowledge
• subjective
• based on experience and redundancy
• simultaneous

Knowledge embodied in products
•Technologies, products
•Components, prototypes
•Manufacturing lines
•Tools

Documented knowledge
•Customer requirement and specification lists
•Construction drafts, blueprints,
•Status reports, clearance requests,
•Minutes, project manuals,
•Handbooks

Experience knowledge
•Procedures, expert know-how,
•Organizational routines,
•Informal coordination

Social knowledge
• Values, standards, culture in association with team spirit and customer focus

Pyramid of Knowledge

Source: Gassmann (1997a: 152).

Fig. II.7.4. Pyramid of knowledge – most of our knowledge is not explicit.

they very often belong to the core capabilities of a company that cannot be imitated in the short term by other companies. New knowledge must always be integrated in an encompassing system of standards and rules as well as adjusted to existing experience and knowledge. Communication in transnational projects is often disturbed by cultural noise, since project team members process their information based on an incommensurable background. A receiver interprets information in a way that was not intended by the original sender. When a German R&D employee is talking about a „problem," his US counterpart understands „issues," and when a Singaporean says „yes" he means only that he understood what his German colleague has said; whether or not he agrees remains open since it was not articulated. In international R&D, these subtleties become heavy-weights, since R&D is mostly concerned about creating new knowledge, about going into new, yet unspoken areas of human artifacts.

Tacit knowledge is difficult to manage, impossible to document, and extremely difficult to transfer. It is often inseparably linked to processes and people, representing a central element of skills and competencies of the team members (Teece, Pisano, and Shuen, 1990).

For instance, rules-of-thumb based on extensive experience support fast evaluation of airframe designs. A certain weight increase is accepted if this is accompanied by a reduce in drag. If the proportion of thrust to a loaded airplane weight is around 0.2 and 0.3, an airframe designer expects a sub-optimal construction or even an outright miscalculation. The aerodynamic design of turbine blades is based on approximate values that resulted from complex iterative computations. The accuracy of such values depends to a large degree on the number of iterations performed in the quest for the optimal design, thus influencing directly development time and costs. These skills of engineers, namely to predict future events based on incomplete data of the past, form a good part of their specialist competence. The phrase „to take an educated guess" refers to the ability to put tacit knowledge based on experience to use.

In lens design, one of the first scientific areas for number crunching because of the availability of very accurate scientific physical models, global sourcing needs at least two to three rounds until a stable, efficient supplier relationship comes into being. One reason is the individual experience and skills-based lens-design of every lens-designer and every lens-shop. The tacit knowledge behind it usually surfaces during these moments of instability and disappears again as soon as it becomes routine.

The generation of tacit knowledge can be supported by words, diagrams or pictures, but eventually must be achieved by a personal and individual cognitive effort. Contrary to explicit knowledge, tacit knowledge is therefore difficult to exchange via teleconferences or videoconferences, and even less successfully transmitted by means of shared databases or e-mail. Personal contacts between the knowledge carriers and the knowledge receiver, as well as the establishment of mutual trust are paramount. The most successful knowledge exchange within an R&D project therefore almost exclusively takes place in a collocated team, in which direct personal communication is dominant.

The stronger the cultural noise in the information exchange, the more likely misunderstandings or misinterpretations will occur in transnational R&D projects. The main problems are less to be found in the transmission of technical specifications (explicit knowledge), but rather in the coordination of various activities, setting project priorities, and the management of the team as a whole (tacit knowledge). Frequent feedback in communication (preferably face-to-face) reduces costs and time-intensive failures in allocation and reduces the risks of pursuing the wrong goals.

The establishment of a collective redundant knowledge base is therefore central to the management of intellectual resources. The intellectual capital of a company in its entirety must be traceable or at least indirectly accessible. Organizational learning and innovation are best achieved when all employees participate. An organization of knowledge is needed. Only through the transformation of the different intellectual „denominations" is it possible to generate a strategic impact for the desired leverage effect on investment of technology and knowledge generation. A major tool in this effort is modern information and communication technologies.

The difficulties with tacit knowledge become clearly apparent in technology monitoring: More than 80% of all technical documentation ever published are patents which still play a decisive role in many industries. Our research has shown that patent-based knowledge is very well structured but not accepted at all within organizations. The main reason is the explicit nature of the knowledge presented. No trust has been built up between the patent-issuer and the patent-reader; the

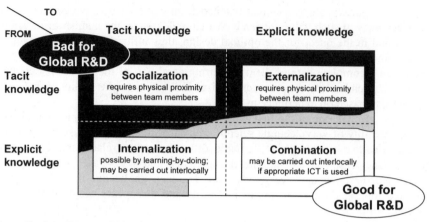

Source: Nonaka and Takeuchi (1995).

Fig. II.7.5. Knowledge transformation between tacit and explicit knowledge Socialization and externalization are difficult in global R&D, internalization and combination are possible.

redundant knowledge base does not exist; the reader does not know how to read between the lines. Even in patent issues, the rule „knowledge travels with heads" holds true (Boutellier and Behrmann, 1997).

2.3   Process of Knowledge Transformation

The separation of knowledge into tacit and explicit knowledge can be reconciled to a certain extent. Moreover, an adequate transition from one knowledge mode into the other is often necessary. Nonaka and Takeuchi (1995) distinguish four modes of knowledge transformation: Socialization, externalization, combination, and internalization (Fig. II.7.5).

- *Socialization* is a process in which experience is shared among team members, thus generating redundant tacit knowledge. The establishment of an idiosyncratic project culture in transnational projects is an important element for their success. Cultural differences between team members at different R&D sites contain potential for serious conflict. Measures to ensure sound team formation, such as informal gatherings and brainstorming meetings, are of high importance especially in the early phase of the project.
- The formulation or articulation of tacit knowledge in explicit concepts, such as specification lists or the construction of prototypes based on mental models, is called *externalization*. This is supported by story-telling, metaphors, analogies, concepts or models.[36] A frequent application is the attempt to articulate or code

---

[36]   See Vincenti (1990: 221) for an example of the aeronautical industry: „Aeronautical engineers... think about directional stability (the stability of an airplane in angular motion about its vertical

experience and practical knowledge of engineers. Another is the integration of new team members from other cultures: There is little use to leave them alone with a stack of 9,000 regulations that are to be followed. Intensive communication is a proven way to create a shared understanding of project procedures quickly and effectively.

- *Combination* is a process of systematizing concepts into a knowledge system like CAD or expert systems in the realm of R&D. Based on specification lists, drafts and first prototypes are created. Different explicit pieces of knowledge and information are reconfigured, i.e. redesigned by means of monitoring, combination and categorization. A systematic analysis of company-internal databases or international patent databases requires the screening of large amounts of data with appropriate tools.
- Learning-by-doing is the prime choice to achieve the *internalization* of explicit knowledge. Team working by project manuals or development guidelines help to „live" such external or explicit rules as part of the project culture.

Knowledge transformation is therefore a process in which experiences are shared in a project team, thus resulting in tacit knowledge (socialization), or in which tacit knowledge is transformed into explicit knowledge such as specification lists or prototypes (externalization). Such transformation processes are fundamental to the execution of transnational R&D projects. Command of such processes in the early phases of a project is a critical factor. Tacit knowledge is required to make use of results in basic research or advanced development in the subsequent product development. „The physico-chemical topography of the object may in some cases serve as a clue to its technical interpretation, but by itself it would leave us completely in the dark... The complete knowledge of a machine as an object tells us nothing about it as a machine" (Polanyi, 1962: 328). When moving a project from advanced development into product development it is required to impart the knowledge created by the former research stage to the often not identically manned development team.[37]

In the early project phases a new project team must get to know each other and develop a common team spirit. Shared tacit knowledge must be built up (socialization) and be transformed into explicit rules (externalization). Geographical distances are barriers to such knowledge transformation. The transformation of one form of explicit knowledge into another explicit form (combination) can be done decentralized and is supported by modern information and communication technology (software tools for patent screening and transfer or CAD data). Internalization of individual explicit knowledge is best done on an individual basis by learning-by-doing on-site: Geographical distance plays a minor role. The geographical

---

axis) as similar to that of a weathercock.... Such stability is (therefore) called 'weathercock stability'...".

[37] Note that we do not recommend to articulate all of the tacit knowledge available, as rigidity would certainly confine the dynamics of knowledge creation processes. By formally assigning and writing down core competencies and key processes there is the danger to wake up „sleeping dogs." In one case we observed a resistance to the authority of a system design head over some marketing people once this fact was tried to be put down in print and formalized, as the marketing head feared a permanent loss of power himself.

origin of explicit knowledge is unimportant for the location where the internaliza-tion eventually takes place. But as soon as routines are involved that have to be carried out by several people like the development of a module or a special manu-facturing process, the collocation of the whole group may speed up the learning process considerably.

Only consequent management of these knowledge transformation processes guarantees a superior knowledge base and consequently a high innovation rate. Due to the increasing internationalization of R&D projects, knowledge manage-ment becomes strategically important. Innovation processes may be substantially improved if the right knowledge is in the right form, in the right place at the right time („knowledge logistics").

In order to carry out interlocal R&D projects, externalization and socialization need the most management attention. The better tacit knowledge is articulated, the better it is coded and transmitted by information and communication technologies. The more shared tacit knowledge can be established, the less communications problems will occur due to cultural differences. This leads to new challenges for project managers: Activating and translating tacit knowledge that resides in team members (individual knowledge) or within a group (team knowledge), but which is not accessible to the project team as a whole.

2.4   Technological Learning as a Driver for International R&D

The establishment of a technological knowledge base is one of the most important rationales for technology-intensive companies to internationalize R&D activities. „It is... the technical action-oriented learning for the company which is the main reason why companies go through the pains of creating an international network... Faster learning of more relevant information is the key to explain the internation-alization of R&D" (De Meyer, 1993a: 111). The ability of a company to link intel-lectual resources into a global learning process defines its future innovativeness.

Technological learning improves future R&D performance and future competi-tiveness of the company. By creating informal R&D networks all R&D activities are integrated such that cross-border learning effects appear across different mar-kets, problems solving techniques, technological sources, cultures, and competi-tors. Porter (1986: 52) emphasizes the advantages of a worldwide R&D network because it is „sharing 'best demonstrated practice' among facilities."[38] Moreover, during the project execution a common knowledge base is established, which supports the construction of shared tacit knowledge (organizational learning).[39]

The MTU - Pratt&Whitney alliance uses iterative and time-consuming compu-tational procedures to define the basic aero-design of a new engine to be devel-oped. These iterations are based on starting parameters derived from the extensive experience of the aerodynamic designers. If these iterations are repeated for sev-eral geometrically different turbine blades, then knowledge is built up that can be shared by engineers of both companies.

---

[38]   See also Kogut and Zander (1993: 631; 1991, 1992).
[39]   See e.g. Nonaka (1988, 1989, 1990, 1991, 1992, 1994), Garvin (1993).

Apart from learning on the organizational level, intercultural learning on the individual level plays an important role. Dispatching personnel to transnational projects are part of intercultural training as it is pursued by more and more companies. While international job rotation has become a standard element in personnel development strategies in companies such as IBM or ABB, other companies have begun to push R&D internationalization by means of cross-border exchange of scientific personnel.

Since 1984, Hitachi has been promoting the exchange of international scientists via its „Hitachi Research Visit Program (HIVIPS)". Foreign researchers are invited to join a Hitachi R&D site for one year. The objective is to expose its personnel of central R&D sites in Japan to an international stimulus, and to create innovative impetus by intercultural interaction. In 1995, more than 450 scientists were engaged in HIVIPS, 35% of which were from the US, 40% from Europe, and 25% from Asia. More than 50 of them were employed in the central research laboratories.

Personnel development through to personnel deployment in transnational projects supports an openness of the employees for internationality as some sort of an intercultural training, thus promoting horizontal mobility across geographical regions and corporate functions.

According to Sakakibara and Kosaka (1991), Japanese companies have internationalized their product development processes primarily in order to achieve breadth learning. A struggle with internal isomorphism and product coherence is, according to them, the principal factor of internationalization. Internal isomorphism refers to the similarity of management systems. This similarity is relatively strong between Japanese companies and is found in a high degree of standardization in recruiting patterns, career development, incentive and sanction systems, and organizational systems. The term product coherence describes the similarity between products of the same product platform. The Japanese economic success may be partially explained by the traditionally high degree of internal isomorphism and product coherence, but has an impeding effect on creativity and adaptation of products to country-specific requirements. Sharp's President Tsuji described this problem figuratively: „The nail that sticks out gets hammered down. But what if the nail doesn't stick out...? It would rot inside. So even if you might get stuck, it's better to stick out than to rot."[40]

3   Managing Cultural Diversity

The internationalization of innovation processes demands an ever higher degree of social competence from project managers. Misunderstandings resulting from language barriers and socio-cultural differences are everyday occurrences and dominate apparently factual discussions.

Such problems become more and more important, because former developing countries from Asia (especially China, Taiwan, and South Korea) have greatly

---

[40]   Tsuji (1991), cited in: Nonaka and Takeuchi (1995: 189).

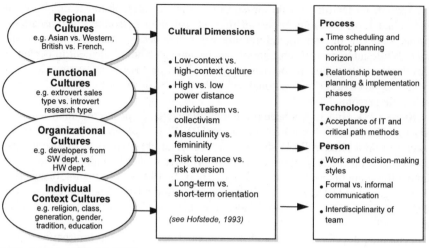

Source: Gassmann (1997a: 216; 1997d).

Fig. II.7.6. Process, technology, and person must be matched to the team culture.

increased their importance as a destination for foreign R&D (Li and Zhong, 2003). As these nations are culturally very different from the West, managing cultural diversity becomes a challenging activity.

Cultural diversity can, however, also open up opportunities. In our interviews it was often mentioned that certain types of abilities are correlated to particular cultures: British inventiveness, Swiss and German systematics, Italian design orientation, or American and Japanese pragmatism. According to the head of R&D at Hitachi Europe the underlying consideration in the internationalization of R&D is the conviction that mixing western and Japanese mentalities achieves high quality R&D results faster.

However, cultural diversity alone is no guarantee of faster innovation. For innovation to be stimulated, culturally sensitive management is also required. „The approach to diversity and not the diversity itself determines the actual positive and negative outcomes" (Lane and Di Stefano, 1992). A first step is recognition of the culturally dependent differences which, however, are not restricted only to regional cultures (Fig. II.7.6).

Of all the various cultural dimensions the context relating to the stimuli accompanying communication is the most significant. In high-context cultures (e.g., Japan and China), the meaning of a message depends heavily on the accompanying stimuli, and implicit knowledge plays a significant part. By contrast, the Scandinavian and German - and especially the Swiss-German - cultures are low-context cultures in which explicit knowledge and verbal information define the message. An increasing distance between the contextual intensity of the cultures of the people involved in a project implies greater cultural diversity, which correspondingly increases the challenges confronting the project leader.

Individuals from high-context cultures have extensive informal information networks and a tendency towards close personal relationships. By contrast, low-context cultures tend to allow only a minimum of informational interference. Language is used more precisely and succinctly, which makes it easier to use information technology tools such as e-mail and fax.

Practical problems can also arise due to different attitudes to time. The Japanese, for example, have a long planning phase and a short implementation phase, whereas for Americans the exact opposite is the case. At MTU, the German manufacturer of aero-engines, this led to numerous misunderstandings when working with the American partner company Pratt&Whitney. Whereas at MTU the first reaction was to carry out a careful problem analysis when a problem occurred, their American colleagues expected immediate shirt-sleeves action and a fast solution. The Europeans called this „nervous, hectic hyperactivity". At the beginning Pratt&Whitney's rough-and-ready project management methods, such as their „problem statistics," were also ridiculed at MTU.

4   Management Concepts are Almost Impossible to Transfer

Japanese team management is strongly characterized by horizontal information flow structures which facilitate integrated working and team decisions. To understand the success of Japanese team management it is important to have some insight into Japanese mentality and logic. Whereas western logic is mainly Aristotelian in its nature, the Japanese way of thinking is based more on a morphogenetic approach to logic which encourages heterogeneity. This enables Japanese teams to see interrelationships between experiences, and overlaps between design concepts, and to achieve conceptual cross-fertilization. It is exactly this difference in thinking that makes it difficult to apply Japanese team management to R&D teams accustomed to thinking in the western manner.

In multicultural teams a clear sense of direction must be established at the beginning of the conceptualization phase (Fig. II.7.7). After an initial period of euphoria over the internationalism of the project there is a drop in team morale; communication problems, and different styles of working and decision-making, lead to a culture shock. If the project leader does not succeed in building up trust in the early phases of the project, and holding the team together by a common vision, there is a risk that the project never gets off the ground. Especially at the beginning of international projects it is important to give priority to trust-building measures and team development. For this purpose a sociable evening out together is usually far more effective than anything that can be achieved with electronic communication.

To turn a working group that merely agrees on the tasks to be done into an efficient team requires cultural assimilation. Team morale can be significantly improved if the team members learn cultural tolerance and acceptance. Seminars for intercultural learning, and training in common methods, carried out before the project starts, can be beneficial for this purpose. If the project leader is successful

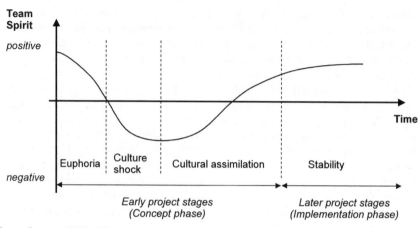

Source: Gassmann (1997a: 219).

Fig. II.7.7. The project leader must manage the culture shock effectively at an early stage.

in stabilizing team morale at a high level, the cultural diversity can lead to totally unexpected impulses of creativity and innovation.

Building up mutual trust and respect is of central importance. Trust is especially significant in development projects, where uncertain information and wild ideas have to be brought in at an early stage. It is essential for the internationally operating team to be protected from in-company conflicts between locations, such as regional budget maximization or individual countries' autonomy. This can only be achieved by face-to-face meetings, which means that, despite all the available information technology, managers of international R&D projects will continue to spend a large amount of their time traveling. From the team management point-of-view information technology can do no more than extend the „half-life of trust".

5   Conclusions

Knowledge management is still in its infancy. As always, when a new management concept is emerging, many old activities are integrated under a new definition: R&D has created new knowledge since R&D is around. But what has changed are two things:

- The amount of resources a company allocates to create new knowledge has increased dramatically. A recent survey in Germany shows (Harhoff and Licht, 1996) that even SMEs in Germany spend five times more on knowledge creation than they spend on capital investment;
- The speed of science and technology is much higher in some fields than it was a few years ago. Fifty years after the invention of the transitor, mankind produced more transistors than calories for food (Bell Lab Journal, 1998).

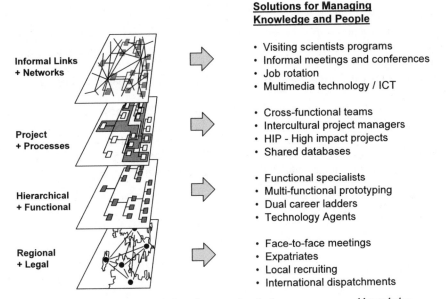

Solutions for Managing Knowledge and People

Informal Links + Networks

- Visiting scientists programs
- Informal meetings and conferences
- Job rotation
- Multimedia technology / ICT

Project + Processes

- Cross-functional teams
- Intercultural project managers
- HIP - High impact projects
- Shared databases

Hierarchical + Functional

- Functional specialists
- Multi-functional prototyping
- Dual career ladders
- Technology Agents

Regional + Legal

- Face-to-face meetings
- Expatriates
- Local recruiting
- International dispatchments

Fig. II.7.8. Finding appropriate solutions for managing the human resource and knowledge.

Some knowledge management patterns are emerging. The most important one is certainly the notion that knowledge creation is completely dependent on individuals, on human beings.

People are the primary source of innovation in high-performance organizations. Cross-functional projects build on formal specialization and hierarchies. Informal networks greatly reduce the need to directly control information flow and know-how maintenance if the appropriate organizational framework is guaranteed (Fig. II.7.8).

Dual career ladders overcome problems of motivation and provide adequate job and reward incentives. Contrary to the current trends in downsizing and reengineering to cut down on middle management levels, it is often these people who fulfill the intermediary roles of communicating between upper and lower levels of the organization (between the „financial" and „concrete" terms). Maintaining this knowledge-base is considered as overhead in good times, but is vitally needed in bad times when business depends on knowledgeable managers. Many R&D projects have stalled because of inexperienced project management and insufficient team working capabilities.

Personnel collocation and job rotation help to build a network of informal linkages that provide information channels often far superior and efficient than formal reporting structures and official message boards. Mutual trust and face-to-face contacts are to be maintained in order to sustain the network. The success of cross-border R&D projects and company-wide R&D programs depend heavily on such networks.

„Knowledge travels with heads" - this notion is confirmed over and over. Technology transfer and management transitions are substantially improved by training programs, temporal job dispatchments, and development collaboration teams. Knowledge that is hard to communicate by formal means is thus easily transferred to colleagues and project partners. Strategic alliances and other long-term commitments provide a framework for sustained know-how exchange and competence leverage.

Integrating project members from different cultural backgrounds requires high cultural adeptness and special personal skills. Cultural differences must not be equalized - each project member will bring in a personal hue and thus redefine team interaction. Project leaders and R&D managers must develop individual strengths and advantages while adjusting intercultural differences.

Part III
Best-in-Class: The Pharmaceutical and Chemical Industry

Industries show big differences in many of their functions: Selling power stations in China needs lobbying at many levels, sometimes preparations going on for many years and sometimes sales can be achieved only by offering concepts like Build-Operate and Transfer. On the other hand, food is sold throughout the US via extensive retailer chains. A Siemens employee selling power stations follows completely different routines than his colleague at 3M selling post-it© notes does.

In contrast, the R&D community shows a remarkable homogeneity all over the world and across different industries:

- Most R&D teams are led by academics who have been trained in natural sciences and who have learned to set up hypotheses and to test them through equipment.
- The prevailing paradigm of R&D work organization is the project: well defined work packages with clearly set goals.
- Technology and technological progress is at least one of the drivers behind most R&D work. Customers can be convinced, but technology can only be applied properly. R&D people are used to accept limits, given by well established natural laws.
- The measure of success is uniform as well: profitability through acceptance by the customer and low internal costs.

Our case studies show this worldwide uniformity with all the subtleties which are mostly due to different products and different cultures. It seems that the biggest differences in global R&D management are not due to differences in industries but follow more the tripartite distinction given by Kodama (1995): Science-driven R&D, high-tech, and dominant design industries clearly follow distinct patterns. The first group, materials, pharmaceutical and chemical industries, is mostly science-driven. R&D is close to top management since the future of the company depends essentially on research results.

All these companies are striving for size in order to compensate for the unpredictable nature of research: The pharmaceutical industry can expect one new drug for every US$500 million spent, but only on average! Before a drug is on the market, it needs worldwide approval by government authorities and worldwide market introduction in order to match the exorbitant R&D expenses. Thus, all these companies go for global products and try to protect their intellectual property through legal means. As the Ciba case study shows, the Kodama criterion is

Table III.1. Benchmark companies in the pharmaceutical and chemical industry (2006).

Company	Sales (US$ billion)	R&D Expenses (US$ million)	R&D Ratio (%)	Number of Employees
Pfizer	48.4	7,599	15.7	98,000
GlaxoSmithKline	42.7	6,360	14.9	99,503
Sanofi-Aventis	35.6	5,561	15.6	97,181
Novartis	36.0	5,349	14.9	100,735
Roche	33.6	5,258	15.6	74,372

Table III.2. Best in class companies in the pharmaceutical and chemical industry (1996).

Company	Sales (US$ billion)	R&D Expenses (US$ million)	R&D Ratio (%)	Number of Int'l Sites
DuPont	45.2	1,032	2.3	35
Roche	16.0	2,400	15.0	5
Schering	3.3	593	18.0	4
Ciba*	17.9	1,723	9.6	6
Kao	7.3	306	4.2	12

*: In the meantime, Ciba has merged with Sandoz to form Novartis.

met: Projects are stopped independently of their size and the money already spent on them.

Knowledge is the main driver for pharmaceutical R&D. Small start-up companies operate quite globally in R&D. They acquire their knowledge through cooperation with other companies and public databases (e.g. Internet). At least in the early pharmaceutical R&D phases, economies-of-scale are therefore less important. However, the knowledge output in early phases can be very valuable: In 1998, Hoechst paid one billion German Mark for a single gene technology patent owned by a small research company. In the later R&D phases, costs can escalate to heights which only multinationals can afford: 80% of the R&D expenditure are caused by clinical research.

All companies have pushed their globalization very far and are tapping knowledge-clusters worldwide. Legal restrictions have had a big influence, especially in biotechnology. Most companies of the group will undergo a profound change in their R&D management style: New scientific progress such as human genomics or anti-fat-pills in the food industry are already changing the pace towards a high-tech style approach. Basic research is increasingly sourced out to big universities and parts of development are outsourced to small specialized companies. The industry is changing from vertically integrated competition towards more horizontal-type competition like the PC industry a few years ago.

Whether this trend will continue on a broad scale or whether changes will be limited to isolated parts of the industry remains to be seen. In any case in-licensing and thus cooperation will become more and more important.

III.1 DuPont: Gaining the Benefits of Global Networks — from the Science Base to the Market Place*

1 Leading in the Chemical Industry - DuPont

DuPont is one of the world's leading chemical companies, and a major producer of oil, gasoline, natural gas and special materials. As a manufacturing and industrial marketing company based on technologies derived from the chemical, material, and biological sciences DuPont applies these to the development of high performance materials, specialty chemicals, pharmaceuticals and biotechnology-based products (Fig. III.1.1). In 1996 the company operated some 17 strategic business units from Agricultural Products, Automotive Products, and Conoco, to Nylon, „Dacron", non-wovens, Specialty Chemicals and White Pigments with a portfolio of more than 2000 registered brands and trademarks (such as Teflon, Silverstone, Lycra, Stainmaster, Kevlar, Tyvek, Conoco, and Corian to name but a few).With 97,000 employees the company operated in every major market of the world. Sales in 1996 were US$ 43 billion; net income was more than US$ 3.6 billion. Market capitalization was in excess of US$ 60 billion and was expected to be US$ 80 billion by 2002 — the two hundredth anniversary of the founding of DuPont as a gunpowder and explosives company on the banks of the Brandywine Creek in Wilmington Delaware.

The chemical industry in which DuPont competed was no longer a predictable mix of products and companies; instead it had become a powerful US$ 1.5 trillion global economic system in the throes of evolutionary change. New competitors were springing up overnight all around the world. The industry was one of fierce competitiveness coupled with tremendous opportunity. Major consolidations were taking place as companies decided that they wanted to be number one or two glob-

---

* This case study was authored by *Joseph A. Miller, Ph.D.*, Chief Technology Officer and Senior Vice-President for Research and Development at E.I. Du Pont de Nemours & Co., and *Parry M. Norling, Ph.D.*, Planning Director in Corporate R&D Planning for E.I. Du Pont de Nemours & Co. This case study was written in 1998: The reader should keep in mind that all numbers, figures, organization charts and forecasts represent the state of 1998 or before. The case study was revised in 2007 by *David Müller*.

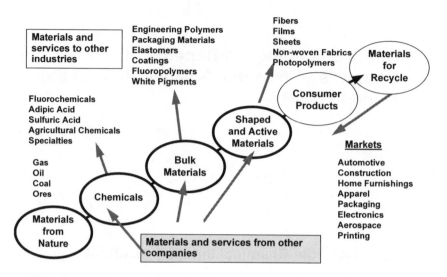

Fig. III.1.1. DuPont's business structure in 1996.

ally in those businesses critical to their futures. The ultimate result of this process was expected to be a further strengthening of the chemical industry globally but near term uncertainties and risks abound.

The industry had achieved its strength through creation and development of large markets around the world, supported by major global investments in both R&D and manufacturing facilities. What gave this industry its opportunities for further growth was the incredible science and technology network that helped create the industry in the first place and to sustain it.

To deal with the uncertainties and new realities in this industry, DuPont developed a strategy with supporting plans to remain a formidable competitor in the next century as the most successful energy and chemistry-based company in the world. This required being number one or two in all our global businesses, being the low cost producer across the extensive product line, and strengthening the technology platforms that support these businesses. This required in addition leveraging our global strengths and technologies as we built on our heritage of inventing, manufacturing and marketing high-technology materials that make people's lives better and easier (in line with DuPont's original advertising slogan: „Better things for better living through chemistry").

This strategy for growth and competitiveness involved creation of value specifically through globalization, development of significantly new products and entirely new lines of business, and partnerships and acquisitions. It was not surprising that science and technology were important in all aspects of this strategy. This strategy was being played out. The globalization strategy for example was leading to investments, new product development, alliances, and joint ventures tailored for each region.

> **Major issues for global R&D management at DuPont:**
> 1. The role that can and will be played by information technology; the extent to which a "virtual" organization can be realized;
> 2. The decisions made today on the extent of structure that should be built into our R&D processes;
> 3. The extent to which we go beyond product tailoring and technical service in our foreign markets;
> 4. The extent to which major new sciences and technologies are not accessible from our home base.

In Europe which accounted for 25% of current sales and earnings, DuPont saw significant opportunities to gain market share, to introduce new applications of existing products, and to make acquisitions and alliances to fill the gaps. DuPont saw re-emerging markets in Central and Eastern Europe and in the former states of the Soviet Union.

In Asia (excluding Japan) rapid growth was in excess of 20% per year; and in South America growth was more than 10% annually. In North America DuPont's home base with nearly 50% of sales, growth was expected to be slower and to depend upon exports; but still 25% of DuPont's workforce could tie their jobs directly to these exports.

The six point R&D agenda supported the overall corporate strategy:

- Revolutionize asset productivity through new process technology and novel facilities engineering;
- Build new polymer platforms capitalizing on new catalyst breakthroughs in polyolefins and new chemistry in polyesters;
- Double new product introductions;
- Commercialize two new businesses each year;
- Integrate the biotechnology platform throughout the company;
- Develop future opportunities through discovery research.

These goals were understood throughout the corporation: within the businesses, corporate labs and among key external collaborators. For the last several years this agenda had guided our efforts and expected to continue in the near future.

2   R&D Organization

DuPont invested about US$ 1 billion a year in R&D in the mid-1990s. This did not include DuPont-Merck Pharmaceutical Company which invested an additional US$ 300 million per year. This billion supported about 3,200 scientists and engineers working with another 1,200 support personnel at 24 major sites (35 total) in 11 countries in both business R&D units and in corporate R&D.

In addition to R&D DuPont spent over another billion on manufacturing technical, marketing technical, engineering and information technology. Nearly ten percent of all DuPont employees were engaged in some aspect of technical work. About 13% of this technical work was conducted outside the US, up from 10% in the late 80s.

3   R&D Coordination

R&D was conducted both in corporate R&D (Central Research and Development) and within individual business units. The R&D head — the Technology Director —was an important person of each business team. The head of R&D in each business also reported to the Chief Technology Officer who had responsibility for the adequacy and vitality of programs across the company. A major initiative involved the development of ten-year technology plans for all the businesses to assure that there was adequate technological support for each business plan and that short term renewal, longer term renewal, and long range opportunity programs were being properly targeted and staffed. With this organizational structure, corporate R&D has both a science and technology mission while the business R&D organizations have a technology and development mission. R&D budgets for the business R&D units are determined by the businesses themselves; corporate R&D is determined through discussions with the CEO and is partially funded by the businesses. The heads of R&D for each of the businesses are responsible for global support of the business with technical and R&D resources.

A Technology Council, led by the Chief Technology Officer, and composed of the heads of R&D for the businesses and the Science Directors in corporate R&D, met monthly with the charter to deal with corporate R&D issues and to oversee the efforts across the company. This included the career management and development of key R&D personnel who were important corporate assets not just individual business unit assets.

In addition, over 300 technology-related networks of scientists, engineers, and manufacturing personnel were effective technology transfer agents as they leveraged technical knowledge and talents across the company globally. A 200 person Technology Transfer Network operated worldwide to scout out technologies of interest to the company and establish working relationships with universities, research institutes, and other companies on a global basis. Major efforts had been launched in Russia, China, and India.

4   Important R&D Instruments and R&D Processes

DuPont processes for managing technology were based on the model in Fig III.1.2 which shows the flow of information from a science base to the market place. This model said that in addition to optimizing current business performance, researchers had to do the work that would expand the technology base and give DuPont the opportunity to broaden the number of businesses.

Therefore DuPont had R&D units which worked to optimize performance of the business units, and in addition a corporate research organization which worked to expand technology horizons. The model also indicated strong connections between research organizations and other functions such as marketing and manufacturing.

The challenge was to create and move information along this chain as fast as possible. To do this DuPont R&D management had to answer the following questions:

- Science Base: Do we have access to the new advances?
- Market Knowledge: How do we maximize this knowledge and test its validity?
- Invention: Do we have the creative climate, tools, and resources that foster the creation of inventions? Do we recognize the importance of a proprietary position? Have we developed a patent strategy?
- Product Development: Do we have a quality process for rapid product development and market penetration? Do we have a stream of product improvements? Are we developing common platforms for families of products?
- Process Development: Are we developing improved processes concurrently with our new products? How do we maintain our manufacturing processes at world-class levels?
- Application development: Do we recognize that key inventions are often made here? Do we learn from our lead end users?
- Customer process development: Do we understand the „technologies of the marketplace"? How can we use this knowledge for obtaining a competitive advantage?
- Plant support: Are we controlling and operating our plants at optimum condi-

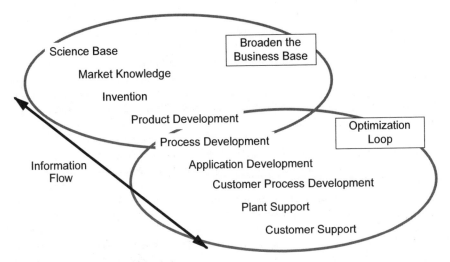

Fig. III.1.2. Technology supply chain.

Levels of Performance	Performance Needs:				
	Context	Goals	Structure	Motivation	Improvement
R&D Organization	Is R&D's role in the business understood?	Are technology plans developed and broadly understood?	Are R&D resources organized in the best way to carry out its mission?	Is the organizational climate assessed?	Does the organization have measures for success? Does the organization learn? Audits in place?
R&D Work Processes	Are R&D practices linked to business practices?	Are work processes those needed to implement the plans?	Are work processes defined, disciplined and structured?	Is the "Human Side" of work practices understood?	Are there metrics related to the goals/ results of the work processes?
Individual Effort	Are global technology networks and collaborations fostered?	Are individual objectives supporting the plan?	Is individual work organized? Are teams adequately chartered?	Are individual motivational factors understood and acted upon?	Are researchers becoming active learners?

Fig. III.1.3. Managing innovation: some key questions.

tions? Do we really understand our processes as a basis for significant improvement?

- Customer support: Are the right people supporting our customers? Are they helping to define further opportunities in the marketplace?

The DuPont technology organization that operated this supply chain was much different from what it had been just five years ago. It was more integrated, more focused, and more responsive to the businesses. It conducted more long term research, necessary for long term survival and growth. About 80% of DuPont research dollars were spent on optimizing current businesses with 20% spent in broadening the overall business of the company.

Fig. III.1.3 points out that R&D needed to be managed at three different levels or in three different perspectives with a focus on the organization, the work processes, and individual effort. There were performance needs for each of the three levels or points of focus, and all three had to be managed simultaneously. A key question (in the middle of the figure) that had to be answered was „to what extent does the different R&D work processes need to be structured?" This was a great challenge for R&D management as each process was assessed, redesigned, and tailored for the particular organization: Too much structure and bureaucracy, too many measures, and policies and procedures that were circumvented. Too little structure and free-for-all effort that could not be repeated and work that was not understood by the participants. Fig. III.1.4 shows the different degrees of structure that were in place for some representative DuPont R&D work processes.

The product development process for example was a highly structured process. Once a potential product emerges from the many ideas developed in discovery research, a DuPont business team systematically plotted its advance to the marketplace, guiding its progress every step of the way.

That approach was relatively new among DuPont's research managers; and owed its popularity to the results of a system put in place since 1991. Since then

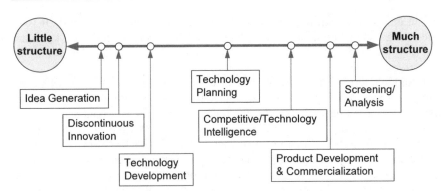

Fig. III.1.4. How much structure?

DuPont businesses had cut typical development times in half. At any one time a business unit may tackle only 40% of the projects it would have taken on in the past, since project efforts are fully staffed. In one business for example, revenues from new products soared in four years from 5% to more than 75% of total business revenue. The new system termed PACE - Product and Cycle Time Excellence, developed by the Massachusetts firm of Pitiglio, Rabin, Todd, and McGrath relied on multi-disciplinary teams to expedite the development, a product approval committee (often the business team) that made sure that the product development met scheduled milestones and made the decision „yes or no" to advance to the next check point. A „PACE engineer" oversaw the entire process to assure that decisions were made in a timely fashion. Key elements of the system are shown schematically in Fig. III.1.5

By setting out clear performance criteria, PACE forced fast decisions while compelling managers to assign the people and fund project needs. Because customers/partners could be involved in setting the milestones that guide the process, the system helped maintain and strengthen customer networks. PACE had redefined - as a business process - the development end of research and development.

In discovery research DuPont used a much less structured approach termed the „Stine Model" - named after DuPont's research head of 80 years ago. Charles Stine laid out broad areas for exploration; set some high objectives; but left it for the researchers to gradually develop the detailed work plan. Back in 1926, when the company's growth began to level off, DuPont family members called for aggressive diversification into new businesses. Charles Stine, wrote to the company leaders: „We are including in the central Chemical Department's budget for 1927 an item of US$ 20,000 to cover what may be called for want of a better name, pure science or fundamental research work... The volume of fundamental work is rapidly losing ground as compared with the volume of applied research. In other words, applied research is facing a shortage of its principal raw materials." Stine fought for that US$ 20,000, and got it.

Several months later Stine pointed out what he meant by fundamental research — „fundamental research is bound to result in the discovery of new highly useful and in many cases indispensable knowledge". He went on to point out: „It is an interesting fact that none of our competitors in this country, so far as we know are carrying out fundamental research... *This should give us increased assurance of the wisdom of our plan to undertake work of this nature.*"

In today's terms, Stine was very bold in going against his benchmarking results; he wanted to follow a different course than his competitors. Stine went further and proposed general areas for the fundamental work — „fundamental work in organic chemistry and in physical chemistry such as catalysis, colloids, and polymerization... also certain physical-chemical work which will involve considerable physics" (this was to lead to major efforts in chemical engineering).

Going back to read his original memo is quite exciting, recognizing that it essentially launched an entire industry. In addressing about polymerization he wrote: „In most cases very little is known about the actual mechanism of the changes that take place... It is believed that a more thorough understanding of polymerization would permit us to develop oil and resin products and similar materials which would possess properties markedly superior to the properties of materials of this sort at present available." — These insightful words were to lead to the hiring of Wallace Carothers from Harvard, the invention of nylon and the creation of an entire new industry.

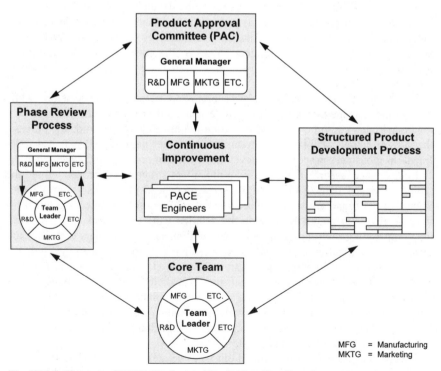

Fig. III.1.5. Elements of PACE (Product and Cycle Time Excellence).

Most important drivers for globalization:

1. Possible limitations in the supply and quality of technical talent in our home country in certain technical fields;

2. The extent of the need to supply new technology to our manufacturing facilities abroad;

3. The extent to which customer needs greatly differ - at home and abroad;

4. The extent to which sciences and technologies being developed abroad are not accessible operating from afar.

One can manage and improve R&D work processes, but for these processes to be truly effective, a primary ingredient must be present — talented people. These are scientists and engineers who:

- Are broadly versed in the needs of their industry, organization, business, or function;
- Have the technical edge to walk with credibility;
- Participate in setting direction;
- Take the steps to ensure adequate resources and preserve skills and abilities;
- Assure that research is productive and effective;
- Are courageous and committed, for research and development is an endeavor filled with risk and failure.

With the help of such individuals R&D managers can look at the extent of structure or discipline to be applied to a number of the other related R&D processes.

5   Example of an International Project

With DuPont businesses being global and with major laboratories in Europe and Japan, much research was global in scope. Numerous developments involved collaborative work between laboratories, customers, and manufacturing sites across a number of continents. One major R&D effort however dealt with a global issue on a global scale and deserves special attention.

DuPont's entire fluorochemicals business had to be remade in the 1980s and 90s as the chlorofluorocarbons (CFC's) were replaced by an entire family of products based on new industrial chemicals — primarily hydrochlorofluorocarbons (HCFC's) and hydrofluorocarbons (HFC's). This transition began with the presentation of the original Molina/Rowland CFC/ozone theory in 1974, accelerated with the enactment of the Montreal Protocol in 1987 (phasing down CFC's internationally) and became a reality with commitments for total and earlier phaseouts (Fig. III.1.6).

An urgent effort was launched to develop alternatives for DuPont's US$ 500 million - US$ 1 billion refrigerant, blowing agent, propellant, and cleaning agent business, then known as the „Freon" family of products. Over a nine year period, with a US$ 400 million R&D and capital program, the Research, Development, Engineering, and manufacturing team in a world-wide effort developed a family of nearly two dozen products with the associated processes and manufacturing facilities. Over 200 patents were granted covering chemical processes, materials of construction, products and product use.

Using state-of-the art computer modeling for identification and design of these new products and processes, the team was able to reduce research, development, engineering, and production cycle time significantly and quickly commercialize the new products. The modeling and simulation included the integrated application to the ecosphere (assure minimal environmental impact), product molecular properties, product applications (e.g. refrigerant energy efficiency) process (flow sheets and dynamic simulation) and plant construction (3-D computer models).

Significant and novel chemical process research identified improved reaction pathways to the targeted products. Data were gathered first in the lab, then at the „bench scale" and then in complex integrated pilot plants running continuously. In each successive stage a significant improvement was made. Three generations of processes had to be developed for one product alone.

When the drive began to find alternatives, DuPont R&D managers knew they

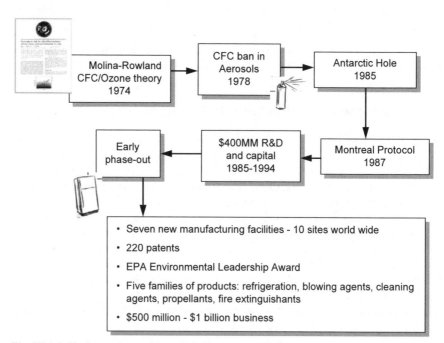

Fig. III.1.6. The journey - remaking of a business.

faced limitations in facilities, time, people, and expertise in many areas of product characterization and process design data. Some of these needs could be met within DuPont laboratories, but many had to be found externally and internationally. An additional factor became important — the realization that mixtures of refrigerants might be beneficial and could be required to replace single compounds. This required development of property information for multicomponent mixtures, then demonstration to the industry that mixtures were viable alternatives. The complete list of research needs was astounding:

- Not many fluorocarbon mixtures exhibit ideal vapor/liquid behavior — all binary mixtures of interest had to be determined experimentally requiring careful lab measurements and computer modeling and analysis.
- In addition the needs included:
- Thermodynamic and transport properties for performance in customer applications;
- Heat transfer coefficients for compounds and mixtures;
- Data on mixture performance in actual equipment throughout many world-wide industries;
- Data on materials compatibility and lubricant solubility;
- Data on toxicity and environmental effects;
- Ability to manufacture small lots of new compounds;
- Support for a very special request for the US Navy on replacing a special compound;
- Vapor/liquid equilibrium data for design of distillation and separation equipment;
- Thermodynamic and transport property data for process design;
- Materials of construction data for plant design;
- Reactor design for alternatives synthesis;
- Significant assistance in catalyst development.

To develop this information DuPont's research management assembled a world-wide network of resources, employing over 24 universities, consortia, institutes, and companies around the world.

For example, when mixture performance had to be demonstrated in actual equipment, the research management went outside DuPont where equipment was located in test chambers. Performances of key alternatives were demonstrated at Oak Ridge National Laboratory, the University of Hannover in Germany, and customers like Tecumseh Products (compressor manufacturer) and Whirlpool (refrigerators). This opened the door to more extensive industry testing and acceptance of the most important mixtures.

DuPont joined with larger world-wide industry groups for sharing costs of evaluating new alternatives toxicity and possible long term environmental effects. These types of test programs cost millions of dollars; here the costs were being shared by over a dozen fluorocarbon manufacturers around the world.

Reactor design for manufacturing facilities involved researchers from the University of Houston, the University of Delaware, City College of New York City,

---

Major innovative break-throughs in DuPont (last five years):

1. Creation of a "food quality management system" - genetics-based machines that can track bacteria to assure the freshness of food products such as milk, meat, poultry (now sold by a DuPont subsidiary - Qualicon (TM));

2. Development of a new catalyst system to produce entirely new types of polyolefins, going beyond metallocenes;

3. Exploitation of "group transfer polymerization" to develop unique architecture in acrylic polymers for next generation ink-jet printing;

4. Development of an entirely new manufacturing process for key ingredient for "Lycra" spandex fiber.

---

and Stuttgart University. Work on materials development for process equipment involved Ohio State University, Oak Ridge laboratory and a joint program on metal alloys with Metallwerk Plansee GMBH of Austria.

The result was the remaking of an entire business with five families of products (a total of two dozen products), seven new manufacturing facilities around the world, a significant patent estate, and an Environmental Leadership Award from the EPA.

In carrying out this work DuPont learned a number of lessons:

- Huge tasks require effective use and coordination of external resources
- Using such world-wide resources saves time, company human resources, dollars, lab space and equipment.
- It is not uncommon to obtain a 5-10x multiplier on each company R&D dollar. (others have the talent, available equipment, and are ready to work so they can do the work more efficiently, effectively and at a lower cost).
- As leverage goes up, control of proprietary information goes down; this has to be managed and risks recognized.
- Partnering with worldwide customers who have complimentary expertise can be most rewarding
- During networking one often gains access to surprising technological expertise
- Leveraging resources can foster industrial teamwork to solve „worldwide problems" and
- Significant excitement can be generated in universities and government laboratories when work is being done on a truly significant problem with international impact.

> **Lessons learned for organizing R&D in DuPont:**
> 1. Maintain a vibrant corporate R&D group for discovery research with a science and technology mission;
> 2. Have a diversity of skills and talents; foster networking and collaboration;
> 3. Develop 10 year technology plans to stretch the business and guide R&D across the company;
> 4. Manage technology platforms across the company - not individual R&D projects.

6   Conclusions

What lies ahead? Two important trends are apparent:

- Research and development resources will be more dispersed, not only within the firm, but around the globe. By 2002 we expect that 20% of the DuPont R&D budget will fund work outside the United States. Science and technology networks will be even more extensive. Managing technology will be a more complex task. Those doing the managing will need to draw on entirely new resources and newer information technologies to make possible additional ways for individuals and groups to work and collaborate with one another while being miles or continents apart.
- Increased attention will need to be given to the capture and retention of knowledge by both the individual researcher and the R&D organization as a whole. If the information and resulting knowledge residing around the world cannot be effectively managed, the productivity and impact of R&D in support of the business can rapidly decline.

Some things however will not change. The basic reason for being, for our R&D, would remain as it had been since the early 1900s. At the heart of this mission was, is, and will continue to be the necessity to understand customer needs and develop solutions linked to business strategies. Having the talent and fostering technical excellence will separate „winners" from „losers". Creativity will be at the heart of research and development processes. The continued development of critical science-based technologies will generate new ways for meeting existing needs and create new opportunities for emerging needs, and technology leaders who are articulate, courageous, and who can deal successfully with change will continue to be needed as an integral part of our businesses.

III.2 Hoffmann-La Roche: Global Differentiation between Research and Development*

1 The Roche Group

Roche develops, manufactures and markets high-quality products and services in the field of health care. The activities of the group's four divisions- pharmaceuticals, diagnostics, vitamins and fine chemicals, fragrances and flavors - focus on the prevention, diagnosis and treatment of disease and on the promotion of general well-being.

In 1996, Roche had 50,000 employees of which 6,000 were working in R&D. The sales of the Roche Group in 1996 rose 11% to approximately CHF16 billion of which CHF10.46 billion was contributed by the pharmaceutical division. Pharmaceutical sales were focused on North America (41%), Europe (36%), Latin America (9%) and Japan (6%).[41]

The Pharma division was divided into three subdivisions: prescription medicines, over-the-counter (OTC) medicines and Genentech[42]. This article will describe only the Pharma prescription market, Genentech will be excluded.

Competitors of the Pharma division of Roche were all major pharmaceutical companies that were active in the same therapeutic areas as Roche at the time. In 1996 Roche was number eight[43] in global terms of pharmaceutical sales (2.7% market share/April 1997) and number one in the sales of hospital products.

The Roche Group relied heavily on investment in research and development to maintain its market position and reputation as a healthcare innovator. Roche was

---

* This case study has been authored by *Dr. Peter Borgulya*, Pharma Research, Hoffmann-La Roche Ltd., Basel, Switzerland. This case study was written in 1998: The reader should keep in mind that all numbers, figures, organization charts and forecasts represent the state of 1998 or before. The case study was revised in 2007 by *Fredrik Ullman*.

[41] In 2005, Roche integrated two divisions: Diagnostics and Pharmaceuticals. The group realized sales of 35 billion Swiss francs being a 25% increase from 2004. The number of employees has increased to 68000 in 2005. Pharmaceutical sales are distributed as follows: North America (40%), Europe (32%), Latin America (6%), Japan (14%) and others (8%).

[42] The Pharmaceuticals division is subdivided -Roche Pharmaceuticals, Genentech, and Chugai- and generated 27.3 billion Swiss francs with an operating profit margin that increased from 25% in 2004 to 27.5%. (Roche Group 2005 annual review)

[43] Roche was ranked number 6 among pharmaceutical companies in term of sales in 2004.

Most important drivers for globalization:

1. Less redundancy due to global R&D coordination;

2. High R&D costs can only be retrieved by launching drugs in a large number of countries;

3. Need for large clinical trials involving different hospitals in various countries.

committed to launch highly innovative products, which were truly novel treatments for diseases and not merely improvements of existing drugs (me-too products). Roche also wanted to maintain its strong position in the hospital market while increasing the presence in the general practitioner (GP) market.

At Roche, the Research (R) and Development (D) organizations were separated and organized in different ways. Research was performed at five major research sites; each site acted as a center of excellence for certain disease areas. Development was globally coordinated with the project leaders located in different areas, mainly at the same sites as the research activities.

The Roche Group produced in-house substantially all of the active ingredients, which form the basis for its pharmaceutical products. Active substances were produced at the group's facilities principally located in Europe, the United States and Japan. Raw materials and intermediate substances were purchased from a variety of sources. Roche marketed and sold its pharmaceutical products through its own subsidiaries in more than 50 countries and through local partners in other countries.

Research and development alliances were entered in order to strengthen the group's competitive position and to establish specific technologies and know-how in its fields. Marketing alliances allowed the Group to obtain rapid market coverage for its new products as well as to utilize its sales force more fully and effectively.

2   R&D Organization

Research and Development were organized differently. Research was organized to allow innovation and maintain a certain degree of freedom necessary for the creativity of scientists in research. Development was focused on the management task of bringing drug candidates to the market as quickly and efficiently as possible.

Research was performed at five different sites that were centers of excellence in their specific disease area. Integrated disease units (IDU) were formed to have all the necessary functions and technologies to bring projects to a state where they can be handed over to development. The IDU had a great deal of autonomy in how they achieve the goals that were set by the Research Board.

The research site in Palo Alto (Roche Biosciences) comprised two business

---

Major issues for global R&D management at Roche:

1. Increasing R&D costs;
2. Cost containment efforts in public health care;
3. Availability of genomics data.

---

units. Roche Biosciences maintained all the functions necessary to achieve „clinical proof of concept" for a compound. This covers discovery, early development and strategic marketing. Roche Biosciences was used as a model for a novel and highly innovative drug discovery organization.

Disease areas were distributed among the sites as shown in Table III.2.1. The geographical research site configuration had mainly historical reasons. The Basel site evolved from Roche's classical research areas such as bacteriology, central nervous systems and cardiovascular diseases. Metabolic diseases and autoimmune diseases were established from the beginning in the US. Japan maintained a large variety of sources of algae, bacteria, plants, etc. which made it an ideal site for drug screening of natural compounds.

Research moved away from the classical concept of being an expert in a certain disease area or field towards increasingly applied research. New expert knowledge and basic research was brought into the research organization by collaborations and interactions with universities and small biotech companies. In addition, more emphasis was put on providing novel tools for research such as high throughput screening, genomics and combinatorial chemistry. Each center had a certain technology in which it excelled and offered this technology as a service to the other centers. Welwyn, for example, specialized in the NMR (Nuclear Magnetic Resonance) technology, while Nutley had extensive knowledge in the genomics area through close links to specialized biotech companies such as Millennium.

Development was globally coordinated with the Project Development Meeting (PDM) responsible for the entire steering of drug development. Projects were developed according to the requirements of the key countries of market interest which, were the USA, Japan and the major European markets. The International Project Team (IPT) was the key organizational group for developing prescription medicines. The International Project Manager (IPM) leading the IPT was usually located at the site where most of the research leading to the development project took place.

3   R&D Coordination

3.1   Centrally Coordinated Research

The central coordination of all research activities took place in an internationally working research board. Representatives of all research areas and therefore from

Table III.2.1. Roche R&D sites and designated research areas.

Sites	Research areas	% of 1997 budget
Basel, Switzerland	Cardiovascular diseases	31
	Bacterial infections	
	Central nervous system disorders	
Nutley, USA	Oncology	23
	Metabolic diseases	
	Autoimmune diseases	
	Inflammation	
Palo Alto, USA	Inflammation	31
	Peripheral nervous system disorders	
Kamakura, Japan	Fungal infections	8
	Screening	
Welwyn, UK	Virology	7
	Inflammation	

all research centers were members of this board. This assured that projects with synergy potential could be identified early on. This also helped to avoid the not-invented-here syndrome, since all research areas took part in the decisions. To include the requirements of marketing and clinical development, the heads of marketing and development were also members of the research board. The function of the research board lied in the planning of research, which consisted of initiation, termination and evaluation of research projects. In addition, the board also evaluated potential research alliances and technologies and steered the allocation of resources to the different research centers

The coarse budget framework (how many percent of sales should be invested into R&D) and the general focus (in which disease areas should research be done) was set by top management in a global way. The budget was then split into a part for research and another for development. These decisions were based on proposals by special task forces who analyzed research potential and market position of the different disease areas. Based on the results of the analysis, the task forces made proposals to the research boards who in turn submitted proposals to the Pharma division management. This procedure intended to prevent potential favorisation of big, established business areas versus new, small areas when financial resources were distributed. The strategic focus then determined the allocation of financial resources to the individual research centers.

Once the research board had approved the budgets, the individual research centers were given autonomy over how they allocated their resources. This meant that the general direction and focus of research was given by the research board, but the research center was free to perform all the necessary work in-house or to decide to complement the necessary know-how by research alliances.

3.2   *Development in International Project Teams*

The balancing of the entire development portfolio, the decision about project continuation at the beginning of the different drug development phases and the monitoring and coordination of all project teams was the task of the internationally acting project development meeting (PDM). Representatives from marketing, production, registration and research were also members of this board. The global budget for development was also managed by the PDM, using project driven budgeting in form of a rolling financial plan. The function of the project development board lied more on the management level in contrast to the research board. Project teams (see below) were actively involved in the decision process, which ensured the acceptance of decisions and increased the understanding for the whole portfolio. Conflicts of interest between teams and line functions could be avoided with this approach.

The development process in the pharma industry is tightly regulated by governmental guidelines. Large volumes of data have to be submitted to the regulating authorities for approval of new treatments. In an effort to bring products to the market in shorter time (time-to-market), the clinical trials measuring the efficacy of the new treatment have to be performed in a highly coordinated fashion. This is reached by clinical trials performed in parallel at different clinics and universities in different countries, so called multi-center studies. Results have to be collected and compiled for submission with the authorities in the different countries. As a result development processes can only be reasonably managed on an international basis.

The international project team (IPT) was the key organizational structure for the management of global development projects. The IPT consisted of one single representative from each function internationally responsible for the development of a compound. Composition of the team could differ during the various stages of development, depending on the needs of the project. IPT members were assigned by their respective head of functions. Team members, together with functional areas, were accountable for the functional expertise of the team, for the quality and international validity of the activities performed and for following PDM-approved development plans with the approved resources. As a team, the IPT was accountable to the PDM for the project. In addition the international project manager (IPM) and team members were responsible for designing the overall development strategies and ensuring the consistent evolution of the clinical development strategy, regulatory strategy and marketing strategy.

The members of the team involved in product approvability and marketability were the driving force of the project. The project leader was primarily responsible for time-to-market planning and assuring resolution of all issues within the project. Project leaders were recruited from a project manager pool, since a team leader was expected to lead a heterogeneous group from different locations, cultures and functions. This could only be done with appropriate training and team leaders who shared their experience with other team leaders from the pool.

In the development area, it was the responsibility of the project team to develop their own budget, since it was the individual members of the team who knew best about the costs of their project (project driven budgeting). The project development board adjusted the project budget for the whole development portfolio. With this approach it was possible to align the money according to long-term success

Major innovative break-throughs at Roche (last five years):

1. International project teams;

2. Independent discovery units;

3. Rolling financial plan.

potentials, since it was the same board that set the priorities between the different projects. The resource allocation by the board was not a one time activity. It had be decided several times per year for each project whether to continue a project and with what intensity.

4   Important R&D Instruments and Procedures

Pharma R&D used the classical controlling of budgets comparing budgeted versus actual costs. Allocation of resources to the different projects was one form of management tool to control the direction of R&D.

The budget for total R&D was set by top management in a global way and then split into a part for „R" and another for „D".

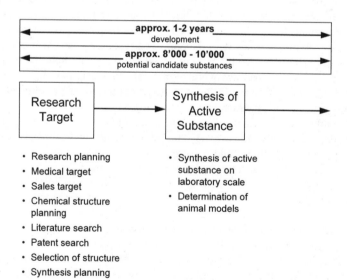

Fig. III.2.1. Research concept and discovery of active substance.

4.1   Research

How the total budget for „R" was allocated to the individual therapeutic areas was defined by Pharma management based on recommendations in the Therapeutic Area Strategy Plans (TASP). The Therapeutic Area Strategy Team (TAST) consisted of specialists in a certain therapeutic area (i.e. antibacterials) from marketing, development and discovery. The TAST analyzed various aspects of the therapeutic area such as market size, market growth, opportunities, competition, current portfolio, pipeline, scientific discoveries, etc. These findings were summarized in the TASP and recommendations were given for a therapeutic area. Recommendations could be to focus discovery efforts on a certain disease area with large growth potential or to investigate the licensing-in of a compound to bridge a gap in the development pipeline. All TASPs together provided the basis for the distribution of the total „R" budget among the different therapeutic areas.

The therapeutic area head was responsible for allocating the therapeutic area budget to individual projects. The therapeutic area head was free to initiate new projects, discontinue existing projects or allocate more resources to a particularly promising project, as long as the total therapeutic area budget was not exceeded. The success of a therapeutic area was measured by the number of Product Development Candidates (PDC) that were submitted to Development and the time it had taken to reach this milestone.

4.2   Development

The global budget for „D" was managed by the PDM (Project Development Meeting), that reviewed also all individual projects and approved new entries to the portfolio. The tools for managing this task were the International Drug Development System and the Project Driven Budgeting/Rolling Financial Plan.

International Drug Development System

For each project a Drug Development Plan (DDP) was set up, describing and defining all activities needed to reach the next decision point. The program each development compound ran through was defined by the International Drug Development System. The program foresaw activities, investigations and further developments for compounds in order for it to reach the market according to a target profile. The program was divided into phases for which clear milestones had to be reached. These phases were:

- *New Product Research Proposal (NPRP) - Phase 0*: preclinical studies had been concluded and the compound was proposed by research for entry into the drug development portfolio.
- *Entry into Man (EIM) - Phase 1*: The compound was ready for testing in humans. The first studies investigated the safety of the compound in healthy volunteers.

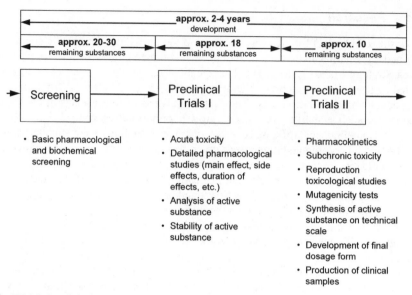

Fig. III.2.2. Preclinical development.

- *Full Development Decision (FDD) - Phase 2*: The compound had been successfully used in preliminary efficacy trials and large clinical trials would be performed.
- Pre-*New Drug Application (NDA) - Phase 3*: Clinical trial data was analyzed and documentation for NDA filing was compiled.
- *NDA filing*: The data on the compound was submitted to the authorities. Additional questions from the authorities had to be addressed.
- *Post NDA filing*: The product had been launched.

Decisions were made at the end of each phase whether the target profile had been reached and the product should be promoted to the next phase.

Project Driven Budgeting/Rolling Financial Plan

The global Development budget was defined without considering the development portfolio. The development activities were adjusted to the financial frame set by the available budget.

Each of the activities according to the Drug Development Plan was evaluated according to resources needed and all other cost elements. Support activities and indirect costs (buildings, informatics, etc.) were included via percent add-ons. The sum was the estimated total costs of the project for the given budget period. This was calculated under the assumption that all milestones would be successfully reached. Since most projects would reach a decision point during the budget period, the possibility of failure had to be accounted for.

The probability to pass a given decision point could be estimated from past experience and was dependent on the phase the project was in. Factoring was the application of the probability percentage to the resources and costs for the time after the decision point. The full budget costs before the decision points and the factored costs after the decision point would provide the budget costs for the project in the given project period.

The sum of all factored project costs would provide the necessary budget and had to be compared to the budget framework. Exceeding the budget framework would result in revision of the portfolio and possibly to the termination of whole development projects.

5   Problems and Challenges of the Existing Organization

All pharmaceutical companies strive for a place amongst the 10 best companies in their field and interpret this goal by mere size. Size very often means profitability, critical mass, etc. and is regarded as necessary in order to afford the ever increasing R&D costs. Some companies try to grow by in-licensed products mainly, some others rely on their own research and complement the in-house efforts with both, early projects from academia and/or start up companies and more established projects in advanced development stages. Roche belongs clearly to the second group.

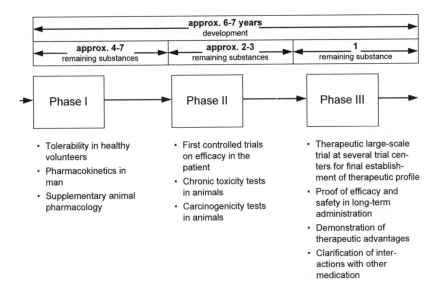

Fig. III.2.3. Clinical development.

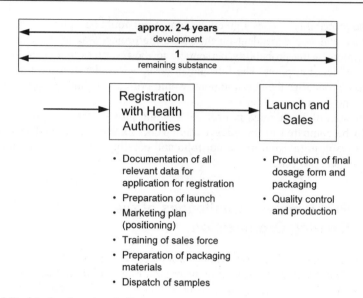

Fig. III.2.4. Registration, launch and sales.

All pharmaceutical companies are aware of the importance to reach the market with *innovative* products and this very quickly, in order to be, at least, among the first three, if not first. Only then market share and price warrant the necessary profitability to finance future research.

In addition of meeting an unsatisfied medical need, the *cost/benefit relation* of a new drug is paramount for its success. If efficacy and safety are given, in most cases it is the innovative character *and* the cost/benefit relationship which make a drug readily approvable and successful. The goal of getting quick and successfully to the market is summarized in the slogan „Time to Market" and implies a continuous shortening of the development time of a project, starting with early discovery and ending with the „NDA" (New Drug Application).

5.1   Research

Basic versus Applied Research

A time span of 8 and more years, before a drug-candidate was offered to Development, used to be acceptable or normal. This time span allowed more 'basic' experiments and studies. Today' tendency was to define and specify such candidates in about 4 years. This trend drives the research organization to more applied research, forcing the companies to look for the 'basic' input at other places.

With increasing speed knowledge about diseases and causes is multiplying, hence it is more and more difficult to fully cover even a single disease area within a specific company. The same is true for the continuously emerging new techniques and tools. All this reinforces the need of the industry to cooperate and ally with all sorts of outside partners. The challenge lies in the management of the new sources of knowledge and their efficient application in terms of projects and time.

Science versus Drug Hunting

Inherent in the trend to more applied research is the need and pressure to find new drugs and not so much to find new insights in the scientific background of a disease. It is understood that one can not happen without the other, but emphasis is clearly put on new drugs. This leads to high pressure on the discovery organization to come up with new development candidates of increasing quality but in a continuously decreasing time-frame. The consequence is a shorter 'turnover' cycle for discovery projects, in other words less time to find 'lead-compounds' and to specify them. The challenge consists of keeping a long term balance between 'good science' and 'timely output'.

5.2   Development

Development in this sense of the word starts with the 'Entry into Portfolio' of a development candidate. Experience tells that only 10 - 15%[44] of Entries into Portfolio reach the market, in other words 85 - 90% of projects fail (attrition) in the development process, which lasts 3 to 5 years and covers several stages.

Global Development (Portfolio) Budget versus Sum of All Individual Projects

One of the challenges is to balance the financial needs of all individual projects with the global development budget. As all project plans and financial implications are based on 'full success', meaning that the project will reach its goals, fully and in time, and disregard the statistical probability of failure (attrition), the sum of all individual projects by far exceeds the global budget frame. The challenge lies in matching the projects needs with the available finances. The tool for it is project-driven-budgeting on a yearly basis and the rolling-financial-plan on an ongoing manner.

International Project Management

The mix between scientific understanding, know-how of the particularities of pharmaceutical development and skills and talent in organizing and managing multifunctional teams in an international, multicultural environment makes the choice of international project leaders one of the most important single elements of success.

---

[44]   Between 1995 and 2000 the cumulative success rate from "Start of Development" through launch was 14%, this number decreased to 8% between 2000 and 2002. (In-vivo: The business & Medicine Report, Bain Drug economics model, in Parexel's pharmaceutical R&D Statistical Sourcebook 2005/2006 p.111).

Co-operation Between Project Teams and Functional Expertise

All teams are composed of various members representing the disciplines and functions needed for the development of a specific compound (project). This composition might vary depending on the stage of the project. Whereas the project team carries the responsibility for the project as a whole, the real activities are performed by the functional departments, which act on behalf of the teams. The efficient interaction between functions and teams is paramount and demands a mutual acceptance and trust.

Co-ordination of Interdependent Functions

The pressure on development time and the continuous shortening of it makes the co-ordination of interdependent functions even more important because more and more activities have to run in parallel. Clear understanding of the tasks and transparency of all activities running and their interdependence is crucial.

'Good Practices' versus Preclinical Investigation

The increasing shortening of development times brings about an earlier start with activities performed under 'good practices' standards, required by the authorities. GMP (good manufacturing practice), GLP (good laboratory practice) and GCP (good clinical practice) are requirements, which involve a high degree of formalities and documentation. Changes are possible, but time consuming, costly and cumbersome. The earlier activities under 'good practices' start the shorter is the time where the preclinical functions are free in experimenting and searching for better solutions.

Flow of Material (Substance)

From identification of a lead compound onwards, more and more substance is required for all sorts of studies, from toxicology, pharmaco-kinetics/metabolism to galenical formulation, etc. Very often the molecules involved tend to be more complicated than in previous times and therefore demand longer lead times in Kilolab (i.e., scale-up) and production at the same time. Process research has less time to improve on synthesis. The challenge lies in balancing an early start of production with the financial risk of having started too early.

6   Conclusion

The pharmaceutical market place has become much more aggressive. The managed care environment in the United States and cost containment in Europe have led to a much more competitive market. Generic market penetration, price competition, and reference pricing have had a big impact on the industry's structure. Discussions on the rising costs of health care and ways to contain the costs are

> **Lessons learned for organizing R&D at Roche:**
> 1. International teams require new organizations;
> 2. Organizations must be flexible to be able to respond to changes.

omnipresent and are demanding for solutions. While the pressure on the price of pharmaceuticals has increased, so have costs for the development of pharmaceuticals. Increasingly complex demands by regulators, an increasing number and complexity of protocols, a rising number of patients enrolled in the studies and a still growing number of files per new drug application are the main factors for the increased costs. The cost of researching and developing a major new product today already exceeds US$ 500 million (US$ 900 million in 2005). The pharmaceutical industry has responded to price pressure and rising costs with a set of approaches:

- Vertical integration through investment in
    1. Distribution and PBMs (pharmacy benefits management)
    2. Over-the-counter i.e. non-prescription medicine, and generic companies;
- Horizontal acquisitions and mergers to reach critical mass;
- Virtual integration through strategic alliances and co-operation in research, development, marketing, distribution;
- Focus on fewer therapeutic areas;
- Efforts to increase productivity.

Productivity Increase in Research

The new paradigms of the industry with advances in molecular biology, genomics, and gene therapy promise breakthrough products and therapies in the future. Research departments will have to change radically. Almost all major companies have already outsourced part of their research and this trend will continue. Because of the high and rising entry barriers to become fully-fledged R&D-based companies, most biotech companies have become part of the supply chain, feeding the development machines of the major players with new promising drugs. In-house research will have to compete with co-operations, alliances, and licensing activities, which will become powerful tools of rejuvenating companies' portfolios. Furthermore, research will increasingly become exposed to the needs of the marketing departments defining the needs of the market and assessing the health economics of a new project early in the process.

Productivity Increase in Development

A main difference between companies has been their respective ability to bring new products to the market quickly. Re-engineering development and faster time to market has become a catchword for almost every single pharmaceutical company. Shrinking life cycles and the need to recoup escalating research and development costs drove companies to seek major improvements in their development time.

Significant improvement has been made by the regulators in the major countries in cutting the review time of medicine approval. The introduction of the user fee act in the United States, the recruitment of new reviewers and a much more performance oriented approach was matched in Europe by agencies competing with each other. The establishment of the European Medicines Evaluation Agency has led to a very healthy competition among the leading European agencies. The beneficiary has been the patient who can now hope to access new therapies faster. There are also ongoing efforts to harmonize the registration process internationally.

III.3 Schering: Synchronized Drug Development*

1   Concentration on Core Businesses

In the early 90s, Schering[1] divested two non-pharmaceutical divisions and bought a third division, its plant protection business, into an independent joint-venture firm with Hoechst AG/Germany.

After these transactions, Schering was a pure pharmaceutical company, based in Berlin/Germany, with a turnover in 1996 from ethical pharmaceuticals and diagnostic imaging agents of DM 5.3 billion. More than 85% of turnover is generated outside the home country, with roughly 45% coming from Europe, 17% from Japan, 16% from the USA and 22% from the rest of the world. The total number of employees was around 21,000, whereof 30% worked in the headquarter's facilities. Employees in the R&D organization amounted to roughly 3,600, with 2,000 working at corporate headquarters in Berlin, and 1,600 in the affiliates' R&D organizations.

Schering's strategic goals have evolved from a classical niche strategy and were to maintain or aspire to market leadership in specialized fields world-wide. The traditional core business areas were diagnostic imaging agents (roughly 33% of turnover), female health care (approx. 29% of turnover) and dermatology (approx. 7.5% of turnover), while more recently added areas include oncology and certain disabling/life-threatening neurodegenerative and cardiovascular diseases (approx. 30% of turnover).

Schering's main competitors were Nycomed, Bracco and Mallinckrodt in the diagnostic imaging field and Wyeth and Akzo-Nobel in female health care. Various agreements and cooperations existed with most of the main competitors and with other pharmaceutical companies, covering a range from shared patent exclusivity and R&D cooperations over mutual supply of goods to regional marketing cooperations.

---

*   This case study has been authored by *Dr. Bernd Müller*, Ph Project Coordination, Biology Research, Schering AG. This case study was written in 1998: The reader should keep in mind that all numbers, figures, organization charts and forecasts represent the state of 1998 or before. The case study was revised in 2007 by *Alexander Schicker*.
[1]   As a result of the take-over by Bayer, Schering AG was renamed Bayer Schering Pharma AG in December 2006.

Schering was traditionally an R&D oriented company (R&D expenditure was 19% of turnover in 1996), which strategically relied on innovation in all its business areas. Generic drugs and over-the-counter medicines were handled as opportunistic areas.

The emphasis in R&D was bifocal. Where leading market positions existed, like in diagnostic imaging and in female health care, R&D on the one hand side strived to be in the lead of all major scientific developments to create true innovations, on the other hand side served needs of the existing market with incremental innovations and product life-cycle support. In therapeutics for disabling/life-threatening diseases the focus of R&D was on true innovation only and unmet medical need besides market considerations which were a major discriminating criterion for R&D project selection.

2   R&D Organization

Schering's R&D activities were concentrated in Berlin (Germany), USA (Wayne, New Jersey, and Richmond, California) and Osaka (Japan). In addition, small integrated R&D organizations existed in two acquired pharmaceutical companies in Germany and Finland, and small clinical units were located in several European countries. R&D functions were organized according to a competence/excellence center work share concept, where all sites were obliged to work under global corporate standards to support global projects. Specific reasons to concentrate US-research in California were the favorable local R&D infrastructure, allowing for efficient scientific networking with top academic and private research institutions. Research in Japan was small, but served as an increasingly important window towards internationally renowned Japanese research institutions. Reasons to establish biotech development in California were the availability of experienced staff, an experienced and pragmatic regulatory environment, and favorable federal and local legislation favoring relatively fast and efficient implementation of the respective facilities.

In research, the headquarters-located sites maintained intellectual leadership in the traditional Schering areas of diagnostic imaging and female health care, while the US-site was focused on the „new" areas of oncology, neurodegeneration, and

---

Major issues for global R&D management at Schering:

1. Globalisation of regulatory environment;

2. Competition for innovation through new enabling technologies;

3. Uniform world-wide standards for R&D through integrated data management;

4. World-wide cost containment in health care.

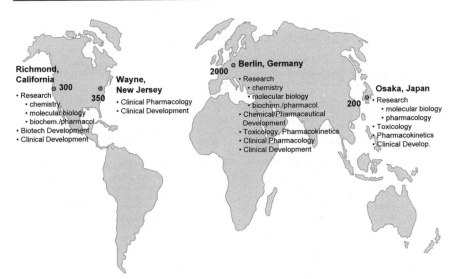

Richmond, California
- Research
  - chemistry
  - molecular biology
  - biochem./pharmacol.
- Biotech Development
- Clinical Development

300

350

Wayne, New Jersey
- Clinical Pharmacology
- Clinical Development

2000

Berlin, Germany
- Research
  - chemistry
  - molecular biology
  - biochem./pharmacol.
- Chemical/Pharmaceutical Development
- Toxicology, Pharmacokinetics
- Clinical Pharmacology
- Clinical Development

200

Osaka, Japan
- Research
  - molecular biology
  - pharmacology
- Toxicology
- Pharmacokinetics
- Clinical Develop.

Fig. III.3.1. Major R&D sites of Schering in North America, Asia, and Europe.

selected cardiovascular diseases. Japan concentrated on specific areas of diagnostic imaging, under the guidance of the strategic business unit in Berlin. Modern compound-finding technologies (for instance combinatorial chemistry, high-throughput screening techniques, molecular modeling and access to genome-libraries) were implemented in Berlin and in California, and were interactively used by all research sites.

3 R&D Coordination and Management

All key features of Schering's R&D management have been established between 1990 and 1994, responding to the business requirement of fast, synchronized global drug development and market entry, to the harmonization of international regulatory requirements, and to resource limitations in R&D, which were a consequence of cost increases due to increased regulatory requirements.

Rather than a clear-cut centralized organization with direct power over all R&D facilities, a decentralized organization coordinated by corporate management processes and a strong International Project Management was chosen, with the hope, to thereby best combine global R&D capabilities and flexible responses to local needs.

Strategic R&D management was looked after at board level in the Portfolio Board and included setting of R&D strategy, decisions on major R&D cooperations, decisions on initiation and start of phase III of development projects, and yearly prioritization as well as continuous adjustments of prioritization for the whole portfolio of development projects (Fig. III.3.2). Portfolio Board decisions

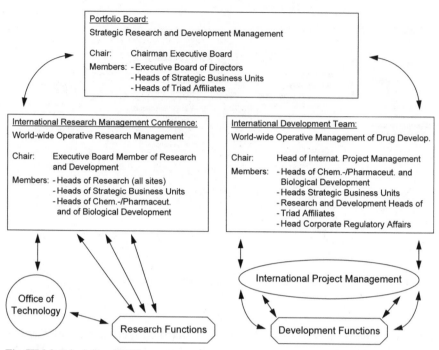

Fig. III.3.2. Principles of R&D management.

concerning research were operationalized by the International Research Management Conference (chaired by the Executive Board Member of R&D), which took care of research budget setting and -control, all decisions concerning research projects and research cooperations (below Portfolio Board -level), and periodical project reviews.

Portfolio Board decisions concerning development projects were operationalized by the International Development Team, chaired by the head of International Project Management and representing all major resource-holders in international R&D. The International Development Team closely interacted with International Project Management and its responsibilities covered development budget planning and -control, all operational decisions concerning development projects, and all operational issues concerning the international R&D organization and management processes in R&D. The International Development Team also monitored composition and performance of the International Project Teams.

Disciplinary and functional reporting lines were dissociated in many parts of the R&D organization. While all headquarters' R&D function reported directly to the Executive Board Member of R&D, functions located in the affiliates disciplinarily report to the local hierarchy. Functional reporting, however, in the case of research, was to the Executive Board Member of R&D and, in the case of development, to the International Development Team.

Core members of the International Project Teams disciplinarily reported to their home-base and functionally reported to the respective international project manager.

Proposals concerning new R&D projects could come from all parts of the organization. They were, however, in case of research projects, subject to formal proposal-agreement processes, organized by the International Research Management Conference, or, in the case of development projects, subject to the formats and processes established by the International Project Management. Decisions on new development projects were recommended by the International Development Team and made in the Portfolio Board. Local projects were possible, but no R&D project may have been conducted without decision by either the International Research Management Conference (research) or the International Development Team/Portfolio Board (development), and all milestone decisions were subject to the respective corporate processes.

- International research coordination below the level of the International Research Management Conference, i.e. on project/program level, was by international research project groups.
- International development coordination was the responsibility of International Project Management, supported by coordinators in the affiliates.

World-wide networking with academic and commercial R&D institutes and, generally, search-activities for project and product opportunities, was supported strategically and had become progressively important and complex. Therefore, an Office of Technology (altogether 15 employees, based in Berlin, USA and Japan) was established, which conducts all scientific intelligence, networking and search activities on behalf of the Strategic Business Units and of the R&D functions. The Office of Technology defined areas of interest with its partners in the R&D organization, and within these areas of interest proactively provided the R&D organization with scientific intelligence and cooperation opportunities. An international management process had been established, along which the Office of Technology interfaces with the R&D organization, with Corporate Licensing and with the decision-making bodies. After identification of concrete cooperation opportunities, the Office of Technology run the initial negotiations and, after contracts have been signed, provided also contract management services.

4   R&D Instruments and Processes

The key features of International Project Management as established at Schering are outlined in Fig. III.3.2. Key tools in the R&D management processes were:

- A global R&D controlling system, which was in the late phase of implementation. It was used by all R&D sites for the purposes of function-wise and project-wise planning and tracking of cost and capacity and allowed for viewing planned and actual resources on the level of individual R&D functions, projects, and specific R&D tasks within projects. This system was also used for project planning and was „owned" jointly by International Project Management and Corporate Controlling.

- Project master plans, which were compiled by the International Project Teams and approved by the International Development Team. Master plans were regularly updated and represented, on a global level, in all details the agreements on how a specific project will be developed.
- A project prioritization scale, used by the Portfolio Board, which ranked all development projects in a scale from low (resource application according to availability) to top priority projects, which were so-called Corporate Projects with the understanding, that resources had to be allocated by all functions as requested.
- Economic project analysis, which was a customized software used for all development projects to support strategic and operational portfolio management.

R&D budget planning was a yearly bottom-up, top-down process, where R&D functions specified their needs, the International Project Management defined the project's needs, and the International Development Team reconciled and proposed a budget to the Executive Board of Directors. After the Executive Board decision, the individual R&D functions (headquarters) or the affiliates became budget owners, but were only allowed to use their resources within the limits set by the project master plans of International Project Management. Responding to day-by-day needs for additional resources or for resource reallocation was a task of the International Development Team.

International Project Management was located at corporate headquarters. The head of International Project Management reported directly to the Executive Board Member of R&D. Full-time project managers were employed on a continuous basis. They could hold even very high ranks in the corporate hierarchy. Project teams incorporated representatives from preclinical, chemical/pharmaceutical and clinical development, regulatory affairs and marketing. The project team members represented their special field on a world-wide basis and worked with international sub teams. Project teams had full access to all R&D functions and data on all levels of hierarchy. They were allowed to use external resources - where appropriate - in agreement with the International Development Team. Although not being the direct budget-owners, the project teams held virtual project budgets, agreed with the International Development Team, allowing for recruitment and control of resources across the international R&D organization.

Further important tools in international R&D management were the global data systems, supporting specific R&D processes, like for instance a global system for clinical safety data reporting, a global system for clinical data administration, and a global document management system. These systems, together with their user standard operating procedures, represented an important clamp across the international R&D organization by safeguarding common working standards and - processes and allowing for efficient execution of corporate processes.

Recruitment and allocation of key personnel in world-wide R&D was considered an issue of utmost importance, where decisions from the level of department head upwards involved the Executive Board Member of R&D. Acknowledging

---

Most important drivers for globalization:

1. Harmonisation of global regulatory environment;

2. Competition for innovation;

3. Global availability of scientific/market information through information technology;

4. Economic pressure for shorter time-to-market and global project launches.

---

the dual reporting lines for core members of International Project Teams (disciplinarily towards home-base, functionally towards project manager), performance assessment and decisions on benefits were shared between the respective line management and the project manager. A good performance servicing in the project management organization (as a core team member or in the sub teams) was considered an important prerequisite for promotion in the international R&D organization.

5 Levovist: Example of an International R&D Project

In 1987, Levovist was invented by a dedicated group in diagnostics research to be an imaging agent for ultrasound diagnostics. It enables for the first time an ultrasound signal enhancement in the heart and in all blood vessels, thus dramatically improving and broadening the diagnostic yield of the ultrasound technology.

The basic principle sounds simple: a mixture of galactose and a small amount of palmitic acid - both natural untoxic substances occurring in the human body - if suspended in water and shaken form small micro particles, to which extremely small airbubbles are bound. Injected into blood vessels, these air bubbles, stabilized by palmitic acid, circulate for a certain time in the blood and effect the ultrasound signal enhancement. In fact, the establishment of a galenic formulation and a production process allowing for formation of a reproducible and narrow range of micro particle size turned out to be quite complex.

Since Levovist represented a completely new technology and, considering the wide-spread use of ultrasound technology, could represent a considerable market potential, management decided to start drug development with high priority. The preclinical development phase went smoothly since, as anticipated, no toxicological problems emerged and pharmaceutical production on a pilot scale was controlled satisfactorily. Clinical phase I and phase II studies (conducted in Europe) were finished within two years and confirmed the anticipated favorable potential. The Japanese affiliate entered into Levovist development immediately after end of the preclinical phase, but due to the necessity to establish all prerequisites for clinical testing and to repeat phase I studies in Japan, lost approximately two years against the European development program. USA initially was reluctant to enter

Major innovative break-throughs at Schering (1991-1996):

1. Ilomedin - first drug therapy for severe peripheral ischaemic disease with proven efficiacy;

2. Betaseron - first medication for multiple sclerosis;

3. Levovist - first ultrasound contrast agent;

4. Mirena - first 5-year hormone-releasing intrauterine device for contraception.

Levovist development due to marketing considerations. When the decision was made to start development also in the USA, 3 years had been lost against the European program. Also, not all features of the European clinical development program met US expectations, necessitating repetition of a major part of clinical phase II and III development in the USA.

After end of phase II clinical testing in Europe, corporate management fully acknowledged the high potential of Levovist and exerted pressure to shorten the remaining development time by one year. Around this time, it was also decided to establish a specialized new production facility at considerable costs.

Clinical phase III development was finished successfully and on time in Europe, and a computerized new drug application was assembled for regulatory submission within approximately one year. Two major issues surfaced around this time. One was, that the clinical evidence from phase III studies, while obviously adequate to support efficacy and safety for regulatory approval, was not necessarily supporting the complete range of clinical indications in the market place, which were envisaged by the marketing and sales organization. This was at least partly due to the fact, that the clinical phase III program had been slimmed in order to save time. A comprehensive multinational „phase IIIb" clinical study was started with the aim to produce, until regulatory approval, the necessary additional data to support broader indications.

The second issue was, that the established production scale turned out not to satisfy the initial needs for the product. Establishment of a second production line initially went well, but soon faced reproducibility problems: due to time pressure, some features of the production process had been transferred to the new scale empirically rather than with a sound scientific understanding of the process. These problems were solved with considerable use of additional resources and some impact on the initial market roll-out of Levovist.[45]

Two major lessons were learned from Levovist development: one is, that desynchronization of clinical development between the Triad (in this case between Europe and the USA) cannot be tolerated, since not only the loss of time to market but also the additional resource-needs to repeat large parts of the clinical develop-

---

[45] Levovist was introduced on the market in the late nineties and was available in more than 40 countries in the year 2000.

> **Lessons learned for organizing R&D at Schering:**
> 1. Synchronisation of international drug development is essential to shorten R&D cycle;
> 2. International Project Management is key to international synchronisation of R&D projects;
> 3. World-wide integrated R&D data management is key to uniform high standards in R&D;
> 4. Acquisition of external ideas and projects is as important as internal R&D.

ment program greatly impact on the profitability of the product. This was later avoided by International Project Management safeguarding regional synchronization of the development programs.

A second lesson is, that time-to-market versus comprehensiveness of the phase III development program must be carefully balanced: a very slim phase III program may well support regulatory approval, but will not necessarily render a marketable compound.

6   Conclusions

The principles of R&D management at Schering have over the last five years greatly improved our capabilities for global drug development in terms of time, efficiency of resource use, quality and transparency. Complex and expensive communication, agreements and decision processes in the international organization are still major drawbacks: Fine-tuning of our management processes is expected to improve this. We do not expect fundamental changes in the R&D organization or in our principal processes of R&D management in the foreseeable future. Rather, a continuous change process has started, where all parts of the organization as well as the management processes are subject to continuous benchmarking, adjustments, fine-tuning, and acquisition of new skills.

Educational aspects will play a great role: to accept continuous change as normality and to accept and use global standards and work processes as necessary clamps across the international R&D organization will be mandatory in the future.

III.4 Ciba: International Research Laboratories in Japan: Practical Validation of a Strategic Concept*

At the beginning of the 1980s, the top management of Ciba-Geigy declared "We have looked into the future, and it lies in Japan and South-East Asia." However, until then Ciba did not have a clue how to get at results of Japanese basic research. Though Japan's universities have long been open, most scientific papers were published in Japanese and thus difficult to access by foreign readers. Japanese technology tended not to be up for sale as much as western expertise was. The Japanese were often reluctant to license out what they considered valuable as a long term asset.

The present study unveils a successful practical validation of a research-related strategic concept of Ciba-Geigy Ltd. in Japan in the years 1984-1996 as well as the sudden and astonishing reversal of this concept as a consequence of the merger of Ciba with Sandoz Ltd. to form the new company Novartis on Dec. 17, 1996.

1 Ciba before the Merger with Sandoz

Ciba was a leading world-wide chemical and biological group, based in Switzerland, dedicated to satisfying needs in healthcare, agriculture and industry with innovative value-adding products and services.

The philosophy of striking a balance between economic, social and environmental responsibilities was Ciba's Vision 2000. Since its introduction in 1990, it had become a major strategic principle in securing further business success and simultaneously in consolidating the company's world-wide leading position in many markets, e.g. crop protection, pigments, additives. The Vision called upon all employees to assume a greater role in the management of the company through empowerment, leadership and teamwork.

---

* This case study was authored by *Dr. Urs Burckhardt*, former Research Liaison Officer in the Corporate Research Units of Ciba, *Dr. Rudolf H. Andreatta*, former Director of International Research Laboratories (IRL) in Takarazuka, Japan, and *Prof. Dr. Daniel Bellus*, former Head of Corporate Research Units. This case study was written in 1997: The reader should keep in mind that all numbers, figures, organization charts and forecasts represent the state of 1997 or before. The case study was revised in 2006 by *Eric Montagne*.

Table III.4.1. Main Ciba businesses and key figures.

		1994	1995
Number of employees	Total	83,980	84,077
	Abroad	63,095	63,674
Turnover CHF billion	Total	22.05	20.70
	Healthcare	8.75	8.00
	Agriculture	4.76	4.80
	Industry	8.54	7.90
R&D expenditure		2.15	1.99
Profit after taxes		1.91	2.16

Ciba maintained international research centers in many countries, the major ones being located in Switzerland, USA, Germany, France, the UK and Japan. Production and selling organizations were located world-wide in 81 countries.

The main competitors were the big pharmaceutical companies (Glaxo, Hoechst-Roussel, SmithKlineBeecham, Roche, MSD), the important agrochemical companies (Zeneca, Bayer, DuPont, AgrEvo, Monsanto) and the leading companies in chemical specialties (DuPont, Monsanto, BASF, Hoechst, Clariant). Partnerships have been established in selected areas with some of our competitors. A very substantial internal engagement in biotechnology was realized and later reinforced by strong minority participation with Chiron USA.

2   R&D Organisation

Ciba's R&D efforts (1995: CHF 1.985 million) were performed mainly in the 13 operating divisions (Ciba-Geigy corporate organization: Fig. III.4.1). Only 6% of the total corporate R&D budget was centrally allocated to the Corporate Research Units. The Corporate Research Units (CRUs) complemented divisional activities

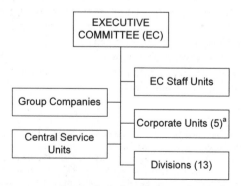

Fig. III.4.1. Ciba's corporate organization including Corporate Research Units (CRU).

> **Mission statement of Corporate Research Units:**
>
> The CRUs create and cultivate Centres of Excellence. Being aware of Ciba's Vision and future market needs they carry out research for the benefit of the company as a whole.
>
> The scientific efforts are focused on future-oriented key technologies rather than short-term needs. A clear priority pertains to the continuous identification and scientific evaluation of carefully selected emerging technologies of outright interest to Divisions of Ciba-Geigy. Promising results are then transferred to the Divisions for development of novel commercial products.
>
> In addition, the Corporate Research Units provide an attractive research environment for top young scientists by
> * performing research in areas at the forefront of science
> * maintaining close contacts with leading academic centres
> * patenting and publishing research results of a high standard.

either in collaborative projects or by pursuing more speculative approaches in fields of potential future interest to Ciba's businesses (see Fig. III.4.2 for comparison of divisional versus CRUs' research efforts and the CRUs' Mission Statement in above box).

Close to 50% of Ciba's total R&D resources were spent in Switzerland, the site of the company's headquarters. 24% were spent in the US, 15% in Europe outside of Switzerland, and 5% in Japan. The main areas of R&D were chosen primarily according to the business interests of the corresponding divisions.

3 R&D Coordination

R&D programs of the divisional R&D units were decided upon by the corresponding divisional management committees who were also responsible for R&D budgets, R&D funding and their controlling.

The Corporate Research Units were funded by the Corporate Executive Committee through a yearly allocated budget. The basic direction for corporate research programs were outlined in the Mission Statement. All corporate R&D projects were decided upon by the Management Committee of the Corporate Research Units after in-depth consultations with the management of divisional R&D units potentially affected by these projects.

The co-ordination of decentralized R&D sites within a division was primarily the task of the divisional head of R&D. As a rule he was also a member of the divisional management committee. The regular R&D co-ordination on the corporate level was taken care of by the Corporate R&D Committee headed by the member of the Executive Committee responsible for R&D matters and manned by all R&D heads of the divisions, the head of Corporate Research Units and the head of Research Services.

4   Example of an International R&D Project

In the 70s and 80s the Ciba management realized that East Asia had a promising economic future and had therefore world-wide the highest potential for a fast growing market for the company. Japan contributed already for 7% of Ciba's global turnover and positioned itself as the number 3 of all countries, preceded only by the US and Germany in importance.

The distribution of Ciba's research sites was a regular discussion point of the Corporate Executive Committee. During 1984 the question was raised if and how the scientific potential of Japan might be used most fruitfully. There was a strong feeling that profiling Ciba's research in Japan in order to show Ciba as a technology-based and research-oriented company might result in a strategically relevant goodwill gain in Japan. Two alternatives were discussed involving the opinions of potentially interested divisions: a gradual increase of Ciba's R&D effort on a divisional level in Japan or the establishment of a centrally managed Corporate Research Unit for long-term projects to the benefit of several divisions. The Pharma division was more inclined to strengthen the Pharma R&D effort in Japan for short-term needs but did not oppose a corporate research endeavour if the right bioorganic projects would be included. The Agro division was mainly interested in increasing development work in Japan and very reluctant to an additional research institute outside of Switzerland. The Plastics and Additives division was positive on a corporate research unit in Japan, which would include projects on Materials Science. The head of Central Function Research expressed himself in a very positive way in favor of setting up a corporate research unit in Japan.

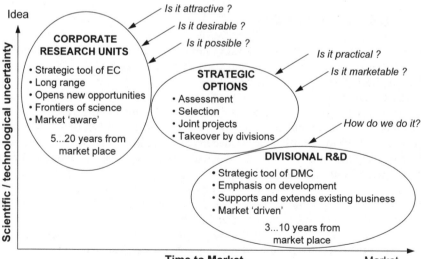

Fig. III.4.2. R&D Organization in 1996.

Finally, the Corporate Executive Committee decided in 1985 to proceed with the planning of a corporate research center in Japan. The research projects were expected to supplement Ciba's world-wide research efforts. A Steering Committee was established with the task to formulate a general concept, to collect and evaluate project ideas, to nominate one leader per project both in Basel as well as in Japan, and to overview the recruitment of the key scientists for the new institute.

Based on the enthusiastic recommendations of the Steering Committee, the Executive Committee decided in 1986 to establish a corporate research unit, later called *International Research Laboratories (IRL) in Japan.* It was foreseen to build up the institute in two phases to an approximate size of 120 persons in 1992. The recommendation was issued, that the envisaged research activities in Japan should reasonably supplement the world-wide research efforts of the divisions and of Central Function Research. It would be up to these units to contribute to the definition and realization of the projects as priority research topics. Enzyme research and research for new materials for the electronic industry were foreseen as main themes for the IRL research activity. The IRL would administratively be part of Ciba-Geigy Japan Ltd., but functionally responsible to the Research Conference headed by the R&D representative in the Executive Committee. The part time delegate in Basel was in charge of the co-ordination for the divisional projects at IRL and an expatriate already working in Japan was nominated as full-time head of the unit in Japan. A scientific advisory council was foreseen to guarantee the scientific competence and to help recruiting high caliber scientists for the new institute. The Executive Committee stipulated that in principle the costs would be allocated to the sectors (divisions and functions) involved in the research projects. To ease the start, however, the costs for the first phase would be borne centrally on the corporate level. Right at the beginning the Corporate Executive Committee made clear that the research efforts in Japan will succeed only if all divisional and functional sectors involved will themselves engage vigorously for the new center. In June 1986 the establishment of IRL as a new research center located at the headquarters of Ciba-Geigy Japan Ltd. in Takarazuka, in the dynamic Kansai area between Osaka and Kobe, was announced to the press.

In addition, it was decided that a foundation would be set up to support research at Japanese universities in the fields of Life Sciences and Materials Research, later to be named Ciba-Geigy Foundation (Japan) for the Promotion of Science. This decision created a lot of goodwill amongst Japanese political authorities as well as influential scientific community.

Provisional laboratories were occupied in a Pharma building in Takarazuka in early 1988 to host the first scientists recruited for IRL. In 1990 a new research building was inaugurated with enough space to accommodate all IRL scientists even those of potential further expansions. With that step the first phase of the build-up was successfully terminated and the critical mass for such a research institute was reached (see Table III.4.2). From 1991 a period of consolidation followed with less emphasis on expansion than on quality improvement of the ongoing research projects at IRL.

Table III.4.2. Personnel and expenses at IRL 1988 - 1996.

	88	89	90	91	92	93	94	95	96
Personnel total	47	63	100	107	112	117	132	128	146
Pers. expatriates	5	3	5	4	4	6	5	5	5
Total expenses in million CHF	7.3	9.8	11.5	17.8	21.7	30.6	31.3	29.9	30.4

The main objectives of the International Research Laboratories (IRL) were finally formulated in a short paper in October 1994 as follows:

- As a unit of Corporate Research Units, IRL performs research in the selected future-oriented fields of chemistry, biochemistry and molecular biology of potentially bioactive compounds, as well as chemistry and physics of commercially interesting functional materials;
- The IRL are Ciba's gateway to the world of Japanese research, therefore the IRL cultivate intensively relations with Japanese universities and other research facilities for early recognition of new scientific concepts and technologies of Japanese origin;
- All IRL projects possess a long term outlook and are earmarked as very attractive by the Ciba's divisions because of their potential for future development;
- The scientists for the IRL are recruited mainly from first-class Japanese universities and research institutes, whereas a temporary staff of about 5% expatriates fosters at any time a good co-ordination between the IRL and the divisional R&D departments at head-quarters;
- Through a first-class scientific approach, the IRL will endeavour to become a respected partner in the Japanese research community, thereby securing the best Japanese scientists for future co-operation with Ciba.

5   Establishing International Research Labs in Japan

5.1   Recruitment: Hiring the Best Scientists

The establishment of IRL was conscientiously seen as a strategic move to allow Ciba-Geigy to hire young high caliber scientists from the best Japanese universities. Only in performing first-class research in fields popular in Japanese university circles Ciba would be taken seriously as a scientific employer by the university community. At the same time easy internal communication and good contacts to the key researchers in Ciba's divisional and corporate research units had to be guaranteed in order to secure the future of IRL in the company. *It was therefore of utmost importance to hire top scientists right from the beginning* to properly man the key positions in the new organization. In addition, it was felt that a limited number of expatriates with in-depth knowledge of Ciba's research departments in

> **Most important drivers for globalization:**
>
> 1. Complexity of emerging technologies;
> 2. Profiting from different expertise / experts available abroad;
> 3. Cost of doing R&D, especially contractual R&D;
> 4. Compliance with local regulatory requirements.

Switzerland's headquarters would be necessary in order to complement the young IRL team. For the recruitment of Japanese scientists Ciba relied on the counsel and contacts of the members of the Scientific Advisory Board, of the trustees of the Ciba-Geigy (Japan) Foundation, and of researchers active in Ciba's divisional or corporate research units. The actual recruitment work was mainly in the hands of the head of IRL, assisted by the delegate of the Basel Corporate R&D Committee.

Special attention was given to Japanese scientists having lived or living as postdoctoral fellows abroad for some time. All candidates for key scientific positions had to be presented to and approved by the Basel Corporate R&D Committee. Of the 90 scientists recruited, 24 had graduated from Kyoto University, 8 from Osaka University and 8 from Tokyo University, the three most prominent Japanese Universities in Science.

5.2 Projects: Cooperating with Divisional Sponsors

First research topics suitable for IRL were suggested between 1985 and 1987 by IRL scientists *via* the IRL-management after in-depth discussions with the R&D departments of the divisions Pharma, Agro and Plastics & Additives as well as Central Function Research as potential sponsors. The final selection was decided upon in the Basel Corporate R&D Committee. After the principal reorganization of Ciba in 1990 (see below) the selection of projects was in the responsibility of the Head of the Corporate Research Units in Basel who had to present new research projects of IRL to the Corporate R&D Committee for ratification. Since 1992 the IRL projects were included in the Global Project Portfolio of the Corporate Research Units, a document which was challenged and updated every year until 1996.

From 1988 to 1996 the scientific progress was reported in semi-annual reports. Formal *project review meetings* were held annually starting in 1989 with participation of the project sponsors and challengers from divisional and corporate research units. In this way it was assured that groups of internal colleagues and selected external experts helped to implant systematically in the IRL projects both the best and most recent scientific knowledge well as the objectives of the divisions. Not all was sweetness and light in such vibrant challenge meetings; the blunt impatience and outspokenness of western participants and the consensus-minded approach of Japanese colleagues sometimes collided. However, as one participant said: "It was a good feeling to know that I have helped to realize a small step in the evolution of a highly promising project."

Following the project review meetings the IRL management committee usually decided upon the suggestions of the challengers. The divisional sponsors had to stay in close contact with "their" project team and especially its leader through frequent visits at IRL, and visits of the IRL-project team members in the sponsor's department abroad. Since a successful project would eventually be taken over by a divisional research unit, the *communication between divisional sponsors and members of the project teams was one of the most important key success factors* (see also in the following box the statement of the Head of Corporate Research Units regarding the project monitoring and reviewing).

1988 IRL started research work on 5 bioorganic projects, 2 of them sponsored by the Agro division and 3 by Pharma division. In addition, the New Materials department took off with 2 projects, both sponsored by the Plastics and Additives division.

In the following years, several projects were terminated and replaced by new ones. However, the approximate allocation of IRL-resources of 75% to life science projects and 25% to materials research remained unchanged.

Since its formation the IRL was integrated administratively into Ciba-Geigy Japan Ltd., a practical and suitable solution, as at the beginning the provisional laboratories and from 1990 the new IRL laboratory building were both at the Japanese headquarters site in Takarazuka. At the beginning, the functional responsibility for projects and scientific staff was assigned to the IRL Basel committee and its IRL delegate as an executive officer. The IRL started with a Bioorganic department and a New Materials department comprising the project teams and a sizeable Analytics and Informatics department taking care of all the supportive scientific tasks.

Changes in Ciba-Geigy's corporate structure in 1990 influenced the IRL organization: Most of the Central Services world-wide were decentralized and became profit centers. The tasks of the divisions and their business units were more strictly focused to the markets and the business needs. The big and heterogeneous Central Research Function was divided. The corporate research activities were globally brought together in the Corporate Research Units (CRUs). *IRL became a part of the CRUs.*

Head of Corporate Research Units, 1994:

"We focus sharply on Ciba's franchises during the design of our future-oriented projects, and we use mixed CRUs/divisional steering committees and project review meetings to systematically detect both, the progress of the science as well as the needs of the divisions, before doing the next costly experiments. In CRUs, the perfection in project challenging is one of the most important parts of quality management."

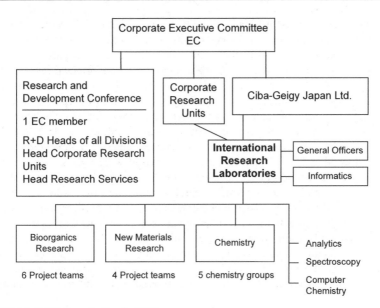

Fig. III.4.3. R&D Organization in 1996.

In the early 90s the project teams at IRL needed increasingly chemical support in synthesis. The chemists, although active in several research projects, were organizationally merged into a new IRL Chemistry department. The Analytics and Informatics department on the other hand was disbanded and most of the scientists were distributed to the project teams. Only expensive high-tech core activities (like molecular modeling by computers, spectroscopy) remained to be performed centrally, by groups directly supervised by the head of IRL.

5.3   Finance: Zero-based Budgeting

During the early discussion phases in the Executive Committee (EC) it was estimated that running costs of about 30 million CHF per annum would have to be taken into consideration for the IRL in Japan, a realistic figure which was very close to the actual expenses in the years 1993-96 (see Table III.4.2). The EC decided to have the costs allocated eventually to the sponsoring divisions and central units but would bear the cost during the first phase on the corporate level to ease the build-up of the envisaged laboratories. This first phase ended when the new IRL building, a four-storey laboratory building constructed at cost of CHF 75 million, was inaugurated in the fall of 1990. Shortly thereafter the world-wide reorganization in Ciba in 1990 caused an enhanced cost-awareness throughout the company and through all levels of the organization. The extreme pressure on the divisional R&D budgets combined with planning exercises like zero based budgeting, brought about a very critical review of all external expenses allocated to the divisional research units. It became quickly apparent that under pressure the heads of research in the divisions or business units would rather shed off some external long-term projects allocated to their units, than to close down part of their own laboratories. In order to save the strategic idea of a future oriented research institute in Japan, the EC had to accept that the cost of IRL would be a part of the Corporate Research Units' budget borne by the EC on the corporate level. The IRL budget for current expenses and for investments was set up on a yearly basis. It was proposed by the IRL management committee and discussed first with the head of the CRUs on the one hand and the head of Ciba Geigy Japan Group Company on the other hand. Then, as part of the world-wide CRUs' budget, it was finally approved or modified by decision of the EC.

The ultimate goal of a corporate research institute like IRL is to bring a feedback in terms of commercially promising, technologically feasible and unique new products and processes to the operating divisions. It is obvious that such a research institute involved in long-term and speculative research for the future benefit of the whole company can survive long enough only if the costs are borne on the corporate level and not directly allocated to the divisions or business units. The fate of the IRL during the Novartis merger proved that point in a very dramatic way.

6   Successes and Failures

Due to the very careful selection of the long-term IRL projects, after the merger the succeeding companies Novartis and Ciba Specialty Chemicals took 8 of 10 IRL projects into their project portfolios.

6.1   Impact of IRL Research Projects on Divisional R&D

In the following paragraphs we have chosen for illustration four IRL projects out of a total of ten in order to demonstrate their interconnection with the world-wide research efforts of Ciba.

Major innovative break-throughs at Ciba (last five years):

1. Antisense oligonucleotides for therapeutic applications and as drug discovery tools;

2. Novel daily-disposable contact lenses;

3. Systematic control of fleas in pet animals;

4. Realisation of catalytic single-isomer technology on a large production scale;

5. New class of non-phenolic antioxidants.

The *Vasomodulation Project*, attracted high attention throughout the existence of IRL. Molecular biologists, peptide chemists and organic synthesis chemists joined the interdisciplinary team at IRL to carve out a novel class of endothelin antagonists possessing interesting possibilities in treatment of elevated blood pressure. The lead compounds, selected at IRL because of their *in-vitro* activity, were later evaluated by *in-vivo* models in the Pharma Research laboratories in Basel and Summit (USA). From 1993-95 at times a group of over 15 synthesis chemists from Summit joined in the effort to optimize the lead structures. Also in Novartis the vasomodulator project played an important role; it was steered by the therapeutic area Respiratory Diseases of Pharma division and transferred to the research center in Horsham, UK.

The objective of another project was to establish a biotechnological process for the production of *human calcitonin* to replace the existing synthetic process. From a technical viewpoint the objectives were fully met. But although the project stayed in close contact with the sponsors in Pharma research, the process was not taken over to Pharma production, since Pharma marketing considered the necessary additional investments as not profitable enough. Apparently the economic factors were not taken seriously enough into consideration at the initiation of the project. However, strong patents were taken and the genuine technology is at the disposal of the licensing department.

A third project had an extremely successful early start. Already within 3 years *inhibitors of histidine biosynthesis* were found with *in-vitro* potencies comparable to the very best herbicide standards. Unfortunately these lead compounds proved weaker and very slowly acting *in-vivo*, on the plants. In spite of the active participation of the chemists in weed control research in Basel no inhibitor could be found with a herbicidal activity worthy of development. For most of the IRL team members it was difficult to understand in the beginning why these early potent lead compounds would not be developed further by the Agro division. Many visits of the Japanese project team members to the screening and field facilities of weed control in Switzerland and many discussions of weed control experts at IRL were needed to appreciate the whole complexity and the pitfalls of the development of a new, superior weed control agent. This educational experience was necessary to refute reproaches of a NIH ("not invented here") attitude of the divisional research unit at headquarters in Switzerland. The project was discontinued at the end of 1996.

A fourth project, one out of the realm of the new materials research, dealt with the *technology of thin film depositions*. It aimed at new methods of non-absorption color generation for a new class of color materials for pigment use. The project had a quick start and showed early on very promising results. However, the massive competition and an unfavorable patent situation soon became apparent, thus rendering a very careful refocusing of the project goals towards not only innovative but also economically feasible processes necessary. Excellent results encouraged the new company Ciba Specialty Chemicals to continue this project on a divisional basis, as the outlook for its commercial realization is considered to be very good.

6.2   IRL as Talent Pool

One important strategic reason for founding the IRL in Japan was Ciba's craving to participate in the Japanese scientific expertise to make best use of Japanese scientists and to incorporate impulses from the Japanese culture. If this task should be performed successfully, good communication and close interaction with Ciba's main R&D centers on an international basis was of utmost importance. It was clearly a very demanding management task to integrate a scientifically motivated but proud crowd of young Japanese scientists into a diversified, western-dominated, Europe-centered corporation.

During the entire period 1984-1996 the nominated heads of IRL were expatriates from Switzerland. The first served from 1986 to 1990, the second from 1991 to 1996, and the third from 1996 until the dissolution of IRL in 1997. Besides the head, one or two members of the IRL management committee were expatriates, too. In addition, scientists from divisional or corporate research units in Switzerland joined the IRL for periods of 1-4 years to strengthen the projects as project leaders, chemists or biochemists - and to help to establish (and to sustain) English as the internal communication language! In total 4-6 expatriates served at any given time at IRL (see Table III.4.2); they guaranteed an international, open atmosphere at the Japanese-dominated institute. On the other hand, a job rotation to the IRL was a welcome management development tool for scientists from the parent company and was seen by them as a chance to prove themselves outside of their own research units.

From the other point of view most of the Japanese IRL project leaders and many team members were given a chance of working for approximately one year in the divisional research unit to which the project was mainly attached, in Switzerland or the United States. This way the scientists of IRL got well exposed first to the objectives of the divisional research and the market needs and second to the way of thinking of their Swiss or American colleagues. Normally 1-2 IRL researchers stayed at headquarters research centers at a time. In general these exchanges were considered successful by both parties. The Big Hanshin Earthquake of January 17, 1995 affected the expatriates in a major way too. As a consequence, for family reasons some assignments had to be cancelled prematurely.

6.3   IRL and Japanese Universities

The IRL mission stated that: "IRL serves as a bridge to link academic research in Japan and Ciba's divisional R&D units. IRL endeavors to be at the cutting edge of modern research striving to produce innovative solutions and concepts that will form the seeds of future commercial Ciba products". In accordance with this mission, IRL had various contacts with top-ranking Japanese universities in order to recruit good graduates, further educate and train its employees, and transfer technology. The contacts were nurtured at several levels:

In 1987 the Ciba-Geigy Foundation (Japan) for the Promotion of Science was established which annually endowed approximately 1.5 million CHF in the form of 50 research grants and 10 exchange fellowships to Japanese professors. The boards of trustees and counselors of the Foundation included many eminent retired professors.

5-10 IRL employees were sent every year for 3-12 month to Japanese universities for further general training and for the acquisition of specific novel techniques useful for the IRL projects. Most projects have been supported by one or several small collaborations with university laboratories. Contacts between companies and universities are widespread in Japan. As a striking difference to western customs, they are always on non-exclusive terms and at modest costs.

On a weekly basis, university researchers were invited to present their work on internal seminars at IRL. Three retired professors were hired to come to IRL on a weekly basis to educate employees and to consult the project teams.

6.4   The Dissolution of IRL

The merger of Ciba and Sandoz to form a new company was announced on March 7, 1996, and came into effect on December 17, 1996. The new giant with a turn-over of 37 bio. CHF and a potential profit of 6 bio. CHF, was later split into Novartis, a life-science pace setter, and into Ciba Specialty Chemicals, a world-wide leading chemical company. In the first month after the announcement it became apparent that no corporate research units were foreseen for Novartis. Apparently the management theories in favor called for distribution of all central units to the operating business sectors at all costs. This preconceived idea affected the IRL in a fatal way: The Agro projects were terminated at the end of 1997 and not continued in Japan. Three Pharma projects were carried on in the Japanese Pharma sector with a reduced work force. Due to the drastic reduction in scientific manpower, the supporting functions (spectroscopy, computer assisted modeling, analytics etc.) continued only on a dramatically lower level of manpower, expertise and competence. The researchers of the new materials department were mostly incorporated into the local divisions of the Ciba Specialty Chemicals, split off from the Novartis corporation.

The new management of Novartis was not willing to appreciate the strategic opportunity offered by a first-class research institute in Japan. Though heavily committed to global innovation - at least judged from interviews in the popular press - it sets no signs for practical steps to achieve excellence in scientific research in Japan. To form a first rate research institute like IRL, employing high-caliber scientists from the best universities, enjoying an excellent scientific reputation, and, above all, producing already outstanding results for the company, is much harder and takes much more time in Japan than in Europe or the United States. The immaterial damage of the dissolution of IRL is difficult to appreciate. The future will tell if the loss of image will complicate contacts of the company with the universities or hamper the further development of its business in Japan.

7   Conclusions

This case is a story of success and failure at the same time. The key factors of success for establishing an international research laboratory in Japan can be summarized as follows:

Commitment

To establish a corporate basic research institute for long-term research projects in Japan a primordial outspoken commitment of the corporate top management is essential. The time horizon for a cost/benefit analysis and the consequences thereof must be at least 10 years. Methods must be found to secure the highest and long-lasting interest of the divisional research units on the general direction of the projects in their realm, whereas the research projects themselves have to be challenged regularly and critically. The existence of the research institute must not be questioned in order to avoid loss of morale and motivation, as well as difficulties in hiring the very best scientists from Japanese universities.

People

Obviously the quality of the research scientists is vital for the success of the research institute. The scientists have not only to be creative researchers but also good communicators to colleagues within the company on the international level (in English!) and to university professors and institutes in Japan. Frequent job rotations to and from the institute are helpful for the communication within the company. Visits of members of the institute to Japanese universities and lectures or consultancies of Japanese professors at the institute are necessary to keep intense contacts with the academic world. The selection of candidates, especially for senior positions, needs excellent connections with the Japanese scientific establishment and the assistance of a large number of international experts as *ad hoc* consultants.

Projects

For a Japanese research venture it seems to be essentially important that the projects have a scientific appeal in the Japanese research scene. Of course it is essential that the members of the institute can identify with the projects they are working on, ideally they are the co-originators of the projects. This is best achieved if the idea and the proposal come from the members themselves. But, *vice versa*, it is also important that the projects are mentally accepted by the sponsors from the divisional research units potentially affected by the projects' results. Ideally both the members of the institute and the divisional sponsors display strong parental feelings towards the basic idea of the project. An early involvement of the divisions is vital since success is secured only if a project is finally taken over by the divisions "into the pipeline" for further development and transformation into a commercial product or process: The corporate push needs the divisional pull for completion. Apart from frequent interchange between project team and sponsor, regular formal review meetings are necessary to ascertain that the project stays on a track acceptable for all parties. Besides the sponsors a selected number of challengers from different parts of the company and a few outside experts have to be actively involved in the reviews.

Finances

A research institute devoted to long-term projects for the benefit of several divisions has to be financed on the corporate level for the whole time of its existence. If divisional sponsors have the option of cutting funds to the institute in order to contain their own research budgets, the days of the corporate institute would be numbered. A budgeting procedure has to be established which allows a steady operation over the years. Dramatic ups and downs in funding are detrimental to morale and continuity of the institute. The basic financial policy determines accountability and responsibility. It is then only an operational decision if finances are actually transferred from corporate headquarters to the institute or if expenses are paid directly by the Japanese group company. This depends also on the tax situation in Japan, which must be carefully considered by the corporate legal department.

Organization

A project organization is probably the most appropriate form. For a research institute devoted to long-term projects a matrix organization which includes functional responsibilities is hardly necessary. Care has to be taken to incorporate the supporting functions (spectroscopy, analytics etc.) in a way to allow a flexible use of their services by all projects according to their needs.

Site

The site of the research institute should be close to both, the main university areas and the international airports, either Tokyo or Osaka/Kyoto. It is of course very

---

Lessons learned for organizing R&D at Ciba:

1. Creation of a research climate conducive to innovation attracts and retains top class scientists;

2. Regular and critical project challenging meetings foster technology and market awareness among scientists;

3. Full attention to bottom-up creativity, followed by clear top-down decisions motivate people;

4. Flexible resource allocation to emerging technologies is a must;

5. Different cultures at decentralized R&D centers require intensive personal interactions.

advantageous if the institute can be incorporated into an already existing important location of the Japanese group company, be it a business center or its headquarters.

What will bring the future? As described above, the merger of Ciba and Santos to form Novartis meant the end of the IRL as a corporate research institute. It is well possible that the pendulum will swing back away from 1997's fascination with extreme focus on research in Europe and in the United States. A few years later the temptation might be overwhelming to tap the rich research opportunities of Japanese science again. Of course, an enormous effort will then be needed to regain the ground lost due to the closing of Ciba's IRL in Japan. It is interesting to note that at the same time several competing companies (Bayer, Pfizer etc.) were announcing their intention to open or enlarge basic research centers in Japan.

III.5 Kao: Localizing R&D Resources*

1   Customer Commitment

Kao's corporate mission is to contribute to the wholehearted satisfaction and the enrichment of the lives of customers and employees throughout the world. We will accomplish this by drawing on our creative and innovative strengths to develop products of excellent value and outstanding performance. Fully committed to this mission, all members of Kao companies are working together as a single corporate force to win the loyalty and trust of their customers. Based on our corporate mission, Kao's activities are as follows:

- Ensure customers' wholehearted satisfaction worldwide;
- Create innovative products based on original ideas and technologies;
- Sustain profitable growth and respond to the trust of stakeholders;
- Leverage the abilities of individuals into a powerful corporate force;
- Encourage close harmony with the environment and the community.

Kao now offers worldwide a wide range of products: Approximately 570 branded package-product items from the consumer product divisions, a wide range of chemicals from the chemical divisions for industrial and institutional uses, and high technology information storage products from the Kao Infosystems group. Kao specializes in consumer products, and chemicals and infosystems products.

Consumer Products

Household products are fabric softener, starch, dish washing and kitchen detergents, bleach, laundry detergents in liquid and powder forms, and a wide range of household cleaners for windows, floors, gas range, toilet room bathtubs, etc. Kao's personal care product lineups include toilet soap, hair shampoo and conditioners, body and facial cleansers, skin care products and hair care items such as hair col-

---

*   This case study was authored by *Dr. Kenji Hara,* Director of Research and Development Division, Kao Corp. This case study was written in 1998: The reader should keep in mind that all numbers, figures, organization charts and forecasts represent the state of 1998 or before. The case study was revised in 2007 by *Wei-Chi Chen.*

Major innovative break-throughs at Kao (1995-2000):

1. Biodegradable ester amide hydrochloride (fabric softener);

2. Quickle Wiper (hosehold cleaning tool);

3. Biore Pore Pack (pore dirt removal).

---

ors, treatment agents, hair styling agents and spray. Additionally, Kao offers bath additives, sanitary products, cosmetics, food and cooking oils.

Chemicals and Infosystems Products

Kao offers a wide range of fine chemicals for various industries, including surfactants, polymers, and fat and oil-based chemicals, fragrance, flavors and edible oils. Kao entered the information technology product industry with floppy disk production. Kao recently diversified into the duplication business to produce formatted diskettes for end-users. Kao is also offering data storage products in other categories such as DAT (Digital Audio Tapes). In 1994, Kao entered the field of optical information media. Other information-related products are toner binders, ink ribbons and thermal paper for office reproduction machines. These are further examples of Kao's state-of-the-art technical applications.

2   Plants and Laboratories in Japan

Tokyo Plant and Research Facilities

The Tokyo plant, the eldest of Kao's plants, commenced operations in 1923 after the successful expansion of the market for the 'KAO SOAP' product throughout Japan. Within this plant site there are varied research sections. Research is divided into three principal areas:

- Personal care and cosmetic products;
- Perfumery and fragrances; and
- Packaging technology.

Wakayama Plant and Research Facilities

The Wakayama plant started in 1942 and is the largest of Kao's nine plants. At the Wakayama laboratories, extensive research is conducted in the fields of material science and chemistry for product development, and in technologies for the production process and environmental concerns. Three research programs in material sciences related to oil and fats, polymers and other organic chemicals provide a strong base for Kao's final consumer products, developing new key substances with revolutionary performance in applications. Research at the Wakayama plant also includes practical studies on laundry and dish washing detergents, household cleaning products, starch and fabric softeners.

Tochigi Plant and Research Facilities

Activities at the Tochigi laboratories are focused on fundamental but applied areas of sciences related to Kao products. In the Biological Science laboratory, research is conducted in physiology and biotechnology. It also includes an environmental and safety evaluation section to ensure that Kao products are safe for the users and the society. Researchers at the Tochigi plant also conduct practical studies on paper wipers, women's sanitary products and diapers. The Tochigi complex includes the Information Science laboratory, where research is conducted in floppy disks and other information-related products.

Kashima Plant and Research Facilities

The Kashima laboratory focuses on biochemistry and bioprocesses, especially in the technological area of fermentation and foods processing. Research in specialty chemicals for foods, margarine and cooking oil, both for home cooking and industrial uses, is a source of current and future business development for Kao.

3   The Coordination and Management Structure of R&D

3.1   Strategy for Corporate Innovation

For corporate innovation in general, Kao has implemented strategies which have become a mainstay of the company. These strategies have been applied comprehensively to business innovation in Kao for decades.

Profit for R&D in its Widest Sense

Perhaps it sounds unrealistic to assert that the primary emphasis of Kao's business is neither profits nor staying ahead of the competition. Yet Kao's mission is to improve and proliferate Kao's services to the customers in a way that will offer truly useful innovative products and services of satisfaction. Financial profits at Kao are regarded as the means to open its future. Former chairman Dr. Maruta once said of profits, „In order to be able to continue providing services to society, a company has to make a profit. The profit should fund the company's research and development, so that the company can develop new products and services that are beneficial to customers. It is my belief that such profit should be regarded as something like alms from customers, and should be returned to them by the company."

He emphasizes that Kao's basic managerial stance is to position Kao's research

> **Major issues for global R&D management at Kao:**
> 1. Strong connection to the headquarters and laboratories in Japan;
> 2. Hold the international R&D strategic meeting.

and development as the pivotal force in developing products that can be innovated through self-generated funds. Kao regards people at any workplace to be an on-the-job study group whose purpose is to develop customer services on an ongoing basis. To be a member of Kao's customer service, everyone needs to question oneself about how to improve performance in his or her respective assignment.

Extensive Research and Study

Kao recognizes that any innovation can be achieved through extensive studies with contemplation of day-to-day life. By being interested with various matters of human affairs, reality will reveal itself and we can apply the wisdom in the form of new products and services. Kao should conduct such studies with a multinational human resource, in accordance with Kao's mission, as business continues to globalize.

Any activity by individuals or a group of people is surely based on the uncertain effect of large amounts of information, but is integrated practically into our thoughts, feelings and will. These can be cultivated by our lifelong aspirations and decide matters of life with greater acuity. Thus, Kao's corporate studies and research include not only natural science and technology, but also socio-psychological studies. The universal studies and research for customer services shall be the hallmark of all Kao activities.

Corporate Creativity

Creativity at all levels is a generic basis of the Kao mission. Creativity should permeate all of Kao's activities, and not just be restricted to the development of new products or to artistic design. It should be exhibited by all the participants in Kao from management to workforce, especially where they interact with customers or consumers of Kao products and services. For example, a decade ago, staff and management at Kao strove to raise productivity to fund Kao's business expansion during an inter-company management campaign called „Total Cost Reduction" (TCR). They eventually renamed it „Total Creative Revolution," as they found that any cost reduction necessarily followed a revolutionary change of the work processes, be it internal or external, that ultimately depended on their own creativity, especially in the use of newly developed information technology.

Domestically (in Japan), TCR heralded reengineering drives of the workprocess by other corporations. Whether in designing a system of management, developing a production technology, serving a new sales channel, or even operating a machine for product quality, it is „creativity" that enables our improvement (kaizen) and innovation (kakushin) in any area of work. TCR has hereditarily become Kao's own banner of self-innovation. The third phase was called New TCR, and aimed at achieving "Vision 2000" as the corporation enters the 21st century.

3.2   Interdisciplinary and Vertically Integrated R&D

Kao has always emphasized R&D as the critical driving force for the evolution of business. In this age of rapid technological development and dependency on information systems, Kao has increased its investment of management resources in R&D, consistent with globalization of the market, deploying more than 2,200 researchers worldwide. Expenditure on R&D totaled 35 billion yen in 1996, or 5.5% of the net annual turnover of Kao Japan.

Emphasis on Fundamental and Interdisciplinary Research

The research and development activities at Kao cover a wide range of areas, centering around fat and oil, surface sciences, polymer science, biological studies and applied physics. These scientific studies are conducted on fundamental research in the nuclear level of the physico-chemical and physiological world. Since the boundaries of chemistry, biology and physics have become blurred, the interactions and influences between disciplines are well infused at Kao's R&D.

Kao recognizes that natural sciences can not be neatly compartmentalized and thus encourages interdisciplinary approaches among its scientific staff and other research institutions. Assisted by the rapid development of computer science and technology, Kao relies on mathematical approaches to facilitate its scientific studies, because they are useful as the common language to all people of diverse disciplines to communicate on non-empirical grounds.

Presently, Kao has 14 research laboratories and research centers in Japan. Some of these are working on innovative product development and improving existing Kao products, while others work on corporate R&D to develop new substances, production processes, packaging, engineering and mechanical fabrication. The former corresponds to Kao's product divisions such as household, skin and hair-care, and sanitary products, as well as to the business divisions of specialty chemicals, foods and data-storage and information media products.

Kao believes that the more widely the „seeds" of R&D are sown, the more productively they will grow to meet the „needs" of the users of Kao products. Over 1,900 researchers work in the four research centers in Tokyo, Wakayama, Tochigi and Kashima. To facilitate product innovations in these R&D centers, activities are focused on finding and developing „key phenomena" and „key chemical" substances that can be extensively applied to final product development, thereby vertically integrating the „seeds" from R&D with the „needs" determined through market research.

Kao also recognizes that no product development can be achieved without an intricate synthesis of science and technology, especially on the frontiers of its real innovation. For instance, if the combined powers of precise mechanical process-engineering and surface science are not fully utilized in the production of Kao's floppy disks, no real accomplishment can be expected in the processing of ultra-thin film materials with the ultra-fine, sticky magnetic particles. So Kao's scientists, working in conjunction with the engineers, are expected to create key technologies which can be extensively applied to other products and processes.

Vertical Integration in R&D

The best service can be provided to customers only if Kao continues to develop its knowledge and technology in all areas, upstream (from primary materials) to downstream (the finished products). Kao thus places great importance on the principle of Vertical Integration, which is reflected in the integration of the „seeds" of R&D with the „needs" of customers.

Kao's floppy disk business is one example where Vertical Integration is applied. Originally, Kao supplied only materials to floppy disk manufacturers. However, it soon became obvious that in order to produce superior chemicals for floppy disks, it would be necessary to go into the production of the disks themselves, as floppy disks are a product of physico-chemistry technology.

Kao subsequently started floppy disk production „vertically", linking the primary key-chemicals, developed by Kao's surface science research, to its high-speed floppy disk production facility, thus entering the worldwide market. To expand its range of information storage media products, Kao's vertical integration strategy urged the scientists and engineers to enter the other information media horizons, such as CD-ROMs (Compact Disk of Read-Only-Memory), which are based on optical-electronics science with Kao's technology of high speed and precise mechanical processing.

Since the „needs" of the customers must be satisfied, researchers work closely with the marketing staff in order to understand the structure and trends of the marketplace. Kao researchers often visit superstores to directly grasp consumer preferences and habits, as well as the places of application for industrial chemicals. R&D staff also work together with production staff to improve the production system and technology, and to help avoid potential problems. Inefficiency in the production process may arise if products are designed inappropriately by researchers. Kao researchers cooperate not only on an interdisciplinary level, but also on an inter-industrial basis, especially in regards to chemical products. Kao believes that real breakthroughs in the creation of new products can be achieved only by mutually combining the benefits of Kao's science and technology with those of other industries. Micro-electronics, new raw materials and biotechnology are popular ventures for corporations and researchers. But these can't be successful without inter-industrial cooperation.

Many of the new chemicals that Kao is developing, lie at the heart of the emerging industries toward the next century. New chemistry is often called „key" science, because new chemical techniques will play a vital role in solving environmental issues such as water pollution and waste disposal in the next century. They will also play an important role in the creation of Kao's innovative products for our lives and in contributing to local cultures on a global scale.

4   Managing R&D: Flat and Dynamic

The four locations in Japan are doing research classified into three main categories: basic research, corporate research and business research. Centralization and divisionalization of the activities of the laboratories within Kao's R&D organization is not as clearly specified as in many Western companies, which is important in understanding the efficient management of innovation within Kao. To accomplish Kao's mission by generating dynamism in the corporate culture, the overall organization at Kao was designed to be flat or non-pyramidal. It is often likened to a flat paperweight with a knob in the center. A cluster of Kao's top management people are at the orchestrating center and other people are at a flat extension to perform their parts around the cluster. Top management people „walk around" the flat stage, holding ad hoc meeting for paperless decision making. Thus they can get a grasp of business issues directly. An extensive communication network to exchange the information and intelligence is indispensable to maintain this flexible management style.

Research is centralized in terms of specific research projects, which are decided upon during various meetings among researchers. Information exchange and sharing is held on a daily basis between researchers in the same laboratories, and two days a month between researchers across different laboratories. Researchers working on related projects have the opportunity to discuss their approaches and findings at these meetings, as well as deciding upon new and emerging research themes. The initiation of new projects and themes of research are further discussed at the R&D directors meeting, which takes place between R&D top managers and directors every month. At these meetings, the decisions to carry out specific research projects are made.

In addition, Kao holds a monthly R&D conference, where researchers can communicate their ideas directly to top management. Finally, two times (two days each time) a year, top management and research directors hold an R&D strategy conference to determine the future focus of research and development and a goal for future R&D spending. The management of R&D in Kao is based on extensive communication between top management and researchers directly, and characterized as being flexible, non-authoritative and favorable towards individuality.

5   International Labs: Tapping Local Resources

Kao strives to globalize its business by localizing management resources such as personnel, finance and materials to be supplied, while sharing management, administrative know-how, business experience and technology throughout the global group of companies. This enables any local business of Kao to be positioned as a globalized business. As well as developing Kao products locally to meet the needs of each market, Kao is strengthening its internationally-oriented research laboratories to adapt them for the globalizing market by investing in their production and marketing facilities. One of Kao's international businesses has been strategically initiated outside of Japan: The technology necessary for producing floppy disks

Most important drivers for globalization:

1. Business strategy;

2. Breakthrough technology;

3. Product development to meet the needs of local markets;

4. Localize management resources.

became a business in itself in 1985. The following year, Kao Corporation of America (KCOA) acquired a production facility in California and purchased Didak, a company producing floppy disks in Ontario, Canada. Soon the business expanded to the entire North American continent and also to Germany.

In Europe, Kao started operations in 1970 with two chemical plants in Spain producing and supplying construction chemicals to European countries. Kao's other business lines have subsequently developed throughout Europe, such as personal care products with Beiersdorf GmbH and Goldwell GmbH in Germany, fragrances in France and the marketing of specialty chemicals all over Europe.

In North America, Kao conducts research on skin care products at the Andrew Jergens Company, which was acquired in 1988. The R&D center at Andrew Jergens also conducts research in product evaluation, sales and marketing.

The European laboratories conduct research on hair and skin care product development, beauty technology development and packaging. The Kao Europe Research Institute (KERI), was established in Germany in 1991, and functions as the link between Kao Corporation (France), Goldwell GmbH (Germany) and Kao Corporation S.A. (Spain). Now this institute is united within Goldwell GmbH, R&D Division. The function of this institute is communication and transfer of technology between R&D facilities to adapt products to the European market. Both in Japan and abroad, the R&D activities of Kao are quite extensive, and the areas of research at each facility appear to be rather broad. As a result, the management of R&D becomes crucial to successful product development and management of diversification.

6   Conclusions

Kao's weakest points are the lack of international experience, limited human resource assets, especially in top management, and little international knowledge and experience of Western markets and consumers. Its international operations were driven primarily along the product division axis. Kao's overseas R&D laboratories were strongly connected to both the product headquarters and the R&D laboratories in Japan through frequent meetings and information exchange.

Kao does not prefer to staff its overseas operations with Japanese nationals. Finding, training and keeping suitable local personnel is a major challenge. Kao

---

Lessons learned for organizing R&D at Kao:

1. Introduction of local culture and know-how;

2. Flat, flexible organization;

3. Localize management resources.

---

strives to globalize its business by localizing management resources such as personnel, finance and materials to be supplied, while sharing management, administrative know-how, business experience and technology throughout the global group of companies.

In addition to developing products locally to meet the needs of each market, Kao is strengthening its multinational research laboratories. These laboratories need to be adapted for the globalizing market by analyzing local market needs and characteristics and integrating them into the product development process.

Part IV
Best-in-Class: The Electronics, Software, and Service Industry

Table IV.1. Best in class companies in the electronics and software industry (1996).

Company	Sales (US$ billion)	R&D Expenses (US$ million)	R&D Ratio (%)	Number of Int'l Sites
Xerox	17.4	1,000	5.8	n/a
Canon	22.1	1,440	6.5	6
HP	38.4	2,700	7.0	27
IBM	75.9	4,700	6.2	10
SAP	3.4	454	13.3	4
Unisys	6.4	349	5.5	250

In our group of electronics, software and financial services we have exclusively high-tech companies: Xerox, Canon, Hewlett Packard, IBM, SAP, Unisys, Huawei, Fujitsu and Swiss Re. Even though Swiss Re is from financial services, it employs hundreds of natural scientists and engineers to model natural and financial catastrophes and risks of new technologies as well. New technologies are the most significant drivers behind R&D in this group. In the electronics and software industries it is still possible to achieve a decisive difference on the market with new high tech products. Since the fundamental components of the technology, electronics and software, are improving very fast, R&D managers must have the courage to slash even big projects as soon as one of the competitors is likely to come up with a next-generation product. And if the big re–insurers say no to a new technology, even the best products will have no chance on the market.

Products are characterized by short life cycles. Platforms and especially product architectures are therefore at the center of most R&D efficiency-improvement programs: Companies try to balance the short life-span of product components with robust architectures and the establishment of dominant designs (e.g. Intel processor standard).

The escalation of R&D costs leads to more pressure towards outsourcing and technology alliances. High levels of modularization and industry-wide standardization facilitate the international division of labour in large-scale R&D projects. The R&D internationalization of companies like IBM has therefore already a long history.

Most of the companies have been forced to concentrate on their true core capa-

Table IV.2. Benchmark companies in the software and office electronics industry 2006.

Company	Sales (US$ billion)	R&D Expenses (US$ million)	R&D Ratio (%)	Number of Employees
Microsoft	44.3	6,584	14.9	71,000
Oracle	14.4	1,872	13.0	56,133
SAP	11.8	1,677	14.2	35,873
Canon	23.5	2,542	10.8	19,707
Xerox	15.9	922	5.8	53,700

Financial Statements 2006, Source: Bloomberg.

bilities and have reduced their internal manufacturing to less than 10% of the total value-added. Thus, most companies are very strong in logistics and have begun to develop logistics concepts in parallel with product R&D. Since all of them are in a fierce cost-competitive environment, they had to balance economy-of-scales with local customization very carefully, they have to manage their global bill of materials on a sophisticated level.

From a research point of view this type of industry is particularly interesting for the academic scholar, but it is interesting for the R&D practitioner as well because of its tremendous learning potential: Since life cycles, on-the-shelf life times and ramp-up times are extremely short, managers in these industries go through dozens of projects during their R&D career. They have to shorten time-to-market and need to cope with unpredictable technology-discontinuities.

IV.1 Xerox: The Global Market and Technology Innovator*

1 Xerox, the Document Company

The Document Company, Xerox, is a leader in the global document market, providing document solutions that enhance business productivity.

A global company in the document processing business, Xerox Corporation offers the widest array of products and consulting services in the industry: publishing systems, copiers, printers, scanners, fax machines and document management software, along with related products and services. All Xerox products and services are designed to help customers manage the flow of information from paper to electronic form and back again. The Xerox customer is anyone who uses documents: Fortune 500 corporations and small companies; public agencies and universities; and home businesses.

Xerox started the office copying revolution with the introduction of its 914 copier in 1959. Today, Xerox stands poised for the continued expansion of the global document processing market, a large and growing market. Xerox Corporation's revenues in 1997 were US$ 18.2 billion. Fuji Xerox, whose revenues are unconsolidated with Xerox Corporation, had revenues of US$ 7.4 billion, yielding a combines US$ 25.6 billion in revenues for the Xerox Group. Fuji Xerox, a 50/50 joint venture between Fuji Photo Film Company, Limited and Xerox, is the hub of Xerox operations in Japan and the high-growth markets in the Pacific Rim. In 1997 Xerox's organizational structure was set up as pictured below.

Business Operations

Xerox Corporation had five business groups organized around the five broad segments of document processing marketplace. The business groups worked closely with each other and with Xerox customer operations around the world to guaran-

---

* This case study was authored by *Mark B. Myers, Ph.D.*, Senior Vice-President Corporate Research and Technology, Xerox, and *Kim W. Smith*, Executive Assistant Corporate Research and Technology, Xerox. This case study was written in 1998: All numbers, figures, organization charts and forecasts represent the state of 1998 or before. The case study was revised in 2007 by *Nicolas Rohner*.

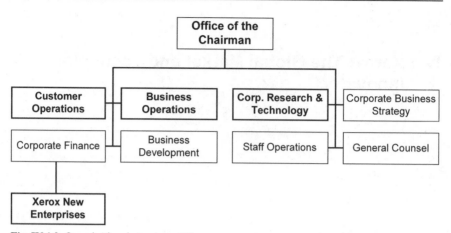

Fig. IV.1.2. Organizational structure at Xerox.

tee an integrated marketing strategy (Fig. IV.1.2 and IV.1.1). The Production Systems Group focused on the high-end printing and publishing needs of large enterprises. The Office Document Products Group handled the company's broad line of office copiers, the products that had been once synonymous with Xerox and which remained a core Xerox business. Also within this group are Document Center Systems, the family of digital networked multifunction devices for work groups, and the Xerox line of full-color digital copiers/printers.

The Channels Group focused on retailers, resellers and distributors, where a growing number of customers were turning for their small office/home office needs. The Document Services Group delivered a broad range of document services, all designed to help customers harness technology to improve document production, from creation and storage to distribution and printing. The Supplies Group had been created to meet increasing demand for various document products, including paper, toner, inks and cartridges.

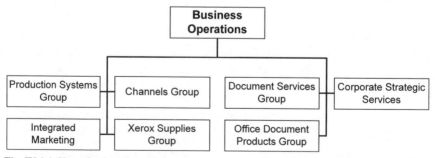

Fig. IV.1.1. Xerox business operations.

Customer Operations

Customer Operations, organized geographically, were responsible for the marketing, sales and servicing of Xerox products and services throughout the world (Fig. IV.1.3).

United States Customer Operations sold and serviced Xerox products and supplies to major accounts and other commercial customers throughout the United States. Americas Customer Operations (ACO) marketed Xerox business products, systems and services through subsidiaries or distributors in more than 30 countries throughout Canada, South and Central America, as well as in the Caribbean. Its largest operating companies were Xerox do Brazil with headquarters in Rio De Janeiro, Brazil; Xerox Canada Inc., with headquarters in North York, Ontario; and Xerox Mexicana with headquarters in Mexico City. Xerox Limited manufactured, marketed and serviced Xerox products in more than 80 countries in Europe, Asia and Africa.

Corporate Strategic Services

Corporate Strategic Services (CSS) were responsible for the manufacturing of Xerox products and consumables. The manufacturing operations had two primary focuses, product/component and supplies/consumables manufacturing. The largest manufacturing site for both product and supplies manufacturing was located in Webster, NY. CSS had sites strategically located worldwide to leverage local resource and distribution as well as trade requirements. Sites were located in Latin America, Canada and Europe.

The Manufacturing Support group (MS) was responsible for worldwide manufacture of all end products and critical components within the Xerox Corporation. Products designed and manufactured by Fuji Xerox further augmented the product portfolio distributed by Xerox Corporation. In addition to its Webster, NY site,

Fig. IV.1.3. Xerox customer operations.

MS had sites in El Segundo, California; Mitcheldean, United Kingdom; Venray, Netherlands; Cairo, Egypt; Toronto, Canada; Rampur, India; Resende, Brazil; Manaus, Brazil; and Aguascalientes, Mexico.

The Supplies Development and Manufacturing Services group (SD&MS) had both the development and manufacturing responsibility for Xerox supplies. These include photoreceptors, toners and developers. In addition to Webster, NY, SD&MS had sites in Oklahoma City, Oklahoma; Oakville, Canada; Salvador; Brazil; Shanghai, China; Venray, Netherlands and Coslada, Spain.

CSS was also responsible for the Integrated Supply Chain with primary responsibility for supply/demand management and forecasting and worldwide distribution services.

Corporate Research and Technology

Corporate Research and Technology had central responsibility for research and technology development in support of existing and emerging Xerox businesses. Its research extended beyond traditional physical and computer sciences to include all aspects of organizational effectiveness, including work practices, customer engagement, and institutional learning. Research was conducted at laboratories and technology centers in the United States, Canada and Europe, in collaboration with research conducted by Fuji Xerox.

CR&T was also home of the Corporate Engineering Center (CEC). The CEC was responsible for defining, developing and maintaining the product development competency within Xerox including work practices, training and development, and tools. The CEC had overall responsibility for the product development process.

Xerox New Enterprises

As the business development arm of Xerox Corporation, Xerox New Enterprises (XNE) was responsible for identifying and bringing to market promising technological breakthroughs that emerge from research and development done by Xerox but fall outside the core business of Xerox Corporation. Xerox New Enterprise Companies were created as independent companies, but with a privileged role under the Xerox corporate umbrella. The companies could tap into established Xerox resources, including corporate engineering, marketing support and professional services - support that was beyond the reach of most start-up companies. Ultimately, XNE companies would either be merged into Xerox Corporation, become majority-owned, publicly traded subsidiaries, or sold. XNE reported to the New Enterprise Board, comprised of senior Xerox executives. At year end 1997 there were eight companies within Xerox New Enterprises:

- Chrystal Software;
- Document Sciences;
- Documentum;
- DpiX;

> **Most important drivers for globalization:**
> 1. Low cost communications;
> 2. Globalization of markets;
> 3. Growth of third world economies;
> 4. Growth of information economies.

- InConcert, Inc.;
- Inxight;
- Semaphore Communications Corporation;
- XE Systems.

Strategic Alliances

In rapidly changing business environment, where strategic collaborations had emerged as a primary means of conducting business, Xerox had continued and strengthened its commitment to the use of alliances to achieve economic success. The largest and most significant example was the strategic partnership with Fuji Photo which had given Xerox a strong market position in Japan and Asia. Xerox recognized early on that the world was being shaped along economic boundaries and that business alliances often would provide the keys to success. They were critical to the future growth of Xerox, they increased its competitive position and they improve the company's ability to meet customer needs.

Xerox' Corporate Alliance Program Directors managed a small number of corporate-wide alliances that provided Xerox with complementary business and product strengths. These alliances included a broad exchange of intellectual property, joint development or joint marketing. Joint strategic planning was conducted on a regular basis.

Examples of these alliances included Adobe, Digital Equipment, IBM, Microsoft, Novell and Sun Microsystems. As both Xerox and the marketplace moved forward, Xerox would identify new alliances to bring added value to its products and its customers. Xerox also had many alliances managed at the Group or Division level that provided similar capabilities for specific product lines.

Competition

Xerox had two sets of competitors. Xerox had traditional Japan-based competitors in the reprographics business such as Canon, Ricoh and Sharp, which were major manufacturers of light-lens copiers. The second set of competitors was focused on the growing domain of network document services. In the production market, there were IBM and Siemens-Oce; in the personal and workgroup markets, there was Hewlett-Packard.

In the United States, large dealer organizations, such as Danka and Alco Standard, which didn't manufacture their own products, were increasingly influential in the marketplace.

2   Research and Development

Since its beginnings as The Haloid Company of Rochester, N.Y., Xerox had always invested a significant portion of its revenue back into basic and applied research. Many of the technologies people then took for granted had their roots in Xerox research laboratories. In 1997, Xerox spent US$ 1.1 billion on research and development, or about 6 percent of its this time US$ 18.2 billion in document processing revenues. The US$ 612 million spent by Fuji Xerox on research and development raised the total Xerox Group commitment to more than US$ 1.7 billion in 1997 alone.

2.1   International Sites of Research and Technology Development

The history of Xerox research dates from the early 1960's. Its growth had been modeled along the lines of the great centralized research organizations such as GE, AT&T, IBM, and DuPont. Meanwhile, the organization had become inherently more decentralized. Geographically distributed centers had embraced the missions, values, and cultures that reflect their particular areas such as imaging sciences in Rochester, digital systems in Palo Alto, chemistry in Canada, information sciences in Cambridge, UK and Grenoble, and low cost design and manufacturing in Japan.

Research and Technology Development at Xerox was centrally managed under the Corporate Research and Technology group with direct line-of-site to the CEO. CR&T had an average annual headcount of 1,320. There were five research sites worldwide, Wilson Center for Research and Technology (WCR&T) in Webster, NY; Palo Alto Research Center (PARC) in Palo Alto, CA; Xerox Research Center of Canada (XRCC) in Mississauga, Canada and the Xerox Research Center Europe (XRCE) with two locations, Grenoble, France, and Cambridge, United Kingdom. Each site had a specific research focus and was strategically located to leverage area industry and academic competencies relevant to that region and research focus.

Technology centers had the primary responsibility for Technology development and delivery to the Business groups. Although management of the technology centers was centralized, resources were located to align with the development groups and manufacturing sites they deliver to. There were three primary technology centers within CR&T. The Digital Imaging Technology Center (DITC) and the Architecture and Document Services Technology Center (ADSTC) had offices in El Segundo, CA; Webster, NY; and Palo Alto, CA; and the technology center within the Wilson Center for Research and Technology had offices in El Segundo, CA and Palo Alto, CA.

Major issues for global R&D management at Xerox:

1. Adapting R&D Management to a worldwide extended enterprise;

2. Adequately trained human resources in systems and software;

3. Creating the 21st century information infrastructure to support seamless worldwide communications.

The *Palo Alto Research Center (PARC)* had been established in 1970. PARC had an average annual headcount of 300. PARC was focused on fundamental research in computer science, document hardware, electronic materials, information sciences, systems study and workgroup practices, that would influence and define the Document Market over the next 10 years. PARC had been responsible for some of the seminal inventions of the computer age: The prototype of the personal computer (Alto). The first Local Area Network for linking office computers (Ethernet) and the first commercial laser printer (the Xerox 9700). Innovations such as icon-based computing - the system of on-screen symbols and a „mouse" pointer to issue commands - and windows-based computing itself also had came into being at PARC. The XNE businesses heavily leveraged PARC technologies as a competitive advantage in their markets. Many of that time XNE businesses were based entirely on technologies developed at PARC.

The *Wilson Center for Research and Technology (WCR&T)* had been established in 1962 in Webster, N.Y. The Wilson Center had an average annual headcount of 424. The center focused on research and technology development that enables digital reproduction of images, known as marking technologies. Scientists at the Wilson Center concentrated on developing better ways to deliver high-quality, permanent images onto paper, with increasing speed, across networks, in black-and-white and color. Their work encompassed the entire scope of document production: the capture of images (from originals in both paper and electronic form); the transfer of images onto paper (marking); paper handling and transport

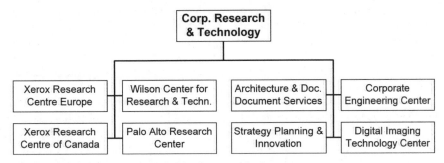

Fig. IV.1.4. Corporate research and technology organization.

(through the copier or printer) and finishing (collating, stapling, binding). The marking technologies developed at the Wilson Center constituted the heart of all Xerox copiers, printers and fax machines. The Wilson Center defines and develops next generation marking technologies 5 to 10 years prior to market realization.

The *Xerox Research Center Europe (XRCE)* had been established in 1993 with laboratories in Grenoble, France, and Cambridge, the United Kingdom. XRCE specialized in the study of human-computer interaction and in technologies for the on-line translation and storage of documents in several languages. XRCE was charged with expanding Xerox' R&D activities in Europe and addressing European-specific issues, a significant proportion of which focused on linguistics. The linguistics technology had a direct market connection via Inxight, one of the XNE companies. XRCE headcount was approximately 75.

The *Xerox Research Center of Canada (XRCC)*, established in 1974, focused primarily on materials research. Staffed by Chemists, Chemical Engineers, the research accomplished at XRCC primarily supports the development and manufacturing of marking materials, such as toner, inks, photoreceptors and developer. The site collaborated closely with the Supplies Development and Manufacturing Services group within CSS. The site included a pilot manufacturing facility that enabled the validation of designs through scale up. Although materials research in support of Xerox consumables was a primary focus of XRCC, research extended to novel materials study in the area of display media (electroluminescent materials, film, etc.) XRCC headcount was approximately 110.

The *Architecture and Document Services Technology Center (ADSTC)* had the primary responsibility for defining the Xerox product architecture. This includes the definition of the Network Document Environment which will define the standard network interfaces, capabilities and relationships of Xerox networked products both as the interface externally via standard communications protocols and as the interoperator with each other. The technology center defined standards internally and seeks to influence the development and publication of external standard bodies. A recent example was the development of the Digital Property Rights Language, which had been adopted by IBM. The adoption and standardization of Xerox developed protocols and standards provided significant advantage to Xerox. ADSTC had an average annual headcount of 125.

The *Digital Imaging Technology Center (DITC)* provided imaging and computational platform technologies in support of Xerox network printers. Focused primarily on Imaging Science, DITC provided Xerox with a significant competitive advantage by enabling benchmark RIP (raster image processing) time through proprietary algorithms and encoded VLSI designs. As Xerox focused primarily on full color images, DITC research in area of color image compression/decompression and color management from creation to storage and print, was increasingly critical. DITC had an average annual headcount of 210.

Xerox research was further extended by leveraging the Fuji Xerox relationship. Fuji Xerox had two research locations in Japan and had recently located a research facility in Palo Alto, CA. Research at Xerox and Fuji Xerox was co-managed by the Technology Executive Committee (TEC). The TEC seeks to leverage research and technology activities within the Xerox Group to deliver a full range of products across the international market. The TEC was composed of senior research and engineering managers as well as senior mangers of strategy and planning.

2.2   *Engineering and Product Development*

Management of development was decentralized to align with the five business groups. Each business group had direct control of development management, spend and focus to address its specific market requirements. Development teams were geographically collocated with the primary manufacturing sites serving their respective product markets. The largest manufacturing site was in Webster, NY responsible for approximately 65% of Xerox manufactured end products (excludes products manufactured by Fuji Xerox). Development teams located in Webster were primarily responsible for the design and development of digital reprographic and network printing products. The second largest manufacturing site in the United States was El Segundo, CA, responsible primarily for component/electronic manufacturing including ASIC and the Raster Output Scanner (ROS) manufacture. Development teams located in El Segundo were primarily responsible for design and development of components as stated, in addition the development resources responsible for the centralized printing products were also located in El Segundo. These resources were predominantly electrical, software and systems engineers. Although there were no manufacturing facilities in Palo Alto, CA, this site was the third largest development center in the United States. Development in Palo Alto focused primarily on Software product development.

Organization of development resources varied by and within business groups (Fig. IV.1.5). Each structure seeks to balance the benefits of a vertical competency based structure (e.g. Mechanical Design and Engineering, Software Engineering, Systems Engineering and Program Support) and a horizontal Product/Program based structure (e.g. Product Team A, Product Team B, etc).

Many groups had evolved a development infrastructure that was a hybrid of these two structures. These groups had established business teams and competency centers to manage their product development and delivery requirements. Large vertical competency centers had been established with appropriate subcompetencies (e.g. Client Applications and Operation System S/W within the Software Engineering competency center). These subcompetencies were then organized by product program. Business teams have been established to address specific segments of the business group market. These business teams were comprised of a product/program management team with product support personnel reporting directly and appropriate development resources 'matrixed' in from the vertical competency centers.

In the case of large multiyear product programs usually surrounding a product platform introduction, supporting development and engineering resources reported directly into the product program team. These programs are large enough to enable vertical competency alignment and resultant benefits within the program team structure.

3   R&D Coordination

3.1   Management of Research and Technology

The senior vice-president of Corporate Research and Technology, was responsible for the corporation's technology management process. As a core member of the corporation's central Strategy Committee the leadership of CR&T had shared responsibility for the corporation's overall strategic intent, direction and resource allocation.

The *Technology Decision Making Board (TDMB)* which was comprised of senior R&D managers from CR&T, the Business Groups, Manufacturing, and Corporate Strategy was a key governance facility in the technology management process. The TDMB oversees the corporation's technology investments. Chaired by the senior vice-president of CR&T, the board established a community of senior managers who held a common understanding of and perspective on technology issues over the entire range of businesses.

The heads of Corporate Research and Technology and the Corporate Strategy Office had provided recommendations to the Corporate Strategy Committee on the level of investment for the corporation's research, development, and engineering operations over a three-year strategic timeframe

Research and technology investments had become a key part of the corporation's strategic planning process. There had been four types of investments in the central research and technology organization: pioneering research, identification of emergent markets and technologies, strategic capability development and core technology.

Investment in pioneering research, funded centrally by the corporation, was characterized by high levels of uncertainty. It had the purpose of discovering emergent technologies that could shape the company's strategic vision and generate future options. Areas of investment were determined by the technical vision of the research management.

Investment in the *identification of emergent markets and technologies* permits the exploration of opportunities and uncertainties associated with markets that were presently outside the scope of existing business divisions but could expand

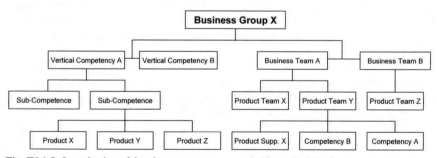

Fig. IV.1.5. Organization of development resources varied by and within business groups.

the company's vision of its role as the document company. Protobusinesses were centrally funded by the corporation and employ technology developed by the research centers.

The third type of investment - investment in *strategic capability* - had the purpose of establishing new technology platforms and skills that were of recognized importance to the company. Strategic capability was responsive to the Technology Decision Making Board. Major technology investments were shared across divisions and charged collectively to them in proportion to the size of their product development and engineering investments. This type of investment was clear on the possibilities of a specific emergent technology but could be uncertain about its technical feasibility and timing.

The fourth type of investment was in *core technology*. This was technology that was ready for use in existing or emerging businesses. Investments were contracted with the responsible business entity and charged to the cost of engaging the opportunity. This type of investment, often premised on learning and experience derived from the foregoing types of investments, has had the lowest level of uncertainty.

Research and Technology investments account for approximately 22% of the total R&D investment. Approximately 50% of that investment was allocated to pioneering research and identification of emergent markets and technology; 25% was allocated to strategic capability, and 25% was allocated to core technology.

3.2   R&D Projects per Site

Research project selections were determined by the Corporate Research and Technology senior management team. Each research site had a broad mission that defines the scope of its projects. Projects were selected within those broad missions as they aligned with the strategic direction of the company, emerging technologies both internally and externally developed, and emergent market requirements. For pioneering research overall strategic vision from the corporate level defines emergent market and technology domains of interest. Three to five year goals were defined within CR&T which were refreshed and restated as annual objectives based on the intersection of the three forces (corporate strategy, market needs, emerging technologies). Within the boundaries of these goals and objectives the local technical contributors have defined specific areas of research. For core technology, projects have been initiated by and aligned with the requirements of business divisions.

Development programs were selected to address the unique market requirements of each business group. Each business group managed a portfolio of products in various stages of development and continuing engineering to meet profit and revenue growth objectives. As there were often competing priorities coupled with resource limitations to support multiple programs, the group presidents and senior VP for manufacturing were the ultimate decision makers for the selection and prioritization as well as the cancellation of product programs.

3.3   Project Rview

Within Corporate Research and Technology, the laboratory site management, the technology platform managers and the senior VP for research and technology (depending on the scope and scale of the program) provided overall review and inspection of projects. Technologies that had been contracted to one or more business groups undergo a rigorous structured review process lead jointly by the appropriate technology center and business group management teams. Review structure and content for projects that had not been contracted was dependent on the phase of research and technology development the project was in.

The transition from research to technology development and finally product integration has occurred in three phases:

- Map the concept space for future options;
- Define Markets and commitment for emergent options;
- Mature and deliver committed technology platforms.

Map the Concept Space for Future Options

In the first phase, the pure research stage, concept space was mapped and scanned for opportunities that would ultimately be leveragable in the market. The mapping of the concept space involved a review of emergent markets and technology and feasible intersections with Xerox Corporation's market and strategy. For example, the intersection of the Internet and resultant capabilities (e.g. electronic commerce) and the document life cycle. Options were defined, studied and matured, however only a small percentage of these options would hold future value for the Document Company. Only these options, following some early validation of concept and definition of broad alignment with strategic vision, would move into the next phase. It was also in this phase of research that predictive concepts of the future were defined, studied and tested.

Define Markets and Commitment for Emergent Options

In the second phase, the option were further matured and tested. Market concepts were defined and early indicators of economic value were measured. The objective of this phase was to develop the concept and technology sufficiently to obtain business sponsorship for further development and ultimately product integration. Options emerging from this phase were of two types: Research that supported and sustained existing businesses and technologies and research that seek to expand existing markets or create new market opportunities for Xerox. The research that supported and sustained existing business and technologies was supported by a well-defined business model and supporting business processes. This research seek to improve upon or completely replace existing technology by uplifting one or more critical parameters. The key questions to be addressed were: Would it work and does the business opportunity support the development schedule and expense? Positive responses to these two questions signaled the transition to technology development. 'Does it work' was usually demonstrable at a lab level with supporting feasibility studies. The business groups determined the business opportunities. When a business group contracted a research project, these questions had usually been answered positively and the research project was formally considered to have moved into the technology development stage.

Research that seek to expand existing markets or create new market opportunities was focused on Xerox broader strategic vision. Business models supporting these research initiatives were undefined; relationships to existing businesses were only loosely mapped. To support the transition from research to technology development the key questions to be addressed were what's the business model and business case, how does that business fit within the Xerox existing businesses and strategic vision and, of course, does it work. The business model definition and business plan development was the primary determinant of transition. The markets and technologies addressed by these research initiatives were still emerging. Therefore, the task of defining and validating business models was significant. Business skills required to support these analyses were traditionally resident to the business groups and were focused on existing businesses. To address this gap CR&T had defined a small group of business principles focused on new business development. Once the key questions were answered and funding was secured the research project was considered to have moved into the technology development stage. Although some were formally contracted with a business group or groups, technologies could also be spun out as new businesses within Xerox New Enterprises, sold or licensed out.

Mature and Deliver Committed Technology Platforms

Technology delivered to the business groups was primarily integrated with existing and commercial technologies to develop new product concepts. The focus of this phase was to mature and demonstrate the technology platform within the context of a system. This phase occurred within the define phase of the Time to Market product development process. During the define phase responsible scientists and engineers from CR&T collaborated with the product development engineers from the business groups to integrate and mature the technology. Prior to entering the Design phase, all products must evaluate technology readiness. This review focused primarily on the new technologies as they integrated to define the product. Technology latitudes, critical parameters, producibility, failure modes and manufacturing/sourcing positions must be well understood and demonstrated before the program could proceed to the design phase. Successful demonstration of technology readiness served as the 'handoff' from technology development to product development. Although the technologists continued to participate as consultants the level of participation greatly reduced as the product matured.

In addition to technology readiness, there were several review intervals or checkpoints required in the Time to Market (TTM) product development process. The primary reviews occurred at major phase-gates in the development process; Define, Design, Demonstrate, Deliver and Delight (customers). These major assessments included a team of subject matter experts, external to the program, who reviewed the program progress to determine readiness to move into the next development stage. Criteria to 'pass' each gate were clearly defined within the TTM process.

4   R&D Instruments and Procedures

By far the most important tool in use was the Xerox Time to Market (TTM) core process. The TTM core process represented a structured approach to product development and delivery from market planning, through product concept, design, development and delivery. Two key elements of the TTM core process were a common phased product development and delivery structure used throughout the corporation and a market oriented front end for developing the Market and Product Strategy Visions and Market Attack Plans with supporting technology and value chain strategies and plans. The TTM program addressed several critical enablers in support of its goals of UMC reduction, New Product Revenue Ratio (NPRR) growth, and of course, reduced Time to Market. These included a focus on the engineering environment both from a skills and tools perspective. The focus on the growth and development of engineering competency had led to the development of the Xerox Engineering Excellence Institute. This program recognized developmental requirements of the engineering community in design practices, systems engineering, critical parameter analysis, etc. that were often not included in the College Curriculum. Previously these basic tools had been acquired 'on the job', which had led to uneven understanding and practice as well as limited competencies in areas of system engineering and design. In addition to the Engineering Excellence program, Xerox was focusing on rapidly maturing its software development environment through the introduction and implementation of the Carnegie Mellon program in Software Process Improvement (SPI). The program includes an assessment of current capability and a structured maturity growth model. SPI was increasingly important to Xerox as the digitization and networking of the Xerox product family required an increasing investment in Software Development.

The selection and standardization of the engineering design environment (CAD/CAM) was the second element of the overall focus on the engineering environment. Prior to this effort each development team had selected their toolset based on program requirements and internal assessments. The result of this method had been often incompatible environments across Xerox and Fuji Xerox. Sharing of engineering files across programs for reuse required additional time for 'translation' of files often manually between the two systems. The standard CAD/CAM toolset, selected in 1997 provided an integrated environment for design analysis through drawing release. The selection of a standard environment enabled the development and maintenance of the engineering database which in turn enabled knowledge sharing across communities, organizations and worldwide. Reduced time benefits were anticipated in multinationalization of products, tooling costs and error reductions.

5 An International R&D Project: XTRAS

The Xerox Palo Alto Research Center (PARC) and Xerox Research Center Europe (XRCE) – Grenoble, were both active in the development of linguistic technologies. PARC had a long research tradition in this area, and XRCE had made linguistic technologies a strategic component of its investment.

It had been natural for the two centers to organize a technical cooperation. Based upon preliminary results of a development project conducted in XRCE, a team had been put in place to develop a product and service offering, a business case and business plan, engaged early customers and found a home for the to-be-created business: this was the project XTRAS (Xerox Translation and Authoring Systems).

Seeking New Opportunities

The XTRAS project had fallen into the category of research that 'seeks to expand existing markets or create new market opportunities'. The technology results, and early customer feedback (internal to Xerox: Xerox Business Services provider of translation services, Xerox Inxight provider of linguistic tools and the internal translation center) from the initial research project had provided indication that a business might be viable. Funding had been required to

- Define the business model and business case;
- Define any alignment with existing Xerox businesses and appropriate organization and;
- Demonstrate the technology ('does it work').

The required funding had been requested from a corporate fund specifically targeted at cultivating research and technology initiatives that extended beyond the scope of existing Xerox businesses. This fund was managed by the Corporate Innovation Council (CIC) co-chaired by the Sr. Vice-President of CR&T and the Executive Vice-President of Corporate Strategy with participation from the Business Group Strategy officers and the Xerox New Enterprises. To gain support of the Innovation Council, a small core team involving the two research centers, the internal business customers, internal business development consultants and external consultants had been formed. This team had been expanded with a number of technologists after CIC approval and a formal project was launched.

Managing the Project

The project had been organized in a straightforward manner: a project leader, a business team and a technical team. No less than seven Xerox organizations had participated in the project distributed across four sites in the United States and Europe. The majority of the management team had participated on a part time basis only, however the distributed nature of the project had offered the most significant management challenges.

> **Major innovative break-throughs at Xerox (last five years):**
> 1. Digital Reprographics;
> 2. Low cost and high quality color;
> 3. Internet enabled documents and work practices.

The main issues to be dealt with in managing the project had been threefold: managing an internationally distributed team; coordinating and collaborating with potentially competing teams (the business to be created could be seen as competing with current product and service offerings, as well as internal translation services); and validating the product / service concept and business models. The management coordination had been done through the use of collaborative tools such as video conferencing, significantly reducing the requirement, frequency and cost of 'face-to-face' meetings. The technical team had been co-located in Grenoble, with the project leader.

Objectives and enablers had been defined from the beginning: available funding, customer engagement requirements and target dates for business proposal delivery. Key actions had been conducted in parallel to enable rapid time to market. An intense effort to recruit early customers had helped to understand the business model and build a business case. These had lead customers contracted with the Xerox Professional Document Services team, the consulting arm for Xerox, with support from the technical team.

The success of the project had been due to the tight coordination between the technical and business teams. It had been key to the evolution of the concepts on which the business was created.

Lessons Learned

The major learning surrounded international project management in a large corporation. In the XTRAS case the establishment and maintenance of multiple collaborations at appropriate levels of decision authority was critical. While at the working level a large number of collaborations were established between the various camps, the business teams management was not engaged early enough through their respective participants in the project, contrary to the assumptions made by the project management team. This gap could have led to delays in decision making and ultimately the launch of the business. The XTRAS management team, recognizing this shortfall, organized a crash program to get the appropriate management levels involved.

The distributed aspect of the project, both geographically and organizationally offered the most significant management challenges however the richness brought by the various viewpoints of the different cultures and organizations was a key to its success.

Lessons learned for organizing R&D at Xerox:

1. Mastering the confluence of emerging business opportunities and emergent technologies;

2. Fast time to market;

3. Architecting technology in order to create new revenue and profit streams in new markets.

---

6   Conclusions

The challenge to Xerox R&D and to all traditionally established organizations was the rapid change of the underlying technologies of the business and the impacts of global shifts in the economy. Xerox, a relatively young company with a worldwide presence and a strong technology leadership tradition, was better positioned with respect to this challenge than many companies. It remained a challenge never the less.

The changes that we were experiencing occurred in timeframes that were relatively short in comparison to traditional organizational growth and human career development. In this environment, the winning organization would be highly innovative across parts of its business and would be a highly adaptive and rapid learning.

Over the next decade the challenge would be the creation of R&D organizations, that serve highly networked and globally distributed inter and intra enterprises, which excel at the creation, development and acquisition of technologies, products, and core competencies and serve customers on a world-wide basis.

IV.2 Canon: R&D –Driver for Continuous Growth and Diversification*

1   Continuous Growth and Diversification

1.1   Working for the Common Good

Guided by the company's „*Kyosei*" philosophy, i.e. living and working together for the common good, Canon has been in operation since its foundation in 1937. In 1997 the company celebrated its 60th anniversary employing more than 75'000 people worldwide.

In the fiscal year 1996 Canon recorded remarkable results: consolidated sales amounted to ¥2,558 billion (US$ 22.054 billion) representing an increase of 18% over the previous year, and net income was ¥94.177 billion (US$ 811.9 million), up 71%. The scope of the company's products was wide ranging: (i) business machine printers and laser beam printers (35% of 1996 sales); (ii) business systems such as computers, including copiers (32%), computer peripherals such as bubble jet faxes and micro-graphics (17%); (iii) cameras including SLR cameras, compact cameras and 8mm camcorders (8%); and (iv) optical products such as semiconductor production equipment, medical and broadcasting equipment (6%). Although Canon initially focused on the camera business, sales in this area dropped to 8% (non consolidated sales in 1996).

1.2   Continuous Growth and Diversification

Canon's evolution was characterized by *continuous growth* and *diversification*. Fig. IV.2.1 shows sales of Canon Inc. for the different product categories from 1980 to 1995. Each product category experienced gradual growth with new product ranges being introduced. The corporation was striving for diversification of business areas (vertical diversification) and of products within an existing business area (horizontal diversification). Research and development has been an important

*   Author is *Dr. Yasuo Kozato,* Manager, Global Research Promotion Project at Research and Development Headquarters, Canon Inc. This case study was written in 1998: The reader should keep in mind that all numbers, figures, organization charts and forecasts represent the state of 1998 or before. The case study was revised by *Ursula Deplazes* in 2007.

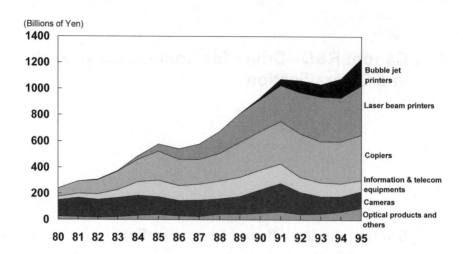

Fig. IV.2.1. Sales by product 1980 - 1995 (Canon Inc., not consolidated).

driver of diversification. In the late 1990s, Canon Inc. was entering the so-called „*multimedia era*" and much R&D effort was dedicated to this very promising business area.

In 1991 „Five Principles for Canon's R&D Activities" were defined:

- We reject research and development for military purposes.
- We do not conduct R&D that is not desirable from an ecological point of view.
- We develop previously unexplored technologies and product categories.
- We respect technologies or products created by others.
- We conduct R&D activities on a global scale and create new business activities where research took place.

No. 1 is obvious. Even if we developed, for instance, technologies for image detection and recognition, we will never use them for producing military weapons. Principle No. 2 may be illustrated with R&D in solar cells. These ecologically desirable products were developed by Canon and passed to business operation in the late 1990's. Principle No. 3 is particularly important as only truly unique technology enables great diversification in the product range. No. 4 is related to Canon's pursuit of its own unique technology, the basis for new alliances. Principle No. 5 refers to global R&D aspects which are the core issue of this case study.

Canon has been very keen on generating unique technology. This is shown in the number of patents the corporation holds. Tab IV.2.1 shows the top 10 corporations that received US patents from 1992 to 1997. Canon has consistently been among the top three companies.

2   R&D Organization

2.1   R&D Resources

In 1996, we spent ¥150,085 million in R&D – the equivalent of 5.9% of consolidated sales or 12.0% of Canon Inc. sales. Fig. IV.2.2 illustrates the development of R&D expenditure from 1983 to 1996. 6,000 employees (33% of the work force of Canon Inc.) were employed in R&D in 1996 (Fig. IV.2.3).

2.2   Company Organization

Fig. IV.2.4 illustrates the organization chart of Canon Inc. as of January 1997. Basically, the whole company was divided into two parts: headquarters and business operations. Headquarters included (i) general administration divisions such as personnel and accounting, and (ii) general service divisions such as quality management, intellectual properties and information systems. R&D in headquarters included (i) Research and Development Headquarters (R&D HQ) and (ii) Product Development Headquarters (PDHQ). R&D HQ dealt with mid- and long-term R&D issues requiring three years or more to deal with. PDHQ dealt mid-range projects aiming at developing a specific product range which could not be attributed to the existing business groups.

As for business operations, there were six major business headquarters. Each headquarter consisted of several business groups. For instance, Office Imaging Product Headquarters covered a Copier Group, a Fax Group, a Scanner Group, etc. Each business group had its own development center whose mission was to design products for the business group. Therefore, time-horizon of these develop-

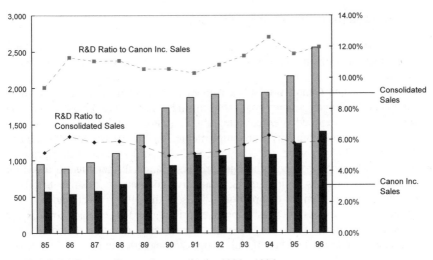

Fig. IV.2.2. R&D expenditure ratio to total sales 1985 – 1996.

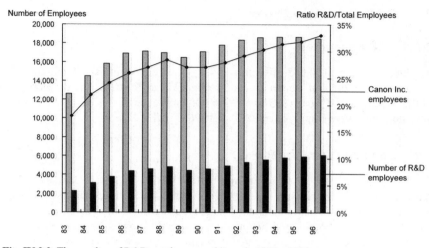

Fig. IV.2.3. The number of R&D employees and its ratio 1983 - 1996.

ment centers was usually one to two years. Fig. IV.2.6 shows the location of Canon's major R&D organizations in Japan in 1997. Although most centers were located around Tokyo with Shimomaruko headquarters as its center, there had been a slight tendency to decentralize the R&D centers. Examples include Fuji-Susono Research Park which opened in 1996 and became a major R&D center for new electrophotographic technologies.

3   R&D Coordination

3.1   Management Direction and R&D Issues

Fig. IV.2.5 illustrates Canon's past activities and strategies for R&D from 1960 onward. R&D sections implemented top management directions by fixing appropriate R&D goals.

In the 60's when Canon was still a camera company, top management introduced diversification as a major goal. Thus business machines such as copiers and facsimiles were developed. Vertical integration and horizontal diversification (i.e. business group reinforcement) were implemented in the 1970's and 80's. *Four Major Product Targets* were set. They covered camcorders, laser beam printers, Japanese word processors and bubble-jet printers. Canon further tried to diversify into new product ranges by integrating innovative components in order to differentiate its products from its competitors'. Thus in the 1980's R&D defined key components and devices such as bubble-jet printing heads, contact sensors for small-size faxes and BASIS image sensors for distance detectors (used in EOS series cameras and high-end faxes) and for optical magnetic memory.

3.2   Planning of R&D Projects

The annual procedure for choosing R&D projects involved mid-term planning where broad objectives for the coming three years were determined for each organization. Mid-term planning was based on a revolving plan: results of the first year determined the budget of the following year; in the second year a new mid-term plan for the following three years was set up.

In the case of R&D centers, a mid-term plan for each project or division was determined. These plans were then combined to form the mid-term plan of the concerned R&D center. This plan was presented to top management for approval. Finally, the budgeting process for the following year took place.

Although the mid-term plan defined main goals and major projects of an organization for the coming three years, it may not have covered all R&D projects undertaken. Usually the details of the projects were proposed to the director in charge of R&D. If he decided that a project was important for the whole company, it was passed on to the top executive meeting. This procedure was very often adapted to each particular project.

The planning procedure described above combined top-down and bottom-up procedures. Projects with significant effects on the company's strategy were decided upon in top executive meetings. The other projects were dealt with locally.

We believe that the coexistence of top-down, i.e. with greater focus and lots of resources, and bottom-up, i.e. broader in scope and with few resources, was very

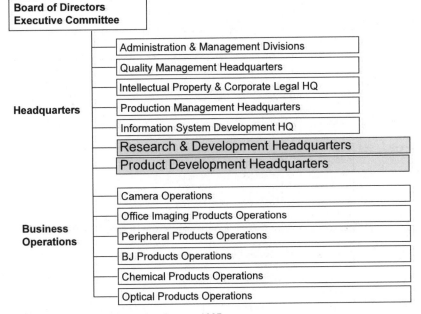

Fig. IV.2.4. Canon Inc. Organization January 1997.

important for corporate R&D. If on one hand excessive focusing and selection of R&D projects had been implemented, many new businesses would have been set up in the mid-term (i.e. in around three years). However, the longer term business performance would have been weakened. If on the other hand too many small R&D projects had been carried out (we call this „sowing the seeds"), it would have been difficult to focus the resources on promising items. Therefore, the emphasis was on focusing and sowing the seeds at the same time.

3.3   Other Means for R&D Promotion

Another important aspect of R&D was the promotion of communication between various groups.

As an example, we organized annual internal exhibitions of technologies, where many engineers and researchers met. It was an opportunity to share new trends in technology. These exhibitions were held around the same time as "global conferences". In theses conferences employees from various business areas such as R&D, sales, marketing and production of the world-wide branches of the Canon group met. These conferences were good occasions for R&D employees to exchange information and ideas with employees of other business areas.

Infrastructure for computer communication had become very important in the 1990's. Canon met this challenge offering (i) access to Internet for communication with non-Canon employees and (ii) Intranet for communication within the corporation.

Table IV.2.1. Top 10 corporations receiving US patents 1992 - 1997.

1992		1993		1994		1995		1996		1997	
Company	No.	Company	No.	Company	No.	Company	No.	Company	No.	Company	No.
CANON	1106	IBM	1085	IBM	1298	IBM	1383	IBM	1867	IBM	1724
Toshiba	1020	Toshiba	1040	CANON	1096	CANON	1087	CANON	1541	CANON	1381
Mitsubishi Electric	957	CANON	1038	Hitachi	976	Motorola	1012	Motorola	1064	NEC	1095
Hitachi	951	Eastman Kodak	1007	GE	970	NEC	1005	NEC	1043	Motorola	1058
GE	937	GE	932	Mitshubishi Electric	970	Mitsubishi Electric	937	Hitachi	963	Fujitsu	903
IBM	842	Mitsubishi Electric	926	Toshiba	968	Toshiba	969	Mitsubishi Electric	934	Hitachi	903
Eastman Kodak	775	Hitachi	912	NEC	897	Hitachi	910	Toshiba	914	Mitsubishi Electric	892
Motorola	658	Motorola	729	Eastman Kodak	888	Matsushita Electric	854	Fujitsu	869	Toshiba	862
Fuji Photo Film	640	Matsushita Electric	712	Motorola	837	Eastman Kodak	772	Sony	855	Sony	859
Matsushita Electric	608	Fuji Photo Film	632	Matsushita Electric	771	GE	758	Matsushita Electric	841	Eastman Kodak	759

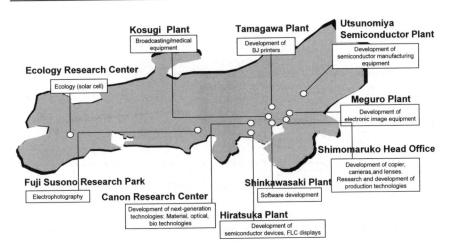

Figure 7 Major R&D Sites in Japan

Fig. IV.2.5. Major R&D sites in Japan, 1997.

4 Overseas R&D Centers

4.1 Overview of Overseas R&D Centers

Canon had six R&D centers outside Japan. Table IV.2.2 outlines these centers. CRE which was located near the University of Surrey, Guildford, UK, was the first overseas R&D center. Its establishment had been announced during Canon's technical expo held in London to celebrate its 50th anniversary. As expressed in the fifth principle for Canon's R&D activities, R&D results were to be exploited in the country where the research took place. An example is Criterion Software Ltd. (CSL) in Guildford, UK. Its mission within the Canon group was to develop and market the interactive 3D graphics software known as *RenderWare*, which was originally an R&D project of CRE. This project will be discussed later on in this case study as an example of an international R&D project. CSL was licensing RenderWare and focusing on producing game software based on its interactive 3D graphics expertise. This expertise opened Canon the door to the multimedia business.

R&D in overseas labs was complementary to the expertise of Japanese R&D centers as overseas labs had been established according to the needs for new technologies manifested by Japanese R&D centers. For example, one of the CIS's areas of expertise was the development of driver software. This software was necessary to connect equipment (e.g. printers, copiers and digital cameras) to a computer or a network. In order to develop this expertise, CIS had on one hand to be informed about new releases of operating and network systems and on the other

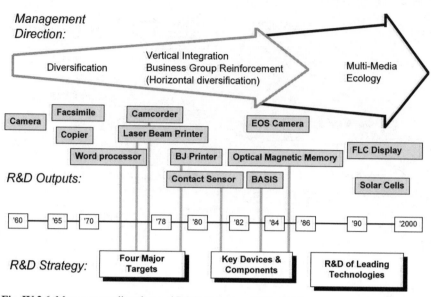

Fig. IV.2.6. Management direction and R&D strategies, 1960 - 2000.

hand work in a fast changing environment where standards changed frequently. Additionally people with good technical skills in very specific domains were needed. These were the reasons why CIS was set up on the West Coast of the US.

Some overseas labs had the largest R&D groups in particular technological areas: CISRA for example had the largest image processing group. In a global corporate structure, cooperation between organizations of different functions and different locations was essential. Thus, clear positioning of each R&D center was necessary. In the late 1990's *One-Lab One-Concept* had been emphasized for overseas R&D in order to clarify their positioning.

Overseas R&D centers tended to develop expertise in software in order to complement Canon's Japanese hardware expertise. However, CRA had planned to widen its expertise in document processing software and systems. It thus opened an R&D center focused on a non-software area. This was a new challenge for Canon which had the potential to change the structure of the corporation's R&D activities. CSME was the last overseas R&D center established in 1995.

4.2   Management of Overseas R&D Centers

The basic aims of overseas R&D centers were:

- To create technologies that will become the seeds of new business by ideas and approaches that do not exist in Japan.
- To satisfy Canon Group's need by research and development utilizing local resources (humans and technologies).

The expression in aim #1, „do not exist", was very important. It represented the company's desire to search for new sources of diversification. Aim #2 can be interpreted as carrying out R&D activities in the most appropriate geographical area in the world. Thus R&D could have taken place not only in advanced countries but also in certain Asian countries where skilled but less expensive R&D resources were available. However, Canon decided to capitalize on R&D opportunities in Asian countries by investing in local companies as opposed to establishing its own R&D subsidiaries.

Overseas R&D centers undertook projects contributing to either of the mentioned basic R&D aims. However, according to their main focus, overseas R&D centers were divided in two groups:

- CRE, CRA, CRF: As the "R"s in the middle of the names suggest, the main emphasis of these centers was on research.
- CIS, CISRA, CSME: Theses centers focused on development to meet the needs of other business groups and sales companies. Thus stronger coordination within the Canon group was important.

Management structure of these two groups of overseas R&D centers is illustrated in Fig. IV.2.7. Two contact points, one in R&D HQ and the other in PDHQ, played an important role in the company-wide exchange of R&D findings. Thus one of the functions of these two window organizations was to transfer R&D results to business groups. Overseas centers were funded according to the following principle: whoever benefits, pays. However, HQ had to contribute some significant funds for the overseas R&D centers. Thus, funds for CRE, CRA and CRF were mainly provided by business groups and R&D HQ - the latter contributing most of the funds. CIS and CISRA were partially funded by business groups and PDHQ covered the remaining financial needs. In the late 1990's a gradual increase in the funding by regional group companies such as Canon USA and Canon Europe took place. CSME was the only overseas R&D center that received most of the funds from Canon Europe and not from HQ. This was due to the fact that the center was established to meet the R&D needs of Canon Europe.

Although the main emphasis of the above mentioned two groups of overseas R&D centers differed, there were increasing needs for inter-organizational cooperation. For example, when a research project of a center in the R&D HQ reached the stage of exploitation, cooperation with business groups became essential. Thus

---

Significant drivers of globalization:

1. Corporate Kyosei philosophy (living and working together for the common good);

2. R&D established in the best places and conducted by the best people;

3. Mixture of talents and their synergy effects.

Major issues for global R&D management at Canon:

1. Global project set-up and optimal resource allocation;

2. Making R&D fruits into the assets of the whole group;

3. Innovation management in a distributed environment;

4. Better coordination, collaboration and communication.

---

a temporary team, a task force, was set up. Working with task forces has a long tradition in Canon's R&D domain. A task force is a cross functional team involving different organizations to pursue a specific purpose. The members of a task force are selected from organizations offering the required competencies, and the chief of a task force is appointed by the director in charge of the task. A task force is set up for a time period ranging from 3 months to two years depending on the scope of the project. Setting up global task forces which involve overseas R&D members was relatively new. Thus new management expertise had to be developed to make company-wide task forces work.

There were several other issues concerning overseas R&D centers. For instance a computer network infrastructure had to be implemented. These common issues were discussed twice a year in face-to-face global meetings where overseas R&D employees met.

4.3   From Overseas R&D to Global R&D

The ten-year history of overseas R&D activities can be divided into three phases:

Phase I (1988 - 1992): Starting-up period

- Build up R&D organizations
- Recruit key people
- Start R&D activities

Phase II (1993 - 1995): Ripening of R&D fruits

- Continue R&D activities and build up technical strengths
- Conduct trial business operations including, e.g. establishment of Criterion Software.

Phase III (1996 -): Transition from overseas R&D to global R&D

- Position each center in a global context
- Conduct global cooperation to follow Canon's strategy and improved improve results

Phases I and II are based on the 5th principle of Canon's R&D activities. Specifically, "We conduct R&D activities on a global scale and create new business

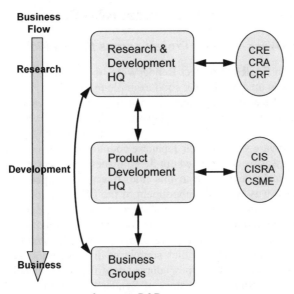

Fig. IV.2.7. Management structure of overseas R&D centers.

activities where research took place". As was mentioned above overseas R&D aimed at two objectives.

However, the company's focus turned to greater globalization. Thus Canon developed more appropriate approaches to exploit R&D findings. The 5th principle stated above became obsolete. The corporation determined that commercialization of R&D results should take place in the most appropriate place in the world, and not in the country where the corresponding research was conducted. There have been three main driving forces responsible for the mentioned change: (i) Canon stressed the importance of near-market development to offer greater benefits to customers. (ii) The trend to increased global cooperation became more apparent when Canon's products shifted from stand-alone products to systems based on networks. (iii) The nature of leading edge technologies was inherently local. Perrino and Tipping (1989) wrote that advanced technologies had been produced in „the pockets of innovations around the world", due to the fact that these technologies were people oriented. All these changes (i – iii) made it more difficult for R&D engineers to foresee the possible uses of items they had developed. Thus, a more market-oriented approach to development was necessary. Additionally, global cooperation was to be emphasized. Under these circumstances the best solution was to develop clearly defined strengths in a certain field of technology and exploit the findings of R&D in the most appropriate place in the world.

5   Example of an International R&D Project

5.1   RenderWare – a Joint Project across the Pacific

We have chosen the R&D project RenderWare, the software technology for fast 3D graphics taken up at CRE, as a good example to discuss.

At Canon an international project was usually a joint project between one of the overseas R&D centers and a related Japanese R&D division. Since many of our overseas R&D centers have had expertise in software, they typically complemented the hardware skills of their Japanese counterparts. Business exploitation of the R&D result was usually carried out by a Japanese business group. The Render-Ware project was an exception to this rule. It was developed and implemented overseas. Thus it was an ideal embodiment of the fifth principle of Canon's R&D activities. It also fulfilled the first aim of overseas R&D, i.e. develop technologies with business potential based on ideas and approaches that do not exist in Japan.

Based on this example we would like to address on one hand the uniqueness of Canon's international R&D, in which sources of diversification are sought worldwide, and on the other hand the procedures and difficulties related to this uniqueness. Fig. IV.2.8 illustrates the history of RenderWare from its early R&D stage onward.

5.2   Selection of the Project

Most R&D projects taken up at overseas R&D centers were based on an entrusted R&D contract between Canon Inc. and the corresponding overseas center. Although the importance of local cooperation had been emphasized and the portion of local funding was increasing, the major funding was still provided by Canon Inc. This was due to the fact that in the 1990's Canon Inc. was the headquarters of the Canon group and corporate R&D of the group was controlled by Canon Inc.

Table IV.2.2. Overview of overseas R&D Centers (end 1996).

Name	Location	Year	Employees	Area of R&D
CRE Canon Research Center Europe Ltd.	Surrey, UK	1988	37	Human Interface Technology
CIS Canon Information Systems, Inc.	California, USA	1990	144	Software Development for Canon Products
CRA Canon Research Center America, Inc.	California, USA	1990	25	Documentation Related Systems
CRF Canon Research Center France SA	Rennes, France	1990	52	Communication Technology
CISRA Canon Information Systems Research Australia	Sydney, Australia	1990	69	Image Processing
CSME Canon Systems Management Europe	Berkshire, UK	1995	63	Software Support and Localization

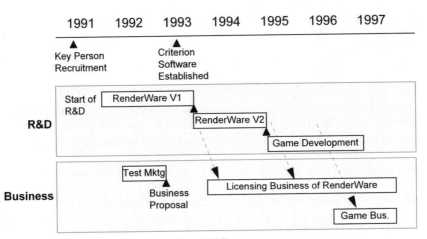

Fig. IV.2.8. RenderWare development (1991 – 1997).

The typical process for choosing an R&D project was initiated by either:

- A request from a Japanese R&D center or business group, or
- A proposal from an overseas R&D center.

There is no need to explain about the former case, since it corresponds to normal practice of entrusted R&D projects. The latter case may need some explanation because it considers overseas sources of diversification. The procedure of selection of an R&D project based on a proposal from an overseas R&D center was as follows:

(i) A proposal was presented to the directors of the corresponding overseas R&D center. A corporate guideline determined that each overseas R&D center should include a related Canon Inc. director, such as the director in charge of R&D, a director of the regional principal company, such as Canon Europe or Canon USA, and a local person who was in charge of the operative business of the R&D center. Thus, corporate as well as local interests were taken into account.

(ii) After approval by the directors, an advisor was appointed. His function was to further analyze the project and make sure that it would not lead to inappropriate diversification of the company. The reason was that the outcome of an entrusted R&D project, such as intellectual properties, belonged to Canon Inc. If the project was carried out in close cooperation with the HQ, the advisor would usually be a manager of the partner department at Canon Inc. However, if the project was a more independent overseas project, a specialist in the corresponding technical area at Canon Inc. would be nominated.

The presentation of the RenderWare project to the directors of the overseas R&D center took place in 1991. The project was accepted and passed on to Canon Inc. that authorized and contracted it in the same year. At that time, Canon Inc. had no appropriate R&D division with expertise in 3D graphics. However, as the directors realized the great future importance of 3D graphics for the corporation, the project continued even though there was no close cooperation with a Japanese counterpart.

5.3   Recruitment of Key People

Qualified employees are a key source of success in R&D. This was particularly true in software R&D as one single innovative person was able to create a new business area with little investment in production and equipment.

The key person with technical expertise in the RenderWare project was a friend of a Canon employee at CRE. As a Ph.D. student, he had been a part-time programmer for Canon. Based on his very good work, Canon was eager to employ him after the completion of his Ph.D. Thus, in 1991 he became a full-time employee of the corporation. Although the company usually applies a more structured way of recruiting good managers, personal acquaintances can be very important in the software area where a promising idea is more important than work experience.

At first he was not assigned to a particular project, but explored some ideas in areas related to graphics, his field of specialization. However, he kept close contact with the technical staff at CRE. Thus, he came up with a new promising idea for reducing computing time in graphics rendering. He produced a prototype and made an R&D proposal.

After approval of the project by the directors, a few more key people were recruited. Even at that time Internet turned out to be more efficient to recruit new employees than ads in newspapers and science magazines.

5.4   Early Marketing and Business Decision

In 1992 an early version of RenderWare was produced. To test its competitiveness and find out areas of improvement, early marketing activities were carried out. The beta version of the software was distributed to a limited number of promising user sites, where evaluation of the new product was undertaken. Since RenderWare was not an end-user application product but a software library which was used to develop end-user applications, the selected beta sites were mainly universities and professional users. The evaluation showed that: (i) RenderWare was based on world leading technologies, and (ii) a number of users wanted to use it.

Based on these promising marketing results, another key member of the RenderWare team with some expertise in business exploitation of a new product set up the business plan. Thus, even in R&D centers it was important to have employees who know how to exploit the center's R&D results. In 1993 the plan was presented to the directors of CRE for approval. Among them, the R&D director of Canon Inc. was particularly important, as Canon Inc. was the legal owner of R&D outcomes. The plan suggested the following: start independent business activities and license the software to third party developers of 3D graphic applications.

The reaction was mixed. The speed in producing new technology was appreciated. However, the concern was manifested that too rapid an exploitation may not

Major innovative breakthroughs at Canon (1991-1996):

1. Surface conduction electron emitter display;
2. Silicon on insulator;
3. Photograde color printers;
4. Large area new MIS sensor & TFT.

be the best option. The director of Canon Inc. intended the RenderWare project to turn into an important business for Canon. Specifically, he wanted to capitalize on the synergy between CRE's software technology and Canon Inc.'s hardware expertise. The suggested rapid exploitation of the new product would not enable the business to grow to a sufficient size to be of interest to Canon Inc. Another aspect of concern referred to the licensing business. Canon had no expertise at all in this area. However, CRE employees stressed that time was critical in the software business. The value of software would not last for long. Thus, only a very quick decision would prevent Canon from losing this business opportunity. Some internal marketing had shown that there were no potential users of RenderWare within Canon Inc. Thus, there were no possibilities for synergies within Canon Inc. in 1992.

Finally, top management agreed to the plan. This decision turned out to be the right one as we will see later on.

A new company called Criterion Software Ltd. (CSL) was set up in 1993. Its objective was to exploit business opportunities offered by RenderWare. There were two reasons to set up a new company: (i) CRE's R&D expertise was not appropriate for managing a software business, and (ii) there was a tax advantage.

5.5 Current Status and Future Outlook

CSL distributed RenderWare software to more than 1,000 users from 1994 to 1997. Although competition with major software companies was intense, the company achieved a good market position in the 3D graphic business. Specifically, RenderWare was taking a very high share in the business of Internet browsing software.

In late 1995, CSL diversified its 3D graphic business into the area of 3D games. This strategic move enabled CSL to take advantage of its good technological reputation.

Top management at Canon Inc. had always been very keen on exploiting synergies between CSL and the Canon group. It was only in the late 1990's that Canon started to change its management approaches in order to participate in the emerging multimedia business, that potential for synergy became likely. Canon had a lot to learn from CSL who had been a forerunner in the multimedia business. It realized the importance of having a forerunner in the group. The forerunner's expertise had the potential to change the main business of the whole corporation.

Lessons learned from organizing R&D at Canon:

1. Make top policy and company direction clear;

2. Adopt an appropriate mixture of top-down (request-based) and bottom-up (proposal-based) procedures when defining a project;

3. Cultivate human networks and find good key people;

4. Develop competitive technologies, adopt the best timing for exploitation.

5.6   Learnings from the Project

We deliberately selected a project which does not involve a number of international parties sharing various roles. The case study deals with an independent project in its various stages: from early R&D to business exploitation. The intention behind the selection was that the project discussion should underline the unique characteristics of R&D at Canon as described in the early section of this case study.

The lessons from the RenderWare project were:

- Forecast the future direction of the company. Thus you might be able to take up promising R&D activities which differ from your existing business.
- Implement both types of procedures (i.e. proposal based and request based) for defining R&D projects.
- Set up a framework to select and determine the funding of an R&D project. It should be based on an entrusted R&D contract. Do this also for technologies that are not (yet) required by the various business groups.
- Set up a human network to select people likely to have new promising ideas that might change the whole business of the company.
- Have the courage to establish business activities which are very different from those of the corporation. Bear in mind that future synergies within the whole company might be realized.
- Employ business forerunners to accumulate new skills and expertise. These might in the future become very important for the company.

In 1997 it was too early to make a final statement about the RenderWare project as it was still ongoing. Lots of challenges still lay ahead. However, the case study illustrated the characteristics of R&D driving continuous growth and diversification at Canon.

6   Conclusions

In 1998, after only a few years of international R&D, it was too early to judge on the performance of overseas R&D centers. This is too short a period compared to the usual R&D cycles. For instance, it took bubble jet printing 13 years to turn from basic idea into the successful business big enough to be of interest to Canon. Nevertheless, several smaller projects created successful business opportunities. A few even appear to have great business potential, for instance RenderWare. Overseas R&D centers are meeting the two aims fixed by Canon. Specifically, meet the R&D needs of Canon and create opportunities for diversification

The main learnings from the Canon R&D case study are:

- Management policy should be clearly defined. This is best illustrated in Fig. IV.2.6 as well as for the setting of our American R&D centers at Canon.
- Defining an R&D project should be based on both top-down and bottom-up approaches. Thus, both projects focused on specific needs and more exploratory (future oriented) projects will be accepted.
- Business exploitation should be timely. Thus, quick action may be required as in the multimedia software area. The establishment of CSL is a good example. However, avoid premature business exploitation. Canon waited for very long before starting business exploitation of bubble jet printers.

Finally, we consider enthusiasm and belief in the business potential of a new technology to be decisive to Canon's successes. Without it, neither management methodology nor R&D organization approaches would bring about Canon's unique characteristics of continuous growth and diversification.

IV.3 Hewlett-Packard: Planet-Wide Patterns in the Company's Technology Tapestry*

1 Preface

In March of 1999, Hewlett-Packard announced the strategic realignment of the company into two independent companies. These have been named, Agilent Technologies and Hewlett-Packard. The then president and CEO, Lewis Platt, said "We are taking this action to sharpen the strategic focus of our businesses, improve their agility and increase their responsiveness to customers and partners. We are creating two distinct and strategically focused enterprises, one focused on the measurement businesses, the other on the computing and imaging businesses."

Agilent Technologies, focused on the measurement business, has its roots in the earliest days of Hewlett-Packard Company, which started as a test and measurement company in 1939 with the production of the company's first audio oscillator. Agilent is the world's premier measurement company and a technology leader in communications, electronics, life sciences and chemical analysis.

Agilent's headquarters are in the Palo Alto, California. The headquarter is in a new building at 395 Page Mill Road, the site of HP's first manufacturing building. Agilent offers its products and services in more than 110 countries. At the time of this writing, Agilent has approximately 42,000 employees in more than 40 countries. The company's 1998 revenues were nearly US$ 8 billion. Edward (Ned) W.

* This case study was authored by *Rosanne Wyleczuk* at Hewlett-Packard. Her sincere thanks go to countless HP webpage authors simply identified as „webmaster" everywhere, and Dewey Baker, Steve Bicker, John Birk, Herb Blomquist, Janice Bradford, Jason Brown, Carolyn Brown, Bill Buffington, Tara Bunch, Leigh Cagan, Jeremy Carroll, Sharon Connor, James Conway, Hoyle Curtis, Margaret Day, Anna Durante, Kathe Gust, Florence Haas, Rob Hamilton, Susanne Helmer, Pamela Hines, George Hopkins, Jim Horner, Toshino Ichino, Rhonda Kirk, Chuck Leath, Daisy Lee, Swee-Kwang Lim, Gerhard Lindemann, Partricia Markee, Hans Mattes, Emily Mathews, Bill McFarland, Rich Marconi, Akihiro Morioka, Richard Moss, Roberto Mottola, Walter Nash, Steve Paolini, My Phan, Eugenie Prime, Cheryl Ritchie, Sylvain Sadier, Bern Shen, Jim Shunk, Polly Siegel, Bess Stephens, Morgan Stewart, Hans Stork, Jim Sullivan, Sally Swedburg, Ju-en Teng, Jeremy Theil, Pat Vinton, Liz Vugrinecz, Tomio Wakasugi, Barbara Waugh, Barry Willis, Hazen Witemeyer, and Al Yuen.

This case study was written in 1998 and revised by the author in 1999: The reader should keep in mind that all numbers, figures, organization charts and forecasts represent the state of 1999/1998 or before. It was revised in 2007 by *Adrian Fischer*.

Barnholt is the chief executive officer. In the organization chart in Figure IV.3.2, the left side of the chart essentially depicts Agilent's then businesses. The significant business units include:

- Test and Measurement: with Automated Test Group, Communications Solutions Group, Electronic Products and Solutions Group;
- Chemical Analysis Group;
- Healthcare Solutions Group;
- Semiconductor Products Group;

The new computing and imaging company continued to operate under the Hewlett-Packard name and include all of HP's enterprise computing systems, software and services, personal computer, and printing and imaging solutions businesses. Under the banner of the recently articulated e-services initiative, all of the computing and imaging businesses capitalize on the opportunities in the second chapter of the Internet, the mass proliferation of electronic services. Carleton (Carly) S. Fiorina was named president and chief executive officer.

In this chapter, the examples are used to reflect the heritage of the combined Hewlett-Packard Company. HP's central research labs, referred to as HP Labs throughout the chapter has also split in two to support the two companies. Agilent Labs pursues research in support of the Agilent Technologies business direction and vision, as the HP Labs organization, vintage 2000, does the same for HP.

2   HP: A Strong Company in Growing Industries

„The character of our company is basically set by the character of its R&D work." (Bill Hewlett). William Hewlett and David Packard founded HP in 1939 while working out of a one-car garage behind 367 Addison Avenue – today a California State Historical landmark and a Silicon Valley cornerstone. The company's first product, an electronic test instrument known as an audio oscillator, was built in a Palo Alto garage. The oscillator improved upon existing audio oscillators in size, price and performance. One of HP's first customers, Walt Disney Studios, purchased eight oscillators to develop and test an innovative sound system for the classic movie „Fantasia." HP incorporated in 1947 and ten years later made its first public stock offering. HP shares have been traded on the New York and Pacific stock exchanges since 1961. At the end of the 1990s, about 92,000 shareholders hold slightly more than one billion shares of stock.

HP designs, manufactures, and services electronic products and systems for measurement, computing, and communication. These systems and services are used by people in industry and in the home, in business and in medicine, in engineering, science, and education. HP's basic business purpose has been to accelerate the advancement of knowledge and improve the effectiveness of people and organizations. The company's more than 25,000 products include computers and peripheral products, electronic test and measurement instruments and systems, networking products, medical electronic equipment, instruments and systems for chemical analysis, handheld calculators, and electronic components. At the time of

Some facts about HP:

2   America's Most Admired Computer/Office Equipment Company,
      Fortune, March 1999
3   Most Admired Company in Asia, *Asian Business, May 1998*
#10   Best Company to Work for in America, *Fortune, January 1999*
#13   Fortune 500 list of US Industrial and Service Corporations, April 1999
#23   Most Admired Company in the World, *Fortune, September 1999*
#41   Fortune Global 500 list of corporations, *Fortune, August 1999*
#42   Global 1000 (based on Market Value), *Business Week, July 1998*

this writing, HP employs 123,300 employees worldwide. Lewis E. Platt is HP's Chairman of the Board, President and CEO. There are more than 600 sales and support offices and distributorships in more than 120 countries; and 101 divisions.

Headquartered in Palo Alto, California, HP is one of the world's largest computer companies. The company had a net revenue of US$ 38.4 billion in its fiscal year 1996 (ended October 31), and US$ 42.9 billion in its fiscal year 1997. More than 55 percent of its business is generated outside the United States, and more than two-thirds of that is in Europe. Other principal markets include Japan, Canada, Australasia, the Far East, and Latin America.

2.1   A Breadth of Products and Markets

Early in its 50 year history HP grew into the world's leading manufacturer of electronic test and measurement instruments for engineers and scientists. These instruments, systems, and related services are used today to design, manufacture, operate, and repair electronic equipment, including emerging global information networks. Besides the electronics industry, the principal markets for HP instruments and systems are the telecommunications, aerospace/defense, automotive, consumer electronics, computer, semiconductor and components industries, and scientific-research programs.

In the early 1960s, HP extended its electronics technology to the fields of medicine and analytical chemistry. At the end of the 1990s, HP medical equipment, including cardiac ultrasound-imaging and patient-monitoring systems, is used in hospitals and clinics around the world, and HP computer systems are used in both clinical and administrative areas. HP's analytical instruments analyze the chemical components of liquids and gases and are used in the chemical, energy, pharmaceutical and food industries, and in environmental monitoring, medicine, bioscience, and university research.

HP introduced its first computer in 1966 to gather and analyze data produced by HP electronic instruments. When HP branched into business computing in the 1970s with the HP 3000 midrange computer, it launched into the era of distributed data processing, taking computing power out of computer rooms and making it accessible to people throughout an organization. In the mid-1980s, HP was the

Major innovative break-throughs at HP (1994-1999):

1. Digital Photography: HP's new HP PhotoSmart digital photography system;

2. HP OpenView Network Management Software/Services: enterprise management solutions available on a variety of platforms, including HP 9000 systems, Sun Microsystems workstations and Microsoft Windows and NT systems;

3. HP AcceSS7 (SS = Signaling System) telecommunications network monitoring system;

4. HP GeneArray Scanner: reads DNA probe arrays.

first major company to introduce a number of computers based on an innovative technology known as reduced-instruction-set computing, or RISC. HP's central research labs (HP Labs) pioneered this technology; Joel Birnbaum, HP Laps director, accelerated the first systems to market. HP is the world's No. 1 revenue leader for RISC systems and UNIX system-based computers and the world's No. 2 supplier of powerful workstations for engineering and business applications.

HP is also one of the fastest-growing personal computer companies in the world. HP's PC products include the Pavilion family of PCs for home users, the palmtop PC family with the recently introduced color handheld, the HP 620LX, and the HP OmniBook notebook PCs. Sitting alongside HP personal computers is a vast array of successful hardcopy products that set the standard for technology, performance, and reliability. HP's market-leading products include LaserJet and DeskJet printers, DesignJet large-format printers, ScanJet scanners, OfficeJet all in ones, and CopyJet color printer-copiers. Most of the company's revenue comes from a broad range of computer products and services, including workstations, personal computers, and peripherals.

Users often link their computers for better and easier access to information. HP is pushing the frontiers of fiber-optic, wireless, and visual communications with more than 9,000 component products that help people communicate quickly, reliably, and cost effectively. HP also manufactures and services networking products to help customers interconnect HP computers as well as those of other manufacturers. The company is a leader in the movement to create standards that will allow all computers – from PCs to mainframes – to be linked in „open systems."

"It is critical to produce core components that snap together easily with other components available in the market to realize the solutions our customers expect from us. We're likely to see more winning combinations of 'off-the-shelf' commodity technologies mixed with HP inventions."

— My Phan, HP Cupertino, USA

HP services facilitate the linkages between HP systems, the people using the equipment, and the business operations being supported. HP has become one of the world's top computer service and support companies. The company's 35 response centers and support offices in 110 countries give customers 24-hour-a-day access to HP anywhere in the world. HP also offers a broad range of consulting, systems integration, management, and finance services to give customers cost effective, timely and easy access to information.

In pursuit of total solutions for HP customers, the software businesses within HP have also grown. HP OpenView is the world's leading network and system management solution. Imaging solutions and electronic business software, alongside other rapidly growing Internet-ready systems and security products, complement HP's services, integration, and outsourcing businesses.

Not to be forgotten, of course, is that HP introduced the world's first scientific handheld calculator – the HP-35 – in 1972, which quickly made the engineer's slide rule obsolete. Many HP engineers joked about the calculator, never believing it could ever take the place of their trusted slide rules. Today, HP makes some of the world's most sophisticated and compact business and scientific calculators.

2.2   HP Presence

HP's objectives, values, management strategies and practices are expected to travel across country borders as easily as people do. HP established its first presence outside of California with a European marketing organization in Geneva, Switzerland, and its first manufacturing plant outside of Palo Alto in Boeblingen, Germany. At the time of this writing, HP has operations, either sales, manufacturing, research, or distribution in over 100 countries around the world. HP manufacturing plants are located in 28 U.S. cities, mostly in California, Colorado, the Northeast and the Pacific Northwest. The company also has research and manufacturing facilities in Europe, Asia Pacific, Latin America and Canada.[46]

From any one of these countries, it is possible to impact the entire HP world, customers worldwide, and even the entire industry. For example, at the first European manufacturing site in Germany in 1967, the medical products division pioneered the concept of flexible working hours, which was adopted at HP facilities around the world. „Flextime" is still so popular that it serves as one of HP's flagship „family friendly" policies, and is now part of dozens of other companies'

---

[46]   HP product development and manufacturing sites are located in: U.S. locations: Cupertino, Folsom, Mountain View, Newark, Palo Alto, Rohnert Park, Roseville, San Diego, San Jose, Santa Clara, Santa Rosa, Sunnyvale, and Westlake Village, California; Colorado Springs, Fort Collins, Greeley, and Loveland, Colorado; Wilmington, Delaware; Boise, Idaho; Andover and Chelmsford, Massachusetts; Exeter, New Hampshire; Rockaway, New Jersey; Corvallis, Oregon; Aguadilla, Puerto Rico; Richardson, Texas; Everett, Spokane and Vancouver, Washington. Non-U.S. locations: Melbourne, Australia; Campinas, Brazil; Calgary, Edmonton, Montreal, Richmond, Vancouver, and Waterloo, Canada; Beijing, Qingdao, and Shanghai, China; Grenoble, Isle d'Abeau, and Lyon, France; Böblingen and Waldbronn, Germany; Bangalore, India; Dublin, Ireland; Bergamo, Italy; Hachioji, Kobe, and Musashino, Japan; Seoul, Korea; Penang, Malaysia; Guadalajara, Mexico; Amersfoort, The Netherlands; Barcelona, Spain; Singapore; Bristol, Ipswich, Pinewood, and South Queensferry, UK.

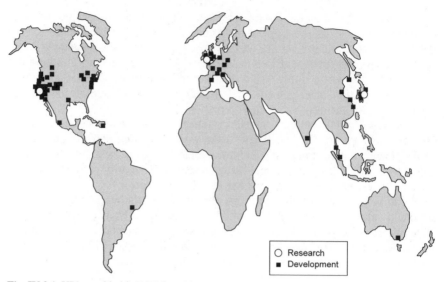

Fig. IV.3.1. HP's worldwide R&D locations.

policies (across numerous industries). Of course, it's a natural way for scientists and engineers to work.

2.3   „We're in the books"

In 1982 HP was included in the book by Tom Peters (1982), „In Search of Excellence: Lessons from America's Best-Run Companies" and twelve years later HP stories were woven throughout „Built to Last: Successful Habits of Visionary Companies" by Collins and Porras (1994). A personal documentary of the company's growth is found in „The HP Way" by David Packard (1995). This is not about bragging – for tens of thousands of employees these books and references are an uplifting experience and an invisible pat on the back because „we" are the company. These books are especially powerful reminders of the big-picture; they give not only the world, but also employees, the „systems" view of our company, a very difficult perspective to keep while focusing on daily challenges and contributions. These books add to this work by providing greater breadth and depth to HP's history, its people, its leaders, its business practices, and its culture.

In „The Death of Competition" James Moore (1994: 42) writes about HP saying, „Its great strengths are in technology and implementation – in being a strong member of an ecosystem..." In the global R&D ecosystem of computer and electronics research labs, universities, standards bodies, industry research teams, government and private consortia, HP has critical roles and leadership positions, and is defining the ecosystem.

3   The WARP Threads: HP's Global Attributes and Practices

The 'warp' threads are placed on the loom first to run *lengthwise* throughout the entire fabric, from one end through to the other. Even though the warp is put on first, it is not until one weaves back and forth with the weft across all of the threads that the pattern becomes apparent. The pattern can actually be created in the warp if the warp is packed tightly; here the weft threads are not visible at all. But even then, no pattern appears at all until you start weaving with the weft. So, it's really the interaction between the two that makes everything apparent.

In this section, the *warp* threads of HP are discussed. These threads are consistent across the HP organization, throughout R&D and beyond. These are the practices that enable continuity, durability and fluid interaction across the various countries and lines of business. Around the world, woven textiles have worn well over the centuries. Similarly, the fabric of HP wears well over time – both in terms of fit and lasting value.

3.1   Values

HP's organizational values and commitment to meeting its corporate objectives color its strategies and practices. These values certainly influence the thinking of all HP employees and give an HP look-and-feel to most of HP's business practices. Essentially, these values describe a system that has high expectations of its people, sets high expectations for its products, and causes customers to have high expectations of the businesses in which it operates, resulting in a company that is a role model in the industry. HP's organizational values include:

- Trust and respect for individuals.
- Focusing on a high level of achievement and contribution: One of the critical questions R&D is constantly asking, „What is the contribution made by this product or technology?"
- Conducting our business with uncompromising integrity.
- Achieving our common objectives through teamwork.
- Encouraging flexibility and innovation.

For the R&D organizations throughout HP the focus on contribution and real added value is integral to everything we do. HP's growth strategy requires a relentless pursuit of new and better products. Each annual report displays proudly

"The sales of digital products are expanding worldwide, while the information technologies we create seem to shrink the world and make its markets accessible to all. So, from the start, we must design and build products that can be localized around the world, including postponement as a strategy to achieve low-cost and time-to-market objectives."

— **Swee-Kwang Lim, HP Singapore**

the company vintage chart showing the revenue contributions from products introduced year by year; within the business sectors, the vintage charts of the various
product lines are closely examined. And all of these products must be making a
contribution to the industry or to the customer. The demonstration of „business
value" is the target for our products and our technologies. Research from the central labs must add business value to an HP product division before it finds its way
out to the marketplace, and the HP product must provide real value to customers.

Folklore retells the tales of battles lost in the struggle to fund developments
when technological contributions were not clearly defined. In a highly networked,
standards-based, open systems world, product contributions may be more ab-
stractly defined or intangible. Contributions can be recognized for the ease with
which the product integrates into the customer's environment, its capability for
working well with other products across organizations, or the total cost of change
or the total cost of ownership.

„Value" is embedded in the minds, spirits, and hearts of HP employees. At the
time of this writing, ongoing process improvement projects are focusing on increasing people's understanding of the „value-chain" for HP's products. „The
search for clarity and real business value" represents the first significant step taken
by scientists and engineers expecting to see their technology succeed as a product.
More than simply defining value, in „The Death of Competition", the author suggests that businesses „need to invest in co-evolutionary sequences of building
capability that establish the elusive trait known as value. ... In the new world, we
need to go from identifying and improving value chains to the active generation of
new value chains. ... You should ask yourself what opportunities there are for
dramatic performance improvements in your business if all the direct and complementary capabilities were reorganized and new technologies, customers, markets,
and regulatory regimes were in place" (Moore 1994: 70). What better place to play
this „what if" experiment than amongst a company's global R&D teams? With
University partners? With standards bodies?

3.2   Corporate Objectives

HP's corporate objectives are seven of the company's most vibrant, eye-catching,
dream-catching, warp threads which weave a pattern that appeals to shareholders,
employees, customers, colleagues, and communities. The company's management
practices are based on the belief that people are committed to doing a good job
and are capable of making sound decisions. It is upon these HP corporate objectives that group and individual goal setting (in which all employees participate) is

*"Pumping money into R&D without both a market and a value proposition is irresponsible.
We are all responsible for providing real value while transforming development
environments from in-house development to 'virtual R&D' where a small core team
architects and orchestrates a network of contributors outside the lab."*

— Roberto Mottola, HP Bergamo, Italy

threaded. Such objectives are of central importance in technology-rich (and driven) enterprises where it is essential to keep focused on business impact and not unbridled research. The HP Company objectives assist hundreds of R&D groups, including the central research labs, to contribute to the company texture and pattern in ways that align with HP's chosen businesses.

- *Profit*: To achieve sufficient profit to finance our company growth and to provide the resources we need to achieve our other corporate objectives.
- *Customers*: To provide products and services of the highest quality and the greatest possible value to our customers, thereby gaining and holding their respect and loyalty.
- *Field of Interest*: To participate in those fields of interest that build upon our technology and customer base, that offer opportunities for continuing growth, and that enable us to make a needed and profitable contribution.
- *Growth*: To let our growth be limited only by our profits and our ability to develop and produce innovative products that satisfy real customer needs.
- *People*: To help people share in the company's success which they make possible; to provide employment security based on performance; to ensure them a safe and pleasant work environment; to recognize their individual achievements; to value their diversity; and to help them gain a sense of satisfaction and accomplishment from their work.
- *Management*: To foster initiative and creativity by allowing the individual great freedom of action in attaining well-defined objectives.
- *Citizenship*: To honour our obligations to society by being an economic, intellectual and social asset to each nation and each community in which we operate.

3.3   Strategies and Practices

There are several key company management practices that are not solely limited to HP's R&D organizations. However they are critical to the R&D organizations, and integrally woven into the development-specific practices. These practices also enable spontaneous generation of ideas such as those spawned within the World's Best Industrial Research Lab program, the Grassroots Basic Research Proposals, the internal conference, etc. These are all discussed below. These practices add texture to the company fabric that makes it „feel good" to work at HP.

Management By Objective (MBO)

Individuals at each level contribute to company goals by developing objectives that are integrated with their manager's and those of other parts of HP. Many objectives are written with a keen focus on effectively meeting (or providing the means to meet) customer needs, with special recognition going to those who demonstrate greater flexibility and innovation in defining alternative solutions. MBO is reflected in

- Written plans that guide and create accountability throughout the organization;
- Coordinated and complementary efforts, and cross-organizational integration; and,
- The sharing of plans and objectives.

Open Communication

At the core of open communication is the belief that, when given the right tools, training, and information to do a good job, people will contribute their best. Open communication leads to strong teamwork between HP people, customers, and others, leads to enhanced achievement and contribution, and leads to customer relationships built on trust and respect. Over the years, colleagues of this author, especially those who have worked at other companies, rave and wax philosophical about HP's great openness and information sharing. Anywhere in the world, in whatever language, if you ask, „gotta minute?" everyone always does. („Gotta minute?" is equivalent to asking whether the individual has a few minutes to talk.) „Anybody will talk to you about anything. There is so much information and access to information that we know so much more than we consciously think we know," concludes a colleague and insightful systems thinker.

Open Door Policy

Open Door means that any individual can speak with any other HP employee/manager about a topic or concern, as schedules permit. Because HP thinks managers and employees should interact and communicate directly, the company has always had an „open door" policy at all levels of management. This requires the assurance that no adverse consequences will result from responsibly raising issues with management or personnel. Trust and integrity are important parts of the Open Door Policy. Open Door may be used to share feelings and frustrations in a constructive manner, to gain a clearer understanding of alternatives, to discuss career options, or to discuss business conduct and communication breakdowns.

Management by Wandering Around (MBWA)

MBWA is an informal HP practice that helps maintain regular communications between managers, individuals, and programs through informal or unstructured interactions. An MBWA might look like a manager consistently reserving time to walk through the department or be available for impromptu discussions, individuals networking across organizations, or coffee talks, communication lunches, and hallway conversations. And now, for example, all employees can review (listen to the audio portion) of informal communication sessions, such as coffee talks, via the internal website – not replacing face-to-face communication, but reaching a broader audience. Trust and respect for individuals become apparent when MBWA is used to recognize employees' concerns and ideas.

3.4   A Unified Organization with Independent Business Units

HP is widely recognized for its form of corporate organization that is melded with independently run business units. Hundreds of decentralized product groups pursue their specific product charters as part of the Hewlett-Packard Company. Such a decentralized organization gives businesses considerable decision-making authority, fostering the company's entrepreneurial flexibility. New businesses and product lines are created as spin-offs from the old ones. These new ventures may happen when separable products reach critical mass, when a start-up business needs dedicated attention, when the timing is right for country expansion, or when a management leader is ready for growth. From the beginning, the company has adhered to a „pay-as-you-go" philosophy, financing its growth primarily from profits. Any new venture start-ups in a specific sector are usually funded from within that sector.

The company's organization is in constant motion as people, projects, and businesses mesh, meld, and move amongst each other. As of this writing, the company is organized into two major sectors under President and CEO Lew Platt. First, there is the Measurement Organization including the Automated Test group, the Microwave and Communications group, the Communications Test Solutions group, and the Electronic Instruments group, as well as the Chemical Analysis group, the Components group, and the Medical products group. The second major sector of the company is the Computer Organization consisting of the Enterprise Servers group, the LaserJet Solutions group, the Consumer Products group (including HP InkJet products), the Information Storage group, the Personal Systems group, the Software and Services group (including electronic business and e-commerce solutions), the Extended Enterprise Business and Veriphone (Fig. IV.3.2).

These businesses do not run wholly independent of corporate headquarters or the middle levels of business management. They operate with access to vast arrays of information, consultants, business process tools and training, the corporate infrastructure for benefits management, recruiting, grants and philanthropy programs, innovations such as the HP E-Mentor program, and more. Some of the warp threads that contribute to company confluence include a Chief Executive Officer Hoshin (company-wide annual plan) which defines breakthroughs or broken fixtures requiring everyone's attention, the 10-step planning process (a methodology for specific business planning), the personnel policies (with localization), the annual financial planning cycle, and the common accounting practices. Some company resources threaded into business plans to varying degrees include the central research labs (HP Labs), the corporate development group looking at strategic partnerships, and the geographic infrastructures. Each new business then proceeds to contribute to the pattern by establishing its unique business strategy and metrics, technology investments, sales and marketing, alliances, and much more. This balanced approach to the organization enables HP to sustain the common core values of the company while promoting standards of excellence, quality, contribution, and commitment to customer value in many different lines of business.

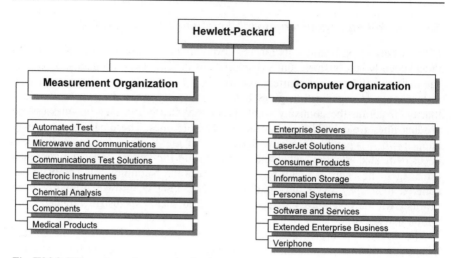

Fig. IV.3.2. HP's sector and group organization.

3.5   Facilities: The Same, but Different throughout the World

Imagine the Ansel Adams photograph "Moonrise, Hernandez, New Mexico," with the moon shining over a small village in the middle of the night. Imagine Van Gough's Starry Night, with windows lit by candle glow. Imagine any Japanese wood block print with a village nestled at the base of Mt. Fuji. Now, imagine that those villages are all HP sites buzzing with sales, manufacturing, and development projects.

Once told that these were all „HP villages," any employee who mentally traveled around the globe while reading these sentences, would immediately become comfortable with the knowledge that these sites all have the same HP characteristics – the warp threads upon which these HP villages would have grown. These HP characteristics allow an HP site to be „the same, yet different" throughout the world's locations. HP facilities around the world are all constructed with a similar external architecture and usually similar internal design. This common HP feel to a facility allows an engineer to walk down cubicle-lined hallways assuming that, if they stop and ask in the local slang, „Got a minute", that they'll get it. They know that making a positive contribution and imaginatively solving customer problems are central to the activities of everyone's daily life. HP people around the world are at ease in the environment with the knowledge that all teammates are working to be the best in their fields of interest.

It takes an HP village to build a successful product and business; HP is nurturing those villages around the world.

3.6   Hiring

With engineers and computer scientists accounting for some 28 percent of its work force, HP annually recruits about 1,500 college and university students, 70 percent of whom have technical degrees. The company's goal has always been to hire only the top 10 percent of the graduating seniors from respected engineering schools. Historically, HP has preferred to not hire experienced engineers from industry, although, increasingly, experience in technologies and industries new to HP are being sought. At over 230 college campuses, in close to 40 countries around the world, HP sends 1,350 managers looking for today's best minds. Any student invited to visit an HP site for a job interview may be introduced to as many as ten HP employees during the interview process. You can see that, by involving thousands of HP employees and managers, the company takes hiring very seriously. And for good reason: Many individuals throughout the company readily admit that, despite an accumulation of degrees, it is one's colleagues that make the difference in meeting daily challenges; people make the difference in creative collaborations, and they make the difference in getting the product out ahead of time and under budget.

3.7   Diversity

HP's hiring goals are tied to our diversity goals, and together they accelerate the company into the future. HP is positioning itself for a planet-wide workforce. For decades, before affirmative action and before equal employment opportunity, Bill and Dave were building a company based on unique individuals. HP demonstrates to all that diversity depends on the existence of many unique individuals in the workplace – men and women from different nations, cultures, ethnic groups, lifestyles, generations, backgrounds, skills, and abilities. Frequently, working at HP, a U.S.-born employee might be the only U.S.-born person on a team.

The genesis of this valuation of diversity was the analytical minds of the HP founders, who truly had a pulse on human nature and were non-judgmental and accepting of an idea, regardless of its source. As the company moves forward, it must continue to reinforce this cornerstone of its employee practices because of its critical contributions to meeting globalization challenges:

- HP's customers, suppliers, and strategic partners are increasingly global and multi-cultural; the company and its people must be positioned to relate to them.
- HP's customers are changing – their needs and expectations for products and services are diverse; HP must be able to understand, interface, and respond.

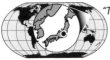 *"The future will be shaped by the human resources within the company. The confidence to become number one in our selected markets, and the key technology developments required, happen because of our people."*

— **Akihiro Morioka, HP Tokyo, Japan**

- Changing work force demographics and projections of a severely limited labor pool contribute to the forecast of fierce competition for talent; HP must be the best place to work for everyone.
- HP's competitive advantage is to become the leader in innovation, creativity, problem solving, and organizational flexibility; the company must be stocked with diverse perspectives, talents, and teams to construct the kind of company that meets this global challenge.

„We believe our diversity represents a tremendous strength for Hewlett-Packard. It allows us to tap a broad range of human potential," states Lew Platt, HP's president and CEO. HP's diversity strategy is working towards a vision of „*an inclusive environment that benefits from diversity at all levels, values individual differences, and enables all employees to develop and contribute to their full potential while meeting the work/life demands of the 21st Century.*"

3.8   Feedback and Performance Evaluations

HP's management practices are based on the belief that people are committed to doing a good job and are capable of making sound decisions. HP's corporate objectives provide a framework for setting goals and its „Management by Objective" process defines the guideposts by which performance is evaluated. HP's openness and informality contribute to a non-authoritarian atmosphere – even during the performance evaluation process. (Employees share in their own and HP's success through regular cash profit sharing and stock-purchase programs.)

HP's performance evaluations consist of three major areas for review and planning:

- The results accomplished by the employee, written based on the last year's objectives and plans, represents „WHAT" the employee got done;
- Performance attributes, making up the body of the evaluation, represent „HOW" the employee accomplished the work, including such key attributes as initiative, technical competence and job knowledge, teamwork, productivity, dependability, and planning and organization skills;
- Lastly, the plan for the future cites the objectives for the year and the employee and emphasizes the skills needing improvement. The completion of the performance evaluation is a collaborative effort of the employee and manager and also frequently includes colleagues who have worked with the employee.

It is key for R&D engineers to manage their own career and development plans. They must request what classes and skills training they need to grow in their job as well as grow as individuals within a company. They are also the ones who must determine for themselves whether they will follow a management track or the technical track for job promotions.

3.9   Obsessed with Quality

By the year 2000, one of the company goals is to become recognized as the leader in quality, where company growth and success are directly attributable to the extraordinary satisfaction and loyalty of HP customers. To fulfill this aspiration, the Corporate Quality function has defined its purpose: *To improve the performance of HP people and organizations as experienced by customers.*

A major factor in Hewlett-Packard's ability to stay competitive in the marketplace has always been this ceaseless focus on managing our processes and building a culture of constant quality improvement. In HP's early years our focus on test-fix-test and „next bench" matured into the Total Quality Control era in which the concepts of customer satisfaction and continuous improvement took root. Now these concepts are fundamental to all of our organizations and are built into everyone's performance evaluations; customer satisfaction has expanded into active customer involvement in many of HP organizations.

This maturity of quality development grew alongside an interest in breakthrough planning and process management. With both these process components in place, the company now focuses on total quality *management.* Businesses and teams immerse themselves in Customer-Centered Quality to achieve the greatest customer enthusiasm and loyalty. A focus on value, value propositions, and value chain definition and creation permeate the company. When groups start looking at influencing customer choices, they begin actively engineering their futures. And so continues the HP tradition: in each HP era, the businesses and the quality teams have built richer and richer sets of tools that have propagated throughout the world.

Discussions around the creation of value-delivery systems trigger thoughts about HP's view regarding building reliable products. Richard Moss (1997) of HP's Corporate Quality function, in his chapter entitled „Electronic Product Design," in the Quality Management Handbook, writes „Reliability is not something that is added by inspection or a burn-in step in manufacturing, or by requiring it in a specification. It is designed in, a little at a time, as each part or process is chosen and incorporated into the design, and problems are discovered and solved. Therefore, every person who makes a design decision has a hand in determining that design's reliability." Most people agree with this, especially with respect to electrical product design. Similarly one might say the same of building in quality or value: everyone who makes product or process decisions has a hand in determining a customer's enthusiasm and loyalty to the product or service. Operating with this understanding, scientists or engineers who are developing technology that might be sequestered within the internals of a product can always connect their contribution to the eventual end-customer.

"People are most creative when operating with the fewest constraints – so let the sources of constraint be natural laws and the competitive marketplace, and not the whims of the corporation. Drive R&D by the need to get diverse input and to utilize increasingly scarce talent."

— Hans Mattes, HP Santa Rosa, USA

 *"I am firmly of the opinion that utilization of the broad perspective of research collaborators around the world is the only path to success in the future. Not only do these cultural differences influence the ultimate goals, but these differences can and do strengthen the range of perspective available for high quality work."*

— Barry Willis, HP Palo Alto, USA

3.10 Folklore, Stories, and Foibles – HP is Full of „Bill and Dave" Stories

Only, these „Bill and Dave" stories are real. There really is a garage in Palo Alto that's now an historic landmark and pictured on thousands of credit cards. A coin toss really did decide the name of the company in 1939. Bill and Dave really did build their first building so it could be converted into a grocery store if the electronics business should fail ... and HP does continue to encourage a healthy amount of paranoia. HP engineers really did design the calculator in response to a challenge from Bill Hewlett, even while marketing reports were claiming there was no real interest in such a product. (The need for a champion was clear decades ago.) Years later a similar story is told about a different R&D manager. During a management review of the active development projects at that instrument division, a strong opinion was voiced by Dave Packard that one of the projects „had better not be in the lab at the next review," the implication being that it should be canceled. The R&D manager followed through, but used an unexpected route out of the lab: he tightened the schedule and got it into the marketplace before the next review – it was a very successful product.

From amongst these stories, one catches a flavor of the „try and try again" philosophy. HP's numerous product successes did not follow, one after the other, a nicely defined set of product strategy roadmaps resulting in revenues of US$ 43 billion at the end of the 1990s. In fact, at the first business meeting held in 1938, the product strategy was discussed. HP history says, „It seemed the general consensus of opinion was that the work should be limited to manufacturing and merchandising our *own manufactured goods* entirely. The question of *what* to manufacture was postponed to a later date." Continuous success did not follow. As HP historians have chronicled, Bill and Dave went on to design a notable number of failures: the automatic foot-fault finder for bowling alleys, an electronic toilet flusher for the dormitories at Stanford, and an electronic lettuce picker that destroyed a farmer's entire field and made spectators run for their lives. Tightly defined and monitored plans were not the norm. From these humbling beginnings, the company culture assimilated the acceptance of failures and the eagerness to learn from mistakes.

These stories have traveled through time and around the world, and they will travel into the future. Many managers throughout the company tell „Bill and Dave stories" without ever having met the principals. Now, one of the local HP internal newspapers has a regular article on „Bill and Dave Stories." This is a great resource for managers who want to sit around the coffeepot and share tales of the company's founders with new engineers. But even without these written resources, the story-telling would continue.

3.11   HP Investment in R&D

HP's continuing growth is based on a strong commitment to research and development. Each year the company invests about seven percent of its net revenue in R&D (US$ 2.7 billion in 1996). HP continues to be ranked among the top 5% of U.S. corporations in R&D investment. 90% of that investment is managed 'locally' within the product lines and businesses. These funds are allocated based on business potential, the current year's results, and the potential breakthroughs sought after within the business plans. The remaining 10% of the funding is allocated to HP's central research labs, HP Labs.

Heavy R&D investment across the entire company – coupled with the ability to manufacture and market leading-edge technology quickly – lets HP provide a steady flow of new and useful products. More than half the company's orders in 1997 were for products introduced during the previous two years. Consistent funding of central research labs also provides those labs with the stability required to maintain a long-term view, the freedom to take risks, the flexibility to move quickly, and the independence to chart a course unconstrained by the dynamics of a particular marketplace. Enabling such an independent course has proven a wise gamble as suggested by the stream of successes, such as the first RISC-based computer architecture, inkjet printing, digital photography, and gene array measurement systems.

3.12   HP Labs – Centers of R&D around the World

HP Laboratories (HPL), the company's central research facility, ranks as one of the leading industrial-research centers in the world. HPL started at its current headquarters location in Palo Alto in 1966 with the objective of helping the company move into new businesses. Now, across all the research centers (in Palo Alto, the UK, Japan, and Israel) researchers are working towards the HPL purpose: *To lead HP in the creation of innovative information products and new business opportunities.* In the '90s this means the labs need to do two things very well:

- Support current businesses through innovative contributions based on core competencies.
- Create business opportunities that exploit combinations of core competencies in measurement, computation, and communications.

To accomplish both of these objectives HP Labs stays focused primarily on applied research with fewer resources on the most basic research or the more targeted product development projects. Flexibility is still essential, as you can see from the Fig. IV.3.3, because the role and goals can shift as the company's business demands.

Funding for the labs has grown in the '90s as have the demands and expectations on it and its peoples. HPL has always prided itself on its applied-research focus, as opposed to a singular pursuit of scientific inquires. In addition to and very often in conjunction with the product development work in the R&D labs at the hundreds of HP divisions, is the product development work underway at HPL. Basic research is also underway at HPL; however, most work is targeted to applied research. Driven by the desire to have a large positive impact on the company by turning ideas into products, many teams within HP Labs have become masterful at partnering and transferring their technologies to the business units for development of the final product.

The worldwide research activities of HP Labs are aggregated within three centers, each focused on one of HP's major businesses. The Enterprise Systems and Solutions Center develops key technologies to provide competitive differentiation in the extended enterprise arena, including next-generation computer systems, distributed systems software and solutions, Internet communications and service management, multimedia, fixed and mobile networking, and system management and security. Research in the Peripherals, Appliances and Consumer Systems Center is primarily focused on peripherals, home personal computers, home networks, digital imaging, displays and digital media appliances. Finally, the Microelectronics and Measurement Systems Center conducts research into solid-state materials and components, silicon ICs, photonics, microwave, and medical and analytical measurements, bioscience, and manufacturing systems.

3.13   HP Visions of Pervasive Information – a Tapestry of Rich and Royal Hue

The director of HP Labs, Joel Birnbaum, has been speaking for years of the day computers will become a pervasive technology, most notable because of their apparent absence rather than presence. Dr. Birnbaum elaborated on his vision for

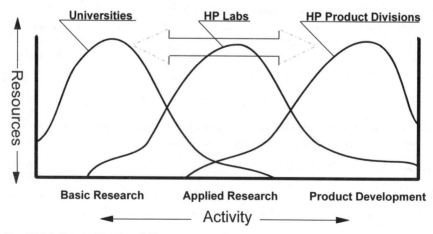

Fig. IV.3.3. Focus of R&D activities.

"It is quite challenging to meet the needs of the world's markets given the priority differences amongst the customers and markets in each country. Because of this, we face difficult tradeoffs between emerging technologies that improve human interfaces and those that provide stricter security in mobile computing environments."

— *Toshio Ichino, HP Kobe, Japan*

the 50th anniversary issue of the „Communications of the Association of Computing Machinery." He looks forward to „a time when computation devices are everywhere, buried in everything, so that people have trouble identifying where they all are." Pervasive computing is likely the next evolutionary step along a path that includes mainframes, minicomputers, microcomputers, and open systems and client/server, continuing on into the era of information utilities and appliances. In this later stage of information appliances, a combination of core technologies is required to make computers small enough to fit into anything, and make computing intuitively accessible and useful to ordinary people. It is up to industrial R&D labs to use the latest technologies to develop the appliances that will fit nicely into our everyday environments, our lives, and our routines, all operating with a consistency of service no matter where it is. This really could be the best of times for technologists, and also the best of times for businesses that are quick to accept, adopt, and deploy these latest technologies.

HP Labs literature says „Just as important as the technology we provide is the vision that underlies it." With a combined emphasis on business conditions, technological and social trends, and customer needs, HP Labs attempts to envision the future and HP's place in it. HPL envisions a world in which information flows as freely and transparently as electricity, consisting of a dynamic and interactive mix of spoken, printed, and written words, images, and video. This information will be there when people need it – no matter where they are – in the form in which they can best use it. Connected via an intelligent communications web, people will navigate information spaces as easily as they drive their cars today.

Pervasive information will have an impact on future generations that is similar to the impact pervasive electricity has had on ours. Pervasive information will come about, in large part, through the convergence of three key areas – measurement, computing, and communications. HP Labs has been in nonstop pursuit of combinations of these measurement, computation and communications (MC²) technologies to accelerate business growth and sustain HP's future position. It is within these three fields that HP focuses its core technologies, as depicted in Figure IV.3.4 Revolutions in any one field transforms all of them and blurs the boundaries between them. The information utility of Joel Birnbaum's vision requires breakthroughs in all of these MC² technology areas (including, for example, security, bandwidth, intuitive interfaces, systems management, and so on), as well as the foresight and/or intuition to refine the organizational and information technology policies and practices that might otherwise create a drag on the future.

4   The WEFT Threads that Add Color and Texture to Local Patterns

Webster's dictionary says the weft threads are the threads that go from side to side, carried back and forth across the warp threads; the weft are the filling. My weaving „coach" also says that it is not until the weft threads are woven with the warp, that the interaction and interlocking of the two creates a stable textile and pattern. Inside HP, it is not until thousands of people and hundreds of organizations interact with the company's basic warp, that the wonder of the corporate pattern becomes apparent. The richness in this pattern becomes even more vibrant and vital as the cultures of the world add their local style and custom threads to the HP tapestry.

This next series of topics describes these weft threads, especially those that have been woven from the basic R&D culture of the company. These programs, tools, or practices may or may not be implemented within a region of the world or within a business unit; they may or may not have had a dramatic impact on the running of a specific company business. Altogether, however, they contribute to the pattern of HP success around the world. Finally, these weft threads may represent the relatively smaller-scale, ever-moving programs – guided within the company context by empowered, enthusiastic, people and teams – that may later result in large-scale, industrial R&D patterns and trends.

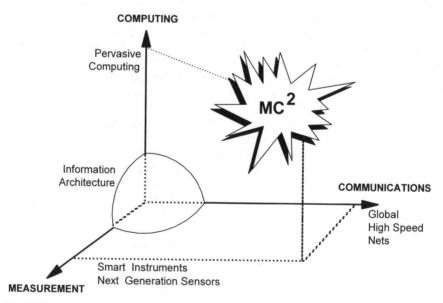

Fig. IV.3.4. Pervasive information systems.

4.1   Accumulating the Best Ideas

The best ideas can come from within HP organizations, such as with the HP Labs WBIRL program, or they can arise as a result of internal competition. Good ideas may come from expansion into other countries and their local markets, or from other companies that are brought into the organization. Regardless of where a good idea comes from, it should not be left alone.

WBIRL - World's Best Industrial Research Lab

The „World's Best Industrial Research Lab" program is broad in scope and vast in its reach, yet loosely and simply structured under one formal manager. Project ideas can come from anywhere, and persons voluntarily and independently propose ways to make HP Labs truly one of the world's best. The program is funded with central HP Labs money, but it also seeks matching funds from many different sources around HP Labs. The program started with the objective „to make HP Labs the Best Industrial Research Lab in the World," but soon stretched towards the greater goal of becoming „the best lab FOR the world." Why? Because that's an aspiration that moves hundreds of people to do and be their best on a daily basis. With this program, employees have the best chance of supporting the overall company objective: „To create information products that accelerate the advancement of knowledge and fundamentally improve the effectiveness of people and organizations." The WBIRL program annually funds about a dozen projects including the Technology Transfer project described at the close of this chapter that has received funding for the last two years.

The Classic Charter Wars?

HP often has multiple development and research projects all heading towards the same goal, and/or multiple product divisions all selling into the same market or account. An early HP technology often has multiple product destinies and, if it doesn't, it should. Why? Because HP is great at evolutionary progress, that is, unplanned progress. Authors have written about HP's unplanned move into the computer business. At that time, the company would state only that it was pursuing technologies that contributed to the management of instrumentation. Then, through a side door, HP entered the minicomputer market.

Just as is true in the market dynamics, it may be true of company dynamics: one project team that acts as a partner today, may be a competing project tomorrow, or a customer the next day. One has to be prepared for multiple possible futures.

Even in this time, HP has continued to develop multiple species of computer systems and operating environments and allows the marketspace to serve as the force of natural selection. Investment continues in each because the products respond to the demands of the customer – the customer decides what system best fits smoothly into their environment, not HP. Such evolutionary R&D continues, and should continue into the future. For example, HP may have several initiatives in the information appliance or home appliance arenas; the company may not rely solely on one group for these product plans. There is such a divergence of industry opinion and predictions regarding the acceleration of digital electronics/computation/ communication into the home, the development of computers for ordinary, non-Silicon Valley individuals, and the wireless world of tomorrow. The best bet, if the organization can afford it, is to be prepared for anything.

Continuous Sprouting and Acquisition

In a recent article in our employee magazine, Measure, Lew Platt discussed the importance of growth for the company. He stated, „We grow in three ways: by the natural extension of our current product lines, by acquiring other companies, and by penetrating new geographic markets." The following announcement appeared recently in HP's internal electronic-newspapers: „Malaysia Expansion. The Microwave Technology Division (MWTD) plans to establish an operation at Hewlett-Packard's existing facility in Penang, Malaysia this fall. Its goals are to develop a presence and accommodate business growth in the fast-growing Asian market. Initially, the new 40-person operation will manufacture microwave accessories and microcircuits for test-and-measurement instruments and systems." This is how HP launches into new countries, and eventually sprouts new R&D organizations – starting with sales, and growing to manufacturing, to perhaps strategic marketing, to ultimately full product development. HP has always encouraged international operations to develop R&D capabilities. Usually this means launching a new product into the marketplace – self-funded as usual. This is how a manufacturing plant might attain full division status and begin to take responsibility for sales and profit contributions.

HP acquisitions are another critical way R&D happens; instead of „birthing" a technology, acquisitions accelerate the generation of entire product families (and the integral core technologies/competencies). The challenge of the acquisition process is the careful and sensitive integration of what is usually a very different research and development culture into an HP culture that shouldn't smother the newcomer. The integration of a company into the HP way requires a slow and gradual integration – if any at all. Knowing when and where to secure key knots is critical bringing the new threads into the HP picture. For example, almost 40 years from the first HP acquisition, the company made one of its largest purchase decisions with the acquisition of Veriphone, Inc. and its renowned electronic-commerce solutions. Veriphone with its leadership position and E-Commerce technologies has strengthened HP's product portfolio in security, financial applications, and the extended enterprise – yet it remains a fairly independent business operation.

4.2   Relationships Enrich the Research and Results

Much of what HP accomplishes is done with others. There are numerous industry and university partners and programs that provide HP researchers and engineers with access to intelligence and innovation around the world.

Partner Companies

In how many countries does HP operate? Across how many business or product lines does the company operate? That's probably the number of business relationships with other companies – sometimes partners, sometimes competitors. On the one side of the planet, the POLO (Parallel Optical Link Organization), a consortium of leading technology companies and academic research groups is aimed at finding faster and less expensive ways to link computers to high-speed optical communications lines. HP is a participant.

For a non-US-based example, HP participates in the activities of the TERATEC consortium in Japan. This group, formed to develop high-speed electronic measuring technology, is funded by the Japan Key Technology Center. The group consists of five Japanese companies along with HP. Members of HP's research labs are involved in two new approaches to the measurement of high-speed, small-size devices. One approach is a new type of wafer testing probe. A complete measurement system is integrated into a very small probe, making low loss, high accuracy and easy measurement possible. The other approach is a new method of measuring high-speed electrical waveforms, combining optical sampling and scanning probe microscopy (SPM) technologies to achieve very high temporal (in the order of pico-seconds) and spatial (in the order of sub-mm) resolutions.

Finally, a useful demonstration of co-opetition (cooperation at one moment, competition at the next) is observable in the Internet Imaging announcements. „Based on the Internet Imaging Protocol (IIP), an interactive protocol jointly developed with Eastman Kodak and Live Picture in collaboration with Microsoft and Netscape, HP's Imaging for Internet architecture supports FlashPix (1), JPEG and other file formats. By recognizing multiple formats, HP's new architecture brings the enhanced utility of the FlashPix tiled-image format to the legacy of images that are prevalent on the Internet today. In addition, the architecture conforms to standard transport protocols. The flexibility of the architecture allows for support of any client as well as interaction with any server in an Internet environment." And another press release referenced „a new architecture that enables end-to-end imaging applications over the Internet. HP's new Imaging for Internet client/server modules, promoted by HP's Internet Imaging Operation and endorsed by Microsoft, Informix, Oracle, Netscape, and Live Picture, Inc., enable rapid viewing and printing of high-resolution images over the Internet. This capability is key to the development of such new Internet imaging applications as digital-photo previewing and on-demand document distribution and printing."

In day to day operations, many of these companies may find themselves competing for significant business while their engineers and developers forge new technical linkages.

Standards Appreciation 101 ...1001

Too numerous to itemize, HP engineers and scientists, as well as thousands more throughout the company are working on standards that enable efficient and effective collaborations amongst persons companies and products. At one point, HP's

Corporate Engineering attempted to enumerate all of the activities, and, before the almanac was complete, it was out-dated. Now a web-search can quickly highlight the enormity of HP engineering involvement in standard-setting groups. Some examples, however, are useful. As part of the Infra-Red Data Association (IrDA), HP, working with other companies (including competitors), helped establish an interface for reliable connections from peripherals (like printers and scanners) to portable computers, desktop computers, and PDAs (Personal Digital Assistants). Proposals from HP Labs in Bristol set the standards for the physical link and management layers of the basic interface, creating an easy-to-use, yet robust data link. Another example consists of HP in the TINA Consortium (TINA-C), which is mapping out the architecture and framework for distributed computing standards. TINA-C uses many ideas developed by the ANSA consortium, of which HP has been an active member for a number of years. ANSA is a major research focus for developing new distributed systems concepts and architectures.

University Relations, Donations, and Associations

HP relies on and funds universities in the areas of basic research critical to its businesses. Universities serve as the beginning of the knowledge value chain as depicted in Fig. IV.3.5. The web of university connections is vast; to highlight and summarize the activities let's look at the activities in just one of the HP Labs research centers in Bristol, England. In Bristol, HP Labs has an extensive network of relationships with selected departments in academic institutions in over 20 countries worldwide. This investment is great, but so are the return and the future potential. Together, HP and the academic community foster innovative research, as well as develop the skills of the people generating those innovations and the people involved in the transfer of innovation from academia to industry.

Every year, the HP Labs site in Bristol hosts about 50 multinational students who work as members of project teams to gain industrial experience for their academic qualifications. Some of them are funded jointly by their government and HP as „industrial PhDs" in a program designed to forge long-term links between academia and industry.

In HP's tradition of „corporate citizenship" HP Labs, Bristol, provides state-of-the-art equipment to academic centers of excellence worldwide in the disciplines that impact its research, and it also collaborates with other HP entities in Europe on broader grant initiatives supporting pan-European consortia. This is only part of the overall HP contribution; because HP considers science and math competence vital in preparing people for the future, it is among the leading contributors to educational institutions. In 1996, HP donated US$ 57 million in equipment and cash to educational institutions. This was 80 percent of the company's total philanthropic contributions of more than US$ 70 million.

Most of the external research with academic partnerships focuses on strategic themes of direct joint concern: Appliance Architecture, Computing Platforms for Telecommunications, Mobile Communications, Multimedia Networking, Pattern Recognition and Imaging, and Security. Each of these is a coordinated program involving one or more of the Bristol laboratories and a small number of Research

Partners collaborating on joint projects funded by HP. For example, the HP Internet Research Institute funds support public domain research on Internet communication and service architecture and technologies. The research is conducted primarily at the Swedish Institute of Computer Science and researchers at HP Labs in Bristol manage the program.

Science Centers

HP Labs has satellite research facilities around the world. A recent article in HP's employee magazine, Measure, provided Lew Platt's views on company growth. „HP has a great deal of experience with entering new markets early, investing in their future and sustaining our pledge to ride out the difficult times. For example, we have a reputation for staying in Russia – for 29 years now – when other companies pulled out. And we've become one of the top ten companies in China because of our long-term resolve there." In both of these countries HP has research programs.

In Russia, the Enterprise Systems and Solutions Center is funding two research activities at the Institute of Thermophysics, which is part of the Russian Academy of Sciences, Siberian Branch. The projects harness a wealth of technical expertise from the forty Russian institutes located near Novosibirsk, Siberia. One project is studying the physics of bubble nucleation and expansion on rapidly heated surfaces, much like those found in HP's thermal inkjet printers. The second project focuses on low-cost, high-density packaging.

In China, HP Labs has established a joint research program with China's State Science and Technology Commission. Several projects in the areas of telecommu-

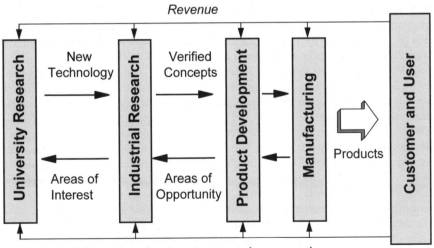

Fig. IV.3.5. The knowledge value chain.

nications and biotechnology are under way at various universities and research institutions across China. A unique feature of the program is that it is funded equally by both partners.

In 1997 the HP Israel Science Center was elevated to full stature as the fourth major center, alongside, Palo Alto, Bristol, and Tokyo. The HP-Israel Science Center was established in 1993 at the Technion-Israel Institute of Technology in Haifa, and has long been recognized as a Center of Excellence in computer science and electrical engineering. Since then, research activities have expanded in the areas of processing data, images, and video, with an emphasis on compression technologies and error control, video storage and networking, graphics and video integration, and database technologies.

HP also has formalized several programs with particular focus on different research objectives of common interest to universities and the company. Three of these are described below.

Basic Research Institute in the Mathematical Sciences (BRIMS): „Over HP's video teleconferencing network or from a vast video library, HPL engineers and scientists can access the work sponsored by HP's Basic Research Institute in the Mathematical Sciences (BRIMS). BRIMS was launched in 1994 as a joint undertaking with the Isaac Newton Institute for Mathematical Sciences (INI) in Cambridge, England. The INI set up a Hewlett-Packard Senior Research Fellowship and HP equipped the INI with a cluster of powerful workstations for high-performance scientific computation and research. BRIMS is also closely affiliated with the University of Bristol and has funded a joint appointment for five years with the Department of Mathematics. BRIMS is based around a core of resident researchers in Bristol augmented by PhD students, post-doctoral fellows, and frequent visitors. The main areas of research include quantum chaos, soliton propagation, dynamical systems, and stochastic modeling. This is a unique and innovative collaboration between industry and academia in developing a sustainable model for basic research. It has the potential to impact fields as diverse as quantum devices, medical instrumentation, and broadband networking. The question of „Can we or anyone build quantum computers more powerful than anything conceivable today?" may be answered with the BRIMS work.

QSRI, the Quantum Structures Research Initiative: Alongside the BRIMS program, HP Labs sponsors the Quantum Structures Research Initiative (QSRI), a basic research program to study the behavior of structures with nanometer dimensions, which are so small that they are dominated by quantum mechanical effects. This program brings scientists across the continents together (virtually) to explore devices with components that are tens of nanometers in dimension. At that size, the classical principles of Ohm's law, upon which most devices are based, are no longer valid, and the Heisenberg uncertainty principle is the dominating influence governing the behaviors of electrons. The QSRI focuses on ways to reproduce uniform quantum structures and study their electrical, optical, magnetic, and chemical properties with a view toward future device applications. Relying on HP Labs' Microelectronics and Measurement Systems Center, our capabilities in lithography, materials growth, and characterization may provide the company with a special expertise in the theory, production, and analysis of quantum structures.

Grass-Roots Basic Research Program: Around an HP coffeepot a conversation once took place: an engineer asked, „Why can't engineers do basic research?" The response was „Why not? Got any ideas on how to make it happen?" From this initial interchange, and a small amount of funding from the World's Best Industrial Research Lab program, the "Grass-Roots Basic Research Grants program" began. It is entirely owned and operated by engineers, soliciting proposals from students at universities and funding six to eight „out of the box" research projects a year. Students are given the opportunity to present to an HP audience, and HP researchers can tap directly into whatever wild and crazy university work they think will contribute to HP and the world. The peer-review process used by the group has since been incorporated into other research, and the program is now formally funded annually.

K-12: Supply Chain Management of Intellectual Capital

„At HP, we recognize that supporting education is one of the most important things we can do to realize success for future generations, for our company, and for society as a whole. I see educating our children as both a business and a social imperative. After all, the young faces we see today are the faces of the workforce and the customers of tomorrow," says Lew Platt in his web-letter to employees. And, in a recent Silicon Valley evening speaker series, one lecturer recalled the brilliance of Fred Terman (the Stanford professor who stimulated the thinking of many key founders of Silicon Valley companies) for his recognition of the value of young minds. This is also HP's vision: to help students be prepared to succeed in the workforce by making math and science exciting and meaningful, giving all students the opportunity to succeed, and helping every child enter school ready to learn.

It's critical for leaders within R&D organizations around the world to realize that, in the time it took to commercialize UNIX® (UNIX is a registered trademark of The Open Group), to widely deploy LAN technologies, to move the Internet from the university landscape to the corporate landscape, the world's educational systems released another generation of students. For R&D teams to devise the inventions of their dreams, they must invest some time in nurturing their future engineers and scientists. Companies must provide the young thinkers with the proper grounding to develop into the problem-solvers industry needs ... the proper „food for thought."

There *are three key goals* in developing future engineers and scientists for HP's research and development supply chain:

- Science & Math Proficiency, to significantly improve science and math achievement;
- Diversity, to increase the number of females and underrepresented minorities studying and teaching science and mathematics;
- Ready to Learn, to ensure that all children are ready to learn when they start school.

In support of these goals, there are dozens of different programs in place to contribute to hundreds of school districts (thousands of students) across the U.S., including the Hands-On Science Program, the Diversity in Education Initiative, and the Ready to Learn Via K-3 Early Literacy Initiative.

Contributions by engineers and scientists do not need to be massive in this arena. The following program highlights a way for even smaller R&D organizations to positively impact their educational supply chains. Many of HP's K-12 programs encourage time away from work but are limited by the number of HP scientists or engineers eager to work with a classroom full of students for an hour or so. Using e-mail, HP and David Neils (the HP employee who conceived and developed the program) found a way to reach students in a consistent, ongoing, one-to-one basis, extending the reach of HP engineers interested in working with young people. „Helping students find what they're passionate about -- and helping them develop skills that will boost their chances of success, especially in math and science – that's what HP's E-Mail Mentor program is trying to do," says David Neils. This program is one of the easier ways to establish connections between a company's current R&D wizards, and these future members of research and development teams. The best topics for discussion are those that generate enthusiasm and the drive to follow through in the student. Even simply writing in English may be a huge benefit for the student. In 1997, more than 2,000 HP employees participated in this e-mail mentor program.

In Europe, projects are underway in 63 schools in 16 countries across the European Community. In its first year alone, the European K-12 program reached more than 50,000 students with early access to emerging information technologies. Especially key to many of the pan-European programs is bringing the power of the Internet to the fingertips of these students. One program that seems readily adaptable to the Internet is the BerMUN (Berlin School's Model United Nations) Program, in which students simulate the work and function of the United Nations by representing the interests of different countries and debating those issues currently under discussion at the U.N. Another program in Geneva, Switzerland partners HP with Lego to help children learn about image acquisition, image processing, and image restoration, along with other image processing techniques. HP's future in digital photography, as well as imaging on the Internet, can only be spurred ahead once these students join the workforce. And yet another program will provide children with first-hand experience with widely distributed but collaborating teams, as each school adopts a monument to describe, photograph and put up on the web.

4.3   Practices and Processes to Improve the Product and Profit

There are many aspects of the product development process that product divisions can learn from each other or improve on. Some of the tools, training, resources, and challenges facing engineers throughout HP are described here. To varying degrees these may be relevant to a product group.

Imaginatively Understanding Customer Needs

Many studies in the academic arena and amongst corporations point to the first critical steps in a project as clear indicators of a product's future market success (Wilson, 1990). These first steps should include: intimately understanding user needs, identifying key stakeholders in the buying process, clearly defining the problem to be solved, assessing the market environment, and translating all these data into product definitions. The risks associated with the product are a function of the risks assumed in these first steps, especially if teams fail to rigorously develop a thorough understanding of these needs. But how does one execute these first critical steps? Process improvements are essential in the areas of market research, scenario construction, metaphor techniques, ethnographic studies (anthropological expeditions into the living culture of the customer), and other creative means of understanding users needs. Empathy with the user world rather than simply relying on users' own articulation of their needs is a requirement.

HP's Corporate Product Marketing organization is looking for ways to help „product designers develop a deeper understanding of the current user environments so that they can better extrapolate how those environments may evolve in the future and imagine the future needs their technology can satisfy." The marketing and the Corporate Quality folks are equipping HP groups with the skills and tools to more rigorously specify the value creation and delivery systems through which HP products will emerge for the customer. Immersion and knowledge of the true added value of each of the value chain contributors helps in fully understanding customer reactions to products.

The danger to all these mechanisms is that R&D may not believe in these tools, until „they see for themselves." Data distrust, unless delivered by a trusted source, has plagued marketing and other business functions for generations. However, skeptical individuals might prosper from the wisdom of recognized high-technology marketing guru Regis McKenna, as he coached a recent meeting of Silicon Valley entrepreneurs: „In this real time world, be prepared for the eventuality of anything." In a world of constantly changing systems, dynamics, and business relationships where keeping up with the speed of light may be too slow, interpersonal relationships amongst marketing, R&D, and other business functions with the strength and trust of steel will define the outstanding product development organizations.

"R&D managers need to stimulate cross-disciplinary activities for real breakthroughs. They also need to be skilled at managing investment portfolios, balancing risk with return, long-term priorities against short-term issues, and measurement of the present vs. vision of the future. "

— Hans Stork, HP Palo Alto, USA

Balancing Creativity versus Planning

HP's organizational values and commitment to meeting corporate objectives shape the company's strategies and practices. Each business engineers its future with a mix of HP traditional management practices, such as Management By Objectives, Management By Wandering Around, and the Open Door Policy and the more structured planning practices, including the Ten-Step Business Planning process, Total Quality Control and Hoshins.

The following excerpt comes from a speech given at the Yale School by Lew Platt. „Bill Hewlett tells an interesting story about the dynamic tension between the creativity that leads to innovation and the hard-headed practicality required to bring a product to market and earn the profit that makes possible the next round of creativity. In a 1986 speech on creativity, Bill recalled the time he quoted Thomas Edison to an HP engineering manager. You've probably heard Edison's famous quip, 'There ain't no rules around here. We're trying to accomplish something.' When Bill said that, the HP manager replied, 'Don't say that. Creativity is what screws up my engineering schedule.' Bill then recognized that 'these two comments say a great deal about the creative process. It works well when it is not too structured. But, in the end, it must be tamed, harnessed, and hitched to the wagon of mankind's needs.'"

Lew Platt retold this story at the Yale School of Business, continuing with a response to the question, 'What about the concerns voiced earlier by the HP engineering manager who told Bill Hewlett that creativity killed his engineering schedule?' Lew replied, „Well, we've got a process in place to make sure that doesn't happen. It's called the phase review process (Fig. IV.3.6). The rigor imposed by this process helps translate creativity into products that can be shipped. Everybody knows what each phase entails, and so they are quite clear about what needs to be accomplished before moving on. More rapid time-to-market is one of the real benefits to having those phases clearly defined. Let's take product definition as an example. Years ago, the company did a major survey of HP engineers trying to identify what caused products to be late to market. The number one cause was unstable product definitions. Said differently, people kept changing the product specifications by adding elegant features that our customers could live without and which increased costs and development time."

Lew continues, „So we spent a lot of time honing our skills in product definition. And we made it very clear that after a project had moved past Phase One, the product definition couldn't be changed. What makes this discipline bearable to our creative engineers is their knowledge that the product under development is just the first of a family. We never design assuming that we won't go back and make it even better in a second iteration. And so, our engineers know that if they couldn't do something in the initial introduction, they can do it in the follow-on product." Getting it „more right" upfront, better secures the likelihood of these future releases. This upfront „correctness" is what was clearly proclaimed as one of the most significant challenges around the globe for HP managers.

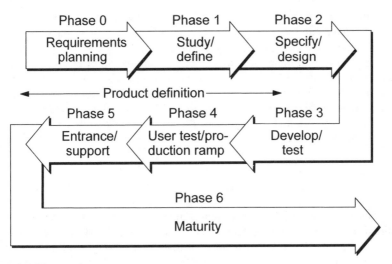

Fig. IV.3.6. Phase review process.

Engineering and Manufacturing Processes (EMP) Organization

One of the corporate organizations critical to streamlining global R&D is HP's Engineering and Manufacturing Processes (EMP) organization which is focused primarily on process improvements. EMP was formed some years ago by an HP management team that desired closer links between R&D and manufacturing organizations. The primary role and responsibility of the department is to drive improvements in HP's conceptual product design and development process, including various disciplines such as electronics engineering, mechanical engineering, and software design methodologies.

The organization's goal is to create an integrated „roadmap" that links product development plans and requirements more closely with manufacturing technologies. Responsibilities include leadership and integration of design improvement goals, such as design for reliability and design for reuse, as well as developing and acquiring methodologies. EMP also has a key role in the evaluation and development of HP's electronic assembly process for which it establishes and maintains standards for design, equipment, quality, and material for selected electronic as-

"Hardware and software innovations enabled localization of HP-UX , including Japanese, Korean, and Chinese input, and Asian outline font. With the emphasis on profitability, we must find ways to meet our goals to be customer-oriented and address the local needs and custom styles."

— Ju-en Teng, HP Taiwan

sembly processes. Other special areas of expertise include software development, project management, CAD design tools, and R&D process measurements.

All of these areas and topics provide an opportunity for EMP to better integrate engineering and manufacturing processes for improved products and product processes across the HP businesses. This organization's contributions are often critical to the quick start-up of a new development operation or the adoption of newly acquired research organizations. Some examples of the resources available from the Engineering and Management Processes team include the Project Management Initiative materials, software tools, training and reference materials, and more.

Project Management Initiative (PMI)

The purpose of the Project Management Initiative is to provide leadership for the continuous improvement of project management throughout Hewlett-Packard. The vision guiding the Project Management Initiative is a future state in which: The practices for project success are being identified, concisely documented, widely understood, willingly adopted, appropriately adapted, and enthusiastically applied, so that HP people managing projects continuously improve how they do their work and lead others to quickly achieve excellent results. In his 1989 Hoshin, then HP Chief Operating Officer, Dean Morton, established the Project Management Initiative. CEO Lew Platt continued this emphasis when he met with the HP Project Management Council in 1993 and shared his vision for project management at HP: „I think project management is a core competence and a real important one. I'd like to see it be best-in-class. To be the best and to stay the best requires continuous improvement." This activity encompasses the development and deployment of many cross-company competencies. Through websites, conferences, training, tools, and consultancy, the PMI team continuously pursues their vision.

Reference Documents and Project Management Resources

A common practice around many functions within HP is the documentation of processes and the development of reference documentation by actual practitioners. Usually the content of process reference documentation builds upon the experience of successful process participants. For example, with process documentation for project managers the goal is to use the experience of successful project managers to guide others in developing and improving their skills and those of their teams. HP teams frequently refer to these writings as „living documents," because they are candidates for modification whenever changes would improve the communication of information to process players. The creation of such documentation is just one of the ways HP teams take responsibility for „sharing best practices". Teams that find themselves working together for the first time, especially across organizational boundary lines, usually make decisions on the ground rules (for working together) and the processes found in these documents, thereby aligning team members or „getting everyone on the same page."

One of the best examples of this activity which grew to become an established part of HP's project manager training is best described in a book entitled *Creating an Environment for Successful Projects*. HP's Randall Englaund described the information resources that were developed as part of HP's Project Management Initiative. The authors write: „Topics scoring the highest, (those identified as the most important to a project manager's success), such as scheduling and estimation, were researched to find ideas and best practices and to share them widely. Both the initiative staff and the project managers around the company document these practices and make them available to others in hard copy and online using a World Wide Web browser. Interested individuals are tracked on a database so best practices and success stories can be disseminated to a known audience of practioners. Preparation of these documents has the added advantage of bringing the knowledge of the initiative staff about each topic to a peak" (Graham and Englaund 1997: 214).

The authors continue with „A project manager's survival kit of instructional materials was assembled to help new and seasoned project managers perform their jobs better. It is recommended that each project manager get a personal copy so the material may be marked up, easily accessed, and used repeatedly."

The description continues: „The survival kit includes the following:

- A computer-based training course on project management.
- An audio cassette program that discusses ways to improve communication, managing, and time management skills.
- Videotapes of interviews with successful HP project managers.
- Books on effective meeting skills, the project manager's work environment, coping with time and stress, and the implementation of project management.
- Bibliography of additional resources.
- Project management training curriculum.
- And much more."

Everyone throughout HP can have access to these materials, yet it is always the responsibility of the individual, the organization, or the team to adopt and deploy the techniques.

Software Initiative

The purpose of the Software Initiative is: To foster sustainable breakthroughs in product generation capabilities for HP's business goals as related to software and solutions. The vision guiding this program foresees an HP where: We build work

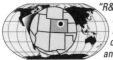 "R&D can't remain isolated in functional structures if it is to become responsive to and knowledgeable about markets, competition, customers, and channel partners. Developing market winning products now means developing a product that is optimal from both the customer perspective, as well as the channel perspective, and this may mean partnering to win."

— *Tara Bunch, HP Greeley, USA*

 *"People who cannot read English and have never used a computer must find our new products not only highly reliable, but easy to use and even intuitive. In a young R&D department such as HP China, more important than language, culture or government are the basics of prioritizing, planning, and schedules."*

— Jim Sullivan, HP Beijing, China

environments for the network age where progress and growth are important and essential; where community and business values overlap in meaningful ways; where change is comfortable and normal; and, where individuals are valued and respected for their own unique contributions. Tools developed and coordinated via the software initiative include the HP Inspection Process, methods for reuse, and numerous tools for software configuration management, measurement and assessment, and maintenance. The Software Initiative also serves as the center of expertise on HP's Fusion methodology for object-oriented software design, one of the technologies investigated as part of the Technology Transfer project described at the end of this chapter.

4.4   Meeting, Growing and Learning

There are many ways to meet other professionals within HP and to learn from them. Access to people, access to information, and access to time is enabled via a variety of mechanisms.

Dual Career Ladder = The R&D Technical Contributor Program

There had to be a way of stopping the practice of turning *great* engineers and scientists into *adequate* managers, and there was. HP needed to provide engineers with a career-path alternative, and thus evolved the dual ladder. The dual ladder was designed to attract, develop, motivate, and retain senior technical contributors. It is the means by which technical contributors can earn promotions and associated salary increases, without moving into the management arena. It is expected that senior R&D engineers and scientists jobs will be highly paid because these incumbents contribute as much to HP as managers in similarly scoped jobs. The role of R&D Technical Contributor was later strengthened and expanded within HP. Technologists who were experienced with many external technologies that were not developed within HP became critical to HP's products retaining profitable, leadership, solutions-oriented positions in the marketplace.

Travel

HP engineers and scientists travel as the need arises. We travel amongst divisions to customers, universities, partner companies, conferences, and research labs. We travel to overcome the challenges posed by the distances … even in the U.S. We plan on travel, fund travel, and optimize all the associated processes to make travel easy. We complement all the new electronic communications media with good old-fashioned face-to-face meetings and discussions. And, we make sure all of the communications technology also works to support the continuation of productive work while traveling. Of course, whenever possible, multiple objectives are combined to make the most of the travel expense. For example, a researcher traveling for a scientific symposium may complement their itinerary with visits to customers or colleagues at other HP sites.

Mobility

HP provides its employees with international opportunities to develop their expertise. In this author's 17 years with HP, she's moved amongst almost a dozen businesses within HP, and across numerous departments including R&D, marketing, and field sales centers. Time has been spent in the U.S. as well as Boeblingen, Germany, and she harbors dreams of her next opportunity to work at another HP location somewhere in the world.

A colleague who developed part of the AcceSS7 telecommunications management system while working in South Queensferry, Scotland is now working in the software applications frameworks department in Palo Alto, that is transferring its technologies to HP's software operation in Bangalore, India. In just a couple of years she's obtained a broad cross-continental perspective of HP R&D around the world. Another colleague who recently participated in a video documentary on technology transfer retold the story of years of project experience gained in HP's divisions in Waldbronn, Germany. While there, for breakthrough technologies germinated, were co-developed with the German team once she returned to the U.S., and now discussions to develop the final product are underway.

Just recently, a few of us were brainstorming some project ideas for a department manager newly transferred to HP Labs in Japan. This manager is eager to make contributions to HP's products and businesses anywhere in the world. As he starts up his group, building a vision of the future, and determining how his team can have an impact on HP's customers, he is business and site neutral; HP's business operations around the planet provide him a field of opportunities.

Within the company there are over 10 different ways of enabling HP personnel movements around the globe: longer term foreign service assignments or even permanent relocations to a variety of extended business trip arrangements. Different sets of employee benefits with varying associated expenses provide a broad range of options to a business trying to find the right people for a job, regardless of their current locations within the company.

Learning Opportunities

A core principle of the HP way is the belief that „men and women want to do a good job, a creative job, and, if they are provided the proper environment, they will do so." HP recognizes that providing a supportive development environment is vital to the company as well as to the individuals. Fundamental to creating and

---

Major issues for global R&D management at HP:

1. Insatiable appetite for intellect: our people will shape our future;

2. Intimate interconnections: across HP businesses, with partners, with customers, especially across the emerging, wired ecosystems;

3. Ingrained HP Way: opening our doors to the input and ideas of others (no matter who or where they are), and management by walking around (around the globe) to enable massively parallel product development to meet our objectives;

4. Increased speed at which we must mobilize ourselves, the rest of the company and our partners, to take advantage of the innovations and ideas.

---

maintaining such an environment is the commitment to lifelong learning – an investment made by HP and its employees in the future of the company. Although lifelong learning is a responsibility shared between HP and the employee, ultimately, the employee is responsible for his or her own development and career management. In this way, development is employee-owned and manager-supported.

Because HP relies on fast-changing technologies, the company promotes continuing education through internal programs, as well as advanced-degree programs with universities. In the same local company newspaper that provides space for selling a car or renting a vacation cabin, employees can find out about after-hours and daytime classes. Thousands of classes, classroom-based, self-paced, and viewable via any of several distance-learning programs are cataloged on HP websites, and are usually focused on a discipline, such as mechanical or electrical design, project management, software, etc. Other more pervasive learning resources, such as the library, the web, and internal conferences are also available.

HP has created several programs in which employees earn advanced degrees part-time, including the National Technical University and its distance learning program. If part-time options do not sufficiently satisfy HP's business needs, full-time fellowships may be awarded. „Resident Fellowship" awards are usually given to employees seeking master's degrees in traditional engineering areas, such as computer science/engineering, electrical engineering, engineering management, industrial engineering, and manufacturing. Employees may attend any U.S. university where HP currently recruits. HP will pay 75% of the employee's base salary and 100% of tuition, texts, and lab fees, plus two roundtrip airfares to the school. These resident fellowships have expanded much beyond the original HP Honors Cooperative Program formed with Stanford University in 1959. Even back then, David Packard writes, „The program made it possible for us to hire top-level young graduates from around the country with the promise that, if they came to work for us and we thought it appropriate, they could attend graduate school while on full HP salary." This kind of program may be found in many other countries where HP has significant R&D resources. Of course, it's designed and managed locally to satisfy the needs of the local employees and local HP businesses in collaboration with their local partner universities.

Team Learning

HP also offers the opportunity for group or team learning. In several classes over the years, this author has seen or been part of intact teams taking the classes together. Very often, during student introductions the members of these teams have cited local HP management's commitment to the skills and concepts that are being taught as the reason the intact team is taking the class together. Some of these classes included „Crossing the Chasm" for newly started business teams, the „Process of Management" (when delivered to newly formed division departments), and „High-Performance Teams" training.

Three additional classes have a broad appeal to teams. Complete teams or cross-organizational partners are encouraged to participate in „Operating Across Organizations" together. During this training, participants identify detailed process steps for operating across organizations, create a plan to address the needs of stakeholders and influential people, and develop approaches to using proven success practices for influencing without authority within entities and across geographical or functional areas.

Another opportunity for group learning at HP is the „Rapid Time to Market" workshop at which existing work teams gain exposure to the best practice techniques for projects with time-constrained schedules. Teams learn how to shorten project times, which may lead to lower costs and improved market potential.

And the last example with broad appeal in many HP organizations is „Working in Groups", which is designed especially for previously formed work teams training. The goal is to improve the teamwork skills of solving problems and making decisions as a group. Together, teams learn to understand the stages of team or group development and to lead or facilitate a group through these stages. With the high value placed on open communications within HP, the team learns to give and receive feedback individually and in groups, and to overcome the common meeting errors such as those made when planning, starting, structuring, controlling and closing meetings.

Conferences - the Internal-Only Kind

Connections and collaborations, especially across distributed and widely dispersed

"The future will only move faster as businesses are driven to release more custom products to market. Speed. Speed. Speed. Speed is critical as we design for local customers and access local technology, talent, and trends."

— Steve Paolini, HP Malaysia

R&D groups, need to be instigated or ignited in some way. One of the early practices was the „chalk talks" in which researchers interested in a particular subject or project could come together and share ideas voluntarily and informally. This has evolved, as those with common and specialized interests became distributed across the large product development landscape, into the grassroots generation of conferences and forums for presentation and discussion of research and technology problems. These are relatively informal, low budget, pay-as-you-go (as always) events, run by and for HP engineers.

In a recent twelve-month period, the conferences targeted for HP-employee only participation included the Distributed Application Developers Conference, HP Portable Design and Low Power Summit, Home Summit, HP Radio Conference, Conference on Optics and Radio Technologies, Silicon Technology Conference, Design Technology Conference, Micromechanics, Micromachining and Miniaturization Workshop, Content Based Retrieval workshop, HP Thermal Symposium, Performance Modeling and Analysis Symposium, Electronics and Packaging Conference, and the workshop on the Automated Analysis of Driven Nonlinear and Stochastic Systems (this one open by invitation to non-HPers). And, as a by-product of a recent conference, there are now web-based registration, feedback, and conference proceeding tools for non-HPers to use, as well as a „how-to" binder for those administrative assistants dealing with the conference logistics.

The best summary of the value of these events can be summarized in one organizer's brief history as recanted over email: Chandrakant Patel says, „The HPL Thermal Symposium has resulted in the HP Thermal Symposium Series. This year's HP Thermal Symposium is at the HP Convex division in Richardson, Texas. The immense interest is due to growing thermal challenges in system cooling design. HP has one to three thermal engineers at each site. The objective of the thermal symposium is to bring all the engineers together to learn the „best practices" at various sites. The first symposium at HP Labs was supposed to be an informal get together of chalk talks from local sites. It resulted in attendance from 23 divisions worldwide. It also resulted in the „HP Cool Team" and the HP Thermal Master Index – a network and web site that helps each other out by sharing thoughts electronically."

Corporate Intranet

The following was written in the January 15 issue of *CIO Magazine* (Field 1997):
    „It's 9 a.m. Monday in Palo Alto, Calif., and Hewlett-Packard Co. is primed to roll out a new company-wide word processing application. But first there are some last-minute details. Brandt Faatz, Fort Collins, Colorado-based head of HP's PC common operating environment team, calls his key players in the United States, Europe and Asia. Together they iron out the final bugs of the rollout and post a synopsis of their discussion on the World Wide Web, alerting thousands of HP employees to the pending upgrade. By 5 p.m., the new software is loaded onto a master server in Palo Alto and from there is transmitted globally to 400 file servers, which in turn distribute the software to more than 100,000 HP desktops

worldwide. By 5 p.m. Wednesday—just 48 hours later—the rollout is complete."
It's true. It works.

The internal support organization at one site even allows for push-button load-
ing of 30 applications. All employees use the network for global electronic communication, software distribution, and personnel training and document management, and to create distributed teams. It was the network that allowed this author
to build the global HP view of R&D issues that contributed to this chapter.

A 1996/1997 snapshot of the core of Hewlett-Packard's client/server Intranet is
a 21-node, global WAN. HP's worldwide server hubs are connected by 64Kbps
T1 and T3 lines. The servers are the system's backbone: each is connected to at
least two others for backup and redundancy. 100Mbps fiber-optic data distribution
interface (FDDI) networks exist in every HP building and transmit data to local
workgroups of ten to 100 desktop PCs. Shared or switched 10Mbps Ethernet cable
connects every PC to the FDDI network, with routing over the TCP/IP network
via Cisco routers. The future may bring a peer-to-peer, multimedia network that
supports video and 3-D graphics. Via this network one HP connects 400 plus sites,
3000 plus servers, 100,000 personal computers and 23,000 workstations. Over 1.5
million e-mail messages travel across the network daily, and it carries over 10
terabytes of data monthly. Special purpose web applications support a variety of
functions such as the sales information tool that reaches 5000 sales representatives
around the world.

Web Sites for New Information Distribution: Everyone knows the web is wonderful for sharing and accessing information – we are reminded of its importance
daily in the press. Rather than preach the value of the web here, examples of
Intranet usage seem more valuable. However, since readers can not browse the
internal sites that support some of the R&D engineers a partial enumeration must
suffice. The HP Intranet connects sites containing information on external contractor management, planning tools, software reuse, manufacturing and R&D processes, university programs focused on manufacturing excellence, strategic alliances (including descriptions of current relationships), software applications (at
various stages of deployment or implementation), HP's standards activities, and
materials to assist with Formal Technical Reviews (FTR).

Local websites provide timely access to opinions and discussions not otherwise
accessible to the broader populations. For example, management discussions during the HP Labs annual review (in Bristol, UK) were posted on a secure website,
enabling HPL employees worldwide to ask questions of management during the
review meetings. Replies were posted as they were written. That day, the website
had 13,000 hits – coming from an organization of just 1,100 people – signaling
individuals keeping abreast of timely business discussions. Over a hundred internal newsgroups provide additional vehicles for contact and collaboration.

Web as a Development Tool: HP is using the web widely as a development
tool. A couple of examples that are talked about publicly follow. The Inkjet Business Unit has 6000 manufacturing employees on six sites. The challenge of publishing the correct manufacturing process documents in a timely manner and to the
right people was improved with the move to a web repository. The web database
provides easy access and tracking of the manufacturing-change documents read by

the various operators. Overnight changes are now possible; the company benefited greatly from this improvement when it moved a manufacturing line from Corvallis, Oregon to Dublin, Ireland in two days.

Another web project provides for web-access to HP's product and parts information. The project was started at one HP location and it spread to 24 other locations around the company. Any authorized user may query the web-site regarding costs, usage, sources, and other useful parts data. The user doesn't have to know where the information is located – i.e., on which of the thirty different HP systems. Tremendous time-to-market can be realized when, for example, design occurs in Santa Clara, California for HP NetServers and the resulting products are built in Singapore; the move from manufacturing release to volume production now happens in one day, not 3 weeks.

Beyond these major development and manufacturing linkage improvements, there are hundreds of distributed development teams operating with websites as their primary means of cross-group coordination, including the Technology Transfer team described at the end of this chapter.

HP Journal

The Hewlett-Packard Journal is published bimonthly by the Hewlett-Packard Company to recognize technical contributions made by HP personnel. Primarily HP employees write articles for the HP Journal, although articles from non-HP authors are also considered for publication when the article deals with HP-related research or when solutions to technical problems are made possible by using HP equipment. Publishing one's research and engineering contributions in the Journal is a source of pride throughout HP's R&D organizations. In a recent twelve-month period, the HP Journal published articles authored by engineers in Australia, Britain, France, Germany, and Japan. Thirty-three engineers and scientists from these countries shared their work with the world. The HP Journal's Advisory Board consists of technical representatives from almost forty different HP R&D organizations, with over 20% from non-U.S. labs.

HP Press

The goal of Hewlett-Packard Professional Books is to give technical people a better understanding of emerging technologies, industry standards, and how HP products and services address a wide range of needs. Books are also a vehicle for HP engineers and scientists to share their technical knowledge and practical know-

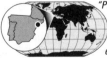

"Phenomenal computing power at insignificant cost, ubiquitous satellite transmission of information to the mobile individual, and transparent computing and unobtrusive ease of use are in our future. To produce these, R&D should retain simple focused organizations with clear objectives and priorities, and create more efficient distributed design processes that work across a global landscape."

— **Dewey Baker, HP Barcelona, Spain**

*"Communication in English, given time differences, is very difficult
but most important. Constant and continual communications is especially
critical as we race to keep up with market dynamics and establish
leadership positions in local markets against worldwide competitors."*

— Tomio Wakasugi, HP Kobe, Japan

how, and to explore the application of new technologies with their colleagues throughout the industry. The books are published as Hewlett-Packard Professional Books, an imprint created by both Prentice Hall Professional Technical Reference and HP Press. HP books on new technologies, standards, best practices, and specific products include: „ATM & MPEG-2: Integrating Digital Video Into Broadband Networks," a detailed look at MPEG-2 and ATM, the key enabling technologies for digital video from two authors in HP Germany. From two Canadian HP authors you can read about practical techniques for securing distributed computing systems in „Security in Distributed Computing: Did You Lock the Door?" And, from one of the HP Labs teams that was interviewed as part of the Technology Transfer case study presented at the end of this chapter, one can find the title „Object-Oriented Development: The Fusion Method."

The Research Library

In a recent report on *Managing In-House Information* by the European Industrial Research Management Association, Working Group 4, it was said „Managing information to make it effective and relevant for R&D and managing R&D to make it effective for the business are but two sides of the same coin – the creation of competitive advantage" (EIRMA 1993). If you want the company to be competitive, you need R&D; if you want R&D to be relevant and meaningful you need an innovative library focused on break-throughs that keep HP's intellectual capital operating on the freshest crude and refined information available. So says Eugenie Prime, the head of HP's Research Library in Palo Alto, California. Joel Birnbaum suggests „Information is no longer simply a strategic asset; it is a critical enabler of success. The future of our company depends, in large part, on how effective we are at accessing, distributing and synthesizing information on a global basis ... the HP Labs Research Library is the nerve center of our organization." In 1997, HP's use of technology finally resulted in the introduction of the Digital Library service which provides HP employees with tools for searching and downloading INSPEC abstracts, IEEE articles, and U.S. patents at their desktops and is one step closer to a true virtual library. This is just one of dozens of on-line search information access tools available at HP and is a result of a collaboration amongst HP, INSPEC, the IEEE, and MicroPatent.

As the HP R&D community faces the challenges of staffing distributed design and development teams, it may take greater advantage of another special library service, CONNEX. CONNEX is a web tool for connecting people to people, by interests and expertise, across departments and divisions. Employees submit their individual profiles to the network, so searchers can look for others at HP with similar interests or with expertise in particular areas. It's not a job requisition system (employees have access to another tool for that); it's really a vehicle to facilitate making connections to other HP employees. As managers work on and recruit for „virtual teams", in which one may not really meet others at morning coffee, people CONNEX-ions will become ever more important. (By the way, CONNEX was funded by the World's Best Industrial Research Lab program also, as is mentioned further ahead.)

5   A Successful Team

5.1   The Technology Transfer Tapestry

It is within the context of this HP fabric that the reader should view the story of the Technology Transfer WBIRL project. The Technology Transfer Project was a grassroots project to examine those key success factors (or barriers) to successful transfer of technologies from HP Labs to HP's product divisions. It was sponsored by a WBIRL (World's Best Industrial Research Lab) grant that started in April 1996 and is ongoing. This project was formed with individuals located in England, US, and Italy from three of the HP Labs research centers and was inspired and coordinated by one scientist who decided it was time for improvements to HP's technology transfer toolset. His observation of the challenges faced when trying to impact HP businesses with new technologies from the research labs, and his firm belief that he could make a unique contribution, raised the interests of colleagues, the support of his management, and the financial commitment of the WBIRL grant committee.

George Hopkins, the team leader, recruited members, and then members re-cruited members. The people involved included individuals from the US, England, and Italy. We worked for over two years and are still working. The team consists of a diverse group of people with dozens of advanced degrees; we are participants in numerous HP advanced education opportunities, engineers, managers, and business-types, with a wide variety and large amount of product development and research expertise.

We worked in a distributed manner, communicating by e-mail or videoconfer-ence most of the time with a few face-to-face daylong meetings that were critical to building a common purpose and vision. The early attempts to „get going on the work" flopped because the distributed team of twelve had not yet established

"To speed our products to market, and to leverage technology, we must generate common product platforms and technologies that enable a variety of end user products while executing as virtual teams. It's unlikely we'll have all the expertise and resources in single locations. So we must effectively organize and execute programs across multiple geographies within and outside of the HP organization."

— **Bill Buffington, HP Palo Alto, USA**

> **Most important drivers for globalization:**
>
> 1. Obtaining the best intellectual capital on the planet to work on HP business problems;
>
> 2. Proximity to the universities that change the way the world looks at the world;
>
> 3. Living and R&D-ing in the markets and ecosystems HP wishes to influence, impact and change;
>
> 4. HP vision of "HP for the world".

common goals and objectives. These early difficulties and frustrations disappeared after the crucial face-to-face 2-day goal-setting/working meeting. We could then proceed with briefer monthly video or telephone project meetings.

We were web-enabled and web-dependent for our working documents as well as our final product. We used the resources of the company in all our work. An information researcher on our team did extensive library research to identify the industries best practices and techniques. Other corporate functions lent a hand by directing us to make „really useful and useable" tools to be sure we understood the needs and expectations of our sponsors and to continually think about the broad variety of product development work taking place amongst the hundreds of HP divisions. The team selected some pre-existing process reference documentation templates for packaging our findings; we thought it was important to reuse any tools available, and this template was already a de facto internal HP „standard" for capturing best practices.

Dozens of HP employees at all levels of R&D and amongst dozens of different divisions gave us time for interviews; dozens more gave us time to present our findings. In the hallways and around the coffeepots, still others supplied additional pointers and references. With the time and talents of the HP people, we were able to exceed our own expectations while incurring minimal expenses.

We scrutinized close to a hundred HP Labs research projects and identified a dozen that deserved detailed study, many of which developed into successful HP products. We accessed individuals throughout the R&D community around the world. One case we inspected involved a team building a Very Large Instruction Word (VLIW) processor for performance improvements in a product developed and managed by a business located in another country.

Another case study involved the development of FUSION, a systematic software development method for object-oriented software that was developed at HP Labs in Bristol, England. Fusion is a full-coverage method, providing a direct route from requirements definition to analysis, design, and implementation. This transfer success story was threaded into the R&D picture around the world (including HP Germany, France, Singapore, and the U.S.). This technology also moved into the marketplace, thanks to HP's tightly interlocking warp and weft threads (HP Labs, EMP, partnerships with software companies and consultants, the HP Journal, internal conferences, and so on).

As the Technology Transfer project makes its contribution it moves HPL further towards fulfilling its aspirations: To have an even greater impact on HP products and innovations. The amount of time invested in this project grew beyond our original proposal, once the team determined what it wanted to do and once we saw what we could accomplish together. All of the team members worked well beyond the call of duty to make sure that the project met its goals and was a product of which they could all be very proud. There were over one hundred project contributors if one considers all the managers, interviewees, and reviewers involved. We couldn't have completed this project without operating across the company terrain created from the warp and the weft of HP. It's a rich environment in which we do our work; it's truly a thriving, vitalizing ecosystem in which we innovate and thrive.

5.2   The HP Future

The pattern in HP's future is already strung across the loom, and the moves to bring forth the HP future are being made as you read these pages. Essentially, only after weaving together many of the essential threads of the HP Company is one able to see the pattern of HP R&D work, as was modeled in the technology transfer case study. To close this HP review, let us take a look at HP's future as seen through the eyes of R&D managers around the world, Lew Platt, and this author.

In the process of constructing this HP chapter, dozens of HP R&D managers around the world were consulted. Because the inquiry was completed swiftly via email, these managers contributed their thoughts without hesitation. Their forecasts unanimously converged in areas of significance and provided the following insights in addition to those already presented in the boxes at the bottom of some pages.

Everybody Is Invited to Comm-In, Communicate and Inform.

All HP locations are experiencing the way information access changes the world with easy global access to information via the Internet. The Internet is a tool for radically changing the way a company does business by linking information to anyone, anywhere, and anytime. Within HP there are global communications tools and a *Global Communication Environment* that helps speed global R&D productivity improvements. Lowered barriers to information access, alongside a growing demand for close regular contact, for alignment of goals and plans, with the „centers of gravity" in R&D organizations, demands that everyone increase investments in their skills development and the discipline required for communications (across the media).

HP R&D Reach Is Stretching

HP businesses must generate product platforms and technologies that enable a variety of end user products and services. For HP, products that appear in cars, bedrooms, kitchens or gardens or even those worn on people represent significant evolution. When HP R&D managers unanimously suggest a shift from technology-oriented R&D to market-oriented R&D, that shift is critical. These managers emphasize that one size does not fit all – HP must know about user needs in each country. The world population is growing and aging fast; HP businesses need to predict where the economic consumption powers will be in the next decades. Local customer needs will drive custom (localized) styles. Many R&D leaders are expecting, and aspiring to make a *fundamental impact* on high complexity problems – those that affect enterprises, countries, and how people live their lives.

More „Joints" in the Future

Finally, the HP R&D managers unanimously see more „joints" in our future:

- More places where informational and organizational structures can connect for the benefit of all (win-win-win-win …HP, customers, partners, shareholders, etc.) will form,
- More physical and informational places where people can gather will be built,
- More concurrent activity will take place, and,
- More shared activities will be sought.

They see more joint development across the continents, worldwide distributed design and development of new products, more integration between labs and businesses, and *the convergence of traditionally distinct technology bases* to provide capabilities and products that are currently hard to even conceive. *Organizational responsiveness* is key. Working across multiple geographies is key. Many said they could no longer act as independent entities in their businesses. Teams everywhere will see ever increasing levels of collaborative efforts. Product groups will need to efficiently link inside and outside resources from and around the world. „Border-less" research collaboration will grow from within some regions and extend into other regions and continents.

How Does this Compare With the Views of Lew Platt?

Nicely. At one of HP's user group conferences, Lew Platt painted a picture of HP's future which could be derived from two significant trends: „The first lies in the development of what we at HP call the information utility. Al Gore and friends call it the information highway. And despite the fact that the hype has preceded

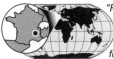

"R&D organizations are building more products around industry standard definitions, and in consort with true alliance partners and cooperating competitors. Yet, we must each deliver products and services in which our customers find true value. Therefore, we shouldn't focus on existing core competencies solely; we must focus on those required core competencies to deliver to the customer's need."

— Sylvain Sadier, HP Grenoble, France

reality, we're convinced the information highway or utility will come to pass in our lifetimes – probably before the end of the decade." (Fig. IV.3.5)

Lew continued, „We prefer the 'utility' metaphor because it suggests the development of the second trend, 'information appliances' that can plug easily into the utility and tap its power – just as today's toasters, coffee machines and televisions plug into the electrical outlet. But tomorrow's information appliances won't have to search for an outlet, because the information utility will include ubiquitous wireless technology."

He continued, „This scenario presents enormous opportunities for HP to help our customers take advantage of these emerging technologies. We see ourselves in two basic roles. First, we'll help build the information utility. We won't try to build it ourselves. That's the responsibility of the telephone and cable companies of the world. We have a lot to offer, however, to customers building and managing their own private networks. Second, we'll create a rich variety of information appliances. We have a culture and organization that encourage innovation – plus lots of experience and an increasing comfort with mass markets."

„In this future era of converging technologies and industries, HP has an arsenal of expertise that few companies possess. We have three core competencies – measurement, computing and communication – something we call MC^2. We're advancing the state of the art in each of these areas. We're also combining them in interesting new ways. Let me illustrate why their combination intrigues us so."

Lew Platt concluded his comments to the HP User group with this forecast: „If

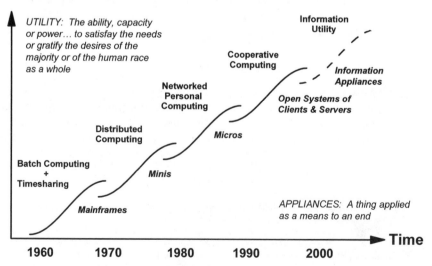

Fig. IV.3.7. Towards pervasive information systems.

Lessons learned for organizing R&D at HP:

1. R&D is part of a team that needs to live and breathe the needs of the customer;

2. Centralized R&D, incessantly seeking breakthroughs while freed from the demands and constraints of the day-to-day business, and product-line R&D, aggressively seeking ways to better meet customer needs, are both required for the long-term health of innovative businesses;

3. An R&D mindset and problem solving persona, mixed with business acumen, can be an unbeatable combination for intrapreneurship within a large company;

4. R&D "renaissance" teams & persons, skilled at mixing know-how across multiple disciplines or sciences will be indispensable to high-technology growth-seeking companies.

---

each field is pursued separately – and if each has one thousand opportunities for innovation and growth – then HP has three times a thousand – or three thousand possibilities for growth. But, if instead of being viewed as three lines going in separate directions – if instead, you think of each them as defining a three-dimensional cube – then the formula to quantify our growth opportunities isn't three times a thousand, but MC^2 – or one thousand to the third order, which means a billion possible ways to innovate and grow."

Summary

This author views MC^2 (measurement, computation, and communication) not only as a potentially explosive combination of HP's technology core competencies, but also a vehicle for capitalizing on the unique HP organizational and people distinctions. It is not only the pattern one sees when the hard technologies are combined for product success, but it is also the subtle pattern rising from HP's people, processes, and personality. It is both the ends and the means.

The Hewlett-Packard fabric is woven from fundamental warp and weft threads. These threads, many of them described within this chapter, enable tens of thousands of HP employees to *measure* and meter the world, to *compute*, that is, to execute the product generation process (enabling the flow of innovative technology to market), and to operate with massively parallel *communications* resulting in quick and flexible responses.

The *Measurement* of the market and customer dynamics and the sensing of global and personal relationships requires a world populated with sensors and monitoring instrumentation – let us call those „R&D systems" – collecting data on everything from personal to enterprise needs, value gaps, and emerging product categories. Simply deploying sales teams around the world is insufficient; the company with a huge growth potential has to be able to see beyond the now, to hear more than what is being said, and to integrate the different signals into the company's product response.

Communications make these market measurements available to teams anywhere and everywhere. Communications coverage must accommodate all the many layers, from the culture and the language, to the interactive and the archival, to the now and the later. HP's natural, embedded, massively parallel, fault-tolerant open communications is constantly recharging the company. Don't forget the HP individual who said the collective company „we" knows so much more than we think we know (or we know who is in the know).

And the very fabric of the HP Company enables the organizational Computation required to provide non-stop market, product, and value creation. The company can do that because it has architected a truly amazing parallel-processing corporate machine. We've hired, trained, and continue to listen to and allow our people to learn how to operate as truly distributed, asynchronous, product development engines. Finally, the company has common business processes (Hoshin planning, business reviews, product life cycles, and quality coaches) to ensure that we synchronize our global processes and we weave together. This is why HP energy = organizational MC^2.[47]

---

[47]   The developments since 2000 bear out the predictions of the R&D managers: Global access to information with adequate means of communication, changes in customer needs due to the demographic development and 'border-less' joints have become more and more crucial for many companies. At the beginning of the 21st century, HP focused on reducing the complexity of information technology systems for business and improving the overall experience consumers have with technological solutions. In 2002, the largest tech merger in history was completed between HP and Compaq. The HP is now a leading global provider of products, technologies, solutions and services to consumers and business. The company's offerings span IT infrastructure, personal computing and access devices, global services, and imaging and printing.

IV.4 IBM: Using Global Networks for Virtual Development*

1 Leadership Through R&D in Information Technology

The International Business Machines Corporation (IBM) is an internationally operating company which strives to lead in the creation, development and manufacture of the information industry's most advanced systems, including computer systems, software, networking systems, storage devices, and microelectronics. IBM translates these advanced technologies into value for our customers through a professional solutions and services business worldwide.

The importance of R&D for IBM is self-evident given this focus on the leadership in the information technology industry and the transformation of advanced technologies into customer value. Research and Development has always been the cornerstone of IBM's success and its research labs have an excellent reputation in the scientific community at large. Among IBM's employees are a number of Nobel Prize winners who received the coveted prize for basic research done on behalf of IBM.

In 1996, IBM total worldwide revenue was US$ 75.947 billion with a distribution over the major product areas as shown in Table IV.4.1. Approximately half of the revenue was generated in the US, with Europe accounting for about half of the oversea revenue (Table IV.4.2).

In 1996, IBM's R&D expenses amounted to US$ 4.754 billion. Of this amount, US$ 3.934 billion were spent for research and development activities covering basic research and the application of scientific advances to the development of new and improved products and their uses. Purchased process research and development was US$ 435 million. The R&D expenses of the corporation thus constituted 6.7% of worldwide revenues or 23.2% of the operating expenses.

---

*   This case study was authored by *Manfred Roux*, at that time Director at IBM's Software Solutions Department, Böblingen, Germany, and *Prof. Dr. Oliver Gassmann*, Institute of Technology Management, University of St. Gallen. This case study was written in 1998: The reader should keep in mind that all numbers, figures, organization charts and forecasts represent the state of 1998 or before. The case study was revised in 2007 by Lukas Weiss.

Table IV.4.1. IBM's product areas and worldwide revenues in 1996 (US$ billion).

Total Revenue	US$ 75.947
Hardware	US$ 36.316
Services	US$ 15.873
Software	US$ 4.082
Maintenance	US$ 3.659
Rentals & Financing	US$ 1.624

2   R&D Organization

Within the IBM Corporation, R&D is separated into Research, being the responsibility of the Research Division, and Development, which is the responsibility of the international Manufacturing and Development organizations.

The research sites devote their efforts to basic and applied research in support of future technology and product development. Key research sites are the Yorktown Research Center in New York, home of „Deep Blue", Hawthorne, New York, Almaden, California, and Zurich in Switzerland.

The development sites work on product and solution development over the entire spectrum of IBM's engagement in the information industry. Locations are spread over the globe with a concentration of the sites within North America. Important sites in North America are

- Poughkeepsie, New York, where the System/390 Enterprise Servers and the OS/390 operating system are being developed;
- Santa Teresa, California, where DB2 database development takes place;
- Austin, Texas, home of the RS/6000 processor family and the AIX operating system;
- Rochester, Minnesota for AS/400 and OS/400 development;
- Toronto, Ontario, Canada: workstation software and languages development.

Many of the development organization also operate development laboratories

Table IV.4.2. IBM's geographic regions and worldwide revenues in 1996 (US$ billion).

Total Revenue	US$ 75.957
United States	US$ 39.592
Europe/Middle East/Asia	US$ 27.735
Asia Pacific	US$ 17.533
Americas	US$ 11.653
Elimination	(US$ 20.556)

Major innovative break-throughs at IBM (1991-1996):

1. Scalable parallel systems;
2. Silicon germanium chips;
3. Thinkpad 701C;
4. Secure electronic transactions;
5. CMOS 7S.

---

outside the USA, like the Hursley development lab in England for transaction systems, and the Böblingen development lab in Germany for System /390 CMOS Servers, OS/390 systems management products, and production workflow.

In addition, a number of Industry Solution Development Centers exist, some which are separate organizations with their own reporting structure within product development laboratories. These centers focus, as the name indicates, on tailored solution development for specific industries as opposed to general purpose product development, which is the focus of the product development organizations.

In former times development was frequently sourced outside the USA in order to sell products in its major markets IBM wanted to present itself as a worldwide development organization: The Company was not just selling in those markets but was also spending money locally on development and manufacturing. Now, the division of labor is driven primarily by business reasons such as competitive pressures, availability of skills, and proximity to the prospective customer.

3   R&D Coordination

The missions of the development organizations is defined by their organizational context. Since each of IBM's international product divisions has a clear mission within the overall context of the corporation's business, spheres of competence and division of responsibility are easily achieved and understood. Close contacts between executives of the divisions ensures that overlapping development, should it occur, is quickly eliminated.

Most important drivers for globalization:

1. Globalization of customers require global actions by IT provider;
2. Regional centers of excellence;
3. Close contact to leading universities and research institutes.

New areas of development activity are defined and assigned to organizations by the executive management of the corporation in response to analysis of industry trends and competitive pressures. Thus we witnessed the establishment of an Internet Division or a Consumer Systems Division, each of them focused on a piece of the business which had not existed before or which had not been adequately covered in the former context. Within the predefined organizational context, development locations receive functional guidance from the division executive management, typically from a Vice-President Development or a General Manager. The division's executive management also charters a committee to allocate development funding to projects. This group of people, which is drawn from the brand management, finance, and product development organizations, has been delegated the responsibility to manage the division's product portfolio and to ensure that the portfolio generates the necessary business results.

To ensure that distributed development locations continue to function within the overall context of the product division as a single cross-location team a number of mechanism have been put in place. They emphasize on regular formal and informal communication between distributed development teams with a common objective.

System Design Councils:

Key developers across locations and divisions meet regularly to discuss key platform design issues and to develop implementation concepts and plans. For example, the OS/390 Software Design Council meets roughly every two months to review key issues facing the System /390 platform, primarily from a software point of view but with close ties to the hardware development groups.

Groupware, like Lotus Notes:

The company-wide introduction and use of Lotus Notes for collaborative purposes begins to shape the communication between distributed development teams. The Notes product is increasingly being used not merely for mail purposes but in the development context to establish distributed databases with project data, technical questions and answers which are needed to facilitate cross-location information exchange. On a broader corporate scale, the establishment of a company-wide technical community helps foster intense communication on technical issues between the leaders within development sites and divisions. The IBM Academy, which consists of about three hundred of IBM's top technical contributors, is one aspect of this. There is also a strong trend towards the establishment of less formal technical communities at a local or European level, focused on closer ties between top contributors and informal information exchange.

Over the preceding years, IBM has focused on bundling its forces and coming to a more focused approach in R&D. The emergence of clear areas of competence within product divisions has helped greatly to achieve the goals. The introduction of the Integrated Product Development (IPD) process with clearly assigned responsibilities for project initiation, funding, execution, and project termination and

> **Major issues for global R&D management at IBM:**
> 1. Creating the industry's most advanced IT technologies;
> 2. Helping customers apply technology to improve what they do - and how they do it.

its focus on availability of resources and skills has significantly reduced the competition and infighting between development locations and has made successful project execution more predictable.

4   Management of International R&D Projects

Traditionally, large-scale commercial software development projects such as the development of the VSE/ESA (Virtual Storage Extended/Enterprise System Architecture) operating system for IBM's S/390 Enterprise Server Family has always been conducted across national boundaries. Already back in the 70s, the division of development responsibility among different product houses required close international cooperation. The demands of customers for integrated solutions has tended to reinforce this trend in the 80s. As a consequence of the environment in which the company operates - IBM as a manufacturer in the IT industry - ICT methods were used in projects very early and to a great extent to overcome the drawbacks of geographical separation by promoting team formation.

In the following sections, it will be described how ICT is being used during the software development process to solve problems arising from the widespread use of dispersed teams. The gathering of requirements, the product planning and design phase play an essential role in the development of products: the aim is to collect customer requirements, to develop adequate responses to these requirements, and to validate the solutions with the customers.

4.1   Gathering Requirements

In system software development at IBM, requirements are brought to the attention of the development organization via a variety of channels:

- World-wide operating user organizations such as GUIDE, COMMON, or SHARE, collect and prioritize requirements and pass them on to IBM. At IBM the requirements are gathered in databases, distributed to the development organizations, where they are analyzed and answered. The time from the entry of the requirement to the answer given to the customer is tracked, measured, and regularly reported throughout the company.
- IBM's service organization is another important channel for customer requests: employees in this function have daily contact with customers who experience

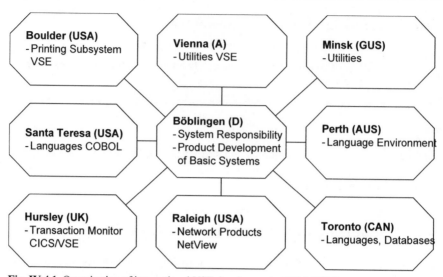

Fig. IV.4.1. Organization of international VSE development at IBM (1996).

problems with current products. These problems are entered into a database (RETAIN) which can be accessed world-wide. Problem resolution is tracked and later on, problems are classified as either „defect-oriented" (cause of the problem was a program defect) or „non-defect-oriented". Conclusions about product deficiencies and new requirements can often be drawn from the „non-defect" problem reports.

The development teams operating world-wide access the available data and define suitable small product improvements in close cooperation with the system house. Significant improvements, especially with impacts on several products, are only introduced in close cooperation between all affected development locations.

For extensive new developments, customers are involved in the validation process after the conceptual design has been created. One or more concepts are presented personally to the customers by R&D members and their feedback is requested and analyzed. This process is used to reduce the number of implementation alternatives. Frequently tools supporting the well-known "rapid prototyping" methodology are employed: In the area of user interface prototyping in particular, programming tools like Smalltalk suggest themselves: Using visual programming methods, product ideas can be quickly prototyped and validated with customers.

4.2   Planning: Requires Intensive Face-to-face Contact

For the subsequent coordination and planning processes both IT-based and traditional methods (travel and meetings) are employed.

- First approaches are often defined in internal face-to-face meetings and conferences. Video conferencing (fixed image and finally full-motion video) is also being used. This medium allows frequent, effective discussions lasting several hours without the stress (waiting periods, travel time, jetlag) and cost of long business trips.
- For later stages of coordination in which details are settled, the possibilities of electronic mail (e-mail) and telephone contacts are sufficient. At IBM, e-mail is preferred over telephone contacts: in the first place it is cheaper, in the second place it has been observed that many German IBM colleagues dislike talking to answering machines and therefore avoid the use of the available voice mail systems.
- For final planning coordination personal meetings are preferred.

These early activities and the close cooperation between the different functions involved lead to a common understanding of the requirements and the content of what is eventually to be produced. At the same time the close cooperation promotes team building in the virtual team.

4.3 Design: Defining the System Architecture

The design represents the first phase of transforming the plan into a product. The design phase is especially critical because during this phase the foundations of the implementation are laid down. Revising them at a later stage of development is only possible at considerably higher expense.

The development engineer views the design process as a creative activity inde-

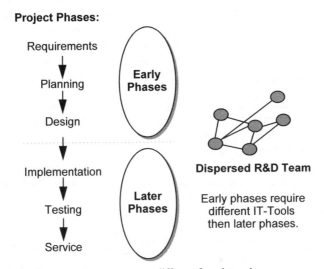

Fig. IV.4.2. Early phases require management different from later phases.

pendent of whether the job is a new product development or an extension to an existing product. In this phase intensive team work is necessary. In the initial phase, all organizations are involved in the definition of system structures and interfaces between components and products. In the second phase of the design process, interface between modules are being defined and component and module structures are developed locally in small teams.

This staging is possible because interfaces between components and products are generally being described comprehensively and completely. The description is written down and published throughout the team: the design document describes the layout of interfaces, all inputs, and outputs. Checking the design for completeness and correctness is labor-intensive, error-prone and requires careful coordination with others.

- Coordination takes place initially in face-to-face discussions lasting several days. Implementation alternatives must be discussed and weighed against one another. The discussions serve to develop a common understanding among the various local teams about the functionality and the implementation.
- In the second phase of design, as the definition process progresses, documents are exchanged via the e-mail system of the IBM Global Network. This phase establishes the normal communication flow between decentralized teams: a common understanding among the teams about the progress of the work is guaranteed.

The component and module design process takes place in the local teams. It is completed with a series of inspections of the overall design. During these inspections the correct implementation of the user requirements, consistency of interfaces, and the clear separation of functions is checked. The inspections take the form of highly interactive face-to-face discussions. Project leaders and those responsible for the design are included. By the end of the design phase all members of the team have a common understanding of the objectives and the project scope. This understanding is supported by intensive daily contacts between all team members via the internal e-mail system of IBM Global Network.

4.4   Implementation: the Role of Pre-versions and Scaffolding

It is frequently desirable to transform the design into executable code and to remove defects in inspections and tests strictly locally. This approach significantly reduces the communication overhead between developers and testers in a development project. The need to transmit large amounts of data over networks can be eliminated, interactive debugging is made easier when developers and testers reside in a single location. In large-scale international projects, especially in operating system development, this division of labor is not always possible, even when clear structuring and separation of functions has been pursued during the design phase. To resolve mutual dependencies and allow work to proceed in parallel, either pre-versions of the code of other teams must be available for test purposes or code scaffolding is utilized.

In large-scale projects the management of dependencies represents the greatest challenge. If several teams are dependent on each other the resolution of these dependencies via pre-versions leads to a high degree of complexity in project management and tends to prolong the project: both results are undesirable.

- *Pre-version of* a product or a component are characterized as code under development which only contains part of the final functional content. In pre-versions a subset of the final functional content can be executed. When the code is passed to others for test purposes, it is „frozen", i.e. no further development takes place with this piece of code.
- In the *"scaffolding"* process software is written which only serves test purposes. The scaffolding code is designed to simulate the existence of missing products or components. The extent of this code can range from small units, so-called „stubs", to complete components. An extreme case are hardware simulators which may take on the size of complete software products.

Pre-versions have the advantage over scaffolding that the same developer provides both the pre-version and the product version of the function. This ensures that misinterpretations of the design or interfaces become apparent at an early stage of development. Scaffolding code is usually written by the person who needs to call the as yet non-existent function. Simulation is based on system characteristics documented during the design phase: Errors in the documentation or failure to communicate later modifications to the design will inevitably lead to extra work.

The disadvantage of the pre-version becomes apparent when complex mutual dependencies exist. Under such circumstances code has to be supplied to other teams for testing purposes frequently and early in the cycle. This procedure tends to put the development teams under substantial pressure. Defects which have occurred in tests at other locations or even in early customer tests with the pre-version must be eliminated by the developer. At the same time, however, he or she is pushing ahead with the development of the final version. Typically, after a short while the two versions will cease to have much in common at all.

Pre-versions are being used for example in a large product release of IBM's VSE/ESA operating system: The release requires the coordinated development of the VSE/ESA supervisor and CICS/VSE (Customer Information Control System/Virtual Storage Extended) transaction monitor. In this case certain functions and interfaces in the VSE/ESA supervisor were developed and frozen and passed onto the CICS/VSE development. These functions and interfaces will allow the CICS/VSE developers in Hursley, U.K. to implement and test their own code. The development of the relevant parts of the VSE/ESA supervisor will be completed and put through a single system test together with the CICS/VSE function at a later date.

"Scaffolding" was employed for example in the development of version 5 of the MVS/ESA (Multiple Virtual Storage/Enterprise Systems Architecture) operating system. In this version a new function of IBM hardware, the so-called Coupling Facility (CF) was supported. A combined hardware/software function, the Coupling Facility provides the means for very rapid communication between different processors in a S/390 Parallel Sysplex™. As the hardware environment for the development of the MVS/ESA components was not available, the corresponding interfaces and functions were simulated on test systems. In this manner the support required in the operating system and in the applications was able to be developed and tested without the need for every developer and tester to have access to the CF resource. In the final system tests the conformity of the simulation with the real CF was validated.

For an international development team the coordination required in the context of mutual dependencies between project activities contains much potential for conflicts. There must be common understanding and trust that all involved are working towards the same goals and are working to the best of their abilities. In this phase of development there is a lot of project management to be done. In complex projects weekly telephone or video conferences with all involved parties are the norm.

In the implementation phase communication between the decentralized teams primarily consist of the transfer of information concerning problems which have arisen with the system structure or the interfaces. In this period the process is conducted more formally than during the development phase. In order to make sure that all problems are pursued further and solutions are found, the teams use a previously defined reporting procedure. Defect reports are documented and passed on to other team members for processing. Problems remain open until all necessary changes have been implemented.

4.5   Testing: Support through IBM's Global Network

The test phases prior to product delivery are subdivided into the system or integration test and customer tests. The objective of system testing is defect removal, the objective of customer testing is validation of product quality commitments and the testing of the distribution and service processes.[48]

System tests of operating system components usually entail intensive use of hardware. Almost every new version of the operating systems contains code supported by new hardware such as new processors or peripheral equipment which must be included in the test environment. As the interaction of the new hardware and the operating system support has to be tested before the first delivery of the hardware, engineering models are usually employed for testing. These devices have gone through a special manufacturing process and are therefore much more expensive than the machines which later go through the normal manufacturing process. These test phases are usually conducted centrally at the location where the hardware is being developed as potential problems with the hardware can be solved easier with locally available know-how.

Before decentralized virtual test teams used to meet centrally in this phase and had to contend for the available machine time, typically in around-the-clock operations. Now nearly all test activities are conducted from the employee's own

---

[48]   In VSE/ESA contexts these customer tests are known as the "Early Support Program" (ESP), in MVS/ESA contexts they are known as "Early Install Option" (EIO) and "Product Introduction Program" (PIP). The purpose of these programs is to gain initial experience in the field in a controlled environment with a small number of customers.

desk via the IBM Global Network, whether the test system is in the same building or half-way around the globe. Almost all IBM test systems are linked into the IBM Global Network and are thus accessible world-wide. This has resulted in considerable improvement in system utilization and at the same time has improved working conditions during system tests.

Test progress is measured in terms of workload completed and number of defects removed. The test workload is planned and prepared using standardized defect-removal models in advance of the actual test activities. Defects occurring in the test are reported and tracked using an online database in the same way as defects in other stages of the implementation: defect report, defect analysis, defect correction, fix validation.

In the late phases of development the development, integration and test teams work closely together. Only a team effort will permit rapid project progress to be made. In this phase the integration team often has to include defect corrections in the code libraries on demand and to build new systems in short intervals. Fast processes which lead to reproducible results are an essential requirement.

The customer tests which follow the system test differ from the internal tests in that the hardware has undergone the normal manufacturing process, and due to different objectives the expected defect rate is much lower. On the other hand, demands made on defect-turn-around-times will be greater: The customer demands rapid problem resolution and the goal of bringing the system into production can only be achieved after a sufficient test period.

The development of system software is increasingly characterized by close cooperation between the development engineers, customers, and independent software companies. The software suppliers are important partners for the system manufacturers as IBM and have to be included in the development processes early on. Customers will only be willing and able to make use of fundamental innovations if the software of the different suppliers has been tested together and runs properly. This means that large-scale system-related projects also have to take the product range of independent partners into account.

Software suppliers receive information at an early stage of development which allows them to adapt their own software to new functions of the operating system. During later development these partners are treated similar to an IBM organization: Support can range from early code shipments to support during tests. With important software firms more extensive agreements usually exist which for example enable defect corrections to be exchanged rapidly and with very little red tape via the company networks.

Close cooperation with reference customers may arise in the context of the migration to new versions of the operating system. The system installation in the customer's firm represents an extension of the IBM in-house test cycles and developers might even have direct access to the customer's systems.

Parallel to the final internal test phases, the latest version of the MVS/ESA operating system and the Parallel SysPlex™ hardware environment it supports were subject of a Joint Customer Study (JCS) with a small number of customers. The objective was to observe and test the system under production conditions.

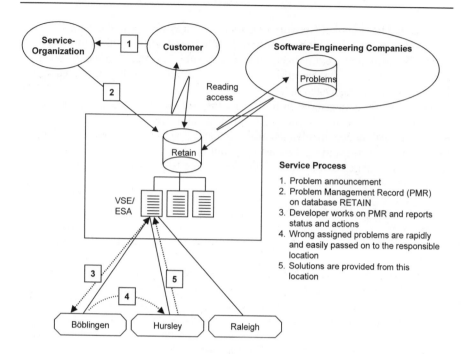

Fig. IV.4.3. The VSE service process - intergration of R&D and service processes.

The year before the Böblingen VSE/ESA software development team conducted a study with one of its largest customers in the USA to determine if a new processor series together with the VSE/ESA operating system was able to satisfy the customer's performance demands. For this study an analysis of system performance was conducted from Böblingen via the link between the IBM Global Network and the customer installation in New Jersey, USA. In the course of this analysis both optimization of the customer's workload and modifications to the operating system were conducted in order to achieve optimal utilization of the processor performance. In all these cases the developers work closely together with other software suppliers and with the customers via the IBM Global Network: The network is used to operate systems in remote control, to analyze problems, exchange information about problems and to distribute corrections. Telephone and the video conferences are employed in conjunction with the IBM Global Network to make arrangements and to analyze problems in the group.

4.6   Service: Maintenance with Help of R&D Centers

The final stage in the software life-cycle is service. During the maintenance phase of a product the developers at different locations and the international service organizations cooperate closely with the objective to deliver best service to the customer. The vehicle of communication is the IBM Global Network and the RETAIN database. The RETAIN database serves as vehicle for problem communication, problem tracking, and the documentation.

5   Conclusions

For dispersed teams the disadvantages of running decentralized projects must be compensated by consistent dependency and project management. This is supported by a number of ICT-based aids:

- The core of the project information is the project plan. It always reflects the current status of the project and the progress of the project so far. It gives a preview of tasks and checkpoints which have yet to be performed. It is maintained online and distributed via e-mail to all functions involved in the project.
- Various tools form the basis of project planning and tracking. These are used for visualizing relevant information in the form of Gantt charts. For instance, Computer Associates SuperProject product is used at IBM for scheduling and project tracking purposes.
- Managing technical, logical and time dependencies between the dispersed team activities require intensive communication with suppliers and customers. The project office makes regular and extensive use of telephone and video conferences. At these conferences several locations with several participants each switch in. To ensure that conferences run in an orderly fashion, meeting agendas are distributed by e-mail in advance. Following the meetings the participants receive minutes of the discussions and „to do" lists.

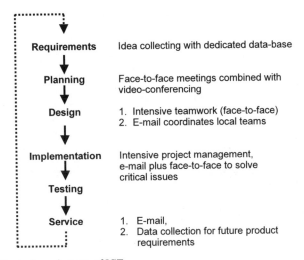

Fig. IV.4.4. Phase-dependent use of ICT.

Lessons learned for organizing R&D at IBM:

1. Market and customer orientation of research and development;

2. R&D structure aligned with a clear business and technology strategy;

3. Strong corporate identity is more important than organization charts.

- To track dependencies the project office utilizes online database systems to which all involved parties have either read access or whose contents are distributed via e-mail. Via the project management online database all employees involved are informed continuously about the current status of the work units. If this is used consistently, it is to generally possible to dispense with conventional release modes with signatures.
- At essential checkpoints in the development cycle the overall status of the project is documented and distributed via e-mail. In this manner the progress of the project can be tracked precisely and evaluated regularly.

IV.5 SAP: Global Intellectual Property Management in the Software Industry Sector*

"Patents are not necessary to build a successful product, but the patent situation in the US made it necessary that we protect our software."
Dr. Harald Hagedorn, Patent Attorney at SAP

1   The Software Company SAP

SAP was founded in 1972 by five former IBM systems engineers. SAP is the world's leading provider of business software solutions. Today, more than 36,200 customers in over 120 countries run more than 96,400 installations of SAP® software – from distinct solutions addressing the needs of small and midsize enterprises to suite solutions for global organizations. Powered by the SAP NetWeaver® platform to drive innovation and enable business change, mySAP™ Business Suite solutions are helping enterprises around the world improve customer relationships, enhance partner collaboration and create efficiencies across their supply chains and business operations.

SAP's growth is based on the development of business software solutions that are designed to meet the demands of companies of all sizes – from small and midsized businesses to global enterprises. Their first product was R/1 in 1972, followed by R/2 and R/3 introduced in 1979 and 1992 respectively. In 2003/2004, SAP brought the business solutions family mySAP Business Suite and SAP NetWeaver to the market. mySAP Business Suite is a complete package of open enterprise solutions which links up all people, information, and processes and thus increases the effectiveness of business relationships. It is based on the SAP NetWeaver technology platform and can be seamlessly integrated with practically every SAP and non-SAP solution. SAP NetWeaver is an open integration and application platform that reduces complexity and total cost of ownership, while empowering business change and innovation.

SAP industry solutions support the unique business processes of more than 25

---

*   This case study was authored by *Prof. Dr. Lutz Heuser*, Vice-President SAP Research, Chief Development Architect at SAP AG, and *Dr. Martin A. Bader*, European and Swiss Patent Attorney, Managing Partner of the innovation and intellectual property management advisory group BGW AG, St.Gallen and Vienna.

industry segments, including high tech, retail, public sector and financial services.

Furthermore, SAP strives to strengthen its position as a technological think-tank. SAP Ventures invests in emerging companies that are developing and advancing exciting new technologies. The goal of SAP Ventures is to grow businesses that create shareholder value for everyone involved.

The main purpose of SAP Labs is to discover and understand new technology trends around the world. The focus is on short-term innovation projects that are closely aligned with current SAP products and customer requirements.

SAP's corporate research organization, SAP Research, prepares the groundwork for future growth by acting as SAP's information technology trend scout. The group focuses on identifying emerging information technology trends, researching and prototyping in strategically important SAP business areas, as well as leveraging entrepreneurial inventive talent.

Headquartered in Walldorf, Germany, SAP is listed on several stock exchanges, including the Frankfurt Stock Exchange and the New York Stock Exchange, under the symbol "SAP".

For the fiscal year ended December 2005, SAP's revenues totaled 8.5 billion euros with a net income of 1.3 billion euros. The company's revenues are derived from four distinct sources: Software, maintenance, consulting and training.

2   SAP Research Organization: The Teams

SAP maintains a corporate research group called SAP Research. SAP Research is headquartered in Walldorf, Germany. SAP Research's mission is to prepare the groundwork for future growth by acting as SAP's information technology trend scout. The group focuses on identifying emerging information technology trends, researching and prototyping in strategically important SAP business areas, as well as leveraging entrepreneurial inventive talent.

Its two key groups are SAP Research Centers & Campus-based Engineering Centers and SAP Inspire; each with a dedicated focus (Fig. IV.5.1). SAP Inspire is the corporate venturing unit with an innovation and project focus from six months to two years. SAP Research carries out applied research with an innovation and project focus of up to three or even five years. Each department is assisted by dedicated support functions, such as research business development and research operations. Internally, these groups seek a research transfer engagement with the business units. Externally, they aim for innovation collaboration as trusted innovators, with governmental organizations and in partner alliances as well as through customer engagement in the industry sectors. Communication, media and event activities round up the picture. Research Operations comprises the functions finance, legal and a project management office.

The vision of SAP Research is to always be a world-class knowledge and thought leadership partner to SAP, and its customers and partners. SAP Research executes its research either on its own, or as is often the case, in collaborative research projects with academia, potential technology partners or potential customers. These kinds of research projects are often partly publicly-funded.

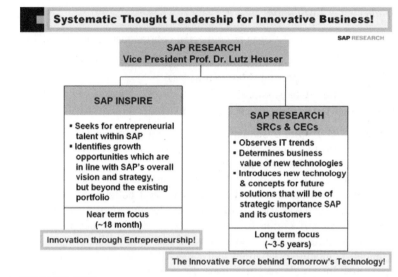

Source: SAP Research (2005).

Fig. IV.5.1. Structure of SAP Research.

SAP Inspire

Throughout its history, SAP has renewed itself and successfully created innovative business in new areas. With the Inspire initiative SAP recognizes that a major part of its renewal process takes place within the minds of its employees. They require the right environment and support to successfully turn creative ideas into winning business.

The corporate research group of SAP includes the internal venturing group SAP Inspire which brings all this together – innovation, the entrepreneur's passion and SAP.

It is dedicated to seeking entrepreneurial talent within SAP and looking for growth opportunities. These opportunities must be in line with SAP's overall vision and strategy, but beyond the existing portfolio. The corporate venturing group manages the full innovation process from idea generation to commercialization and incorporation into businesses.

SAP Inspire contributes to SAP's long-term growth and leadership through business and technical innovation. The venture business process is based on four process steps:

- Idea gathering & evaluation;
- Prototype building;
- Transition.

Idea Gathering & Evaluation

Ideas that fit into the SAP vision are collected continuously from internal sources using tools such as:

- An intranet-based capturing solution for ideas;
- SAP Inspire think-tank sessions;
- Special initiatives such as idea contests (NextGeneration@SAP).

Furthermore, SAP Inspire systematically scans emerging trends. The knowledge gained from these two perspectives identifies potential new business ideas that might result in successful Inspire projects.

Once an idea has been submitted, the SAP Inspire team begins with the idea evaluation by gathering additional information, and collaborating with experts. The SAP Inspire reviewer tries to find answers for questions such as innovation substance, existence of similar solutions within the SAP product portfolio, potential technical feasibility, and strategic fit with SAP core business, high-level market potential, competitive situation and capacity for execution. Based on these questions, SAP Inspire decides to pursue the due diligence process by building a business case which aims to justify the investment.

Prototype Building

The business case describes problem and background, solution, innovation degree, strategic fit, project planning and estimation, benefits and go-to-market. Only the most promising ideas are developed further in the SAP Inspire incubator, which offers necessary development resources to build prototypes as the basis for further product development. Furthermore, SAP Inspire helps with access to SAP's support system, e.g. legal, communications, and human resources. This uniquely combines the best practices of internal corporate venturing and venture capital activity. In comparison with other research projects, however, the Inspire projects have a much shorter project time scope for prototype building, i.e. only nine to twelve months duration. The business lines get actively involved and can expect results for their business and product development process.

Transition

The Inspire team provides proactive support to successfully re-integrate the idea prototypes into the organization and optional to pilot customers. This transition phase normally requires three to six months. As a basic outcome, SAP seeks to either merge the Inspire results into existing business units or creating new ones.

SAP Research Centers and SAP Research Campus-based Engineering Centers

The SAP Research Centers (SRC) and Campus-based Engineering Centers (CEC) are corporate technology research locations that support SAP's long-term strategy of establishing SAP as a leader in the area of innovative and breakthrough information technology. They monitor current and upcoming information and technology trends. They determine the business value of new technologies for SAP and introduce new technology and concepts for future solutions that will be of strategic importance to SAP and its customers.

The SAP Research location strategy follows two approaches: either the research team is hosted by an SAP subsidiary (SAP Research Center/Group) or SAP Research founds a Campus-based Engineering Center (CEC) in close vicinity to a university. Existing research locations are:

- Karlsruhe (CEC), Germany;
- Darmstadt (CEC), Germany;
- Dresden (CEC), Germany;
- Belfast (CEC), UK;
- Sophia Antipolis (SRC), France;
- Montréal (SRC), Canada;
- Palo Alto (SRC), USA;
- Pretoria (CEC), South Africa;
- Brisbane (CEC), Australia;
- St. Gallen (CEC), Switzerland.

The research branch has identified long-term research programs with a focus on technologies, platforms and business solutions. They act – if necessary – on trend-driven information technology or market changes.

SAP RESEARCH

	Focus topics
Smart Items Research *Enabling the real-time enterprise by bridging the gap between the real and the digital world*	Focus topics • AUTO-ID, Sensor Nets & embedded systems technologies • distributed hierarchical Auto-ID infrastructure
Security & Trust *Provision of user-centric security solutions for dynamic, collaborative, and adaptive inter-enterprise business scenarios*	Focus topics • authorization and trust management • secure services & composition • security engineering
Knowledge People Interaction *Integrated knowledge-intensive collaborative working environments*	Focus topics • e-learning and KM technologies • knowledge integration and innovation • smart human computer interaction
Software Engineering & Architecture *Computer assisted engineering practices for SAP's standard development processes*	Focus topics • Model-driven SW development • SW quality and non-functional aspects • SW architectures for virtualization
Business Process Mgmt & Semantic Interoperability *Highly configurable process-oriented applications and semantically enriched service-oriented composition of applications*	Focus topics • Collaborative bus. processes between enterprises • Model-driven architectures & engineering • Semantic Web Services; • SoA • Interoperability of applications & enterprises

Source: SAP Research (2005).

Table IV.5.1. Research programs @ SAP Research.

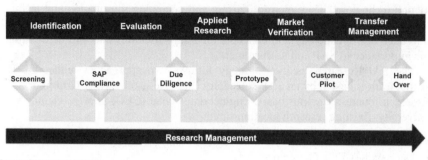

Source: SAP Research (2005).

Fig. IV.5.2. Research process @ SAP Research.

Research Programs

SAP Research runs various research programs conducted by global teams across the various research locations (Table IV.5.1). The research programs establish a vision for how to address the challenges of an area of strategic interest for SAP. The program provides guidance for individual researchers on one hand and for research projects or proposals for implementing the vision as part of the project charter and avoiding duplication of effort on the other. Furthermore they help to challenge individual research contributions such as invention disclosures, while also setting up doctoral theses and internships within the different projects to provide synergies between the stakeholders involved.

3   SAP Research Coordination: The Research Process

SAP Research is closely following the technology market and academic trends in order to identify those of strategic relevance for SAP within the next 3 to 5 years to be prepared when the market is ready and the customers request it.

The applied research process of SAP Research is rather a classical stage gate process but a lively process with manifold interaction between the various research phases, the overall SAP Product Innovation Lifecycle as well as with the necessary feedback loops within the engagement with the product groups. The main focus is on new technology concepts and their potential integration into the SAP software environment (Fig. IV.5.2):

- *Identification:* Screening of technology and research dialog with the research community will lead to the identification of opportunities that will be expanded by a research outline.

- *Evaluation:* The research outlines are then validated with the state-of-the-art, technology providers and their prototypes and academia as well as initial investigations into the business relevance. A research proposal is written to enable the start of a collaborative research project, white papers or conference papers are being submitted for further dialog with the scientific and the real world.
- *Applied Research:* This stage can mark the start of the collaborative research project and may include the preparation of an initial feasibility study, anticipated usage cases, business scenarios and technical concepts, for example technology evaluation studies, technology due diligence studies, research concepts, guides, recommendations, good practices and methodologies. Moving on with the project, demonstrators and prototypes will be built to show the technical feasibility, or e.g. the ease of use or the novelty of the concept.
- *Market Verification:* The prototype will be taken out of the lab into real life environment; customer-specific requirements will be applied to the prototypes or demonstrators. A trial or research pilot will evaluate the business potential and may result in a customer requirement study.
- *Transfer Management:* Throughout the research process transfer is driven by Research Business Development communicating and engaging with the SAP internal development or solution management teams. Whitepapers, technical concepts, forums or workshops facilitate the know-how transfer and/or technology decision processes. When the product decision has been made a dedicated transfer project, based on terms of engagement, is being carried out.

SAP Research executes its research either on its own, or, which is more often the case, within collaborative research projects with academia, potential technology partners or potential customers. These kinds of research projects are often partly publicly-funded.

4   Global Collaborative Research Activities

Partnering has traditionally played an important role for SAP. The company works together with numerous partners on various engagement levels.

To build further on this, the Research Business Development team moderates collaboration with partners from industry and academia as well as other research organizations. It also drives the generation of joint research roadmaps with partners of strategic interest to SAP Research. Typical characteristics of collaborative research projects are: duration of two to three years; competency augmentation through diverse consortia; risk sharing through cost sharing and joint applications for partly governmental funding.

A research partner network is important because it speeds up the value of the innovation process and monitors the competitiveness of SAP's research focus. Before a collaborative project starts, SAP Research assesses potential partners. Sometimes, competing partners come together and discuss these issues in a steering committee, striving to manage the co-opetive situation for the benefit of joint research.

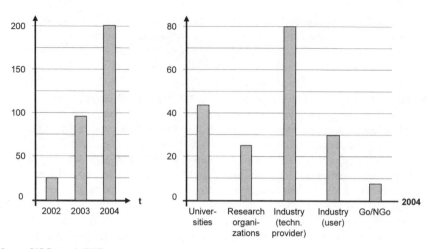

Source: SAP Research (2005).

Fig. IV.5.3. Evolution of the SAP Research network.

The total number of partners has consistently doubled during the last few years, to reach about 200 collaboration partners in 2004 (Fig. IV.5.3). The main collaboration partners for SAP Research are:

- Academia;
- Technology partners; and
- Customers.

Academia. Academic partners are mainly involved in joint innovation sourcing projects and provide the basic research within the collaborative projects. The goal is to make SAP Research a strong partner for collaborative research and to manage the development of the research partner network: public calls for proposals are introduced, opportunities are identified, the proposal process is facilitated and reviewers are provided.

SAP Research maintains research agreements with leading universities worldwide.

Technology Partners. Strategic research alliance partners help to align research roadmaps and prepare future product synergies. SAP Research applies joint technology validation projects with strong use cases. Strategic research collaboration includes well known SAP alliance partners but also technology providers that are new to the SAP community.

Customers. Existing and potential SAP customers act both as pilot project partners as well as a target for innovation marketing. Facilitated by Research Business Development SAP Research demonstrates thought leadership to the SAP community and invites them to join in future research to be prepared for upcoming technology potential and to by themselves be perceived as thought leaders.

5   Intellectual Property Management at SAP

5.1   IP Management in the Software Industry Sector

The development of software began 40 years ago, in the 1960s (Boehm, 1976). The early stages of software development focused mainly on mainframe and mini-computer computing, whereas today's software development differentiates between personal-, pervasive-, and embedded computing. Formerly, the legal protection covering software in practice was provided by copyright. Many enterprises also protected their ideas and products through the patent process. An unprecedented judicial ruling in the United States called the *Freeman-Walter-Abele*[49] test, allowed for the patenting of algorithms created during various practices in the US, including software.

This test was then replaced in 1998 by a similar judicial ruling called *State Street Bank*[50], which was reconfirmed in 1999[51]. It stated that mathematical algorithms became patentable automatically if it was proven that the invention led to a concrete and understandable result. This ruling was the beginning of the *Business Method Patents* era, which established patents for commercial purposes. In addition, banking and insurance products also display relatively passable qualities of this rule. Thus, competitors can glean advantages through imitation of products. Latecomers can simply wait until a trend asserts itself, and then jump on board to reap the advantages (*Second Mover's Advantage*).

As a consequence, this practice becomes intertwined with patents for business practices and software solutions. Accordingly, it opens up new possibilities for financial service providers and insurers (Lerner, 2004).

In the software and financial services branches, the numbers of patents and patent applications have risen sharply in recent times (Fig. IV.5.4), along with a rise in the criticism of the patentability in these sectors (Coriat and Orsi, 2002).

The following challenges and risks of handling patents are prevalent in the software industry:

- A high and increasing number of patents on software and business model methods, which requires constant supervision and corresponding expenses;
- Questionable quality and legal validity of patents, due to well-publicized lack of sufficient and relevant state of technology of applicants and patent offices;
- Difficulties in establishing one's patent, due to inexperience in dealing with inventions;
- High risk from third parties in the high cost and time intensive patent infringement process, especially in the United States market;
- Enforcement of one's own patents is associated with high financial risks, most notably in the US;

---

[49]   Arrhythmia Research Technology, Inc. v. Corazonix Corp., 958 F.2d 1053 (Fed. Cir. 1992).
[50]   State Street Bank and Trust Co. v. Signature Financial Group, Inc., 149 F.3d 1368 (Fed. Cir. 1998).
[51]   AT&T Corp. v. Excel Communications, Inc., 172 F.3d 1352 (Fed. Cir. 1999).

- Uncertainty regarding the general rights development of the different legislations concerning the patentability of software applications.

Although the above points appear in other industries, where other patenting trends occur, inventions in the software industry may be particularly critical. In particular, the United States Patent and Trademark Office (USPTO) have had difficulties maintaining the proper level of quality for the procedure of patent distribution. This is due to the codified documentations that are made available for software algorithms and the economic state of art. These difficulties stem from the applicant's appreciation and understanding of patent registrations (60% of US patents quote only patent documents as state of the art), and the quality of resources and equipment made available for examiners in the patent office (Aharonian, 2004).

Patent infringement complaints in the software industry have become more prevalent, especially in the United States. This is particularly true with large organizations: the software giant Microsoft has filed more than three dozen patent infringement complaints since 1988. Often companies terminate judicial proceedings, such as with Time Warner and Netscape, with Immersion Corporation, or with AT&T. To Java-based Sun Microsystems, Microsoft paid out 1.95 billion US dollars. The world of patent law does not escape small companies, as evidenced by Santa Clara California-based Inter Trust Technologies Corp. They filed a suit pertaining to a set of 30 patents relating to DRM Technology (Digital Rights Management) against Microsoft in 2001. The result of this suit was a 440 million US dollars payout by Microsoft to Inter Trust Technologies Corp., and a user license on the patent portfolio for Microsoft and the end users of Windows operating systems.

Currently in Germany and the European Union (EU), there are legislative procedures underway to determine in what respect computer patents could protect implemented inventions in the future. Supporters of this movement include the

---

IP Risks in the US Software Market:

A small company called Patriot Systems, claimed to have written to 155 IT companies as part of its patent infringement fight against PC vendors. The firm sent letters warning of potential infringement of its US Patent number 5,809,336. Patriot did not provide company names in its announcement, but it is widely expected that nearly every large IT company received a letter. The small IT firm asserted it contacted the world's largest electronics firms in the semiconductor, communications equipment, computer hardware, electronic instruments, computer peripherals, scientific and technical instruments, computer storage, computer networks and office equipment industries. Patriot said microprocessors operating at speeds above 110 to 120 MHz are in violation of portions of its patent portfolio. From the time its patents were issued, Patriot estimates that more than 150 billion US dollars worth of microprocessors have made use of its technology. It has given no indication as to what compensation it is seeking for a license.

Source: SAP info / Edittech International (05.05.2004).

Issuing Trends for Computer Implemented Inventions in the US*

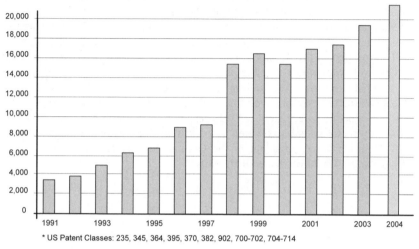

* US Patent Classes: 235, 345, 364, 395, 370, 382, 902, 700-702, 704-714

Source: Aharonian (2005).

Fig. IV.5.4. Number of patents for computer implemented inventions in the US.

European Information & Communications Technology Industry Association (EICTA), the ZVEI associations or Bitkom in Germany; they all focus on providing "a valuable service for the innovation area called Europe".

The Open-Source, the network Attac, the Linux association, the Chaos Computer Club or Free Software Foundation Europe are examples of groups belonging to this movement. These groups foresee any patenting of software to be "an existence-threatening disaster for independent software developers and small to medium-sized software enterprises" (Welt, 2004).

The current debate on software patents in the EU is centered on a policy decision originally due a year ago. The European Commission (EC) has announced a directive on software patents. However, thanks to significant lobbying efforts by Linux activists last summer, which garnered support from many non-Linux companies; politicians and economists have been forced to postpone this decision.

Behind the scenes, significant infighting is taking place. The battle lines have been drawn through the governments of member states. As a rule of thumb, the pro-patent faction consists of patent lawyers and patent officials, and extends to ministries of justice and the EC's DG Internal Market. The anti-patent faction comprises economists, programmers, ministries of economics and the DG Infosociety.

Macro-economists have remained skeptical about the benefits of the patent system ever since it was introduced internationally in the late 19th century. Their objections stem from the fact that the incentive for invention made patents unnecessary, and a patent system would therefore be too high a price for society. Eric Maskin, a professor at the Institute for Advanced Study in Princeton New Jersey, states that while patents may encourage research in some sectors – pharmaceuticals for example – in his opinion the opposite was true about software: "Software innovation is sequential [each new improvement builds on the last] and complementary [different firms pursue different research lines]". His economic model shows that in this situation, patent protection "can reduce overall innovation". One well-known effect of the patent system is that it discourages developers in certain patent-covered fields. This effect gets exponentially worse in industries where small, incremental innovations are the rule rather than the exception.

On the opposite side, patent lawyers respond by pointing out that software is not the only sector where innovation is sequential. Their main argument is presented by Heinrich Mayr, president of the German Society for Computer Science: "Why software should be treated differently?"

Patent Loss Causes Worry (Eolas v. Microsoft)

Due to a patent infringement decision in August of 2003, Microsoft must pay out more than a half billion dollars. A US Federal Court awarded Chicago-based Eolas Technologies and the University of California upwards of 520 million US dollars (460 million euros); Microsoft immediately announced it would appeal.

The court found that Microsoft had infringed on a patent for its browser Internet Explorer, which had been co-developed between Eolas CEO Michael Doyle and the University of California. In essence, the case concerns a technology, one that enables access to interactive programs imbedded in the webpage. Eolas was established in 1994, specifically to distribute the software, over which the University had an appropriate patent. Eolas and the University of California accused Microsoft of having integrated their technology into Windows. There are more than 30 complaints against Microsoft for infringements on patents pending.

Eolas' victory over Microsoft and its Internet Explorer browser has sent shockwaves through the Web and the software industry. Microsoft has vowed to fight the judgment; however the standards body World Wide Web Consortium (W3C), is not waiting for the appeal. The W3C is investigating whether the venerable Hypertext Markup Language (HTML) is also infringing on a patent. It seems the 'object' and 'embed' tags in HTML may fall under the wording of the Eolas patent. The word is that the W3C is on the verge of funding a "patent advisory group" to determine if there is a problem. Eolas certainly thinks there is: "If you read the trial testimony, you'll see references several times to experts who testified that browsers that support the 'object' and 'embed' tags are covered by the patent," said Eolas founder and lone employee Mike Doyle in an interview with News.com. He added: "You have to look at the details on a case-by-case basis, but the testimony at the trial was pretty complete."

Source: Edittech International (Sept. 24, 2003).

Table IV.5.2. History of the opinion and legal formation of the patentability of computer-implemented inventions in Europe.

Date	Event
September 2003	Acceptance of a draft directive on the patentability of "computer-implemented inventions" is passed by the European Parliament. Strong restrictions on patentability.
May 2004	A strong protest was raised about a resolution by the European Union Council of Ministers concerning the contractibility of computer-implemented inventions by patents. Patentability is again supported.
September 2004	Decision by the European Parliament.
July 2005	Idea of a law that would harmonize software patenting practices across the EU finally dies after rejection by the European Parliament.

5.2   Intellectual Property Strategizing

Twenty-five years came and went before the German software giant SAP established its own patent division in 1998. During its globalization process, SAP experienced stronger competitiveness, with patents playing an increasingly important role. This was mostly due to stronger activities in the US market, where the company became aware of its risk exposure resulting from conflicts with third party intellectual property. Furthermore, the patent situation in the United States also made it necessary for SAP to protect its own software (FAZ, 2001).

Hence, SAP has recently undertaken the usual practice in US industry – to generate its own patents so that it has a trade currency if competitors sue for infringements of theirs. Today, SAP takes numerous measures to protect its intellectual property. These include written notification of copyright infringements, registration of patents, trademarks, and other marks. This also entails the conclusion of licensing and confidentiality agreements, and the installation of technical precautions against infringement. Today, SAP is confronted with the following situation:

- Offers for patent cross license agreements are received;
- Critical reflection of own patent portfolio;
- Decisions are made early enough with respect to time requirements.

SAP therefore follows the main strategy of growing a large and valuable patent portfolio. An important action that reduces the risk of patent conflicts is reaching patent cross license agreements with major competitors. As such, SAP has not to have significant conflicts with other parties' patents yet.

As a comparison, competitor Microsoft is estimated to file 2,000 to 3,000 patent applications each year. However, with the current application procedure before the United States Patent and Trademark Office, it takes about five years for software applications to be issued.

Patent protection, however, is not always considered to be the best solution, especially in cases of hidden functions inside SAP products. An infringement would be very difficult to pinpoint, let alone to prove. Hence, secrecy is sometimes considered to be the far better alternative. While coding or algorithms are generally not patented either, strategic issues are filed with a very broad protective range in different countries in order to secure a competitive advantage over several years. Due to its high impact leverage, it would therefore be desirable to file software-related patents therefore mostly for user-computer interfaces (interaction).

SAP focuses its patent portfolio on main markets. All of the patent applications are filed in the US. One half are then selected to be filed in Europe, with about 10% in Australia, Canada, China, and Japan.

SAP has been striving for a greater number of patent applications. In 2002, SAP filed 350 patent applications, followed by 750 in 2003. Due to the late start of its patent activities, SAP has issued 49 patents in the US so far (Fig. IV.5.5).

The direct effect of the SAP patent portfolio on the software market is still unclear. For example, various small and medium software enterprises with no more than 50 employees regularly adapt to SAP software and reprogram certain functions that have proven to be successful. By reprogramming they avoid conflict with copyright laws.

The temporal distance between SAP original modules and reprogrammed versions currently ranges between two to three years. A patent protection with a maximum of 20 years, however, would severely disrupt the current equilibrium. But in general, most small and medium software enterprises still doubt that an investment in the protection of intellectual property would pay off, nor do they monitor the intellectual property of others. So the passive power of SAP's patent portfolio likely has a significant influence in this industry segment.

5.3   *Organizing and Coordinating Intellectual Property*

Intellectual property management has increased in importance for SAP over the past ten years. While SAP started with only two patent attorneys, today the intellectual property office employs numerous people. The Global Intellectual Property Department is situated in the United States, in Palo Alto, California. The United

---

Patent Cross Licensing Agreement SAP – Microsoft

In 2004 SAP and Microsoft entered into a patent cross-licensing agreement to provide a better environment for joint technical collaboration and solutions development.

During discussions with Microsoft regarding the joint development partnership for Web services, SAP confirmed that it had been approached by Microsoft in 2003 about a potential merger. The preliminary talks stalled, with no plans for their resumption. However, the two parties entered a joint development partnership for Web services and a patent cross license agreement. The joint road map for both technology deliverables and business engagement is designed to deliver significant business value to customers, enabling the extension and connection of SAP deployments using SAP NetWeaver and Microsoft.NET.

Source: SAP Press (June 07, 2004, May 12, 2004).

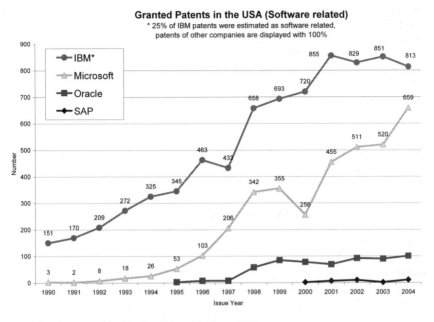

Fig. IV.5.5. The emergence of SAP's patent portfolio (issued software related US patents).

States department houses about six US patent attorneys supported by three paralegals, while the German headquarters in Walldorf has eleven patent professionals and six paralegals.

The Global Intellectual Property Department reports directly to the head of the board of directors of SAP and is legally separate from the legal department, yet there is strong cooperation between the two entities (Fig. IV.5.6).[52]

Each patent professional has dedicated internal customers, whether it is a certain lab site, unit or location. There is specialization in various fields, e.g. one patent officer in the US specializes in risk management in patent conflicts. Other fields of competence include:

- Administration;
- Contracts;
- European law;
- Remuneration;
- Searching;
- Standard committees.

---

[52]   In 2005 the SAP organization was restructured with an organizational model following the value chain.

The global intellectual property department manages the intellectual property budget and takes necessary decisions. The idea-to-invention process at SAP is kept on a simple level:

- Idea;
- Invention;
- Search procedure;
- Prosecution.

SAP actively lobbies experts to divulge the number of inventions being disclosed. There is a first monetary award given for each invention disclosure being filed as a patent application and also a second monetary award given for the issuance of a patent. In countries such as Germany, where invention remuneration is required by law, these awards are accounted against the legally necessary payments.

The corporate research department, SAP Research, has even established an average invention deliverable value for its research teams. It demands a certain delivery target concerning invention disclosures per research group per year. In general, SAP Research delivers a number of inventions that is significantly above the overall SAP average per person.

SAP uses a software and intranet-based portal to gather invention disclosures. The global patent department becomes involved, as soon an invention disclosure is internally published. The anticipated economic value of the invention is estimated by the inventor and is approved by the supervisor and the patent department.

The search for state-of-the-art is carried out by the patent department with the help of the inventors. A substantial portion of the reported inventions are filtered out in this process step, reflecting high standards.

Drafting, filing and prosecution of the patent applications is largely outsourced to private practice law firms. While in the US branch of the Global Intellectual Property Department all inventions are prosecuted externally, the German branch does some internally.

5.4   *Intellectual Property Management in Collaborations*

Generally, SAP insists on its own standard agreements for collaborative projects. This is where it is decided whether intellectual property, in the specific context, refers to patents, trade secrets, copyrights, brands (seldom), etc. Furthermore, they state that intellectual property belongs to the inventor, while joint intellectual property will be shared.

However, this may vary depending on the interests of the partners. Generally, SAP tries to gain the ownership rights to the whole intellectual property. This is often difficult to achieve, especially with large companies looking to make their own stipulations. Here, factors such as company size, relative power and the broader network surrounding the partner, will all have an influence on the collaborative agreement. In some cases, SAP has even paid for the intellectual property rights when a close analysis indicated good market potential.

Since SAP is an international company that often gets involved in cross-

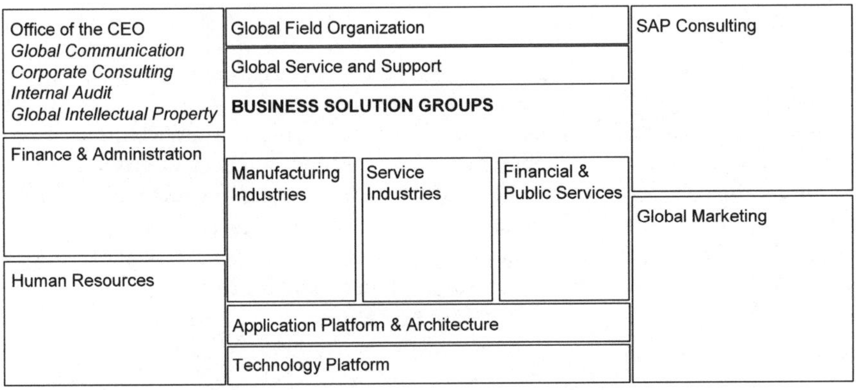

Office of the CEO	Global Field Organization			SAP Consulting
Global Communication				
Corporate Consulting	Global Service and Support			
Internal Audit				
Global Intellectual Property	**BUSINESS SOLUTION GROUPS**			
Finance & Administration				
	Manufacturing Industries	Service Industries	Financial & Public Services	
				Global Marketing
Human Resources				
	Application Platform & Architecture			
	Technology Platform			

Source: SAP Annual Report (2004).

Fig. IV.5.6. Global Intellectual Property Department as part of the CEO's office.

national development projects, additional questions regarding intellectual property typically come into play. For instance, the partners have to decide which laws should be applied. It is common to choose the legal system of the county where the larger or more committed partner is located. In any case, the system that is more beneficial for the parties is most often the one that is used. Jointly developed intellectual property is considered the main source of disagreements. Where previously joint patenting was sometimes used during transition phases or to access certain markets, today SAP generally avoids joint patent inventions with third parties.

Licensing agreements can take different forms. Occasionally, the partners decide on a 50%-rule, which means the product and maintenance revenues are shared. Licensing-in contracts only exist for software from third parties integrated in SAP's own products. Furthermore, patent protection is not always considered to be the best solution, such as in cases of hidden functions inside SAP products.

General Rules for Collaborating

A typical SAP collaboration project distinguishes temporally between created knowledge and the related intellectual property of each of the partners. There is the knowledge and intellectual property that is created during the collaboration phase, and pre-existing knowledge and related intellectual property that was owned by the parties before joining the collaboration. For SAP, it is important to keep its pre-existing intellectual property and knowledge exclusive, where it relates to their standard products, e.g. SAP NetWeaver. Collaboration partners or other parties are generally denied rights of access to these products and tools. On the other hand, SAP does provide the preexisting knowledge of the open interfaces, which are necessary to access their standard tools and products. These are oftentimes published via a special internet address (http://ifr.sap.com/).

Access Rights

As described in Fig. IV.5.7, party *A* could receive access to intellectual property and pre-existing intellectual property of the other partners *B* to *E*. Access will depend on the nature of the project, and, if granted, it means they would not have to pay royalties. After the collaboration, however, only intellectual property created during the collaboration may be used for internal or non-commercial research. If access to pre-existing intellectual property is necessary, party *A* has to apply for a license. The other partners cannot deny this application so long as party *A* does not use its part of the collaboration results without using the license.

Externalization of Rights

Party *A* may grant access rights for its pre-existing and intellectual property to third parties (*3rd party*) outside the collaboration. They can do so without having to notify, account for, or compensate the other parties. Furthermore, ownership of rights cannot be transferred to third parties, unless there is no limitation of the rights of the other collaboration partners. Party *A* may even externalize the access rights of collaborative intellectual property of its partners *B* to *E* to third parties (*3rd party*). This would only be done if party *A* seeks to use the intellectual proper-

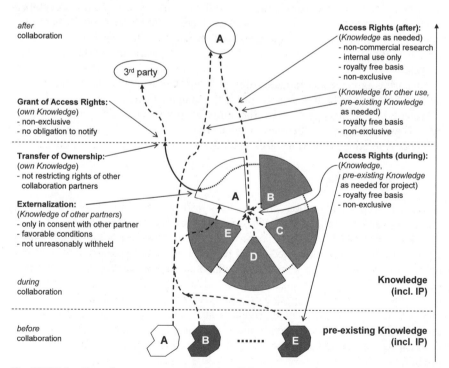

Fig. IV.5.7. Intellectual property management in collaborations.

Table IV.5.3. SAP's collaboration partners in the CoBIs project.

CoBIs-Partner	Country	Function
SAP*	Germany	Software
HardwareCorp	Austria	Technology (hardware)
NetCorp I	The Netherlands	Hardware/network/SME
TransportCorp	United Kingdom	End user/application
University I	Germany	Research network
University II	United Kingdom	Research network
University III	Netherlands	Research network

ty within other research activities, to enter into other technical collaborations, or if licensing arrangements and affected owners *B* to *E* agree.

Joint Inventions

A joint invention takes place if two or more collaboration partners contribute to one invention (Fig. IV.5.8). The parties have to inform each other if they receive such an invention disclosure, and a decision has to be made as to whether they want to file a jointly owned patent application. All costs are shared equally between the parties. The joint owners have a right to use and to license without any obligation to inform, to compensate or to account to the other owner(s). The right to license may even include the right of a licensee to grant sublicenses.

Litigation against third parties may be conducted jointly, which would result in sharing costs and recovery payments. If one party would like to litigate on its own, there is the obligation to inform the other partner that it may still join. Otherwise, costs and recovery payments remain with the litigating party.

5.5   Collaboration Coordinator: Case Study Examples for Intellectual Property Management in R&D Collaborations

CoBIs

This project aims to improve smart items peer-to-peer communication for transport pallets, including a search for new business models. Project duration is two and a half years, stretching from August 2004 to February 2007 (Table IV.5.3)

R&D: The technical areas were easily divided between the partners. Only HardwareCorp is focusing more on software. The project outcomes will be very conceptual, meaning that it might take four to five years for commercialization. Success will be based on whether results can be used by project partners.

Intellectual Property Management: Each partner keeps the intellectual property created by its team. Thus, intellectual property created by SAP remains exclusively with SAP. Hence, partners try to avoid joint inventions (case-by-case basis).

A general research agreement with the University I, states that inventions will be transferred to SAP.

Before starting with the project, the preexisting know-how is evaluated and distinguished between inclusion and exclusion items as part of the collaboration contract. SAP's philosophy is to exclude their standard products. As interfaces are made public, they can be included into and improved within the collaboration.

Consensus

This project focused on mobile web applications. It aimed to create application software that would be independent of the end device, and it would simplify the interface with the end device, e.g. mobile phones from various manufacturers. The EU-funded project started in April 2002 and ended in March 2004 (Table IV.5.4).

R&D: The project partners were chosen on the basis of trust, along with technical and market experience.

- MobileCorp was chosen as a producer of mobile end devices to represent the device market. These partners possessed large market share, EU nationality, strong EU project experience, membership of the E3C standardization committee, and turned out to be very active and collaborative partners.
- TechnologyCorp was chosen as a partner for infrastructure and service area for providing and distributing information. This partner was also a member in the E3C standardization committee, was seen as close to development but not as a competitor. TechnologyCorp also provided strong human resources, including good research management and the ability to play the role of an active collaboration partner.
- As project coordinator, SAP Research provided the environment for software development and worked on the business cases for the visualization of data on end-devices.
- Validation of pilot projects was provided by a system integrator. TestCorp was chosen to perform the independent testing on SAP software-based applications for various end devices.
- Usability experts needed to be independent, e.g. a research institute such as ExpertCorp in Austria to develop test cases with pilot users for mobile devices.
- Support for voice-based applications like VoiceXML, e.g. CommCorp in Belgium.

Competitors were not chosen; also no third German enterprise due to an otherwise uneven distribution of European countries.

The work packages were divided between the partners. Work packages were completed together, e.g. problem definition and analysis, first construction of solution and architectural design. The implementation and integration of the results in the work and product environments would be carried out separately by each of the partners.

Intellectual Property Management: Various inventions were filed as SAP patent applications. The specific results for each of the collaboration partners were:

- SAP Research is currently working on an internal transfer of the project results into the business lines.

- TechnologyCorp has placed the applications on its servers.
- MobileCorp has not pursued the issue since it wants to refocus on its customer base of end consumers.
- TestCorp has tried to use the results with the customers of its larger mother company, which involves the open source modules but nothing that is the intellectual property of SAP.

The project was considered to be a success. Overall solutions could be retrieved, standardization was brought forward, and the application development costs were reduced (two test applications). Also, the interface software component for the servers was published as open software modules in order to speed up distribution and provide accessibility for further evaluation. Furthermore, the results, including the problem description and solution areas, were presented to the W3C standardization committee.

Mosquito

Mosquito is a follow-up project partly funded by the 6th EU framework program within the SAP research program Security and Trust, which is based on the results of the former 5th EU project Witness (Table IV.5.5). SAP Research filed about four patent applications on the basis of the former project. For the new project Mosquito, the partner selection was based on criteria as follows:

- Former active collaboration partners were reselected;
- Formerly passive, inactive or unfit collaboration partners were not selected again;
- Each selected former partner brought in its own results from former projects, which form pre-existing knowledge that could be used by all partners;
- New partners replaced the updated work packages of the de-selected partners.

There might be certain risks in using the collaborative results from a former pro-

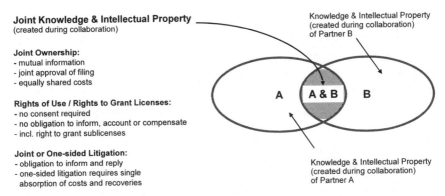

Fig. IV.5.8. Management of joint inventions.

ject, as the contract was still open with the de-selected former partners. The replacing new partners therefore might not be able to use their exclusive project results. Also, the re-selected partners might only be able to do so after requesting a license, which may not be royalty-free (Fig. IV.5.9).

MobileCorp

In 2000, the first initiative for a bilateral collaboration between SAP Research and MobileCorp was undertaken. MobileCorp was contacted in the USA via an external SAP Research consultant based in Palo Alto, California. With this partnership, SAP Research wants to build an interface from SAP to MobileCorp devices by creating a development infrastructure for Wireless Application Protocol (WAP) enabled enterprise software solutions. The goal is to provide easy "data on the fly" deployment of handheld WAP enabled devices, with the SAP enterprise software mySAP.com Mobile Workplace. Customers and partners of SAP would benefit from being able to develop mini-applications (MiniApps) that can be deployed on mobile devices. Companies can tailor MiniApps for internet economy workers who rarely stay in their office and rely on mobile phones and handheld devices to accomplish their work.

SAP approached MobileCorp because the mobile company's WAP server is the most widely used WAP server technology. Interfacing this widely accepted server technology with SAP's enterprise solutions, enables users to access and update enterprise information online from a WAP enabled mobile device. Customers get flexible access to critical inter-enterprise data and applications, enabling them to conduct business activities from virtually any location. In addition, they can take advantage of internet-enabled mobile computing capabilities and wireless information management as quickly and productively as possible. Further reasons why SAP chose MobileCorp:

- SAP wants to grow with the help of partners, especially in the US market;
- MobileCorp is a large customer of SAP;
- MobileCorp would serve as a pilot to test the systems, which would be a significant advantage.

Table IV.5.4. SAP's collaboration partners in the Consensus project.

Consensus-Partner	Country	Function
SAP*	Germany	Software
ExpertCorp	Austria	Usability expert
TestCorp	Finland	System integrator/ testing
TechnologyCorp	Germany	Technology
CommCorp	Belgium	Voice applications
MobileCorp	Scandinavia	End user/ applications

* Collaboration coordinator

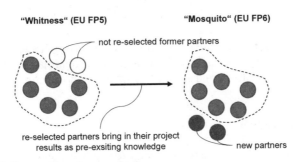

Fig. IV.5.9. Challenge with partner re-selection.

Advantages for MobileCorp from this partnership include:

- Opportunity for MobileCorp to sell more devices;
- MobileCorp can create its own distributable middleware;
- The interface between SAP and MobileCorp, i.e. Application Program Interface (API) might be certifiable but would stay non-exclusive and open to users, so customers could still create their own interface connections to personalize their systems.

In 2000, the field of mobile computing was very tangible, but moved quickly toward Radio Frequency Identification Device Technology (RFID). It took some time for both companies to individually develop competences in this field. Today, SAP has an RFID architecture with strong potential.

Intellectual Property Management: The parties do not grant any intellectual property rights to each other, e.g. know-how and patents.

Notably, the pre-existing knowledge of parties' hardware, software solutions, and interfaces will remain exclusive. However, strictly for the purpose of the project, the partners provided each other with a limited, non-exclusive license to remotely access the hardware and software solutions of the other party.

As the existing knowledge is developed by the parties during the collaboration, a concept design is to be provided. It describes the functional specifications of the

Table IV.5.5. SAP's collaboration partners in the Mosquito project.

Mosquito-Partner	Country	Function
SAP*	Germany	Software
ChipcardCorp I	Germany	Chip cards
ChipcardCorp II	France	Chip cards
SoftwareCorp	Germany	Software
ResearchCorp	France	Research
NetCorp II	Finland	Networks
TelecomCorp	The Netherlands	Telecommunication
ConsultCorp	Germany	Consulting

respective party's interface, which is necessary for the linkage between the two interfaces.

Both parties accepted that any unexpected knowledge, e.g. independently developed software that may not be based on confidential information, might end up competing with the hardware and software solutions of the other party.

6   Conclusions

SAP Research currently conducts numerous research collaborations with more than 200 collaboration partners. Through its intellectual property strategy, the company aims to create:

- Freedom of action;
- Establishment of own patent portfolio;
- Risk reduction;
- Design access.

Due to the recently confirmed European legislation SAP patent applications in Europe focus on software related patent applications with attributed technical effects. SAP thereby focuses specific attention on e.g. user-computer interfaces that have a high impact for customer related value creation. The majority of the patent applications are categorized among three sub-classes of the patent classification group "G06F". SAP tends to avoid including coding and algorithms in patent applications, and instead maintains secrecy for these kinds of trade secrets. The most often selected countries for patent protection are the United States, with a significant portion in Europe. SAP also seeks protection in Japan. In general the selection of first and second filings depends on the business and legal situation.

The central Global Intellectual Property Department takes care of SAP Research. In addition, within SAP Research there is a legal support function that at times also takes care of intellectual property issues, for example during contracting. The invention protection process starts with idea generation, invention disclosure submission, and search procedure for prior art, followed by drafting, filing and prosecution. For idea submission there is an intranet-based portal for gathering inventions that can be accessed by a wide range of inventors. The prosecution process is largely outsourced.

Within SAP Research there is a quantitative target for the research teams per year. Furthermore, there is a monetary incentive system that awards the inventors for filing an invention and for issuance of a patent. Within R&D collaborations, SAP generally provides an open interface for their collaboration partners relating to intellectual property, but ensures to keep own core products proprietary.

SAP looks to develop a large patent portfolio, which thus far has mainly focused on reducing risk, such as patent cross-licensing agreements, e.g. with Microsoft. A major goal for SAP in conducting collaborations is to in-source innovative capacity. Henceforth, SAP tries to gain the sole ownership rights of collaborative intellectual property within collaborations. SAP generally tries to in-source intellectual property on a proprietary level.

To summarize, the motivation-, structure-, and performance-related aspects of managing intellectual property in the software industry sector from the SAP perspective are being described as follows:

6.1   Motivation-Related Aspects

SAP Research maintains strong partnerships with various universities, e.g. University of Karlsruhe and various customers, e.g. BP. The research collaborations are based on the belief that customers do not strategically consider the impact, opportunities and risks of new technologies. Therefore, SAP Research's main goal for collaborative research is to find a way to gain new customers and to motivate the existing customer base to join into the research projects.

Partly government-funded projects help to involve new partners that would otherwise not have been involved. These projects stimulate experimentation, and facilitate the creation of internal know-how with a two to three year vision.

Non-government funded projects, in principle, have the same objectives. As opposed to funded projects, however, the project management can be done at the research team level.

SAP Research always tries to find suitable partners. While universities fill the role of basic knowledge suppliers, industrial partners tend to provide business scenarios that are expected to influence product development.

The current collaboration projects are often established with a technology research perspective. However, the business perspective is becoming increasingly important. Collaboration provides the opportunity to work with both partners and potential customers.

SAP Research often takes the lead in its collaborations as project coordinator. Very profound and trustful relationships form the basis for partner selection with various research institutes and universities.

6.2   Structure-Related Aspects

The compatibility between the partners depends on the anticipated deliverables of each partner, and their compatibility. It is important to ensure that there is no overlap in the usage of research results post-collaboration. At this stage, there is a need to have a look into technical content and details. Very often strong efforts have to be taken to jointly develop an agreement that mutually ensures each others interests and defines suitable exit criteria for the case of an earlier termination of the agreement. In principle, each partner may use the joint research results, but only on basis of its own research contribution and intellectual property.

The selection of collaboration partners is based, on the one hand, on existing relationships. On the other hand, an overall fit must also be reached. In partly government-funded projects this means to determine the ideal firm size and country portfolio. At SAP Research, partner selection criteria could follow any of the following strategic aspects:

- Reaching potential SAP customers that are interested in collaborating with SAP on research level;
- Approving research relationships;
- Contributing to own research and business agenda.
- It also has to find good answers for these questions:
- To what business activities does the collaboration topic really fit into?
- What does the intended consortium look like?
- The research proposal finally has to get accepted by the EU.
- How can win-win-situations be found, while staying within the core competencies?
- How can it be avoided that partners do not significantly enter into each other's core competencies?
- How shall the achieved research results be divided between the collaboration partners?

Non-government funded projects normally are based on similar research road maps between the research partners.

An example is MobileCorp's search for mobile phone based applications. On the one hand, MobileCorp and SAP have a similar research road map and their collaboration makes sense. On the other hand, there is the risk that MobileCorp might be getting too much access to SAP's software competences. This differs from the general case where customers such as hardware companies hand over some of their hardware to be used by SAP for software development and testing. Both parties would not fear any overlap of competencies. SAP would not expect the hardware partner to move into software applications and vice versa. Under these circumstances the clients approach SAP for such collaboration.

6.3   *Performance-Related Aspects*

Patents play a relatively important role within collaboration projects. The quantity of achieved invention disclosures has even become an indicator of project success. SAP Research sets a quantitative invention goal measured per project, which is included in personal target agreements and effects salary bonuses. Within SAP Research, the research groups are still developing a sense for which aspects might be patentable and which not. Within the invention process it is crucial to place basic ideas into an application context to evaluate the potential of each idea.

Next to general enhancement of rough ideas, a focus on enrichment also is an important issue. Typical further characteristics for idea selection and for detailing encompass:

- Potential usage by third parties and the anticipated blocking value towards competitors;
- Enrichment of varieties to avoid obvious design errors;
- Enforceability of patent (legality, quality of prior art search).

The current process in the patent field is to secure internal ideas as early as possible by patenting them. At a later stage, more prior art could weaken the scope of the patent applications. SAP therefore aims to multiply and sharpen inventions by categorizing them into three classes:

- Protection of standard products (internal impact);
- Impact on customer development groups (focused external impact);
- Impact on technologies (broad external impact).

At SAP Research, it is the responsibility of each researcher to enhance the research work with valuable intellectual property. It is used to protect existing standard products against copying, help to block competitors and even claim future areas that might become import business fields for SAP. The research project leaders have also to assure that no exclusive intellectual property from collaboration could infiltrate the company's outlined research fields.

IV.6 Unisys: Localization of Software Development*

1 Main Business Information Technology

Unisys serves organizations in 100 countries. Their 50,000 clients around the world include financial services, banking, airlines and transportation companies, government agencies, communications providers, and other commercial market leaders. Unisys is one of a select group of companies with the broad portfolio of services, technologies, and third-party alliances needed to deliver the benefits of information management – helping clients use their information assets to enhance their competitiveness and responsiveness to customers. Their expertise in information management is founded on the strengths of our three global businesses:

- Consulting, outsourcing, solutions, and systems integration;
- Industry-leading technologies; and
- Comprehensive services and products supporting distributed computing environments.

Based on years of research and development, Unisys offers a range of powerful hardware and software technologies, including desktop, client/server, and enterprise server systems that run all the popular, open business software applications. Unisys and its predecessor companies have over a century of technology leadership, and Unisys is one of the largest holders of patents in the information technology industry.

Unisys competes internationally with other major information technology product and services providers like Hewlett Packard, Digital Equipment, EDS, and Andersen Consulting (today Accenture). We have hundreds of partnerships and alliances in hardware and software R&D, systems integration, consulting, and others. Major partners include Intel, Oracle, Microsoft, Motorola, IBM, NCR, EDS, BEA, and Hewlett Packard.

---

* This case study was authored by *Arnold Winkler*, Standards Management, Unisys Corp., and *Michael P. Edgar*, Engineering Manager, Unisys Corp. in 1997. This case study was written in 1998: The reader should keep in mind that all numbers, figures, organization charts and forecasts represent the state of 1998 or before. The case study was revised in 2007 by *Berthold Barodte*.

Most important drivers for globalization:

1. The global market;

2. Emerging markets in developing countries;

3. Emerging suppliers / work forces in developing countries;

4. Internet-based global communication driving the world to a 24-hour / 365-day open market and bringing customers to businesses they would never see otherwise.

As a global company, Unisys is involved in R&D activities around the world. Major sites are in Europe, Asia-Pacific Rim, and the United States, and include North Ryde, Australia; Milan, Italy; Amsterdam, The Netherlands; Roseville, MN, Tredyffrin, PA, and Mission Viejo, CA. Major production centers include Rancho Bernardo and San Jose, CA. Selling locations dot the globe.

Unisys employs more than 32,000 people, including thousands of engineers, technologists, developers, and researchers. There are more than 4,000 engineers of various disciplines on staff worldwide.

The R&D focus clearly is on applied technology for the business-critical requirements of our clients, helping them manage information as an asset. Unisys currently has an active patent license program based on approximately 2,000 U.S. and 1,000 foreign patents, among which is one of the most widely licensed technology patents in the world, U.S. Patent No. 4,558,302 known as „the Welch patent." We base our future on the R&D we are doing both alone and with our R&D partners. For the future, we recognize the crucial importance of R&D partnering and our programs reflect that. Totally open network computing, the Internet/intranet, electronic commerce, Year 2000 issues, object-oriented programming language, telecom, and the overall challenge of IT asset portfolio management are just a few of the key trends on which we chart our direction.

2   Research and Development Organization and Coordination

2.1   Unisys Main Research and Development Sites

The Unisys Computer Systems Group (CSG) and the Unisys Information Services Group (ISG) research and development sites and their general areas of work are organized in a matrix (Tables IV.6.1 and IV.6.2). This chapter will only address activities in these groups. Aquanta, ClearPath, A Series, and 2,200 are brand names of Unisys computers.

Unisys is a large international company with R&D sites in many areas of the globe. The present R&D configuration is designed to take advantage of technical expertise and skills, as well as intimate knowledge of local regulations, language, and cultural conventions for the development of international products. For example, the International Engineering Center was established in Brussels, Belgium, as the lead plant for internationalization, localization, and translation.

Development projects include large data bases, reliable high-throughput transaction systems, fourth-generation programming languages, advanced networking, high-speed printers, storage solutions for many terabytes of data, „open systems," and powerful applications. For example, the new technologies of object orientation and graphical interfaces to legacy applications are developed by the innovative smaller divisions in all geographical locations.

Unisys develops international applications in Atlanta, GA; Brisbane, CA; Milan, Italy; Roseville, MN; and in Uxbridge, United Kingdom. Additional sites for local development are in Brazil for the South American market, in Hong Kong for the East Asian market, especially China, and in Villers Escalles for Europe.

A joint venture operation with Nihon Unisys Ltd (NUL) in Tokyo develops and localizes products for the Japanese market. NUL's Tokyo Development Center site houses software, hardware, and computer center groups. It creates technology for the most advanced computer systems. Research areas include large-scale computer systems, basic software for servers, language development, transaction monitors, object-oriented software development systems, knowledge systems, office automation, and telecommunications applications. The JV operation is involved in every Unisys hardware and software product marketed in Japan.

Table IV.6.1. Computer System Group – research and development sites.

	North Ryde AUS	Amsterdam NL	Brisbane CA, USA	Brussels BE	Tredyffrin PA, USA	Mission Viejo CA, USA	Plymouth MI, USA	Roseville MN, USA	San Jose CA, USA	Salt Lake City UT, USA
Aquanta PCs & servers									L	
Check processing						L				
HMP-Clearpath H/W 2200								L		
HMP-Clearpath H/W A Series					L	C				
HMP-Clearpath S/W 2200								L		C
HMP-Clearpath S/W A Series					C	L				
Imaging Systems							L			
I18N and L10N	C		L		C	C		C	C	C
NT Enterprise Technology					C	L		C	C	
OO technology						L				
Mass. par. proc. UNIX systems										L
Security systems					L					
SMP / UNIX						L			C	C
Software tools	C				C	C		L		
Storage solutions						L	C			
USoft systems		L	C							
VoiceSource - Telephony					L					

Legend: L: Leading plant in an R&D project
C: Plant contributing to R&D project

Major innovative break-throughs at Unisys (last five years):

1. Biometrics enabled systems security;

2. Natural Language Processing technology;

3. Large-scale SMP system architecture;

4. Universal Repository / Object-Relational Databases.

Overall, the current configuration of Unisys R&D efforts is a result of heritage, available skills, and strategic product decisions. The best example of how strategy drives the geographic location and organizational distribution of product development is „Internationalization and Localization," with its center in Brussels and contributions from practically all hardware and software development sites.

High impact projects dominate the main areas of research in Unisys. They establish leadership in cutting-edge technologies and/or apply them in mission-critical, high-throughput applications to solve real world problems. Examples are heterogeneous multi-processing systems for enterprise solutions, NT Enterprise Technology, systems, and applications, „open systems" technology for mainframe systems, telephony products such as large voice mail systems, natural language processing, Single Point Security technology for large computer networks,integrated imaging systems, internationalization technology, localization of worldwide software products, massively parallel processing UNIX systems, high reliability, resiliency, and recovery in distributed systems, high-performance I/O systems and storage technology, object technology, retail and wholesale banking systems, and publishing systems.

In the solutions that follow, we look at the localization issues in more detail.

2.2 R&D Project Selection and Site Assignment

The vice-president of the Advanced Technology Group is responsible for the strategic direction of the international research and development in the Unisys Computer Systems Group. The appropriate marketing organization decides, on the division level, which kind of R&D programs will be carried out. The selection is based on business plans and strategic reviews for the required markets. Product and technology strategies are taken into consideration.

The decision about which project will be assigned to which R&D site depends mainly on the skills mix needed for successful completion of the project. R&D management decides on the optimal site for each project.

While the program management organizations in marketing drive the program on a higher level, the R&D managers develop and carry out detailed project plans. Periodic review meetings and appropriate tools ensure immediate recognition of deviations from plans and commitments and allow corrective actions.

2.3 Project Funding

The R&D budget is assigned to target market programs within the business groups, based on business model profit-and-loss calculations. Program managers consider multiple markets for the target product.

These managers of the target market programs decide the use of R&D funds to make the most cost-effective use of the available budget. Allocations to specific R&D projects are made by R&D management.

Projects normally originate in a market analysis by the target market program groups. Innovative ideas from the development staff and recommendations from customers are carefully considered. Unisys also has a very active program to stimulate new product ideas from employees. For example, the company has developed an award-winning internal website called the Idea Factory, where technologists can present and share ideas.

Synergy between decentralized activities is managed within the R&D organization. Unisys has developed a highly effective and sophisticated online Research and Development Planning System (RDP) software tool that provides high visibility to the key people involved in projects. Periodic meetings of R&D managers further support the exchange of information.

The Technology Competence Program is a forum in which Unisys technical Special Interest Groups collaborate on the productive application of emerging information technology. Chat Groups using the Unisys intranet are an integral part of the information sharing process.

The Information Technology Professional Forum is a periodic event held via multi-site video conferences involving Unisys engineers and technologists. It is designed to encourage innovation and professional pride and development within worldwide information technology organizations. Papers presented during the IT Forum are available on the Unisys intranet.

Table IV.6.2. Information Services Group - research and development sites.

	Atlanta GA, USA	Blue Bell PA, USA	Milan Italy	Plymouth MI, USA	Roseville MN, USA	Uxbridge UK
Construction management						L
Financial systems	L			C		
Airline management systems					L	
Publishing system			L			
NT applications		L				
Wholesale banking						L

Legend: L: Leading plant
C: Plant contributing to R&D project

Table IV.6.3. Computer Systems Group - Research and Development projects.

ISO 9000 Site	Research and Development Projects
North Ryde, AUS	Software tools, fourth-generation programming languages
Amsterdam, NL	Software development management systems
Brussels, BE	Internationalization and localization engineering
Milan, IT	Publishing system
Uxbridge, UK	Wholesale banking
Atlanta, GA	Financial systems (retail banking)
Blue Bell, PA	NT Applications
Brisbane, CA	Software development management systems
East Coast Development Center (ECDC), Tredyffrin, PA	Heterogeneous Multiple Processors (HMP)-ClearPath software and hardware, Telephony products, Single Point Security systems
Mission Viejo, CA	HMP-ClearPath software and hardware, NT Enterprise Technology, Object-oriented technology, UNIX, storage solutions
Plymouth, MI	Imaging systems, printer technology, high-speed check sorter, banking systems
Roseville, MN	HMP-ClearPath software and hardware, software tools, fourth-generation programming languages, airline reservation and freight management systems
Salt Lake City, UT	Communication software, massively parallel processing UNIX
San Jose, CA	Aquanta PC programs, client/server development, Symmetric Multi Processor (SMP) UNIX, NT Enterprise Technology

2.4   Technology Transfer

An extensive network, effective tools for communication of large amounts of data, and a centralized, image-oriented engineering data base, support the transfer of technology between sites. Unisys has state-of-the-art business video conference sites in more than 100 locations worldwide. Interactive Distance Learning is provided to all Unisys employees via Unisys Business Television.

R&D organizations report their success and share information and technology at the annual Unisys Technology Conference.

The Unisys Applied Technology Awareness Program ensures continuous exchange of new technologies, and a generous Unisys Authors Sponsorship Program, in collaboration with Addison Wesley Longman, Inc., assists employees in publishing their books.

The lead organization for each project coordinates between geographically distributed sites. The Unisys Research and Development System software planning tool (RDP) helps to recognize interdependencies and to ensure that they are eliminated. Every employee is connected to the Unisys internal electronic communications network and uses the same tools, national and international sites alike.

The Research and Development Planning System is the single most important tool at Unisys for the coordination of activities in international research and development.

3   Important R&D Instruments and Procedures

3.1   R&D Tools

To complement the Computer Systems Group in controlling and coordinating R&D projects, Unisys has developed its proprietary Research and Development Planning System. It is a network-based system for entry, consolidation, and reporting of research and development planning information. The Research and Development Planning System is used for gathering top level R&D funding and schedule projection from the Computer Systems Group for use in finalizing the annual product budgets. It is also used to provide deliverable strategies from the Computer Systems Group to key market sectors such as banking, communications, government, and transportation. In addition to providing a consistent format for requirements, the Research and Development Planning System enables users to perform various real-time „what-if" scenarios to analyze and adjust R&D priorities and schedules to fit market program requirements.

Unisys uses its proprietary Research and Development Planning System exclusively to provide project control in these key areas:

- Project maintenance;
- Funding summary;
- Revenue summary;
- Product attributes;
- Development milestones;
- Interdependencies;
- Reports and checklists;
- Achievement metrics.

3.2   Personnel Management in R&D

The capabilities, vision, and expertise of our R&D employees contributes directly to the success of our R&D activities. We are committed to rewarding and recognizing these key resources at levels demanded by the marketplace, and in providing career growth and development opportunities that continually improve professional satisfaction. In addition to base compensation, R&D employees are eligible for various forms of variable and incentive pay, company stock grants, and specialized achievement awards.

The Unisys Fellow's designation for extraordinary excellence and achievement in R&D is among the highest honours at Unisys, recognizing engineers who have made major contributions to Unisys technology and served as technical leaders.

Unisys has a powerful workforce. PeopleSoft and PRO software gives Unisys managers and employees access to personnel information from *one* worldwide employee information database. This capability gives Unisys a competitive edge in managing its global operations.

> **Major issues for global R&D management at Unisys:**
>
> 1. New European Union and its requirements on companies of the EU to do business within the EU;
>
> 2. Overall technology and business climate worldwide, and market requirements;
>
> 3. Networks and tools to connect virtual offices to R&D centers;
>
> 4. Supply of skilled work force.

3.3   Functional Integration

Researchers access required resources such as marketing, competitive analysis, and purchasing through project management. Unisys state-of-the-art network allows various centers to participate in R&D simultaneously, share information, and integrate locally separate functions in the process. The Research and Development Planning System software tool records and tracks interdependencies with these functional areas.

4   URBIS Localization

4.1   IEC and Project Introductions

The Unisys International Engineering Center (IEC) was established in 1993. In addition to offering software localization and documentation/on-line help translation, it provides two capabilities that differentiate it from other localization businesses. First, it offers internationalization services. Second, it has a wide range of services including internationalization training, product support, and product customization for local market requirements. Internationalization is the process of creating software that will work for any language without modifying source code. The IEC analyzes the product and makes recommendations to the development team and/or implements these changes in the base product.

The IEC performed software localization, on-line help, and documentation translation services to fulfill the native language support portion of the contractual agreement between Unisys and its European customer for the URBIS product. The following describes the project's key characteristics and the lessons learned.

4.2   Project Requirement and Size

The project requirement originated with a signed contract between Unisys and the European customer. While the contract was to provide a general wholesale international banking solution, it also called for a local language version of URBIS' graphical user interface (GUI), 4th generation language reports, documentation, on-line help, and environmental software support of the local character set and cultural conventions (such as date, time and number formats, proper alphabetic sorting). Unisys internal European marketing organizations asked the IEC to provide services to meet these requirements.

The software localization consisted of 870 PowerBuilder objects (which comprised 301 screens), 432 text message strings embedded in the source code, and 172 reports.

The translation work consisted of an English language glossary creation and translation, 5,600 error messages, 1,300 pages (290,000 words) of documentation, and creation of the on-line help from the documentation source. A previously nonexistent glossary of terms, required for defining new terms in the local language was created as a single reference point for consistent translation between the GUI, documentation, and on-line help translations.

4.3   Product, Market, and Financial Characteristics

URBIS is a client/server wholesale banking software product developed by the Unisys International Banking Service Center (IBSC). The server portion of the product is written in a 4th generation language (LINC), with approximately two million lines of code. It runs on UNIX SVR4 using an Oracle database. The GUI client portion of the product is written in PowerBuilder's PowerScript language and runs on Microsoft Windows.

Unisys decided to expand URBIS' market penetration from its traditional UK market base to a broader Europe-wide presence. This necessitated providing a local language version to meet both market and customer requirements. The continental European market was viewed as having good potential for growth as many of the countries had not been actively marketed to and others were just starting to redevelop their banking systems in the post-cold war period.

The project was funded by the Unisys European Marketing headquarters in Uxbridge, England. This project was viewed as one of many in the future, and so it made economic sense to create a centralized method and knowledge base in the IEC rather than undertake one-off projects by local project teams spread around Western, Central, and Eastern Europe. In the past, local project teams seemed to reinvent the wheel each time they had a localization requirement, with no knowledge, documentation, or utilities passed from one project to the next. By being centralized, the IEC could invest in the procedures and tools while it performed the localization task.

The organizations and sites involved, and their areas of responsibility, are described in Table IV.6.4.

4.4   Planning

The IEC project manager initiated planning for the localization project upon notification of the contractual agreement with the customer, Unisys European marketing localization financial funding sign-off, and receipt of more detailed require-

Table IV.6.4. Unisys sites involved in the URBIS project and their responsibilities.

Organization	Location	Area of Responsibility
Country Marketing Org.	Continental Europe	Local country marketing and support
Overall Marketing Org.	Continental Europe	Overall program management
Customer	Continental Europe	Customer qualification
IBSC, ISG	Slough, England	English language version of URBIS
IEC, CSG	Brussels, Belgium	SW & documentation localization/translation
Customer Project Team	Project at customer site	Delivery of URBIS solution to customer
Unisys Marketing Europe	Uxbridge, England	Funding centralized localization

ments from the country marketing organization. The ideal implementation plan, given the organization structure, would have been for the IEC to complete the localization and translation work prior to commencement of the customer project team efforts. Unfortunately, the contractually agreed upon delivery date meant that the two organizations would have to work in parallel.

Additionally, prior to the signing of the contract, the IEC director, IEC project manager, and the European Marketing manager held several meetings with the IBSC development director, program manager, and project leader to establish a relationship, and to define the working model, roles and responsibilities, and overall project schedule. Upon completion of an initial product analysis, the IEC project manager created a project plan and schedule.

4.5   Responsibilities

The country marketing organization was responsible for selling the product to the customer. Because they were focused mainly on the sales activities however, the overall program management responsibility went to an assisting country marketing organization that had experienced and resources available in the area. The IBSC was responsible for delivering English language product to the IEC, and the IEC was responsible for delivering localized software, translated documentation, and on-line help to the customer project team at the customer site.

4.6   Project Working Model and Coordination

The development model was to have one base product source site - IBSC - and two development sites - the IEC and the customer project team - that would work in parallel. This was possible because the customization work performed by the customer project team was almost non-existent and the localization work done by the IEC was not going to be affected by their work. Also, the model controlled base product distribution in that the IBSC shipped only to the IEC, and the IEC then shipped to the project team.

The IEC project manager led the coordination between sites to ensure successful management of expectations, continuous communication, and synchronization of the sites schedules. The IEC project manager established a weekly conference call between himself, the customer project team manager, and the program manager. He distributed a report prior to each conference call which contained the project's current status, working model definition, phased delivery definition and information, a list of dependencies, questions/requests, and general and future considerations. The conference call and updated report were the key mechanisms for keeping these three sites well connected and synchronized. The IEC also had many communications with the IBSC regarding product shipments, contents, customer project schedules, and product support issues, and often involved the program manager and customer project team manager.

4.7   Engineering Task and Quality

The initial IEC engineering task was to attain the software and hardware products required, install them, analyze the English language software product (UNIX, 4GL, and GUI) from a localization standpoint, and size the effort involved to create the local language version of the product. The IEC then created utilities to automate the process of GUI translation (no industry tools were available for this specific GUI development platform), wrote guides to perform localization and testing of the local language product, used the utilities and guides to create the local language version of URBIS, and documented the UNIX server installation and administration operations for current and future reference.

The IEC and IBSC are ISO 9000 certified organizations. This requires the IEC to adhere to strict engineering processes to help produce a higher quality product. As part of the localization process, the IEC conducts internal beta tests, field tests, customer acceptance sign-off, and translation review both internally and with the customer.

4.8   IEC Team Creation and Description

The IEC project team was formed by the IEC localization project manager. Due to URBIS's large size and complexity, it required a wide variety of technical skills. As a result, the eight engineers came from six different organizations in six different countries. The IEC put considerable effort up front into analysis and procedure creation to ensure efficient localization by the incoming L10N engineers (whose skill level was unknown at the time) as well as for future projects. This initial investment was also an insurance against any unknown issues that might arise.

4.9   Management Issues

Each of the significant management problems experienced during the course of the project is described below. While all these issues existed in previous projects they stood out in this project because of their magnitude.

Initial Organization Synergy

Most new projects involve groups with no prior relationship, be it the IEC and another Unisys group or a third party. As with most new organizational relationships, the relationship between IEC and IBSC was difficult to establish, but became very close and efficient over time.

Initial difficulties were due to the IEC's being an outsider to the IBSC's business practice, and that IEC participation, by introducing a new site in the development process, could jeopardize the success of the project. In addition, IEC had no previous experience with URBIS or with the people at the IBSC. The IEC would do the localization and the customer project team would do the project specific work. In the past, any localization to URBIS had been done by the local project team, but the GUI had never been localized. Some previous projects with substantial localization requirements had been very costly in terms of time and reusability of the localization work performed. In fact, although previous projects had spent many months performing localization, there was no documentation or other information to be salvaged or leveraged.

Finally we were able to define a development working model acceptable to the IBSC and IEC. Specifically, the IBSC would deliver product only to IEC (not the customer project team) to prevent confusion between the sites, the IBSC would support only the English language version of the product, and the localization would be done in Brussels. Due to facility and logistical problems at the customer site (no electronic data connection such as e-mail or Internet), IEC could not establish a team there and still deliver a localized product as well or as quickly as it could from Brussels.

As the project progressed, the IEC and IBSC relationship grew closer. An IEC engineer actually joined the IBSC development team for a short period.

Multiple-site/Just-in-time Software Component Delivery

Another challenging management area was created by having multiple sites working in parallel on the same product base, and by having the two sites on a tightly interdependent component-based and phased delivery schedule. The IEC was to deliver the critical path components of the localized product to the customer project team in order for them to meet their scheduled milestones and planned delivery date.

The phased delivery was necessary because the entire localization effort could not be completed before the project team's effort began. The idea was to identify independent components of the base product which could be localized individually by the IEC and shipped to the customer site as they were completed. This is similar to the just-in-time delivery system developed by Toyota Corporation, but for multiple site interdependent software development.

As this structure increased the risk of delays, the challenges created were increased management attention to coordination, communication, and schedule synchronization between Brussels, the customer site, and IBSC.

Fast-cycle/Geographically Diverse Personnel

Although new to the product, the IEC had a project manager and lead engineer for the GUI but had to look outside to fill the other positions. The complexity of the product and requirement for local language support demanded a breadth and depth of experience that required more than one person. The project manager used his international connections from previous projects to assemble a team from five different organizations in four different countries within six weeks.

Locating the personnel with the correct skills was challenging. Even though people were located and qualified for the job, their availability was in some cases limited due to visa restrictions and/or other project schedules. This created discontinuity and required a transfer of knowledge between personnel. Redundant effort was reduced by requiring the engineers to document their activities performed before departure. This happened with the UNIX, URBIS, and Unisys Skills Center engineers.

New Terminology

Many terms were specific to wholesale international banking and URBIS itself. They literally did not exist in the local language and had to be created and verified by universities and national institutes, obviously slowing down the translation effort.

Training

Product and software training were required since the IEC had no previous experience with URBIS and some of its technical components. The project manager and lead engineer attended courses covering some basic material, but due to time and money constraints, the majority of training took place on the job. Experts were brought in to the product and technical environment and required to document their activities so that a common knowledge base could be established.

Moving Target

The number of URBIS releases from IBSC during the project was an issue for both the IEC and the customer project team. For a project of this kind, the software version would be fixed upon starting localization; any changes to the base product would be limited in number and frequency. In this case, there were four upgrade versions of the product. This created a moving target for both sites and brought with it the inefficiencies of having to install each release and, in some cases, having to stop the localization work altogether. The solution was to selectively install the versions and determine which work could continue independent of the new versions being received.

Communications

The customer site didn't have e-mail or electronic file transfer capabilities. Especially in a multiple site environment, e-mail is a very convenient way to keep people up-to-date, but the customer site had only a fax and a limited number of phones. Often, software was shipped by express mail or hand-carried by employees driving for five hours to the site. These limitations created further distance.

Another communication issue was the linguistic problems within the IEC team. Some had very little experience speaking English in a business setting and occasionally interpretation was required. While this wasn't a critical problem, it did create some distance and inefficiencies between the IEC team members. Fortunately, the lead engineer was bilingual.

IEC Distribution

Since the IBSC shipped the base product only to the IEC, the task of distributing standard product to the project team fell to the IEC. The IEC wanted to keep its focus on the localization task, but was often side-tracked into distribution issues due to the agreed-on working model. This would have been less of an issue if the released version had been more stable at the beginning of the project.

Additionally, several urgent requests for delivery of the localized components prior to their completion arose from the project team, diverting the localization team from their main task. Given the working model between the IBSC, IEC and the project team, the distribution issues could not easily be solved. The requests from the project team could not be ignored (although they could possibly be reduced) since the customer was requiring proof of the localized product.

Extraordinary Events

The instability of the UNIX server created a crisis situation on several occasions. There were over 20 system crashes during the project, resulting in lost translated reports, hardware component investigations and replacements, and at times a complete shutdown of work. The entire URBIS system required up to 20 hours to regenerate, and some failures occurred during these generations. This created the very difficult task of recreating a stable software environment after thorough investigation of what had been damaged.

4.10 Lessons Learned

The complexity of the project provided many lessons that can be used for future projects. The following describes those lessons in both general and specific terms.

Centralized Localization

Provided you have a certain volume of work required, it is efficient to centralize the task of localization in an organization such as the IEC (even though the funding might better come from the software product developer). In this way, the benefits from the investment in the creation of procedures, processes, documentation, and tools will far outweigh the cost.

Initial Relationships

The IEC learned that you can expect initial relationship problems between new groups (internal to your company or external). There are varying degrees of this initial adjustment period but it usually exists, and the main issues behind this are control, trust, and confidence. The base product developers naturally want to control the product to ensure its success, retain ownership, and not be responsible for the changes of others, e.g., IEC, to their product. They must be convinced that the outside organization can be trusted not to adversely affect product reputation or customer satisfaction before they will work it. Often the base product software developers are „forced" to work with organizations like the IEC due to a contractual agreement for local language support and their own inability to provide such a product. In these cases, the issue of trust is slightly reduced.

One way to gain the trust and confidence of the software product provider is for the outside organization to know the product, document its findings and provide constructive design and implementation improvements. Any design improvements are more likely be implemented. In the case of the IEC, we documented all occurrences of inappropriate coding for easy local language support and presented these to the IBSC. This then turned into a joint development effort to internationalize the base GUI product, solidifying the relationship and benefiting both organizations.

Experts

The IEC hired product and system experts at the beginning of the project. Although they were more costly than the other engineers and not available for the entire project, they provided a significant benefit. Gaining their expertise up front put the project on a solid foundation and guided course for the less experienced people to follow. This initial investment helped avoid many mistakes and inefficiencies.

Tools

It is efficient to develop or use tools for automation of translation and other activities on big projects. Doing them manually on a project of this size would be prohibitively costly and time consuming. Whether the investment would be worthwhile on smaller projects would depend how much on the tools could be leveraged in other projects.

Local Personnel Involvement

It is a very good practice to have people from the customer and/or local operation involved in the project in a multiple site environment. This creates an instant communication link between sites that provides invaluable information for project execution, greatly increases customer satisfaction by creating a feedback loop for requirement definition refinement, and builds a path for future support and projects. Conversely, if the IEC were to hire people exclusively external to the local operation on short-term contracts, the knowledge base would be lost from the company and the link with the customer would have to be created.

Localization and Learning Curve

We have discovered that localization projects are very good for engineers new to particular products and tools. Since they only focus on one aspect of the product, they are not overwhelmed with new technology, and can be productive very quickly for localization purposes. Also, since localization issues tend to be scattered throughout the product, these engineers get a broad base of exposure. With this experience they can then move deeper into the product's design and functionality.

Documented Procedures

Creating documented procedures reduces the effort required for localization. The documented procedures act as an expanding knowledge base that can be passed from project to project and from engineer to engineer. This makes sense if the process will be repeated for other projects, but is rarely done by a project team since they are completely focused on delivering a specific product on time to a particular customer. The outcome of this focused approach is that knowledge is not recorded or reusable, and „the wheels must be reinvented" by the next project team.

Identical Environments

In a multiple-site development project the sites must have identical hardware and software environments. This was not the case with our project; the hardware at the customer site was slightly different and the software installation/configuration was done for an English language environment instead of the local language environment. Identical environments require very close control. For our project, software deliveries from the IEC were intended for installation on a local language environment that didn't exist at the customer site.

Localization Timing

Ideally, the localization should be completed before the project team starts, but a phased component delivery is also possible. Horizontal and non-customized software products (such as Microsoft Office) are relatively easily localized before implementation, but it is much more difficult to achieve this with vertical and customized products.

Developer Global Responsibility

The software product development organization should take global responsibility for its product, including internationalization, localization (coordination at a minimum), and support on a global basis. This will help avoid the difficult task of multiple site parallel customization and localization, or at least reduce the complexity involved. If the software product developer does not assume global responsibility, the push for this support will have to come from outside organizations, including the customer, which can create a customer or language-specific effort.

Post-mortem Meeting

A post-mortem meeting was held at the IBSC with the program manager, customer project manager, IEC project manager, IBSC development director, IBSC support manager, IBSC GUI engineer, URBIS marketing representatives, and European marketing manager. The IEC reviewed the project, the future benefits of leveraging this work, proposals for improvements to the process in the future, and specific technical improvements required to internationalize the URBIS GUI. This was the starting point of the joint development project between IEC and IBSC to internationalize the GUI and helped all parties involved understand what was involved in the localization project. The IBSC could use this information to better understand the IEC localization issues, and the marketing people could use this information in future bids.

Underestimating Translation

The local operation underestimated the time and commitment required for managing the documentation translation. This is common when local bilingual people are available in the local operation but are neither experienced translation managers nor industry-specific translators. Additionally, these people must give their regular job top priority. The translation effort should have a single group (internal or external) committed to performing this task and ensure that reviewers are able to meet the scheduled deadlines. In the case of URBIS, there were great delays in getting the documentation reviewed locally due to other local projects taking priority, even though the skill was available.

Terminology

The translation manager and team has to be very careful when considering the translation effort involved in a project like URBIS. The terminology was very specific and terms in the local language simply did not exist. This added complexity and time to the schedule, as well as the need for a higher level of industry specific expertise and research.

5 Conclusions

5.1 Planning

At present, the planning for the localized versions is handled by the marketing or local organizations, with little or no input from the primary organizations responsible for the product. The positive aspects of this approach include:

- Staff that are physically close to, and very knowledgeable about, the local target market are making the key decisions as to whether a product should be localized.
- The „primary" program management and engineering staff remain focused on the responsibilities and deliverables for which they have the experience and skills.

The drawbacks to this approach include:

- A weakened sense of ownership may adversely affect timely delivery and the repair of deficiencies in the localized versions of a product. The organizations best placed to address these issues, the primary program management and engineering groups responsible for the product, may view their responsibility as ended when the English version of the product is delivered.
- Localization is performed as an extension to the product rather than as a key element of the product.
- Many products are released later in local markets than they would be in the U.S. (or English language speaking countries).
- Local operations responsible for the sale and support of the product in non-U.S. markets feel that their commitment is secondary to that of the U.S. (or English language speaking) markets.
- Project-specific localization can be expensive, poorly managed, and incapable of being leveraged in future efforts.

5.2 Engineering

The engineering process to produce the localized versions of products is sound. The design of any changes required for localization is not done in a vacuum but in collaboration with the primary engineering group, and there is a good level of cooperation to integrate these changes into the standard product. The localization work is performed by engineers who come from the destination country of the product who know the language as their mother tongue. They are also very familiar with the market requirements for that country and are either experienced or have received extensive training in the product to be localized. The International Engineering Center retains the basic skills necessary to support the product after release. The product is supported at the same level and using the same corporate error-reporting procedures and systems as those used for the English language version of the product.

> **Lessons learned for organizing R&D in Unisys:**
>
> 1. Design products and services for the global market;
>
> 2. Structure organization to focus on competencies;
>
> 3. Train our people in the skills they will need for their work;
>
> 4. Leverage previous work.

The major disadvantage of this approach is due to the view that localization is an extension to the responsibilities of the primary group(s) responsible for the English version of the product, it takes longer to localize a product for the first time. Much time is required to obtain:

- Essential information;
- On occasion, the source code;
- Access to knowledgeable engineering staff at the primary engineering location;
- Other resources needed to achieve a level of quality comparable to that of the English-language version.

These obstacles are overcome with varying degrees of difficulty, but the time required to resolve them delays the release of the localized version. This in turn has a negative impact on the overall product program. Where a group has performed localization on a given product in the past, the impediments listed above normally have been resolved and the localization can be performed efficiently and cost-effectively.

5.3   Financial

The most positive financial aspects of the methodology in the case study include:

- Localization is performed only for those markets where it is considered imperative; little or no money is expended on localization in a market where it is unnecessary.
- Financial planning is simplified at the headquarters level because the funding and costs are absorbed by the local operation.
- From a tax perspective, it is typically better to record the cost as an operational expense by a profitable operation in the highest tax rate jurisdiction.
- Some of the negative aspects include:
- There is no overall view or control of how much localization should cost.
- Consequently, there is little or no concern whether investments in product improvements to simplify localization would result in lower overall costs for future localization projects, which in turn would improve the gross margins and (conceivably) the marketability of a product.

- The funding for localization tends to be project, and/or client-driven rather than market-driven. The net result is that few if any products are localized for announcement and initial release. This affects the competitiveness of a product when compared with other vendor products that have support for local requirements from the outset.

Addressing the Issues

At the time this case study was undertaken, Unisys had already initiated a review of its localization processes, especially the planning and funding aspects, and was addressing whether the model for software localization should be changed. Any changes being made are expected to become operational in late 1997 or early 1998.

Remaining Challenges to Be Overcome

The key challenges are to address planning (and with it the ownership aspects) and the methods of funding software localization projects in Unisys. When the planning and ownership considerations are addressed, the coordination and logistical issues currently being experienced during the engineering phase for new products are expected to be resolved.

Main Trends Regarding Globalization of R&D at Unisys

Unisys is committed to being a major player in delivering IT services, products and solutions worldwide. For many years, all our programs have recognized the need to design and deliver products and services that can be marketed, sold, and supported worldwide.

How Will the R&D Organization Change in the Next 10 Years?

We periodically review our processes and make changes to them in order to be more competitive and more responsive to the needs of our current and future clients. We were involved this type of self-evaluation and review at the time of this case study.

- We anticipate that changes will be made to our planning and financial processes.
- We also anticipate that, as the Unisys markets in Southeast Asia, Central and Eastern Europe, and Latin America expand, more R&D work will be done in these markets than is currently done today.

There are both cost advantages and practical advantages to increased R&D. The pace of this trend will vary by market and will likely be related at least partially to the rate of our growth and the economic health of these markets. We already have established R&D projects in both Southeast Asia and Latin America.

IV.7 Huawei: Globalizing through Innovation

1 Who is Huawei?

1.1 Huawei's Profile

Huawei Technologies is a private high-tech firm based in Shenzhen, China focusing on the provision of next generation telecommunications networks. By the end of 2006, Huawei served 31 of the world's top 50 operators, along with over one billion users worldwide. Since 1999 Huawei experienced a CAGR (compound annual growth rate) of 30% in sales, and 110% in international sales alone. With over 61,000 employees, of whom 48% are dedicated to R&D (although this percentage seems to include product development as well), Huawei generated contract sales of US$ 11.0 billion in 2006, of which US$ 7.48 billion from international markets.[53]

Huawei is committed to providing Internet-protocol (IP)-based fixed & mobile communication (FMC) solutions to ensure that end users are able to experience consistent communication services at anytime, anywhere. Products and solutions include wireless products (HSDPA/WCDMA/EDGE/GPRS/GSM, CDMA2000 1xEV-DO/CDMA2000 1X, TD-SCDMA, WiMAX), core network products (IMS, Mobile Softswitch, NGN), network products (FTTx, xDSL, Optical, Routers, LAN Switch), applications and software (IN, mobile data service, Boss), as well as terminals (UMTS/CDMA). Major products are designed based on Huawei's proprietary ASIC chipset and utilize shared platforms to provide quality and cost-effective products.

Huawei's vision is "to enrich life through communication," and its mission is to "to focus on our customers' market challenges and needs by providing excellent communications network solutions and services in order to consistently create maximum value for customers." Competing domestically with e.g., ZTE, China Putian, and Datang, and internationally with e.g., Cisco, Ericsson, Alcatel, or Nortel, Huawei's strategy is to build on customer focus, giving priority to high quality, excellent service, low operating costs, competitiveness and profitability.

---

[53] Unless otherwise noted, the information is taken from Huawei's press releases, annual reports, websites, or other forms of public communication. The case was authored by *Dr. Maximilian von Zedtwitz*, Professor of Technology Management at Tsinghua University, Beijing (PR China).

1.2   Origins of Huawei

Huawei was founded in Shenzhen, Guangdong province, in the south of China, by Ren Zhenfei in 1988, as a small distributor of imported PBX products. However, by 1990 there were more than 200 agents in the telecom equipment reselling market in China, and profit margins had become slim. Ren thus decided to gamble all of Huawei's earnings into product development, with the only alternative being to wait for inevitable industry consolidation and eventual acquisition or extermination of the new firm. Ren once told his R&D staff on one occasion that "if the development had failed, I would had no choice but to throw myself out of this window".[54]

Luckily, Huawei's R&D team was successful, and soon Huawei manufactured its own PBX products. Initially a private company, it was restructured in 1990 into a share limited company. Huawei continued to develop new products for the Chinese market, and in 1993 broke into the mainstream telecommunication market by launching C&C08 digital telephone switches with a switching capacity of over 10K circuits. Until that time, Chinese domestic telecom companies were not able to build switches with such capacity. Huawei's switches were first deployed only in small cities and rural areas. Ren applied Mao's famous "encircle the cities by winning the countryside" strategy and used his strong position from the rural markets to make inroads in the foreign-supplier dominated cities, focusing on third and second-tier cities first. Ren, a former army officer, was very adept at deploying this strategy that was often compared to guerilla tactic. Huawei eventually gained market share and then made its way into major city switch offices and toll services.

In 1994, Huawei established its long distance transmission equipment business, launching a HONET integrated access network and SDH product line. In 1996, Huawei captured its first overseas contract, providing fixed-line network products to Hongkong's Hutchison-Whampoa. One year later, Huawei released its first GSM product and eventually expanded to offer CDMA and UMTS. In 1999, it was selected as the principal supplier for China Mobile's nationwide CAMEL Phase II compliant IN, currently the largest and most advanced network of its kind in the world.

The success at home has been the base for Huawei's international expansion. By 2000, Huawei had developed a noticeable global presence, with contracted sales of US$ 2.65 billion and overseas sales of about US$ 128 million. The contribution to the all-important standards discussion, it became a member of the International Telecommunications Union (ITU) in 2001. In the same year, according to market research firm RHK, Huawei became the largest provider of optical line products in Asia-Pacific. It also commercially deployed a 10Gbps SDH system in Berlin, Germany. To gain more focus, it sold its telecom and data power conversions provider subsidiary Avansys to Emerson for US$ 750 million. In 2002, it achieved a growth of 68% in international sales from US$ 328 million in 2001 to US$ 552 million despite a global decline in the investment of telecom infrastruc-

---

[54]   Private communication to the author by a former Huawei employee.

ture by 50%. It was also selected by China Mobile to launch one of the world's first mobile wireless LAN.

While continuing growth in Europe and the Middle East, Huawei was faced with a lawsuit in 2003 by Cisco Systems, claiming that Huawei infringed Cisco's intellectual property to develop a line-up of routers and switches. Huawei immediately stopped selling the relevant products in the US market and then agreed to modify its command line interface, user manuals, help screens and portions of its source codes in some of its products. As a result, Cisco dropped the lawsuit. Both sides paid their own court fees (The Register, 2003).

In 2004, Huawei was awarded "Most Promising Vendor of the Year, Asia Pacific, 2004" and "Asia Pacific Broadband Equipment Vendor of the Year, 2004" by Frost & Sullivan. It was selected by China Telecom to optimize China's national Internet backbone, and won several other major contracts that established Huawei as the market leader in China. It also established a joint venture with Siemens to develop TD-SCDMA mobile communication technology targeted for the China market.

In 2005 and 2006, Huawei saw more development in Africa, Thailand, Australia, Japan and Europe. Huawei was selected as a preferred supplier of communications equipment for BT's 21CN network. Motorola and Huawei teamed up in collaboration to develop UMTS and HSPA infrastructure equipment. Motorola would also distribute and install Huawei's 3G equipment. Huawei also won a Global Framework Agreement with Vodafone for mobile network infrastructure.

In 2006, Huawei succeeded in growing the European business, signing deals with German operator Versatel to build a fiber-optic communication network, and with France Telecom to supply UMTS mobile equipment for its third generation network. Huawei also replaced Alcatel/Motorola in Romania, and Nortel in Belgium.

For the past 20 years, China's telecommunication industry has been growing twice to three times as fast as China's GDP. Huawei's strengths used to be greatest in selling to new entrants where its lower costs and shared platform design (to enable fixed-mobile convergence) were particularly attractive (Huawei's prices are about 50% below Western competitors). But Huawei is now becoming a leading overall vendor in the industry. By the end of 2006, Huawei ranked No. 1 in the global NGN market, the MSAM market, and the IP DSLAM market (all according to Infonetics), No.1 in Mobile Softswitch (according to In-Stat), No.2 in broadband convergence routers (according to Gartner), and No. 2 in Optical Network (according to Ovum-RHK). Huawei has also become one of the few vendors in the world to provide end-to-end 3G solutions.

1.3 Management Systems

Since 1997, Huawei has been working with leading consultancies such as IBM, Towers Perrin, the Hay Group, PricewaterhouseCoppers and the Fraunhofer-Gesellschaft (FhG) to carry out management and process transformations in order to keep abreast with international industrial benchmarks, particularly in the areas of integrated product development, integrated supply chain management, human resources management, financial management, employee stock option plans, and quality control.

Starting from the product lines, Huawei's Executive Management Team and "Strategy and Customer Standing Committee" strengthened the decision-making ability of the marketing system for understanding customer requirements and planning Huawei's strategic direction and business development. With the help of the Investment Review Board (IRB), Marketing Management Team, Product System Management Team, Operation & Delivery Management Team and various other supporting teams, Huawei is concentrating on efficient implementation of an overall strategy that is driven by customer needs.

Huawei has established a financial management and monitoring system, implemented and unified financial regulations, procedures, codes and monitoring, and established a system for worldwide financial monitoring and management. Huawei is nearly 100 percent held by Huawei Investment, a company in which employees participate through an Employee Stock Ownership Plan.

In managing people, Huawei formulated the "Three-High Policy": high efficiency, high pressure, and high salary. While Huawei's engineers have still lower salaries than their US or European counterparts, they are generously paid by Chinese standards, amounting to several thousand dollars per month. A significant portion of this income is derived from the Employee Stock Option Plan, linking payments to profitability (Zhang, 2006). However, salaries in China are above the same for foreign and Chinese telecom companies (although a recent study by Norson (2005) estimated that Huawei pays an average of US$ 38,000 to their managers, US$ 8,000 more than the average for foreign firms, and more than US$ 10,000 than the average for Chinese firms). Many of Huawei's employees are young – a result in part of the fast growth and recruiting highly qualified engineering graduates from top universities. This also extends to their management teams: The heads of Huawei's R&D as well as their pre-R&D group were still in the mid-30s (BusinessWeek, 2004).

In terms of quality control, Huawei's production process system includes the 3D warehouse, the automatic warehouse and the entire production line layout designed by FhG of Germany. The new system reduced the need for transportation of materials and decreased production time, thereby increasing the all-round efficiency and quality of production.

Huawei developed a flexible supply chain, in order to provide fast, cost-effective and quality supply. Striving for customer orientation, it formulated pertinent supply guarantee strategies and built flattened manufacturing organizations. Quality engineering technologies were introduced to improve supply chain capabilities and customer service. Huawei also developed partnerships with principal suppliers, enhanced purchase performance management, and carried out supplier certification procedures based on the industrial TQRDCE benchmark.

2   International Expansion of Sales and Services

2.1   Seizing the Opportunity

After years of hard efforts, Huawei is becoming more and more internationalized. To some extent Huawei was benefiting from the telecom crisis of the early 2000s: While foreign rivals such as Nortel, Ericsson and Lucent were distracted as they went through massive restructuring in the early part of the decade, Huawei was able to focus on the market and build new solutions. As of the end of 3Q 2006, 68% of contract sales was from the international market, served by more than 100 branch offices worldwide.

To fund its expansion, Huawei is actively raising capital to carry out their international expansion plans. Among its largest deals, Huawei signed a financing agreement with the China Development Bank (CDB) in December 2004 under which CDB supports Huawei's international expansion with a massive credit facility of US$ 10 billion for both Huawei and its customers abroad until 2010.

Huawei's products and solutions are deployed in over 100 countries and serve over one billion users worldwide. Its rate of internationalization outpaced its overall growth by a significant margin. Since 1999, Huawei doubled its overseas sales every year (see Table IV.7.1).

Huawei also established more than a dozen R&D centers around the world and engaged in international partnerships with key industry partners and customers. In addition, Huawei has 28 training centers worldwide to help customers and local people to study advanced management, technologies, and related subjects. A confessed believer in localizing global operations, Huawei has increased hiring of local employees. In 2005, approximately 29% of its employees were non-Chinese nationals (IDC, 2006). Huawei also hired hundreds of Indian software engineers to work for them in Shenzhen, thus increasing the internationalization of their Chinese R&D headquarters.

For a telecom start-up from a developing country, it is particularly important to develop a track record with tier-1 carrier in developed markets. Huawei has thus invested particular attention to win leading telecom companies such as Vodafone or France Telecom. Instrumental to gaining 'attention space' in the minds of established telecom firms, Huawei pursued a dedicated brand developing strategy involving heavy investments in international fairs and exhibitions. Huawei's exhi-

Table IV.7.1. Key economic and R&D figures about Huawei, 1999-2006.

	1999	2000	2001	2002	2003	2004	2005	2006
Sales	$1.93bn	$2.29bn	$2.13bn	$2.67bn	$3.83bn	$5.58bn	$8.20bn	$11.0
Int'l Sales	$53mn	$128mn	$328mn	$552mn	$1.05bn	$2.29bn	$4.76bn	$7.48bn
Int'l %	3%	6%	15%	21%	27%	41%	58%	68%
Staff	13,000	16,000	n/a	22,000	24'000	35,000	44,000	61,000
R&D Staff	5,200	7,200	n/a	10,100	11,500	16'800	21,120	29,280
R&D Invest't	n/a	$180mn	$342mn	$355mn	$398mn	$480mn	$820mn	$1.1bn

---

Most important drivers for globalization:

1. Globalization of customers require global actions by IT provider;
2. Attractive markets and customers;
3. Locally developed technologies;
4. Attaining size and competitiveness.

---

bition platforms would have to be bigger, better designed, and flashier than its rivals. The latest technologies and products would be on display to attract attention. As Huawei was virtually unknown until just a few years ago, this approach to brand building was key to be taken seriously abroad.

In addition, Huawei targeted several countries step-by-step to expand international sales. First, it focused on countries of similar economic development and conditions, i.e. other emerging countries. Later, as Huawei had built up a stronger international market base and experience, it entered the more advanced markets of North America and Europe.

2.2   Russia

Huawei started working in Russia in 1996, which made it one of its earliest international forays. One year later, Huawei established a representative office in Moscow and a joint venture BETO-Huawei in UFA. Although the initial period was challenging and marked with much learning, the company's presence in the region has been growing remarkably since from year to year and the CIS has become a very important market for Huawei. One key to success was better service during network failure: Huawei was able to distinguish itself from competitors by have much larger technical support staff available, which reduced the average time to respond to complaints, and significantly lowered network down times. In 2005, Huawei has branch offices in 14 cities in Russia and in another 8 cities in the CIS. 80% of their employees in the CIS are locals.

2.3   Latin America

Latin America is one of the most important markets for Huawei. Since entering the market for the first time in 1997, Huawei has been consolidating its position as one of the main vendors in the region. In Latin America, Huawei's development strategy focuses on establishing strong partnerships with customers through innovation and customization of its solutions. As early as 2000, it established a technology training center in Brazil for the whole region.

Huawei's working environment is highly multicultural. Localization has always been at the core of its expansion in Latin America, including local legal entities and investment, local staff, local partners and local logistics and support infrastructure. Headquartered in Sao Paulo, Brazil, Huawei has successfully established a network of 11 offices covering almost all markets in Latin America.

2.4 Africa and the Middle East

Given the exploding telecommunications infrastructure and handset markets in Africa, Huawei has turned to this continent already in 1998. Headquartered in South Africa, Huawei's regional division covers 39 countries throughout the whole continent with the exception of North Africa. More than half of its employees are locals. Huawei established a Talent Training Center in cooperation with TELKOM, one of Africa's largest telecoms companies, and the Telecommunications Ministry of South Africa.

The Middle East and North Africa (MENA) are managed as a separate region from continental Africa. Headquartered in Egypt, Huawei MENA has 20 representative offices covering this region. Here too more than half of the staff is local.

Huawei has set up a regional technical assistance center in Egypt with over 50 technical support engineers and a network extending across the whole region. In cooperation with its customers, Huawei has established a regional training center that can take up to 120 trainees at the same time and deliver training in Arabic, French and English.

One of the biggest achievements in the region is the industry-leading commercial GSM/UMTS dual-mode network deployed by Etisalat in the UAE. Launched in December 2003, it is the first UMTS commercial network in the Middle East and the first commercial R4 UMTS network in the world. UMTS trial networks were deployed in Tunisia, Saudi Arabia, Bahrain and Algeria. GSM/GPRS/EDGE products have been widely deployed in MENA and the total capacities have reached more than 8 million subscribers. Huawei has become the Number 1 CDMA total solutions provider in the region.

2.5 Europe

Huawei first entered Europe in 2000. It had branch offices in 26 European countries by 2006, and maintained collaborations with top-tier operators such as Vodafone, British Telecom, Telefonica, Orange, KPN, T-Com and T-Mobile.

In recent years, Huawei has passed audits of a large number of major operators such as British Telecom, France Telecom and Vodafone. These strict audits involve reviewing the company's strategic planning, process, management system, quality control, and human resources. It thus proved fortunate to have invested much time and effort in developing modern corporate governance and operations, product quality control and service delivery in the years before in part with the assistance of foreign consulting companies.

As a result, Huawei is an approved global UMTS supplier of Vodafone, winning its Spain project and signed contracts for ODM handsets. Huawei is also a preferred supplier of BT 21CN, which includes MSAN and optical transmission products. Huawei has also been cooperating globally with Telefonica on mobile and fixed/broadband and been its major IP DSLAM vendor.

2.6   North America

Huawei's expansion in the US has been met with some challenges. While some of them can be attributed to Huawei's inexperience with high-cost developed markets, others are more peculiar.

For instance, there was the problem of pronunciation. Although Huawei is pronounced 'hwa-way', potential customers, clients, and even some of its own American employees called it 'hoo-way', 'high-way' or 'how-way' (AWSJ, 2005). The company thus decided to adopt another name for its US subsidiary, cooperating with a Dallas-based advertising firm in the search and selection process. The results is 'Futurewei', now officially Huawei's North American subsidiary. It was founded in March 2001 and is headquartered in Plano, a suburb of Dallas, Texas, in the heart of the Telecom Corridor.

While Americans can now pronounce the new name, questions remain over the choice of the name. Huawei employees almost always have to explain to customers the relationship between Huawei and Futurewei. Huawei itself has perhaps done too little to promote the new name, and some ads appearing in US trade magazines even bear the worldwide Huawei name. The Futurewei name appears on its booths at trade shows, brochures and other materials. Clearly, Futurewei is not fully benefiting from the increasing global brand value and name recognition of its parent company.

Futurewei's ambitions were further imperiled by other setbacks. 2003 saw Cisco's lawsuit, which put Huawei into a negative light in the US. At about the same time, rumors emerged over Huawei engaging in unethical information collection practices, including a Huawei employee taking pictures after hours of the insides of competitor's technical equipment, and Huawei's alleged detailed technical examination of candidates it had invited to China for job talks (AWSJ, 2005).

Nevertheless, from its Plano headquarters, FutureWei conducts research and development in wireless networks, optical transport and broadband networks. Moreover, product development, customer service, technical support, sales and marketing are based in Plano. Additional R&D and technical offices are in Santa Clara and San Diego, both in California. In just a few years, the Plano office grew to 150 employees, and Futurewei established a network of branch offices across the US; it also commercially deployed all the major Huawei product lines – including wireless, optical transmission, and VoIP solutions – in North America.

3   R&D at Huawei

3.1   From Technology to Customer Orientation

Huawei invests about 10% of its revenues in R&D every year (with 10% of that investment used for early stage research to stay abreast of new technologies and breakthroughs), engaging nearly half of its employees in R&D.

> **Major issues for global R&D management at Huawei:**
> 1. Availability of talented engineers and scientists;
> 2. Technical standards;
> 3. Internationalization of business and staff;
> 4. Accountability and customer-orientation.

In the 1990s, Huawei's R&D was characterized as highly competition-oriented: externally as well as internally. For instance, Huawei would assign the same task to two teams that would work on it concurrently and independently. Once completed, the results would be compared. The winning team would be given awards and extra recognition, while the losing team would be penalized. In those days, the focus was on advancing the state of technology as much as possible.

Like many other telecom companies, the collapse of the New Economy bubble in 2000/2001 meant a serious challenge. For Huawei it was clear that the entire information industry was threatened by a conflict between limited demand and limitless supply. As a result, Ren Zhengfei established a strategy focused on quality, service, cost-effectiveness and customer satisfaction. His vision was that customers not only need products and technology, but more importantly, they need solutions that bring them success in their business. Huawei thus engaged in a transition from being technology-oriented to being driven by customer requirements, from solely providing products to offering complete end-to-end solutions, allowing the development of products to be driven by customer success.

This did not mean that R&D became less important. What changed, rather, was the focus of R&D activity. If it was on product development and the acquisition of technological competence and know-how before 2000, then it was on the integration and packaging of R&D into solutions and systems after.

Huawei also adopted standardized, component-based and platform-specific management in R&D, and simplified the structure of systems and organizational frameworks to prevent the leakage of technology. Modern concepts such as concurrent engineering and the capability maturity model (CMM) were introduced. Using CBB (a hardware and software sharing module), Huawei established a technology sharing system that comprises various layers such as system design, platform, modules and components. With the experience gained from eight years of CMM implementation, it established a large and sophisticated software engineering management system. Huawei also introduced the fundamental ideas of CMM into its hardware quality management system. Most of its software development R&D institutes have already passed CMM level-5 certification.

By focusing on key network technologies, Huawei has formed core technology systems for systems architecture, hardware, software and ASIC design. Huawei developed over 100 types of ASIC chips including UMTS baseband and HSDPA chips, optical network chips, router chips, and broadband access chips. Huawei also holds strong technology positions in mobile softswitches and other network technologies.

All of these efforts improved time-to-market of products and sped up response times to market demands. But essentially it spelled a directed transition from providing products to providing solutions, i.e. a transition from a focus of copy and imitation (adequate for Huawei during the catch-up period in the 1980s and 1990s) to a new era of creation and collaboration.

3.2   Patents and Standards

Huawei set up an intellectual property rights department as early as 1995. Given annual investments of at least 10% of sales in R&D, Huawei has been able to concentrate hundreds of million of dollars on developing key network technology for nearly two decades, and by 2005 held 5% of the world's 3GPP essential patents, ranking amongst the top five worldwide. In September 2006 Huawei had applied for a total of 14,252 patents domestically and 2,635 patents overseas (of which in total 2,528 had been eventually granted, see Table IV.7.2). In 2005/2006, Huawei was applying for about 20 patents every day, making Huawei the most prolific patent producer in China, and putting it on par with leading Western technology MNCs. Huawei has also registered more than 600 trademarks in more than 90 countries.

Although Huawei has received hundreds of patents, just a handful came from the all-important US market. To crank up the pace of innovation, the company recognizes employees who come up with patentable ideas as "Huawei Innovators", and rewards them with a medal and cash awards of as much as US$ 1,200.

Huawei understands the significance of standards in the technology industry, and has participated in 70 international standardization organizations including ITU and 3GPP. Huawei's representatives have been elected to positions in various organizations, including vice president of ITU-T SG11, president of ITU-R 8F

Table IV.7.2. Patents filed for by Huawei and granted, 1999-2006.

Year	Patent Applications	Patents Granted
1999	131	n/a
2000	226	n/a
2001	504	n/a
2002	1,199	n/a
2003	3,888	686
2004 (June)	4,628	1,127
2004 (Dec)	6,500	1,400
2005 (June)	8,000	1,600
2005 (Dec)	11,000	1,844
2006 (Sep)	16,887	2,528
2006 (Dec)	19,187	2,742

Technology Group, vice president of 3GPP TSG SA2, vice president of OMA MCC as well as vice president of OMA GS. Through their active participation in these groups, Huawei is committed to realizing the vision of network convergence, where communications and networking services are genuinely merged together, as well as China's contribution to international technology and innovation.

4   Internationalization of R&D

4.1   Domestic R&D Centers

Huawei started organized R&D activity in the late 1980s, when it decided to become independent from foreign suppliers. Its first R&D center was established in Shenzhen. In line with domestic expansion of the business, it established its Beijing R&D center in 1995 (when it also set up its intellectual property right department). A Shanghai R&D center followed in 1996, and in Nanjing in 1998. R&D centers in Hangzhou, Xi'an, Wuhan and Chengdu followed later.

The Longgang high-tech industrial park, in the northeast of the Shenzhen Special Economic Zone, is home to Huawei's research and development headquarter facilities. The company's new facilities, built at a cost of 65 million RMB (about US$ 8 billion), comprise a three-story production plant and an eight-story research lab. The building, covering 1.3 square kilometers, is also Huawei's most wired property. Sophisticated consoles with LCD touch-screens are scattered throughout the Longgang facility, enabling staff to get in touch with anyone in the company worldwide and connect to the company's databases.

As Huawei was branching out its domestic R&D network, it located R&D labs close to the wells of technology talent. Cities such as Beijing, Shanghai, Xi'an, Chengdu and Hangzhou are hosts to leading universities that produce capable telecom engineers. Huawei has set up the joint R&D institutes at Zhejiang University in Hangzhou, at both campuses of Jiaotong University in Shanghai and Xi'an, Chengdu's Science and Technology University, and Fudan University. These collaborative R&D institutes help Huawei to leave a mark on the next generation of China's telecom graduates. Most technology students are proud of being considered by Huawei, and in some cases entire classes have been recruited by Huawei after graduation.

In software R&D, Huawei's Central Software Department in Shenzhen and both the Shanghai and Nanjing R&D labs have been awarded CMM5 certificates, which shows that Huawei's software development process management and quality control have reached the highest level. The Beijing R&D lab, which is one of the largest with about 2,500 engineers, covers the entire technology spectrum of Huawei's business. The other R&D centers tend to focus in scope: Shanghai on mobile communications in 3G (with about 1,000 engineers), Nanjing on network management, Chengdu on optical transmission, Hangzhou on data communications, and Xi'an on wireless technologies.

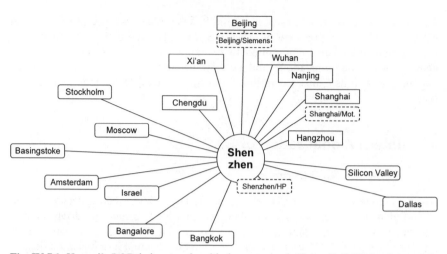

Fig. IV.7.1. Huawei's R&D hub network, with the center node Huawei's R&D headquarters in Shenzhen, PR China. R&D centers include domestic and foreign centers, R&D as well as major product development units, technology listening posts, as well as major joint-venture R&D labs (HP, Motorola).

4.2   Global R&D Centers

As Huawei entered foreign markets, R&D centers were established in Bangalore (India, 1999), Stockholm (Sweden, 2001), Dallas (USA), Silicon Valley (USA) and Moscow (Russia). Smaller R&D units were set up in Israel and Amsterdam, and at the time of writing two R&D units were under construction in Bangkok and Basingstoke, UK.

Each of those R&D centers has dedicated technology missions, concomitant with their chosen locations: For instance, Huawei R&D in Stockholm has about 60 engineers and focused on CDMA base station architecture and system design, radio technologies and RAN algorithm. Many telecom engineers were recruited from Ericsson and other local companies when they underwent difficult times in the early 2000s. Despite the relatively high taxes, the standard of living is high, too, which is attractive for highly educated employees. The overall cost level is acceptable in European comparison. In addition, government agencies are quite welcoming and flexible in making things happen.

Huawei was also the first Chinese company to set up a R&D center in Bangalore in 1999, earmarking over US$ 100 million for the Indian R&D site, which it expects to serve the Indian subcontinent, the Middle East, and Africa as strategic markets. With 1,200 engineers working in three labs in 2006, it was expected to grow to a staff of 2,000 eventually. 85% of the R&D staff were Indian nationals, as the purpose was the tap into the rich Indian expertise in software design, software testing, 3G mobile communications, VoIP, wireless infrastructure and network management. India is famous for its software talents and India government encourages foreign investments on developing software by offering preferential policy. India engineers speak fluent English and have strong dedication to quality. In August 2003, Huawei's Bangalore R&D center achieved a CMM Level 5 certification, which demonstrates the excellent quality of Huawei's software process. By 2005, the Bangalore lab had already contributed more than a dozen technology patents to Huawei's IP portfolio.

North America is the most important IT market in the world, and it is the leader in many telecom technologies. Setting up R&D labs there enabled Huawei to keep abreast with the most advanced technology, and to interact with other famous centers of research and innovation. Huawei's US R&D centers in Dallas and California (engineers in Santa Clara and San Diego) thus focus on fundamental research, i.e., technology that will take considerable time before it can be turned into new products. Still, the US R&D labs also have the mission to support the local market and to help Huawei compete with Cisco, its biggest competitor, on its home turf.

In order to strengthen its position in Russia and the former Soviet region, and to localize both products and services, Huawei has set up an R&D center in Moscow. From the very beginning the Moscow R&D centers was set up to be as local an institution as possible, promoting active collaboration and joint training with major local institutions in the telecoms industry such as the Ministry of Informational Technologies and Communications, the Central Research Institute of Communications and the St. Petersburg Research Institute of Communications.

In August 2005, to service the European market better, Huawei opened a fully-functional, industry-leading Technical Assistance Center (TAC) at its headquarters in Basingstoke, UK. The TAC is open 24/7, 365 days per year, and is fully supported with trained product engineers ensuring service commitments are met. It is also the site of its new UK R&D center, which at the time of writing was nearing completion.

As part of its contract with Dutch operator Telfort, Huawei also agreed to set up an R&D center in Amsterdam to focus on end-user services (China Business Weekly, 2005). The Amsterdam R&D lab also serves as a test bed and customer showcase in the Netherlands.

Huawei's Israeli R&D center, numbering no more than fifteen employees and costing only US$ 2 million to set up, is mostly used to gain better access to the Israeli market (Norson, 2005).

In Thailand, where Huawei has already an R&D team working jointly with AIS technicians to provide customized network solutions, an independent R&D center is currently set up to support customers with new high-tech equipment in the six Southeast Asian countries of Laos, Cambodia, the Philippines, Vietnam, Burma, and Thailand (The Nation, 2007).

4.3 International R&D Collaboration and Partnerships

Now that Huawei has an international R&D network that rivals many Western

---

Lessons learned for organizing R&D at Huawei:

1. R&D should feel what impact their work has on products and profits;

2. Focus on efficient and high-quality R&D processes;

3. Strong internal R&D investment allows fast acquisition of new technologies and own production of intellectual property;

4 Partnerships are important for the direction of future technology standards.

MNCs, it is beginning to take advantage of its multicultural dimension. Huawei has formed a rotation scheme of sending engineers to work overseas, which helps them to learn how to work in different cultures and environments and to understand international quality control practices and project management.

But even before establishing its own R&D centers overseas, as early as 1997, Huawei began collaborating with local research institutes abroad and invested in joint R&D activities with foreign MNCs. As of June 2005, Huawei Technologies had a total of 10 joint research labs, notably with Texas Instruments, Motorola, IBM, Intel, Agere Systems, Sun Microsystems, Altera, Qualcomm, Infineon and Microsoft, mostly focusing on next generation mobile communication technology. It also engaged in a number of joint R&D partnerships, e.g. with Lucent, Philips and NEC, with some starting back in 1997 as well.

In the related domain of technical training, Huawei also invested in overseas training institutes. For instance, in 2002 Huawei set up a joint lab with Pakistan's Lahore Polytechnic Institute, providing telecommunications training to the carriers in the country. Also, Huawei established a training center in Malaysia to provide customer training, product demonstration and technical seminars.

Among the latest R&D collaborations at home in China is a joint venture with Siemens which focuses on the research, production, sales and services of TD-SCDMA in order to further advance its development. In March 2006, HP, one of the lead global players in telecom OSS software, formed a global partnership with Huawei to "help the world's telecom carriers manage their networks more efficiently and continue to provide the best possible quality of service to their end users" (press release). The two companies established an OSS lab in Shenzhen for joint R&D, testing and validation, and pre-integration of OSS solutions.

Also in 2006, Motorola and Huawei decided to collaborate on UMTS development. Central to this UMTS venture was the creation of a joint R&D center in Shanghai, where employees from both companies work on the development of UMTS architecture and a portfolio of related products and services. Motorola contributed services expertise in network design, deployment and integration as well as providing value added services such as network performance, network security, network management and Operation Support Systems (OSS), while Huawei provided its increasing expertise in technology innovation, research and development.

5   Conclusions

Expanding its R&D locations and setting up local sales branches all over the world attest to Huawei's ambition of becoming an internationally recognized player. In line with this strategy, Huawei will seek to increase its R&D focus and is determined to win premium-priced projects by providing extensive onsite support services, customized solutions, and operating expenditure savings for its customers. These will be possible by collocating local R&D and technical expertise with customers and centers of innovation.

Note that despite all the R&D effort, Huawei is still relatively small compared with its competitors (some of whom outspend Huawei R&D by a large muliple), and none of the Huawei innovations developed so far have been considered "radical" (CLSA, 2006). Huawei has been particularly good at driving successful improvements in existing products and technologies – it remains to be seen whether it will be able to break new ground with truly innovative technologies. However, doing so may not even by Huawei's ambition: After all, it fully endorses the customer-focused innovation philosophy, and the economic difficulties in which quite a few technology-driven telecom firms have found themselves in the past years (e.g., Lucent, Ericsson) may indicate that an over-reliance on technology competence does not translate into market success.

In a conclusive characterization of Huawei, it is perhaps most important to note that Huawei is building on market-driven rather than technology-driven innovation. The transition was accomplished in the early 2000s and marked a switch from a purely technology catch-up firm to one that pursues independent R&D and innovation. This also means that Huawei's emphasis is on R&D speed rather than the functionality and performance. Optimization of functions and performance can be done once a product has been developed and is already in use.

Unlike many Chinese firms to date, Huawei invests a large share of its revenues in R&D, resulting in hundreds of millions of dollars and tens of thousands of engineers to form China's largest R&D group in the telecom market. Huawei's R&D effort is also extremely well organized and efficient, applying many Western models of management and organization. Some specification lists have up to 2,000 items to check—little is left to chance here.

However, Huawei's future is not without risk or uncertainty. One element is Huawei's own cultural identity as a risk-taking company (e.g., Ren Zhengfen's bet on own R&D in 1990, or its ambition to invest in fundamental R&D). At some point Huawei will experience a slow-down induced either by the increasingly difficult advancement of technology to support innovation, or the natural limitations of having expanded into all geographical markets possible, coupled with a saturation of the telecom market. Many other companies have struggled through these periods, having to cope with the fact that growth slowed down from 40-50% per year to more 'normal' levels. To make matters worse, this period may coincide with Ren Zhengfen's retiring from Huawei, and the identification of a suitable successor – or team of successors – in founder-led firms is always problematic. The slow-down of hyper growth often lays open shortcomings in areas that need to be resolved in order to turn into a mature global organization.

Major innovative break-throughs at Huawei (last five years):

1. All IP fixed-mobile convergence solutions;

2. Mobile softswitches;

3. TD-SCDMA (co-developed with Siemens);

4. Next-generation networks.

One of these shortcomings is related to Huawei's limited share structure, which has served its staff so well during the start-up period and still is as a major motivation for R&D and innovation (R&D staff bonuses are sill partly based on product profits generated). Independent observers have noted, however, that these scattered shareholdings might ultimately be detrimental in taking Huawei public, which would be a natural step in helping Huawei access international capital markets and independent sources of financing its growth.

None of these are insurmountable problems—they have been solved many times before. However, they present challenges that even the best of Chinese firms will have to face as well as they enter the coveted circles of truly globalized multinational firms.

IV.8 Fujitsu: Solutions for the Ubiquitous Networking World*

1 Fujitsu

Providing enabling technologies for global networking and innovation, Fujitsu is one of the catalysts for global innovation, an excellent example for global research and development.

Following the "Fujitsu way" means to contribute to the networked world, in which societies, firms and individual persons are linked to each other. The "Fujitsu way" was introduced as the company-wide mission, value definition and code of conduct in 2002: "Our forward-looking technologies are creating tomorrows ubiquitous networking world." Fujitsu perceives the ubiquitous networking revolution as the result of changing business models and contexts. The activity fields of Fujitsu Group are "Enabling a more comfortable society, communicating anytime, anywhere, supporting safe and secure lifestyles, making interfaces effortless".

Fujitsu provides hardware and software solutions. The firm has been changing towards a solution providing and customer oriented business strategy. This implies investments in market know-how, resulting in slightly decreased R&D investments, 5% of sales were invested in R&D in year 2006, compared to 7% about 10 years ago. As information and communication technologies converge, Fujitsu benefits by offering complete solutions. System integration services and after sales services are increasing.

The global research organization of Fujitsu consists of research activities within the business segments, the Fujitsu Laboratories, virtual research centers and outside innovation partners. Today, Fujitsu has a hub model R&D organization, combining decentralized R&D units with the head office of Fujitsu Laboratories, in order to realize optimal synergies by exploiting all best available resources, and avoid redundant R&D.

The R&D activities of Fujitsu Group are global. Fujitsu Laboratories' basic and

---

* This case study was authored by *Karin Löffler*, Chair of Technology and Innovation Management, Swiss Federal Institute of Technology, ETH Zürich, with contributions from *Fumitaka Abe*, General Manager R&D strategy and planning office, Fujitsu Laboratories Ltd., Japan.

applied research teams are working closely together in applied technology and product development across the Fujitsu Group worldwide. Today, R&D capability includes 1,500 research scientists at Fujitsu Laboratories in Japan, the United States, in China and the United Kingdom. Some 14,000 development engineers work at locations worldwide. Innovation projects are organized in seven Research Laboratories, seven virtual Research Centers, and one Project Group.

Fujitsu Laboratories Ltd. is a 100% subsidiary of Fujitsu Limited. Fujitsu Laboratories' mission is to contribute to Fujitsu's technology value chain. One of the Laboratories' aims is to promote the creation of new businesses for Fujitsu Group. Individual research programs are decided by a technology management committee and the Fujitsu Laboratories. Research centers "virtually" unite researchers working on the same research topics in different laboratories. One research center has about 30 to 50 members.

1.1   Global Network of Research Laboratories

In 1962, the Fujitsu laboratories were created by merging R&D departments previously managed by the technical divisions. Soon, the laboratories were spun off as 100% subsidiaries of Fujitsu Limited, named Fujitsu Laboratories Limited. The head office of Fujitsu Laboratories is located in Kawasaki, Japan. The internationalization of R&D started with the foundation of Fujitsu Laboratory in the USA in 1993, with head office in California. The Fujitsu Research and Development Center Co. Ltd. was established in Beijing, China in 1998. In 2001, the Fujitsu Laboratories of Europe Ltd. were founded in London.

Fujitsu extended its research organization with the construction of Yokosuka Research Park in Japan in 1997 and in 2000 with the creation of Akiruno Technology Center in Akiruno, Japan. For a long time, R&D spending of Fujitsu used to be 7-8% of sales. Because of Fujitsu's strategy change towards solution provisioning, research expenditure is reduced to about 5% of sales today. In 2006, overall R&D spending was around 255 billion Yen, including the 40 billion Yen Fujitsu Laboratories spent on R&D. The percentage of R&D spending varies amongst the research fields significantly.

Today, 80 researchers work for Fujitsu Laboratories of the USA. The Fujitsu Research and Development Center in China is fast growing with about 60 employees in 2006. Fujitsu Laboratories of Europe has 30 employees beginning of the year 2007.

The aim of the global innovation network is to realize synergies on a global scale. The choice of research laboratories' locations was done in order to be close to the best research talents and to relevant markets (see Fig. IV.8.1). The Fujitsu oversees research laboratories were established step by step.

USA

Fujitsu Laboratories of America, Inc. (FLA), a wholly owned subsidiary of Fujitsu Laboratories Ltd., was established in 1993, headquartered in California. FLA focuses on research and development on Very-Large-Scale Integration computer-

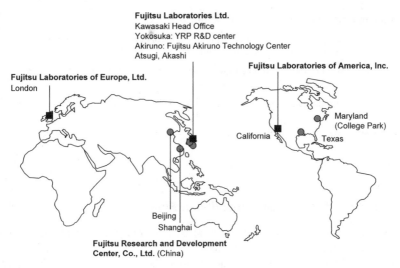

Fujitsu Laboratories Ltd.
Kawasaki Head Office
Yokosuka: YRP R&D center
Akiruno: Fujitsu Akiruno Technology Center
Atsugi, Akashi

Fujitsu Laboratories of America, Inc.

Fujitsu Laboratories of Europe, Ltd.
London

Maryland
(College Park)

California   Texas

Beijing
Shanghai

Fujitsu Research and Development
Center, Co., Ltd. (China)

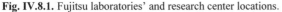

Fig. IV.8.1. Fujitsu laboratories' and research center locations.

aided design, Network management, Broadband applications over the Internet, Software agents, Pervasive computing, Low-power high-speed CMOS circuits and all-optical switches.

Europe

Fujitsu Laboratories Europe was established in London area in 2001. The aim of the foundation was to carry out basic and applied research activities throughout Europe in Fujitsu's then key business areas, including information processing, telecommunications, electronic devices, services and software. In 2006, the London laboratory is focussing on topics like biotechnology. Together with Cambridge University Fujitsu conducts research on quantum computing, with Heinrich-Hertz-Institut (member of Fraunhofer Gesellschaft, Germany) research on optical signal processing, and with ETH Lausanne (Switzerland) research on circuit design.

Asia

Founded in 1998, Fujitsu Research and Development Center Co., Ltd. (Beijing) is focussing on communication systems and web services. Fujitsu will expand the daughter laboratories in Shanghai and in Beijing to provide solutions to local businesses. The two China laboratories are the fastest growing laboratories of the worldwide network. Beginning of 2007, 60 researchers work for the Fujitsu Research and Development Center Co. Ltd.

Most important drivers for globalization:

1. Reach and maintain leading technological position by attracting best research talents available worldwide;

2. Direct personal contacts are necessary to access the knowledge of the leading research talents worldwide;

3. Support overseas' Fujitsu business via proximity to customers;

1.2   Drivers for R&D Globalization at Fujitsu

In every technology field Fujitsu tries to quickly reach and maintain a leading technological position. Contacts to research talents who are located in leading research institutions worldwide are necessary to be able to access the knowledge. Virtual connections cannot replace the personal contacts. Therefore, Fujitsu R&D has to be present in leading research clusters worldwide.

Today, 67% of Fujitsu's revenue is created in Japan. The international business is growing. In June 2006, Fujitsu decided to set up new overseas groups in Asia / China, the Americas and Europe, with the intention to support the increase of sales in the four regions from actual 33% (of total sales) to 50% in 2010. Therefore, the importance of the global innovation network is increasing as well. The global research principle matches the global market concept of Fujitsu. Global customers need global suppliers. To be able to provide networking technologies and solutions for customers who are present worldwide, research has to be present in many regions as well. R&D in overseas' locations supports the overseas' business of Fujitsu.

One challenge and sometimes even inhibitor of global innovation is the protection of property rights. Therefore, the overseas' R&D units have specialists for intellectual property protection, steered by the global R&D department on-site. Key are foreign patent applications. Fujitsu owns over 34,000 patents. Fujitsu's foreign patent application rate is higher than 60% at present. Foreign applications in Asia show the biggest growth rate. The total amount of annual foreign applications rose from 2000 patents in the year 1996 up to over 7000 patents in 2005. Global research collaboration needs open communication and idea sharing. In addition to patent application, other findings, which should not be patented, are published in publicly accessible journals, like the Fujitsu Scientific and Technical Journal, the Fujitsu Ten Technical Journal, local Fujitsu publications or world leading technical journals.

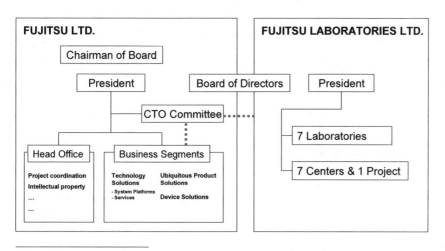

■■■ : Technology Management

Fig. IV.8.2. Fujitsu units involved in innovation projects.

2 Global Collaboration of Fujitsu Units in Innovation Projects

2.1 Structures

Today's challenges ask for close collaboration between laboratories and business units. Fujitsu research activities in business units and research laboratories are organized in virtual research centers. All units collaborate closely in projects at Fujitsu in order to quickly bring to market innovative and highly reliable products and services. This requires a constant and well-coordinated flow of information and innovative ideas amongst the worldwide operations.

Fujitsu technology planning is conducted by the chief technology office (CTO) committee, consisting of about ten committee members: the leaders of the business units and the president of Fujitsu Laboratories. The research laboratories, with 100 to 200 researchers each, operate semi-autonomous, steered by "the Board of Directors" and "the CTO committee". Technology projects can be initiated by the research laboratories, the CTO committee, or by business units.

Projects at Fujitsu Laboratories are business unit-commissioned (55%) or head-quarters-commissioned (45%). The budget is allocated on different types of re-search projects: Development Research: 15%, Advanced Research: 35%, Com-mon Base Technologies: 30%, and Exploratory Research: 20%. This allocation was chosen in order to create business and technology ideas for tomorrow, as well as supporting the further development of existing product families.

Fujitsu Laboratories are oriented to specific technology fields. Besides six Laboratories with technology focus, a seventh Laboratory, the "Business Incubation Laboratory" was founded. It creates technologies for future product platforms. Because research projects require the combination of various fields, the virtual organization of "Research Centers" has been created.

2.2   Collaboration with Universities and Research Institutions

Fujitsu Laboratories conduct joint research with leading universities and leading independent research institutes in Japan and abroad, in order to enhance technology and products. Replacing contract research, Fujitsu invests in joint research projects and personnel exchanges. There are various examples for successful research collaboration with Japanese, American, European and Chinese universities.

As other Japanese High-Tech companies, Fujitsu intensified the collaboration with foreign universities in the 1990ies. Fig. IV.8.4 displays the investment in university research by Japanese companies, citing Kimura and Schulz (2004).

Since the foundation of Fujitsu Laboratories of America, Fujitsu intensified the collaboration with many foreign research institutes and universities. Most of the Fujitsu Laboratories are based next to a campus of leading universities, with the aim to foster joint research with universities worldwide.

One of the very successful global research collaborations is the joint work with Heinrich-Hertz-Institut in Germany (Fraunhofer Institute for Telecommunications). Fujitsu and Heinrich-Hertz-Institut developed the world's first high-speed optical fibre switch with power amplification features. The new switch enables high-speed switching at over one terabit per second. This research collaboration started in 2001 with the goal to develop super high-speed optical signal processing technologies.

One recent example for a successful collaboration with a university is "QuantumDotLaser". New technologies utilizing quantum dots were developed through an academic-industrial research collaboration by Fujitsu Laboratories and Professor Yasuhiko Arakawa's laboratory at the University of Tokyo. The collaboration

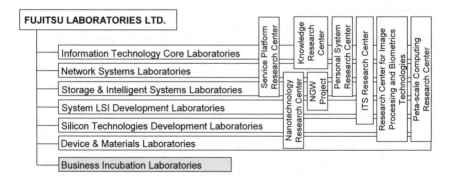

Fig. IV.8.3. Organization of Fujitsu Laboratories and Research Centers.

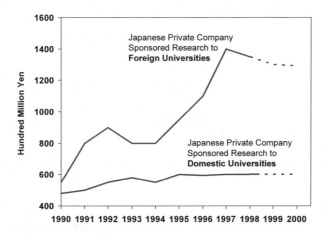

Adapted from Kimura and Schulz (2004: 30), based on METI data.

Fig. IV.8.4. History of research sponsoring, to domestic and foreign universities.

resulted in the launch of the new venture company QuantumDotLaser in April 2006. Today, QuantumDotLaser is supported by Fujitsu's corporate venture capital fund. In addition to providing technical support through joint research with Fujitsu Laboratories and QuantumDotLaser, Fujitsu will also offer business management support. Through commercialization of its world-class technology, Fujitsu's aim is to enhance its competitiveness in the optical access market. Recently, QuantumDotLaser Inc. and the University of Tokyo have won a Runner-Up award for the Semiconductor category of The Wall Street Journal Technology Innovation Awards 2006.

2.3 Research Collaboration with Firms

In addition to collaboration with universities, Fujitsu collaborates with private companies, in joint research projects, by founding joint ventures like Fujitsu-Siemens JV or through cross-licensing deals with other firms. There exist cross-licensing agreements with companies like Lucent Technologies, IBM, Microsoft, Intel, Texas Instruments, Motorola or Samsung. Since 1998, Fujitsu's licensing revenues have exceeded licensing payments.

Grid computing is an example for successful radical innovation in global collaboration with France Telecom: In 2006, Fujitsu Limited, Fujitsu Laboratories, and France Telecom co-developed a grid service platform. This platform allocates resources automatically in response to application loads, using grid technologies to virtualize and integrate 24 servers located in three locations, Paris (France), Tokyo, and Kawasaki (Japan).

In Japan, regional collaboration is fostered. Recently, the Kawasaki area hosting the Fujitsu Laboratories' head office, has become a base for numerous other

> **Major issues for global R&D management at Fujitsu:**
> 1. Collaboration between research laboratories and partner research organizations worldwide;
> 2. Customer orientation in research;
> 3. Flexible structures for cross-divisional innovation projects.

high-tech companies such as Ajinomoto or Canon. Today, many R&D bases and research institutes are clustered along the coast of Kawasaki and Tamagawa.

3   Flexible R&D Structures and New Innovation Approaches

The Fujitsu R&D organization consists of laboratories and virtual research centers. The research activities are organized according to specific project structures. Three approaches exist how to run an innovation project at Fujitsu Group. The linear model represents the classical sequential approach. In "Akiruno-style", the sequence of units involved in a linear project structure can be adapted to project needs. The third approach, called "New Business Development", is used for new business creation projects at Fujitsu.

3.1   The Linear Innovation Model

For product improvement projects, Fujitsu applies the conventional linear innovation approach. Researchers present and hand over completed research projects to the business units. The business unit commercializes the new technology or the new product and cares for product improvement in cooperation with the laboratories.

3.2   The Akiruno-style Approach

Cross divisional project ideas require the involvement of many different resources, which are dispersed in the Fujitsu organization. In these cases, the "Akiruno-style" approach is chosen at Fujitsu: Fujitsu Laboratories work closely together with the business units. Formal boundaries are neglected. Fujitsu Laboratories and the business units work together as one team. The Laboratories can be involved in the commercialization phase as well as in product customization and further product development.

Promising projects with a high degree of novelty and cross-divisional characteristics are candidates for Akiruno style management. One example is the 90 nm Large Scale Integration (LSI). Fujitsu was the first company to successfully

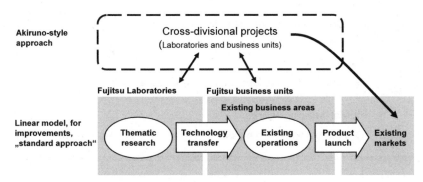

Fig. IV.8.5. Akiruno-style approach.

mass produce 90 nm LSI devices. Other successful examples are the Hard Disk Drive technology projects or the 3rd generation mobile communications base stations projects. These projects were concentrated at the Akiruno Technology Center. The name "Akiruno-style" was given after the Technology Center, where the new project style was used for the first time.

3.3 The New Business Development Approach

Whereas the linear model and Akiruno-style approach represent methodologies and structures specific for R&D needs, there is need to identify break-through new technologies and to transform those into new products. This exploratory research has been institutionalized in a project organization called "New Business Development". A "Business Incubation Research Laboratory" has been established in October 2005 to foster radical new business development at Fujitsu, independent of short & medium term needs of the business units. Examples are Grid Comput-

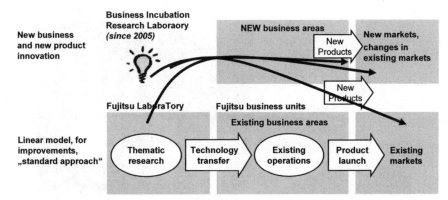

Fig. IV.8.6. New Business Development approach.

Major innovative break-throughs at Fujitsu (last five years):

1. Electronic Paper: First bendable colour display;

2. Palm Vein Authentication;

3. Semiconductor micro fabrication: Mass production of 90 nm Large Scale Integration devices;

4. Optical switching devices;

5. Grid computing: Automatic work allocation among multiple computers.

ing or Palm Vein Authentication technologies. The project form is more flexible than others. The Business Incubation Laboratory supports the fast realization of new ventures (Fig. IV.8.6).

Palm Vein Authentication as an example for successful new business creation

One example for a successful cross-divisional new business development and breakthrough innovation project at Fujitsu laboratories is the palm vein authentication technology. Various business units, including the Business Incubation Laboratory, collaborated in order to realize the project. Authentication is one of the technology bottlenecks in mobile commerce.

The Fujitsu Palm Vein Technology turned out to be superior to the existing authentication technologies. Palm veins are unique, even among identical twins. Each hand has a unique pattern. Reduced haemoglobin coursing through the palm veins absorbs near-infrared light. The pattern is scanned by a contact-less scanning device and analyzed. 150.000 vein patterns have been tested with the new technology, and the method turned out to be most reliable. The probability of false acceptance is lower than 0.00008 %. Therefore, the technology is superior to most

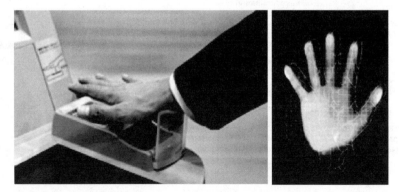

Fig. IV.8.7. Palm vein authentifcation.

> **Lessons learned for organizing R&D at Fujitsu:**
> 1. Global cross-divisional projects require flexible structures;
> 2. Worldwide research collaborations in form of joint research with leading institutions are key for successful R&D;
> 3. Service products require the same global R&D network as devices;
> 4. Business development should be supported by R&D structures.

other biometric authentication technologies. The technology is easy to use and hygienic. Today, the technology is in use in many banks, universities, and security services. Application examples are room access control, ATM authentication systems and IT security. The first customer was Bank of Tokyo-Mitsubishi. In March 2006, Fujitsu started the worldwide sales of the Palm Vein authentication system (Fig. IV.8.7).

Collaboration among business units, R&D, sales, engineering, and affiliates was necessary to realize the project. In the incubation phase, limited funding was adequate. In the later phase, "fast track" funding supported the project to be realized in time. Because no strict stage gate process had to be followed, the developers were not hindered by formal restraints in the project realization.

Flexible project forms, like the one applied in the later stages of the Palm Vein project, will be employed in many more projects in future. Fujitsu works on improving the technology by scaling down the Palm Vein scanner. A Palm Vein scanner incorporated in mobile phones might extend the range of mobile applications drastically.

4   Outlook and Conclusions

The case underlines the advantages of a global innovation organization in multinational firms. As well as in solution provisioning, Fujitsu succeeds by focussing on successful technologies - the critical technologies in ubiquitous computing, networking and in fields like data security. Excellent coordination and steering is a precondition for efficient and effective collaboration in global project organizations. Fujitsu is successful in using flexible project approaches to push radical innovations to market.

Trends

Information, communication, devices, services, and content are converging. Fujitsu will contribute to the construction of the next generation of information and communication technology - with its strong background in the mixture of these areas. Fujitsu will be able to vertically integrate the value components. The firm's strategy is to change its business model towards solution provisioning. Combination of integration and cutting-edge technologies will be key for Fujitsu's competitive position. Global presence will help Fujitsu to understand its customers' needs worldwide.

In future, Fujitsu will apply even more flexible structures for successful global innovation. The IT market has become very competitive and fast-changing. But still, new challenges, e.g. in the area of data security, provide new business opportunities for Fujitsu. The early identification of these chances is crucial. Fujitsu is investing into the future of the company itself, by creating new business fields like the Palm Vein Technology applications. Fujitsu's investments in New Business and New Technology creation, including the foundation of the Business Incubation Laboratory, are very promising.

IV.9 Swiss Re: Global Intellectual Property Management in the Financial Services Industry*

"You don't know how lucky you are if you know where your inventors are!"
Dr. Frank Cuypers, Head of Global IP Group at Swiss Re

1 The Reinsurance Company Swiss Re

The Swiss Reinsurance Company (Swiss Re) is one of the leading reinsurance organizations, and the world's largest life reinsurer. Swiss Re was founded in 1863 in Zurich. Today, the company has more than 70 offices in 30 countries worldwide. Swiss Re has maintained the highest official security rating, "AAA", for decades. The reinsurance business is about insuring primary insurance companies, and therefore a business-to-business activity. The insurance business is based on managing the volatility of risks, i.e. to decrease probability of ruin, decrease tax burdens and cost of capital, and to secure returns to shareholders. Traditional reinsurance products therefore cover the entire spectrum of underwriting risk in the life and non-life areas. Examples of such products include accident, property, third party, car, and travel insurance. In addition, Swiss Re offers insurance-based solutions for enterprise financing and support services for risk management (Swiss Re 2004b). To absorb risk volatility without endangering itself as a reinsurance company, Swiss Re has to be big, diversified and – most importantly – has to understand the insured risks. These three aspects drive globalization. Swiss Re runs three divisions: Property & Casualty, Life & Health, and Financial Services, offering a wide variety of products and services to help manage capital and risk. The business group Property & Casualty offers "non-life" reinsurance products as they are termed, Life & Health contains products related to human life, and Financial Services is responsible for investments, credit and art. There is also a Corporate Center that hosts an IT group, a finance group and the Group Intellectual Property Department.

---

* This case study was authored by *Dr. Martin A. Bader*, European and Swiss Patent Attorney, Managing Partner of the innovation and intellectual property management advisory group BGW AG, St.Gallen and Vienna, and *Dr. Frank Cuypers*, Head of the Group Intellectual Property Department of Swiss Re, Zurich, Switzerland.

Major issues for global R&D management at Swiss Re:

1. Get access to new resources, particularly new technologies;
2. Long-term perspective philosophy;
3. Collaborative research activities with external partners.

At its headquarters in Zurich, Switzerland, Swiss Re announced a fiscal profit of 2.5 billion Swiss francs for 2004. Swiss Re employs over 8,000 employees, 3,000 of whom are based in Switzerland. Notable competitors include Munich Re, Hannover Re, and GeneralCologne Re. Swiss Re ranks second to Munich Re in terms of premium volume, with 29.4 billion Swiss francs (2004).[55]

2   Research and Innovation

Within the (re–)insurance business, there are no classical research and development activities. Instead, there are numerous decentrally organized and conducted technical projects. Their goal is to develop in-house information technology solutions, especially if there are no outside, off-the-shelf products on the market. These types of research and development activities are important for Swiss Re to defend itself against attacks by hackers, to simulate natural catastrophes as well as develop epidemic models, pricing models, tools and reserving methodologies. Further targets are e-business solutions and specific product developments. These project activities absorb significant human and financial resources. In the (re-) insurance business, the engineer's function is therefore replaced by the actuary's function.

(Re–)insurance products are, however, often characterized as possessing a relatively easy imitativeness. Competitive advantage can thus be achieved by emulation of existing products. This is often described as the second-mover advantage. Furthermore, first-mover activities, e.g. the introduction of a new product on the market, are considered to involve high-risk components and hence lack attractiveness.

3   Global Collaborative Research Activities

Primarily Swiss Re gets involved in innovation collaborations in order to gain access to new resources, particularly technologies. The sought after technology plays a decisive role in partner selection. The basis for choosing a partner there-

---

[55]   In November 2005 Swiss Re announced it had agreed to acquire GE Insurance Solutions, the fifth largest reinsurer worldwide, from General Electric Company. GE Insurance Solutions had net premiums earned of US$ 6.2 billion in 2004 advancing Swiss Re to the world largest reinsurance company.

> **Major issues for global R&D management at Swiss Re:**
> 1. Get access to new resources, particularly new technologies;
> 2. Long-term perspective philosophy;
> 3. Collaborative research activities with external partners.

fore boils down to the technologies and subsequent intellectual property that can be gained by collaborating.

For Swiss Re, collaborations are designed and aligned to the company philosophy taking a long-term perspective. Often a long-term intensive partnership results in a win-win situation for both sides.

Swiss Re has had collaborations with a number of partners in the past. Essentially, the common invention mindset of both parties has played a supporting role in these partnerships. Swiss Re never signs licensing contracts with more than one party at any given time.

As an internationally active enterprise, Swiss Re has entered into collaborations with a wide array of partners worldwide. For a major part, collaborations are formed with research institutes and universities. There are also collaborations with competitors; but, those arrangements are dependent on the decision of the respective department within the company.

Innovation collaborations led Swiss Re to work with their partners up to a certain point. This solution is obvious, since the greater number of partners requires a more complex set of contract rules, resulting in a substantial rise in costs to Swiss Re.

4   Intellectual Property Management at Swiss Re

4.1   *IP Management in the Financial Services Industry*

Intellectual property strategies are increasingly based on the protection of service innovations. Astonishingly, only 50% of companies are aware of the protection of services by commercial patent rights (Gassmann and Bader, 2007). The protection of services is a relatively new phenomenon, especially for European organizations. Especially Anglo-American and Japanese entities serve as examples of predecessors that incorporated intellectual property into business activities. At the European Patent Office 75% of patent applications in the bank and (re–)insurance industries originate from companies in Anglo-Saxon countries like the United States, Canada, and Great Britain. (Fig. IV.9.1). Only 10% of all patent applications come from European organizations. Despite the fact that the European Patent Office is more restrictive with respect to the protectability of new business models, it is clearly evident that US-based service organizations are more patent aware.

In the financial services sector, banks and insurances companies are increasingly becoming aware of the opportunities created by patent innovations. In particular, they are looking to patent business models that run off of computer systems: business models and software solutions are more patentable, something that has become common practice in the United States and Japan. Meanwhile, the application for pure business models is rare, as even in the United States the granting process for submitted inventions must be both tangible and comprehensive. Typical titles of specifications for patents include, for example: systems and methods for user authorization, verification and audit systems, devices and process for calculating options, and internet-based insurance products. Following the US trailblazers (e.g., Citigroup and Merril Lynch,) Swiss Re and UBS have caught on to the trend: establish dedicated patent departments and announce in-house patents. Swiss Re is one of the first (re–)insurance organizations that created its own patent department and carries out a consistent internal strategy. Hence, the following sections look at the problems faced by Swiss reinsurance firm Swiss Re, in dealing with patent rights and patents in the financial services sector.

In the following graphic, the published patent applications and prominent patents of insurers and reinsurers are displayed (Fig. IV.9.2, as of October 2003). The graphic also specifies Swiss Re's as of yet unreleased patent applications. It is evident from this, that other than Swiss Re, Converium and ERC, no other reinsurer has produced patents internally. Yet, there are such capabilities from insurers. The world's largest reinsurer Munich Re has no internal published patent applications. According to the data, Japanese insurers are strong in this area, occupying the first three places. The Swiss Re data shows how sizeable the difference is between published patents or patent applications, and unpublished patents. This means there are a great many applications in the pipeline that are highly guarded, until some time in the future when they are revealed publicly.

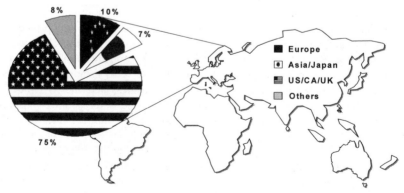

Source: Bader (2006a).

Fig. IV.9.1. Patent applications in the financial services sector in Europe.

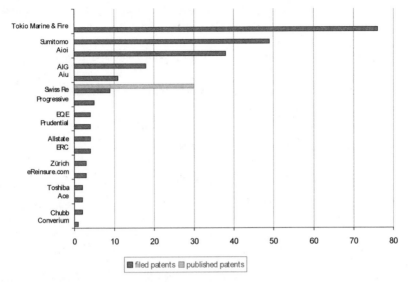

Source: Swiss Re, Intellectual Property Report 2003 (Swiss Re 2004a).

Fig. IV.9.2. Published patent applications of large insurers.

A large number of patents in this industry can attributed to original patent holders and large companies that have many years of patent experience, characteristics not often associated with the (re–)insurance industry. This situation stems from the New Economy hype from a few years ago, when the dot-com companies were vying for patents on software and business practices. They were doing so to make their financial situation more attractive to investors (Cuypers, 2003).

Beginning of the Intellectual Property Era. The introduction and establishment of intellectual property within Swiss Re can be traced to the introduction of e-business-based reinsurance products. The goal of these e-business solutions is to achieve high efficiency in the processing of reinsurance transactions. In this framework, one can see how the internet- and browser-based IT solutions disrupted and altered competitors' specifications. This has been legitimized by the State Street Decision[56] in the United States, which followed a large and sudden growth in business model patent applications. Swiss Re, whose core competencies lie in the evaluation of risk and chances, is significant for two facts:

- At one time there was a risk of the infringement of patents from:

a) Competitors;
b) Other third parties not in direct competition with Swiss Re.

---

[56] State Street Bank and Trust Co. v. Signature Financial Group, Inc., 149 F.3d 1368 (Fed. Cir. 1998).

- Swiss Re faced more than just risk, as simultaneously there were other opportunities:

  a) Publishing of trade secrets that until recently had been protected by patents;

  b) Hedging of investments and income from research and development activities;

  c) Greater autonomy from key knowledge sources;

  d) Maintaining and taking stock of internal know-how.

This scenario led management to set up a task force in fall 2000 that had to investigate the potential of an in-house intellectual property department. The establishment of the central intellectual property department, called Group Intellectual Property Department, was finalized in August 2001, and it was placed under the Risk & Knowledge Division at the Swiss Re corporate headquarters in Zurich. This new department supports a division that already provides a number of services in the firm.

At the time of the new department's establishment, no patent infringement complaints or their like had been submitted. The Group Intellectual Property Department's initial focus was on the generation and supervision of patents. The legal department already handled copyrights, and external lawyers handled trademarks on a regional basis. The goal of the intellectual property department was and still is primarily to minimize risk.

Initiation of Intellectual Property Activities. With the initiation of patent activities, the Group Intellectual Property Department launched an awareness program. Activities related to the program included: internal and external publication of articles relating to intellectual property, a company intranet site with information on intellectual property, active participation in international conferences; and internal and external interviews on intellectual property in order to establish a bilateral dialogue and team meetings. The Group Intellectual Property Department also specifically created a new pamphlet called Welcome on Board for incoming employees. The following graphic (Fig. IV.9.3) displays the cumulative activities and promotion of the patent department in 2003.

The specific challenges facing Swiss Re's intellectual property department during the initial stages of establishing patent activities included:

- Sufficient sensitivity towards patents and intellectual property. The first challenge was to raise awareness within Swiss Re and help employees to understand the new issues surrounding a new patent department.
- To deal with supposedly "unimportant" ideas that the public could access and that could have an impact on patent protection. Even if internal experts knew about the Group Intellectual Property Department, their inventions were not always properly acknowledged and recognized. Inventors still lacked the specific ability to identify and evaluate their inventions.
- The acceptance and perceived value of intellectual property for (re–) insurers.

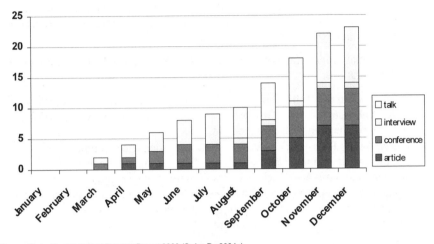

Source: Swiss Re, Intellectual Property Report 2003 (Swiss Re 2004a).

Fig. IV.9.3. Intellectual property initialization activities at Swiss Re in 2003.

- The ability to point out improvements and changes that could be achieved through the internal Group Intellectual Property Department and its related patent activities.

4.2   Intellectual Property Strategizing

Swiss Re pursues an internal patent application and activity process to protect its intellectual property, while building up a respectable and well-diversified patent portfolio to protect itself against potential conflicts. Where reinsurance products are concerned: the better the statistical findings on risk are, the easier that premiums can be calculated. Hence, a good model focuses squarely on profit.

Reinsurance products are especially easy for competitors to copy when the development steps and related know-how are done by different parties. This means exposure to those handling or accepting the contracts distributed to customers. There is thus an incentive to protect this model with a patent. The advantages of such protection include:

- Product development or subtasks can be split into separate parts internally, ensuring that competition is not exposed to sensitive information. The development process can therefore be streamlined and costs lowered.
- R&D collaborations can be entered into in respect of patents; something that was not possible before without the additional protection of intellectual property.
- In addition, products can be passed on to customers without fear of being copied by third parties. This also frees up their use in other contexts and situations.

Previously, projects (especially smaller ones) were not pursued vigorously if their application and project range were too small, since there was no incentive to develop and exhaust all the project's possibilities.

The intellectual property activities of Swiss Re are based on the three strategically aligned foundations:

- *Defence:* (Patent-) Infringement against Swiss Re should be anticipated, prevented and handled. The Group Intellectual Property Department maintains a strategic partnership with management.
- *Action:* Swiss Re's R&D activities should be identified, promoted, protected, and then used to the firm's advantage. The Group Intellectual Property Department maintains a strategic partnership with management.
- *Leadership:* Swiss Re wants to become an industry leader in handling intellectual property. The central Group Intellectual Property Department maintains a strategic partnership with management.

The above strategic points were developed by the central Group Intellectual Property Department with the insight and understanding of Swiss Re's corporate leadership. These points are in agreement with Swiss Re company policy. A strong and diversified patent portfolio is a necessary prerequisite for successful strategy implementation.

The following guidance rules were derived from the intellectual property strategy that is available to any Swiss Re employee. These fundamental points are of particular importance to key employees who have frequent contact with third parties.

- *Novelty:* Novelty is a fundamental criterion for having an invention patented. Inventions, before they are registered via patents, may not take on a publicly recognizable form to avoid the risk of losing patentability. Beyond this, there is the danger of a damaged reputation if the object to patent has already been revealed or inferred to by internal or external publications.
- *Identification and proof of patent infringement:* In some cases where it is difficult to prove patent infringement, it is better to classify the invention as a trade secret.
- *Usefulness for third parties:* If the patent application is too specified and for the benefit of Swiss Re only, the potential economic usefulness is questioned. Hence, the protected technology should be of use for other organizations as well.
- *Relevance to Swiss Re:* If an invention falls within the core competencies or other important areas of the firm's business, and if it can be avoided, competing firms should not be allowed to establish their own patents. In such a case, classifying an invention as a trade secret would be a dangerous option. The registration or publication of the patent is more advantageous than other strategies that could be detrimental to its novelty.

Swiss Re first registers inventions with strong distribution potential in Europe. As a rule, patent applications with reference to information technology are usually

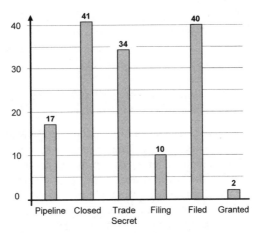

Source: Swiss Re Group IP (2005).

Fig. IV.9.4. IP activities of Swiss Re: building up a patent portfolio to defend and leverage.

referenced with a higher level of technicality. Swiss Re systematically places patent applications in India and China, as patent applications procedures there are not too expensive and these countries with their many inhabitants are considered emerging markets. However, the emphasis on application activities generally still resides in the United States.

Today, Swiss Re files about 30 patent applications per year. The company's intellectual property portfolio has increased significantly, thanks to approximately 100 inventions and more than 40 submitted patent applications (Fig. IV.9.4). Another ten were classified as trade secrets, while fifteen others were deemed not new and hence rejected. Two US patent rights stem from the acquisition of Lincoln Re in October 2003.

4.3   Organizing and Coordinating Intellectual Property

Organization. The central Group Intellectual Property Department, i.e. Group IP (GIP) at Swiss Re is staffed by three intellectual property managers and a part-time administrative officer. All Swiss Re patent activities at its headquarters and worldwide are coordinated from Zurich. The GIP is responsible for patents, trade secrets and innovation. Lately, the GIP has also taken over responsibility for trademarks, domain names and copyrights.

For decentralized support, Divisional Intellectual Property Officers (DIPOs) make themselves available to the patent departments in larger local offices (Fig. IV.9.5). They devote about 5% of their time to interests relating to intellectual property. There are three major task areas:

- *Identification of potential patent infringements:* The DIPOs compare the patent activities of third parties with the business activities of their own division.

- *Identification of inventions:* Firstly, the sensitization for intellectual property interests is increased through consultation with inventors. Secondly, the DIPOs develop a network with numerous inventors and oversee their R&D activities.
- *Identification of business opportunities:* On the one hand, the DIPOs must investigate possible patent infringements by Swiss Re. On the other hand, licensing opportunities with other parties should also be sought, as long as they fulfill a need or have a use for Swiss Re products.

The DIPOs are specifically responsible for adherence to the principles of defense and action within the Swiss Re intellectual property strategy. "DIPOs should be aware of any new development or invention at the earliest stage, preferably at conception" (Swiss Re, 2004a). In order for DIPOs to be effective, they must be accepted throughout the organization. In addition, they must be well versed and connected within the various business areas, and have a strong contact network that includes many key partners. Importantly, DIPOs must have substantial knowledge in their area of market expertise. Hence, they are often placed in hot spots, which are highly concentrated areas of knowledge and show a great potential for the development of patentable inventions. At the moment, Swiss Re employs 13 DIPOs, eight of whom are stationed in Zurich. Other locations that have key function areas and are in need of invention support are Germany, Great Britain, and France. For all of Asia there is only one DIPO, since there are no predicted future activities in this area at this time.

The internal structure of Swiss Re has turned out to be particularly favorable when it comes to the protection of intellectual property. The structure allows for

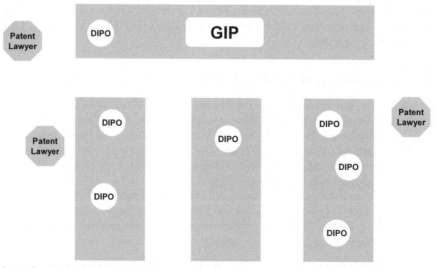

Source: Swiss Re Group IP (2005).

Fig. IV.9.5. IP infrastructure at Swiss Re.

an overall view of the projects, and can decide upon the proper resources, including project leaders, for worthy and appropriate projects. As a rule, DIPOs interact with project leaders on site – for the most part this occurs at the GIP. The goals and objectives of a project are discussed, and a general discussion is held to inform all sides and determine the possibilities of future actions; including patenting if necessary. The number of projects that concern the development of software is rather remarkable. Other internal target groups include actuaries and risk engineers whose job it is to simulate and analyze risk. All together, the internal client team is made up of close to 100 people.

The integration of the locations might optimize the central patent department even more: DIPOs' mandates can at present only be fulfilled to a certain extent. Thus, DIPOs undertake their tasks at various levels of commitment and engagement. There are power conflicts between the GIP and line management concerning the amount of work that DIPOs can allocate to intellectual property activities.

Processes. An important component of intellectual property management is the identification of inventions. Swiss Re sees itself first as a knowledge organization: the decision-making capabilities that are found within the minds of the employees (Swiss Re, 2004b). In order for inventions to be properly identified and duly protected, Swiss Re has introduced a number of processes and instruments:

- *Integration of larger projects into the project management organization process:* The decision as to whether an invention is patentable depends on the project manager and the project review committee. If the project introduces novel components, the central GIP is notified and henceforth involved in the decision-making process.
- *Responsibilities of DIPOs in smaller projects and local development:* Since the DIPOs have a good network of business units at their disposal, potential inventions can be identified relatively quickly.
- *Informal network of the central patent department:* Through conversations with employees, intellectual property managers attempt to identity the current status of inventions at the company.

The most effective instrument in the identification of inventions has by a large margin been the GIP informal network: "I find out about most inventions during my coffee break" (Cuypers, 2003).

A significant problem in the implementation of this strategy is that the patent department is often notified too late about patentable inventions. The reason for this often stems from premature disclosures of inventions, for instance at talks and conferences or during casual discussions with third parties.

The inventions are reported to the GIP either directly by the inventor or through the DIPO. The GIP verifies the invention and evaluates the related business opportunities on the basis of the aforementioned evaluation criteria, i.e. novelty; detection and proof of infringement; importance to third parties; importance to Swiss Re. The outcome is either to patent, to classify as trademark, to publish, or to provide no protection (Fig. IV.9.6.).

During the invention verification process, the GIP looks for relevant prior art. At the moment, however, Swiss Re does not undertake complete patent analyses, due to a lack of resources. The GIP is still in its infancy, which is why there is still difficulty in discerning between tasks of equal and similar importance. In five to ten years, fully established patent analysis of (re–)insurance activities should be well underway. And with it, an ability to properly detect market trends and potential infringements. The need for and pursuit of potential collaboration partners will also be an indispensable attribute of this process. The first step of this process occurred in spring 2003, with the acquisition of multi-functional search classification instruments. With these instruments, refined analyses will now be possible in the future.

The planning of patent applications and management of procedures before contacting patent office are prepared for Swiss Re with the help of two external patent law firms. For registration and application procedures for US patents and brands, external US patent lawyers are used. Nevertheless, Swiss Re will endeavor to be more independent in this area in future: for proceedings before the European Patent Office, internal Swiss Re employees are increasingly formulating the company's applications.

Cultural Aspects. Intellectual property is a new phenomenon in the financial services sector. Up until recently, intellectual property was perceived to be only for industries, with technology-intensive products such as mechanical engineering. However, the methods and approaches that origin from these industries were never transferred to service sectors, such as the banking and insurance industries. For a reinsurance firm, the interaction with intellectual property has been a new and revealing experience. Hence, for many employees, especially mathematicians and engineers, it is difficult to understand why business methods and software applications are no longer just part of regular activities, but are now identified as intellectual property that has to be protected.

Swiss Re's intention is not to elevate the role of intellectual property in its regular employees' every day activities. It will, similar to IT, be seen as a support-

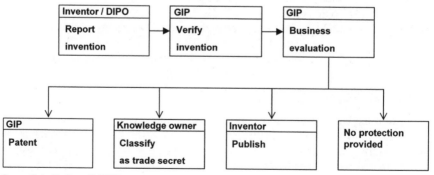

Source: Swiss Re Group IP (2005).

Fig. IV.9.6. IP workflow at Swiss Re.

ing element. Nevertheless, the challenge will be to educate the majority of employees that are not sensitized to or educated about intellectual property. Due to an information overload at work, most workers are not aware of or misinterpret the key information and activities that permeate their day-to-day activities. This makes it difficult for the DIPOs to ask employees to spend 5% of their day undertaking tasks that are not directly related to daily activities in the narrowest sense. For that reason, Swiss Re introduced a revised incentive system for inventions. The system includes monetary and non-monetary components. With regard to the monetary award, an inventor receives a monetary lump sum that is dependant on the stage that the invention reaches in the patent application and granting process. For example, an inventor receives a higher sum for the granting of a patent than for the preceding patent application. The steps of the reward process are:

- Decision to patent;
- First filing;
- First grant; and
- Technology transfer (license out).

The non-monetary components of the incentive system include:

- Hall of fame on the intranet: Inventors are identified and honored in a special area of Swiss Re's intranet;
- Silver dollars;
- Inventor lunches and dinners;
- Letter of appreciation from a member of the senior management;
- Other small gifts.

Swiss Re has focused on establishing an invention culture, with a focus more on non-monetary compensation. At the same time, it is considered important to garner feedback on issues such as perception and recognition. Once a year, a special dinner is held in which all inventors are invited.

4.4 Intellectual Property Licensing Activities

Swiss Re follows an open licensing philosophy and aims to license its technology to third parties. However, within the insurance business and particularly within the reinsurance business, the big players still do not follow an open approach and do not look to adopt a competitor's technology. So, as a first approach, Swiss Re has initially focused on making contact with smaller players.

Swiss Re therefore expects that even though it might still take some time for patent portfolios to grow, technology transfer and licensing models will find entrance to the financial service industry (Fig. IV.9.7). The company has already gathered various experiences with licensing internal technology to third parties, as for example:

- A software solution invented by a Swiss Re contractor during his appointment. This was licensed back to his software company so that he could implement it with other clients;

- An artificial intelligence tool invented by a Swiss Re colleague and an external scientist. This was licensed back to their software company so they could implement it with other clients;
- A mathematical tool invented by a Swiss Re colleague and two ETH researchers. It was licensed back to the ETH where it should commercialize a software application using the method;
- An e-business application invented by Swiss Re colleagues was licensed to the software development company that programmed the implementation, in order to market it to other reinsurance players.

4.5   Intellectual Property Management in Collaborations

If an external third party is involved in a collaboration or R&D project with Swiss Re, it requires the signing of a non-disclosure agreement (NDA). The agreement document lays out and regulates any and all potential intellectual property developed during the project. Afterwards, the NDA is examined by the Group Intellectual Property Department.

Swiss Re attempts to justify, in principle, the exclusive ownership of the patents: "The patent should belong to only one party, preferably Swiss Re". If it is not possible for Swiss Re to be the sole owner of the patent, then it is conceivable that the partner will be given sole ownership. Under no circumstances does Swiss Re want to share ownership of a patent. The advantages of the sole ownership of a patent for Swiss Re are the following:

- *Simplicity:* The administration of patents as well as the patent application process is substantially simplified;
- *Transparency:* Swiss Re's patent activities can be stated openly and clearly to external and internal stakeholders;
- *Strong position in cases of patent infringement:* If a Swiss Re business unit

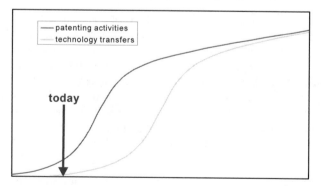

Source: Swiss Re Group IP (2005).

Fig. IV.9.7. Swiss Re expects licensing activities to grow within the financial services sector.

concerned about a patent infringement accusation, the entire patent portfolio can be used, independent of the particular business unit, as an instrument in cross-licensing negotiations;

- *Taxes:* The expected future profit of a larger and more diversified patent portfolio is gained within a tax-favorable area, especially with sole ownership. With the patenting of technologies that are used worldwide by Swiss Re, there is a strong potential tax-optimizing source of income.

In return for giving Swiss Re patent ownership, partners are often given the opportunity to receive rights of use. Swiss Re has a relatively open licensing policy, which means the company wants to use the technology itself, without having to always resort to licensing. A licensing option that is not often mentioned or used, is cross-licensing. The requirement for this option is a strong and diversified patent portfolio. If it were to establish such a portfolio, Swiss Re would have a significantly stronger bargaining position in collaborations.

Swiss Re often takes on all patenting costs, which can be an enticing offer, particularly for smaller partners with fewer resources.

The benefits of the licensing go directly to the business unit from which the patent originated.

Swiss Re has been involved in three cases in which patent aspects were regulated. The three partners in these cases were AlphaSoft, CreativeTools, and CompuSpec (Müller, 2004). The three collaborations focused on the development of a software solution.

4.6   Case Study Examples for IP Management in R&D Collaborations

Alphasoft Case. Since AlphaSoft developed the product on behalf of Swiss Re, the handling of patent ownership presented few problems. Swiss Re assumed exclusive patent rights over the computer program.

Swiss Re did, however, offer AlphaSoft a basic license. That meant that there was no material, location, or temporal exclusivity. Swiss Re could give away as many licenses in this area as it saw fit. It was also negotiated that AlphaSoft would have no rights to sub-licenses, but they were allowed to offer basic licenses to the end user. Furthermore, both Swiss Re and AlphaSoft could use developed versions of the product free of charge, this would also include all subsidiaries of Swiss Re.

Given that Swiss Re owned the exclusive patent rights to the product, it was assumed that Swiss Re would undertake all the patenting costs. Included in these costs would be lawyers' fees, registration costs, and certain maintenance costs. If AlphaSoft so chooses, it could register Swiss Re granted license rights. But this would normally be done at AlphaSoft's expense. However, since AlphaSoft is a small company with a minimal budget for patent applications, it was decided that Swiss Re would pay these costs. With regard to licensing income, it was agreed that AlphaSoft would pay Swiss Re a certain percentage per license agreement. This ended up being 35% of the net royalty, with a minimum payment of 2,500 Swiss francs.

Creative Tools Case. The intellectual property regulations with CreativeTools, as it concerned patent ownership, usage, license rights, costs and other aspects; were almost identical to the AlphaSoft case. Therefore, this case is not delved into any deeper separately.

CompuSpec Case. The arrangements and contract for the CompuSpec case turned out to be much more complicated than in the CreativeTools or AlphaSoft cases.

Within the context of their collaboration, CompuSpec and Swiss Re developed a software-based product that analyzed risk. Without contacting the GIP, a project manager from Swiss Re coordinated a contract with CompuSpec in which the intellectual property aspects were regulated. When the GIP read the contract after the fact, it became evident that Swiss Re had delivered on all their rights regarding intellectual property at CompuSpec. The GIP initiated another meeting in which Swiss Re invited CompuSpec to new treaty negotiations.

The patent ownership originally belonged to CompuSpec, and during further negotiations it was agreed that Swiss Re would eventually gain sole ownership of the patent. Obviously, concessions had to be made in order to make this happen, and they are described below.

CompuSpec received a basic, non-exclusive license in which Swiss Re could not stipulate further restrictions of location, matter or time. As long as Swiss Re was not involved or threatened by an intellectual property complaint, CompuSpec would normally be allowed to license the patent to business partners. CompuSpec, however, did not have rights to sub-licenses.

For the symbolic amount of one US dollar, Swiss Re took over all patenting costs, including potential process costs during a patent infringement. In order to achieve the licensing benefits, Swiss Re had to make compromises to receive sole patent ownership and the corresponding rights. CompuSpec did not have to pay any royalties to Swiss Re, essentially making their license royalty-free. In addition, CompuSpec received a portion of Swiss Re's licensing receipts. CompuSpec receives 30% of Swiss Re's license income from third parties outside the Swiss Re Group that which are acquired through Swiss Re endeavors. Seventy percent of the license income achieved outside the Swiss Re Group activities, and directly caused by CompuSpec, goes to CompuSpec.

InsureWell and SafeFinance Case. A practical possibility for intellectual property regulation, and one that as yet has not been attempted, is one that was tried by another enterprise in the insurance industry. The idea would result in Swiss Re examining geographic licensing.

An American insurance company called InsureWell, operating within the United States, patented an insurance product in the United States and Europe. At the time of patenting the product, for varying reasons, was considered a flop. At some point, the British direct insurer SafeFinance was approached by InsureWell about licensing the patent for this product. InsureWell gave up its exclusive license, and possibility for sub-licensing, to SafeFinance. The British direct insurer placed licenses in Great Britain and sublicenses via subsidiaries throughout Europe. InsureWell could thus garner benefits from licensing, while SafeFinance found new markets in Europe. The two insurers do not compete with each other due to their different business activities, providing a win-win situation for both parties.

Although, the above example is not based on real innovation collaboration, it is, however, a collaboration that could be entered into given the current environment of intellectual property protection. Based on this environment, Swiss Re can enter into patent collaborations today that will open up new markets that would not have been available without intellectual property protection.

Due to protection of intellectual property, new market growth can be realized by expansion into various niches. Without intellectual property, collaborations within such niches could not be carried out, as there would be the problem of knowledge dilution.

5 Conclusions

The financial services industry is marked by companies that can look back upon long and storied histories. Now this industry is confronted by prospects and risk scenarios relating to business protection rights, specifically patents. This trend dates back to the mid-1990s in the United States and Japan. Anglo-American and Japanese entities served as the predecessors of financial service providers that are incorporating intellectual property into business activities. European companies have neither recognized the major risks relating to intellectual property, nor have they taken countermeasures or actions to protect their own prospects.

The intellectual property strategy of the reinsurance peer company Swiss Re has the following aims:

- Risk reduction;
- Freedom of action;
- Establishment of own patent portfolio;
- Licensing income; and
- Design access.

Swiss Re has furthermore identified the following emphases for future intellectual property management:

- Greater sensitivity to intellectual property interests in the organization.
- Swiss Re is pursuing an open license policy and seeks to work cooperatively with third parties instead of monopolizing these areas.
- Maintenance of relationships with banks and assurance firms, in particular in the area of development of computer inventions in Europe (software patents).
- Independent formulation and planning of patent claims, in particular the applications made to the European Patent Office.

The focus for patenting is on business models that run off computer systems, for example the e-business-based reinsurance products. Their characteristics have not necessarily been associated with (re–)insurance products. Whether a patent application is filed or not depends on certain criteria, including novelty, identification of infringement, usefulness for third parties, and relevance to Swiss Re. The country selection focuses on Europe, the USA, India, and China; with the latter two being relevant emerging markets with many inhabitants and potential customers.

The Swiss Re intellectual property activities are internally organized as central Group Intellectual Property Department (GIP). This central entity is supported by decentralized, part-time Divisional IP-Officers (DIPO). Swiss Re considers it essential to integrate larger projects into the project management organization, which is of paramount importance when seeking inventions. The DIPOs' responsibilities are focused on smaller projects and local development with respect to identification of potential patents and risk of infringements, identification of inventions, and identification of businesses and opportunities. Legal activities are largely outsourced to external law firms.

Swiss Re has an internal patent awareness program with monetary incentives on four levels (disclosure, application, issuance, licensing). As far as remuneration is concerned, there are non-monetary incentives that reflect the inventors' cultural and regional backgrounds.

Swiss Re follows an open licensing policy. The company is becoming very experienced and successful in out-licensing technology to third parties. The first approaches are focused on small external business entities that are interested in in-licensing technology.

For Swiss Re, internal intellectual property is often the only guarantee to prevent dilution within collaborative technology development activities; and to secure potential new market segments. An important goal for Swiss Re in collaborations is to gain access to new resources, especially new technologies. Due to protection through intellectual property, collaborative growth can often be realized by expansion into various new niche markets.

Based on the case of the reinsurance firm Swiss Re, the following success factors for intellectual property management are presented, with a particular emphasis on the financial services industry:

- *Support from top and middle management:* While support from the top management and the patent department is vital, much depends on the interactions that middle managers and employees have with third parties. If these parties are dedicated and loyal to the company's intellectual property, inventions can be protected before secrets reach the general public.

- *Awareness program:* A sensitization with regard to the topic of intellectual property is necessary. A well-arranged awareness program, one that reaches as many employees within as many years as possible, can create this awareness. Such measures should be implemented unconditionally over the long term. This is due to the fact that in industries such as the service industry sector with dominantly only a short tradition or ignorant of patents, active interaction must be launched for counteraction.

- *Incentive systems for inventions:* The introduction of an incentive system for inventions is a proven aid to help support a patent department's activities. An important point here is that in order to assess the workforce's view of inventions, it is necessary to understand their underlying perceptions. Without an effective incentive system, or a proper perspective on inventions, there is a danger that inventions will not be declared or will be done so too late. This can happen even if there is a general understanding at the firm about the importance of intellectual property.

- *Identification of inventions:* The identification of knowledge residing in employees' minds will largely depend on the presence of informal contacts within the organization. Subsidiaries can use integrated processes and mechanisms to support projects, which helps to facilitate their identification.

- *Local investigative and discovery partners:* Another important area of knowledge identification comes from middlemen, e.g. the DIPOs at Swiss Re, who are found between the business units and the patent department. There should be a set of criteria established for this position, including: interactions with employees, market knowledge, understanding of intellectual property issues, and sensitivity towards innovation and inventions. In organizations where there is no concentrated R&D department and potential inventors are scattered throughout the company; companies like Swiss Re rely on decentral intellectual property officers to identify and isolate hot spots within the organization.

- *Establishment of defense position:* A large and diversified patent portfolio is the best defence against intellectual property attacks from third parties. One's bargaining position can be greatly strengthened and enhanced with such an arsenal. There is, for example, the option to conclude cross license agreements.

- *Sustainability of intellectual property activities and sufficient budget:* The establishment of an internal intellectual property portfolio is a time-consuming and complicated matter; especially in the service industry sector. Therefore, it is advantageous if the intellectual property department can absorb some of the operating costs, and takes a leadership role in the application and process phases of the patent application process.

- *Use of external expert know-how:* The presence of skilled and experienced external patent agents is vital, especially for those organizations that have little experience in dealing with intellectual property.

Companies that are looking to take initiative and seize the opportunities present in the financial services industry should heed some advice. In an industry that does not handle intellectual property in an expedited manner, sustainability and cultural factors inside the firm will play determining roles in the success of an intellectual property management program. The qualities of those working in the intellectual property area of a firm should not only include solid technical knowledge, but they should be able to handle and thrive in a collaborative work environment (Gassmann and Bader, 2004b).

From a wider perspective, the overall importance of intellectual property for companies should be understood and well communicated. In the service industry sector and particularly in the (re–)insurance and banking industry sector, software solutions and business practices have strong business relevance. Only time will tell what the current various differences in legal protection for processes, business methods and software-related inventions in Europe, Japan and the United States will lead to in practice.

Lessons learned for organizing R&D at Swiss Re:

1. Support from top and middle management;
2. Local investigative and discovery partners;
3. Use of external expert know-how;
4. Protect (service) innovations with intellectual property rights;
5. Reduce second-mover advantages with intellectual property rights;
6. Use legal protection instruments to open up new markets;
7. Anticipate technology transfer and licensing models.

The security of a company's research and development investments in intellectual property will become of increasing strategic importance for companies in the service industry sector. Increasingly protected service innovations will lead to imitation and second-mover advantages being reduced if not terminated. Furthermore, legal protection instruments anticipate the potential for financial services enterprises to open up new markets. One could thus expect that it might still take some time for patent portfolios to grow, but that technology transfer and licensing models will find entrance to the financial services industry sector.

Part V
Best-in-Class: The Electrical and Machinery Industry

In our case studies, electrical and machinery industries belong to more or less the dominant design industry. ABB, Mercedes (DaimlerChrysler), MTU, Schindler and Leica are to a great extent operating with a mix of new and mature technologies. They are continuously improving their existing products, have only a small number of big competitors on a global scale, and have to distinguish themselves not only through better products but through better services as well.

R&D projects are usually large ones, well distributed over different knowledge centers. The Kodama criterion for stopping projects is met: Big projects are duly completed even if one of the truly global competitors launches a better product onto the market. The customer does not become aware whether his product uses the latest technology or not; branding is often more important than technology.

Most of the companies make a clear distinction between the development of technology and the development of new products: The external customer does not buy technology but products, technology is driven more directly by the internal customer and by cost reduction programs. Therefore, we see sophisticated approaches to align research with overall business strategies especially within this group.

Companies like MTU in the turbine industry had to face the decline of comfortable military projects where every fancy technology had been paid in advance according to cost-plus procedures. Today, most of the projects are conducted in an extreme competitive civil aircraft industry, where an ROI of 20 years or more is quite usual. This trend required a radical change towards careful evaluation of new technologies and international high tech cooperation.

Despite heavy cycles, cut-backs and many restructuring programs, the electrical and machinery industry is still growing: We live in an age of machines! "The house is a machine for living, the chair is a machine for sitting," the famous Swiss architect Le Corbusier once remarked. But most of the companies still struggle with the structural change from a metal-basher tradition towards technology fusion: In the 1950s, thousands of Schindler employees were proud of the superior mechanics in their products. Today, mostly cost reduction projects are conducted in the pure mechanical area; the powerhouse China takes over more and more manufacturing.

Deregulation in the 1990s initiated major innovation pushes. Mechanical safety devices will be replaced by new multi-group controls, new information systems combined with mechatronics. R&D is confronted with the old trial-and-error mentality that is substituted through sophisticated computer-aided methods like finite elements and system design. Mechanics is a commodity: New technologies are driven by new materials, smart software packages, and electronics together with new approaches like e-tailing in the distribution channels.

V.1 ABB: Management of Technology: Think Global, Act Local*

1 The Transnational Company ABB

1.1 ABB in 1996

ABB is a global US\$ 34 billion electrical engineering Group serving customers in electric power generation, transmission and distribution, industrial and building systems, and rail transportation.

Created in 1988 to better anticipate and capitalize on new and changing opportunities in an increasingly competitive international market, ABB takes full advantage of its global economies of scale in technology development, financing, purchasing, distribution and production to deliver greater value to its customers.

The phrase 'think global, act local' reflects ABB's fundamental idea of strong local, regional companies working together across borders to gain economies of scale in many areas. ABB has tried to recreate small company dynamism by breaking down a large organization of more than 200,000 employees into 5,000 local, flexible and entrepreneurial profit centers and 1,000 legal entities. Local companies use the Group's total resources in research, distribution, supply, information technology, benchmarking, and access to capital markets and international financing.

ABB does not have one single major national presence. The country with the largest number of ABB employees is Germany, with about 30,000 people, Sweden is next with some 27,000. In recent years, there has been a large change in the geographical distribution of ABB's employees. Although the total has remained about the same, ABB has added around 56,000 new employees in Asia and Eastern Europe, and has reduced almost by the same number the employment in the US and Western Europe.

---

*   The part 1996 of this case study was authored by *Prof. Dr. Maurice Campagna,* Senior Vice-President & Director of ABB Corporate Research, and *Dr. Tony Roeder,* SVP Technology Planning & Administration Corporate Staff Research & Development, ABB. This case study was written in 1998: The reader should keep in mind that all numbers, figures, organization charts and forecasts represent the state of 1998 or before unless otherwise mentioned. The part 2006 was revised by *Markus Stocker,* ETH Zürich, based on company reports and other public information.

For ABB, multicultural-multinational management is another organizational lever to achieve improved competitiveness. Although it takes time and persistent effort to develop successful multicultural teams, the payoff is considerable: combined understanding and insight into global business problems and needs is deeper, benchmarking on an international scale promotes world-class performance standards. The rotation of specialists across borders makes it easier to transfer best practices within the company, and international cooperation such as supply contracts across borders and joint development projects, becomes reality and the norm.

An important additional benefit is the ability to recruit, develop and maintain (future) global managers from around the world, all sharing the ABB mission, policies and values towards a sustainable growth for an advanced global society.

ABB's world-wide business activities are grouped into four Business Segments comprising 37 Business Areas, out of which the ten largest received about 50% of the total ABB new order volume in 1996. This group of large Business Areas is based on some of ABB's most prominent technologies, such as gas turbines, low emission combustion, power electronics, process automation, drives, and robots.

The company aims to be a technology leader and to respond to the continuous demand for new technologies for present products. Microelectronics and information technologies have a dominant impact on products and systems. The fastest growing demand from traditional markets is for intelligent, integrated systems. This demand strongly drives product innovation and aggressive use of emerging technologies.

ABB's technology strategy derives directly from ABB's business strategy, and it must match and support the objectives described above, including profitable growth. There are two key elements to this strategy, namely:

- Develop technology that helps protect ABB's leading position in traditional markets in Europe and the US, and

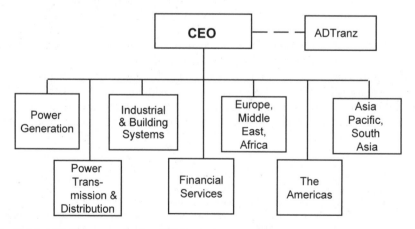

Fig. V.1.1. ABB Group organization (1996).

ABB   561

> **Most important drivers for globalization:**
> 1. Globalization of business;
> 2. Re-use of technologies adopted to local needs;
> 3. Information technologies (IT).

* Support business growth in the emerging markets.

ABB is committed to sustainable development. Efficiency in all form of human activities is the key to both improved environmental technology and business success. In the case of natural resources, increased efficiency lets consumption fall, and the same is true for waste and harmful emissions. Efficiency is the key to survival in deregulated markets. Improving environmental performance is a win-win opportunity for business partners and society.

1.2   ABB in 2006

ABB in 2006 is a global US$ 23 billion engineering company in power and automation technologies that enable utility and industry customers to improve performance while lowering environmental impact.

Originally a US$ 34 billion company with more than 200,000 employees, ABB disinvested some of its businesses to find a better match between global size and concentration on promising technology sectors. In 1999, ABB outsourced its electric power generation activities into ABB ALSTOM POWER, sold its part of the rail transportation company ADTranz and sold as well its nuclear technology sector. In 2002, the remaining divisions were restructured: ABB concentrated on power and automation technologies. The oil, gas and petrochemical activities were not further pursued.

As per end of 2006, ABB employs about 107,000 people. The country with the largest number of ABB employees is Germany with about 15,000 employees; Sweden is next with some 12,000, followed by the US with about 10,000. In recent years, there has been a large change in the geographical distribution of ABB's employees. Ten years ago, 67% of the employees were working in Europe, mainly Western Europe, and only about 15% was engaged in Asia, Middle East and Africa. Today, about 55% of ABB's workforce is employed in Europe, with an increasing part in Eastern Europe. Already 25% of ABB's staff is working now in Asia, Middle East and Africa. ABB has added around 30,000 new employees in Asia and Eastern Europe, and has reduced almost by the same number the employment in the US and Western Europe.

ABB's world-wide business activities are grouped into five business divisions: Power products, power systems, automation products, process automation and robotics. These divisions have 30 business areas. The ten largest received about 50% of the total ABB new order volume in 2005. This group of large Business

Areas is based on some of ABB's most prominent technologies, such as power transformers, high voltage power transmission, SF_6 breakers, network control and automation substations, drives, process automation, robots, and information technology.

2   R&D Structure

2.1   The 1996 Situation

The 8% of revenues invested in technology development are an average valid in the electro-technical industry. At ABB the level of investment has been quite consistent from year to year, also during recession periods, like 1991 or 1996. Due to the growth of the company, the absolute amount of R&D dollars has nearly doubled in the period from 1988 to 1996 (see Fig. V.1.3).

Slightly more than one half of the R&D funds go to customer-specific technology development. Again, this is rather typical for most large companies in the electrical industry. One billion US$ discretionary expenditure was spent in 1996 in ABB's business segments, for product development. About 200 million US$ were spent through ABB's corporate research laboratories. As we shall see, the laboratories are involved in product and process development for products and technologies up to two generations beyond current products and technology.

ABB has somewhat more than 20,000 scientists and engineers, that is, people with very solid technical education and training, who one way or another are in-

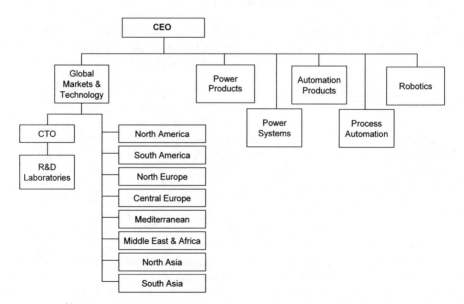

Fig. V.1.2. ABB Group organization (2006).

ABB   563

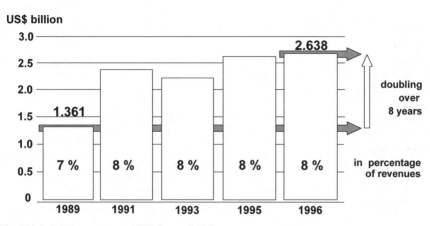

US$ billion

Fig. V.1.3. R&D expenses at ABB Group (1996).

volved in technology development. 95% of these employees are located in our business areas around the world, main development centers being located in Europe and US.

About 1,100 employees work in ABB's eight corporate research laboratories located in the US and in European countries, plus two small groups in Poland and Japan (see Fig. V.1.4). A special feature of these laboratories is the multinational origin of the employees. Thereby, ABB uses the known fact that for complex problem solving, a multicultural approach is often more advantageous.

ABB inherited the present geographic R&D configuration with the merger of

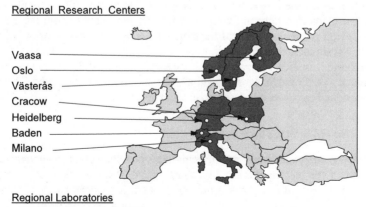

Regional Research Centers

Vaasa
Oslo
Västerås
Cracow
Heidelberg
Baden
Milano

Regional Laboratories
• Windsor, Connecticut, USA
• Raleigh, North Carolina, USA

Fig. V.1.4. Geographic configuration of ABB Corporate Research (1996).

Table V.1.1. ABB corporate research programs (1996).

Systems	
Industrial Systems Engineering	Electrical Systems Engineering
Electro Magnetics & Systems Simulation	Engineering Systems Integration
Software Engineering	
Products	
Man Machine Communication & Control	Sensors & Instrumentation
Current Conduction, Interruption & Limitation	Insulation Systems
Technologies	
Combustion Technology	Power Fluid Dynamics
High Temperature Materials	Power Electronics
Air Pollution Control & Waste Treatment	Mechanics
Electronics, Signal Processing Communication	

the Swedish company ASEA and the Swiss-German company Brown-Boveri, and with the series of major acquisitions made after the merger. It is ABB's policy today to locate development centers in all major growing markets.

ABB is a technology based company. Technological competence determines the quality, performance and cost of the products, and thereby establishes ABB's competitiveness in the marketplace. Innovation is essential to secure ABB's future. This holds particularly true for ABB's key technologies, such as gas and steam turbines, low emission combustion systems, power transformers, High Voltage power transmission, SF_6 breakers, network control and automation substations, drives, process automation, robots, and information technology.

ABB's key technologies, defined by 16 Corporate Research Programs or disciplines, are the main areas of research in the corporate laboratories (see Table V.1.1).

Depending on their size, on competence profile and partly on local customer needs, the Corporate Labs are working with different emphasis on the 16 Corporate Research programs. Most of the projects are however multinational projects, involving team members located in Labs.

Corporate Research programs are terminated or created depending on the business needs, as provided by suggestions coming from the so called Technology Management Team, we will describe in a next paragraph.

2.2   The R&D Structure in 2006

The 4-5% of revenues invested in technology development is a modern average for firms in the electro-technical industry. At ABB the level of investment has been consistent for the last five years and was not influenced by short-term structural changes in the group. Due to the increasing turnover, the absolute amount of R&D investments is close to one billion US$ (see Fig. V.1.5).

ABB has some 6,000 scientists and engineers, people with solid technical training, who in one way or another are involved in technology development. 80% of

ABB 565

these employees are located in ABB's business areas around the world. The remaining employees, about 650 people, work in ABB's corporate research laboratories. These are located in Switzerland, Sweden, US, Finland, Poland, Norway, China and India. In the last years, the main focus was given to the development of the Chinese, Indian and US laboratories. It is ABB's policy today to locate development centers in all major growing markets.

ABB's key technologies are developed within 10 Corporate Research Programs or disciplines, which form the main areas of research in the corporate laboratories:

- Control and optimization
- Software architecture and processes
- Sensors and microsystems
- Power electronics
- Advanced industrial communication
- Mechatronics and robotics automation
- Power device technologies
- Power transmission and distribution applications
- Manufacturing technologies
- Nanotechnologies

3 R&D Coordination and Integration

3.1 *Matrix and PIPE in 1996*

ABB is well known for its matrix-management. Reporting to the CEO of the com-

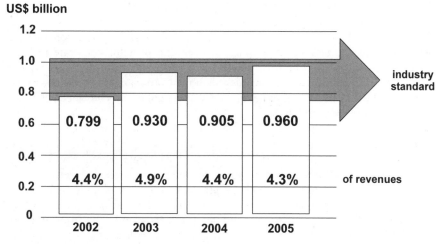

Fig. V.1.5. R&D expenses at ABB group (2006).

> **Major issues for global R&D management at ABB:**
>
> 1. Business impact of innovative ideas and project;
> 2. New markets;
> 3. Proximity to customers;
> 4. Multinational / multicultural / cross-border teams.

pany are three senior executives who have world-wide product responsibility in their respective area of Power Generation, Transmission and Distribution, and Industrial & Building Systems. They have explicit responsibility for the technology strategy of their businesses and for its implementation. Also reporting to the CEO at the same level are three regional executives who have actual operating responsibility for all businesses in their region (see Fig V.1.1).

The key players in the management of technology in ABB form the Technology Management Team. The team is lead by the Corporate Technology Officer (CTO) of the company. The team includes the senior vice-presidents (SVP) for technology of the corresponding three ABB Business segments and the research directors for the corporate laboratories (see Fig. V.1.6).

We briefly explain the role of the Senior Vice-Presidents for segment technology. Business and technology strategy is a clear responsibility of the business segments. To assure a top-down approach and a reasonable degree of control, ABB has a senior technical officer for each of the three business segments, Power Generation, Transmission & Distribution and Industrial & Building Systems. These three senior vice-presidents report simultaneously to the segment business executive and to the Corporate Technology Officer. They therefore have two reporting lines and *two bosses* determining their bonus, as it is the case for many ABB managers. Their main responsibility is to assure that the segment has a consistent technology strategy and the resources to implement it.

The Technology Management Team brings the R&D organization together. The team has the task of developing an operating plan for corporate research, securing resources from both corporate funds and funds from the businesses, to guarantee its implementation. One mission of the Corporate Research Laboratories is to help ABB fulfil its goal of being the most technologically advanced engineering company in the world, today and in the future.

The corporate research activities (the corporate programs) are managed by program managers. A program manager typically has a budget of several million dollars and will have people from several of the corporate centers working in his program. A program manager is truly an international research manager.

Once a year each program manager presents to the Technology Management Team his program proposal and budget request for the following year. The program proposal includes all R&D activities (projects) within the respective program. Major projects are specified with objectives, milestones, technical risks,

ABB 567

resources and payoff. The proposal must fit the ABB business strategy. It identifies critical technology issues and proposes how to resolve them.

Each program manager has the task to develop a strategic technology plan and to review it once a year. This document describes the business context, the technology trends, the competitive situation, and it develops on that basis specific technology roadmaps in line with business/products or technology roadmaps. It is imperative that the program manager develops his strategic plan together with the colleagues from the business units and, preferably, with major customers. In the ideal case the business unit R&D manager and the corporate program manager develop jointly one integrated strategic technology plan.

The Technology Management Team with the CTO as chairman reviews, modifies and finally approves the strategic technology plans and the program proposals. The CEO of ABB approves the consolidated budget request for Corporate R&D.

Corporate R&D projects are in most cases jointly funded from corporate sources and from businesses. We have learned from experience that R&D funding is not an issue in cases where the idea is sound, where the project has a high business impact potential and where adequate resources are available for project execution and for fast transfer of the results to the market.

The real issue is the *project creation*. Each program manager is responsible, together with the department heads in the corporate labs, to drive this process. The best ideas for new R&D projects are generated when scientists are exposed to the real business world, in meetings with people from the businesses, other disciplines, and with ABB's customers. A very effective way of exposing especially

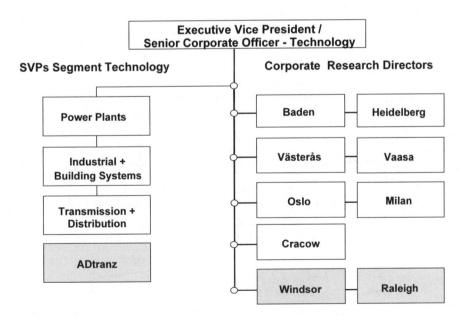

Fig. V.1.6. Technology Management Team TMT (1996).

new employees to the business environment is job rotation. This is where the scientists and engineers from Corporate Research get to know the daily business, the end customers needs and priorities.

Since each scientist in ABB Corporate Research has Lotus Notes on his or her desk, they can communicate, share knowledge and access relevant databases independently of the platform: Macs, PCs or UNIX workstations. The same holds true for many ABB colleagues in the businesses, Lotus Notes being the ABB standard tool for communication. For specific core processes of the corporate research organization, a software tool (work flow application) called PIPE based on Lotus Notes applications has been developed (see Fig. V.1.7).

It consists basically of three main applications: creation of ideas and projects, portfolio planning and project execution. A scientist can create an idea any time, test it, i.e. discuss it with suitable, selected colleagues around the globe. He then seeks support either from business area colleagues or from corporate research management, e.g. the program manager. Upon positive feedback a project is generated and it flows into the portfolio planning stage. After a ranking process it flows into the execution phase, if resources are available. Otherwise it is put into a „project storage" data base.

Often, such a local project becomes part of a global project. This is the case when resources for execution are not exclusively available in one lab. In such a case colleagues are working as members of a global virtual team on various aspects of a main problem.

The process dramatically helps:

- Forming cross-border project teams.
- Overcoming multicultural barriers.

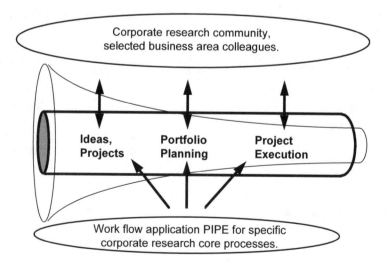

Fig. V.1.7. PIPE - 'Project Idea, Planning, Execution, and Reporting' (1996).

ABB   569

Major innovative break-throughs at ABB (1990-1996):

1. New gas turbine family concept 'GT 24/26';

2. Power electronic modules with integrated gate bipolar transistor;

3. New control platform for process automation;

4. High temperature superconducting fault current limiters and transformers.

- Improving transparency and trust in collaborations.

Each program is steered by a committee of business representatives, to ensure that the program is well focused on business needs. The chairman of the program steering committee is usually the senior vice-president of one of the three ABB business segments. The steering committee members from the businesses create contacts with the operating units, care for business commitment to the projects and help arranging the transfer of results.

The Technology Management Team connects the responsible persons for the decentralized R&D activities, the senior vice-president for segment technology and the CTO of ABB. With the help of advanced IT tools the world-wide R&D activities and resource allocations are completely visible and transparent to the management team. Redundant efforts in the projects within the corporate research organization can more easily be avoided because the program managers have control over the funds.

ABB's experience confirms the so called modified form of Einstein's „golden rule", which says that „He, who owns the gold, rules".

In summary, however, one can say that in a multinational-multicultural company like ABB, the most important coordination tools within international R&D - besides control of funds - is openness and transparency of all R&D activities and resource allocations through one common database and groupware applications.

ABB promotes the view that to measure R&D performance is to assess how fast and successful the results are transferred to the business and implemented in customer products or processes.

Since ideas and concepts are strongly linked to individuals, the most effective way of transferring know-how from the research lab to the market place is clearly to transfer it with the people themselves. The mobility in term of job rotation and transfer of people is a crucial task of the corporate research labs. It will be an ever more important task for the business units for guaranteeing life-long learning. It needs continuous management attention, especially in decentralized, matrix type organizations. When successful this creates opportunities for hiring young engineers and scientists and maintains a flow of excellent people through the organization. This is essential for a dynamic organization as a corporate lab must be.

3.2   R&D Coordination and Integration in 2006

The most important key player in the management of technology in ABB is the Head of Global Markets & Technology. He is not only conducting the eight regional executives, the Chief Technical Officer (CTO) is as well reporting to this function. The different R&D laboratories are reporting to the CTO (see Fig. V.1.2).

4   Conclusions

4.1   For the 1996 Company

The necessity for a so-called „intelligent switching machine" for the distribution of electrical energy and line protection in the medium voltage range was identified in various European countries early in 1992. A multidisciplinary team of researchers, engineers and marketing colleagues was first formed to define - in close contact with the end (lead-) customers - the functional specifications and business concept.

A multinational group of engineers from ABB companies from Germany, Italy, Norway and Switzerland as well as members from the corporate research organization was assembled in September 1992 as a team in the Corporate Research Center located in Switzerland. The location was chosen so as to allow the team members to work undisturbed on the details of the product specification. The next goals were the prototype, then the presentation of the prototype at the Hannover fair (April 1993), accepting first orders from lead customers and field trials. A year after the starting of the teamwork the product called „intelligent switching machine" was ready to be delivered in series to the customers.

Each member of the team was chosen according to his or her capabilities, and was also expected to contribute according to his special skills. Accordingly, the Italian member gave crucial input for the final design ('look and feel').

A characteristic for the success was that the team was „empowered" primarily in terms of setting its own schedule. The ABB Technology Management Team was overviewing the progress based on regular reports of the main project leader and providing support in the case of technical- or resource-bottlenecks.

Lessons learned for organizing R&D at ABB:

1. After dissolution of the global team, the members back home take over the local role in a natural way as technology transfer specialists;

2. A strong motivation leading to better team performance is automatically generated with improved cross-cultural communication;

3. A successful team builds up long lasting relations long after dissolution, helping international / group integration.

ABB   571

Key problems to be overcome in such multinational projects are:

- Take a clear decision to go ahead with the project (management commitment) and a critical mass of resources (task of the Technology Management Team);
- Initial financing when small business units are involved. Here help from the corporate fund is important;
- Set the proper conditions to be able to assemble a multinational team in one location (provide proper logistics for cross-border family moving!).

4.2   Conclusions in 2006

By comparing ABB's situation 1996 with 2006, the following observations can be made:

- R&D expenses differ significantly between the different business areas.
- The amount of R&D synergies in a diversified company is limited.
- Progress in R&D is not only a question of the number of R&D employees and of the size of investments into these activities. It depends heavily on the dynamics of the field.

V.2 Daimler: Global Knowledge Sourcing and Research*

1 Daimler-Benz's R&D Organization in Overview

1.1 The Daimler-Benz Group before the Merger

Between 1997 and 2007, Daimler-Benz went through several major mergers and demergers. In 1997, before the merger with Chrysler, Daimler-Benz turned over more than US$ 69 billion (DM124 billion) and employed a work force of more than 300,000 world-wide. There were 23 business units in four divisions: Passenger Cars, Commercial Vehicles, Aerospace, Services, as well as in the directly managed industrial business units (rail systems, microelectronics, diesel engines and others). Eight years later, in 2005, DaimlerChrysler AG turned US$ 176.7 billion and employed a work force of more than 380,000 world-wide. After the divestment of its Aerospace business, DaimlerChrysler had four divison again: Mercedes Car Group, Chrysler Group, Commercial Vehicles and Financial Services. In 2007, Chrysler was sold to Cerberus, in a move that raised share prices for the new Chrysler and Daimler.

Unless otherwise noted, the focus of the subsequent description is Daimler-Benz in 1997. Daimler-Benz made 75% of its revenues with automobiles: 43% with passenger cars and 32% with commercial vehicles.[57] The main market was Europe, accounting for 64% of total sales (German sales were US$ 23 billion or 33%). North America contributed 21% to the total sales of Daimler-Benz. Between 1996 and 1997, automobile sales expanded by 18%. Among the principal regions, sales in North America grew with a rate of 26%, and sales in Europe with a rate of 21%, as compared with 1996.

Daimler-Benz's main vehicle lines are luxury and high-class passenger cars,

---

* This case study was authored by *Dr. Maximilian von Zedtwitz* when he was a research associate at the Institute for Technology Management, University of St. Gallen, Switzerland. The case study is based on Vöhringer (1997: 330-335) and a number of research interviews. In 1998, Daimler-Benz merged with Chrysler. This case study was written before this merger: The reader should keep in mind that all numbers, figures, organization charts and forecasts represent the state of 1997 or before. The case study was revised by *Tamara Iskra Alcántara Concepción*.

[57] In 2005, revenues were 90%: Mercedes Car Group generated 31% , Chrysler Group 33% and 26% with commercial vehicles.

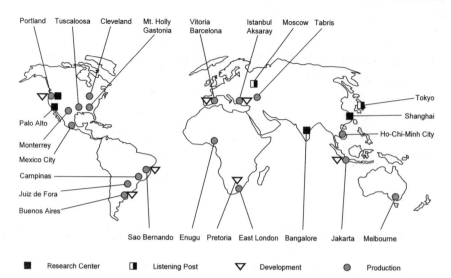

Fig. V.2.1. International research, development, and production locations of Daimler-Benz.1998. The largest share of research (see Fig. I.3.9), development, and production is carried out in Germany, particularly in Stuttgart. Major German development locations were Hamburg, Munich, Ottobrunn, Bremen, Ulm, Friedrichshafen, Unterschleissheim, Berlin, Dachau, Mannheim, and Stuttgart.

off-road vehicles, sports cars, and commercial vehicles. In 1997, a total of 715,000 passenger cars and 417,000 commercial vehicles were sold.[58] The product ranged expansions included the V-Class and the SLK roadster to the traditional model series comprising the C-Class, E-Class and S-Class. The CLK coupe followed the M-Class produced in Tuscaloosa, USA and the A-Class produced in Rastatt, Germany. Together with the Swiss company SMH, Daimler-Benz had launched the two-seater city car Smart in late 1998, which were produced in Hambach, France. Product launched in the commercial vehicle lines included the Actros truck, Sprinter, and Vito.[59]

Daimler-Benz has undergone a number of reorganizations since the merger of two German car manufacturers; the two major ones being Daimler and Benz in 1926, and the transatlantic Chrysler merger in 1998. In the 1980s, 1990s, and 2000s, Daimler-Benz/DaimlerChrysler acquired several industrial companies in order to establish itself as a major „integrated technology group" with technological foundations in automobiles, aerospace, microelectronics, and defense systems.

---

[58]   In 2005, DaimlerChrysler sold a total of 4.8 million vehicles; Mercedes Car Group 1.2 million, Chrysler Group 2.8 million and 0.8 million commercial vehicles; 4,029,831 passenger cars and 824,867 commercial vehicles.

[59]   The products in 2005 included 17 new models: Mercedes-Benz brand launched four new models, the S-, B-, M- and R-Class; while ChryslerGroup launched the Dodge Charger, the Ram Mega Cab, the Viper Coupe, Jeep Commander and SRT vehicles; the commercial latest vehicles were the Axor and Atego families, the new Mercedes-Benz and Setra Buses and the Fuso Canter.

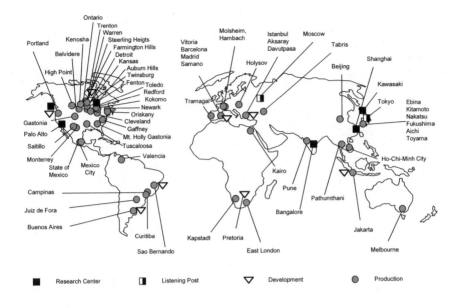

Fig. V.2.2. International research, development and production locations of DaimlerChrysler in 2005.

Some of these businesses were sold later, when under new leadership Daimler-Benz began to concentrate on specific competencies and competitive strengths. R&D units that had been acquired in the wake of the diversification were brought under centralized control (see Fig. V.2.1 and Fig. V.2.2). They remained with Daimler-Benz's R&D after their former parent companies were divested. For instance, the Frankfurt Research Center was brought in by AEG, and Friedrichshafen was the site of the Dornier R&D center.

During the strategic change of Daimler-Benz towards reinforcing its automotive business, many internal customers for corporate research were abandoned. In a corporate-wide reorientation, the impact of the Research & Technology Department (R&T) was carefully evaluated. Redundancies were detected, and it was found that R&T units competed with each other in an often non-productive manner. Given a tightening budget situation and a conservative R&T organization determined mainly by historic and internal-political motives, it was realized in the mid-1990s that major decisions were to be made to render R&T as the strategic technological weapon for Daimler-Benz's competitive future.

1.2 The Organization of the Research & Technology Department

Daimler-Benz was one of the highest spenders on R&D worldwide. Total R&D

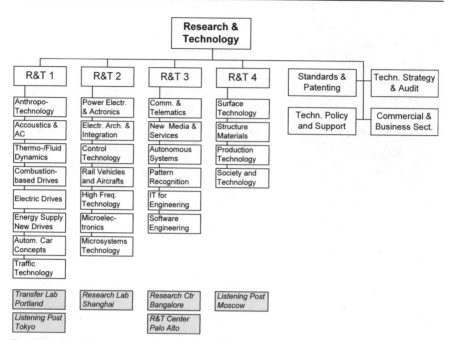

Fig. V.2.3. Functional organization of Daimler-Benz's Research and Technology Department in 1998.

expenditures in 1997 amounted to US$ 5.4 billion (DM9.8 billion), which resulted in an R&D intensity of 7.9%.[60] About three quarters of R&D was vehicle-oriented (Fig. V.2.3), supporting the main businesses of Daimler-Benz.

Daimler-Benz did not heavily engage in basic research as it considered this task a responsibility of national institutes and universities. Daimler-Benz's R&D included product development, advanced development, and fundamental research. Research and development were clearly separated from an organizational point of view as well as its underlying strategies and missions. Development was almost exclusively carried out by business units and accounted for US$ 5.1 billion.

The Research & Technology Department was centralized for all business units and covers research activities for a wide range of potential products, e.g. passenger cars, commercial vehicles, aerospace, microelectronics, and rail systems. In 1997, R&T had a budget of US$ 280 million. About half was contracted directly from business units and aims at transferring new as well as mature technology for a particular business unit. The other half was provided by the Daimler-Benz group and aimed at the creation of technology with a wide applicability in several business areas. Overall, this represented a ratio of 0.4% of research expenditures to sales which stayed relatively stable over those years. Research activities were

---

[60]   In 2005, R&D expenditures amounted to US$ 6.6 billion and R&D 3.8% of sales.

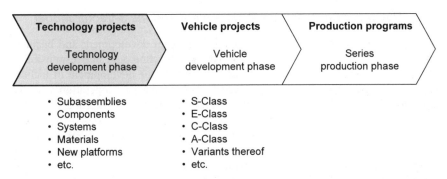

Fig. V.2.4. Research & Technology at Daimler-Benz focuses on the technology development phase.

increasingly financed by business units but selected long-term projects which were of importance to more than one business unit and which were also of strategic importance for the future competitiveness of the Daimler-Benz Group tended to be financed by corporate funds. Examples of such projects are multimedia, satellite based navigation and communication, and environmental production processes.

In 1997, 1,300 patent applications were filed in Germany alone. Outside Germany, 4,400 new patents were filed, almost twice the number in 1996.

R&T was organized within four research units (see Fig. V.2.4). Again, their main research areas followed their historic origin. For instance, the first R&T unit (R&T-1) originated from the former Mercedes-Benz research institute and is still mainly active in automotive research. Each research unit was divided into several „labs" and led by a director who reported directly to the Chief Technology Officer (CTO). Mainly due to historic acquisitions and/or relocation, there are currently six German research locations, with the main one still being in Stuttgart, close to the company's headquarters. Other locations are Frankfurt, Ulm, Berlin, Munich and Friedrichshafen. The main research areas of these locations still reflect their origin. Frankfurt has a strong focus on rail related topics, Friedrichshafen and Munich on aerospace due to their Dornier and MTU heritage, and Stuttgart and Berlin on automobile research. Only Ulm was established from scratch and focuses on information technology. Four international research sites had been established in the 1990s, and two listening posts exist in Moscow and Tokyo. Their management and organization are the focus of the subsequent sections.

In Germany, the total number of scientists added up to over 1,400 including Ph.D. students and other trainees as well as administrational staff. There was also a comparatively high number of temporary employees increasing the work force in R&T by about 800 people. With less than a hundred overseas researchers, the international R&T work force was relatively small but growing strongly.[61]

---

[61]   At the end of 2005, corporate research employed 2,600 people and development units employed a further 25,600. Together with the development departments of business units, they employed a total of 28,300 scientists, engineers and technicians worldwide in R&D activities.

1.3   Downstream Research Management and the 3-Vector Model

The main purpose of R&T is to provide downstream development and business units with reliable and high-quality information and technology. The responsibility of R&T is essentially the support of business units in the development of technological strategies through networked and knowledge-based cooperation with the units. R&T aims to be an integral part of all product development processes within business units. Therefore, scientific know-how of R&T employees is the crucial success factor and requires constant training along with continuous personnel exchange programs. This know-how can only be sustained via the establishment of international networks and sites which is directed towards global know-how centers. Consequently, world-wide appraisal of technological developments and their benefits for Daimler-Benz is one basic task of technology management.

Since the transfer of research results to business units is R&T's yardstick for success, all potential projects are expected to contribute in some way to a future product in one of the business units and are more likely to be financed if the business unit has already signaled their interest.

Based on the understanding of the key success factors for industrial research as:

• Close interaction with internal customers at divisions, and
• Goal-oriented and time-managed projects based on these areas,

a culture had to be created in which employees realize that cooperation across regional and departmental boundaries is essential to the continued success of the company. The entire value-creation process had to be supported by the use and integration of information technologies.

Two core processes were identified to help R&T achieve this aim:

• Technology strategy, innovation planning, project work, transfer of results: Two project teams mainly investigated technology management and innovation planning. Measures agreed upon are: (a) technology management and research know-how are now united, not only in terms of organizations structures, but also in terms of employees. (b) cooperation with business units will be determined in individual organizational agreements (c) the process „transfer" will be dealt with separately.
• Staff selection, staff development, staff transfer: Critical success factor for R&T and technology transfer are skilled and motivated employees.

The first core process is directed at creating a value-added process perspective for all of R&T research activities. Three main goals were defined:

• Reinforced integration of R&T in defining the overall technology strategy of Daimler-Benz and the innovation strategy of the business units.
• Transition of all research programs into research projects, i.e. shift from a functional to a project organization.
• Concentration of distinct capabilities in research laboratories designated as competence centers that serve to consolidate internal and external knowledge.

Table V.2.1. Classification of A, B, and C projects at Daimler-Benz.

Project type	Project volume	Number	Approved by	Reviewed by
A Projects	> DM16 million	~30	CTO, KAMs, other R&T Directors	CTO, KAMs, other R&T Directors
B Projects	DM5 – 16 million	~100	KAM	KAM
C Projects	< DM5 million	~240	KAM	Lab Directors

In accordance with 'structure follows processes', a new business system for R&T management and organization was proposed and implemented (Fig. V.2.5). It consists of three dimensions representing customer, research product, and technology.

- Vector 1 is the customer representing all business units of Daimler-Benz, their technological strategies and research programs. On the basis of this technological strategy, central R&T defines a customer-oriented research program. Eleven research program managers support the four research directors to stay in close contact with internal customers.
- Vector 2 represents the research product, i.e. all projects conducted within R&T. For each project not only the targeted scientific result is defined but also the added value it might provide to the final customer in at least one business unit. Each project falls into one of the 20 core research areas.
- Vector 3 is the technological and scientific know-how of R&T. In order to fulfill all tasks, competencies in defined fields of technology have to be gained and maintained. The so-called „Labs" belong to one of the four departments of central R&T, serve as centers of competence for different fields of technology and are responsible for technology monitoring, networking and benchmarking.

As a „Key Account Manager" (KAM), each of the four R&T area directors is to link research laboratories with business units. He is not only responsible for transfer-oriented cooperation with these business units, but also represents R&T in the determination process for innovation and technological strategies. Due to his close contact to internal customers he is in an ideal position to integrate all customer-specific demands in the strategic planning process of R&T and to report about major developments in the cooperation with leading customers.

The research labs are not necessarily located in the same place. Spatial separation is not the paramount problem at Daimler-Benz R&T: It is more difficult to cooperate between different business areas than between different sites. Coordination of such projects is more demanding, as different (business and division) cultures and rules are involved. Typical problems of matrix organization occur, as project members are engaged in several projects or functions. Different locations do increase coordination problems, but they are secondary compared to cross-functional issues. Hence, Daimler-Benz makes little difference in the management of spatially dispersed projects as compared to collocated projects.

Dispersed project management has to deal with the following problems:

- Coordination costs;
- Information costs (which are usually neglected);
- Project management costs are higher and must be accounted for accordingly.

The organization of a project with distributed resources must therefore be defined properly at the beginning. At the individual level, project managers should be educated in human resource management and cultural management. People combining technical knowledge, managerial talent, and good networking skills are generally hard to find.

A major problem with multilocal research is that external partners within Daimler-Benz are considered as competition. The NIH-syndrome occurs between different locations, and especially between international sites. A potential solution is found in the new structure with labs as competence centers. Each lab has a research focus, which reduces intersection and redundant research and increases mutual interdependence. The labs form a resource pool for project teams, hence matrix problems have to be dealt with. Some technology monitoring will also be carried out by the individual labs. Labs are clustered with R&T directors managing the cluster. This is the central platform for all projects in the labs. Projects may be aggregated at the top, and there are almost 300 projects per year to be reviewed. R&T distinguishes between three types of projects (Table V.2.1). Many projects are co-funded by a business unit and R&T. Early projects are typically funded from corporate money, but ideally, with increasing interest of a business unit, the funding ratio shifts. Eventually, when a project is funded completely by a

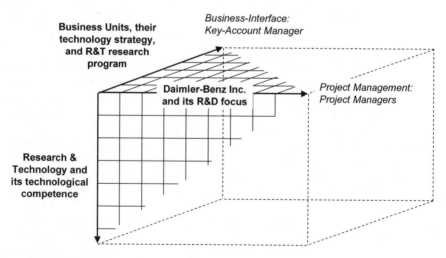

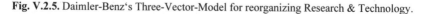

Fig. V.2.5. Daimler-Benz's Three-Vector-Model for reorganizing Research & Technology.

business unit, it is transferred out. Projects commissioned by business units take about 3-5 years to carry out, while internal R&T project duration may exceed 5 years. For comparison, development projects in the business units average about one year.

In conclusion it should be restated that R&T is obliged to fulfill the requirements of advanced development and product development. Two core processes have been identified which are currently being implemented. The new three-dimensional business system aims at integrating the research product, scientific know-how, and the customer. The R&T organization has been restructured featuring 25 research laboratories, each of which has particular research competencies. Designated interface managers ensure the cooperation with internal and external customers. The cooperation between R&T and other R&D units becomes closer because of the reduction in time-to-market and in overall project duration.

1.4   International Research Expansion

The internationalization of R&D encompasses more than establishing R&D sites overseas. Home-based cooperation with leading international centers-of-excellence are just as important. This includes:

- Cooperation in projects with leading universities world wide;
- Cooperation with specialized research institutes;
- Strategic cooperation with other companies, or in international research programs;
- Participation in high-tech venture-capital funds;
- Participation in sponsorship programs.

At Daimler-Benz, the main reasons for the establishment of international R&T sites were market access, costs, technology monitoring, and management of overseas cooperation. Spatial separation of R&T calls for improved coordination and harmonization. International separation requires even more harmonization than internal (i.e., within Germany) distribution of R&T. Corporate R&T must thus consciously internationalize to locate its activities in the best possible places, as has been done when the Palo Alto research center was opened to gain access to the immense human capital in the Silicon Valley, or in Bangalore where costs and software expertise played a dominant role.

Yet, there is no permeating internationalization strategy for research, while manufacturing and production is able to internationalize with a plan at hand.

A major constraint in developing a strategy for internationalization is the often simultaneous restructuring of the corporation as a whole. For instance, during the dissolution of the AEG Daimler-Benz business unit, it was a difficult to conceive a long-term research strategy since it was unknown for how long this unit would still be with the rest of the group. It was learned that an open information policy and the fast reduction of job and business uncertainty helps to create a more encouraging working environment to the individual scientist.

Contrary to development, research follows the internationalization of produc-

---

Most important drivers for globalization:

1. Monitoring technology trends in high-potential regions;

2. Sourcing know-how in centers of technology excellence;

3. Supporting local development;

4. Developing Daimler-Benz to a global company.

---

tion more easily. Development requires a higher critical mass (number of people) for sound operation, which is why it is less quickly internationalized. Research may be conducted with around ten people already. Technology monitoring and cooperation with local universities and companies are at the beginning of this process. Hence, research is more internationalized than development, which at Daimler-Benz is concentrated in Germany (except for automobile development in some overseas locations).

At Daimler-Benz, R&D was still relatively little internationalized in terms of overseas personnel and international research investment, although in recent years the number of international R&D sites has grown. Germany is not the one and only hub of knowledge. Knowledge centers for specific topics can be found on a global scale. If a company wants to stay internationally competitive with its products, it must align its product development process with global needs from the very beginning.

1.5   Special Features of the R&T Organization

At Daimler-Benz, five features support international R&T operations:

- Technology Monitoring
- Research Project Coaching
- Circle Member Group
- Exchange Group R&T
- Research auditing

They are explained in this section in more detail.

Technology Monitoring

In 1990, Daimler-Benz created a technology observation unit to systematize its global technology monitoring. Between 1988 and 1997, technology liaison offices were established in Tokyo, Boston, Moscow, and Palo Alto, and group representative offices in Singapore, Beijing, and Washington.

The mission of technology management is to maintain and strengthen the technological competitiveness of the business areas. Its task is to conduct a business oriented analysis of relevant technological developments and to support corporate or business area specific technology strategy development and to counsel the R&T board. A six-step process includes the following tasks:

- *Identify customers and their needs*: Scientists want detailed technical data while senior executives require technical overviews and business news.
- *Design of a monitoring plan* includes a list of technology fields to be monitored, information sources, and available resources.
- *Information acquisition*: Use of formal sources such as patents, licenses, publications, press releases, and business reports; use of informal sources such as personal networks of researchers, development engineers, and corporate technology management. In specific projects, telephone interviews, visits and consultants may be necessary. Electronic databases, netsurfing, and reverse engineering become more important. Personal networks must be continually sustained. The circle member group and the research audit team are further information sources.
- *Data storage* takes place in computerized databases and original material. Knowledge management is important as much of the relevant information is stored in the heads of the people involved.
- *Analysis of the material* encompasses the identification of substitutes and competing technologies, as well as activity patterns of competitors, suppliers, and customers. Internal technology is benchmarked to the state-of-the-art.
- *Dissemination* depends on the result of the analysis. Briefings are given to the executive board and department heads. Evaluations and reports are conveyed to senior management and expert groups. Presentations and workshops are carried out with researchers and scientists.

In 1998, the technology observation unit was dissolved and the technology monitoring offices were linked to individual R&T units (see Fig. V.2.3). An intranet will assume many of the former technology monitoring responsibilities. By means of new information technologies, the exchange of know-how about new technologies and information will involve all researchers and become a more interactive instrument.

Research Project Coaching

Daimler-Benz established commercial project controlling in R&T in 1991. Its traditional task was to introduce project management and to establish project controlling processes in parallel to some more intangible objectives like establishing a homogenous project culture. Another central task of this unit (FTK/P) was to offer project management support and coaches to project managers. Project coaches were service providers and support project managers by providing project management instruments, project administration and coordination as well as fulfilling the traditional controlling task.

FTK/P had grown from 11 people to almost 40 by 1997. Thus, a critical mass for effective operations had been achieved. In 1998, the project management support function was split from the others and organized as a service center. This service was not only used by R&T but also by Daimler-Benz development units, although a similar service was offered internally. In this way FTK/P was less dependent on a single client.

FTK/P focuses on strategic or special R&T projects, i.e. not all R&T projects are controlled by a dedicated person within the service center or receive project coaching support. Its services are engaged in projects were particular problems are expected or already occur or in projects where project managers ask for support because of a particular high complexity and amount of managerial and administrational tasks he has to take care of.

One example for projects with higher management complexity are international projects or those which are conducted with partners from different companies dispersed in various countries. Here, tasks like the establishment of a communication platform, reporting procedures and team building across borders demand special skills, since so-called „soft factors" are often considered to be the real key to success. In numerous cases, members of the FTK/P service center establish and manage project offices of international R&D projects and are therefore engaged with the whole range of management and coordination issues, sometimes up to the point where coaches represent the official project manager in selected meetings and consortia.

Circle Member Group

The exchange of information is of crucial importance for R&D intensive companies: Not only must scientists in central research keep abreast of major trends in their specialized fields, as 'service providers' for development they also must stay on top of the latest technologies and their potential for realizing new products. In order to intensify information exchange within the corporation, two initiatives have been launched, the Circle Member Group and the Exchange Group R&T.

The circle member group (CMG) was an information network consisting of distinguished scientists from all over the world. The know-how flowed from top scientist into Daimler-Benz's research departments and its researchers could keep abreast of the latest research results and applications world-wide. 23 leading scientists were chosen as CMG members in 1996. They were selected from a broad range of disciplines, also ensuring a good regional mix. Besides a proven academic excellence, they are expected to:

- Demonstrate in-depth appreciation for international state-of-the-art developments, and
- Bring along excellent contacts to other institutes worldwide.

Their activities range from regular informal information exchange to the undertaking of joint projects. Each CMG member had a mentor within Daimler-Benz, but dialogues and information exchange was on a personal basis. This did not constitute an exclusive consulting agreement: The main function of the circle member group was the integration of top people from leading institutes who, in this way, also gained insight into Daimler-Benz's research activities and assessed its R&D projects as experts in their field.

Exchange Group R&T

The second initiative aimed at „transfer through people" within the Exchange Group R&T and was based on an individually-tailored job-rotation system. The objective was to train staff that would have a comprehensive and closely-meshed communication network within Daimler-Benz, thereby serving as communicators between research and the business units. Exchange group members spent one to two years engaged in one or more projects before moving on to their „final destination". Those destined for a research post spent their project phase working in a division, i.e. for a client. Reversibly, staff envisaged for entry into one of the groups divisions would participate in a project at central research. The benefits were many:

- Development and production profit from personal know-how and expertise of researchers;
- Transfer of know-how from research to the divisions is ensured;
- Central research is able to recruit people from former „customers" who know about particular needs of business units;
- Engender greater customer orientation among research personnel.

About two-thirds of the exchange group members had been financed by Daimler-Benz's operating units - an indication how well they value this scheme. The remaining members are being sponsored either by the project areas or their eventual 'final destinations.'

Research Audits

In order to get direct feedback concerning quality and competitiveness of Daimler-Benz's research activities, a network of more than 60 external research auditors was established. These experts evaluate projects or research fields. The research auditing system is an ambitious policy that applies total quality management principles to research. This move to audit research reflects a global trend in industry to justify costly in-house research. Firstly, external top-range scientists judge about the quality of research work and compare it with the world-wide leading technologies and state-of-the-art. Secondly, assessments by internal „customers" within business are taken into account. Four or five research audits are carried out each year. Each audit is performed by a group of ten experts, including five business managers from the Daimler-Benz manufacturing divisions representing customers and five outside scientists serving as independent experts. Normally, between 20 and 30 researchers are involved in each audit.

The research audit is geared to give Daimler-Benz research and division executives a feeling for where they stand in the international scientific community and what the demand is for a new innovation. The basic idea is to bring together the people who can best analyze new science: the researchers themselves, the acknowledged international experts in the field and the business managers who will be commercializing it. It is not a mathematical formula or a controlling instrument, but rather a process to discuss the international position in a selected area of research. During the two-day audit, the research program is evaluated according to technology uniqueness, market potential, expertise of researchers, and management strategy.

Exceeding the original intention at its conception, this network of auditors has in the meantime turned into a circle of first-class advisors and consultants for Daimler-Benz R&T.

2   Management of International R&T Sites

When in 1986 Daimler-Benz decided to expand its traditional automobile businesses, R&D backed up this effort by establishing technology monitoring units to scan external technology development in other markets and regions. Research by the MIT in the automobile industry competitiveness revealed serious backlogs in Western car manufacturers, as compared to Japanese producers. The long-held belief of German superiority was badly damaged. It was shown that Western manufacturers could not keep up with international competitors in terms of productivity and quality. Daimler-Benz became aware that it had not systematically followed technology development in Japan. Hence, a technology liaison office was created in Tokyo as early as 1989. More listening posts were established in Boston, Moscow, and other places, and eventually research centers were set up in the US and Asia.

Two strategic reasons were paramount in deciding about location and staffing of the new international R&T sites:

- Proximity to market: Physical collocation with principal markets and internal customers facilitates the learning and understanding of the needs of downstream functions.

Major issues for global R&D management at Daimler-Benz:

1. Soft and informal coordination means are important in transnational R&D projects;

2. Building a global mind-set for R&T employees;

3. Overcoming inherent difficulties in international R&D operations such as high costs, different languages and cultures, and long project execution times;

4. Interfunctional differences are as important obstacles to global R&D as geographical distances.

Reason for
International Location

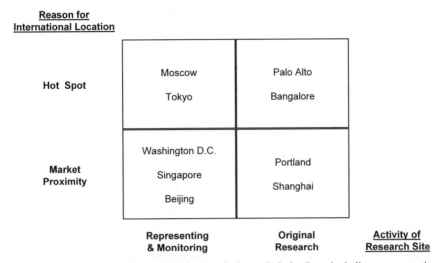

Fig. V.2.6. Classification of international research sites at Daimler-Benz including representative offices, technology liaison offices, and research centers.

- Presence in hot-spots: Critical know-how is created in just a few places around the globe. It is important to access this knowledge through local people and participation in local research in order to stay abreast of the latest technology developments.

This has led to the establishment of three types of international R&T sites: Strategic listening posts, research centers for development support, and research centers for technology sourcing. Representative offices in Washington, DC, Beijing, and Singapore are not part of the international R&T network (Fig. V.2.6).

Listening posts are technology units composed of small teams of three to five employees in Japan, the USA and Russia. These teams are charged with observing core technology areas, identifying trends, initiating corporations, and establishing and maintaining networks. Listening posts clearly fulfill the role of being present in hot-spots.

Research centers were established where there was a growing need to combine Daimler-Benz's internal expertise and know-how with that of top-performing research facilities world-wide. A central criterion when it comes to establishing research facilities in other countries is availability of assistance locally for the increasingly global activities of development, production and sales. Great importance is also placed on gaining direct access to the focal points of technological developments. Since 1994, two institutes were founded, one in the USA and one in China. In 1997, an information technology research center was opened in India. This enabled Daimler-Benz to take advantage of India's excellent software-development know-how and allowed to build long-term business relationships with subsidiaries in Asia.

2.1   *Listening Posts for Technology Monitoring*

Technology listening posts were established in Japan, Russia, and US. Relatively small teams of three to five people are responsible for:

- Technology monitoring, i.e. observation of key technology areas and identification of new trends;
- Establishing research cooperation;
- Establishing and maintaining expert networks;
- Technology and market intelligence service.

The Tokyo Listening Post

In 1990, a technology liaison office was established in Tokyo to find out about Japanese automobile technology. Reasons for choosing Japan as a location for the office were twofold: One was the monitoring of the Japanese automobile market, the other was to get pre-market and first-hand data in order to improve Daimler-Benz's competitiveness on this strategically important market. Administratively it was part of the sales and technical support of Mercedes-Benz of Japan.

In the beginning 10 people were employed: Three Germans and seven Japanese. Their job description listed basic monitoring and project work. In order to cover a large number of technology fields and organizations each member of the unit specialized in a specific technology field and worked on building his specific network. Its foundations usually reached back to the school he attended.

Basic monitoring consisted of keeping track of daily life in Japan: Newspapers, press conferences, annual reports, research reports and conferences were monitored. All institutions which could affect the automobile industry were included: automobile manufacturers and suppliers, industry associations, research institutions and governmental agencies.

It was quickly shown that a deep understanding of the Japanese culture was a pre-requisite for the job as not only fluent Japanese but rather the ability to read „between the lines" brought vital information.

The information gathered was translated and put into a newsletter which was structured according to technology fields. This newsletter was sent to Stuttgart, split up according to end-user profiles and forwarded to identify decision makers. Breaking news such as the establishment of a joint research facility by car manufacturers were transmitted directly to the Board of Daimler-Benz.

Beginning in the 1990s and under constraint of saving costs additionally to this basic monitoring specific projects have been triggered by a client (researcher or research department head) with Daimler-Benz or its divisions. These projects have involve identifying a research institution or a researcher in Japan who might contributes to a problem the client was working on. They would also include making contact and/or facilitating a visit of the client.

These projects required a lot of resources as making (and maintaining) contacts in Japan tends to be a time consuming business. It was calculated that for each day a Daimler-Benz researcher spends with a Japanese institution, a full week of preparation by the technology liaison office was necessary. The positive aspect of making a contact in Japan was that once established it can last a lifetime. After the end of the Daimler-Benz project the link to the institution/researcher is kept alive by the technology liaison office. Additionally, the former client in Germany keeps track of his Japanese source.

The financing of the technology liaison office is jointly provided by the central R&T department which pays for the basic monitoring service and by the projects which are marketed in a way towards research units within the Daimler-Benz conglomerate. The project cost (1996 approximately DM200 per hour) are paid by the research or development project the client is working on. In 1997, the technology liaison office was working on 10 to 20 projects simultaneously with a mainly Japanese staff.

The Boston Listening Post

In 1992, Daimler-Benz set up another listening post in Boston. Boston was chosen because of its excellent research institutions and universities, particularly the Massachusetts Institute of Technology (MIT). The former MIT liaison officer joined Daimler-Benz. After the research center in Palo Alto was opened in 1995, the objectives between the Boston listening post and Palo Alto were delineated, and the Boston group was spun off into a consulting company with Daimler-Benz as its main client.

The Moscow Listening Post

Following the opening of Eastern Europe and several visits to high technology centers within the former Soviet Union, Daimler-Benz also established a technology liaison office in Moscow. Founded in 1992, six employees (one German and five Russians) try to establish contacts to research institutions and companies involved with material sciences, information sciences, and mathematics. The fact that one of the group was a relative to an influential figure in the Russian science community proved to be very valuable.

The results of these activities varied substantially. While a lot of the activities did not result in an immediate benefit for Daimler-Benz, the discovery of a titanium alloy with good welding characteristics marked a major achievement.

The work of the office was greatly influenced by the erratic reception western visitors encountered. A research institution might open its doors to visitors one week and block any overtures the next. Other than in Japan a contact once established might not last very long. It was for that reason that thoughts on a joint venture in Russia were not further entertained. The integration of a research center in the local scientific community is much more difficult to achieve in Russia and Japan because of their particular cultural and social constraints.

Lessons Learned

Running (or better coordinating) the technology liaison offices led to some insights on who should be gathering information overseas. The characteristics sought in technology scouts usually pointed to more experienced people, as well as to a more mature, widely interested and perhaps colorful personality with a broad engineering or scientific background, and one that has the confidence to liaise with high-ranking counterparts. The last characteristic is most important in Japan and Russia. In these cultures a junior technology scout is not taken seriously as seniority is of major importance.

Running a technology liaison office also asks for reviewing the efforts. As the task description for the offices is rather vague, reviews depend to a large degree on rough assessments of the quality delivered (number of reports, timeliness, accuracy) and on comparisons done with similar offices run by other companies. In Japan for instance Siemens, Volkswagen and BMW have liaison with whom Daimler-Benz was in contact.

The reception or assessment of the activities at technology liaison offices „at home" vary strongly: Depending on whether a project turned out well or not, reactions range from „vitally important" to „a waste of money". Calculating expenses versus impacts from information or joined efforts with a new contact gives no final result. On the other hand it was found that one real „hit" could finance running the program for 10 years or more.

Generally the actual costs of the offices are calculated and then put into perspective to the overall research and development investments. Running an office in Japan costs depending on the size approximately DM2 million per year. Compared to exceeding DM9 billion on research and development it seems reasonable to invest a small fraction on collecting information on present and future activities within the technological environment.

The question is not so much whether the program pays itself in the short term, it is whether Daimler-Benz would still be competitive a few years down the road. For now the management has decided that timely information on technological developments are an important contribution for them.

2.2   Research Centers for Local Development Support

Two research and technology centers had been established in Shanghai and Portland to support local development and manufacturing activities. In this case, Daimler-Benz followed a market-driven internationalization for R&D as sales and production departments had done for decades. The trend to collocation with lead customers and presence in important markets had become more apparent in the 1990s. Besides on-site support of distribution, production, and development, learning from lead-users and adaptability to local customer requirements gains in importance.

The Shanghai Institute of Metallurgy

The research center in Shanghai is a joint research venture with the Shanghai Institute of Metallurgy. Since 1995, the Shanghai center supported the Daimler-Benz-subsidiary Temic, a microelectronics company expanding its Chinese business significantly through a number of joint ventures. The research center focuses on 'electronic packaging', a key research area in microelectronics. Its research is tightly integrated with microelectronics research undertaken in Germany, and there is intense communication between researchers in both countries, involving the frequent exchange of Chinese and German scientists.

The Portland Vehicle Systems Center

Since 1996, Daimler-Benz was engaged in vehicle system research in Portland, Oregon. The Vehicle System Technology Center was established to support the Freightliner subsidiary with the early integration of specific technology and market know-how into their product development. Moreover, short organizational and geographic distances facilitate the cooperation with leading key partners and scientific institutes engaged in system modeling and simulation research. About a dozen experts in mechanics, electronics, information and control theory support freightliner engineers in their design of electronic systems and on-board driver assistance instruments. Another focus is on human factors engineering: The evaluation and optimization of manipulating technical instruments is crucial to produce user-friendly car controls. The Portland center closely cooperates with vehicle research units in Germany and other international R&D teams.

2.3　Research Centers for Technology Sourcing

Much of the most exciting technology is created in relatively small regions of the world. In order to keep track of these developments and to reduce internal R&D efforts for late internal technology acquisition, research is often located away from national headquarters and close to regions of innovation. For information technology, these regions are the Silicon Valley in California and Bangalore, India.

The Daimler-Benz Research and Technology Center in Palo Alto

In 1995, a research and technology center was established in Palo Alto, California. The mission of the center was to help keep Daimler-Benz in the forefront of the accelerating revolution in transportation, communications, and related new technologies and services. A growing number of scientists conduct original research, forge joint projects with researcher from US, host scientists and engineers from Daimler-Benz laboratories world-wide, and foster relevant research at universities and independent research institutions, encouraging promising proposals and ideas. The key challenges are the management of an internationally diverse interdisciplinary project team, and the integration and leverage of Daimler-Benz's automotive expertise from Germany.

Originally designed as a technology listening post, it was enlarged to a self-supporting research center as a critical mass and competency was necessary to understand and absorb the technological innovation in the surrounding area. In 1997, the center's scientists came from all continents of the world except Africa. The intense personnel turnover in Silicon Valley was seen as an asset rather than a problem. Frequent job moves of employees means that companies retain high resource flexibility and may recruit new engineers with fresh ideas.

One of its most vital tasks was to help intellectual exchange flourish between US universities and research institutes and Daimler-Benz researchers around the world. The Research and Technology Center returned a direct benefit to the Bay Area through the development and sharing of innovative transportation management solutions that combined Daimler-Benz expertise with ideas and technological advances originating in California.

In the beginning a newsletter resembling the Japanese was compiled. After some time it was halted. Most of the press releases which make up a fair portion of the Japanese original could as well be retrieved in Germany: The use of the Internet and the lack of a language barrier seemed to make the task obsolete. Now the „Automobile Technology Newsletter USA" is again available. The rationale is that not the retrieval of the information is vital but the selection. Selecting which information could be important depends on an intimate understanding of the developments in the target region.

The Daimler-Benz Research Center India

The research effort was not restricted to Silicon Valley in California. In 1997, Daimler-Benz established another research center in a crucial location for information technology and communications research where exceptional scientific progress in the software sector was being made, namely in the region around Bangalore in India. Both international location strategies were pursed in its establishment. Not only was Bangalore one of the world's leading high-tech regions, but also a prime market with a great number of local Daimler-Benz operations.

The main objectives of the Bangalore center were:

- To be part of the global Daimler-Benz Research and Technology network,
- To act as a bridgehead for the Indian scientific community, comprising the nations reputed universities, software industry and research establishments, and
- To benefit from the cost advantages of doing research in India and to serve the needs of the business units and sister companies of Daimler-Benz in the Asian region.

A key component of this concept was the integration of Indian scientists from leading institutes such as the Indian Institute of Science in Daimler-Benz's research projects. This includes sponsoring Ph.D. dissertations and Master theses of Indian students. Entire projects were contracted out to Indian institutes and other research companies. Another key field lies in reverse engineering, an area in which Daimler-Benz expects to help shorten development cycles significantly. The research center, which is to employ up to 50 scientists by 1998, is headed by an Indian scientist who had already been with Daimler-Benz for a long time.

The acquisition of Daimler-Benz subsidiaries in South-east Asia as potential customers for research activities is reflected in the composition of the research center's board of directors consisting of representatives from Mercedes Germany, Mercedes India, DASA, Debis, and R&T-3. The first project was initiated in January 1997 in a step-by-step procedure and was a mainly internal project which was later followed by projects commissioned by DASA and Dornier. The Bangalore scientists visited the customer in order to familiarize themselves with the particular problems for about 4-6 weeks before returning to Bangalore with a very detailed „job description" and profound knowledge about the customer's expectations. As necessary, the Indian project leader returned to the customer for optimal integration of the product.

2.4 Coordination and Control of the International Research Network

Most of Daimler-Benz's R&D is located close to the headquarters in Stuttgart or in Germany. At R&T, only about 4% or less than one hundred scientists work abroad, although their number is growing at a much faster pace than in Germany.

R&T still has to develop a truly global mind-set. The international way of thinking has not yet reached every scientists and engineer in this Germany-rooted R&D organization. Daimler-Benz has been a company with a strong home base, with the main foreign markets being nearby European countries. Production was internationalized early to reduce logistics and manufacturing costs.

International R&D operations are centrally controlled by budgets and reporting to the headquarters. Auditing is organized centrally, as is the assignment of local management. Integration of R&D activities at the project level is ensured by frequent and intense exchange of R&D personnel between Germany and international research centers, as well as the competence center organization with responsible interface managers. Central control and coordination facilitates the steering and controlling of basic strategies and research projects. In theory, no strategy contradictions should evolve. Responsibilities do not overlap and distinct core competencies are identified. Communication patterns are clearly defined. Synergy effects are exploited, and complementing research is integrated on a higher level.

The laboratories' technology strategy formulation has been transferred to the lab director and his team. Hence, coordination between each lab has become more competitive and requires frequent communication and meetings. Due to the geographical distances involved, these integration processes are more difficult to carry out with international sites. Additionally, hierarchical and functional distances restrict creativity and hinder efficient communication since communication channels are too long and too slow.

The reorganization and reorientation of R&D towards business units and downstream customers is not completed and remains a continuous challenge. Some work of R&T will always be removed from direct market contact in order to guarantee radical innovation and completely novel business opportunities.

3   R&D Projects in an International Context

Projects put R&D organization into action. In this section, three projects illustrate some of the key issues of international R&D:

- Knowledge transfer across functional boundaries;
- Integrating expertise across multiple competence centers;
- Accelerating technology development through lead-user cooperation.

3.1   Transferring Knowledge Across Functional Boundaries: Emission-free Fuel-cells

One of the main challenges in R&D management is the transfer of know-how from research to development. Researchers rarely or unsystematically accompany their projects into development. Personnel fluctuation in research is typically less than 10% per year. Especially in US and European companies, research is better paid and more esteemed than development or production. A researcher will move to development or even further only if the benefits of doing so exceed those of staying within research. These incentives might include:

- Image of new project;
- Self interest;
- Opportunity for new challenges;
- Broadening of perspectives.

Under these circumstances, extraordinary measures are needed to ensure the tight cooperation, and hence a constant flow of know-how and technology, between development and manufacturing.

The recent reorganization at R&T aims for the integration with the product, away from the former functional organization. A principal distinction between personnel in research and development has to be overcome: Scientists aim for functional improvements and look at details, while engineers are the integrators of technologies, looking at the entire system. One way to ensure this integration is to give the scientists a vision in order to think product-oriented. The vision in one of the most prestigious Daimler-Benz research projects, the development of alternative fuel-cells, was a environmentally friendly car which would produce no fuel-based emissions.

Research in alternative fuels has been carried out in R&D centers of many automobile manufacturers and space research institutes. In 1990, scientists at Dornier, a Daimler-Benz company, suggested to utilize fuel-cells, which due to the high manufacturing costs had previously been used in space technology-related projects only, to power ordinary automobiles. The idea was successfully pursued and funded directly from the corporate budget. When the strategic nature of the project was recognized, research in fuel-cells for use in automobiles was given full top-management support.

In these early phases of the fuel-cell R&D, the project was managed by R&T. After the first technological breakthroughs and the successful demonstration of fuel-cell powered automobiles (No-Emission Car 1 i.e. Necar-1 in 1994), a concept car was jointly developed between R&T and Mercedes-Benz Advanced Development (Necar-2, 1996). Project management and a large part of the project responsibility was assumed by development. Nebus, suitable for operation as a normal city bus, followed in 1997. Necar-3 (a fuel-cell based A-class vehicle) was went into production in 1999.[62]

R&D on the fuel-cell was further concentrated and emphasized by concentrating all 42 scientists and engineers in the so-called 'Project-House Fuel-Cell' near Nabern, about 30 km away from the headquarters in Stuttgart, but close enough to Mercedes-Benz development. R&D teams of cooperation partners (DBB Fuel Cell Engines and others) are collocated with the Project-House, such that almost 200 R&D people are working on fuel-cell development in Nabern. This centralized organization fosters informal contacts and information exchange, motivating all project members. Also, it offered a centralization compromise for the dispersed R&D activities in the Daimler-Benz research centers at Stuttgart, Ulm, and Friedrichshafen.

Technology transfer is best achieved by transferring the people associated with the critical know-how. Therefore, a large part of the scientists involved in the fuel cell project moved along when the project was handed over to development. These scientists are now enhancing fuel-cell technology for use in automobile application. Intensive collaboration not only guarantees the exchange of information but also makes sure that only mature and extensively tested technology will be used in the design of the new fuel-cell car. Since the fuel-cell is considered as one of the most promising R&D projects at Daimler-Benz, almost 20 different central boards are to be informed, and several steering committees supervise the R&D activities.

Internal technology hand-over was not the only challenge faced by Daimler-Benz: Missing infrastructure poses a serious problem to the market success of fuel-cell based vehicles. Cars operating with traditional gas can be fueled at every gas stations and can be serviced by any auto shop. Due to the high degree of standardization, little extra training to deal with automobiles from different manufacturers is needed. Fuel-cell based cars do not enjoy the same ubiquity of complementary infrastructure. Moreover, the fuel methanol can be obtained only in a very limited number of places. Mechanics are not trained in dealing with fuel cell-related failures. Uncertainty about such standards are best tackled by international cooperation involving a significant part of the value-adding chain.

Hence, Daimler-Benz had to make sure that their technology would find worldwide acceptance and support. One piece in the puzzle to establish their design of the fuel-cell based vehicle is a strategic collaboration with the Canadian firm Ballard Power Systems, a global leader in fuel-cell technologies and a spin-off from General Electric's former fuel-cell research. Daimler-Benz brings in

---

[62] Subsequent successes show the effectiveness of the program: Powered by liquid hydrogen, Necar 4 had a top speed of 145 km/h; Necar 4a, developed also in 1999, had been redeveloped to run on compressed hydrogen, making it much more compact. Necar 5, suitable for practical operation fuelled by methanol; reached speeds of up to 150 km/h. In 2002, Necar 5 clocked up a long-distance record for a fuel-cell-powered vehicles of 5,250 kilometers when it completed a trans-American journey from San Francisco to Washington. In 2000, Jeep Commander 2 had shown hydrogen fuel cell to be suitable for larger cars. Hermes Sprinter was the first vehicle under day-to-day operating conditions. The "Natrium" runs on sodium borohydride (NaBH4). Fuel cell powered urban buses were adopted by public transport operators around Europe as well as the Australian city of Perth (Citaro, 2002). On the "F-Cell", the entire fuel-cell system was integrated into the sandwich floor of the long-wheelbase Mercedes-Benz A-Class (2003).

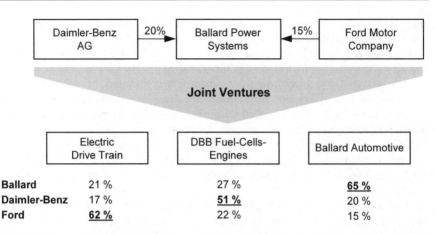

Fig. V.2.7. International initial collaboration between Ballard, Ford, and Daimler-Benz. Ballard was the world leader in the development of proton exchange membrane fuel cells. Daimler-Benz has unique expertise in research into alternative drive systems and automotive fuels. Ford was highly regarded for its advanced electric vehicle power train technology.

extensive system know-how of integrating engines, drives and vehicles. With Daimler-Benz's help, Ballard has the strength and the resources to bring the fuel-cells to volume commercial production.

The cooperation with Ballard, entered in 1992, accelerated the fuel-cell technology development to such a promising degree that in early 1997, Daimler-Benz further intensified their stake in Ballard: One joint venture was founded to develop the entire fuel-cell system, and another joint venture was created for distributing the fuel-cell powered engines. In December 1997, Ford joined Daimler-Benz and Ballard. Ford secures the fuel-cell access to a gigantic mass market while participating on Ballard's and Daimler-Benz's R&D efforts (Fig. V.2.7). Ford's total investment in the partnership will be around US$ 420 million. However, Daimler-Benz retains a leading role in the partnership concerning management of R&D and exploitation of results. In 1998, Ballard Automotive was established as a third joint venture.

Ford and Ballard have moved R&D teams to the Project-House in Nabern and will establish their own R&D laboratories on-site. Daimler-Benz, on the other hand, will dispatch some of their own R&D personnel to Vancouver to collaborate closely with Ballard. Project-internal meetings to coordinate technical issues take place regularly with participants from Daimler-Benz, Ballard, and Ford.[63]

---

[63]   The cooperation with Ballard continued into the 2000s. In 2006, Ballard was extended another contract valued approx. US$ 40 million. In a separate deal in January 2006, Ballard signed an $8.3 million contract to service 27 Mercedes-Benz Citaro Ballard fuel cell-powered buses that will run on European roads this year as a one-year extension to the CUTE (Clean Urban Transport for Europe) / ECTOS (Ecological City Transport System) Project, the two-year fuel cell bus demonstration that began in late 2003.

Smooth project hand-over processes and leveraging external technological capabilities were two important lessons to learn for Daimler-Benz's R&T management. A significant portion of the fuel cell scientists moved along with the project into fuel cell development. Moreover, cooperation with external technology companies and with direct competitors are two key strategies to be pursued on an international scale in order to establish a dominant design to ensure the creation of complementary services and technology by third parties and the market.

3.2 Integrating Expertise Across Multiple Competence Centers: European Projects

Daimler-Benz was engaged in a number of international projects carried out within and sponsored by the 4th framework program of the European Commission. Daimler-Benz's shared ranges from applied research in technology fields to the implementation of new technology management concepts.

R&D activity in European projects is extremely decentralized (see Fig. V.2.8). Reward, a one-year project aimed at designing and implementing re-engineering methods in R&D, was formed by teams from Daimler-Benz, Philips, Nokia, SEC Electrocom, and Thomson-CSF, teams from smaller companies (GSM Software Management, ATM Computer, Planisware) that ensure exploitation of the project results for a wide range of companies in Europe. Teams from research and consulting service providers (KMPG Management Consulting, University of St. Gallen, and Fraunhofer Institute for Industrial Engineering) provided the required theoretical background.

A total of 25 researchers were involved. One of the partners (SEC Electrocom) assumed coordination responsibilities to organize and administer start-up workshops, regular face-to-face meetings, and intensive e-mail communication. His central location was important for frequent personal contact between contributing partners the coordinator himself. Apart from managing a highly dispersed research activity, the management of different cultural backgrounds not only by ethnic but also by professional standards posed a key challenge to the success of the project. Much patience and sensitivity was required to align the individual objectives of each partner team to agree on a shared understanding of what was to be achieved, and how each partner would contribute to this goal.

The entire project work was split into small work packages to be executed by each team. Three problems occurred. First, hand-over of preliminary and final work package results was often complicated by incompatible computer and information systems. Second, after a team had concluded its part of the work, the entire project was given a lesser priority, thus hindering the efficient project continuation for the rest of the teams. Third, the project coordination office responsible for coordination and control was given only weak influence and decision power, thus lacking the strong authority needed to keep decentralized activities on track.

It was learned that decentralized project work involving several partners required a different mind-set from the efficiency-oriented work routines used in single-location projects. Every individual at each partner had to gain an understanding for his collaborators needs and weaknesses. Communication between

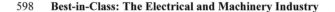

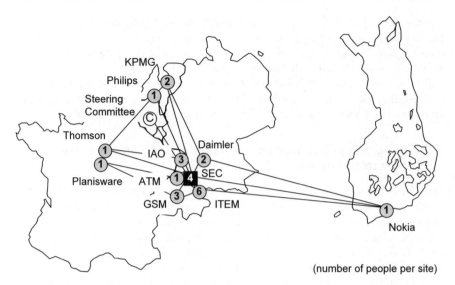

(number of people per site)

Fig. V.2.8. Decentralized R&D in an European project.

teams was essential; the change of intensity often provided a clue when a particular sub-task was delayed or the anticipated outcome could not be reached.

Due to the distances between the teams, initial workshops were designed to last at least two days. Time is required for future partners to build up a relationship of trust and respect. This can be best achieved during the time aside from the formal meeting. The project office must be aware of such needs and consequently arrange appropriate start-up meetings, face-to-face meetings, and regular events to strengthen team culture and team spirit.

Since much of the effective communication takes place by modern information technologies, the access to shared databases and the error-free operation of e-mail and file transfer exchange must be ensured at the beginning of the project. Too often, project members are frustrated when communication breaks down during the critical ramp-up phase of a project. Personal friendships will last longer than the original project, spanning across corporate boundaries to form an informal network by which much of the know-how and technology transfer will take place for which European projects are initiated in the first place.

3.3   Accelerating Technology Development: The Intelligent Traffic Guidance System

The Intelligent Traffic Guidance System (ITGS) is a tool designed to piloting motorists through congested areas and reducing travel times. It includes an electronic street atlas and a device that proposes routes with fastest journey times. It also supplements data on the existing road network with up-to-the-minute information on the traffic situation.

> **Major innovative break-throughs at Daimler-Benz (last five years):**
>
> 1. Fuel cell car;
>
> 2. Intelligent Traffic Guidance System;
>
> 3. Swatch car and A-Class automobiles;
>
> 4. F200 - Drive-by-Wire car.

The ITGS is the product of a rich technology mix. As well as cooperating on conception, various units in Daimler-Benz, Debis, and Mercedes-Benz worked together to advance the necessary vehicle technology and devise the route planner. Bosch and Nippon Denso developed the vehicle terminal. The Tokyo traffic police supply real-time data on the current traffic situation via a state-of-the-art traffic information system. ATIS - a joint venture between the City of Tokyo and a private consortium which includes Debis Systemhaus, a Daimler-Benz subsidiary - is responsible for marketing the data. A mobile radio network provided by NTT is used to transmit data back and forth between service center and vehicle. Daimler-Benz InterServices Telematics Japan operates the service center and markets the ITGS service. An innovative satellite-aided sensor to determine the position of a vehicle is currently designed at Daimler-Benz's research center in Bangalore.

This cooperation of various stakeholders of the new technology pushed forward the development and commercialization. Because such a multitude of political, technological and product integration issues were involved, the competence-based collaboration of all involved was needed to manage the system complexity.

4   Conclusions

4.1   Reviewing R&D Internationalization at Daimler-Benz

With a new, competence-based organization Daimler-Benz R&T expected to serve the needs of its business units better. The underlying business model focused on internal work processes, knowledge flow processes, and R&D staff development.

While sales and production were highly internationalized, R&D had remained relatively centralized in Germany. International research centers have been established in hot-spots and close to market opportunities. Listening posts were created where Daimler-Benz needed to observe important technology and market trends.

Five practices that support the productivity of international research operations were described: Technology monitoring, R&D project coaching, external scientist networks, internal expert networks, and research auditing. The motivation and establishment of technology offices, technology centers and research centers were fundamental for supporting the establishment of an international R&D network.

Moreover, three R&D projects described key challenges and important lessons learned in international R&D. These projects highlighted issues such as know-how transfer from research to development (fuel-cell), the establishment of international R&D alliances (fuel-cell), the integration of key customers in lead markets (ITGS), the operation of multilocal research teams (Reward), and the integration of local expertise with home-base strengths (fuel-cell).

4.2   Lessons Learned from International R&D Projects

The management of transnational R&D projects is more complex than the management of local projects. Despite improved information and communication technology, face-to-face meetings are not replaceable. Communication is more important than believed. Since different languages and different cultures are involved, even if English is chosen as the language of operation, more communication between the project team members is needed to ensure that the information and knowledge is understood. Projects tend to be lengthier and almost always create additional time pressure towards the end.

Nevertheless, cultural diversity gives an intangible but very essential input to project work and overall success. Because objectives often differ between different countries and national interests interfere, a common understanding of the project goals is more important with an international consortium. The responsibilities and competencies of the project manager and the team members must be clearly defined at the outset. Careful selection of project partners and the establishment of a comprehensive communication and cooperation infrastructure help to avoid management overhead and project failure risks. International cooperation and integration of local experts is often unavoidable because the required level of know-how and expertise is rarely found at home. Human and social factors are more important there than on a national level.

4.3   Trends and Upcoming Challenges

The merger with Chrysler and the reinforced globalization were two prime challenges for Daimler's R&T in the late 1990s. The 1998 Daimler-Benz CTO Klaus-Dieter Vöhringer assumed overall R&D responsibility for the DaimlerChrysler company; two large R&D organizations with a history of strong central orientation had to be aligned. Key challenges included the exploitation of technological synergy and competencies, the autonomy and independence of R&D units, and the development of a global perspective on external know-how sourcing and supply management.

Business units have to be convinced that global R&T is a benefit and not a higher expense. R&T must think more globally and attract more globally thinking people. Personnel exchange among global sites and between R&T and external partners is essential to build international networks. A competitive advantage is to identify international know-how centers before others do. In general, an increasing number of R&D sites and R&D people will make global R&T management more complex.

> **Lessons learned for organizing R&D at Daimler-Benz:**
> 1. Balance downstream orientation while securing long-term innovation;
> 2. Aim for a competence-based organization;
> 3. Integrate global competencies and know-how;
> 4. Ensure interdisciplinary and international cooperation through improved communication.

4.4 Implications

Integration of product development processes and globalization are two means to reduce development times and production costs, while simultaneously improving product quality. In order to handle such complexity, a culture has to be created in which employees realize that cooperation across regional and departmental boundaries is essential to the continued success of the company. The entire product development process must be supported by the use and integration of information technologies.

Some of the measures that have to be taken or have been taken already to reduce costs, and to concentrate on speeding up processes are:

- Concentration on core competencies;
- Definition of technological priorities or research and development strategies;
- Realization of innovations;
- Optimization of development integration;
- Definition of core processes:
- New approach to development processes and shortening of the development time;
- Embarking on cooperation;
- Move of development capacity to foreign markets.

The creation of a multi-cultural environment cannot be restricted to international sites. Through job rotation, transnational projects and other means to support cross-functional and international networks, a multi-cultural organization can be created that goes beyond mere orientation towards external markets. At the heart of this strategy lies open communication between Daimler-Benz employees and their partners world-wide.

International projects teach how important it is to work with local experts without losing sight of the final customer. The good practices that Daimler-Benz achieved in some of these projects must become the standards for all of their R&D activities. High standards for processes, technology, and people are global qualities and will earn the customers respect everywhere in the world.

As companies overcome geographical distances, they must also overcome cultural distances. The increasing importance of cooperation forces Daimler to consequently exploit the potential of information technology. The internationalization of research will be understood, in the near future, as the internationalization of cooperative structures.

V.3 Schindler: Institutionalizing Technology Management and R&D Core Competencies*

1 Schindler - the Elevator and Escalator Company

Every day, elevators, escalators and railway cars made by Schindler transport 700 million people worldwide. In 1998, Schindler received orders of CHF6.6 billion, providing work for 38,500 employees.

Schindler Group's headquarters were and still are located in Ebikon, central Switzerland. In 1998, as a result of consequent globalization, Schindler had 30 manufacturing plants and more than a thousand representative offices located in over 100 countries worldwide. The company grew primarily through acquisitions. Schindler operated in South America since 1937 and initiated its first joint venture with Jardine Matheson in Hong Kong in 1974. Today, Asia accounts for more than 50 % of the global new-installation market for elevators and escalators.

Schindler is the worldwide market leader in escalators and second in elevators. Other major global players, and hence also major competitors to Schindler, are Otis (USA), Mitsubishi and Hitachi (Japan), Kone (Finland) and ThyssenKrupp (Germany). In order to improve profitability, a program called SPRINT - 'Schindler's Program for Radical New Thinking' - was initiated in 1995. Since then, the Schindler Group had been reorganized considerably in order to meet the growing challenges of the price-based competition in the elevator and escalator business. These challenges included:

- Strong customer focus;
- Globalization of markets and therefore increasing global competition;
- Deregulation of national codes and standards;
- Shorter innovation cycles;
- Higher product complexity and product variance;
- Separation between commodity and high-end modular products;

* This case study was authored by *Dr. Oliver Gassmann*, Head of R&D Technology Management, Schindler, Switzerland, 1998 and *Martin Bratzler*, Research Assistant, Institute for Technology Management, University of St. Gallen. This case study was written in 1998: The reader should keep in mind that all numbers, figures, organization charts and forecasts represent the state of 1998 or before. The case study was revised in 2007 by *Michael Styger*.

- Increasing pressure to reduce costs and to maintain high quality and reliability at the same time.

In 1998, Schindler's R&D was responsible to meet these challenges by introducing innovative products. This required an efficient product creation process and a focused R&D organization. A major reorganization of Schindler's product creation process led to improved market orientation, stronger concentration on core competencies, clear system engineering responsibility and the establishment of technology management as a new competence center. Schindler decided to move the responsibility and accountability for product creation closer to the customer. This improved output effectiveness by sharpening the market focus, increasing the speed to market and becoming a more effective organization. At the same time, Schindler was then in a better position to integrate product and process work and to reduce the complexity of processes and the organization.

2   Former Innovation Examples

A major breakthrough innovation was the machine-room-less SchindlerMobile elevator. Based on a totally new engineering principle, this elevator consumed less energy, required less building space, simplified jobsite preparations, and therefore reduced the overall investment, and thus costs, of installing elevators. Since SchindlerMobile was systematically developed to address customer needs, it was suited for a broad market. A key characteristic of the new design was that it dramatically sped up the delivery and installation process. The entire assembly process together with commissioning took only 2-3 days (compared to a few weeks for traditional elevators).

Schindler developed this new passenger transport system in a strategic alliance with Porsche and Alusuisse. It was composed of a self-supporting vertical track and a self-propelled vehicle. Two freestanding aluminum pillars with integrated tracks served as the roadway and channeled all forces of the transport system vertically to the foundation. The advantages for architects were tremendous: Unlike conventional elevators, SchindlerMobile required no machine room and no load-bearing shaft walls to absorb static forces. This gave the architect freedom to

---

Major innovative break-throughs at Schindler (1993-1998):

1. Schindler Mobile, machine-room-less elevator with a self supporting structure, self-propelling car and radical new installation principles;

2. Destination call control for significant improvement in passenger traffic (Miconic 10);

3. Micro drives with ropes of totally new composite materials;

4. New elevator safety systems.

place the elevator in the building wherever he liked. The space saved as well as the significant simplifications in shaft construction and jobsite assembly could reduce the builder's elevator costs by as much as 80%.

SchindlerMobile had been developed in a small venture team located at the headquarters in Ebikon. Due to the extreme novelty of the concept, it was separated from the Schindler Corporation as a spin-off company. SchindlerMobile was launched in Germany, Austria and Switzerland in 1997. Market response and feedback were extremely good.

An example for a major cost reduction project was the Miconic TX 5 controller system. This system was based on the first 'global' elevator microcontroller platform. The project involved the international R&D locations at Ebikon (CH), Morristown (USA), and Locarno (CH), as well as a management buyout in Livingston (UK). The project began in 1996 when both Morristown and Ebikon started radical cost reduction projects. In order to reduce redundancy, so-called 'core components', i.e. major parts of the software, PC boards and load measurement equipment, were identified and developed jointly. Only zone-specific components such as boards, safety circuits and production specific components were developed independently. In order to manage such a global project it was necessary to assign clear responsibilities and make use of an efficient R&D organization and process.

3   Organization, Process and Infrastructure of R&D

All R&D activities took place in three groups:

- Corporate R&D;
- Manufacturing R&D;
- Field Operations Engineering.

Resources for new technologies and new product development were focused on Corporate R&D. Therefore, Corporate R&D was to be the main topic of the subsequent analysis.

3.1   R&D Mission

In order to meet Schindler's challenges, Corporate R&D had a clearly defined mission. Schindler's Corporate R&D met and supported the defined corporate priorities below:

- Be a service company;
- Focus on profitability;
- Management resource planning;
- Maintain high level of skills in defined core competencies;
- Effectively use state-of-the-art technologies and methods;
- Use technology and innovation in state-of-the-art development environments;

- Create competitive products and services in transportation which excel in safety and reliability while meeting codes, directives and standards to benefit and delight our customers.

This mission provided a framework for managing and organizing R&D resources as well as a guideline for the daily work of R&D project teams.

3.2   R&D Organization

A series of past acquisitions and expansions had led Corporate R&D activities to be distributed across many locations:

- Switzerland (Ebikon and Locarno);
- Germany (Berlin);
- France (Mulhouse and Melun);
- Spain (Zaragoza);
- USA (Morristown, New Jersey).

Each of the locations brought an individual background and culture to the overall R&D congregation. Although this diversity could have been a prime source of innovation, it also gave rise to redundant development, the NIH syndrome, turf politics, and inefficiencies in collaboration. Schindler therefore chose to change to the current R&D organization with a network based on R&D core competencies. This meant not only eliminating some of the R&D locations, but also reassigning the resources of some R&D labs towards new objectives. Within the mentioned reorganization, some of the more incremental innovative work such as line maintenance or continuous improvement of the manufacturing process had been moved from R&D to the production groups / operations. In order to remain close to the main markets and to the main sources of innovation, the remaining Corporate R&D locations were located in the following countries:

- Europe (Ebikon)
- USA (Randolph, Gettysburgh)
- P. R. China (Shanghai)
- Brazil (Sao Paulo).

Based on a bottom-up identification of core competencies, two sites in the US and Europe had been selected for future technology development. The R&D presence in Asia-Pacific was crucial because of the growing significance of the region as a lead-market. Market criteria would have been dominant in selecting the final location.

The new Corporate R&D organization of 1998 was characterized by:

- An organization based on product modules instead of development disciplines;
- Concentration of Corporate R&D on new technologies and key components;
- Transfer of process development into manufacturing units;
- An empowered and strengthened systems engineering unit;

- Technology Management and Innovation Marketing as new organizational units.

The modular organization of R&D represented a tribute to market-orientation (see Fig. V.3.1). R&D organization along development disciplines such as mechanical, electronics and software engineering were no longer adequate when interdisciplinary requirements dominated functional and specialist know-how. A module-oriented organization better captured technical interfaces and promoted the manufacturability of products.

R&D systems had been empowered to build up systems engineering to ensure system integrity and to design elevators with optimum cost performance ratio. A major goal had been the reduction of life-cycle-costs by eliminating complexity and the number of variants of components. This was achieved through strong interface management and implementation of corporate procedures to promote systems thinking.

Cross-border activities such as technology management, innovation marketing, services & quality and test & trials supported innovation in development centers.

- *Technology Management* was established as a competence center in its own right; it will be described in further detail below;
- *Innovation Marketing* drove the product planning process between R&D and field operations, sold R&D output to the field operations and represented the 'voice of the customer' within R&D;
- *Service & Quality* promoted product data management and quality monitoring and coordinated the tools and infrastructure for R&D development staff;
- *Test & Trials* focused on elevator analysis and measurements as well as field support and documentation.

3.3 R&D Process

The main drivers for innovation were market and customer requirements which were channeled in field operations on the one side (market pull), and skills, technologies and resources of R&D on the other side (technology push). Experience showed that successful innovation could be triggered by both. Finding the right

---

Major issues for global R&D management at Schindler:

1. Systematic management of new technologies;
2. Stronger integration of decentralized technology and application knowledge;
3. Concentration on the technical core competencies;
4. IT-infrastructure, suitable and supportive of the concurrent engineering process.

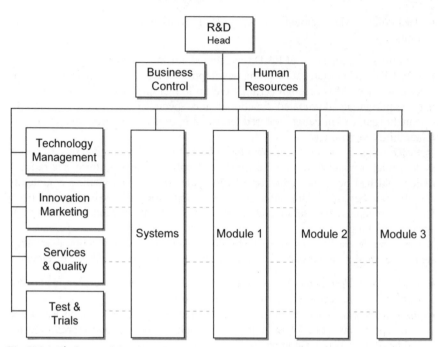

Fig. V.3.1. Product module oriented organization of Corporate R&D at Schindler in 1998.

balance between the two was a major challenge for R&D management. Product planning therefore needed systematic product and technology management in order to manage both inputs (see Fig. V.3.3).

Product planning was based on the two main sources market requirements (pull) and technology core competencies (push) filtered through corporate strategies, e.g. Schindler's Navigator Handbook and Group Product Strategies. In order to reduce variants and concentrate resources, the plans of different field operations had to be harmonized with each other. A project was started only when the availability of the necessary resources was assured. Especially in the engineering phase, the whole product creation process was measured intensely in order to reduce cycle times and to increase quality; dynamic cycle times, on-time-delivery and first pass yields were the most important measurements applied (Fig. V.3.2).

3.4   IT Infrastructure and Development Environment

The creation of innovative products and application of new technologies required state-of-the-art development tools and working environments; four domains were of vital importance:

- *Rapid development environment*; supporting full and consistent connectivity from design and modelling (3D CAD) through integrated analysis (FEM, thermal, kinematics) and simulation tools to rapid prototyping and manufacturing.
- *Product data management (PDM)*; providing the supporting infrastructure for product related workflows and document management with full change management and version control functionality. The access to and distribution of documents / product information uses distributed databases and the latest web technologies.
- *Project management*; supporting project managers and their teams with tools that provide visibility and control for schedule and cost performance (i.e. elaborated hours, expenses, project status information). The purpose was early warning signals and appropriate corrective actions on project activities.
- *Communication technologies*; enabling communication across all Schindler locations worldwide. A major base was the corporate network S-Net which connected more than 40 Schindler locations including field operations, manufacturing and R&D with over 12,000 PCs, workstations or server systems. Every week new locations were connected to support the inter company business processes like order-processing, e-mails, internet and SAP/R3. R&D teams often used media such as RAS (remote access server), FTP (file transfer program), telnet sessions via modem, tele- and videoconferencing.

The global product development which teams mostly included manufacturing and marketing people from locations worldwide, worked on the basis of this infrastructure. Since communication was recognized as the most important success factor in R&D, Schindler promoted an excellent working environment for R&D teams. Concurrent engineering across locations was strongly enabled by the global IT infrastructure.

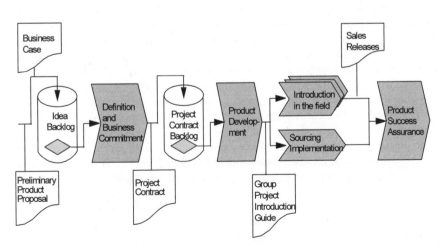

Fig. V.3.2. The product creation process at Schindler in 1998.

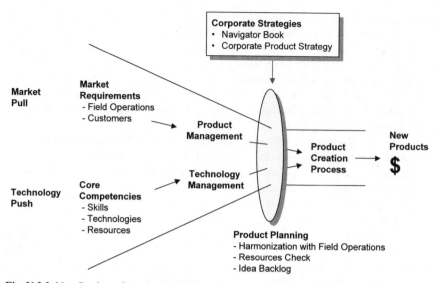

Fig. V.3.3. New Products from the pipeline - market and competence driven.

4   Identifying Core Competencies in R&D

The move towards a more efficient and integrated R&D network organization required the identification of Corporate R&D's core competencies. In 1997, a small team consisting of internal and external experts identified those Schindler competencies which were deemed as world-class in the industry. The goal was to concentrate scarce R&D resources on those areas where Schindler is in a good position to exploit its competitive advantage. All other development activities of lesser significance could have been procured externally. In this resource-based view, it was the company specific technologies and skills that were the most important sources of corporate success (Wernerfelt, 1984). At Schindler, it was recognized that successful exploitation of short-term opportunities was detrimental to the long-term survival of the company.

The identification, cultivation and exploitation of its core competencies allowed Schindler to distinguish itself from competitors and to prevail in global competition. Some technologies could have been easily bought externally; company-specific skills however were very much embedded in the whole organization. They had to be developed in long-term processes and therefore represented the real critical elements of internal competencies. The identification of technical core competencies was a prerequisite for any strategic decision concerning technology, make-or-buy decisions, organizational issues and technology planning.

Core competencies created competitive advantage, were developed over a long

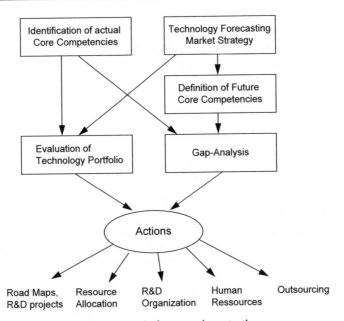

Fig. V.3.4. The core competence process: Actions were important!

period of time, were difficult to imitate and were based on internal, protected know-how (tacit knowledge). Core competencies could have been seen as a market-oriented bundle of technologies enriched with skills and values which created a gateway to new opportunities (Leonard-Barton, 1995).

The entire process for identifying core competencies and deriving competence-based action criteria is depicted in Fig.V.3.4: First the actual core competencies were to be identified. This step required most of the effort because time-intensive workshops and analysis had to be conducted at all R&D sites. Second, the future targeted core competencies were defined on the basis of systematic technology forecasting / evaluating and the product-market strategy.

Based on a gap analysis between actual and future core competencies, actions were defined in order to develop the required competencies (technology, skills and knowledge). These actions comprised of road maps, resource allocation, R&D (re)-organization and human resources.

The most important advantage of this method was its flexibility and efficiency. It was originally developed at the Institute for Technology Management at the University of St. Gallen and adapted to Schindler's special requirements (Boutellier et al., 1998). The process of the identification of core competencies comprised the following eight steps (see Fig. V.3.5).

1. Strategy

At the beginning of every strategy project, it was indispensable for all participants to be aware of the normative management level. At Schindler, those visions, values, mission and midterm goals were documented in the so-called Navigator Book. It proved to be very helpful to remind all participants of these long-term goals in order to get them into the „strategy mood".

2. Goals

In accordance with this top-level strategy, all participating managers had to agree upon the goals of the core competency project. It was extremely important to communicate the goals and potential outcomes of a strategy project as early as possible. Otherwise, the input of the participants could have been greatly biased by self-interest and department thinking.

Furthermore, the early communication of the goals of the project helped to lay the grounds for subsequent actions and implementation.

3. Analysis of Actual Projects

An analysis of actual projects helped to identify the key persons in R&D that should have been involved in the strategy process. A list of the current projects represented the actual allocation of the R&D budget. From this analysis, current as well as future competencies were to be derived. Further issues that should have been examined at this point were:

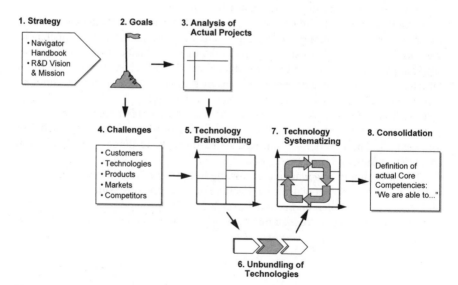

Fig. V.3.5. One day workshop: core competence identification.

- What development activities were external?
- Why were they outsourced?
- Who was the gatekeeper of the project?

4. Challenges

Step 4 and 5 were usually organized as brainstorming sessions because they profited from a multidisciplinary perspective.

In this step, the technological challenges that confronted the company were discussed with participants from R&D, manufacturing, marketing and top management. Based on Porter's scheme of the five forces of competition, all major areas of external influence were analyzed. The exploration of the strategic environment of R&D included competitors, customers, suppliers, new entrants, and substitute technologies. All relevant changes that were expected to take place within the next

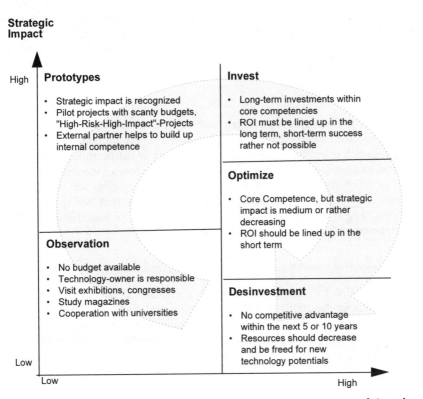

Fig. V.3.6. Portfolio of technical competencies in 1998.

five to ten years were considered from an interdisciplinary perspective. It was therefore essential to invite technological gatekeepers who entertained close relationships with external information sources such as suppliers or the science community.

Furthermore it was helpful to present the latest information from competitor analysis prior to this workshop.

5. Technology Brainstorming

In step 5 the participants sought technological competencies which provided answers to the identified challenges. These technologies and skills were then organized into a portfolio of technical competencies (see Fig. V.3.7). The participants of the workshop should have reached consensus on the position of every competence in this portfolio. It was therefore extremely important to understand the significance of the two dimensions of the portfolio correctly. The vertical axis reflected the strategic impact of a technical competence: long-term importance of the technology or skill, its contribution to meeting the challenges were previously defined. The horizontal axis reflected the internal perspective of resources: the company's technical resources such as patents, know-how, infrastructure, human resources and experience were considered and evaluated relative to competition. The resource axis also represented the availability of a technology for the company and its internal strength.

6. Unbundling of Technologies

When certain technologies were overly abstract (i.e. software technologies) they had to be specified more clearly (i.e. object oriented programming, UML, C++). This step therefore made sure that all competencies in the portfolio were on the same level of aggregation. Abstract or redundant competencies were eliminated.

As Fig. V.3.6 shows, the portfolio of technical competencies was divided into five fields denoting the norm strategies for observation, prototyping, investing, optimizing, and divestment. As depicted by the arrow, technical competencies were supposed to follow a 'natural' lifecycle.

7. Technology Systematizing

At this step, a first version of the technology portfolio was completed. Usually, it represented rather the status quo of the technological competencies of the company. Therefore it was the goal of this step to revise the position regarding where it should be in 3-5 years. This future perspective therefore might require input from forecasting such as technology and product roadmaps.

8. Consolidation

The last and most demanding step was the definition of core competencies. The goal was to find all technologies and skills belonging to the same core competence

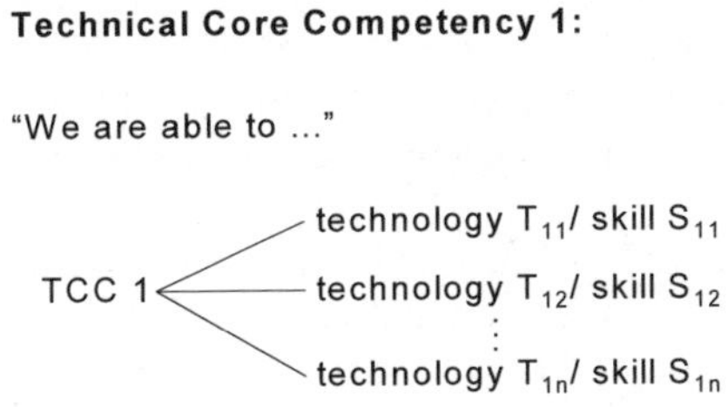

Technical Core Competency 1:

"We are able to ..."

$$\text{TCC 1} \Bigg\langle \begin{array}{l} \text{technology } T_{11}/ \text{ skill } S_{11} \\ \text{technology } T_{12}/ \text{ skill } S_{12} \\ \quad \vdots \\ \text{technology } T_{1n}/ \text{ skill } S_{1n} \end{array}$$

Fig. V.3.7. Definition of a technical core competence.

and to describe them coherently. Moreover it had to be made sure that the following criteria were met by every technical core competence (Prahalad and Hamel, 1990):

- Does it create customer benefit?
- Is it difficult to imitate and therefore build barriers to competitor entrants?
- Does it provide potential for application and exploitation in new products?

It was obvious from these criteria that the technologies and skills which defined technical core competencies were mainly located in the upper right-hand corner of the portfolio, which was characterized by high strategic impact and a high level of internal resources. The competencies had to be defined both verbally and in terms of the relevant technologies and skills that belonged to the particular technical core competence (Fig.V.3.7).

In order to avoid 'paralysis through analysis,' every core competence analysis had to lead to actions. At Schindler the core competence project led to:

- Rethinking of existing road maps and resource allocation;
- A major reorganization in order to concentrate R&D resources and eliminate overlapping competencies in several R&D locations;
- An action plan in the human resource area in order to develop future skills.

The core competence project led to a very positive impact on efficiency and effectiveness of Corporate R&D. But competencies had to be refined, updated and further developed. It was an ongoing process. Therefore the project was just a start into a more systematic technology management.

5   Technology Management as an Ongoing Process

Technology management was not just a one-time project but rather an ongoing process. Schindler therefore established technology management (TM) in a competence center. This center combined the two traditional departments Advanced Development (R&D-AD) and Competitor Technical Observation (CTO), along with what was known as strategic technology management. The mission of TM was 'the integrated management of new technologies for the maximum benefit of the Schindler Corporation.' More precisely, Schindler's Technology Management (TM) was responsible for the following tasks (Fig. V.3.8)

Advanced development: The competence center R&D Technology Management aimed at quantum leap developments in elevators through new radical approaches. New product concepts were defined and studies showed the feasibility of such concepts. Examples of former studies and prototypes were a new elevator control generation (destination control Miconic 10), radical new drive concepts and breakthroughs in safety systems. Multimedia as well as the integration of information and transport systems created new functionalities; an elevator would not be restricted to the basic requirement of vertical transportation.

Advanced development was undertaken in very close cooperation with universities and external technology leaders in clearly defined areas. A highly skilled team was developing totally new concepts and prototypes for vertical mobility. Active ride control systems, touch-free destination control, use of intelligent materials and radical new drive concepts were developed here, leading a trend to multi-car-systems, where several independently controlled cabins moved in an integrated shaft system vertically and horizontally.

Technology & industry monitoring: Technology Management promoted systematic scanning and evaluation of new technologies which arose in other industries (i.e. automobile, aircraft and computer). According to the 'cherry-picking-principle,' Technology Management evaluated new technologies in terms of their applicability to elevators and escalators. In times of scarce R&D resources, Schindler did not want to re-invent the wheel. According to the core competence philosophy, Schindler was increasingly engaged in strategic technology alliances with suppliers who were technology leaders in their fields.

Competitor technical intelligence: Technology Management identified technological activities of competitors. The main competitors like Otis, Kone, Mitsubishi, Hitachi and ThyssenKrupp were observed on a regular base. So-called weak signals were identified with a systematic analysis of patents and publications. In order to stay technology leader in the elevator and escalator field Corporate R&D had to plan and develop new products proactively.

Knowledge management: 'If Schindler only knew what Schindler knows.' Information flow and the knowledge base of people had to be optimized. The goal of Technology Management was the development of organizational learning at

---

Most important drives for globalization:

1. Acquisition of elevator and escalator companies lead to foreign R&D sites;

2. Customer orientation in innovation process, fast shifting of market focus;

3. Country specific regulations and standards in elevator business;

4. Effective IT-infrastructure as enabler.

Schindler's R&D. One person within the competence center was responsible for knowledge management. Several state-of-the-art methods and instruments were used in order to make knowledge management operational: knowledge maps, who-is-who lists and gatekeeper meetings. Gatekeepers in R&D teams were identified and brought together in interdisciplinary technology forums. Know how only travels with heads!

Core competencies: Technology Management was responsible for updating and developing technical competencies and technology portfolios in close cooperation with the development centers. This way Technology Management also promoted the deployment of core competencies in the R&D organization and the development of skills in accordance with the human resource department. The above described core competence identification was not just one project, but an ongoing process.

Technology Liaison Officer: Schindler's Corporate R&D had become more concentrated with the reorganization in 1998. Yet, the problem of coordinating the R&D sites in the USA (Morristown, Randolph and Gettysburgh) and the central R&D unit in Ebikon (CH) remained. As Japanese companies had successfully demonstrated, a Technology Liaison Officer can fulfill an important interface role. At Schindler, this contact person fully belonged and reported to the competence center TM in Ebikon, but was located in Morristown. The first experience had been very good: Operational work and transatlantic projects had been significantly improved.

Benchmarking, R&D tools: Schindler's R&D compared itself with world-class R&D in leading technology intensive companies such as ABB, Electrolux, Bühler,

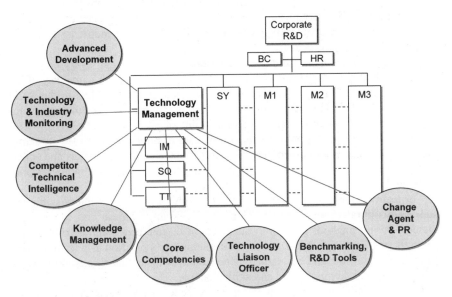

Fig. V.3.8. Technology Management as a new competence center.

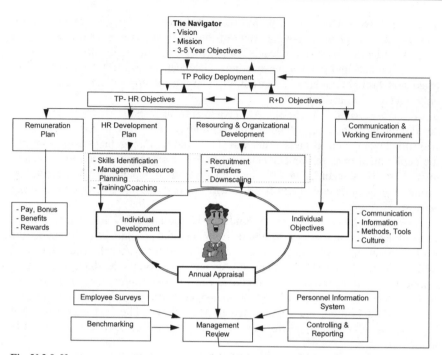

Fig. V.3.9. Human resource management model of Schindler's R&D in 1998.

Leica and Hilti. Technology Management promoted learning from 'best practice' across industries in order to improve its R&D organization, processes and tools. The experience of benchmarking with companies from other industries had been very good.

Change agent & public relations: According to 3M's model, every employee should think about new technologies and radical innovations for some part of his time. This time was not booked on running projects and not tracked in the R&D controlling system. This required cultural change! Internally, Technology Management acted as a change agent to open the mind of every R&D employee.

Externally, Technology Management took care of public relations for attracting the best graduates from universities. Through contacts with universities and scientific publications, Schindler wanted to be clearly identified as a technology leader in its field.

The team of Technology Management was highly skilled, very interdisciplinary and multicultural (Swiss, French, German, Egyptian, Chinese and Malaysian). State-of-the-art methods given into the hands of these creative and diverse people strengthened Corporate R&D and therefore Schindler's position as a leading company in the elevator and escalator business. It was clear that this could only be achieved with highly motivated and skilled people.

First experience with the new competence center R&D Technology Manage-

---

> **Lessons learned for organizing R&D in Schindler:**
>
> 1. Business and market orientation of R&D;
> 2. Competence-based R&D network with clear concentration of R&D resources in order to maintain critical mass for new technologies;
> 3. Definition of clear technical interfaces are reflected by R&D organizational interfaces;
> 4. Strong focus on system management as an organizational R&D unit.

ment had been very good. Several breakthrough developments have been made; the market feedback so far was excellent. The combination of creative chaos and systematic planning led to a successful management of new technologies. According to a former study of the benchmark center TECTEM at the University of St. Gallen, Schindler was best-in-class in strategic technology management.[64]

6 Managing Human Resources in R&D

People are the most important asset in the product creation process. New technologies can be purchased in, but the skills to develop new technologies are difficult to source. The critical know how of an organization is mostly based on key people. Know-how travels with heads. A long-term commitment to the employees is required.

The human resource management model for technology & production (TP) was an attempt to consider this requirement. It was clearly characterized by an object-oriented incentive system. Fig. V.3.9 gives a short overview on the overall human resource process in 1998.

Because of the importance of the human skills much attention was spent on managing the human resource. Substantial efforts were undertaken in technical training and personal development. As outlined in the R&D mission, state-of-the-art tools and excellent working environments should make Schindler's R&D an attractive place for young engineers.

Dual career ladders and empowerment of development teams made project work more attractive. Project managers became more important. Instead of narrow chimney careers Schindler promoted cross-functional experience. The career web showed a typical path of a high-potential, who started in R&D and then gained experience in different areas like sales, finance, new installations and regional management. The whole career web was well adjusted to the core competencies of the individual (Fig.V.3.10).

---

[64] Other companies awarded this recognition were Ford, 3M, Bosch, Canon, NEC, Phonak Semiconductors, and ABB, based on a survey covering 400 companies worldwide with strategic technology management practices.

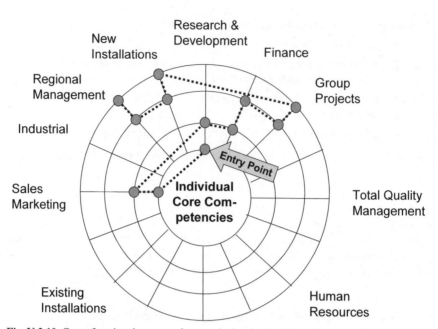

Fig. V.3.10. Cross-functional career web – a typical path of a high potential employee.

7   Conclusions

The trends in the elevator industry were characterized by a stronger customer focus, increasing market globalization, global competition and shorter innovation cycles. Since the elevator industry had been quite stable in the last 100 years, leap frogging and a series of breakthrough innovations were expected for the next coming years. The merge of telecommunication, computer and entertainment (multimedia) and the increasing integration of information and transport systems would have an impact on the elevator industry. Moreover the building interfaces would undergo further standardization and the complete "building and elevator system" would gain importance. High speed and high rise machine-room-less elevators with double deck cabins and touch-free individual destination control were challenging the leading elevator companies. R&D was thinking of integrated multifunctional transport systems where several cars would be moving independently in vertical and horizontal integrated shaft systems (multi-mobile).

These trends became even more challenging as pressure for cost reduction continued and high quality and reliability had to be maintained. These trends required a concentration on the core competencies. The selling of Schindler's wagon business to Adtrans in 1997 had been a consequent step. Corporate R&D would even more concentrate its scarce resources on those fields where competitive advantages could be created. Other peripheral activities were outsourced. The geographic concentration on less R&D locations went in the same direction.

New, innovative and cost competitive product solutions could be achieved with Schindler's new R&D organization. Investments in IT infrastructure such as groupware and product data management was the basis for efficient innovation processes. Yet, as every R&D manager knew, doing things right was not enough - doing the right things was equally important. Projects on new technologies and products had to be carefully selected. The project portfolio kept the balance between well defined product improvements and high-risk-high-impact projects.

With the establishment of Technology Management as a competence center, strategic planning and organization of new technologies could be done more efficient and effective. The outlined technological challenges in the elevator industry could be met best by such an integrated technology management. The strict concentration on core competencies would be maintained and even enforced within Corporate R&D. Knowledge management would change Schindler into a dynamic learning organization. Competitor technology intelligence ensured external orientation of the innovation process. Technology Management as a change agent was the main driver of cultural change and for the integration of decentralized sites. Continuous benchmarking of R&D processes in other industries kept Schindler's R&D in steady improvement.

V.4 Hitachi: Management Practices for Innovation in Global Industrial Research*

1 Three Major Issues for Global R&D

Global collaborative research is now the well-recognized, common and definite necessity among high-technology industries world-wide, because of the following reasons. First of all, the rapidly changing advanced technologies require all participants to be constantly prepared to be competitive at the front-end of such new technologies. High-technology industries must always face the serious issue of continuous huge investment in R&D in the very competitive technology area, in order to survive and especially in order to extend and strengthen their business in the future. This is, however, becoming quite harsh for many industrial companies, who are experiencing great pressure after the breakdown of the bubble economy. In the case of Hitachi, approximately US$ 4.1 billion (consolidated figure; assuming US$ 1 = 124 Yen,) were invested in R&D during the fiscal year 1996 while the sales were US$ 68.7 billion. R&D was about 6% of consolidated sales of Hitachi Limited. However, in this period, profit percentage was much less than the R&D percentage. In 2005 and 2006, around 4.5% of consolidated sales were invested in R&D within the Hitachi Group. In the future, since competition will be more severe and advancement in technologies will become faster, it is possible that investment in R&D will become more important for the survival of industrial companies, even though their profit rate may remain small like today.

Secondly, the social role and responsibility Standards of industrial companies is inevitably becoming more global, because the problems to be solved in the society are rapidly becoming more complex and global. Industries must provide solutions to such complex issues in the global society either by direct endeavors or by sharing created values, such as patents. More and more, the issue to be solved are global in nature, ranging in such areas as environment, energy, health-care, new-media, consumer goods, transportation, telecommunications, as well as new means for sharing intellectual property.

---

*   This case study was authored by *Dr. Yutaka Kuwahara,* General Manager Research and Development, Hitachi Europe Ltd., Maidenhead, Berkshire, United Kingdom in 1998. The case study was revised with the support of *Mr. Hirose, Dr. Abe,* and *Karin Löffler.*

Major issues for global R&D management at Hitachi:

1. Synergy in multi-dimensions;
2. Be prepared at competitive front-end of R&D;
3. Social role and responsibility becomes more global;
4. World-wide standardisation of specifications and protocols.

Thirdly, for the benefit of both customers and vendors, it is becoming more common to standardize the specifications and protocols world-wide, especially those facing the customer, not only in consumer products but also in telecommunications and in the software industry. This is achieved by various world-wide consortia among key concerned vendors or users in the related technology area, to make new proposals for „de-facto" world standards of the new product or new system. This new style of global team-work is rapidly spreading in all technology areas. Among them, those in telecommunications and multimedia are virtually leading the world.

2   New Innovation Processes for Global R&D

Considering the above key issues in the globalization of today's and future industrial R&D, innovation processes are determined mainly by five dominant factors. As Peter F Drucker says in his „Managing for the Future", „technological streams no longer run parallel, and they increasingly cross each other, with frequent spillovers from one to the other." He suggests the simultaneous interactions among various concerned technologies and related issues. Concretely, the new innovation processes considering such „synergistic" interactions among various concerned parameters was proposed by Dr. Y. Takeda, now Senior Executive Managing Director, of Hitachi, and was discussed with his staff including the author of this paper.

The five key factors are as described in Fig. V.4.1:

- Trans-sectors: close and simultaneously existing inter-relationship among industry, academia, government;
- Trans-disciplines: hardware, software, human ware concurrently integrated into the same product or system;
- Concurrent management in a high-tech industrial company: R&D, manufacturing, design, marketing, sales simultaneously involved in the same strategic product development project team;
- Global society;
- Global culture.

In Fig. V.4.1, three steps of progress in relationship to the above five factors can be seen. In each factor, more and more „synergy" interaction is becoming the key. In order achieve such „synergy" for innovation, covering five dominant factors, it is natural that industries enhance more R&D collaboration on a global scale. This enables sharing of risk and resources with other industries, academia and governments. Accordingly, Hitachi has been enhancing such „synergistic" global R&D collaborations with organizations world-wide.

3   New Directions in Hitachi's R&D

3.1   Basic Philosophy of R&D for Innovation - Odaira Spirit

Since the establishment of Hitachi in 1910, the company has always put importance in establishing its identifiable technologies, by creating its own technologies without assimilating other imported technologies. This, in turn is extremely important for global technology alliance or global collaboration, because „give and take" is the base of such global partnership, and no partner would like to co-operate with the other party having no „identifiable" technology. Mutual trust, as the basis of partnership, will essentially occur only when there are high quality & high level technologies on both sides.

Creation of such original technology was especially stressed by the first president and founder of the company, Mr. Namihei Odaira, who proposed and established the Central Research Laboratory in 1942, with only about 20 researchers, expecting that it would create trunk-line key technologies in 30, 50 or 100 years in the future. The year 1942 was a year after the outbreak of the Pacific War and the country was totally in confusion; therefore people could think only of that year or at best a few years in the future. However, Mr. Odaira wrote a proverb in 1930 which reads literally „although a human being can live less than one hundred years, we have to be concerned with 1,000 years hence". This „Odaira" spirit has

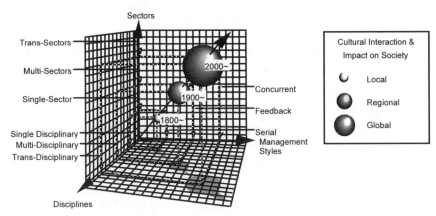

Fig. V.4.1. Innovation processes in five dimensions.

Most important drivers for globalization:

1. Global business;
2. Major innovation through partnering.

---

been the basis of R&D for more than 65 years in Hitachi and is still now highly respected and is faithfully observed. Moreover, this spirit is the most crucial backbone of the globalization of R&D.

3.2   Key Strategy Features for Innovative Global R&D: Balanced and Strategic Resource Allocation

In line with the above „Odaira" spirit for creating original technology, as the basis of global partnership, the following key features in management for innovation have been devised and implemented:

*   Balanced and strategic resource allocation;
*   Strategic Business Projects;
*   Semi-autonomous distributed organization.

A balanced and strategic resource allocation is concerned with the following four issues.

Effective Allocation of Resources

Investment in R&D has gradually increased year by year. During the 90ies it was about 9% of sales. This figure is the overall average in non-consolidated Hitachi; therefore, in high technology areas such as semiconductors, computers, telecommunications, the ratio is much higher than this average percentage, reaching 15-20%. Ten years before, these figures were about half. Since 1993 the figures have not been increasing, showing the saturation of the R&D investment ratio. This concept is important in pursuing various projects around the world simultaneously, and later on combining into a more strategic commercial product.

Four Layers of Research

Among the R&D resources, at present more than 80% represents product development performed at business group development centers, while less than 20% is performed at seven corporate research laboratories. In corporate research laboratories, half of the research is „commissioned" or „sponsored" research, and the remaining half is „corporate" research or „Objective Fundamental Research" (OFR). About 1% of R&D is oriented to „far-future" research which is called „North Star Research (NSR)". The NSR is naturally a part of „corporate" research.

Spiral Migration of Research Types

These four layers of research - NSR, corporate research (OFR), commissioned research and product development - are connected by a multiple tree-like projects scheme, so that the very first tiny seed of a new concept will spirally grow into the final trunk-line technology many years later, and finally into the commercial product.

Government Support

Today, about 90% of R&D financing is obtained from the company's own money. About 10% of the funding comes from the Japanese government, such as NEDO projects, or from EU Funds via EU projects. The government funds are used for very long-term future-oriented research, such as future energy sources, exploration of human brain mechanism, environmental issues, health-care technology, atomic and quantum device technology or high temperature superconducting technology.

3.3 Key Strategy Features for Innovative Global R&D: Strategic Business Project (SBP)

About 20% of total R&D resources are put into the SBP, which is the scheme to carry out both strategically important product development and assessment of emerging new technology which will be a major impact on business in the future. (Fig. V.4.2) The former is proposed and led by the business group and the latter is led by the research laboratory, while both include all the key related people from manufacturing, design, marketing, sales, and corporate planning group. Selected members of the Corporate R&D Planning Office perform a key role in the basic planning and co-ordination of the SBP. One SBP will involve 50 to 150 personnel, and will continue, on average, 6 months to two years. It is given high priority in getting the necessary investment and any other necessary issues. Accordingly, the result is presented and discussed at board member meetings. This mechanism is very important to transfer the technology from one research group of global R&D to strategic commercialization.

3.4 Key Strategy Features For Innovative Global R&D: Semi-autonomous Distributed Organization

In 1995, the company re-structured itself into five major business groups which can contain business activities from R&D to sales. These are: Power & Industrial Systems & Equipment Group, Computer & Telecommunications Group, Electronic Device Group, Consumer Products & Information & Image System Group, and Automotive Products & Instrument Group. In 2001, the Design Center becomes the Design Group, placed directly under the president. The first four business groups have development centers which are responsible for business-oriented product development for their specific business area. (Fig. V.4.3)

In addition to them, there are six corporate research laboratories. These are:

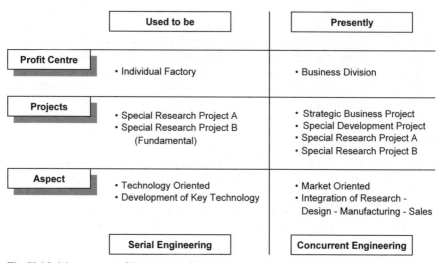

Fig. V.4.2. Management of Strategic Business Projects (SBP).

Central Research Laboratory, Hitachi Research Laboratory, Mechanical Engineering Research Laboratory, Production Engineering Research Laboratory, Systems Development Laboratory, and Advanced Research Laboratory. Each research laboratory has its own technological area of responsibility which it pursues for imminent development to long term future research. However the distribution of them differs from laboratory to laboratory. In an extreme case, Advanced Research Laboratory pursues only corporate research (OFR), including North Star Research. (The overall distribution was already described in the resource allocation section.) There are about 3,000 researchers in these laboratories. In the business groups there are many development centers, with about 9,000 engineers and researchers.

In addition to the said six corporate domestic research laboratories, there are five corporate research laboratories outside Japan. These are the European R&D Center at Hitachi Europe Ltd., Hitachi America Ltd., Hitachi GST Inc. (San Jose Research Center), Hitachi Asia Ltd. and the Hitachi China Research and Development Corporation. The European R&D Center started with focus on new computer technology and industrial design, in the United States Hitachi R&D started with new-media technology and semiconductor devices. Over the years, the research topics have changed according to Hitachi's research plans. Today, Hitachi conducts research on future-oriented semiconductor or quantum devices, Organic Electronics, Numerical Analysis, Mobile Communications, Security and Automotive Systems in Europe. The laboratories closely collaborate with European research organizations. In the United States, research on the practical development of automotive components, advanced wireless systems, and storage area network solutions are performed by closely cooperating with the manufacturing sites in the US. The Hitachi GST conducts research on the next generation of HAD and on its

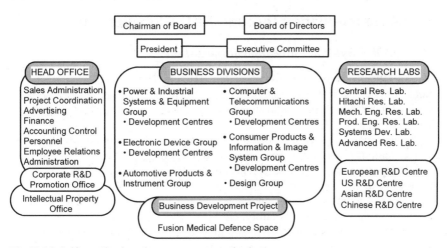

Fig. V.4.3. Self-contained semi-autonomous organization.

applications. The Hitachi Storage Mechanics Laboratory was founded in Hitachi Asia Ltd. in 2005 in Singapore. The laboratory is focusing on hard disc drives. The first Research Center in China was set up in 2000 under Hitachi (China) Ltd.. The Research Center was split-off independently in April 2005 as the first specialized company within Hitachi for R&D, named Hitachi (China) Research & Development Corporation. With its technologies, the company supports the entry to the Chinese market. In 2006, the Digital Appliance Development Center at Hitachi China Research & Development Corporation was founded. With 80 researchers, the laboratory is conducting research on IP Networks, Digital TVs, and Innovative Software and Materials. In Beijing, Hitachi works on IP networks and cutting-edge software, in Shanghai on digital TV and home networks.

The restructuring did not change the total R&D resource. What happened was the application of the more distinct definition and practice of four layers of R&D at the most suitable sites. This new style of organization has clearly strengthened the more product-oriented development layer, so that such strategic development can be accelerated.

Two research centers in Europe and USA continued to operate in the same strategy as originally planned and established in 1989. Since these two overseas research centers were set up with a full global perspective in mind, they are actually showing the right direction of industrial global laboratories and becoming the leading example which domestic R&D units must follow.

4   More Innovation through R&D Globalization

4.1   HIVIPS System - Internal Globalization

In 1984 Hitachi devised a program called HIVIPS (Hitachi Research Visit Programs, a system to invite foreign researchers to Hitachi's Japanese research laboratories for periods from several months to a few years) at Hitachi's Central Research Laboratory (HCRL).

The main purpose was to realize real „synergy" for innovation, through heterogeneous cultural interactions, to create new technology, by assigning the most capable Japanese and foreign researchers to the same projects. HIVIPS was gradually expanded into the whole company scheme involving all corporate research laboratories, Central Research Laboratory, Hitachi Research Laboratory, Mechanical Engineering Research Laboratory, etc.

Foreign researchers were specifically invited, through various channels including universities, government and private companies, to Hitachi's corporate research laboratories in Japan, by reimbursing the whole expenses incurred and giving them the same level of benefit that Hitachi's own researchers receive. This HIVIPS system has achieved enormous success and the number of foreign researchers has increased steadily year by year.

So far, more than 500 foreign researchers, who came from industrial research laboratories, universities and government research institutes, have stayed in Hitachi's corporate research laboratories in Japan, on average about one year per person. Roughly speaking, 35% came from the US, 40% came from Europe and the remaining 25% came from pacific-rim countries and other areas of the world. Quite a lot of HIVIPS graduates are still maintaining their good relationship with Hitachi.

In several important technology areas, innovative concepts were proposed and successfully assessed. Positive experience from HIVIPS gave new confidence in global R&D collaborations in a more extensive way. This 'internal globalization' indeed gave the firm confidence and belief that Hitachi could now actually advance in the direction of global R&D.

4.2   Global Research Collaboration

In parallel with HIVIPS, Hitachi has been promoting research collaboration with various institutes of the world. Partners have included industry, academia and government research laboratories in the areas of microelectronics, energy, telecommunications, medical electronics, neural networks, artificial intelligence, computer-aided design, production engineering technology, etc. (Fig. V.4.4).

Through the experience of these global research collaboration, the teams have found that heterogeneous interactions among researchers with different cultural and technological backgrounds, under certain conditions, can create more 'revolutionary' innovations than homogeneous ones, because they can discuss and analyze the matter from different aspects, deepening the level and increasing the quality of research. It is also true that most high potential research groups are distrib-

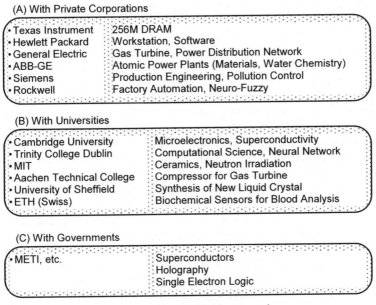

(A) With Private Corporations

• Texas Instrument	256M DRAM
• Hewlett Packard	Workstation, Software
• General Electric	Gas Turbine, Power Distribution Network
• ABB-GE	Atomic Power Plants (Materials, Water Chemistry)
• Siemens	Production Engineering, Pollution Control
• Rockwell	Factory Automation, Neuro-Fuzzy

(B) With Universities

• Cambridge University	Microelectronics, Superconductivity
• Trinity College Dublin	Computational Science, Neural Network
• MIT	Ceramics, Neutron Irradiation
• Aachen Technical College	Compressor for Gas Turbine
• University of Sheffield	Synthesis of New Liquid Crystal
• ETH (Swiss)	Biochemical Sensors for Blood Analysis

(C) With Governments

• METI, etc.	Superconductors
	Holography
	Single Electron Logic

Fig. V.4.4. Some examples of trans-sectoral global R&D cooperation.

uted world-wide, and it is quite unrealistic to try to perform research in a certain geographically confined small area, by collecting the most capable world researchers there. It is much more practical and sensible to do research in a high potential area on the globe in collaboration with a high quality research group, by mutually extending the best technologies, best knowledge and best people.

5 Establishing Corporate R&D Center Outside of Japan

Since the globalization of business naturally needed R&D to operate on a global scale, and since the technological challenges to the globally more complex needs requires the international team to overcome them, Hitachi seriously started the preparation of corporate R&D operation overseas, especially in Europe and the USA. In 1998, the team started visiting various science parks, universities and industries in Europe and USA, with the specific purpose of determining the R&D site, establishing laboratories and starting their operation.

5.1 Establishment of Hitachi's R&D in Europe and the US

Successful experiences with the HIVIPS system and various research collaborations with foreign research organizations have been made. This was the basis and backbone of the planning for the establishment of R&D centers in Europe. Through extensive discussion and surveillance, Hitachi concluded that the firm would start it's R&D operations rather differently in Europe than in the US. The reason is: In Europe, there were not enough of Hitachi's manufacturing operations at that time. Therefore Hitachi could pursue more fundamental research with universities, while in the US the firm could support the manufacturing operations by providing a development team in the closely related areas of technology.

However, it was exactly the very same „synergy" which led Hitachi to establish the research laboratories in Europe, in Cambridge, Dublin, etc. For example, in autumn of 1988, during a discussion with Professor Sir Sam Edwards, director of Cavendish Laboratory, Cambridge University, the Hitachi team found out that the Hitachi philosophy of global R&D from the standpoint of industrial research exactly coincided with the mind of Sir Sam Edwards in the new global collaboration from the academic standpoint. Both were most excited, optimistic and confident that „together we can achieve wonderful innovations". It was indeed „synergy".

Similar „synergy", for more practical technology, was experienced at Trinity College Dublin (TCD), involving Provost Watt of TCD and the Irish government. Thus, the R&D Center in Europe started, pursuing mainly fundamental research, at least in the starting stage, in collaboration with Cambridge University, Dublin University and European design institutes. While in the USA very near-future product development relating to actual manufacturing and business operations at nearby sites was started. However, in both research centers, it was planned that in the long future, both would grow into R&D centers with an appropriate balance of research and development projects.

In the Hitachi Cambridge Laboratory (HCL), the focus was on the future 'revolutionary' innovative semiconductor device. Research on quantum devices has been vigorously pursued, especially involving challenges such as use of the quantum „particle" nature of electrons, as well as ultra-high speed transmission of signals by using the probabilistic transmission of „quantum wave function".

Hitachi's Dublin Laboratory (HDL) was established within the campus of Trinity College Dublin, in the building of Innovation Center - TCD-industry collaborative incubation center - researching advanced computing, especially ultra-parallel computing, and advanced recognition, including opto-neural networking.

Both laboratories put great importance on the collaboration with universities, especially with on-site ones. HCL has been collaborating with the Microelectronics Research Center of the Cavendish Laboratory, Cambridge University, while HDL has been extending partnerships with Trinity College Dublin, Imperial College London and Oxford University.

Later on, in late 1989 and in 1990 two other locations were added to the research sites in Europe, to do innovative work on industrial design, using the „synergy" between Hitachi's technology and European design sensibility & useware, as well as the fusion of East and West cultures. This occurred at Munich in Germany and Milan in Italy.

5.2   Progress of Hitachi's European R&D Center

Since the establishment of the R&D Center of Hitachi Europe Ltd. in April 1989, with a total membership of less than 10 persons, R&D in Europe has gradually and steadily been strengthened to today's level of over 30 staff and over 40 collaborators. In total there are about 80 staff members in search of new frontiers of technology at the European research laboratories, located in four countries (UK, Ireland, Germany, France) with their headquarters in Maidenhead, UK.

Objectives of the R&D Center in Europe

Goals were set to create new concepts and new technologies which will open a new avenue for electronics industry in the future, by fostering and transforming such new technological concepts into actual trunk-line technologies or commercial products in the future - extending to even ten to twenty years - although the time frame is not necessarily restricted to the „only long-term" future. The research types are mainly „Objective Fundamental Research (OFR)", but also include „Applied Research", especially in the area of advanced computing and industrial design. The goals also include Hitachi's efforts to contribute to the progress of European technology and science as well as the identity as part of Hitachi.

At the same time Hitachi has envisaged that the collaboration with European research institutes and universities would be mutually complementary. Therefore, every careful consideration was taken so that the „reciprocity" and „mutual benefit" would be clearly felt and understood not only by both parties but also even from a third party in Europe. For example, special care was taken over intellectual property rights so that the benefit will be fairly shared. In fact, in the European R&D, patent rights obtained remain in Europe.

Present Status and Some Topics

Since the establishment of the R&D Center in Europe in 1989, about seventeen years have passed. During this period, the company has rather patiently pursued it's research consistently and vigorously on the focused key technology areas. Also, Hitachi has carefully chosen the direction of research concentrating on the most promising and competitive, but most difficult technologies.

In 1997, there are four research areas being pursued in the European R&D Center. The UK headquarters located in Maidenhead is responsible to centrally manage all of the R&D undertaken in Europe.

In Cambridge, the Hitachi Cambridge Laboratory (HCL) located on the campus of the Cavendish Laboratory of Cambridge University, has been researching quantum devices, such as „Single Electron Memory", „Single Electron Logic", and „Femto-second Ultra-high Speed Quantum Devices". This research is in synergistic collaboration with the Microelectronics Research Center (MRC) of the Cavendish Laboratory. In this collaboration, Hitachi is strong in measurement technology and device conceptualization, while MRC of Cambridge University is strong in physics, process concepts and technology. Both HCL and MRC are located in the same adjacent building, with their doors open to the partner, and discussions taking place every day involving both parties. Thus, quite complementary collaborative research is being performed.

In Cambridge, collaboration on high-performance computing started in 1996, in computational science & engineering, to explore and unveil the complicated and complex structure and mechanism of materials, fluid dynamics, atomic behavior, aero-dynamic noise, etc., by the effective use of high-performance computing. The collaboration included the Dublin Laboratory (HDL), domestic laboratories in Japan, and various departments at Cambridge University.

As the third major partnership with Cambridge University, in 1997, Hitachi started another a new collaboration in telecommunications by partnering with CCSR (Center for Communications Systems Research) of Cambridge University, in the area of „security of data on the network" such as „watermark", post-ATM, etc. Today, Hitachi Cambridge Laboratory focuses on Spintronics, Quantum Communications and Organic Electronics as well.

In Dublin, Ireland, Hitachi Dublin Laboratory (HDL), has been pursuing advanced computing and intelligence amplification. Research on advanced computing, especially high-performance computing including super-parallel computing, case-based reasoning and numerical computation. Intelligence amplification covers sign language interpretation system and neural networking, including optical neural networks. Today, Hitachi Dublin Laboratory is conducting research on numerical analysis. Collaborations are extended not only extended to Trinity College Dublin, but also to Cambridge University, Imperial College London, Oxford University and Sheffield University. Until today, neural network and case-based reasoning were transferred to Hitachi.

Presently, Hitachi Limited Europe is focusing on fundamental device physics, organic electronics, numerical analysis, mobile communications, security and automotive systems. Also, HDL has embarked on telecommunications research, such as network modeling and architecture.

The design team started its first work in Düsseldorf, Germany in December 1989, and soon added the Milan operation in 1990. However later on, the team moved the Düsseldorf operation to Munich and furthermore they merged the two operations and started unified HDCE (Hitachi Design Center Europe) in April of 1997. From the early stage of design operation in Europe, Hitachi had partnerships with European designers, especially with those in Munich and Milan. Indeed, the teams could achieve the most synergy between Hitachi's technology/design/culture at the European Design team with European design (useware)/beauty/culture.

With German partners in Munich, several projects involving the innovative industrial design of electric heavy industrial products, such as the high-speed train, medical systems, electron microscope, elevator/escalator, etc. have been carried out, while with Italian design partners in Milan, the design team pursued innovations in mobile, desk-top or interior-type information systems and equipment. Through such synergistic collaborative efforts, several new innovative designs were created, proposed and some accepted for commercialization. Hitachi's visual identity has been definitely refined and enriched in the global sense.

In April 1997, Hitachi started a new Virtual Laboratory named HETL (Hitachi European Telecommunication Laboratory). HETL has three research groups in Cambridge, UK, Sophia-Antipolis, France, and Dallas, USA. It is called a virtual laboratory, because HETL is the grouping of collaboration projects which are operated dynamically and can change in locations and partners in the future, although basically the present collaboration is expected to continue to be stable.

Cambridge team is doing collaboration with CCSR of Cambridge University, as explained above. Sophia-Antipolis group is collaborating with a telecommunication research laboratory as a member of a European consortium, in order to participate in determining the „de-facto" standard of new architecture for future telecommunication systems. The Dallas group is involved in the actual development of the required software for high-speed optical systems to be installed at telecommunication carriers.

In October 2005, the Automotive R&D Laboratory has been established in Europe, with laboratories in Munich and Paris. The team designs complex mechatronics control systems for motor cars. The European team collaborates with the Automotive Products Research Laboratory (APL) which was set up in 1989 in the USA. As the previous examples, the APL, based in automotive clusters, shows how Hitachi makes use of the special regional characteristics of the overseas research centers.

6 Examples of Innovations Achieved in European R&D Center

6.1 Promising Devices for the 21st century

Single Electron Memory

In February of 1993, Hitachi Cambridge Laboratory (HCL) succeeded in the demonstration of the world's first „Single Electron Memory", a most promising future semiconductor device in the 21st century, especially in 'tera-bit' or more scale LSI chip age. Although the operating temperature at that time was very low (milli-Kelvin order), the physics principle clearly indicated that the operating temperature will naturally increase, eventually to room temperature, as the size of nano-fabrication advances into the more atomic scale. Indeed, in 1995, the team could observe the Coulomb Blockade phenomenon, which is the basis of „Single Electron Memory", at higher temperature.

It is well accepted that the present semiconductor industry will face deadlock in the early part of the 21st century because of the possible quantum fluctuations effect naturally occurring in too miniaturized scale devices and the difficulty of decreasing the current in a giga- or tera- scale chip. (Fig. V.4.5) the „Single Electron Memory" concept is the memory device consisting of „bits", each of which consists of a small number of electrons, such as 100 electrons, and the flow of electrons into and out of the bit is controlled „one by one".

This Single Electron Memory unit cell was implemented and successfully dem-

Major innovative break-throughs at Hitachi (last five years):

1. B-H (Buried hetero) laser;

2. Super TFT;

3. Single electron memory;

4. IAP (Integrated array processor).

onstrated by the HCL research team in collaboration with the University of Cambridge, Microelectronics Research Center of the Cavendish Laboratory. The control mechanism became possible by using the „Coulomb Blockade" phenomenon, which was proposed by Prof. Rikharev of Moscow State University in 1986.

The breakthrough by the HCL team opened the avenue for future semiconductor industry. Especially in the year around 2010 or later, 16 gigabit or larger scale DRAM will be needed in order to cope with the ever-increasing needs of computer memory, as much as the human brain, for many multimedia applications such as virtual reality on lap-top PCs. (Fig. V.4.6)

The success of this breakthrough came from the tight team work between HCL and MRC. That is, a new „Single Electron Memory" concept was proposed by HCL researchers and was discussed at the weekly collaboration meeting with MRC staff. This frank and serious discussion was one of the most important parts of the collaboration. The experimental memory unit cell was implemented using the fabrication process of MRC. And then, the cell was tested at HCL at mili-Kelvin temperature to confirm the essential characteristics of a memory cell unit - observation of controlling the flow of electrons one by one. This whole cycle was

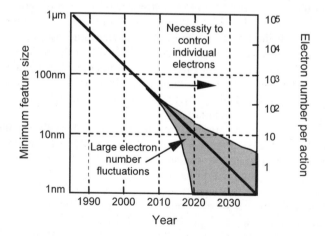

Fig. V.4.5. Operation limit of conventional semiconductor devices.

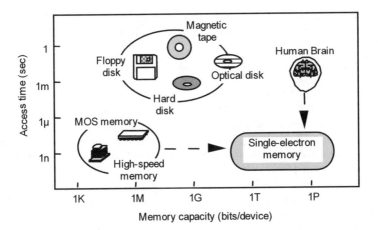

Fig. V.4.6. Memory devices.

repeated several times until the targeted observation was obtained. It is a great tribute to the collaboration that the research team could complete such a new device proposal cycle quite quickly, much faster than in the rather elaborate cycle of the own domestic research laboratory.

Quite possibly, this new concept and new technology could not have been proposed and demonstrated so quickly if Hitachi and Cambridge University had pursued this separately. It was indeed the „synergy" which made the whole stage of this challenge progress speedily and deepened discussion.

Since the first successful demonstration in February 1993, research on single-electronics has risen tremendously. Now, in many international conferences, such as IEDM (International Electron device meeting), single-electronics is an important topic and has been discussed at some sessions.

A European government project FASEM (FASEM=Fabrication and Architecture of Single Electron memory) has started in January of 1997, as a three year project, in a consortium of eight European research organizations including the HCL.

The Japanese project „Single Electron Logic" funded by MITI (Ministry of International Trade and Industry, today "METI")/NEDO started in April of 1995 as a six year project with the HCL, targeting the demonstration of the logic at 77K by the end of the project duration.

The world-wide attention has increased tremendously in recent few years, and Mr. Bill Gates has heightened this awareness by writing in his best-seller book „Road Ahead" that a single electron transistor will be a promising future semiconductor device.

It should also be noted that a new device concept for „Single Electron Memory" gave a wonderful hint of near-future „giga-scale" semiconductor devices which will come into market in the foreseeable future. HCL has proposed such innovative devices which are much more advantageous, having a simple flat structure, simple processes, higher reliability, and overcoming many difficulties of devices proposed as the extension of conventional 'mega-scale' LSI devices.

Femto-Second Ultra-Fast Quantum Device

Femto-second ultra-fast quantum device is the challenge of using the „wave" nature of an electron, to achieve future ultra fast switching devices for both high-end telecommunication and ultra-fast computing in the 21st century – an integrated information network age. This challenge requires extremely demanding and disciplined patience in accumulation of repetitive experimentation using extremely accurately controlled laser systems.

In August of 1995, the team of HCL, however, could succeed in creating and demonstrating the coherent „Femto-second" pulses, by the innovative scheme named „Coherent Destruction" and „Coherent Construction". Here again the „synergy" between the Hitachi team and Cambridge University was a key. European ESPRIT network named „Phantoms" has invited the HCL team for future mutual research communication.

6.2   Key Technologies for Advanced Computing

Opto-Neural Network: Optical Neural Network

Neural network is very useful for a future human brain-like computer system - for computers which learn by experience rather than by memorizing. However, rather slow interconnections among neurons have been the problem to be overcome, in order to accelerate the real application of neural network to important computing or advanced perception. Parallel optical interconnection paved the way to solve this problem by increasing the speed of the inter-communication of many neurons to the speed of light.

In HDL, collaboration with the Physics Department of Trinity College Dublin (TCD) has started right from the beginning of the laboratory in 1989. TCD's strength in opto-electronics well complemented HDL's high technology in neural networks. Some possible applications of optical neural networks are intelligent retina to keep track of the objects even in the hidden area. Future intelligent robots will be able to implement such artificial retina.

Middle Software

In high-performance computing, „middle software" is becoming more and more important for customers, and so for vendors, as the most strategic competitive products. „Middle software" will effectively extract and use the parallelism of the computer and operate the customers' application programs most efficiently at the machine (computer), regardless of the difference of the vendors.

Since „middleware" is a sort of „de-facto" standard, and the specifications are discussed and determined at regularly held international forums, this kind of R&D is more suitable at the European laboratory, especially HDL, rather than at the domestic laboratory in Japan. Therefore, Hitachi focused the research efforts on this software, such as Message Passing Interface (MPI), by attending and contributing to the „MPI Forum", as well as participating in the important EUROPEAN consortium in high-performance computing applications, such as HIRLAM - a European consortium for weather forecast modeling and simulation, and in medical computing applications, data mining, etc.

The teams succeeded in receiving very competitive MPI software to be installed in the high-performance computer and to be installed at the customers' including European sites. The success comes from the competitiveness of the team in HDL, in high quality technology, speedy R&D, and efficient new challenge.

New Concepts in Industrial Design

In the world of industrial design, Europe is exceeding in various aspects. For example, Italy is excellent in its historically renowned sense of art. This is why Milan was chosen as the Hitachi's unified central design research sites in Europe. Partnerships with a German designer in Munich were also another important aspect for Hitachi products.

In Milan, collaboration with Italian design houses has been successfully performed to create various new visual identities for Hitachi's information systems, such as information servers, workstations and mobile information systems. In collaboration with the Italian partner, the design team has received „G-Mark" recognition from the Japanese Government (METI) for four years consecutively until 1996. On the other hand, the collaboration with the German design partner, challenged the innovative designs in electric heavy industrial products such as elevators, escalators, high-speed trains (Shinkansen), medical equipment, such as MRI or blood analyzer, and scientific instruments like electron microscopes, resulting in various successes including two Minister of METI awards in 1997, in the design of Shinkansen and TEM (Transmission Electron Microscope).

More Usable Electron Microscope

In the past, Hitachi's electron microscope was nicknamed „Awaodori" style, a somewhat derogatory expression, because of its too many adjusting screws and buttons. A user must use his two hand and two feet, stretched completely, and adjust simultaneously. It means quite user-unfriendly.

In the design team, the concept of electron microscope was discussed and new proposal for completely 'user-friendly' interface and style was proposed. It was indeed fortunate that the key manager of the business group accepted it „100%."

More Attractive and Comfortable High Speed Train

Design of train systems has been done for almost eight years in the Hitachi design center team. Proposals on new Tokkyuu and Shinkansen were done by the Hitachi team and were accepted, although there were various modifications until they were actually produced and running on the railroads. Designers have always discussed from the standpoint of what is the best design of mass transportation system running with high speed in the urban area, fields, forests, across the rivers, through tunnels, etc. Considerations were severely done for the harmony and acceptance of environment and people.

It is a wonder that the design proposed from such professional industrial design standpoint well matched to the computer simulation using a super-computer system.

7   Management of Global R&D as Practiced in European R&D

The author has been involved in general management of the European R&D Center. He was also responsible for establishing the R&D laboratories in Europe and has experience in solving some difficulties occurred in the early stages of operation. Based on this experience, some concrete management systems as applied effectively to the promotion of innovation and the underlying special features will be explained.

7.1   Special Features of the European R&D Center

The R&D Center was established as a sort of test case for future industrial laboratories in the global arena. So, it is quite natural that there are various essential differences from domestic research laboratories. The special features below are quite unique to Hitachi, especially to those who are accustomed to the domestic corporate research laboratories.

Organization

Organizationally, the R&D Center is one division of Hitachi's European representative company HEL (Hitachi Europe Limited) whose headquarters is located in Maidenhead city, UK. The R&D Center has its headquarters at HEL headquarters in Maidenhead, and its laboratories are located in geographically distributed locations - Cambridge, Dublin, Milan, Sophia-Antipolis, Munich and Paris. Although research laboratories are situated at distributed locations, the management is centralized. At Maidenhead, a general manager is working to manage the whole organization, together with his staff - manager of strategic planning group, an administrator, and a secretary.

In each laboratory, the laboratory manager is in charge of the management, in addition to main responsibility of conducting actual research. That is, each laboratory manager is a „playing manager". Each Laboratory consists of one laboratory manager, one secretary and researchers or designers. In HCL and HDL, there are group leaders who manage the specific research group such as single electronics, Femto-second device, or high-performance computing. Today, Hitachi Europe Limited has it's own Corporate Technology Group.

Researchers

Researchers were recruited mainly through job advertisements, through newspapers, professional magazines, the Internet and through the private human network. Fortunately, more than 100 applicants have applied to just one vacancy. Therefore, Hitachi could recruit top class, fully capable, and young individuals having an excellent track record. Indeed, the researchers are world top level.

Collaboration

The firm carefully chose partners from amongst the brightest and most successful. Hitachi also assigns the best research member, so that the most capable researchers will interact to produce new concepts and new technologies.

Hitachi always emphasizes the close collaboration with the partners, in such way that the parties can mutually trust each other and discuss issues frankly without hesitation, but always to the benefit of the other party (professional friend) and for the advancement of both parties. Moreover, the firm is careful that the management is also of high quality, so that the managerial actions are quite advanced and modernized to attract the partner to be able to willingly work with the research organization.

Research Funding

The major funds come from Hitachi's business group and corporate laboratories. However, gradually, funding from European government, in the form of EU projects such as ESPRIT projects, as well as Japanese government project, such as NEDO projects, are increasing.

Today, Hitachi has about 10% of fund coming from EU and Japanese government. This figure will increase more in the future, to the level like 20%. Especially, EU projects are giving more self-support and autonomy which is one of the most important fundamental factor in global R&D.

7.2   Some Examples of an Effective Management Scheme

Hakuraku Management

Since the laboratories are geographically distant and distributed from the Japanese laboratories and European management headquarters, and since the research subjects are essentially fundamental, special attention was made to cultivate and nurture the potential and level of every individual researcher to the utmost height first, and then, if necessary, to organize them into a team to perform in a research project.

For this purpose, every possible opportunity was provided to encourage the researcher to increase their level, for example, an opportunity to visit Hitachi's research laboratories in Japan, submitting a paper to a high quality professional journal, giving a speech at a major international conference, etc.

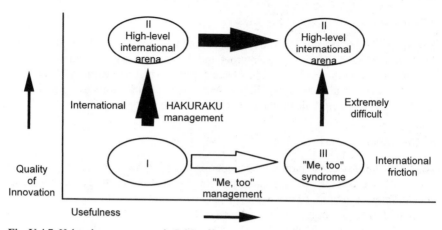

Fig. V.4.7. Hakuraku management in R&D effect.

Also, special emphasis was placed on having the best communication, both for telecommunication and human communication. Especially, the latter is stressed in such way that the General Manager can find „Hakuraku" features (distinguishing features) in every researcher and extend the best support to help enhance these Hakurakus. Some researchers are very suitable for rather individualistic research, in creating a revolutionary concept, other researchers are best fitted to the leading role of a project team to push innovation.

Holonic Management

„Holon" is an elemental biological unit which knows the integrated whole. So, the „Holonic" system is the integrated whole of such „holons". Thus, the „holonic" management adopted at European R&D is the management to give each researcher the maximum power and freedom to exert his/her maximum performance, instead of directing him/her by the manager. To do this, it is vitally important to let the individual researcher know the total objectives of the research laboratory, the relationship between his/her research and the other projects, what the impact of his/her research will be in the future. That is, „holonic" management is a sort of autonomous research laboratory. This management concept is especially suitable for the management of the research environment as a sort of model of future more extensive scale globally distributed virtual laboratories.

On-Site Policy

In spite of requesting the researchers to come over to the room of a general manager or laboratory managers, Hitachi always request the general manager or laboratory managers to visit the actual working area in the laboratories and discuss issues with researchers there.

This helps a lot to improve the communication between the managers and researchers, and researchers will sincerely make efforts to apply their maximum potential. This is a scheme to recognize the importance of human ware in research.

7.3   Five-Dimensional Synergy

As was introduced in the beginning part of this paper, the „synergy" in five dimensional scales is the basis of innovation - trans-sectoral, trans-disciplinary, concurrent managerial, global cultural, global societal. They are the key of innovations for today and tomorrow.

7.4   Special Prioritization on Intellectual Capital and Asset

Since the researcher's potential for innovation is the most important factor for innovation, especially for „revolutionary" innovation expected in global R&D, special care has been taken to always give highest priority to researchers. Since the intellectual asset includes not only researchers, but also management, it is very important that the quality of management must always be at the highest. Also, intellectual asset includes knowledge and culture bases which are accumulated in either digital data or in other form.

Although the evaluation and accounting of an intellectual asset is not yet formulated, that does not justify the overlooking of R&D management on this crucial new direction. Definitely, it is necessary to establish new evaluation formula to assess such intellectual capital and assets.

8   Experience of Practicing R&D Management in Europe

8.1   Overcoming Difficulties

Hitachi encountered difficulties in establishing researchers' career path, both in Europe and in the world-wide scale. Although Hitachi's business operations in Europe is quite sizeable, it still is not suitable for the researchers to find some interesting position or experience subject there. Also, within the R&D Centers in Europe and in the USA, such migration is not planned well. However, some concrete migration could start between Hitachi's European and domestic research laboratory, especially Central research laboratory.

Since Hitachi researchers are extremely capable people, there are always some outside temptations to usurp them with much higher salaries. Since their interests in Hitachi is to experience the most front-end technology and deepen their understanding and technical level, most of the researchers are not influenced much. But some are seriously affected. Hitachi always discuss these matters with individual researchers so that the best possible support and remuneration can be provided, and the researcher understands that the firm is caring for him/her.

8.2   New Impact

Cyber-Space

Cyber-space is really changing the concept of time and space in the conventional environment. Now and in the future, difference of time can be the advantage, because by effective use of time difference Hitachi can achieve a „twenty four hour laboratory". Time can be more dense, that is „time-density" concept will be needed.

Since Hitachi started the research team stationed in Dallas, Texas, USA, the research organization is able to work as a „16 hour laboratory". Quite possibly, new competitive edge will be a function of both, „Intellectual Asset" and „Time Density".

New Definition of Competitiveness

Two key factors will be the most influential parameters in the future information network society. The first factor is „new capability (C)" defined as the combination of intellectual assets, communication quality, global management skills.

The second factor is „time-density (D)" created by the effective use of cyber-space on the globe such as „24 hour laboratory". New competitiveness will be a function of these two factors:

New Competitiveness $= f (C \times D)$

R&D asset is a new concept to assess and measure the competitiveness of R&D in the future. Since the author has studied this in the past and is now practically quite interested in the new R&D environment where cyber-space is giving new parameters to change the paradigm.

8.3   Real Communication - Mutual Understanding

Real communication is „mutual understanding" based on „mutual trust". And the basis of trust is „sincerity". Therefore, it is crucial that management directly discuss the matter with researchers, by listening intently, and by asking questions, with „sincerity", without any hesitation. Achieving real communication for „mutual understanding" is most crucial.

In this sense, cyber-space communication alone cannot solve everything, and face-to-face conversation is indispensable. Visiting researchers by general managers through „On-site Policy" is indeed necessary.

9   Conclusions – Across the Boundaries of Nations and Multiple Cultures

As the global society is rapidly changing, through the impact of the revolutionary

> **Lessons learned for organizing R&D at Hitachi:**
>
> 1. Capabilities of the R&D laboratory director are extremely important;
> 2. Manage cross-company strategic projects with top-down priority;
> 3. Involve all related people in a project from the start.

explosion of information networks, a new paradigm of technology management suitable for the company in the coming century, must be formed. The aim is to cope with the complexity and dynamic changes of the fundamentals and frameworks. Especially, impact of cyber-space is changing the meaning of „space" and „time" which are now becoming important keys to globalization.

Since the establishment of the R&D Center in Europe in 1989, the author has been practicing new schemes of R&D management. Through the actual hands-on experience, as applied to European Research Laboratories, some significant innovations were born. Indeed, innovations are the outcome of both researchers and management. This will become more true in the company of the future.

Since the world will become more complex and therefore the problems to be solved become harder, the challenge is to overcome them through the 'best team' on the globe, across the boundaries of nations or cultural differences. Synergistic global co-operation is crucial, in forming a strong team with the highest technical and managerial potential and skill. Global R&D, featuring the trans-sectoral co-operation of industry, academia, and governments is necessarily becoming more and more the pillar of research, rather than the domestic homogeneous single sector research team, which is more suitable for 'evolutionary' technology rather than 'revolutionary' technology. Following are the key points concluded in this paper.

- In Hitachi, HIVIPS system was the very beginning of major R&D globalization, especially for 'internal globalization'. It has provided good experience and confidence of success in global research collaboration, especially for R&D outside of Japan.
- Some special management schemes and methodologies, such as Hakuraku management and HOLONIC management, were found to be most suitable to the „revolutionary" type research team. Also, these management methods are suitable for a geographically distributed R&D environment, and look more so in the „Virtual Laboratory" which is already structured in the European R&D organization.
- European research laboratories (HCL, HDL and HDCE) have consistently and patiently continued to foster the tight interactions with European collaborative partners, by providing the best possible technologies and human resources (researchers and management), which have led to the creation of innovative and revolutionary new concepts and new technologies.

- Cyber-space is changing the key factors of competitiveness. New capability as the combination of intellectual asset, communication quality, global management skill, and time-density are the two new keys.
- Communication by both cyber-space telecommunications and direct face-to-face human conversation are vital for the advanced innovation process, especially for concurrent management in geographically distant and culturally different global R&D environment. In fact, human communication is vitally important and must increase as cyber-space sends more information to the other party.
- Sharing the benefit through collaboration, in the fair way, is the key issue; especially care is needed when the partnership will commonly extend to the level of collaboration from where both parties can apply mutually competing technologies or commercial products.
- The most important factor for success, in R&D management, is 'mutual trust', especially between management and researcher. „Trust" among partners is also crucial. „Sincerity" penetrates across the boundary of nations and cultural differences.

V.5 Leica Microscopy: International Transfer of R&D Activities*

1 Leica Microscopy and Surveying

Leica was formed by the joint venture of Wild-Leitz and Cambridge Instruments in 1990. Together, they have a history of some 180 years. Today three independent companies share the Leica brand: Leica Camera AG, Solms, Germany; Leica Microsystems GmbH, Wetzlar, Germany and Leica Geosystems AG, Heerbrugg, Switzerland.

In 1997 there are two major businesses under the Leica group of companies; namely Leica Surveying Group, which is today Leica Geosystems, and the Leica Microscopy Group, called Leica Microsystems now. The business groups are bonded by the same vision, established with the formation of the corporation. The vision of Leica is to be totally focused on customers, core competencies and business processes, to be more flexible in meeting customers' buying criteria and faster in the innovation process, lead and delivery times, to be friendlier to our allies, suppliers and partners because the resulting success will create more fun for stakeholders. In line with its vision the mission of Leica is to be the world's first choice provider of innovative solutions to customer's needs for vision, measurement and analysis.

The Microscopy group with an annual turnover of CHF600 million is recognized as a leading international supplier of instruments, systems and applications for histology, specimen preparation; microscopy; measurement, analysis and documentation in life sciences; education; medical research; microsurgery; forensic analysis; flat panel display inspection; industrial research; precision assembly and quality probes. It therefore provides solutions for the complete range of microscopic observations. The group is organized around strategic business units which have the responsibility for defined areas of competence.

Product research and development are decentralized and located in the individ-

---

* This case study was authored by *Ah Bee Goh*, Managing Director of Leica Instruments (S) Pte Ltd., *Ruedi Rottermann*, Director R&D of Leica Stereomicroscopy, *Luitpold Schulz*, Manager Stereomicroscopy, and *Clement Woon*, Business Director at Leica Geosystems. This case study was written in 1998: The reader should keep in mind that all numbers, figures, organization charts and forecasts represent the state of 1998 or before.

Most important drivers for globalization:

1. Market-driven needs;

2. Decentralization of R&D sites;

3. Corporate support and drive;

4. Customer proximity.

ual business units which are located in various countries; Buffalo (USA); Cambridge (UK); Wetzlar, Heidelberg, and Nussloch (Germany); Heerbrugg (Switzerland); and Vienna (Austria). Each location focuses on its key competence in support of the business units.

The microscopy group also maintains selling units and/or representatives in 22 countries establishing a presence in Europe, North America and Asia-Pacific. Selling units support the sales for all Business Units. They are therefore organized on the basis of country and/or regional coverage.

A particular Business Unit for stereomicroscopy has an annual turnover of CHF65 million. It provides high quality stereo-microscope systems and accessories to aid visual inspection and documentation for industrial and biomedical purposes. It has R&D facilities in Switzerland and Singapore. Its main competitors are Nikon, Olympus and Zeiss.

Leica Instruments (Singapore) Pte Ltd, a manufacturing subsidiary, was established in 1971, as an extended workbench of Leica AG, Heerbrugg. It manufactures optical and mechanical components and the assembly of less sophisticated instruments. With the transfer of R&D competence and assembly for stereomicroscopes from 1993, it enjoys growing importance as a manufacturing plant for microscopy and surveying products. It has now become the main factory supporting the manufacturing activities of the Stereomicroscopy Business Unit.

2   R&D Organization

Leica has developed a corporate strategy as guidelines for business activities valid from 1995 to 1999. A supporting document of this strategy is the Leica Innovation Process manual. It defines the guidelines for the transformation of customer needs into products. The objectives of the innovation process manual are:

- To define a common understanding, terminology and methodology;
- To identify key issues and key measures for the innovation process;
- To initiate a benchmarking and improvement process.

The manual defines the process for innovation within Leica and is made compulsory for all R&D activities. The manual establishes the milestones for decisions and release of budgetary expenditures according to the progress of any innovation.

Although the microscopy business is very much international, most of the R&D facilities are integrated in the decentralized business units in Europe and USA, whereas the most important competitors are all located in Asia. However, since 1996, an R&D team is established in Singapore following the transfer of R&D activities from the Stereomicroscopy Business Unit to the Singapore factory. This represents the first R&D effort in the Asia by the group.

The specific duties of the focused R&D department in Heerbrugg are project management, concept development, optical systems design, product development, industrial design and testing of prototypes. A project team, headed by a Project Manager, is responsible for each defined project. A kind of matrix organization is adopted for each innovation. The project team included, besides the R&D elements, members from marketing, product management and manufacturing. However, it has not been necessary for all the members to be located together.

The R&D department in Singapore was built up from 1993 - 1996 to act as an extended branch of Stereomicroscopy R&D in Heerbrugg. Eight engineers learned design duties by providing support to the factory and local suppliers during the 'zero' series (pre-production) production for a completely new line of stereomicroscopes and accessories which was developed in the same time as the transfer of R&D activities.

Historically, before 1993, all stereomicroscopy products were developed and produced in Switzerland. Transferring of production to another location was normally considered only when it was no longer cost effective to produce in Switzerland. This was normally during the maturity phase of the product life cycle. Lower cost is then necessary to extend product life. The transfer would include existing process plans and devices for assembly. No new development in product or process was carried out. R&D competence and sustaining engineering were still maintained at Heerbrugg.

With the introduction of the new stereo-line a decision was made to run this production from the very beginning in Singapore. The rational for this decision was to force the adoption of local suppliers and the R&D engineers to learn more about the international environment rather than the industrial conditions in the vicinity of Heerbrugg. The Singapore factory became for Leica, from 1994, the major and most important manufacturing plant for the mid-range stereomicroscopy. An estimated 80% of Business Unit's products are now produced in Singapore.

Major issues for global R&D management at Leica Microscopy:

1. New technologies;
2. Global market driven strategies;
3. State-of-the-art 3D CAD/CAM;
4. Capable engineers.

Major innovative break-throughs at Leica Microscopy (last five years):

1. New stereo-microscopy product line;

2. Improved manufacturing process.

The main responsibility for product development is to translate successfully customers requirements into products which will be superior to alternate solutions by competitors. The following are specific aims of R&D coordination:

- Development of new processes, e.g. a computer aided adjustment device for semi-automatic centering of optical systems.
- Design of components with new materials, e.g. housing of the basic microscope's structures in plastic injection parts instead of metal.
- Higher performing mechanical and optical systems.
- Increase application of ergonomics to make microscopes more comfortable - a focus on the user.
- New geometry on optical parts to increase optical image quality and to simplify optical mounting procedures to minimize variation from this process.
- Re-design of the optical layout to obsolete lead-based glass material.

2.1 R&D Project Management

Twice a year the Business Units hold a Market Performance Committee meeting. Participants are product managers from the most important selling units, project managers from the actual running projects, as well as marketing and R&D staff from the business units. The agenda usually includes reports on the performance of the existing products on the markets which will provide information about new needs from customers or information on new product releases from competitors. Emerging technologies are reviewed to project the impact they might have on existing markets. With these inputs, new suggestions for products originating from selling unit are proposed from R&D are evaluated. The confirmation of new projects and determination of priorities for the projects are then carried out. The decisions on new projects or cancellation of running ones, are made within this Market Performance Committee meeting which is chaired by the general manager of the Business Unit.

Table V.5.1 illustrates the milestones according to the Leica innovation process for applied research projects. For small innovation projects, the milestones for product engineering and design approval may be combined as the output requirements for both milestones may be achieved simultaneously. Similarly, the milestones for the product announcement and release may also be combined. In this manner the innovation cycle for smaller projects may be shortened. However, each milestone has to be passed by a milestone meeting, in which the go/no-go decision has to be made. Fig. V.5.1 shows the flow of the Leica Innovation Process.

2.2 Reporting Structure, Budget Decisions and Technology Transfer

A project team member is working within a matrix. He reports within the project to the project manager, and as a member of a functional department, to his intermediate superior. A project manager reports directly to the R&D manager. The R&D manager reports to the general manager of the Business Unit Manager. The budget is defined by the management according to the needs and priorities determined at the Market Performance Committee meeting. R&D expenditures are normally in line with priorities of the Business Unit.

There are two types of s in the Leica context. The first is the production transfer and the other the transfer of basic R&D competence. Prior to 1993, only production transfers took place. In this process, a transfer team identifies the technologies and skills that are needed for running the production successfully at the new site. The gap between technologies needed versus technologies available will be closed. The main focus was on the transfer of assembly. Usually the main components were shipped from the existing supplier base because production tools had been built. In this scenario it is often not viable to start new tools because, the product is in the mature phase of its life-cycle. The gap for production is usually closed by a delegate of specialists for coaching and management at the new site. A targeted group of employees such as engineers and production operators are put through a short learning cycle which is followed by on-the-job training which is supervised by the expert trainers. The transfer is usually accompanied by tools, devices, instructions, process plans, and QA procedures. The success of the transfer is usually determined upfront by supervising the pilot run at the new place. The transfer process is considered complete on the acceptance of pilot-run units.

The know-how transfer to build up a new competence at an alternate site is more complex. In this case the key focus is to transfer the activities prior to pro-

Table V.5.1. Milestones in the Leica innovation process.

Phase	Milestone
Innovation justification	Approval for new projects are allowed based on the market justification and viability.
Business Plan	The business aspects of the projects are reviewed and approved.
Product engineering	The product is designed with the critical aspects tested.
Design approval	The design concepts are approved.
Prototype acceptance	The fully functional prototype is built.
Product announcement	The product is announced to the marketing and selling units.
Product release	The product are ready for launch.
Product validation	Feedback from the market are collected to assess the effectiveness of the product to meet customers' needs

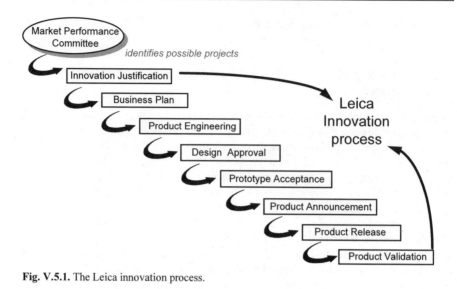

Fig. V.5.1. The Leica innovation process.

duction so that the targeted location will eventually be able to manage the development cycle in the innovation process. This process requires the transfer of product application know-how. The creativity process required in each phase of the innovation cycle has to be transferred.

A particular decision for projects to be transferred is made by the Business Unit Management, whereas the manufacturing process is organized by the management of the targeted site. Key resources are usually identified in each location to act as a single point of contact for all transfer activities between sites. This is especially important for key decisions and milestones.

Information technology is an important tool to overcome distances and it has to be coordinated so that the international R&D cooperation between two sites can occur. (same CAD modules, on line link of CAD systems, Email, ISDN link, e.g. configuration management between Leica sites.) Fig. V.5.2 illustrates the communication tools used by Leica.

3   Example of an International R&D Project

This example refers to the project of building up an R&D department in Singapore which involves the transfer of development know-how as well as production. This project was carried out from 1993 to 1996 in a close cooperation between the Singapore factory and the Stereomicroscopy Business Unit in Heerbrugg. The project resulted in a successful transfer of know-how. Even till today, this factory is still the only one in Singapore engaged in the manufacturing of stereomicroscopes. Some of the products manufactured successfully are the MS5, MZ6, MZ8 and MZ10 and MZ12 stereomicroscope carriers.

3.1 Situation in 1992

The Singapore factory had build up its competence in mechanical and optical component manufacturing over a 25 year period. It also had some capability in the assembly and adjustment of low-end stereomicroscopes as well as low-end surveying instrumentation. All these products were designed and manufactured in the European plants of Leica. When they were transferred, all existing process plans and manufacturing devices were transferred as well. Transfers happened mainly for cost reasons and to extend the life of these matured products in the markets.

The Business Unit was working on the conceptualization and design of a new generation of stereomicroscopes and accessories; altogether a family consisting of 27 instruments. It was planned to introduce all these products into the market between 1995/96 (start of production 1994/95). Furthermore, the production should start from the very beginning in Singapore. This was a task which had never been done before. The successful production of the new instruments requires specific activities to strengthen the process engineering capacity in production and assembly and the build up of local R&D capability.

Since the expertise of design and development of stereomicroscopes was not available in Singapore, an expatriate manager was decided as the best way to develop the required capability. The role of this manager was to build the necessary R&D infrastructure as well as being the coach and mentor to a group of local engineers who would be given R&D responsibility. The position was filled by an existing development manager who was willing to take up this challenge, despite the negative atmosphere generated in the parent company by the decision to effect the transfer. The on-the-job-training program for local R&D engineers was created according to the needs of the start up of the new products.

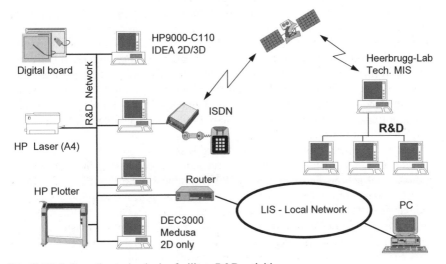

Fig. V.5.2. Information technologies facilitate R&D activities.

3.2   Transfer Plan

Year One - 1993

The first task was to recruit and train a pool of engineers in Singapore and to bring them to the level of competence where fruitful discussions could take place between the two sites involved in the transfer. The R&D organization and culture had to be integrated into the Singapore operations. Since the start-up was from zero-base, communication lines and procedures had to be established. Basic infrastructure such as computer-aided design stations, documentation procedures, engineering change request management and configuration control had to be established. In addition, new employees had to learn the technology and physics in the design of stereomicroscopes. This means the working principles of the instrument including applications, the assembly process and the basic production techniques for parts. The latter means that the engineers have to acquire, as examples, design and manufacturing knowledge in castings, plastic injection and metal forming techniques. They had also to consider the behavior of materials with these techniques and to factor these into the design process. All the development efforts had to be done within the framework of the innovation process. The adoption of this procedure is best learnt through first hand application of the procedure itself. Engineers are trained to apply this knowledge by supporting the operations in prototyping, pre-production and production stage by doing engineering change requests, sustaining engineering, review of product documentation and optimization of components and parts based on design and documentation that had been already developed in Heerbrugg.

Year Two - 1994

The next step required the Singapore engineers to redesign the existing products to make them more cost competitive by using local partners in parts production. In the second year the basic design of some products in the new product line was completed. Swiss engineers sent detailed design of parts, components and sub-assemblies on drafts. The engineers in the Singapore factory converted these designs to formal product documentation, designed and toleranced for manufacturing. This step demanded for the first time a close and critical cooperation between the R&D engineers and the process engineers. The Swiss partners now had the opportunity to focus their attention more on the conceptualization work and to complete the entire product line.

The next competence level was transferred when basic concepts were delivered from a Swiss R&D engineer for the conversion of products in Singapore. This required joint actions between a Swiss R&D engineer, who was temporary delegated to Singapore for six months and his local colleagues to develop a series of modular products. The joint effort allowed an additional channel for training and learning and to understand customers' needs in the application of stereomicroscopes to solve specific problems. Intensive discussions were held with local suppliers who, after a selection process, were integrated into the design team.

Year Three - 1995

The third year was a period of consolidation of the knowledge base. Engineers participated in the process to transfer the design to manufacturing. This included the design of production tools and devices. The development of an optical adjusting concept and the design of the related adjustment tool were completed. The R&D scope was enlarged to surveying projects. Although the content was similar, the application was however, completely different. This expansion of scope also required new members for the team which would lead to capabilities in electronics, including hardware and software for surveying products.

The completion of the product line required a new focus on the augmented products. The new accessories for the new stereomicroscope line needed special attention. Since backward compatibility was assured, the new industrial design also meant a redesign of the existing accessories to extend compatibility to all instruments.

The final touch to the transfer process was the localization of the R&D Manager position and the reintegration of the expatriate manager into the R&D team in the headquarters in Heerbrugg. Both steps are important for management to maintain the continual trust of employees which is essential for globalization efforts.

3.3 Key Success Factors

It was important to motivate the Swiss R&D engineers to participate in the transfer of technology and to explain the reasons to build up the local R&D team in Singapore. It was also important to help them understand the advantage for themselves and for the success of the products by having local support in the remote location. Furthermore, the communication between Switzerland and Singapore becomes much easier and more efficient with direct link between R&D colleagues of both sides. This was necessary to ensure a free flow of information between the two teams. The criteria for the selection of local engineers were therefore also important. The new engineers selected to join the team were graduates with some years experience in design and development. It was also important that the recruits did not have a history of job-hopping. All the R&D engineers joined the team with a three year working contract to avoid interest in short term engagements.

At this time, R&D jobs were attractive for local Singapore engineers. Many of the applicants already had some experience in product transfer from the USA, Japan or Europe to Singapore. However, these were mainly in production transfers. They were also interested to do product design and development.

3.4 Special Situations in this Project

The expatriate manager was originally the project manager under a matrix organization and therefore was designed to report to the Business Unit Manager in Heerbrugg as well as to the local Managing Director in Singapore. Subsequent events resulting from the re-organization that took place in Heerbrugg lead to a single line of report; to the local Managing Director. This proves to be the better solution in the end, as clear and constant support was obtained to facilitate the application of resources for the successful implementation of the projects.

Under the new reporting structure, the role of the expatriate manager was expanded to include surveying products as well. Soon the local R&D team who was mostly exposed to microscopy technology was faced with requests from the Geodesy Business Unit for product improvement and redesign. This tough situation (managing two technology sets) was handled with a very close cooperation among the Singapore R&D team and the timely recruitment of electronic engineers for R&D, which were available in the Singapore environment. Another example was the ISO 9001 certification, which was requested as a consequence of starting R&D work in Singapore. In a joint effort between R&D and production, the factory passed the first external audit successfully after only six months of preparations and got the ISO 9001 certificate. This was possible because of the continuous commitment of the factory to document processes under the previously held ISO 9002 certification.

The building up of R&D activities in Singapore needed a careful balance between the expectations from Heerbrugg (on-the job training and coaching of microscopy projects as seen from the Stereomicroscopy Business Unit) versus the challenging ambitions of the local management team. This became the most motivating aspect of the expatriated Swiss R&D Manager. Aside from the defined job, he was also exposed to the Asian style of management as well as the associated cultures in this foreign land.

Besides the pre-defined R&D projects, several other product development projects were also organized in a matrix. The overall responsibility was carried by two Swiss project managers in each of the two locations. The two project managers were direct discussion partners and steered the projects jointly. In the first year, the local Singapore team took over responsibility for projects in pre-production or in prototype stage. In the second year, Singapore became responsible for the design and development. In the third, the first conceptualization work was done in Singapore for a small project besides the ongoing duties from the other projects.

The Business Unit in Heerbrugg and the Singapore factory held joint responsibility for the R&D set-up in Singapore and the development of the new product line. The need to be successful on both accounts generated ownership and a will to succeed. The progress for the stereomicroscopy project was monitored by periodic and annual reviews in Singapore by the Leica Corporate Management and the Business Unit's representatives. The contribution of the local R&D team was compared with the training program, which was defined as a measure of the project in 1993.

Product development projects were coordinated within the two remote teams via the project managers. In the factory, team meetings were conducted on a weekly basis. Where necessary, additional effort was taken to avoid troubles by identifying the problems early and executing on time corrective actions. During the initial three years, most of the involved engineers and managers had the opportunity to visit other plants, R&D engineers and process engineers were participating in important actions and decisions in Switzerland, e.g. prototype testing and definition of revision before production whereas Swiss engineers came to Singapore for technical discussions with local vendors, or to get feedback from a design review, made in Singapore.

4   Most Important Lessons Learned

Knowledge is embodied in people, and people have emotions. The management of this emotions is the key to unleash a cooperative effort in the development team. The leadership of the team may provide either a powerful stimulus or depressant to the performance of the team. A determining factor for success of the transfer of R&D is the appropriate selection of managers who are willing to lead and manage these global resources for maximum results. In the early periods following the decision to transfer, it was important to overcome the inertia that was created by such high emotional stress. Constant communication was necessary to sell the idea to key resources who had eventually to conduct the transfer process. Management in all earnest does not possess the ability to effect the transfer himself. The decisions of management had to be manifested in the discrete steps of these resources to ensure that the transfer would indeed take place. Management, however has the important role of orchestrating, motivating, coaching and even to certain extent dictating the steps through a powerful reward and recognition process. Know-how transfer will not happen just because a decision was taken.

4.1   Significant Achievements in the International Transfer of R&D Projects

The achievements and benefits gained are varied and it is not possible to list each and everyone. In a general sense, we can say that the corporation as a whole has gained tremendously in the following areas:

- Knowledge;
- Problem solving capabilities;
- Time-to-Market reduction;
- Manufacturing costs.

The benefits in these areas are explained in the following chapters.

Knowledge

The product and design knowledge has been increased with the successful transfer of stereo-microscope to the Singapore subsidiary. Although the Singapore factory had over the years developed a core manufacturing know-how, it was lacking product knowledge particularly in product designs from conceptual stage. Fig. V.5.3 shows the activities and the upstream knowledge that has been strengthened and enhanced as a result of R&D cooperation. Fig. V.5.4 represents the knowledge accumulation in the factory over a span of 25 years, particularly the steep increase in the last 5 years. The process of technology transfer may be considered in several stages. The first and easiest stage was to transfer an assembly process to take advantage of low cost labor. As the operation matures, the technology recipient usually does not maintain its low cost advantage but rather evolved into an establishment with higher value-adding potential. This means an excursion into sustaining engineering for product life-cycle extensions, product development, given specifications, and then finally the mastering of product realization from market or technology research. Fig. V.5.4 illustrates the progress of the Singapore factory as it climbs the know-how ladder. The knowledge link with the Swiss R&D engineers has enabled the Singapore engineers to gain access to skills, know-how and capabilities which were virtually untapped before. The link played an important supporting role in the factory's effort to renew and reshape its core capabilities.

Problem Solving Capabilities

Before the R&D cooperation, the downstream problems especially in the manufacturing stage had faced with tremendous difficulties. There were so many engineering changes that quality and deliveries suffered. With the „upstream" knowledge enhanced, engineering changes and technical problems could be reduced significantly. We had experienced three capabilities:

- *On-time „upstream" solutions would ease the workload „downstream":* The process engineers in production worked closely with the R&D engineers at both locations, to detect problems and limitations which would possibly occur at a later stage. Therefore, the R&D engineers continuously learnt possible constraints which would impact the downstream activities. The removal of constraints „upstream" made life easier „downstream". Time and money is saved.

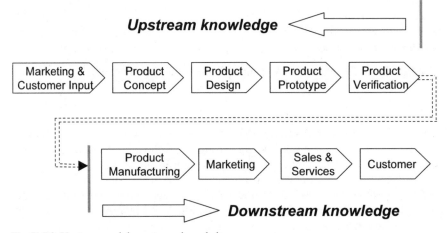

Fig. V.5.3. Upstream and downstream knowledge.

We realized that often the constraints and the difficulties discovered „down-stream" were mostly due to the ignorance of the R&D engineers on manufacturing constraints.

- *Outsourcing:* The participation of procurement engineers was crucial in the development of suppliers. Suppliers need relevant inputs before they can commit themselves in price and delivery schedule. The procurement engineers served as a link between the suppliers and R&D engineers. Knowledge transfer was made easier and confidence in the suppliers was strengthened. The factory therefore gained the confidence and commitment of the suppliers. We experienced that in some cases, the knowledge contributed by the suppliers had helped us to eliminate unnecessary costs.
- Effective communication and teamwork: The team spirit lives through effective communication. When the language of communication is clear, there is little argument over meaningless issues. This is because „downstream" engineers have faith in „upstream" engineers and vice-versa. 'Moving quickly' has been the motto of the team - whether in building a prototype, running a test or trouble shooting a problem. Whenever an engineer discovers a problem, it is communicated quickly to the other relevant members, and it is resolved in the spirit of the team.

Time-to-Market Reduced

It is an undeniable fact that R&D Departments should work closely with manufacturing operations to achieve the best results. Our experience is that we are able to reduce time-to-market by at least 50% as a result of this cooperation. Prior to the cooperation, the factory faces tremendous difficulties in getting products out to

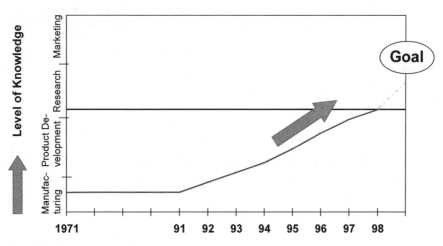

Fig. V.5.4. Accumulation of knowledge.

the market on-time. We are even proud to boast that our high-end microscopes i.e., MZ12 and MZAPO were introduced in record time to the market. Of significance is the point that the products were greatly accepted by the customers in terms of quality and price.

Low Manufacturing Costs

As soon as R&D, development and process engineers were close to manufacturing and to suppliers, significant cost reduction in component sourcing and assembly was achieved. Targeted assembly times were attained quickly and the learning curves of the operations were shortened. Therefore, the factory operations reached the efficiency level of the Swiss counterparts within a short time.

5   Conclusions

Design to manufacturing can only happen through the intimate understanding of the manufacturing conditions. If manufacturing is to be in Singapore, an extended R&D facility is compulsory for maximum effectiveness. The successful achievement of the schedules and budget of the new product line is a proof of this effectiveness. In the first year of introduction of the new stereo-line, Leica Instruments was able to match the increase in market demand by more than 50% of the original budget.

What were the possible achievements within a three years R&D build up project? Considering important differences between Singapore and Switzerland, the expectations in such an R&D build up has to be realistic. It is not possible, to „copy and paste" a department within three years. The success of the project is the establishment of a nucleus, which can only grow further by ongoing involvement and joint actions within the two plants. Further growth in competence will only happen over years, which needs commitment between employees and employer. Table V.5.2 shows the comparison between the profile and market conditions for R&D and/or process engineers. The significant difference between the two locations has to be managed for the continued development of the R&D capability in Singapore.

Lessons learned for organizing R&D at Leica Microscopy:

1. Lack of leading precision engineering technologies;

2. Weakness in electronics and software design and development capabilities;

3. No 3D CAM/CAD for quick prototyping;

4. Weak market-driven activities.

Table V.5.2. A comparison between the profile and market conditions for R&D and/or process engineers.

Criteria	Switzerland, Leica BU-SM	Singapore, LIS
Education:		
Apprenticeship with practical experience in manufacturing environment	Normally Yes	No
Bachelor of engineer	Yes	Normally yes (5/7)
Master degree	No	Often available (2/7)
Experience:		
International exposure at Leica or other Employers	Low, except the build up project	High, product transfer from other countries to Singapore
R&D experience for Leica or other employers	Extremely high, the 7 R&D engineers at BU - SM representing 168 years, averaged 24 years of experience, mainly contributing to Leica Microscopy	Relatively low because of the low rate of product transfer to LIS in the past
Opportunities in the local labor market	Medium	Extremely high, 3 year working contract at LIS enforced to maintain labor stability
Labor turn over, probability for a change of jobs	Low	Extremely high, a unique characteristic of the Singapore environment

Note: BU-SM: Business Unit - Stereomicroscopy

LIS: Leica Instruments(S) Pte Ltd

Strong personal ties between the two R&D departments have been major success factors. The closed cooperation over three years in certain projects has established a good relationship between the two teams. It is very easy now to work together and to complement each other within a larger framework with the individual strengths on both sides. Engineers should appreciate the competence of each other as a criteria for future success.

What are the trends for R&D in Leica? The Leica Corporation has decided in 1997 to convert the „battle ship" Leica AG, Heerbrugg, into an armada of individual and independent acting „fast speed boats", called Leica Microscopy Group, Leica Surveying Group and production companies for Mechanics, Optics and Electronics. Global R&D will happen only within the main contributors Microscopy and Surveying.

The need to merge customer needs in the growing Asia-Pacific markets with design for manufacturing (in Singapore and other places in Asia) to achieve the most competitive products, requires that product development activities are close to the markets. Sharing of responsibilities between Europe and Asia may form the powerful combination for Leica to emerge as a global player and be ahead of its competitors.

V.6 MTU: Partner in International High-Tech-Cooperations*

1 Profile of the Jet-Engine Industry and the Joint „Advanced Ducted Propfan" Program

Jet engines are an example of high technology products with extreme safety standards to the benefit of the airline customers. The resulting high development costs and the technical and financial risk lead to international corporations for the development and production of jet engines. As a consequence this worksharing has not only been limited to real engine projects but it has also been applied to the predevelopment phase of advanced future turbo fans. As an example for such an approach in the following contribution the international „Advanced Ducted Prop Fan" cooperation between Pratt&Whitney, MTU München, Fiat Aviazione and Hamilton Standard is described with respect to motivation, organization of the program and the everyday work.

1.1 The General Market Situation

Modern jet engines for commercial airplanes are high technology products. They combine high pressure ratios and high rotational speed with extreme temperatures. Furthermore the reduction of engine weight is an important development issue. Absolute requirements are the extreme safety standards to the benefit of the airline customers.

Regarding military applications the advanced jet engine technology is the backbone of today's and future airborne defense systems and consequently it has a strong strategic component. This strategic importance is also related to the spin of effects in the fields of materials, combustion, aeromechanics, safety standards and so on. The long term profit of the industry branch and this strategic aspect result in a complex international industry structure with a turnover of about € 38 billion only with respect to jet engines. The expected turnover shares of the main engine

---

* This case study was initially authored in 1997 by *Prof. Dr. K.-D. Broichhausen* and *M. Renkel* of Daimler-Benz Aerospace, MTU Aero Engines GmbH, Munich. The case was revised in 2007 by *Prof. Dr. K.-D. Broichhausen* and *Patricia Hurschler*.

Most important drivers for globalization:
1. Jet engine business is a global market per se;
2. International partners help to open international markets;
3. Risk-sharing in large-scale projects;
4. Economies of scale and scope in development.

manufacturers are € 9.7 billion for Rolls–Royce, € 9.6 billion for General Electric, € 7.5 billion for Pratt&Whitney, and € 4.5 billion for Safran. MTU Aero Engines comes in fifth position with about € 2.2 billion.

On the other hand the severe competition in the jet engine market and consequently moderate profit margin in the original sales business result in a late payback of the high investments during the development phase. To reduce these financial and technical risks, development and production of jet engines is increasingly performed in cooperations and joint ventures with sharing of risk among partners or suppliers. This was valid for the predominant European military engines such as the RB199 for the Tornado, the EJ200 for the Eurofighter and the MTR390 for the anti tank helicopter. This also holds true, however, for the civil jet engines: Examples for joint ventures are the V2500 and the CFM. Other engines like high thrust class PW4000–Growth, the GP7000 for the A380 and GE90 are developed and manufactured in transatlantic or even global cooperation with risk sharing partners being responsible for the development and the production of engine modules.

1.2   The Joint „ Advanced Ducted Propfan" Program

Obviously the risk for the development of a totally new generation of jet engines on a pre-advanced technology-level is even higher. Such a new generation of turbofans has been regarded feasible with respect to the basic technologies in the late eighties. The new concept - a combination of the advantages of propeller engines and modern jet engines - promised a further reduction of fuel consumption and emission (Fig. V.6.1). As a consequence numerous concept studies of these environmentally friendly engines with shrouded or unshrouded propfans have been evaluated and a lot of isolated research activities exploring critical components and feasibility studies have been started. The basic idea of all these developments has been the increase of the cold flow with low energy level in the bypass by increasing the fan diameters.

To focus these isolated activities with respect to product definition and the development of a prototype engine demonstrator the companies Pratt&Whitney, MTU München and Fiat Aviazione decided already in 1985 to join their activities in an efficient and open cooperation.

1.3   The Competition

Already in the early 1980es a comparable cooperation with the goal of building an in-flight engine demonstrator for an advanced propulsion system has been established in an international cooperation by the American company General Electric Aircraft and Snecma (France). They succeeded in presenting the first Ultra High Bypass (UHB) engine flight demonstrator, which has been technically a great success, drawing a lot of attention by the public. However, with respect to the final customer, the realized principle of an engine with two counter-rotating propellers and no casing (shroudless fan) proved to have some disadvantages regarding perceived noise and safety. So, at the end, this engine had no real customer perceived value.

In addition, because of low fuel prices and an unsatisfactory financial situation of the customers (the airlines) the market was not open for new concepts in these years. Thus, being the first in the market or the first in the air with this advanced technology did not lead to an advantageous market position because of the conservative customer behavior and the complex interaction of all technical and financial aspects. Also in other industries (for example in the field of copy machines) being the first at the market is not necessarily corresponding to success.

This experience to a great extent influenced the decision of Pratt&Whitney and the advanced propulsion system team to concentrate on a shrouded propfan, i.e. a fan with a casing. The cooperation established can be used still today as a case study.

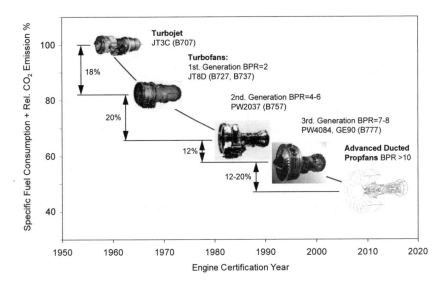

Fig. V.6.1. Reduction of fuel consumption for different engine generations.

> In conservative and complex markets in connection with complex technologies: Too advanced and too early is as dangerous as too little and too late.

1.4   Future Market and Development Costs

The market requirements for jet engines are extremely complex. Due to the extreme safety standards, the market itself is not primarily technology-driven. In contrast to the high fidelity market and the motor car market, technology by itself has no primary customer perceived value in the aero business. Airplanes and aero engines are not ordered because their technology is progressive or trendy. The application of new technologies is only appreciated by the airlines if at the end the life cycle costs of the whole system, the safety of the system and / or the comfort of the passengers are improved. As a consequence, each new concept has to make its breakthrough against reliable engines on the market. This effect is even increased as the engines on the market are developed further on an evolutionary and continuous basis.

The major advantage of the Ultra High Bypass (UHB) or Advanced Ducted

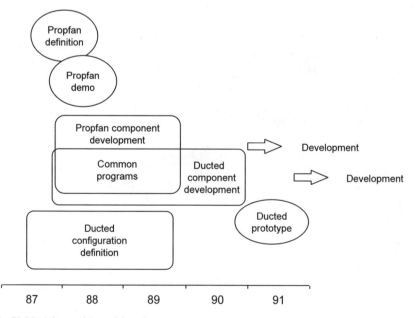

Fig. V.6.2. Advanced Propulsion plan.

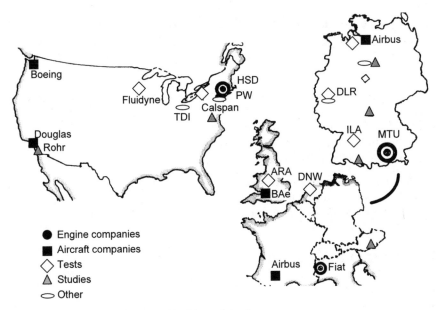

Fig. V.6.3. Ducted Technology, world-wide participation.

Propfan (ADP) engines is the dramatic reduction of fuel consumption. The disadvantage is that nearly all new engine concepts are more complex than the standard jet engines. So for a success on the market, the reduction of fuel costs has to compensate the increased product costs because of the engine complexity.

1.5 Focus and Vision

As described the market situation is extremely complex with a strong interdependence of different aspects extending from fuel prices to passenger behavior. In addition the cost for the development and certification of an „Ultra High Bypass" or „Advanced Ducted Propfan" engine is in the order of a billion US-Dollar. In such a situation it is nearly a question of surviving to proceed in well defined steps separated by technical / financial or market relevant milestones and gates. For this reason the „Advanced System Partnership" management decided a stepwise procedure:

- *Step 1:* Studies and basic experiments referring to the engine configuration.
- *Step 2:* Technology readiness for a full engine ground test demonstrator for feasibility studies of the whole system.
- *Step 3:* Demonstrate feasibility of all new components in a ground test demonstrator including windtunnel tests (flight test consciously have been renounced in this phase of the program).

Take the best ideas or skills from each country / partner.

- *Step 4:* Detailed analysis of all deficits with respect to an on wing demonstration.
- *Step 5:* Close all systematical or technological gaps in a continued, strongly product focused technology readiness program.
- *Step 6:* Be ready for the market.

A rough idea of the structure of step 2 and step 3 of the program is given in Fig. V.6.2 This includes the complex decision process, which started with the possible configurations mentioned above and finally ended with a demonstrator.

2   R&D Organization

2.1   The Sites

As already mentioned the Advanced Propulsion System Partnership has been carried out as an American / European approach by the companies Pratt&Whitney (USA), MTU (Germany) and Fiat Aviazione (Italy). These core companies themselves are involved with a national network of supporters and suppliers. In some high technology fields also universities and research institutes have been consulted. Windtunnel tests of different engine models and component tests studied in the Step 2 phase have been performed at Fluidyne (USA), Calspan (USA), ARA and BAE (Great Britain), DNW (The Netherlands) and DLR and ILA (Germany) .

The reason for this widely spread activities primarily was the number of possible engine configurations which had to be investigated in parallel. Secondly these institutes have special unique skills which had to be introduced to the benefit of the project. And, finally, the program was based on three independent companies and partly sponsored by national technology programs. In a situation like this a two team approach with competing teams is sometimes a natural consequence, for example as long as national interests are involved. This is beneficial to the project as long a clear gating is able to focus on one single approach or technique if it is necessary.

High investment requires a clear screening and gating process and not necessarily a direct approach to the market (technology ready but product on hold).

> Continuous involvement of the top-management is an absolute prerequisite.

Of course the continuous contact to the customers, the aircraft companies Boeing, McDonnell Douglas and Airbus Industries, has been an essential part of the program. Each year in a customer conference the progress and the status as well as the market situation has been discussed. The resulting network of world-wide participation is shown in Fig. V.6.3

2.2   The Organization

Very important for the success of a big program like the described one has been the commitment to a real team approach. This has been done in spite of a difference in the size of the partner companies. The partner companies consisted of Pratt&Whitney, Fiat Aviazione, United Technologies, Hamilton Standard, and MTU.

The highest decision level was the „UHB-management board". The members of this board have been high level representatives of the main involved companies. An appropriate level proved to be for example the vice-president of advanced programs or the company board member for engineering. This Top-Level Management Meeting took place twice a year in the partner companies in an alternating sequence. Participants have been the board members, the program managers and members of engineering. A special attention has been paid to the specialists of the host company and their work progress and ideas. The technological progress is reviewed and corrections for the future have been made. The presentations have been mainly done by specialists and not by management. By this procedure a close coupling between the decision level and the engineering level was guaranteed. In critical situations additional, independent reviewers have been consulted.

It is important to mention that the described appreciation of the achieved results and the close contact between management and the specialists as well as the team approach proved to be absolutely necessary for continuous motivation in this extreme complex international environment.

In parallel to the technology meetings it has been a focus to evaluate the financial value of the work done during the last period. This proved to be impossible on a purely financial basis. The way the consortium had chosen was „technology for technology". The basis for balancing these shares has been the workshare, which is corresponding to develop the final components of the ready-to-market product.

> Exchange "Technology for Technology" for the benefit of the resulting product.

> Use a product focused concurrent technology approach.

Of course the variation of exchange rates during time and determination of price escalation in the different countries also has been taken into account. A basic cooperation contract addressing these financial and technical issues has been agreed on at the start of the project. Every year this initial basis has been updated. These updates have only been negotiated on a „Delta" basis with respect to the basic cooperation contract. By this procedure these negotiations have been reduced to a minimum.

In case a partner wishes to terminate the contracts one-sided all the technology developed so far by this partner has to be given to the other partners disposal.

As already mentioned the financial value of the technology work performed has been closely coupled to the final engine concept. For this purpose just after the gate of „fixed concept" has been passed a realistic engine configuration was established. In the discussed example this was the „Advanced Ducted Propfan Demonstrator". The development costs for the different components of this technology demonstrator engine in case of technology readiness then have been fixed. Depending on their ability and their interest the different partners chose their preferred components. Correspondingly they took over the responsibility for the technology development of this specific component. An example of this worksharing approach is given in Fig. V.6.4, showing the responsibilities of the program partners for the different components of the engine.

This procedure has proved to work quite satisfactorily. A new evaluation is only necessary if the engine configuration changes dramatically.

Below the UHB-Management board so called Integrated Product Management Teams have been responsible for the technical progress within budget and time. They reported to the board members in a three month time frame.

3   R&D Coordinator

Within the three companies a project manager has been established as the carrier of the program. This project manager coordinated the Integrated Product Management Teams and different local teams related to different topics. These topics can be general issues as for example the engine performance. Another topic is the development of a test bed for a special component. In addition teams related to special technologies for example related to fiber reinforced materials have been created. Generally the members of these teams have been chosen from different disciplines. A team for example developing a component consisted of designers, aerodynamical and mechanical engineering staff, test engineers and so on. By doing this the final product and not a special technology has always been the focus.

Each partner is responsible for its component, starting from the technology until the final product definition.

International phone conferences together with fax and datanet exchange became routine. These multifunctional teams met every week in each company. International video conferences were arranged if necessary. The progress of the work in the different teams was presented every three or four months to the Integral Product management teams. This procedure guaranteed that the different technology paths at the end will lead to the engine.

Accompanied was this procedure on the international platform by regular internal reviews in the partner companies themselves.

4   Important R&D Instruments and Procedures

4.1   Concurrent Engineering and Costs

A satisfying time to market or time to demonstration during product development is closely coupled to a development in multifunctional teams (integrated development or concurrent engineering). On the contrary, the development of basic technologies in the premature phase very often eludes a decisive time controlling. Furthermore the danger to develop technology for the sake of technology cannot be neglected.

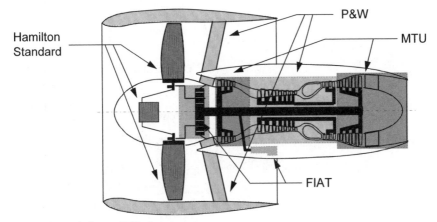

Fig. V.6.4. Work share - ADP -demonstrator.

To combine the necessity of a straight forward development of the demonstrator engine with the high risk of the basic technologies being necessary for this development, the following measures have been taken:

- Even the basic technology was developed in a concurrent way. By this „concurrent technology development" it has been avoided that single techniques have been developed being not the optimum for the demonstrator engine.
- The technology development in the before mentioned step 2 phase has been run like an engine program being based on mature techniques. This has been possible, by defining risk levels for each field and care for fall back solutions or alternative technical measures.

Using this procedure, by the way, a healthy competition between the teams has been created. Each teams' goal was to see its technical solution being a part of the demonstrator engine. The importance of this straight forward procedure to meet critical milestones and gates is demonstrated in Fig. V.6.5, which shows the dramatic increase of costs in the early phase of a ground demo-program. It can be easily imagined that a careful multipath management of the technology topics with parallel approaches and early fall back solutions is more cost effective in comparison to a single iteration with double efforts during the demonstration or testing phase.

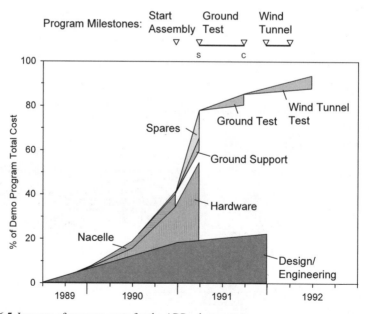

Fig. V.6.5. Increase of program costs for the ADP - demonstrator.

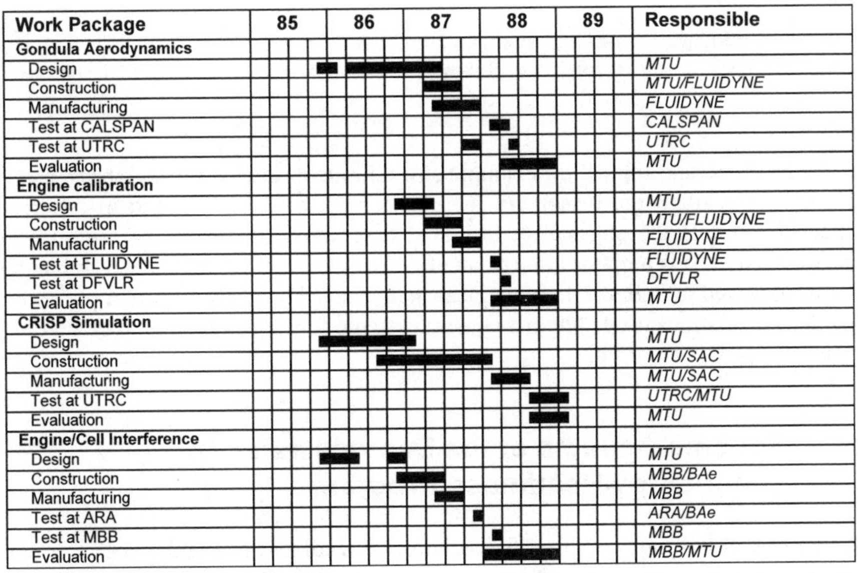

Work Package	85	86	87	88	89	Responsible
Gondula Aerodynamics						
Design						MTU
Construction						MTU/FLUIDYNE
Manufacturing						FLUIDYNE
Test at CALSPAN						CALSPAN
Test at UTRC						UTRC
Evaluation						MTU
Engine calibration						
Design						MTU
Construction						MTU/FLUIDYNE
Manufacturing						FLUIDYNE
Test at FLUIDYNE						FLUIDYNE
Test at DFVLR						DFVLR
Evaluation						MTU
CRISP Simulation						
Design						MTU
Construction						MTU/SAC
Manufacturing						MTU/SAC
Test at UTRC						UTRC/MTU
Evaluation						MTU
Engine/Cell Interference						
Design						MTU
Construction						MBB/BAe
Manufacturing						MBB
Test at ARA						ARA/BAe
Test at MBB						MBB
Evaluation						MBB/MTU

Fig. V.6.6. Milestones for fixed work packages (German contribution „Nacelle Aerodynamics").

4.2 Coordination Techniques

To succeed in comprehensive programs like the described one, it is absolutely necessary to use the optimal planning instruments for each program phase:

For planning and controlling the general technology strategy, a gating process with different alternative ways and branches proved to be the adequate tool. These gating plans, however, are already rather complex.

Regarding the single issues and the single work packages a mapping technique or a gating process for the controlling of the work in the different teams have not been established. With rather fixed goals for these teams a simple controlling or planning by milestones proved to be more efficient. Fig. V.6.6 shows as an example the original milestone plan for different work packages with respect to the German nacelle aerodynamic studies. The reviewed results of these work packages were input to the overall gating process.

4.3 Communication

A general experience made during this multinational project is that communication *must* be managed. In our context the focus is not on the ability to have a discussion on a high technical level in foreign languages. Communication is understood here as technical communication. It proved to be a major hurdle during the whole project that very often the engineers and scientists had deep and long dis-

> Use adaptive controlling / managing methods.

cussions on certain topics, for example stress limits or engine reverse thrust capabilities. Very often the reason for these differences has been found in different understanding of the physical or technical description of parameters they use in the discussion. It is a major issue of an effective program management to force the teams involved to define extremely clear the technical scope and content of formulas and correlations used. Again a general extreme formalism proved to be ineffective.

5   Specific Aspects of the Demonstrator and Technology Readiness Program

As described the joint program for technology readiness and technology demonstration of a new generation of jet engines has been performed in an international approach of different companies. Various management tools have been used being adapted to the appropriate level of controlling for each process.

The ground demonstrator has been realized and tested in time and within the budget. All goals have been reached. The demonstrated fuel consumption and especially the noise reduction have been extraordinary. In addition to it the tests helped to define the technologies needed for a future real flight engine.

This financial and technological success in combination with the extraordinary high technical level of the work being performed has only been achievable because of the extremely high motivation of the people being involved in the project.

Looking backwards this leads to a specific problem which is perhaps inherent to gating processes like the described one:

- Big demands for the teams.
- The teams themselves working highly motivated with extreme personal identification to their goals.
- These goals are additionally separated in work packages focused on companies or nations.

These different factors necessarily lead in case of gating or „go and no-go" decisions to the creation of „losers". Only quite seldom decisions in the high technology area can be based on simple criteria. Like the technology itself the decisions and the argumentation they are based on are extremely complex. So it is very often difficult for the different teams to understand why a special solution is accepted and another route is no longer followed. A „stop decision" leads to remarkable frustration and demotivation for teams having struggled about a year to prove that the worked out solution is the best. These bad feelings are even increased if national or company identification plays a part.

> **Major issues for global R&D management at MTU:**
> 1. Managing technology alliances on a global scale;
> 2. Balancing market-/project-orientation and innovation;
> 3. Creating real international partnership.

As a consequence the past experience showed that it is extremely important from the beginning not only to put enough emphasis on the goals but also on the „units of measure" these goals are valued by. And again these „units of measure" must be accepted by both, the program management and the working level.

6   Conclusions

Generally the successful realization of the „Advanced Ducted Propfan Demonstrator" performed by a joint effort of the companies Pratt&Whitney, MTU München, Fiat Aviazione and Hamilton Standard has been an effective demonstration of an international high technology cooperation. A technological cooperation between different nations and partially competitive companies can be successfully managed. The aspect of appropriate management tools for each phase and each level of the work has been a decisive success factor.

Looking backward, however, in addition to a clear management of the process itself (including a variety of process management tools) the creation of a joint team spirit proved to be the most important issue. This team spirit is continuing to last even if the project itself should be finished and thus it is in addition to the product or the achieved technology level an invest into the future of the companies itself.

About ten years later exactly this point has been proved to be a driving factor: The research effort has led to a ground demonstrator engine and based on that to a continuous work towards this new generation of aero engines. As already indicated in Fig. V.6.1 a marketable engine can be available in 2010. The long timeframe covered in this contribution dramatically proves the need for long term technology and cooperation planning in aero-engine business.

V.7 BMW Group: Strategic Framework for Global Innovation to Enhance the Efficiency of Global R&D*

1 At a Glance: The BMW Group in Today's Automotive Industry

The performance measures of most of today's cars have started to converge and nowadays design and brand are often the only real differentiators. However, innovative technology can still make a difference. The BMW Group therefore has a strong focus on design and brand but has ever since given much attention to R&D in order to keep its advantage and remain in the pinnacle position in the automotive industry's stiff competition for innovation. International R&D has been an issue for quite a while since innovation does not only happen in the labs of the car manufacturers. It emerges from various sources and those sources increasingly spread globally. The challenge of this situation lies in the seamless integration and the coordination of all those efforts with only one thing in mind: to build the ultimate driving machine.

1.1 Past to Present

The BMW Group began its success in the sixties when it started to produce a modern range of sporty limousines. BMW became to be known as the "ultimate driving machine" and this image was founded by cars like the BMW 1500 or later in the early seventies BMW 2002ti. In this decade the BMW Group established a typology for its products that is still in place today: The 3, 5, 6, and 7 series. BMW constantly extended its product range throughout the nineties and the new millennium. This heritage allowed BMW to grow to one of the strongest brands in the world.

Today the BMW Group offers automobiles under the brands BMW, MINI and Rolls-Royce. The successful recent product offensive led the brand BMW to offer

---

* This case study was written by *Dr. Martin Stahl*, BMW Group's central marketing department, and *Marc-Michael Bergfeld*, Ph.D. candidate at Manchester Business School.

Most important drivers for globalization:

1. Localization of products.

2. Sourcing local market knowledge.

3. Reducing costs.

4. Accessing globally dispersed pockets of knowledge and technologies, esp. upcoming in the emerging markets.

---

nearly a dozen different models with a variety of engines, ranging from fuel efficient 1.8l Diesel engines to state-of-the-art high performance engines with over 500HP in the new BMW M6 sports coupé.

The brand MINI has done very well in establishing the new MINI as a successful new interpretation of the iconic MINI, designed by Sir Alec Issigonis in the fifties. While supporting the traditional roots of the MINI, the brand was developed even further into one of today's most desired lifestyle brands. This move was supported by the launch of the MINI convertible in 2004.

In the same time, Rolls-Royce reclaimed the pinnacle position in the international automotive society by launching the new Rolls-Royce Phantom. The Phantom sets the pace for the ultimate luxury car, far ahead of its competitors.

From a financial perspective, the BMW Group is one of the most successful automotive manufacturers. Constantly focusing on premium products, the BMW Group continued its successful growth and achieved new record figures revenues in 2005. Despite adverse currency factors, Group revenues in 2005, at € 46.656 billion, were 5.2% higher than in the previous year. The EBIT-margin of 7% reflects the competitiveness of the BMW Group in the automotive industry.

1.2   Global R&D at the BMW Group

All brands of the BMW Group are facing great expectations concerning the quality of engineering and innovation. To live up to these expectations, BMW Group is bundling all R&D activities in a high performance R&D organization. This organization has its core in the Munich R&D center FIZ ('Forschungs- und Innovationszentrum'). To have an intake for innovation from innovative clusters around the world, the BMW Group has established several units, which are described below.

Accessing Silicon Valley Innovation

The BMW Group Technology Office in Palo Alto (PATYO) lies in the heart of Silicon Valley. It was founded in June 1998 and employs about 16 highly qualified specialists from different technical areas. Half of the staff is locally hired and the other half are expatriates from Germany. PATYO's employees continuously monitor Silicon Valley's start-up landscape, attend venture capital meetings, conferences, and maintain extensive networks with local scientists and engineers. The immediate proximity to neighboring electronics and software companies in Silicon Valley as well as close contacts to Stanford University and the University of California at Berkeley enable the BMW Group to rapidly take up and commercialize new ideas. The Palo Alto Technology Office helps BMW Group to outpace global time differences through steady presence in the Silicon Valley and to foster direct 'trans-Atlantic' communication of the company with this globally leading cluster. Even in today's picture of the global interconnectedness through the World Wide Web, precisely such personal contact between innovation experts (from FIZ and PATYO as well as PATYO and the Silicon Valley community) remains crucial in the creation and implementation of new ideas.

The mission of the Palo Alto Technology Office has evolved over the last years. At first, the office was to look for new technologies and send ideas to Germany. That meant searching for advances in telematics, vehicle computing and electronic commerce. Over time, in addition to those duties, PATYO engineers started developing innovation in form of hardware prototypes. Tody, its mission is thus (a) to permanently be on the look-out for new trends, highly specialized and unique technical knowledge as well as technologies and (b) to deliver (applicable) innovation concepts for BMW Group's advanced development.

An innovation team at PATYO typically comprises three people and has 90 days to identify, explore and develop new innovation concepts. The teams are cross-functional so that each project has the perspective of a marketer, an engineer, a strategist et cetera. If the team determines that a technology has a chance, the engineers begin to work on the components and finally build a working prototype. Once the design and prototype are finished, the innovation concept is tested on-site in the interiors of several production cars. If the concept survives the rigorous testing procedure, it is transferred to Munich for further evaluation, development and final commercialization.

Asian Encounter: Technology Office Japan

In 1981 BMW Group began its operation as the first wholly owned subsidiary of a European car manufacturer in Japan with only five models (318i, 518i, 528i, 633csi and 733i) in the product lineup. At that time the only reason for choosing Japan as a location was getting market access. Despite the limited number of models and difficult conditions for selling imported automobiles, the market developed so rapidly that BMW Group soon added three additional functions to the BMW Group Technology Office in Japan: technology observation and contact facilitation, development as well as testing and validation.

The Japanese development and purchasing unit comprises 26 employees of whom 3 (Japanese and German engineers) work in technology observation and development. The mission of the technology observation function aims at gathering application knowledge and providing BMW Group's headquarters with interesting contacts to Japanese companies and/or research institutes.

In order to cover a large number of technology fields and organizations, each R&D staffer in Japan is specialized in a specific technology field and works on building his external network. Technology observation consists of keeping track of daily life and upcoming trends in Japan. The information gathered is screened and weekly filtered by so-called technology circle members before it is translated and forwarded to BMW Group's innovation management department. Trends are forwarded on a regular basis and selected topics are introduced in the Technology Reports (approximately 10 reports/year). The innovation management makes all trends and reports available to BMW Group associates via a searchable Intranet database called TECHNIS. In exceptional cases the information is also split up according to end-user profiles and forwarded to identified decision makers in the appropriate innovation council. Beneath the gathering and assessing of trends as well as application knowledge, mainly Japanese employees act as door openers towards the local scientific community and competing as well as non-competing companies with the aim to tap tacit and embedded knowledge or establish contacts. The R&D employees must have strong networking capabilities, communication skills and a thorough understanding of the Japanese culture and language. These are the pre-requisites for the job as the ability to read „between the lines" returns high-quality information.

Future Steps: China

The Chinese market is growing in volumes and is only in its early stages with respect to automotive demand. Due to this, the BMW Group established a technology office within its national sales company in China. The technology office facilitates four major tasks related to a successful distribution of BMW Group products in China:

- *Homologation*: Homologation describes the process a car runs through in order to be approved for the use on public roads by the government. The homologation process in China is particularly complex due to the variety of involved authorities. In addition a homologation takes comparatively long (up to 9 months) and involves intense testing of cars and components.
- *Vehicle Testing*: A variety of environmental factors require local testing of the vehicles. Such are the different quality of fuels, the demanding environmental conditions like humidity, high temperatures and the high air pollution.

Major issues for global R&D management at BMW Group:

1. Cross-industry innovation / collaboration;

2. Environmental requirements and eco-friendly technologies;

3. Continuously tapping best sources of emerging technologies globally and choosing the relevant ones;

4. Securing core knowledge in locations with clear IP legislation whilst integrating research results from additional regions.

- *Market research*: As mentioned, the Chinese market is gaining importance. Therefore it is important to understand the needs of Chinese customers somewhat different: it is for example much more important to state one's personal success with the car. In addition people do much more often have drivers than in the western world, therefore the rear seat environment. The technology office gives the BMW Group a first hand view on the development on the Chinese market and allows to quickly adopt to the emerging market demands.
- *Purchase*: China is not only an important sales market, it is an important supplier as well. The technology office therefore establishes links to the Chinese supplier network.

Summarizing one can state, that the BMW Group's technology office in China builds a beachhead into the attractive and growing Chinese market and adds a important function to the international technology network.

1.3   Think Tank FIZ: Where it Comes Together

The heart and soul of the BMW Group's R&D is the Research and Innovation Center 'FIZ' in Munich. This facility houses everything that is required to develop a leading edge automobile. This does not only include the engineering but also the workshops for prototypes, design, research and even a small pilot plant for the training of new model launches. Approximately 8,500 people work on all aspects of the cars of the future. Looking at innovation management, it is the place where everything comes together. Interdisciplinary teams consisting of engineers, designers, production and marketing managers (so called councils) are constantly assessing the innovations in close cooperation with the centers of competence. An innovation management process ensures that innovations are channeled into car projects. This process was awarded by the Product Development and Management Association (PDMA) with the Outstanding Corporate Innovator Award (OCI) in 2002.

2   Taking Advantage of Global R&D

Oftentimes, development follows decentralized structures in production whilst research is retained in central entities. This causes different organizational approaches in the various phases of the overall innovation process and thus a high degree of co-ordination efforts for multinational companies. Today, driving innovation from pure research to de facto development and eventual commercialization of products requires considering the entire innovation process on a global scale. Herein, two questions are dominating discussions on global innovation management in practice (see Bergfeld and Stahl, 2005):

- Where and how to find promising technical inventions and market trends anywhere in the world – earlier than others in order to 'drive global innovation leadership' ?

- How to transform inventions into innovation in global structures and processes – under the maxim of 'managing process and network structures' towards maximum efficiency and enabling 'local innovation leadership' when the market context calls for specific solutions ?

As explained above, the automotive industry faces this challenge to a particular extent because of the global character of its business. Not only are the latest cars constantly sold across all continents. Car manufacturers also maintain strong interrelations with supplying companies which innovate themselves and are also located globally. In addition, innovations in adjacent industries (e.g. multimedia) increasingly influence innovation management in the car industry. Car corporations are therefore already tied into innovation networks that spread globally and across industries. In the presented cases, we look into the ways in which intra-corporational innovation networks and processes can be designed and managed accordingly - on a global scale.

The first question of 'listening' to the global context for cutting-edge trends and technological developments through dedicated foreign entities and 'Corporate Sensing' of upcoming market and technology opportunities is being looked into academically.[65] Organizational and process related issues of managing innovation in the global context have been widely addressed.[66] The aspect of 'local innovation leadership' through intra-company technology transfers in international R&D structures and factors relevant to the exchange of knowledge and technology herein has been looked into in detail (see Bergfeld and Malik, 2004).

2.1   Four Types of Global Innovation at BMW Group

In today's management decisions, additional trade-offs add an extra 'twist of complexity' to global innovation management:

- Increasing corporate concentration on core capabilities *versus* outsourcing R&D on a global scale for cost reasons and due to political 'local content' requirements.
- Tapping best human resources around the globe *versus* leveraging labor cost deltas between industrialized and emerging economies.
- Using ICT for improved decision making in networks *versus* sharing rich, tacit and quickly changing knowledge.
- Maintaining an equilibrium in international innovation actions in the trade-off between home-base augmenting *versus* home-base exploiting activities.[67]
- Allocation of scarce resources to divisions, corporate labs and regions *versus* establishing new business endeavors.

From the perspective of the BMW Group, *market and technology settings* are

---

[65]   See e.g. Gassmann and Gaso (2004), Sofka (2005), Lichtenthaler (2004).
[66]   See e.g. Gassmann (1997a) for four archetypes of international innovation processes, or Gassmann and von Zedtwitz (2003) for transnational innovation processes.
[67]   See e.g. Kuemmerle (1996) and Dunning / Narula (1995)

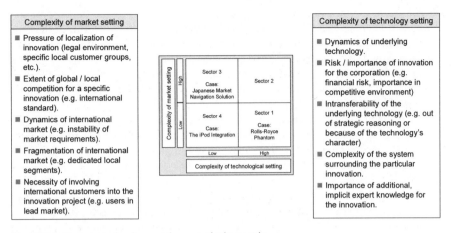

Complexity of market setting	Complexity of technology setting
■ Pressure of localization of innovation (legal environment, specific local customer groups, etc.). ■ Extent of global / local competition for a specific innovation (e.g. international standard). ■ Dynamics of international market (e.g. instability of market requirements). ■ Fragmentation of international market (e.g. dedicated local segments). ■ Necessity of involving international customers into the innovation project (e.g. users in lead market).	■ Dynamics of underlying technology. ■ Risk / importance of innovation for the corporation (e.g. financial risk, importance in competitive environment) ■ Intransferability of the underlying technology (e.g. out of strategic reasoning or because of the technology's character) ■ Complexity of the system surrounding the particular innovation. ■ Importance of additional, implicit expert knowledge for the innovation.

Fig. V.7.1. Market / technology setting complexity matrix.

essential factors for the selection and management of the appropriate innovation network design. Both settings can be of high or low complexity. Formulated as two axis, this spans open a matrix of market setting complexity (MSC) and technological setting complexity (TSC) with four sectors:

The complexity of an innovation's market and technology setting is characterized by five factors each (see Fig. V.7.1). In general, Market Setting Complexity is per se an externally driven factor. Corporations can only slightly influence market situations and will thus have to be responsive to the market setting as a contingency factor for their innovation projects. Technology Setting Complexity is only partly externally driven. The question whether a technology is defined as part of the core competencies of a corporation is rather a decision of corporate strategy. Equally, the question of interdependence of various technologies within a product are influenced by the product portfolio offered by the innovating company. Technology dynamics can be handled within a corporation e.g. by the definition of clear interfaces and standards which gives the company more freedom to act in the TSC context.

The combination of MSC and TSC generates four types of global innovation. For each one a dedicated approach to efficiently managing global innovation networks and processes exists (Fig. V.7.2):

The particular characteristics of these innovation network archetypes are exemplified with practical cases of the BMW Group:

2.2   Rolls-Royce Phantom: Global Innovation Leadership of the Corporate Center

Radical innovations or premium segment products are often examples of high technology setting complexity and low market setting complexity .

In the case of radical innovations, the technological nucleus is often still *highly dynamic* and the innovation project bears a *large inherent risk* for the corporation because it is either radically new to the company or even to the world. In the case of premium and luxury goods, the innovation project is most likely in the area of the company's *core competence* and will subsequently be used in lower segments of the portfolio after a successful introduction in the 'high-end'. The sophistication normally targeted by an innovation in the top segment of a company is most likely to cause *high interdependence of numerous technologies.*

At the same time, *low pressure for local product adaptation* is most likely for radical and globally leading innovations and customer requirements in the luxury segment can be seen as fairly homogeneous in the global context which assures a *low instability of market requirements* and a *low fragmentation of the international market demands.*

As a logical consequence the major part of the innovation process will take place in the corporate headquarters and adaptation to local markets will not be an issue. In order to integrate latest technologies or market trends into such premium products, these will have to be identified and 'brought to the center'. The adequate network will focus on the early phases of the innovation process and mainly source global market and technology intelligence in a 'global to center' mode. The development of the present Rolls-Royce Phantom gives a good understanding, how external entities can be used gainfully in complex development process.

In 1998 a new era for Rolls-Royce began holding chances and risks. The BMW Group had taken over Rolls-Royce. A cooperation between the BMW Group and Rolls-Royce had been established for a while. The BMW Group supplied a variety of components to the Silver Seraph, especially engines. This high-technology transfer contributed significantly to the strength of the brand Rolls-Royce. In the new ownership structure the development of the Phantom was a significant step

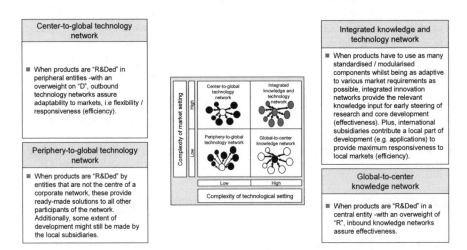

Fig. V.7.2. The BMW Group's approaches to manage global innovation: Complexity and corresponding network archetypes.

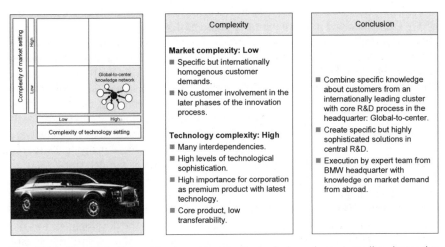

Fig. V.7.3. The Rolls-Royce Phantom. Complexity analysis and corresponding innovation network.

for the BMW Group. It was the first Rolls-Royce to be developed entirely by the BMW Group. In addition, authenticity was a crucial challenge: Managers at the BMW Group where wondering how a modern interpretation of Rolls-Royce could be built whilst maintaining the spirit of the Rolls-Royce heritage.

Evaluation of market setting complexity: Customer integration was a big issue in the development of the new Phantom, in order to design the car to the needs of this very specific customer group that was not too familiar to the BMW Group at this point in time. The luxury segment of the car industry is a very special market. Thus BMW Group faced a novel product with very specific characteristics. However, market setting complexity was comparatively low because the luxury car segment addresses a globally fairly homogeneous customer group (i.e. low pressure for local adaptation, stable market requirements, no international fragmentation of markets, low customer involvement in the innovation process). Market setting complexity was therefore low.

Evaluation of technology setting complexity: The technology setting complexity of a car can generally be rated as high. Today's cars consist of a variety of subsystems, which are highly interdependent (i.e. low transferability of core competences, interdependence of numerous technologies, importance of tacit knowledge). In combination with the high expectations of customers in terms of the sophistication of the products, the seamless integration of those sub-systems becomes an even more critical issue. Therefore a modularization is hardly possible. Technology setting complexity was therefore high. Thus, the challenge was to bring the established product development process together with the direct input of very specific customers that were not necessarily present in the company's national home turf, Germany.

The expectations towards the new Phantom were huge. Especially the design had to fit to the status of Rolls-Royce as an icon of British culture. Therefore the BMW Group decided to place the early phase of development where this culture is alive. A profound field study was conducted in the precise living environment of the end users: A team of engineers and designers was sent to London where they rented an old bank building in Bayswater Road directly in the heart of Kensington. The natural presence of vintage Rolls-Royce cars predestined this place for the development of the new Phantom. In addition the team emerged into the lifestyle of traditional Rolls-Royce customers: They visited traditional Rolls-Royce deal-ers, in order to understand how buying decisions for such luxury product are made. They spent time in traditional clubs in London, where many Rolls-Royce customers are present. This experience for example led to the decision to design the interior of the new Phantom with highest craftsmanship, noble atmosphere but no visible technology.

Conclusion: The successful introduction of the new Rolls-Royce Phantom showed that the use of the "global-to-center" approach in the development was the appropriate way to reinvent this legend in an environment of very specific but still fairly stable and predictable market conditions and high technological complexity. Thus, it was possible to have the development of the car in one team, being able to handle the technological complexity and ensure the smooth hand-over to the fol-lowing development process in the BMW Group's R&D center in Munich where the eventual 'center of gravity of product development' was located. The devel-opment team itself sourced knowledge from the leading market through temporary personal presence. Due to this direct input from the customers the team was able to integrate precise requirements into the development process. The case shows that in the early phase of the development process, an input from foreign subsidi-aries (in this case a temporarily set up one) can generate high value and improve the performance of the development process.

2.3   Japanese Navigation Solution: International Technology Transfer for Local Innovation Leadership

In a sector 3 situation (see Fig. V.7.1), a corporation is facing a low complexity of the technology setting whilst the market setting complexity is high. This is the case for an innovation project that strives for 'local innovation leadership' con-cerning mature technologies.

In the case of rather incremental innovations, the technological core is likely to be *less dynamic*, being rooted in established dominant designs and standards. Interdependence with other technologies might remain considerable, but due to standards, dominant designs and established interfaces the systems *complexity is likely to be reduced*. As a continuous improvement of existing product there is *low risk* in terms of the underlying technology and *transferability* of the projects is *high*.

At the same time, *pressure for local product adaptation* is most likely to re-main high because the innovativeness of incremental product improvements de-pends strongly on the local market context. *Market requirements* are likely to be *highly unstable* and *international markets* are likely to be *considerably fragmented*

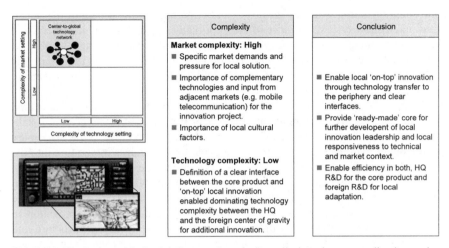

Fig. V.7.4. The Japanese Navigation System. Complexity analysis and corresponding innovation network.

because of the underlying technology's maturity. Further, the integration of customers and even local infrastructures can be of high relevance in order to be perceived as local innovation leader by the respective markets. The adequate network will therefore focus on enabling local entities in the periphery of a corporate innovation network to innovate for local innovation leadership.

The development of the Japanese Navigation System gives a good understanding, how enabling local innovation can lead to innovation leadership in complex market settings.

The Japanese market is different in many ways. For example the perception of customers: The most prestigious cars are often ordered in white, a color that comes across as old-fashioned in most of the western countries. Generally, the perception of status symbols is different from Europe or the US: Status is communicated with much less understatement. For this reason, very dominant cars have great success in Japan. When it comes to customer expectations in terms of technology, one can state that Japan is one of the most demanding markets in the world. Looking at telematics and navigation for example, Japan is one of the most advanced countries in the world. The traffic density demanded for technological solutions since the beginning of the 1980s. This demand led to the development of a unique telematics infrastructure that is superior to most other systems in the world. The infrastructure is limited to the metropolitan areas and uses a huge number of sensors to detect the actual traffic situation.

Evaluation of market setting complexity: Looking at the worldwide market for telematics one can state that there are a variety of country specific and proprietary solutions. The situation in Japan is a good example for such a country specific situation. Due to the specific telematics infrastructure pressure for local adaptation was high. Additionally, complementary technologies such as e.g. the field of mobile communication was very particular and important for the design of the 'localized' navigation system. Because of the importance of human-machine interaction in using the navigation system, even cultural factors (such as language, symbols et cetera) had to be taken into account and thus the end-users had an important role in innovating the navigation system for local innovation leadership. Therefore market setting complexity was high.

Evaluation of technology setting complexity: Certainly the technologies behind the Japanese telematics systems are high-tech. But those systems are not a substantial part of the car. The advantage of developing them close to the market are much higher than the effort that has to be made for a seamless integration into the car's infrastructure. Interfaces can be clearly defined and separated from the rest of the car's infotainment / navigation system. The integration of the navigation system's core into the car's infotainment / navigation system is a core competence of the R&D headquarters in Munich. Still though, 'on top' local innovation in terms of e.g. applications and linking the system to the local infrastructure and technology context is essential. The opportunity to define clear interfaces between the core of the navigation system and localized innovations for Japan lead to the conclusion that technology setting complexity was 'low'.

The BMW Group has been developing specific Japanese navigation and telematics units for ten years. The specifications for the units are raised by the BMW Group's Technology Office in Japan. The specialists there have a thorough knowledge of the Japanese market and the relevant technological trends. Therefore they can precisely define the requirements of the next generation telematics / navigation units for the Japanese market. The development of the telematics / navigation units takes place in the product development department of the Tokyo office. This process is linked closely to the development of more general car systems like the MOST-bus system that takes place in the R&D center in Munich. The strict management of clear interfaces was a key enabler for this very successful international co-operation for innovation.

Conclusions: The fact that the BMW Group is present in the Japanese market with competitive telematics / navigation units shows that transferring technologies and responsibility for further application in a "center-to-global" approach is a viable way to achieve local innovation leadership. In this way, the leading entity in the respective market can act self-managed in order to transform core technologies into respected products for the local market – in the course of the rear end of the overall innovation process. In the past, fulfilling those local requirements contributed significantly to the positive development of the BMW Group's sales in the Japanese market.

2.4   *iPod Integration: Sourcing-in Technologies from Globally Leading Clusters*

In a sector 4 situation (see Fig. V.7.1), a corporation is facing low complexity of the technology and market setting. This can be the case for innovation projects add features to the core product but are not necessarily core competence. In this article we focus on 'add-on innovations'.

Characteristics of such innovation projects are: Low *dynamic of the core technologies, low risk, low interdependence and low stickiness* (e.g. to the headquarters) because of the 'add on character' and thus high *transferability* of the project.

In terms of market setting complexity, the market setting of the core product does not have direct influence on the 'add on innovation' project. It can thus be conducted *wherever the market environment is best* for it – ideally in the lead market for the topic.

The integration of the Apple iPod into the car infotainment system through a foreign entity in a leading innovative milieu gives a good understanding, how leveraging technology 'hot spots' provides corporations with 'on-top' innovations that fascinate the customers.

The digital age has altered many things. In recent years, the digital revolution has reached the music industry as well. Data storage capacity grew and space requirements of music dropped dramatically by the introduction of file formats like mp3. Therefore it was just a matter of time that the old-fashioned Walkman was replaced by small digital devices like the iPod presented by Apple in fall 2001. Apple provided a Windows version of the iPod in 2002 that finally created the breakthrough. The iPod in its latest version is able to carry 80GB of music, which equals about 15,000 songs. This means having your complete selection of all the titles you ever bought with you at any time. It is obvious that this situation demands for a solution for the most common place to enjoy music on the way: the car.

Evaluation of market setting complexity: For the iPod, market requirements are pretty much the same all over the world. Today, the iPod is seen to be the dominant design of an mp3 player. The core product is the same in all countries and equally are the use cases. iTunes sells music for the iPod over the most global platform to date – the world wide web. In terms of the innovation 'integration of

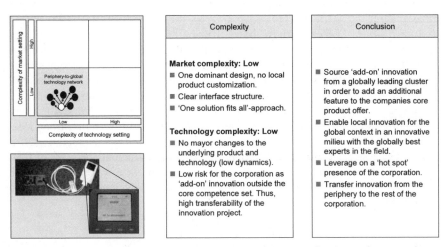

Fig. V.7.5. The iPod Integration. Complexity analysis and corresponding innovation network.

the iPod into the car infotainment system', pressure for local adaptation was thus low. As the first company to work on such an integration BMW Group did not face high competition either. Nor were market requirements instable or internationally fragmented. Thus, market setting complexity was low.

Evaluation of technology setting complexity: Looking at the iPod itself, refreshes are presented regularly but the core product concept is not changed dramatically. The underlying technology is thus little dynamic. As an additional but not essential innovation of the BMW Group, the iPod integration project bared little risk. In addition, there was no knowledge involved that is connected to the core competencies of the automotive industry. Thus, transferability was high. Technological interdependence - the interface between the iPod and the car - was low because of clear interfaces. Overall, technology setting complexity was therefore rated as low.

Following our approach, this suggests that the iPod integration should be handled according to our "selected-periphery-for-all" archetype. For the selection of the adequate foreign entity to execute this innovation project, it was essential to choose the best innovative environment – in this case the PATYO Office in Silicon Valley.

Ideas for the integration of the iPod into a BMW were born at PATYO as early as 2002. At this point in time, there was no interface provided to connect the iPod to the car. The close interaction of the PATYO and Apple led to the definition of a protocol for the iPod's serial interface that was introduced with the 2003 iPod. The collaboration between Apple and the BMW Group was informal and flexible. There were no formalized processes or the like. It was all about using the local Silicon Valley network to get the right people together and an idea on track. The entire innovation process was straight forward and goal-oriented with focus on a precise topic. There was no wide front-end nor a large degree of customization in the rear end of the process. The BMW Group's Palo Alto Technology Office handled this process, being the 'center of gravity' of this project specific network. When the product was launched in June of 2004, the reaction exceeded expectations.

Conclusions: The case study shows that the "selected periphery for all" approach was an efficient way to implement the iPod integration. The low technological complexity allowed the implementation of the interface without intense contact to the BMW Group's R&D center in Munich – the transfer of responsibility to the innovative milieu that was closest to a trend- and technology-setting environment was the most efficient aproach under the given market and technology setting. In addition the development was able to benefit from the strong local network that allowed to develop the interface quickly and unbureaucratically. It was not necessary to integrate a variety of market requirements because of their global homogeneity. Therefore no input from other markets was required which kept the team small and flexible resulting in an overall development time of only six months.

2.5   Simultaneous Global Co-operation on Knowledge and Technology: An Open Issue

In a sector 2 situation (see Fig. V.7.1), a corporation is facing both, high complexity of the technology setting as well as high market setting complexity. This is the case for innovation projects relating rather dynamic technologies on the 'cutting edge between global and local innovation leadership'.

Within the scope of the conducted cases there was no example for widely spanning global-to-center-to-global innovation networks in which the entire innovation process is a globally networked constant exchange of knowledge and technologies. However though, additional discussions shed light on this archetypes when it was stated that especially highly dynamic industries such as mobile communication devices, where market dynamics are extreme and technological complexity is on the cutting edge are intensively looking into such structures in order to dominate an environment characterized by change, ambiguity and uncertainty. Further research will have to look into this area which promises additional insights on the structure of global innovation networks.

2.6   Integrating Global R&D into the Core Process: Taking Ideas to Market Success

The above presented cases have shown that valuable innovation can be created by using global innovation networks in precise designs according to the needed type of innovation and a clear recognition of the market and technology context. As mentioned, such innovation can only be transformed into a competitive advantage by integrating it into the core projects. In order to achieve this, the BMW Group has established a innovation management process that takes care of three core issues:

- *Strategic alignment of innovation:* In order to ensure the selection of innovations that support the strategic orientation of the BMW Group, several topic clusters have been defined. An example for such a topic cluster is "driving experience": Any innovation that supports the genuine driving experience would be supported by this strategic setting.
- *Funding of innovation:* In order to control the innovative projects and ensure their alignment, any project needs to apply for funding. The funding for the projects is allocated by interdisciplinary teams, called "councils". Councils prioritize innovation according to the strategic alignment in a fair competition between global inputs, "home-made" innovation and supplier innovation. These committees have a heavy weight project champion from top-management who acts as a promoter for the innovation within the R&D process.
- *Transfer of innovation:* To make sure that innovations end up in a car project, innovation transfer management has an early involvement into the pre-development. This enables an early understanding of which innovation might fit to which car projects and allows a smooth transfer to series development even for innovations originating from R&D subsidiaries abroad.

Major innovative break-throughs (last 5 years):

1. Active Steering

2. Valvetronic (cold start and smooth running)

3. xDrive (variable four wheel drive)

4. iDrive (simplified steering)

3   Conclusion: Balancing Inside and Outside Innovation in Global Network Structures is the Future Challenge

Today, continuous innovation has proven as a basic requirement for competitiveness and market success not only in the automotive industry. The value of existing international R&D structures for sustainable innovation leadership increasingly depends on an overall strategic orientation for their precise utilization. Managing innovation in the international context becomes a balancing act between market and technology complexity in a very diverse international setting.

- *Choose appropriate innovation structures:* The appropriate innovation network structures and processes need to be identified and applied on a case to case basis. Eventually an adequate usage of global R&D structures gives additional leverage to innovation performance in MNC. The above presented strategic framework for global innovation networks aids to take the appropriate decisions on how and where to locate innovation projects within global innovation networks of MNCs.

- *Benefit from better innovation results:* The cases show that the appropriate use of the innovation structures can create sustainable competitive advantage in different innovation situations: The *Rolls-Royce Phantom* is the most successful car in its segment. The "global to center" knowledge network in the early stages of the car's development had a major stake in that, since it allowed to create a authentic Rolls-Royce and include the latest automotive technology. Similar with the *iPod*: The "selected-periphery-for-all" technology transfer network allowed a fast integration and enabled the BMW Group to be the first car manufacturer to offer a seamless integration of the iPod into the car. And finally the *Japanese navigation unit*: In this case it is not so much about competitive advantage, offering such a system is a entry ticket for a premium car manufacturer in the demanding Japanese market today. Therefore an innovation approach like the "center-to-global" technology transfer network is a commodity in today's competitive automotive industry.

- *Allow the subsidiaries to evolve:* In future times international subsidiaries will be increasingly working as independent units that are aligned by a common strategy. Therefore companies need to *build up interfaces* that *allow the sub-sidiaries* to not only give input in the form of technology trends but enable them *to contribute complete innovation modules* to the core development process. However, this trend should not be overrated since the majority of all development and innovation activities in the automotive industry will still take place in the centralized R&D structures of the OEMs.

In summary, global innovation is developing beyond mere R&D management and increasingly includes issues of strategically steering global network structures with knowledge and technolgy flows in these. Thus, a consistent usage of a strategic framework for global innovation might enable MNCs to enhance innovation performance and thus create and / or maintain sustainable competitive advantage in the global context.

V.8 Siemens: Flying with the Dragon - Innovation in China*

1 The China Magic

At the beginning of this century, China has started to fascinate everyone: everyday people and industrial corporations alike. With continuous annual growth of its GDP of more than 8% since 1978, China is changing rapidly and the world as a result is changing along with China. From 1984 to 2005, utilized Foreign Direct Investment increased at an average rate of more than 20% per year. By 2004, China had become the world's 3rd largest exporting nation after the United States and Germany (Zheng, 2006).

However, the super fast growth in China has also raised many challenges for China to sustain further growth. Some of them are:

- Deteriorating environment
- Lack of energy
- Traffic congestion in the cities
- Ability to provide adequate and affordable healthcare
- Balanced living conditions in big cities
- Wealth gap between rural and urban areas

To continue a stable and sustainable growth path, China must solve these challenges. The only alternative to returning to an agrarian state is that China moves to the next level and becomes an innovation-based economy. The Chinese government has recognized this and is setting "Endogenous Innovation" as one of the most important goals for the current 11th 5 year plan. China achieved the worldwide "Made in China" recognition with global collaboration. To achieve "Invented in China", open and win-win international collaboration is even more important. By doing it in the right way, China has a high chance not only to achieve "Invented in China", but also to establish an innovation system of the future that will change the world game on innovation.

Throughout Siemens' 160-year history, innovation has always been the soul

---

* This case study was authored by *Dr. Richard Hausmann*, President & CEO of Siemens Ltd., China and *Dr. Arding Hsu*, Sr. VP & Head of Corporate Technology.

Most important drivers for globalization:

1. Overall tendency in politics to open economies domestically and internationally;

2. Advances in technology (e.g. information technology, logistics, transportation);

3. Access to talents on a worldwide basis;

4. Market power of newly rising countries (e.g. China and India);

5. Cost differences (labor, services);

6. Mobility – flow of goods, capital, data, and knowledge.

---

and key success factor of the company. From the invention of the first point tele-graph in 1847 to today's Transrapid train in Shanghai, Siemens has achieved many "number ones" on innovation, and from its experience recognizes that inno-vation is a continuous change. One of the most interesting innovation potentials of the 21st century are innovations initially based on an emerging market (such as China) which then move up into the global market. Combining the systematic innovation structure of Siemens with the talent and the market of China, may lead to a very powerful system of innovation for the future. In this chapter, we would like to sketch some elements that need to go into building this innovation system.

2   Innovation in China: Yesterday, Today, and Tomorrow

2.1   Yesterday

China used to be a great country of innovation. For instance, the compass, wheel-barrow, gunpowder, paper-making, and the printing press were all invented in China and then exported to Europe, or at the very least developed much earlier in China than in the West. Along with its history of innovation, China was also an economic powerhouse with about a third of the world's GDP until the year 1600.

But science and technology were never given high social status in China, and centers of science and learning were not institutionalized. The industrial revolu-tion in the West was very much a development of its innovation institutions, just as the renaissance of the 16th century was an accomplishment of free scientific discourse and discovery, based on universities that were established just before and during this period. In just 150 years of industrial innovation, China lost its economic frontrunner position and dropped in its international GDP share to 4.5% by 1950 (all world GDP share are at Purchasing Power Parity) (Maddison, 2001).

With the founding of the new China in 1949, innovation has become an item of China's government agenda again. However, to conduct innovation in China, it is important to understand the overall background and environment of the Chinese innovation system. Two major phases in China's innovation system can be discerned. Incidentally, it is now, in the mid-2000s, that Chinese innovation structure – China's innovation producers, innovation users, and the link from producers to users – is making a transition from the second to a third phase.

2.2   1949 to 1978

In the first decades of the People's Republic of China, the innovation system was basically centrally planned with little direct interaction and accountability between innovation producers and users (Gu and Lundvall, 2006).

R&D institutes were organized and managed under related industrial ministries with direct funding. The ministries also managed all production enterprises, and were responsible for the coordination of R&D institutes and enterprises. This is very similar to the former West's model of 100% centrally-financing industrial R&D organizations – a model which has died out some time ago. With this structure, China was able to quickly build up an innovation system and accomplish a number of important national projects. But just as with the old industrial R&D system, this centrally directed system led to researchers separated in their ivory towers away from the real world and its real needs.

2.3   1978 – 2005

With the opening up of China, the new leaders promulgated a new innovation system that was partially market driven and that allowed companies to spin-off from research institutes (Gu and Lundvall, 2006).

Since 1978, market-oriented reforms on innovation were launched with the objective to increase direct interaction and accountability between innovation producers and users. A series of reform policies were implemented:

- In 1985, research institutes were encouraged to seek direct funding from commercial enterprises.
- In 1987, reform policy was designed to encourage the merger of R&D institutes into commercial enterprises.
- In 1988, the Torch Program was launched to spin-off companies from research institutes.
- In early 1990s, reform policy was released to support changing individual R&D institutes into production entities.

During this period, the main objective was to improve the direct link between research institutes and commercial enterprises. Significant progress was achieved when a number of newly created enterprises became globally competitive, e.g., Lenovo. But, with research moving down the value chain into production, innovation teams became production teams and lost the innovation sustainability. Research institutes easily become extended engineering enterprises with negative impact on the quality of innovation.

2.4   2006 Onwards

To counteract the trend of cannibalization of research, and to stimulate innovative forces again, the government decided to change the system of innovation again. The new paradigm is endogenous innovation that puts enterprises in the driving seat of innovation.

Previously China has been named the "world's factory" based on its huge cheap workforce. This keeps China growing at a high speed for a long time, but at the same time, it builds up serious challenges, such as resource restrictions, environmental pollution, reliance on overseas markets, etc. It is obvious that just being the "world's factory" can not sustain China's development. The time to change may be now, as various indications from the political, social, and scientific community suggests. As a consequence, the Chinese government launched a campaign for 2020 to be focused on "Endogenous Innovation." The goal is to change China from the world's manufacturing center to a world-class innovation center.

In early 2006, "The National Guideline on Medium- and Long-term Program for Science and Technology Development (2006-2020)" was released by the Chinese government. In the guideline, "Endogenous Innovation" was put forward as a strategic element of sustainable and harmonious development. According to the guideline, China plans to become an innovative nation in the next 15 years. By 2020, China's entire investment in research and development is expected to reach 2.5 percent of the GDP, with at least 60 percent of the country's development due to the progress of science and technology. Meanwhile, the country's reliance on foreign technology is slated to decline to 30 percent or less. The number of patents granted to Chinese nationals and the number of scientific publications are expected to rank among the top five in the world (State Council of China, 2006).

According to this guideline, an important change in the innovation system is that enterprises will play a leading role in innovation and become the main body of its propagation. The government will push enterprise to spend more on research and development and support enterprises to take part in national R&D projects. A great transformation is expected to take place when the country's innovation system will gradually move away from a producer-focused innovation model to an end user-focused one.

For a long time, China has been a country where copying of products and solutions was not seen as illegal or unethical. Recently, the rules and regulations have been updated and reinforced to protect IPR more effectively. This is a key factor for any innovation culture and strategy. If ideas and innovations are not protected, the incentives to create and disseminate them commercially are not present in the first place. Therefore, this is a major boundary condition for further strengthening the endogenous innovation system, as well as demonstrating to multinational companies that the appropriate investment and R&D conditions are present.

3   Siemens and Siemens in China

Siemens is one of the largest electrical and electronics companies in the world, and one of the most well-known, liked and respected corporate citizens in China. This is not surprising given Siemens' long history of cooperation with China dating back to 1872 when Siemens supplied China with the first pointer telegraphs, the world's most advanced telecommunication technology at the time. Since then, the partnership between Siemens and China has steadily been extended and strengthened.

Today, Siemens is an integral part of the Chinese economy and a reliable, committed and trustworthy partner of China, actively contributing to major infrastructure developments and industrial modernization. Siemens helps to supply power that is affordable, efficient and environmentally friendly. Siemens provides automation solutions for every branch of industry to increase productivity, profitability and competitiveness. Siemens public transportation system is fast, safe and of high capacity; Siemens communication equipment is reliable, fast and cost competitive. And Siemens medical facilities help provide rapid, accurate and effective diagnosis and treatment. The business portfolio of Siemens covers energy and the environment, automation of public and private infrastructures, and healthcare, which match very well with some of China's megatrends, like the ongoing urbanization and demographic change. In short, Siemens is deploying systems and solutions to China that make up the core of any advanced society in the world.

At the end of Fiscal Year 2006 (30 of September, 2006) Siemens' total long-term investment exceeded RMB 11.6 billion and sales reached RMB 50.4 billion in China. Currently, Siemens has more than 75 operating companies and 60 regional offices in China. These offices form the backbone of Siemens' regional marketing strategy and ensure that the company is close to its customers so that it is able to respond quickly and efficiently to customers' needs. With a workforce of over 43,000 people in China, Siemens is one of the largest foreign-invested employers in the country.

Table V.8.1. The three phases of modern China's innovation system.

Time Period	Innovation System	Achievements	Weaknesses
1949 - 1978	Centrally planned	Quickly built up an institutionalized innovation system with success on several national projects.	No direct link between innovation producers and users resulted in ivory tower kind of innovation
1978 - 2005	Partially market driven with spin-offs	Research institutes were encouraged to look for funding from enterprises and a few companies were established with global competitiveness.	Innovation mostly driven by public research institutes. The transition has a negative impact to the innovation quality. Protection of intellectual property rights was rather weak. The system cannot provide sustainable and high quality innovation.
Since 2006	Endogenous innovation with enterprises as the main driving force for innovation		Increased effort to enforce protection of intellectual property through existing rules and regulations

4   Siemens R&D in China

The history of Siemens started in 1847 with the invention of the world's first pointer telegraph, a quantum-leap in telecommunication at the time. Innovation remained at the heart of Siemens in 159 years of development since. It is this dynamic and enterprising spirit that has been the driving force behind its growth and accomplishment, making Siemens one the world's most successful companies. Today, Siemens is uniquely equipped to offer innovative products and solutions for nearly every aspect of our lives, and is therefore in an ideal position to shape the trends and set the pace for the 21st century.

When Siemens entered the "land of the dragon" 134 years ago with pointer telegraph, terms like "innovation" did not even exist yet and "R&D" was hardly a household name. Yet, since then, Siemens has been committed to delivering to China the latest in global technology and has expanded China's position in their whole value chain from "manufacturing made in China" to "innovation made in China." Today, Siemens China is already an important research and development base for global operations, a role that will be further strengthened by taking full advantage of abundant local talents and market power. Great importance is attached to the local design and development of products suited to the needs of the Chinese market, and also to using the advantages that China has to offer to develop technologies here for global business.

To drive innovations "Invented in China" forward, Siemens China has established R&D centers covering all areas of its business. More than 1,000 patent applications filed in Fiscal Year 2005 offer concrete proof of the extent of innovation activities, making Siemens one of the top patent producers in China. In Fiscal Year 2005, Siemens' R&D staff in China increased by 50% as overall R&D operations were extended, particularly in terms of corporate technology, software development, automotive, medical and industrial solutions. Local R&D centers have been established in all business segments in which Siemens is active.

One example is the R&D center of Siemens Shanghai Medical Engineering (SSME), which was started in 1999. It is Siemens' only overseas Computed Tomography R&D center outside Germany. In a very short time, SSME completed major achievements in its R&D activities, with two locally developed Computed Tomography systems for China and the global market. In September 2000, the new spiral Computed Tomography system — SOMATOM Smile — was introduced in China and globally. This is the world's most compact and cost-effective spiral Computed Tomography device, and is specially designed to meet the requirements of private radiological practices. Many small hospitals are eager to invest in Computed Tomography technology. SOMATOM Smile also won the Design Prize of the Federal Republic of Germany in 2002 and the iF Design Award China in 2003. Even more innovation took place with the launch of the locally-developed SOMATOM Spirit, an entry-level dual-slice Computed Tomography system, which has been very well received in both the domestic and the global market.

Siemens is also closely cooperating with China's leading universities, setting up partnerships that are proving to be truly mutually beneficial. So far Siemens is engaged in comprehensive cooperation with 16 of China's leading universities to promote research and development, foster the sharing of knowledge, and contribute to the development of higher education in China.

5   Siemens Corporate R&D in China

5.1   Siemens Corporate Technology

With more than 2,500 employees in Germany, the U.S., China, UK, Russia, India and Japan, Siemens Corporate Technology (CT) acts as an international network of competences and a worldwide partner for innovations for Siemens Business Groups and regional Siemens companies.

The mission of Siemens Corporate Technology is to secure the technological future and to increase the competitiveness of Siemens in cooperation with its operating groups. In detail, it includes:

- Research, development and consulting for strategically important technologies (core technologies)
- Development of future scenarios in the company's areas of activity and development of new business opportunities
- Protection of intellectual property (patents, company names, brand names), and processing of all intellectual property activities of Siemens AG
- Central tasks in connection with standardization and regulation, information, research center and environmental affairs and technical safety
- Development of future technical managers

The innovation focus of Siemens CT is addressing well what scientists have been calling the global megatrends of urbanization and demographic change.

Urbanization: Today, there are 280 million people living in megacities larger than 10 million inhabitants, and by 2015 the population of the world's megacities will have grown by 25 percent. By 2007, for the first time in human history, more people will live in cities than in rural areas.

Demographic Change: By 2025, the Earth will have some 8 billion people – around 30 percent more than today – many of whom will be living in megacities. Not only is the world population booming, the age pyramid is also shifting as a result of demographic change. Life expectancy increases. For the first time in human history, there will soon be as many people over 60 years of age as under 15 in this world.

These two megatrends will have profound consequences. For example:

- Efficient utilization of scarce resources
- Development of infrastructure
- Protection of the environment
- Quality of life through advanced medical engineering and affordable healthcare
- Mobility: increasing traffic volumes, both public and private
- Growing need for security

Major issues for global R&D management at Siemens:

1. Rise of science and technology in emerging countries (e.g., China);

2. Speed;

3. Global portfolio management;

4. IP management with open innovation.

Innovative technologies are the key to mastering these challenges of the future, and Siemens CT researchers and developers around the globe are trying to realize these technologies. Siemens is ideally positioned to deliver single-source solutions for the world's megatrends: the enormous concentration of people in urban areas and the growth of the world's population due demographic change. Not by chance the research fields of Siemens CT cover:

- Energy and Environmental Care
- Automation & Control, Industrial & Public Infrastructures
- Healthcare

5.2   *Siemens Corporate Technology, China*

The origins of present day Siemens CT in China go back to a very successful joint program started with Beijing's Tsinghua University in June 1998 to develop highly advanced, animated multi-media user interfaces for mobile applications. The fruitful partnership continues to this day. Subsequently in 1999, Siemens established a local Corporate Technology unit with focus on intellectual property, standardization and regulations, and user interface design. In 2004, Siemens decided to dramatically expand Corporate Technology in China (CT China) to reach 300 people in 2008 in Beijing and Shanghai.

With the mission to develop unique innovations for Siemens businesses in China and worldwide, CT China is working closely with private and public research institutions in China to develop innovations jointly to create long-term win-win partnerships. Today, CT China already has 200 top notch researchers working in the areas of energy and the environment, automation and public and private infrastructures, and healthcare.

5.3   *CT China's Innovation Strategy*

As we always say, *a success on innovation is not about what we think up, but rather who we think about*. Meaning, of course, our customers. As shown in figure V.8.1, CT China is working on four types of innovations targeted for three markets.

High End Market

In this market, the need in China is more or less similar to the need in the developed countries. The goal here is to develop mainstream innovations that offer better products for this market. In addition, to align with Siemens business direction, focus areas are determined with the consideration of talent, know-how, and market in China. The following are some examples of these focus areas:

- *Leapfrogging innovation in which China is investing heavily:* To become an innovation power house, China has to invest carefully its limited resources into the areas where China has a reasonable chance to take a lead. Emerging technologies like life science, nanotechnology, clean energy, biotechnology, etc. have become the focus. The Chinese government invests heavily in these areas and CT China is working closely with research institutes in China.
- *Innovation with unique Chinese know-how:* China is a country with more than 5000 years of history. For most of this time, China was leading the world in innovation. As a result, there is a great deal of unique expertise and know-how in China. For example, TCM (Traditional Chinese Medicine) was the unique medical solution for Chinese before western medicine was introduced to China. To better incorporate this kind of unique local expertise, CT China is pursuing innovations like Chinese-Western Medical Fusion technology.

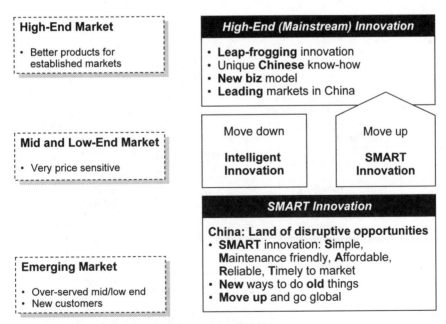

Fig. V.8.1. Mainstream and SMART innovation at CT China.

- *New business models:* Technology innovation alone does not make a successful business. It must be coupled with the right business model. Chinese are very open to new ways to do business. Along with the huge and diverse market, it is certain that many new business models will be developed. As one example, CT China is working together with Chinese partners to provide Internet-based machine maintenance and monitoring.
- *Innovation for leading markets in China:* With its huge market, China is the leading market in the world for many products and services. For instance, up to January 2006, there were 400 million mobile phone subscribers in China (National Bureau of Statistics of China, 2006). As a result, there are many innovation opportunities, for example, innovations for 3G or beyond 3G markets in wireless communication.

Mid/low End Market

For mid/low end markets, adequate products with reasonable pricing are the key. Multinational companies (MNCs) are intelligently moving down their high/mid end technologies, adopting local materials and doing manufacturing in China to produce good enough products with reduced cost. At the same time, Chinese companies that are mostly following a "learn and improve" path with existing products have been quite successful. No doubt, there is fierce competition at this level. Moving down alone is not enough, and sooner or later the possibilities to adapt even more are exploited.

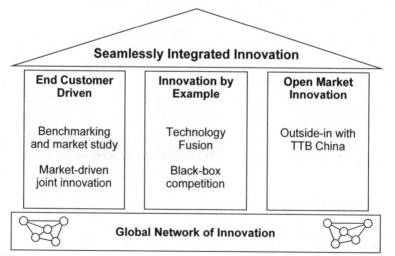

Fig. V.8.2. "House of Innovation" with P (Public), B (Business), R (Research) and D (Development).

Emerging Market

Innovating for the emerging market may well be the most dynamic and attractive opportunity for everyone in China. This includes both the overly served and the new customers, whereby the goal of innovation here is to find new ways to do old things. When it comes to old things, customers do not need to be convinced why they should buy them. With new ways, they could be continuously improved on and move up into the higher market segments. A good example is the Graphical User Interface (GUI). When it was invented by Xerox PARC, the initial version did not have all the features that professional computer users were used to with their standard user interfaces, and hence were not ready to accepted it. Apple took it and used it for non-computer experts, still continuing to improve it and move it further up. Today, the Graphical User Interface is on every computer used by both consumers and professionals. A similar story can be told about the Personal Computer. CT China calls this **SMART** innovation: Simple, **M**aintenance friendly, **A**ffordable, **R**eliable, **T**imely to market. SMART innovation has to be market driven with plenty of end customers (Christensen, 1997). China is the ideal place for SMART innovation.

To summarize the innovation strategy as depicted in figure V.8.1, CT China has devised a "sandwich" approach. From the high end, leapfrogging innovation is performed with moving down intelligent innovation into the mid/low end. At the emerging market end, SMART innovation has the key and potential to move innovations up.

5.4   CT China's Innovation Implementation Strategy

CT China follows a systematic approach that helps connecting ideas and innovation with markets and customers. As we say, "ideas are worthless unless they are used". Innovations are needed that can significantly benefit current and future customers. Although there is a feeling of magic in great innovation, innovation itself does not happen magically.

Figure V.8.2 illustrates how CT China builds a "House of Innovation" with P (Public responsibility) & B (Business) & R (Research) and D (Development of prototype). The foundation of the house is Siemens' global network of innovation: With research labs in all major locations around the world, CT China works together inside and outside CT to produce the best innovation in the most suitable market at the best time. The roof of the house is a seamlessly integrated innovation system that combines market study, technological innovation, product development and customer piloting in parallel to speed up time to market.

Inside the house are three major innovation pillars, starting with the understanding of customer/end user and competitors. Innovations are designed with end users in mind, and they need to be much better than competitors to advance the overall innovation landscape of Siemens. Benchmarking of competitors is a common practice. But, in addition to have this done regularly by product development teams in business units, CT China conducts benchmarking with a deliberate view from another angle. The purpose is to stimulate thinking outside the box. This is

> **Major innovative break-throughs at Siemens (last five years):**
>
> 1. Piezo-Injector for car;
>
> 2. Syngo / Soarian for healthcare;
>
> 3. FET-Gas sensors;
>
> 4. Lab on a chip.

achieved by working closely with Siemens' current and potential customers in China with joint innovation activities to advance China's innovation system and to better serve Siemens' customers.

Generating original innovation has always been a challenge. Some people would say that if you hire the best people and give them freedom, magic will happen. But an industrial research lab must to be able to successfully produce useful and unique innovations at a high and predictable rate. This requires a systematic approach. CT China rigorously practices "Innovation by Example" with content mix and context shift. Examples include technology fusion that mixes the best (including east meets west) to produce new ideas, and a Black Box competition in which people are challenged to produce new ideas to do old things with existing products. In a short period of time, we have been able to produce several successful examples, for instance, innovation in computer gaming has simulated several interesting new technologies for industrial automation.

Last but not least, CT China also practices open market innovation. In this method, the external research community is considered as an extended virtual lab. In 1999, Siemens established an innovation lab, called Siemens Technology-to-Business (TTB) center in Berkeley, California. TTB serves as a technology-to-business factory by working closely with universities, early stage start-up companies, and individual entrepreneurs to bring their innovations into successful business. Up to now, 8 new Siemens products have been developed and 12 start-up companies are working closely with Siemens. With this experience, a TTB in Shanghai was established in 2005 to further expand open market innovation practice in the Asia Pacific region.

5.5   Example: Chinese-Western Medical Diagnostic Fusion

Traditional Chinese Medicine (TCM) has a history of about 5000 years. It was the unique medical solution for Chinese before western medicine was introduced to China about 200 years ago. Today, it is still a key part of the Chinese healthcare system, with about 2600 recognized TCM ranked hospitals. The diagnostic approach of TCM looks a little bit like magic to the layman. The basic concept is to use body sensors, like pulse, tongue, meridian, voice, sound, face, hand, etc., to collect information of a patient's internal condition. A TCM doctor combines the diagnostic information from these sensors and draws a diagnostic conclusion.

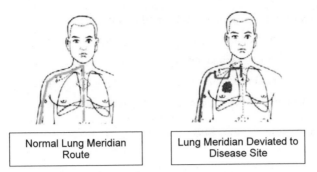

| Normal Lung Meridian Route | Lung Meridian Deviated to Disease Site |

Fig. V.8.3. Meridian change on early stage lung cancer.

CT China is now working on technologies to combine TCM with western devices for early diagnosis of diseases, especially for the most challenging diseases, such as cancers, stroke and heart diseases. Figure V.8.3 shows an example.

"Meridian will deviate from the normal route to the site of diseases" has been a basic principle in TCM for a very long time in guiding doctors during diagnosis and treatment. One potential innovation is to develop a special device for detecting acupoints or meridian passageways, and determine the deviation from the normal route. This deviation will provide useful information for the disease diagnosis, and even early diagnosis. As shown in figure V.8.3, the meridian in the left picture is the normal route, and the meridian in the right picture shows a deviation to the lung, indicating that there may be disease in the lung area. Since the meridian is sensitive to the body functional change even before anatomic change, this provides an opportunity to do early diagnosis in the phase of body functional change.

6   Flying with the Dragon: China and Siemens, Perfectly Together

In less than 30 years, China has achieved unprecedented success in becoming the 4th largest economy in the world. It is anticipated that China becomes the 2nd largest economy behind the U.S. by 2020, assuming that the growth rates of China and the US (and most other major countries) continue as they did over the past 20 years. Considering recent history, the shifting of economic power from the UK to Germany, and then to the US, was based on superior innovation. Looking into today's China, this great country has gone through scattered innovation, centrally planned innovation, and partially market-driven innovation. Observers are unanimous that for the past 200 years China had little to do with superior innovation. Since 2006, the push for endogenous innovation aiming to transform from "Made in China" to "Invented in China" will hopefully reintroduce those qualities.

Will China make it? Before we answer this question, we need to identify first

Lessons learned for organizing R&D at Siemens:

1. The customer stands at the beginning and the end of each R&D-cycle;

2. R&D has to be managed systematically;

3. Old technologies strike back. Always attack them via new applications;

4. At the end of the day it's always the excellence of the employees that counts.

what are the important factors for successful innovation. At the very high level, they are: people, money, market, and process. Money is always important, but a recent study (Jaruzelski et al., 2006) released by Booz Allen Hamilton also found that an increase in R&D investment alone does not guarantee business success. China definitely has a huge market advantage at all levels, as pointed out in Section 5. Regarding people, there is no doubt that Chinese are smart and are generating more and more original ideas. But, that is not enough to reach the top. A very important factor in the US innovation system is the injection of new talents. In US engineering and science graduate schools, more than half of the students are from abroad (National Summit on Competitiveness, 2005). The remaining factor is innovation strategy and process. While it is not so difficult to set up great strategies and processes, innovation is not an assembly line. By following a defined process, one can reach an average level. But to reach the top, one must apply the right strategy and the right process at the right place at the right time – we call it smart experience.

Siemens is a truly international company with employees in over 190 countries. Just taking Siemens Corporate Technology in China as an example, we are bringing in experienced innovation managers and innovators from the US, Germany, and many other countries to work together with Chinese colleagues. That is, we constantly inject new talents into the innovation system in China. Furthermore, with more than 150 years of innovation tradition, Siemens has mastered the end-to-end innovation to business strategy and process with continuous improvement.

For Siemens, the importance of China is far more than today's Chinese market. SMART innovation driven by the emerging market needs in China has a high chance to change the world. By growing the Chinese talent in Siemens' innovation network, we have also achieved new talent injection. Furthermore, by collaborating with Chinese companies on joint innovation, a trusting win-win relationship can be developed for a very long time.

We are living in an exciting period of time in which boundaries among regions and countries seem to be disappearing. Innovation will result from people working together in new ways. We call it "global collaboration with totally integrated innovation". China is the best place to achieve this model. By "flying with the dragon," Siemens and China will spearhead this new type of innovation into a new era.

Part VI
Implications

VI.1 Implications for Organizing Global R&D

„Organizing an R&D department is much like mixing oil with water.
It is easy to describe the intended product, less easy to produce it."
H. A. Simon, 1997

1   Organizing Global R&D

Research and development, and as a result technology, have improved the quality
of human life tremendously over the last six decades. For the first time in the
history of humanity it appears technically feasible to eliminate poverty and diseases for large masses of the population. But are we happier than earlier generations? No, it seems that human aspiration adjusts to opportunities. We know more,
produce more externalities and become more sensitive to the indirect consequences of organizational activity. Today's R&D has to take into account not only
customers and economical issues, but ecology and society as well. DuPont's „Better things for better living through chemistry" tries to catch this spirit. Kao's
„Safety for society and users" incorporates the critical customer into its vision.

Fig. VI.1.1. Today's R&D has an overall responsibility.

But what are the challenges for global R&D organization that result from considering economical, ecological, and societal issues (Fig. VI.1.1).

1.1   *From Historical Growth to Strategy*

Most R&D configurations are a result of mergers, acquisitions and manufacturing-location decisions. Also, criteria for what constitutes a good R&D location or a good R&D environment have changed over time. Therefore, most MNCs have R&D locations due to different reasons, most of them outdated but some of them still valid. For instance:

- Cheap shop labor in Singapore has slowly grown into an R&D center;
- Strong mechanical departments near European universities have in the past attracted R&D centers in their neighborhood;
- Localization was overemphasized, R&D centers have moved to emerging Southeast Asian markets or to Japan for pharmaceuticals.

But by the end of the 20th century it became clear that „more and more of the human work becomes work of thought and communication" (Simon, 1997: 238). Metal basher criteria, cheap labor and development units located right in the target market lose importance compared to:

- Concentrating on core capabilities;
- Outsourcing R&D on a global scale;
- Insourcing of outside ideas and innovations;
- Tapping the best human resources;
- Building up ICT for improved decision making in networks;
- Allocating scarce resources to divisions, corporate labs and regions.

All these challenges are about decisions: How to set up structure, processes and support mechanisms to secure timely decisions with respect to new technologies and new products. These challenges are reflected in the following table listing the main issues for global R&D management of our case study companies (Table VI.1.1).

Table VI.1.1. Major issues for global R&D management mentioned in the cases.

Company	Issues
DuPont	• Impact of information technology; Virtual organizations; • Structure versus processes in R&D; • Going beyond product tailoring and technical service in local markets; • Accessibility of new sciences and technologies from the home base.
Roche	• Increasing R&D costs; • Cost containment in public health care; • Availability of genomics data; • Increasing regulatory intensity.
Schering	• Globalization of regulatory environment; • Competition for innovation through new enabling technologies; • Uniform worldwide standards for R&D through integrated data management; • Worldwide cost containment in health care.
Ciba	• Country selection for global project responsibility; • Coordination and exploitation of synergy between distributed R&D centers; • Identification and use of third party research centers; • Aggressive scouting for emerging technologies.
Kao	• Strong connection to the headquarters and laboratories in Japan; • International R&D strategy meetings.
Xerox	• Adapting R&D management to a worldwide extended enterprise; • Adequately trained human resource in systems and software; • Creating an information infrastructure to support worldwide communications.
Canon	• Global project set-up and optimal resource allocation; • Making R&D fruits into the assets of the whole group; • Innovation management in a distributed environment; • Better coordination, collaboration, and communication.
HP	• Recruiting the right people who strive for knowledge and capabilities; • Establishing networks across businesses, partners, customers, and HP; • Openness to outside ideas and local management to support parallel R&D; • Increase of mobilization speed.
IBM	• Creating the most advanced information technologies; • Helping customers to apply technology to improve what and how they do it.
SAP	• Efficient reconciliation and decision processes; • Knowledge transfer between different sites; • Roll-In (customer to SAP) and Roll-Out (SAP to customer) processes; • Process adjustments.
Unisys	• Requirements and constraints of European Union to do business; • Worldwide technology and business climate and market requirements; • Networks and tools to connect virtual offices to R&D centers; • Supply of skilled work force.
Huawei	• Availability of talented engineers and scientists; • Technical standards; • Internationalization of business and staff; • Accountability and customer-orientation.

Table VI.1.1. Major issues for global R&D management mentioned in the cases. (continued)

Company	Issues
Fujitsu	• Collaboration between research laboratories and partner research organizations worldwide; • Customer orientation in research; • Flexible structures for cross-divisional innovation projects.
SwissRe	• Get access to new resources, particularly new technologies; • Long term perspective; • Collaborative research with partners.
ABB	• Business impact of innovative ideas and projects; • New markets; • Proximity to customers; • Multinational/multicultural/cross-border teams.
Daimler-Benz	• Soft and informal coordination means in transnational R&D projects; • Building a global mind-set for R&D employees; • Overcoming high costs, different languages & cultures, long project duration; • Overcoming interfunctional as well as geographical distances; • Integration of Chrysler.
Schindler	• Systematic management of new technologies; • Integration of decentralized technology and application knowledge; • Concentration on technical core competencies; • IT infrastructure and their role in concurrent engineering.
Hitachi	• Synergy in multi-dimension; • Be prepared at competitive front-end of R&D; • Social role and responsibility becomes more global; • World-wide standardization of specifications and protocols.
Leica	• New technologies; • Global market-driven strategies; • State-of-the-art virtual product development tools; • Capable engineers; • Coping with different owners.
BMW	• Cross-industry innovation / collaboration; • Environmental requirements and eco-friendly technologies; • Continuously tapping best sources of emerging technologies globally and choosing the relevant ones; • Securing core knowledge in locations with clear IP legislation whilst integrating research results from additional regions.
Siemens	• Rise of science and technology in emerging countries (e.g., China); • Speed; • Global portfolio management; • IP management with open innovation.
MTU	• Managing technology alliances on a global scale; • Balancing market-/project orientation and innovation; • Creating real international partnership.

1.2   From Function to Integration

Most R&D work requires the input of specialists; hence, R&D is often carried out in projects: Some form of matrix is needed to balance between scientific and engineering skills and team performance. Modern project organization theory distinguishes between matrix organization and the heavy-weight project organization. In the matrix structure, the project team is subject to directives from the project coordinator and functional managers. In the heavy-weight project organization, the decision authority completely shifts from line management to the project manager. Especially when the project is of strategic nature, time is critical, and resources are sufficiently available, companies resort to heavy-weight project management. The project manager becomes an internal entrepreneur. He has unrestricted access to critical resources and to top-management. On the other hand, he is fully responsible for the success or failure of the project: *Vertical integration* of all hierarchical levels becomes crucial to catch all the different points of view to solve a problem (Fig. **VI.1.2**).

Integrated product development requires more than just increasing authority and responsibility of the project manager. Increasing variety and scare resources necessitate the intensive coordination of all R&D projects in a company. This commitment is still rarely the case even at many renowned companies. Leading automobile companies such as BMW and Volvo thus introduced a vision-based platform management to reduce R&D redundancies: In *object integration*, all products have to be seen as a whole in order to realize the synergies needed to achieve short lead-times and high reliability of R&D processes. DaimlerChrysler is also considering this holistic approach.

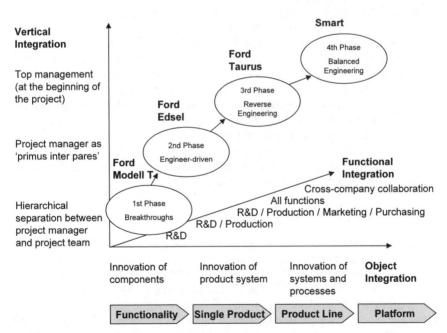

Fig. VI.1.2. Integration along three dimensions.

Integration along objects and hierarchical levels leads to working in parallel with a heavy load of information interchange, i.e., simultaneous engineering. But simultaneous engineering means more than the parallelization of development activities. The goal is a full *functional integration*, which is coupled with early supplier integration and a process coach who accompanies the entire process from procurement, R&D, logistics, marketing to distribution.

In multi-project management, project selection is determined by mechanisms that equally consider marketing and technology requirements. Technology-intensive multinationals further differentiate between types of projects. A small number of projects may be classified as strategically important. Bosch calls them 'Top projects', Sharp 'Gold badge special projects', Hitachi 'Strategic business projects' and 'North star research projects'. They are all under direct supervision of top management. The number of technology development projects with multiple business unit involvement steadily increases, mirroring the significance of multiplication effects in R&D. Since new technology development is risky and expensive, cooperative R&D and technological alliances are often called for to efficiently and quickly integrate external know-how. Such undertakings are called 'Core R&D projects' at Hitachi and 'Core projects' at NEC and Siemens. They are based on contractually defined, internally coordinated project funding and a differentiated allocation of property rights at commercialization.

Traditional R&D management thus evolves into integrated innovation management on a global scale. In step with the innovation of the core product, all concerned business processes are redesigned. Product innovation gives rise to a logistic innovation such as the creation of completely new forms of distribution. Hewlett-Packard develops a global parts list for each new product, along with new logistics channels for its distribution. This new kind of R&D project management transposes concepts from product R&D into new business processes.

Innovation is no longer restricted to creating new knowledge (research) or new products or production techniques (development). Integrated innovation also includes the design of all of the concerned business structures and processes. The core competencies of the company not only consist of technology bundles but also encompass service-related fields such as logistics and distribution. Only with focused bundles of products and services can the company create high customer linkage. Methods as applied in business reengineering bring internal business processes to the highest level of efficiency. These processes are global since the special know-how needed is available only in just a few locations.

1.3   *Centers of Knowledge Creation*

The internationalization of R&D is likely to increase with the multinational firm's experience-based organizational learning as a function of operating a decentralized and dispersed network of foreign affiliates (Belderbos, 2003). Some multinationals already show a remarkable degree of R&D internationalization. Large multinationals with small domestic markets and a relative lack of qualified R&D personnel at home were among the first to establish international R&D sites. Still, on a national or regional level, R&D internationalization remains significantly

lower than sales internationalization (von Zedtwitz, 1999). The asymmetric allocation of knowledge clusters worldwide happens in parallel to a geographical concentration of R&D activities. Our research on international R&D activities of
those technology-intensive multinationals clearly indicates an agglomeration of
knowledge creation in four centers of excellence (Fig. VI.1.3).

- Western Europe (mainly Germany, France and Britain);
- USA (concentration in California, Michigan, and several east coast states);
- Japan (agglomeration around Tokyo and Osaka);
- China & India (plus increasing R&D efforts in the tiger countries).

Europe had been the dominant knowledge center during the 19th century before
the US became the leading knowledge power in the middle of the 20th century.
Today it seems obvious that the 21st century will be dominated by Asian economies, if by their sheer number of people alone. While it is already clear that global
competition will take place in those emerging Asian markets, it could also be that
Asia becomes the dominant knowledge creation region of the world. Still, we
expect it will take 30-50 years, i.e. two generations at least. Even Japan, the Asian
forerunner, who has beaten all other nations with respect to speed in building up a
modern society, still needed one hundred years (Thurow, 1996: 52).

   A major R&D attractor is the market: During the past three hundred years,
product development, technology development, and sometimes even research has
followed markets in the long term. Whether this will change through new means

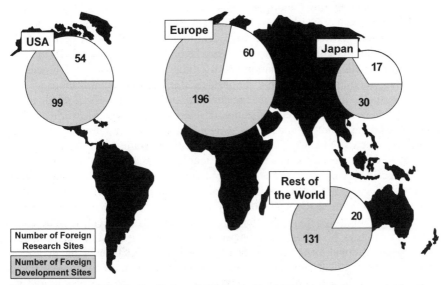

Fig. VI.1.3. The worldwide distribution of 601 international research and development locations
of foreign companies from our research base of 1021 R&D locations indicates that foreign research is mainly attracted to the Triad regions (von Zedtwitz, 1999).

of telecommunications and convergent media remains to be seen. For the moment, the existing knowledge centers have not lost their momentum. These clusters exhibit increasing returns-to-investment: Every additional company that joins an existing cluster receives a higher return on investment than the preceding one. Clusters grow faster than new regions. Only completely new and stand-alone technologies have a chance to outgrow existing centers.

Locating R&D sites in East Asia and India is a trend that has just started. Compared to the R&D power in the established R&D centers, international R&D in the four tiger nations (Hong Kong, Singapore, Taiwan, South Korea) and the BRIC countries (Brazil, Russia, India, and China) is still in its infancy. Companies built up R&D locations in Asia because they expect the future market to be even bigger and local science and engineering to be world-class. The phenomenon is not restricted to the four tiger countries as well as China and India but also includes Malaysia, Thailand, and a few others.

Often, international R&D sites are a consequence of non-R&D related corporate decisions such as mergers and acquisitions, and tax optimization. The main rationales to set up R&D sites abroad are proximity to other corporate activities (e.g. manufacturing), proximity to local customers, and the quest for technical know-how available in only a few centers-of-excellence around the world. Efficiency-related criteria such as development cycle time reduction and multiple time-zone projects play a role as much as cost-considerations for personnel and logistics, although they frequently favor centralization. Protectionist, legal and cultural constraints imposed by national governments, however, often requires a company to establish local R&D units.

Internal forces such as a business unit's striving for autonomy and the build-up of local competence alter the original mission of a local R&D unit. This evolution may take place unnoticed by the headquarters particularly in strongly decentralized companies. Synergy and scale considerations, supported by central controlling and striving for communication intensity favor a centralization of R&D in one place. Coordination and information costs, cultural and linguistic differences as well as the individual's immobility are obstacles for R&D decentralization.

It is virtually impossible for management to anticipate the effect of all these factors when considering a reorganization of international R&D. Measuring actual and potential R&D output under these circumstances is often a sensitive political issue. The success of an R&D unit may be estimated to some extent by a weighted balance of downstream process efficiency, technical feasibility of its output, and market-acceptance of its products, but more and more the speed by which R&D reaches its decisions is put forward as a strong benchmark of efficiency.

Jungle-growth internationalization is certainly not an appropriate R&D decentralization strategy. Location decisions must be made with the entire value creation chain in mind. Short-term and long-term considerations must be balanced out. Often, organizational forms are imposed on international R&D units that do not fit with the local political and cultural environment. Only if the new foreign R&D unit can leverage local competencies, investing time, capital, and people into its establishment makes sense.

Table VI.1.2. Drivers for globalization.

Company	Drivers for globalization
Pharmaceuticals, Chemicals, and Food	• Collaboration between research laboratories and partner research organizations worldwide; • Limitations in quality and supply of technical talent in home country (DuPont); Different expertise available abroad (Ciba); Localize management resources (Kao) • Supply new technology to manufacturing facilities abroad (DuPont) • Different customer requirements (DuPont, Nestlé); Meet local market requirements (Kao) • Better access to local science and technology (DuPont); Availability of scientific and market information through information technology (Schering); Complexity of emerging technologies (Ciba) • Pay-back of R&D costs by simultaneous launching (Roche); Global project launches (Schering); Breakthrough technology (Kao) • Clinical trials are carried out in various countries (Roche) • Harmonization of global regulatory environment (Schering); Compliance with local regulatory system (Ciba) • Competition for innovation (Schering); Business strategy (Kao) • Less redundancy due to global coordination (Roche); Costs of doing R&D, especially contract R&D (Ciba)
Electronics, Software, Services	• Globalization of markets (Xerox, Unisys, Huawei); Living in the market (HP); Globalization of customers (IBM, SAP, Fujitsu); Global legal and business processes (SAP); Understanding local risks (SwissRe) • Growth of information economies (Xerox); Internet-based global 24-hour communication (Unisys); Low costs of communication (Xerox) • Growth of third world economies (Xerox, Unisys); Emerging supplier and work forces in developing countries (Unisys) • Spreading/diversification of risks (SwissRe) • Corporate philosophy (Canon); Corporate vision (HP); Growth and size (Huawei) • Tapping the best R&D people and mixing their talents (Canon, SAP); Obtain the best intellectual capital (HP, Fujitsu); Regional centers of excellence (IBM); Enabling personal contact to research centers (Fujitsu) • Proximity to universities (HP); Contact to leading universities and research institutes (IBM); Seeking local technologies (Huawei).
Electrical and Machinery	• Globalization of business (ABB, Hitachi); Localization of products (BMW); Customer orientation (Schindler); Market-driven needs (Leica); Customer proximity (Leica); Economies open up (Siemens); • Monitoring technology trends (Daimler); Re-use of technologies to satisfy local needs (ABB); Sourcing know-how in centers of technological excellence (Daimler, BMW); Sourcing local market knowledge (BMW); • Complementary skills of strategic partner (MTU, Hitachi); Taking the best ideas and skills (MTU); International partners help to open international markets (MTU); Access to talent (Siemens) • Supporting local development (Daimler); Decentralization of R&D sites (Leica); • Risk-sharing in large-scale projects (MTU); Economies of scale and scope (MTU); Reducing costs (BMW, Siemens); • Country-specific regulations and standards (Schindler) • Developing the global company (Daimler); Corporate support and drive (Leica); Some businesses are a global market per se (MTU); Acquisition of local companies (Schindler); Market power of local countries (Siemens); Mobility (Siemens); • Information technologies (ABB, Schindler); Advances in logistics, transportation and IT (Siemens);

1.4   Concepts of Organizing International R&D

We analyzed R&D organizations by the degree of cooperation between individual R&D sites and the dispersion of their internal competencies as well as knowledge bases and identified five organizational concepts for organizing international R&D.

- *Ethnographic centralized R&D* is characterized by strong inward orientation of all R&D processes. No international R&D activities take place. R&D is tightly coordinated and centered in one place. Technology needs to be kept safe at the headquarters. The R&D culture is strong and homogeneous. Ethnographic centralized R&D can be very efficient: Due to the high degree of centralization and control, cycle times and R&D costs are low. Critical know-how is better protected at the parent location than abroad. However, ethnocentric centralized R&D lacks sensitivity for foreign markets. Due to the strong inward orientation, external technology and market signals may be missed. NIH syndromes occur even within the same company.

- *Geocentric centralized R&D* is open for external input but retains a centralized R&D structure. External scientists visit the R&D center, and internal R&D employees are sent abroad for study and collaboration. The R&D center is in close and frequent contact with the company's international production and marketing locations. Geocentric centralized R&D couples efficiency through centralization with market sensitivity through foreign cooperation. It is a relatively cost-efficient way of R&D internationalization. There is a danger of neglecting a more systematic outward orientation. Local content restrictions and market specifications may be missed. It is difficult to exploit local technical and know-how competencies.

- *Polycentric decentralized R&D* puts local effectiveness before global efficiency. Customization is more important than standardization, product-related R&D is dominant. International R&D sites act highly autonomous, and their activities are not coordinated. Polycentric decentralized R&D is characterized by a strong degree of local market sensitivity: it also makes good use of local resources and technology. From a corporate-wide point of view, polycentric decentralized R&D is inefficient because redundant R&D activities and parallel development are likely to occur. Economies of scale cannot be won because of the often critically small size of local R&D units. Due to strong customer-orientation, corporate-wide technological focus is lost.

- The *R&D hub's* decentralized R&D units are strongly controlled by the R&D center. The center strives to have a dominant lead in all corporate technologies. International R&D sites are coordinated by clear directives and budgets. The R&D hub achieves high efficiency due to the central R&D coordination. Redundant R&D is avoided and synergy can be exploited. Local capabilities are recognized to achieve a predefined goal. However, central coordination involves high costs in time and resources. Local creativity and flexibility is oppressed by central directives and control.

- The *integrated R&D network* has no unique R&D center: Each R&D unit is a competence center and assumes technological leadership in transnational R&D processes. Based on individual strengths, each R&D site is an equal partner in a global network. Important information flows freely between the R&D sites. The integrated R&D network tries to merge the advantages of specialization with synergy effects. Global efficiency is more important than local effectiveness. Local strengths are refined and put to use for the entire network. Multidimensional coordination and information flow incurs high coordination costs. Institutional rules and decision processes may be complex; high standards of collaboration and coordination are required.

1.5   Trends Towards the Integrated R&D Network

Depending on markets, products, technologies and, last but not least, history, companies organize their international R&D activities differently. Each concept has strengths and weaknesses; there is no „best-practice concept" that works for all companies, there is no best organization (Fig. VI.1.4). Since every organization tends to wear out, changes will move it back and forth, often unpredictably due to many centrifugal forces.

Specific environment, strategic direction, historical structure and the individual corporate culture of a company determine the benefits and costs of implementing a

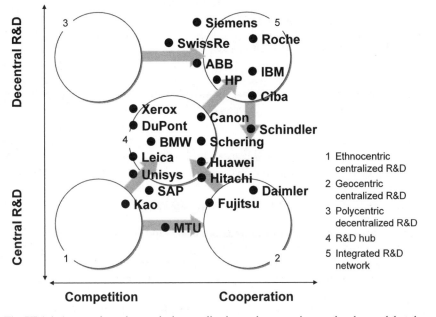

Fig. VI.1.4. A general trend towards decentralization and cooperation can be observed, but there is no single best form.

certain international R&D concept. However, based on our empirical findings we observed seven general trends which drive the evolution of international R&D:

Trend 1 is the *external orientation* of ethnocentric centralized R&D. Externally oriented companies realize better alignment between international market needs and local R&D competencies, e.g. through product localization and integration of external information.

Trend 2 is characterized by the *establishment of listening posts* in international technology centers. Tapping foreign technology and know-how becomes an important impetus for internal technology creation. Listening posts assume local market and technology monitoring responsibilities in order to identify ways of making new technological trends and developments usable in a company. Companies weak in basic research established research units near leading universities and research institutes.

Trend 3 is the *empowerment of foreign R&D sites*. R&D units that have built unique technological competencies are given a lead-role in the R&D organization. Increased autonomy and self-dependency improves creativity and flexibility in local R&D units. Japanese companies like Canon and Sony clearly empower their foreign technological listening posts to become R&D centers with an active strategic role in the corporation.

Trend 4 is the *integration of decentralized and uncoordinated R&D units*. Based on local strengths and competencies, the individual R&D activities are integrated and fine-tuned to eliminate redundancies and exploit synergy effects. Centers of expertise and mechanisms for controlling transnational R&D processes are created. Exploiting synergies between international R&D units becomes important. In the 1980s, Philips moved from a typical polycentric decentralized model in the direction of an integrated network in order to reduce redundancies and prevent re-inventing the wheel.

Trend 5 is a *re-centralization* of overly decentralized R&D organizations. Based on global efficiency programs, several multinationals have been reengineering their international R&D organization. Costs and coordination complexity forces these companies to concentrate on a small number of leading research centers. ABB started to reduce its enormous complexity by concentrating R&D activities and reducing the multidimensional reporting (move from a tensor to a matrix organization, and in 1998, to a divisional structure). Roche has closed overseas R&D sites to improve overall efficiency, and Intel and Sun have done so because the international R&D sites in question did not perform up to prior expectations.

1.6   *External Drivers of R&D Internationalization*

Access to markets and customers on the one hand, and access to leading technologies on the other hand, are fundamental external drivers of R&D internationalization. They differ from the five trends in the previous model as those are primarily internal drivers, determined by the degree of competition and cooperation between and among R&D partners.

We have identified four typical forms of global R&D organization from this external perspective on R&D internationalization:

1. *National Treasure* R&D: Research as well as development are carried out in the home country as both the key technologies and the key markets are available at home.
2. *Technology-Driven* R&D: Research is global while development is at home, mostly when the home country has a relative weakness in the technologies important for the company, or if key players are developing important piece of these technologies elsewhere in the world.
3. *Market-Driven* R&D: Development is located with the market/business organizations, while research is centralized; a configuration that is very frequent as most companies are market and customer oriented, with too little investment in early-stage R&D to have critical size for more than one research center, let alone one abroad.
4. *Global* R&D: Both research and development are located around the world, either because markets and technologies are widely dispersed, or because the company has grown through acquiring competitors with their respective R&D bases abroad.

Two additional observations play into external drivers of R&D internationalization: One is the increased relocation of R&D into developing and emerging markets. R&D activity is no longer limited to the triad of well developed economies of Europe, the United States, and Japan, but in developing countries such as China and India as well. Reasons for this shift lie in limited resources and comparative cost disadvantages in the home countries of the companies that relocate their R&D. China for example is currently attractive due to the large market and the availability of human resources at low cost. India has become a de-facto base for software development outsourcing, but is catching up in pharmaceuticals, electrical and automotive R&D as well.

Open networks and open innovation offer benefits of scale to an R&D organization not to be measured in the number of employees but instead in their factual influence. Small and highly specialized companies are able to multiply their core competencies through a global network; they perform better and are more flexible. At the same time, open architectures and reduction in proprietary development result in a higher division of labor in the global competition for knowledge and innovation.

Overall the various trends in organizing international R&D seem to mirror the mega-trends in a global economy: the move from hardware producers to knowledge creators, globalization of markets and value chains, cultural openness and external orientation, efficiency-focus and cost-cutting programs. The trend towards R&D internationalization will continue. Most of the observed companies have increased their foreign R&D share noticeably in the past ten years and are likely to continue to strengthen their foreign R&D engagements even more. On top of it, the growing number of R&D centers emerging from firms from developing countries invalidates models such as Vernon's product life cycle and will increase the division of labor in the global competition for innovation.

1.7   Establishing Overlaying Structures

The role of communication in R&D is crucial. While much of the information transfer and coordination work carried out in centralized units is done when the need arises, communication between dispersed R&D teams requires explicit management attention. Looking at international R&D organization from four different perspectives, namely geographic distribution (the regional and legal structure), formal reporting and specialization organization (the functional and hierarchical structure), overlaying cross-functional R&D activities (the projects and processes structure), and overlaying informal communication and relationship networks (the informal links and networks structure) provides a framework for classifying the principal issues and solutions for managing international R&D.

Changing behavior, culture, or strategy in a company is much more difficult than redefining organizational charts. Tomorrow's R&D will be even more based on international project work, cross-functional teams, efficient use of communication channels, key scientists, engineers and research leaders. Since conventional R&D organization is constrained by hierarchical and regional barriers, it is often inadequate for the requirements of modern global R&D management. The most important challenges are managing cultural diversity, coordination of decentralized processes, global R&D project management, and integration of dispersed know-how. The overlaying structures in our four-layer-model as we used it in Part II of this book address these requirements.

1.8   Virtual R&D Teams and Decentralized R&D Projects

Increasingly, it seems that much of the creative input to the corporation comes from outside the company. Interorganizational networks bring business partners closer to each other. At the same time, outsourcing of creative and innovative processes to external experts from customers, suppliers, academic institutions will take place: A rethinking of corporate innovation strategy is necessary. Already Patel and Pavitt (1992, 1994) observed a trend towards a more virtual company. Strategic alliances between partners anywhere in the world have become a key competition factor.

However, not every project can be organized in a virtual way: According to our research the benefits of physical collocation of decentralized R&D teams are constituted by four fundamental determinants:

- Type of innovation: incremental versus radical;
- Nature of the project: systemic versus autonomous;
- Knowledge mode: explicit versus tacit;
- Degree of resource bundling: complementary versus redundant.

Interlocal execution of projects is favored if the innovation is incremental, project tasks are relatively autonomous, explicit knowledge prevails and redundant resources are available. The collocation of the project team in one place is favored if a radical innovation is pursued, project tasks are systemic, tacit knowledge plays a central role and complementary resources are deployed.

We have identified four concepts of organizing such virtual R&D projects: In the *centralized venture team*, all project members are collocated in one place. In the *core team* as a system architect, all relevant team leaders and project managers meet in one centralized location. The *system integrator* moves between geographically dispersed R&D teams trying to coordinate them. There is little centralized decision making in *decentralized self-coordinating teams*.

The R&D project organization has to be specifically tailored to the project tasks. Not every project can be carried out virtually: Breakthrough innovations are much more likely to succeed in centralized venture teams than in fully decentralized project organizations. In addition, international R&D meets more and more the Jaikumar-Upton (1993) criteria for virtual corporations:

- Reliability: The more R&D units focus on core capabilities, the more they rely on scientific models, the more predictable they get.
- Management information: If projects can be split into independent work packages, i.e. modules, local teams are able to give precise delivery dates.
- Brokerage: R&D projects need system integration and a system integrator who splits the work into manageable chunks.
- Commodity-type transaction: The system integrator needs more protection against failure. The more „black-boxes" on the market which he integrates, the more robust his products and processes will get.

Virtual R&D is already successful in autonomous modules. Whether „virtual will be virtuous" (Chesbrough and Teece, 1996) in systemic products remains uncertain. Yet, in our research we have identified the following five trends regarding virtual R&D teams:

- Continued internationalization of R&D will further increase the importance of and the reliance on virtual R&D teams.
- Virtual R&D teams will better integrate talent in newly industrialized countries.
- Advances in information and communication technologies will further enhance the functionality of virtual R&D teams.
- Relative costs of running virtual R&D projects will decrease due to learning curve effects.
- Highly decentralized virtual R&D teams will gain importance in open system architectures such as Internet-based applications.

Virtual R&D especially helps in technology development or large and costly projects by spreading the risk and distributing the cost among a network of stakeholders. Nevertheless, not every project or innovation is suited for virtual execution; traditional coordination methods and tools are still necessary. Therefore, the decision about using virtual R&D or traditional R&D has to be made case by case.

1.9   Market-Orientation in R&D

„Customer-focus programs" in several companies indicate that the link between business and R&D strategy still needs to be improved. The alignment of R&D

activities to downstream operations of business units is not good enough. The market-pull versus technology-push discussion does not solve the problem of R&D ineffectiveness: Customer requirements have to be translated into technical specifications. The problem becomes even more complex on a global scale: Regional operations often compete for scarce centrally-allocated R&D budgets or, in the case of business unit financing, are fighting over who has to foot the bill for the project.

But market-orientation in R&D can be promoted and facilitated by

- The establishment of innovation marketing as a competence center (e.g. Schindler).
- An intensive dialogue on the basis of multiple generation product planning and core technology road maps can establish the required link between product and technology strategy.
- The promotion of interdisciplinary teams: The project manager belongs to the marketing department, project members form cross-functional teams.
- Problem-driven R&D projects: Not a fancy technology but a customer's problem gives rise to a product development project.
- Local lead users from the regions who work together with R&D engineers to design future products.
- New organizational forms separated from the main R&D organization that improve market proximity and maintain the entrepreneurial drive (e.g. Canon).
- Tools like QFD and conjoint analysis that support the translation from marketing language to technical language. However, it is important to keep the relation between time and benefit of such workshops.

Technical success of a project is not sufficient: The uncertainty of commercialization has to be reduced. Thinking in terms of the customer's problems must be enforced all over the R&D organization. Even in research and technology development scientists must keep in mind who uses their results.

1.10 Using Technology Listening Posts to Tap Local Knowledge

Technology listening posts used to be small one or two man offices trying to snatch up interesting technology leads and feed them back to R&D headquarters. Modern listening posts not only support global knowledge sourcing, they have become key parts of global R&D networks.

We have identified three types of listening posts:

1. The Trend Scout: Trend Scouts focus on technological mega trends, new application areas and future potential, triggered by a changing society. Their mission is to gather and transfer trend and application knowledge from centers of excellence, lead users or other stakeholders to the company home-base R&D.
2. The Technology Outpost: Technology Outposts focus on specialized technological knowledge. A technology outpost's mission is to gather sophisticated technological knowledge and transfer technologies from centers of technological excellence to the home-base R&D.

3. The Match Maker: Match makers have pure diplomatic functions and act as ambassadors of a company. Their mission is to initiate, leverage and establish cooperation between local R&D providers and the home-base R&D.

As with other R&D units, one critical success factor is a designated and clearly understood mandate from the R&D headquarters, another one is the relevance of results it is capable of delivering to R&D and product development teams around the world. If either of those two is missing, the listening post in question won't exist for long.

1.11 Managing the R-to-D Interface

R&D is often treated as one organizational unit, but differences in the time-horizon of R&D projects and R&D activities suggest a separated organization.

Research is long-term oriented and triggered by technology; the goal is knowledge creation and its achievement within a typically non-linear chaotic process is highly uncertain. Development has a business-driven short-term orientation. Internationalization of product development mostly follows international manufacturing plants. Clear objectives regarding product, costs and schedule have to be met within a highly structured process supported by sophisticated controlling.

The transfer of concepts from research to development involves a paradigm shift and often results in the occurrence of the not-invented-here syndrome. Management of the R-to-D interface is required, especially on the international scale. Successful mechanisms and approaches include the following:

- Technology development has to be completed before product development projects start. Otherwise, cost-intensive project phases get out of time control.
- The institutionalization of technology management as a competence center with integrated research brings more focus into R&D. Such a center is the glue between R and D. The emphasis is on pursuing new technology development and strategic technology planning at the same time.
- Research is sponsored by business units: These are only willing to pay for research if its results help to solve their problems.
- Personal continuity ensures know-how transfer. Tacit knowledge can only be transferred by moving people. Key know-how carriers of applied research projects have to support product development teams.
- More and more companies outsource basic research to universities and try to buy intellectual property from universities at the "right moment".

The struggle between free-wheeling scientists and tightly controlled product development engineers should belong to the past. Intensive job rotation between different functions creates more mutual understanding. However, a good scientist is seldom a good project manager: Individually-tailored approaches are required.

1.12 Processes in Transnational R&D

Managing the R&D process is not just the task of the project manager. Top management has to define the framework for the processes and commit to it. This is even more difficult for global R&D processes: Not only invention, production and markets are geographically dispersed, but also the knowledge creation itself is distributed worldwide. Regardless of the degree of internationality, innovations can be done much faster and more customer-oriented by dividing the innovation process into three phases: (1) pre-project, (2) project and (3) market-introduction.

(1) In the *pre-project phase*, system architectures are defined and key ideas are promoted around. While sourcing for new technologies may be global, the invention is typically a local act. Using global knowledge and creating new ideas locally seems to be the best combination. Although modern groupware supports the idea generation process, the use of computer conferencing and decentralized idea generation is still limited. Tacit knowledge is hard to share on a global scale. The process in the early R&D phase is highly non-linear. Also, finding internal champions for a new idea or project is quite difficult. Workflow systems support this search independent of the location of the idea and the potential champion, but ultimately personal contact is a far better guarantor for project support. The NIH-syndrome and the free-rider behavior are two additional phenomena that inhibit engineers and researchers to share their ideas too freely. In most companies, competition between R&D teams and R&D units still prevail over cooperation.

(2) The *development phase* has to be carried out with rigor and efficiency. In this phase global team work is possible. Clear definition of work-packages and interfaces is required. System integrators and core teams play an important role. Contrary to the pre-project phase, modern information and communication technologies provide better support in this phase. R&D processes become highly structured. Instead of creative, free-wheeling research teams trying to increasing idea diversity, strict milestone management combined with sophisticated controlling is required. ISO certification does not guarantee the implementation of an efficient process; it is an illusion that all critical innovation factors are measurable and structured. Therefore, a good solution for many companies is the introduction of stage-gate processes that provide a flexible approach to passing through milestones: Gates are more flexible in terms of time and content, but stricter in terms of commitment: „You can get around a milestone, but you must go through a gate."

(3) In the *market introduction phase* different strategies are possible: Entering new markets one by one (waterfall strategy) or spreading the product coordinated at the same time (big bang, simultaneous launching). The waterfall strategy is recommended if the product has to be tested in terms of customer acceptance. A cautious market introduction in markets with resembling characteristics increases the learning curve. Product improvements and cost reductions can still be made. While introducing a product in Scandinavia, the R&D team might already be working on an application for the Asia-Pacific region. Simultaneous launching in lead markets is a risky but also a very effective approach in building market barriers. Large R&D expenditures are recouped quickly and the own standard is pushed and established. Imitators will have difficulties to enter the market. Using this strategy requires a very strict milestone management: Stage-gate processes are again an adequate approach.

1.13 ICT as Enabler for Dispersed R&D Projects

Modern information and communication technology is vital for any international R&D project characterized by a high degree of division of labor. The efficiency of transnational R&D processes can be tremendously increased with the use of electronic conferencing, e-mail, shared databases and communication platforms, and remote login possibilities. Videoconferences are a useful complement to face-to-face meetings.

However, ICT cannot substitute for traditional project management. The lack of personal contact cannot be compensated for by even the most skillful project leadership-based ICT. Bridging cultural differences becomes much more difficult without face-to-face communication.

The organizational form of virtual teams must be tailored to the project. The core team of the project has to be brought together in one place. Breakthroughs are only possible in one location („think tank", "R&D center") — even the torchbearers of open systems like Linux have been designed around a kernel developed by one person or one centralized group. Integrated problem-solving strategies still require interpersonal communication within traditional team organization.

A critical issue is the building of trust at the beginning of the project. Without team members knowing each other a project group can hardly develop the required team spirit. An atmosphere of trust can best built up by starting a project with the project team assembled in one place. After the team members return to their dispersed working locations, ICT can be used more efficiently to manage the decentralized team. However, trust diminishes with time during the execution of decentralized cooperation and must be continually revived („half-life of trust").

The use of ICT becomes much more difficult if the project requires complementary resources, high interdisciplinarity and sharing of tacit knowledge. However, the longer the R&D project lasts and the greater the continuity of the team, the easier face-to-face communication may be replaced by ICT-based communication.

Global knowledge creation cannot function without ICT. But technology itself cannot sufficiently cope with the challenges of bridging geographic distances, with time differences, and not at all with cultural differences.

1.14 Leading R&D Labs

Directors of R&D units, particularly of newly established R&D units, share a particular responsibility: They define the culture and future of the R&D lab. It is thus extremely important to select the right person for this crucial position.

Most companies will still intuitively chose one from the inside ranks to be posted abroad to assume this important linkage and control role. But the decision is not as easy today as it used to be, with highly qualified R&D managers available in many countries, thus providing a good pool of local leadership talent.

We have identified eight leadership roles for R&D directors:

1. The expatriate director who is not familiar with local customs but nevertheless dispatched from the parent's R&D unit to run the new site;

2. The expatriate director who is already familiar with local customs is dispatched from the parent's R&D to the new lab;
3. The expatriate director who is promoted from the local country organization and familiar with local customs;
4. The expatriate director who is recruited from outside the company but brings in a substantial local network and familiarity with customs;
5. The national director who is recruited internally and assigned from the parent's R&D unit to return to his home country;
6. The national director who is hired abroad from outside the company to return to his home country;
7. The national director who is hired externally in the host country;
8. The national director who is hired internally from the host country organization.

Often forgotten in the selection of R&D directors are interpersonal and entrepreneurial skills. Technical expertise and administrative experience are not enough. In particular, directors of newly established R&D units must be able to create something out of nothing within a short period of time. This requires a set of skills more easily found among start-up entrepreneurs than R&D staff.

1.15 Managing Knowledge and Human Resources

At the core of every innovation are ideas created by people. Creative ideas cannot be replaced by modern information technologies. The rapid increase and continuous globalization of technological information requires more attention to the management of knowledge and people.

People management begins with the training and selecting project managers. Although more and more companies conduct complex cross-border R&D projects, they lack qualified project managers to do this job. Technical knowledge is by far not enough for transnational projects. Such R&D projects require highly skilled, professional project managers. As long as the line functions still carry higher status than project managers, there will be little incentive to aspire to a project manager career. Therefore, dual career ladders are required.

In the long term the rate of innovation can be increased by multilateral learning. Learning is helped by redundant information which allows analogies and comparison. Redundant resources, however, are at odds with efficiency programs.

Visiting researchers are pure knowledge workers. If managed right they become the nodes of the international R&D network. As gatekeepers, they source, filter and disseminate technological knowledge. Despite the high costs, expatriates have to be systematically supported, as only they can acquire the required intercultural competence. Global R&D processes need expatriates as global change agents.

Managing the „knowledge pyramid" becomes critical in transnational R&D processes. Tacit knowledge is difficult to transfer since „know-how travels with heads." Job rotation across departments, functions and locations enables the spread of tacit knowledge. Technology agents support hand-over processes to production and transfer knowledge throughout projects from development to production.

The nature of tacit knowledge and the „half-time of trust" are currently the principal limitations for a further exploitation of modern information and communication technologies. Regarding the knowledge transformation processes of Nonaka and Takeuchi (1995), socialization and internalization are most important in global R&D management. „Learning by doing" in a global team is more important than all the efforts put into excellent guidelines and project handbooks accessible via intranets. Many companies try to learn from other management styles – and fail miserably. Management concepts cannot be transferred like technology. The cultural context must not be neglected.

Technological learning is a major driver for the internationalization of R&D processes. Diversity of ideas and different thinking are potential sources for innovation. But cultural diversity is not easy to manage: Practical problems with language, misunderstandings and context orientation lead to project crises. Therefore, the project manager has a difficult task in the early project phases: Overcome the culture shock and facilitate cultural assimilation. This requires tolerance and willingness to learn within the project team and high project management qualifications in terms of intercultural competence.

To a great extent, global R&D management deals with contradictory requirements, necessities and trends. In this book we have tried to bring all the different issues in global R&D into a bigger context. Yet, principal questions remain.

2   Some Dilemmas in Global R&D

Management tasks do not have unique solutions. Global R&D problems are not well-structured problems. Too many trade-offs between costs, speed, and quality, together with our bounded rationality lead to dilemmas, i.e. situations in which the decision maker has the choice between two contradictory but equally appropriate alternatives. The manager is forced to make an inconsistent choice: Is it better to concentrate R&D in one location to improve efficiency, or is it better to decentralize to be closer to customers? Many managers chose the „Golden Mean," thereby losing the creative tension so vital for R&D (Pascale, 1990).

The case studies in this book show many creative trade-offs. In our research we have met with many R&D managers still looking for a single best solution as Taylor put forward in manufacturing. Western engineers favor one-to-one relations and unique solutions, they do not like Ying-and-Yang-like situations, the coexistence of contradictory patterns. Although we collected many suggestions for overcoming these dilemmas, we feel it is important to manage rather than to eliminate them. First of all, it would not be possible to eliminate these dilemmas because they are inherent to global innovation. Second, it would be detrimental for the strategic flexibility of a company as a whole if creative tension—considered by many as the engine of technological and corporate renewal—was crudely eradicated. Based on our research, we found six principal dilemmas of global innovation:

1. Local versus global
2. Processes versus hierarchy
3. Creativity versus discipline
4. Control versus open source
5. Face-to-face versus ICT
6. Long-term versus short-term

2.1 Local versus Global

Strategic decisions have to be made on local-versus-global considerations (Bartlett and Ghoshal, 1989): How much autonomy is granted to a local or regional R&D unit? Too much freedom leads to unintended redundancies and re-inventing-the-wheel. Not many companies can afford such luxury in times of scarce R&D budgets and escalating development costs. Overly tight control might hinder creativity and optimal exploitation of local competencies.

Global sourcing is not only limited to purchasing departments. Since the widespread use of the Internet as an external information pool, information has no longer geographic limitations. Even very small companies can afford to source knowledge on a global scale. This sourcing is mainly restricted to more or less highly structured data and information, i.e. explicit knowledge. Experience and know-how of researchers cannot be accumulated by downloading publications from the Internet. Tacit knowledge resides with the person. Successfully tapping of this knowledge requires direct personal contact and local presence. The global village has its limits in the diffusion of tacit knowledge and trust.

On the market side the same principle applies: „Our markets are different"

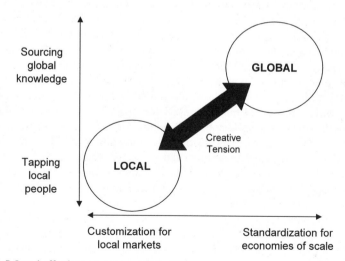

Fig. VI.1.5. Local effectiveness versus global efficiency.

seems to be the most often used argument to support local autonomy. Product management has to decide how much a product has to be adapted to regional market requirements. Customization and tailored products for every specific market segment or even customer might increase the turnover. However, such specifications lead to high costs. Not only does R&D have to develop different products for each wish – the main cost drivers are hidden: variant costs. Therefore, many companies have standardized hidden key components and only adapt visible parts to regional markets. But there is no single solution to the goal conflict between local effectiveness and global efficiency.

2.2 *Processes versus Hierarchy*

The transfer of R&D activities abroad has led to duplication of development and global inefficiency in many companies. To reduce this effect, R&D locations begin to concentrate on their individual core capabilities and cooperate more closely. Each location focuses on the components or technologies for which it possesses the highest level of competence in the R&D network. The greater division of decision processes - in which each location no longer develops everything itself - permits the concentration of resources to reach critical size and economies-of-scale. At the same time, however, this leads to an internationalization of innovation processes. To develop a new system, several locations must pool their resources.

Within projects there is more interdisciplinary cooperation than there has been in the past. Process-oriented teams must be able to overcome boundaries of location and specialization, and yet keep their focus on their own special competence. These teams form an overlaying organizational structure which ensures a company's long-term innovative capability. At the same time the teams create conflicts with classical line organization structures. Open communication and common values (vision/mission) can reduce these conflicts which are difficult to manage on a global scale.

Process structures and information technologies which reach beyond national boundaries are essential prerequisites. However, tailor-made processes and extensive use of state-of-the-art communication technologies do not lead to the desired project success if the human factor is neglected. Based on Van de Ven (1989) we know that innovation cannot be seen as a linear process. Deterministic models of managing innovation processes have given way to models incorporating chaos theory and randomness. R&D processes cannot be managed and measured like repetitive routine processes in the production. But most of the times it is possible to restrict chaos to the early stages of innovation: Chaos and people management lead to innovative new concepts and well-suited processes while adhering to discipline yields the efficiency needed in the later stages.

2.3 *Creativity versus Discipline*

Most large companies spend more for the creation of new knowledge than they spend on investments (Kodama, 1995). R&D management increases in signifi-

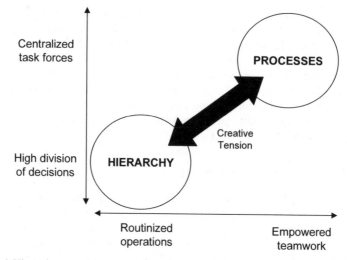

Fig. VI.1.6. Hierarchy versus processes.

cance and, at the same time, in complexity. Ingenious planning procedures often stifle creativity. When it comes to balance between creative chaos and efficient execution, a project management adapted to the respective situation is necessary.

Most small companies control R&D by their annual R&D budget alone. As long as the composition of the R&D team does not change much, and the number of product variants and designs is limited, no major planning support tools are necessary. In such incremental innovation environments, customer-specific adaptation and development projects do not require sophisticated project organization or teams. Process innovation is based on externally acquired production technology and machinery.

Increasing complexity and product variety demand improved coordination of diversified project activities by formalizing the project process. Globalization often aggravates this problem: Companies try to overcome geographic distances through intensified controlling. Many R&D departments therefore support planning by an almost unbelievable amount of formal control mechanisms like form sheets, multiple signatures, project plans, extensive specification lists, etc.

Product liability requirements and misinterpreted ISO certification have led to detailed documentation of the internal R&D process. These efforts are often counterproductive; large volumes of development manuals dust away in bookshelves of project offices. In many companies abridged versions complement excessively detailed handbooks. ISO 9001, when properly understood, allows a case-by-case approach.

Confined planners repeatedly attempt to transpose the reliability and controllability imposed on routine processes (as in manufacturing) into innovation processes. The results often do not match their expectations. Because R&D is constantly operating under time pressure, tight control and regulation lead to deadlocks which induce the growth of uncontrollable „gray zones" and further lengthen development cycle times. Most experienced engineers therefore disapprove of such over-regulation. „True innovation depends on creativity which cannot be controlled by formal criteria. Top-down planning of innovation is not possible." This provocative statement highlights a survey conducted in central Europe: Project management tools are applied in most companies, but their efficiency is below average. Traditional planning methods solely based on complexity reduction, work break-down structures and task simplification are not appropriate any more in a dynamic and interdisciplinary project environment.

Modern operative R&D management consists of control tools that consider performance, deadlines, costs and resources, and continuously adapts its methods to reach these project goals. Modern ICT supports most of these tools. Their prudent application prevents over steering which would make a flexible approach to new situations and events impossible. Milestones are not, as a common practice, interpreted as fixed deadlines, but are driven by extra-ordinary events such as prototype failures, superior competitor products, new market segments, early feedback of dissatisfied customers. The variety of available methods allows a flexible deployment of management tools. In general, the planning effort decreases while the controlling and steering effort, and the integration of functions and management levels increases.

When designing R&D project management, one must always balance between discipline and creativity, standardization and variety, organizational slack and cost-cutting. The more project management focuses on planning and standardization, the better efficiency and cycle time reduction will be accomplished, but the less there is freedom for creative chaos. The stronger integration of project management along objects, functions and hierarchies will increase management complexity, but at the same time improve R&D effectiveness and efficiency. The stage-gate concept considers all of these contradictions and attempts to integrate project management along the three factors market, specialization, and technologies. These factors determine the choice of project management methods.

Fragmentation of the market increases the amount of variants and enlarges the number of parallel projects in a company. Customer focus requires the integration of multiple value-adding activities in the R&D process. For example, the timely consideration of after-sales service is central in the development of new aircraft engines. Basic utility and additional service to the customer must be bundled into a consistent package. Integrated process orientation and a flexible deployment of project management tools increase the efficiency of R&D.

The know-how explosion that we witnessed in recent years has been responsible for the specialization of organizations and individuals in smaller and smaller knowledge areas, leading to an increased division of labor, and to a division of decision processes in R&D. This division of decision-making induces strong cooperation on an individual level between members of separate departments, locations and functions in the project team. Specialization also induces cooperation at the macro level, and we observe the increase in strategic alliances and other inter-organizational collaboration on an international scale. Interface management becomes more and more of an issue, along with its support processes and systems.

Besides information technology, local concentration of product and process technology are other important determinants for the development of R&D project management. Technology fusion in particular forces high-tech companies to globalize their innovation processes, leading to increased coordination intensity. In extreme cases, a company skips an entire product generation and acquires the necessary technology in a fraction of the time to develop it oneself from somewhere else. Newly-hired R&D employees build up new competencies and quickly eliminate established ones. Besides learning, 'unlearning' of so far successful concepts becomes important.

Every company must be aware of how well it can access the technology necessary for survival. Not every company needs the same degree of integration and process orientation. Nevertheless, many companies operate in businesses and markets characterized by different dynamics and technological requirements. The project manager and top management must carefully select their project management tools. The company must differentiate between innovation processes and innovation phases. The development of the Smart-Car by Swatch and Daimler-Benz followed a different set of rules than the internal refinement of a Mercedes rear axle generation. Experienced managers optimize the subtle balance between freedom and discipline, and between creative chaos and well-defined processes.

2.4   *In-house Control versus Open Source R&D*

R&D labs have limited capacities. R&D depth was reduced in the 1990s and 2000s like manufacturing depth in the 1980s. R&D labs are productive when they are selective, when they do what they have already done many times and when they focus on core capabilities. The organizational emphasis is shifting from self-

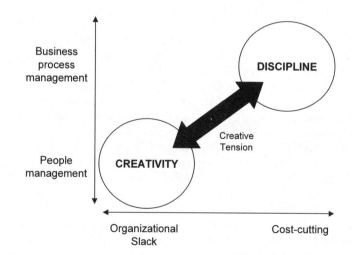

Fig. VI.1.7. Creativity versus discipline: The old organizational dilemma between individual initiative and coordination.

made to bought-in: suppliers, independent laboratories, IP intermediaries, the creative commons, and universities are typical sources.

Under the technological core capability paradigm the new operating tenet is to "own only what you must; influence all you can" (Harris et al., 1996). The most successful virtual companies are at the center of networks that are far from egalitarian (Chesbrough and Teece, 1996). They retain control over the network of their partners. This position cannot be maintained unless the company directly controls some key technologies. Companies need a process to discriminate between "must have" (technologies that must be owned) and "nice to have" technologies.

Schindler also discerned among its „must-have" and „nice-to-have" technologies. As described in the Schindler case study in this book, in 1997 a small group of experts analyzed Schindler's core competencies in order to subsequently concentrate scarce R&D resource in those areas where Schindler was believed to be best-practice. All other activities have been outsourced since: a significant step towards a more virtual R&D organization. The entire process started with the identification of actual competencies based on the analysis of R&D projects in workshops carried out at each R&D location. The main competence criteria for R&D projects were whether

- they created customer benefits;
- they were difficult to imitate by competitors;
- they provide potential for future products.

Projects and activities that survived this elimination process were grouped and defined new competence fields, crucial to the long-term success of the company, the new main activities of Schindler's R&D.

However, in order to prevent information to leak out and to be able to retain critical know-how internally, many companies refrain from partnerships or joint ventures during the early stages of R&D. Some companies, like DaimlerChrysler, are more inclined to start joint ventures than rely on pure partnerships or supplier-to-vendor relationships. These companies usually try to achieve maximal performance with the R&D they have. They control secrecy through ownership.

Most companies apply portfolios to better manage their outsourcing decisions: Portfolios provide standard strategies for well defined situations. For basic technologies at moderate strength the company is best advised to minimize R&D investments and leverage the technology externally. Because the technology life cycle follows the stages of 'embryonic' – 'emerging' – 'key' – 'basic' – 'commodity,' major investments in technologies after the key technology phase make little sense regardless of the relative strength of the company in this technology. But the decision to give up existing technologies is one of the most difficult management decisions as the example of Intel with its data storage chips shows (Grove, 1997).

All this portfolio thinking is very theoretical: It is extremely difficult to make a distinction between key technologies and basic technologies. In the case of the often cited S-curve, psychology is playing a much bigger role than pure technical calculation: Whenever engineers come under pressure and are shown new technologies, the impossible becomes possible. When Edison came up with the electric light bulb, gas-lamps improved efficiency five-fold within a few years after no significant improvement took place for decades (Utterback, 1994). APS cameras emerged as a reaction to the threat of digital photography. At many car manufacturers, outsourcing meets its stiffest resistance within the engineering community: If system-suppliers develop modules themselves, R&D at the car company has to be downgraded! Virtual R&D and in-house capabilities should have some redundancy but some complementary strengths as well.

Equally difficult is the decision to engage in open source innovation. Without being able to control many of the elements that are necessary to succeed in networked innovation, companies shy away from investing resources and time. A permanent danger is the loss of proprietary intellectual property through leakages and open communication in such networks. Worse, sometimes, are the prospects of sponsoring innovations that the company can eventually not exploit oneself because someone else in the network (perhaps a competitor) has assumed control. While it becomes increasingly clear that a single company cannot develop all the technologies it requires in competition, senior R&D directors realize that the management of international standards, open source networks and dominant designs must be added to their repertoire.

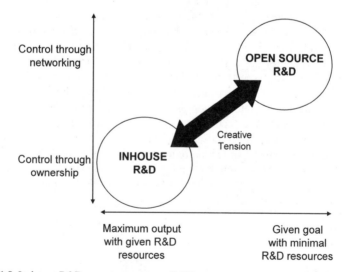

Fig. VI.1.8. In-house R&D versus open source R&D.

2.5   *Face-to-face versus ICT*

R&D is the most important element in technology intensive organizations to source, filter, generate and diffuse knowledge. R&D also greatly depends on advances in technology and information sciences. „Science does not advance by piling up information – it organizes information and compresses it" (Simon, 1997: 226). ICT is almost a "must" in R&D organizations. Access to e-mail, video- and teleconferencing, and groupware is possible almost everywhere. The rapid increase of performance compared to costs leads to the paradoxical phenomenon that some R&D sites in developing countries leapfrog technological generations and install more advanced infrastructure than the R&D headquarter.

Although ICT is a necessary tool for global knowledge management, it is not yet a sufficient one. ICT can support the exchange of explicit knowledge, but learning between individuals requires a basis of trust not easily facilitated by ICT (De Meyer, 1991). Engineers and scientists must be allowed sufficient freedom to build up a network of informal contacts for sharing such knowledge (Allen, 1977; Katz and Tushman, 1981). Managers realize that the procedural and tacit know-how of the project team members is at least as important as the documented and explicit knowledge. But tacit knowledge is almost exclusively shared face to face.

Even face-to-face contact does not ensure perfect communication. Language problems and different cultural frameworks make communication less straight-forward. Communication must be maintained at a regular frequency, as otherwise the trust level between two partners is too low to allow meaningful communication. Face-to-face communication does not need to be exclusively verbal—it may include drawing and demonstration. Some of the latest ICT tries to convey haptic and sensory information as well. No satisfactory means of effective tacit long-distance communication is in sight. Additionally, the amount of explicitly transferable knowledge has tremendously increased: The challenge will not only be to manage face-to-face communication, but also how to manage and make sense of millions of documents and other pieces of information collected in projects, on the Internet, or from specialized information service providers.

Internationally dispersed R&D operations require strong leadership. Geographic distances between local R&D managers and the R&D head who is usually located in the R&D headquarters makes the implementation of strategy difficult. Local R&D managers who administratively report to regional management often have to report to a second manager at the corporate level. The integration of those managers is difficult because they have different interests. Plant managers aim at cost reduction; they are less concerned with innovation and strive for economies-of-scale. R&D staff often fancy technologies. The integration of decentralized R&D can be done in different ways. ABB has a strong Technology Management Team to assure a top-down approach in technology strategy and clear responsibilities in business segments. The team has to develop an operating plan for corporate research. Thereby, it has to align different interests of the business units. The chairman of this management team is the chief technology officer and reports directly to the CEO.

IBM's Investment Review Board for the System/390 division in New York is a

similar team. This board is a steering committee responsible for resource allocation and budgeting of large R&D projects. For those projects, in which several
business units and R&D locations are involved, the board is the final decision
body for resolving escalating conflicts.

At ABB as well as at IBM, teams at different hierarchical levels work face-to-
face within the team and coordinate themselves with other teams more by means
of ICT and less through personal contacts. The direct contact between the different
levels takes place in an efficient Likert-like structure: One member of the local
team is member of the global team. Schindler used to conduct large R&D management meetings with all managers of decentralized R&D sites. This meeting
took place every three months and offered the opportunity for exchanging latest
information. With the new organization of corporate R&D since 1998 according to
product modules, these formal meetings are less needed. Instead, R&D management meets on a more informal basis in so-called „interface meetings." These
meetings are more frequent but much smaller than the previous ones. Schindler
has good experience with this network approach; the political character of R&D
meetings decreases, consensus is reached faster, and the cooperation between
corporate R&D and R&D units in the decentralized plants has improved.

The concentration of locations on core capabilities together with the increasing
complexity of modern products leads to sophisticated forms of knowledge management in multinational companies. The availability of ever more powerful information and communication technologies opens new means for managing projects in the decades to come. Access to electronic conferencing, e-mail, video- and
teleconferencing has become ubiquitous, thus enabling the management of decentralized R&D processes including the exchange of crucial audio-visual information.

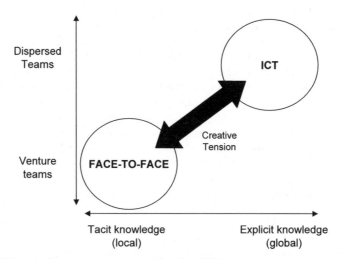

Fig. VI.1.9. Face-to-face contact versus use of modern ICT.

Without these new technologies it would be impossible to coordinate the many strategic alliances and the increased international division of labor. For example, videoconferences play a central role in developing new civil aircraft engines in the transatlantic strategic alliance between MTU and Pratt&Whitney. A permanent connection was established and intensively used for their PW 4048 turbine development to be used in the current Boeing 777. MTU's videoconferencing room is used up to 90% of capacity.

Informal contacts only help to bridge gaps if both parties are inclined to this kind of information exchange and, importantly, if they speak a common language. Only then can tacit knowledge be codified and transferred. In the MTU turbine development example, hard to codify knowledge was initial mass requirements for turbine blades, based on estimates and experience of an aerodynamics engineer. Still today, appropriate starting parameters are crucial for finding the optimal solution, despite advances in the utilized computing power. It is this kind of knowledge that is so hard to transfer between people over short distances and near to impossible over larger geographical and cultural gaps.

R&D managers thus try to foster organizational learning by all means. This includes substantial investments in simulation programs interconnecting long-grown experience knowledge and learned theory. Both 3M and Hewlett-Packard employ a wide set of tools and instruments to detach tacit knowledge from selected individuals and to disseminate tacit knowledge around the company by implementing central information offices and project management departments. They support informal contacts by means of extrovert engineers, shared communication platforms, shared coffee corners, and frequent job rotation. The project management department at Hoffmann-La Roche facilitates the learning transfer between projects. This department supervises a group of world-wide dispatched project managers who after termination of their assignment return to this department. Roche deliberately avoids to reintegrate project managers back in the hierarchy in order to optimize knowledge transfer between projects.

Knowledge management also facilitates the creation of new ideas. This can be implemented by means of time budgets, according to which every R&D employee is allowed to use a certain amount of time for creative activities as he wishes. At 3M, this time („boot-legging") is set to 15%, employees are required to report at the end of the year about how they used this time. Before its merger, Ciba used to conduct an idea auction once a year, at which internal and external participants collected and prioritized unusual ideas. For the rapid realization of the selected ideas, Ciba provided a small amount of seed-money. Most of such activities do not work without friction. They are difficult to match with the highly-acclaimed business process redesign concept. Much of it runs along informal contacts and rests on personal connections between all hierarchical levels, thus playing an important role for horizontal and vertical integration in a company.

In many western companies, consultants suggested to rationalize and eliminate middle management. This may however have a detrimental effect. Primarily middle managers are responsible for carrying out projects, thus ensuring that the necessary knowledge is being reapplied. They mediate between the 'language of money' and the 'language of facts' at the base and therefore assume a significant integrative function. Middle managers are young enough to understand the latest technology and old enough to have the business experience to grasp the goals and visions the top management is promoting. The often reiterated complete rationalization of hierarchical levels and elimination of middle management will most likely also eliminate the knowledge base of many companies.

Strictly hierarchically managed companies such as Kao - with their centralist organization focused on efficiency in their core businesses and operative processes - try to stimulate innovation by generating openness and an informal information culture. In spite of several management layers, Kao succeeds in being highly innovative. By supporting cross-functional and cross-departmental communication, middle management know-how is efficiently implemented throughout the company. Know-how maintenance is thus becoming a core activity for modern R&D project management.

2.6   Long-term versus Short-term

There has always been a gap between long-term and short-term pressures in R&D. Critical in successful innovation is the timing of the new product or service to be introduced in a market. Early or late introduction is equally detrimental (e.g., Foster, 1986). Products offered too late usually face stiff competition from similar products, and customers may have adopted a competing design or product architecture. Profit margins for late products are thus significantly lower (e.g., me-too drugs in the pharmaceutical industry). Products offered too early may fail because customers do not yet experience the need for them, and these products cannot benefit from complementary offerings (e.g., Beta-Max versus VHS, Rosenbloom and Cusumano, 1987). Companies therefore often invest in educating the market about the benefits of its product (additional investments in advertising and marketing) to convince the potential customer of the anticipated long-term benefits of the new product (e.g., failure of the Apple Lisa, or the Apple Newton). Introducing the right product at the right time (rather than just as quickly as possible) is critical in innovation.

The danger of missing this window of opportunity is great, as numerous examples of new product introduction failures document. There are two principal approaches how innovating companies attempt to cope with this problem:

1) Researching future customer benefits and assessing emerging technology potentials: Using various forecasting and monitoring techniques, companies predict changes in both the technology pull as well as the technology demand side, and derive strategic implications how long-term innovation efforts in their R&D organizations can meet these expected customer benefits. The goal is to see farther and more clearly what is ahead.

2) Speeding up new product development and decreasing time-to-market: Customers identify suppliers that can deliver the best solutions to their current needs nearly real-time. Long innovation times are a competitive disadvantage, especially in industries with rapidly changing requirements and thus moving targets. Companies therefore try to reduce R&D cycle times and speed up the

innovation process. Ideally, R&D would be an instantaneous process; practically, one has to beat competition by a time frame that is equal or exceeds in value over the costs of identifying, negotiating and switching to a new supplier. The goal is to be as fast as possible.

However, these two strategic paradigms of innovation have led to a disintegration of the overall R&D effort. As a consequence, R&D departments have been compartmentalized and functionally isolated. Communications between research and development units and the alignment of overarching innovation objectives have suffered. At a global level, research is building capacity abroad to source and absorb scientific and long-term technology information. Development, on the other hand, is following market potentials and localizes new products to customer needs. This adds a global dimension to the problem of disintegrated innovation.

Moreover, the gap between these two critical R&D capabilities is widening. While new product development has to deliver in shorter and shorter time frames, sustainable innovation is increasingly based on integrated technology planning and the phased introduction of compatible modules and systems that extend the usefulness as well as economic and environmental sustainability of products. This is a fundamental dilemma that some companies have tried to address by reintegrating R&D departments, or by establishing special liaison officers between short and long-term R&D teams, or by imposing technology roadmaps and scenario planning on R&D departments. None of these approaches has produced thoroughly satisfactory results so far; the dilemma of diverging short and long-term innovative capabilities continues to persist.

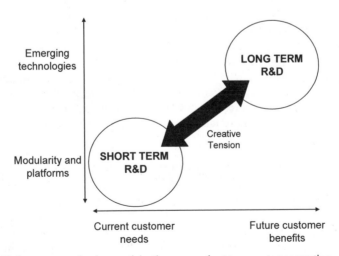

Fig. VI.1.10. Long-term technology anticipation versus short-term customer reaction.

3   Looking Ahead: Organizing Global R&D Ten Years From Now

The case studies in this book have shown how companies manage their technology in the long term. Sophisticated processes of creating, transforming, and implementing technology strategy were presented. Still, we actually know surprisingly little about the systematic relations between firms' innovatory capabilities and the extent of their international innovation activities.

Academic research has focused on inter-firm organization of R&D activities by alliances and networks – almost to the exclusion of intra-firm organization, and scholars have devoted relatively little attention to the relationship between internal organization structure and innovation outcomes. This neglect is at least in part due to a simple lack of appropriate firm-level data on the intrafirm organization of R&D (Argyres and Silverman, 2004). As a result of this missing data, we do not know whether or not firms that have internationalized their R&D activities have actually enhanced their technological capabilities (Penner-Hahn and Shaver, 2005). Major theoretical gaps in our understanding of the firm-internal factors that drive R&D location choice remain (Feinberg and Gupta, 2004).

In one of our own studies of 39 multinational companies we found that just slightly more than half of the investigated companies had a formally written-down technology strategy at corporate level and defined technical core competencies. But especially in small and medium sized companies an explicit technology strategy is very often missing.

Technologies are handled reactively: The three most important drivers for innovation are customers, suppliers, and employees. As small companies are more and more targeting global markets, these companies will need simple, efficient concepts that are not yet available. The rather complex, historically grown R&D patterns of the large multinationals will need simplification which itself cannot be done without better theories on global R&D.

The trend towards a service society progresses at ever greater speed. But, „services are simply too heterogeneous to be an interesting category," remarked L. C. Thurow (1996: 27). For instance, modern hospitals belong to the service industry. They are bundles of high-tech yet poorly managed in many regulated economies. The share of manufacturing will decrease, but the significance of R&D will grow as customers become more and more demanding and technology potential develops even more. Yet, R&D will be different: more system orientation, more reductionism, more telecom-driven, more open networking, and more harmonization.

3.1   More System Orientation

The border of modern products is vanishing: What is the border of a mobile telephone system? Is it the phone, or the phone plus transmitter, plus server, plus camera, plus...? Where to draw the line? Some advanced companies are transferring R&D engineers from corporate labs to module-producing business units.

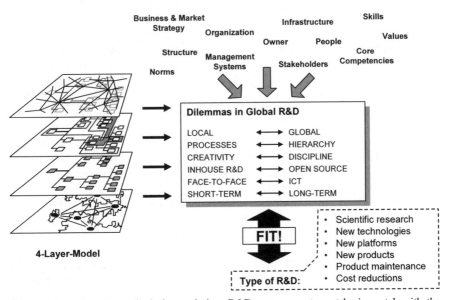

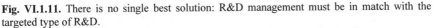

Fig. VI.1.11. There is no single best solution: R&D management must be in match with the targeted type of R&D.

Sociologists, language specialists and psychologists take over their jobs in corporate research: These companies want to understand the trends of modern society in the long term. They want to have answers, at least tentative ones, to questions like: Will DaimlerChrysler sell cars or integrated mobility by the year 2020? Already in the 1950s Frank Lloyd Wright dreamt of building one mile high. These dreams can only be realized with new technologies and new system concepts for elevators, buildings and traffic management. Elevator companies like Schindler and automobile companies like DaimlerChrysler thus study the same trends in technologies and society: Will future cities look more like 'Technopolis' or more like 'Waterfront' or 'Comprehensive cities'?

Globalization plays an outstanding role in this process, since taste differs to a great extent from region to region. Television has homogenized many things but we are still far away from a global uniform society.

3.2 More Reductionism

According to Popper, reductionism has been the most successful scientific approach since Newton. All the holism so important for systems has not changed engineering. Today's physical models are far more powerful than just a few years ago. Material parameters have improved accuracy since manufacturing processes have gained reliability. Well defined parameters combined with high-speed computers allow calculations where trial-and-error had to give answers in cumbersome and time-consuming experiments.

At the moment, pharmaceutical research is being changed dramatically by the human genome project. Illness is not considered anymore to be a sign of too many bacteria as in Pasteur's time or a faulty chemical process but rather an information defect in the human genetic code (Drews, 1998). Illness is reduced to mathematics and can be understood by the help of computers, a trend we also see in more and more R&D fields like stress analysis, material sciences, and electronic circuit layouts. Mathematics is already evolving as the common empirical language in companies like Kao. But the models behind these mathematical computations are so complicated that only a handful of specialists fully understand them: The race for the brightest heads has not only started, it is already under way. Specialized small research centers will be leading the way, like the optical design industry in the US has done already for more than a decade. This trend will be supported by the third big change we see happen over the next decades.

3.3 More Telecom-driven

The Internet started within the scientific community to diffuse new knowledge as quickly as possible. The more that science comes into engineering, the more easily it is to communicate over the Internet. Brain power has to move less often, hence re-centralization of brain power will be possible again. Global competition increases in these fields: R&D will be more evenly spread over the globe. Indian software specialists, Russian scientists and Chinese engineers will team up virtually and compete with R&D specialists in the traditional centers of the US, Europe and Japan. Telecommunication allows virtual team-building.

But we are still in the early stages of the telecom revolution. We still haven't seen many multi-media convergence technologies deliver on their promises. It is expected that virtual teams will become more popular in all industries with the coming large improvements in groupware. Group coordinating processes are already well supported, but most non-linear chaotic knowledge-creation processes between decentralized teams are still handled insufficiently. Electronic brainstorming has its limits in transmission and sharing of tacit knowledge. With better real time exchange of visual and even haptic information, it is only a matter of time until global R&D processes can be supported by ICT during any R&D phase. The driving force behind that development is the entertainment business linked with the computer industry.

The critical size of R&D units decreases, small teams will have the entire globe as their market, and they will specialize even more. The main burden for new products will move to dedicated system groups which are able to manage global projects. Whether this will be accepted socially in the engineering community will be shown in the next few years. In any case, telecommunications will change our R&D sites dramatically over the next decades.

3.4 More Open Networking

With the increased availability of modern ICT, the „global village" will become reality. Even small companies are now able to access the latest research results of the scientific community fast and cost-effectively. With 'tele-presence' they are able to actively participate in the scientific network. Economies-of-scale in R&D will further decrease. Large R&D budgets will be no guarantee for successful breakthrough innovation. Instead, the company making the best use of others will survive in competition.

As knowledge is more and more publicly available, companies concentrate on R&D projects with a short-term ROI. Research is delegated to publicly funded universities. This principle also applies to countries (Thurow, 1996): „A global economy encourages free riding. Why should a country pay for basic research and development if its firms can use whatever new technologies are developed elsewhere in the world?" Even a highly advanced country like Japan displayed this behavior of concentration on product development while sourcing basic research know-how from Europe and the US until the late 1980s. Long-term evolution of industry might be jeopardized by such behavior.

In the future, the ability to concentrate on core competencies and to find the right partner with complementary resources will become even more important. If the concept of the virtual knowledge factory becomes more popular, the merger and acquisition mania of last decade might be substituted by a flexible network of partners with complementary resources who cooperate temporarily on the basis of shared interests. As such, new forms of alliances of the kind we already find in open source projects with sophisticated multi-partner communities will evolve.

3.5   More Harmonization

The European Community, ISO and NAFTA are promoting standards in technology and even standardized business models. Global products developed by R&D centers in different regions will benefit from increased harmonization of technical norms and worldwide standardization. Fast standardization enables the early establishment of a dominant design, a prerequisite for realizing economies-of-scale and cost reduction, one of the main drivers behind economic activity. Today's mobile telecommunication is a typical example for increased competition within such a deregulated market.

The international harmonization of patent laws leads to more protection for multinational companies against cheap local imitators, like pharmaceutical companies have prospered at the end of the 19th century Europe. Strategic patenting on a global scale will promote transnational knowledge generation processes.

In society, two trends can be seen: On the one hand, regionalism and diversity are on the rise. On the other hand, different cultures are assimilated and converge through television and global products. Economies and industries are becoming interdependent. This presents a fundamental challenge for the technology-intensive company: Satisfying the increasingly diverse needs of the local customer with ever more complex technologies in a rapidly globalizing market.

English as the common language in science facilitates communication – the critical success factor in R&D. Scientists and engineers are trained the same way everywhere in the world: Scientific laws and fundamental engineering principles know no national boundaries. With their strong intrinsic motivation and similar backgrounds, researchers everywhere think alike and work alike more than people in others professions. Knowledge redundancies further promote cross-border communication and mutual understanding: a first step to reducing the not-invented-here-syndrome.

3.6 Conclusion

As R&D organizations have developed from centralized and geographically confined towards distributed and open structures, these dilemmas have risen in urgency. Yet dilemmas are not negative per se. On the contrary, in a dilemma both alternative courses of action are equally valuable. The various approaches to managing these dilemmas—including those that attempt to eliminate them altogether—have given rise to an impressive body of know-how among R&D managers and R&D scientists. One thing has been confirmed in every single one of our research studies: Looking ten years ahead, regardless of the rapid evolution of modern technologies, new organizational concepts and even more efficient tools, the individual and teams will remain at the core of international management of innovation.

Table VI.1.3. Lessons learned in managing transnational R&D projects.

Company	Lessons learned
DuPont	• Maintain a vibrant corporate R&D group for discovery research with a Science and Techno-logy mission; • Have a variety of skills and talents; foster networking and collaboration; • Develop 10 year technology plans to stretch the business and guide R&D across the company; • Manage technology platforms across the company – not individual R&D projects.
Roche	• International teams require new organizations; • Organizations must be flexible to be able to respond to changes.
Schering	• Synchronization of international drug development is essential to shorten R&D cycle; • International project management is key to international synchronization of R&D projects; • Worldwide integrated R&D data management is key to uniform high standards in R&D; • Acquisition of external ideas and projects is as important as internal R&D.
Ciba	• Creation of a research climate conducive to innovation attracts and retains top-class scientists; • Regular and critical project challenging meetings foster technology and market awareness among scientists; • Full attention to bottom-up creativity, followed by clear top-down decisions motivate people; • Flexible resource allocation to emerging technologies is a must; • Different cultures at decentralized R&D centers require intensive personal interactions.
Kao	• Introduction of local culture and know-how; • Flat and flexible organization; • Localize management resources.
Xerox	• Mastering the confluence of emerging business opportunities and emergent technologies; • Fast time-to-market; • Architecting technology in order to create new revenue and profit streams in new markets.
Canon	• Always make top policy and company direction clear; • Appropriate mixture of top-down (request-based) and bottom-up (proposal-based) in project definition; • Keep good human networks and find good key people; • Competitive technology and the best timing for exploitation.
HP	• R&D must experience and understand the needs of the customer; • Centralized R&D, seeking breakthroughs while freed from the demands and constraints of the day-to-day business and product-line R&D, seeking ways to better meet customer needs, are both required for long-term health of innovative business; • An R&D mind-set and problem solving persona, mixed with business acumen, can be an unbeatable combination for intrapreneurship within a large company; • R&D „renaissance" teams and people, skilled at mixing know-how across multiple disciplines or sciences, will be indispensable to high-technology and growth-seeking companies.
IBM	• Market and customer-orientation of R&D; • R&D structure aligned with a clear business and technology strategy; • Strong corporate identity is more important than organization charts.
SAP	• Communication is key: too much information is as expensive as not enough information; • Understand and take into account cultural differences; • Cooperation with customers is a win-win situation; • Decentralize the responsibility, but centralize the synchronization; • Flexibility is based on an atmosphere of mutual trust and learning.

Table VI.1.3. Lessons learned in managing transnational R&D projects. (continued)

Company	Lessons learned
Unisys	• Design products and services for the global market; • Structure organization to focus on competencies; • Train people in the skills they will need for their work; • Leverage previous work.
Huawei	• R&D should feel what impact their work has on products and profits; • Focus on efficient and high-quality R&D processes; • Strong internal R&D investment allows fast acquisition of new technologies and own production of intellectual property; • Partnerships are important for the direction of future technology standards.
Fujitsu	• Global cross-divisional projects require flexible structures; • Worldwide research collaborations in form of joint research with leading institutions are key for successful R&D; • Service products require the same global R&D network as devices; • Business development should be supported by R&D structures.
SwissRe	• Support from top and middle management; • Local investigative and discovery partners; • Use of external expert know-how; • Protect (service) innovations with intellectual property rights; • Reduce second-mover advantages with intellectual property rights; • Use legal protection instruments to open up new markets; • Anticipate technology transfer and licensing models.
ABB	• After dissolution of the global team, the members back home take over the local role as technology transfer specialists in a natural way; • A strong motivation leading to better team performance is automatically generated with improved cross-cultural communications; • A successful team builds up long-lasting relations after dissolution, helping international / group integration.
Daimler	• Balance downstream orientation with securing long-term innovation; • Aim for competence-based organization; • Integrate global competencies and know-how; • Ensure interdisciplinary and international cooperation through improved communication.
Schindler	• Business and market-orientation of R&D; • Competence-based R&D network with clear concentration of R&D resources in order to maintain critical mass for new technologies; • Definition of clear technical interfaces are reflected by R&D organizational interfaces; • Strong focus on system management as an organizational R&D unit.
Hitachi	• Capabilities of the R&D laboratory director are extremely important; • Manage cross-company strategic projects with top-down priority; • Involve all relevant people in a project from the start.

Table VI.1.3. Lessons learned in managing transnational R&D projects. (continued)

Company	Lessons learned
Leica	• Invest in leading precision engineering technologies; • Build up electronics and software design and development capabilities; • Deploy quick prototyping based on new information technologies; • More market-driven activities.
MTU	• In conservative and complex markets in connection with complex technologies: Being too advanced and too early is as dangerous as being too little and too late. • High investment requires a clear screening and gating process and not necessarily a direct approach to the market (technology ready but product on hold); • Organizing in A,B,C-Teams ensures differentiation between technical specialists and project champions; • Take the best ideas or skills from each country/partner; • Continuous involvement of the top management is an absolute prerequisite; • Exchange „technology for technology" for the benefit of the resulting product; • Beware of continuously getting lost in contracts; • Each partner is responsible for its component, starting from the technology until the final product definition; • Use a product-focused concurrent technology approach; • Use adaptive controlling / managing methods.
Siemens	• The customer stands at the beginning and the end of each R&D-cycle; • R&D has to be managed systematically; • Old technologies strike back. Always attack them via new applications; • At the end of the day it's always the excellence of the employees that counts.
BMW	• Have clear processes for the (re-)integration of the R&D results into core processes; • Assure clear communication of corporate strategy & R&D strategy alignment; • Apply a strategic approach to designing the global innovation network / building centers of innovation excellence abroad; • Maintain overall direction and control while decentralizing certain R&D tasks.

Bibliography

Abernathy, W. J.; Utterback, J. M. (1978): Patterns of Industrial Innovation. Technology Review, 80(7): 40-47.

Adler, P. S. (1990): Shared Learning. Management Science. 36(8): 938-957.

Adler, N. J. (1991): International Dimensions of Organizational Behavior (2nd ed.). Boston.

Aguilar, F. (1967): Scanning the Business Environment. New York: NY: Macmillan.

Aharonian, G.: Software Patent Statistics 1976-2004; http://www.bustpatents.com/softpats.htm; January, 2004.

Albers, S.; Eggers (1991): Organisatorische Gestaltungen von Produktinnovations-Prozessen. Führt der Wechsel des Organisationsgrades zu Innovationserfolg? Zeitschrift für betriebswirtschaftliche Forschung, 43(1): 44-64.

Allen, T. J. (1977): Managing the Flow of Technology - Technology Transfer and the Dissemination of Technological Information within the R&D Organization. London: Cambridge University Press.

Allen, T. J.; Lee, M. S.; Tushman, M. L. (1980): R&D performance as a function of internal communication, project management, and the nature of work. IEEE Transactions on Engineering Management, EM-27(1): 2-12.

Almeida, P. (1996): Knowledge Sourcing by Foreign Multinationals: Patent Citation Analysis in the US Semiconductor Industry. Strategic Management Journal, 17: 155-165.

Ambos, B. (2005): Foreign Direct Investment in Industrial Research and Development: A Study of German MNCs. Research Policy, 34(4): 395-410.

Amstad, M.; Arvanitis, S.; Hollenstein, H. (1996): Wie innovativ ist die Schweizer Industrie im internationalen Vergleich? In Gassmann, O.; von Zedtwitz, M. (Eds.): Internationales Innovationsmanagement: München: Vahlen. 231-258.

Andersen, O. (1993): On the Internationalization Process of Firms: A Critical Analysis. Journal of International Business Studies, 24(2): 209-231.

Anderson, P.; Tushman, M. L. (1990): Technological Discontinuities and Dominant Designs: A Cyclical Model of Technological Change. Administrative Science Quarterly, 35(4): 604-633.

Anderson, K. M.; Dean, B. V. (1998): Factors That Contribute to the Success of Hewlett-Packard's Distributed Collaborative Work Groups. In Lefebvre, L. A.; Mason, R. M.; Khalil, T. (Eds.): Management of Technology, Sustainable Development and Eco-Efficiency. International Conference on Management of

Technology Proceedings: Amsterdam: Elsevier. 1034-1043.

Ansoff, H. I. (1975): Managing strategic surprise by response to weak signals. California Management Review, 18(2): 21-33.

Archibugi, D.; Michie, J. (1995): The Globalisation of Technology: A New Taxonomy. Cambridge Journal of Economics, 19(1): 121-140.

Archibugi, D.; Immarino, S. (1999): The policy implications of the globalization. Research Policy, 28(2-3): 317-336.

Archibugi, D.; Iammarino, S. (2002): The globalization of technological innovation: definition and evidence. Review of International Political Economy, 9(1): 98-122.

Argyres, N. S.; Silverman, B. S. (2004): R&D, organization structure and the development of corporate technological knowledge. Strategic Management Journal, 25(8-9): 929-958.

Argyris, C.; Schön, D. A. (1978): Organizational learning. London, Reading: Addison-Wesley.

Arthur D. Little (1993): Results of the Arthur D. Little International Survey on the Marketing/R&D Interface. Wiesbaden.

Arthur D. Little (1995): Best of the Best - Colloquia Series. Wiesbaden.

Arthur D. Little (1997): Priority Issues in Technology and Innovation Management: An Arthur D. Little Survey of Management Agendas. Wiesbaden: Arthur D. Little.

Asakawa, K. (1996): External-Internal Linkages and Overseas Autonomy-Control Tension: The Management Dilemma of the Japanese R&D in Europe. IEEE Transactions on Engineering Management, 43(1): 24-32.

Asakawa, K. (2001): Organizational tension in international R&D Management: the case of Japanese firms. Research Policy, 30: 735-757.

Ashby, W. R. (1956): An Introduction to Cybernetics. London.

Ashton, W. B.; Klavans, R. A. (1997): Keeping abreast of Science and Technology. Battelle Press. Columbus, Richland.

Asia Wall Street Journal (2005): Chinese Telecom Firm gets Lost in Translation When Making U.S. Pitch. Asia Wall Street Journal (July 28): A1+A5.

Bader, M. A.; Bischof, D. (2005): Intellectual Property Management in der Finanzdienstleistungsbranche. Wiesbaden: Gabler.

Bader, M. A. (2006a): Intellectual Property Management in R&D Collaborations. The case of the Service Industry Sector. Heidelberg: Physica.

Bader, M. A. (2006b): Risikominimierung durch Intellectual Property Management. (2 ed.). Berlin: Springer.

Bader, M. A. (2006c): Riding the Value-chain Upgrade – Patents as a Means of Boosting your Factual Protection Strategies. epi Information. 2006(3): 94-98.

Bader, M. A. (2007a): Extending Legal Protection Strategies to the Service Innovations Area: Review and Analysis. World Patent Information (forthcoming).

Bader, M. A. (2007b): IP Commercialization in Germany. iam Intellectual Asset Management Magazine, (21): 60-64.

Bader, M. A. (2007c): Managing intellectual property in a collaborative environment: learning from IBM. International Journal of Intellectual Property Management, 1(3): 206-225.

Bader, M. A. (2007d): Managing intellectual property in inter-firm R&D collaborations in knowledge intensive industries. International Journal of Technology Management (forthcoming).

Baldwin, J.; Lin, Z. (2002): Impediments to advanced technology adoption for Canadian manufacturers. Research Policy, 31: 1-18.

Bartlett, C. A. (1986): Building and Managing the Transnational: The New Organizational Challenge. In Porter, M. E. (Ed.): Competition in Global Industries: Boston, MA. 367-401.

Bartlett, C. A.; Ghoshal, S. (1986): Tap your Subsidaries for Global Research. Harvard Business Review, 6: 87-94.

Bartlett, C. A.; Ghoshal, S. (1989): Managing Across Borders: The Transnational Solution. Boston, MA.

Bartlett, C. A.; Ghoshal, S. (1990): Managing Innovation in Transnational Corporation. In Bartlett, C. A.; Doz, Y.; Hedlund, G. (Eds.): Managing the Global Firm: London, New York. 215-255.

Bartlett, C.; Ghoshal, S. (1995): Transnational Management: Chicago.

Becker, B.; Gassmann, O. (2006): Gaining Leverage Effects from Knowledge Modeswith Corporate Incubators. R&D Management, 36(1): 1-16.

Beckmann, C.; Fischer, J. (1994): Einflußfaktoren auf die Internationalisierung von Forschung und Entwicklung in der Chemischen und Pharmazeutischen Industrie. Zeitschrift für betriebswirtschaftliche Forschung, 46(7/8): 630-657.

Beckmann, C. (1997): Internationalisierung von Forschung und Entwicklung in multinationalen Unternehmen. Aachen: Shaker.

Behrmann, J. N.; Fischer, W. A. (1979): The Coordination of Foreign R&D Activities by Transnational Corporations. Journal of International Business Studies, 10(3): 28-35.

Behrmann, J. N.; Fischer, W. A. (1980a): Transnational Corporations: Market Orientations and R&D Abroad. Columbia Journal of World Business, 15(3): 55-59.

Behrmann, J. N.; Fischer, W. A. (1980b): Overseas Activities of Transnational Companies. Cambridge MA.

Beise, M.; Belitz, H. (1996): Internationalisierung von F&E multinationaler Unternehmen in Deutschland. In Gassmann, O.; von Zedtwitz, M. (Eds.): Internationales Innovationsmanagement: München. 215-230.

Belderbos, R. (2003): Entry mode, organizational learning, and R&D in foreign affiliates: Evidence from Japanese firms. Strategic Management Journal, 24: 235-259.

Belitz, H.; Beise, M. (1997): Internationalisation of R&D in Multinational Enterprises: The German Perspective. Conference on Investment, Innovation and Diffusion of Technology in Europe: German Foreign Direct Investment and its role in European Growth. London.

Bendler, A.; Kluge, J.; Stein, W.; Licht, T. (2004): Knowledge unplugged. The McKinsey & Company Survey on Knowledge Management. Palgrave.

Benito, G.; Grogaard, B.; Narula, R. (2003): Environmental Influences on MNE Subsidiary roles: Economic Integration an the Nordic Countries. Journal of International Business Studies, 34: 443-456.

Bergfeld, M.-M.; Malik, K. (2004): Conceptualising the process of intra-corporation technology transfers – a support to managing technological knowledge across multinational corporations. Sesimbra, Portugal.

Bergfeld, M.-M.; Stahl, M. (2005): The role of foreign subsidiaries in the innovation process of German high-tech corporations: A support to building global innovation networks. Proceedings of the R&D Management Conference. Pisa, Italy.

Bergfeld, M.-M. (2006): The MBW Group: Innovating complex systems, core components, peripheral solutions and complementary products in the global market and technology context, working paper, Institute of Innovation Research, Manchester Business School.

Bidault, F.; Butler, C. (1996): Early Supplier Involvement: Leveraging Know-how for Better Product Development. Target, 12(1): 20-26.

Birkinshaw, J.; Nobel, R.; Ridderstrale, J. (2000): Knowledge as a Contingency Variable: Do the Characteristics of Knowledge Predict Organization Structure? Organization Science, 13(3): 274-289.

Boehm, B. W. (1976): Software Engineering. IEEE Transactions on Computers, C-25(12): 1226-1241.

Bosomworth, C. E.; Burton, H. S. (1995): How 26 Companies Manage Their Central Research. Research Technology Management, 38(4): 32-40.

Bosshart, O.; Gassmann, O. (1996): Management Strategischer Technologieallianzen. In Gassmann, O.; von Zedtwitz, M. (Eds.): Internationales Innovationsmanagement: München. 187-211.

Boutellier, R.; Seghezzi, H. D.; Bodmer, C. E. (1995): Produktivität am Standort Schweiz, Studie des ITEM im Auftrag der Schweizerischen Akademie der Technischen Wissenschaften (SATW). Lausanne.

Boutellier, R.; Bodmer, C.; Kloth, B. (1996): Denkplatz Schweiz - Alternative zum Werkplatz Schweiz? io Management, 65(1/2): 67-71.

Boutellier, R.; Kloth, B.; Bodmer, C. E. (1996): Neue Organisationsformen globaler F&E. Zeitschrift für Organisation, Mai 96: 282-287.

Boutellier, R.; Gassmann, O. (1996a): Generationenwechsel im F&E-Projektmanagement. Projektmanagement-Forum '96, Essen: GPM.

Boutellier, R.; Gassmann, O. (1996b): F+E-Projektbewertung führt zu erfolgreichen Produkten - Weichenstellung in der Entwicklung für raschen Marktzutritt. Technische Rundschau, 19: 10-14.

Boutellier, R. (1997): Integration neuer Technologien. Manager Bilanz. III(7/97): 6-11.

Boutellier, R.; Baumbach, M.; Schwarz, G. (1997): Erfolgreiche Praktiken statt „Best Practices". Absatzwirtschaft (6/97): 48-52.

Boutellier, R.; Behrmann, N. (1997): Quellen technischen Wissens. Wissenschaftsmanagement (3/1997): 123-129.

Boutellier, R.; Corsten, D.; Lach, C. (1997): Neue Ansätze im Projektmanagement der Produkteinführung. Thexis Fachzeitschrift für Marketing, 3: 13-20.

Boutellier, R.; Gassmann, O.; von Zedtwitz, M. (1997): Innovation and Phases in Transnational R&D. 7th International Forum on Technology Management, Challenges for the 21th Century - Networking East and West. Kyoto (Japan):

481-488.

Boutellier, R.; Gassmann, O. (1997a): Das Generationenkonzept im F&E-Projektmanagement. Wissenschaftsmanagement (1/1997): 34-42.

Boutellier, R.; Gassmann, O. (1997b): Wie F&E-Projekte flexibel gemanagt werden. Harvard Business Manager, Apr 97: 69-76.

Boutellier, R.; Behrmann, N.; Bratzler, M. (1998): Patentsystem als Wissensfundus. Wissenschaftsmanagement, 1 (Jan/Feb): 50-60.

Boutellier, R.; Bratzler, M.; Hallbauer (1998): Bei KMU Kerntechnologien bestimmen. Technische Rundschau (2/98): 38-42.

Boutellier, R.; Gassmann, O.; Macho, H.; Roux, M. (1998): Management of Dispersed R&D Teams. R&D Management, 28(1): 13-25.

Boutellier, R.; von Zedtwitz, M. (1998): Ensuring an Effective R-to-D Interface by Managing Knowledge Transfer through R&D Individuals. In Xu, Q.; Chen, J. (Eds.). Management of Technology and Technological Innovation. Proceedings of the 2nd ISMOT Conference. Hangzhou: 150-161.

Boutellier, R.; von Zedtwitz, M.; Gassmann, O. (1999): Fine-Tuning R&D Processes to Overcome the R-to-D-Interface. Paper presented at the Civilization, Modern Technology and Development. Proceedings of the IAMOT 1999 Conference. Cairo.

Bower, M. (1979): Perspective on McKinsey. McKinsey & Company, Inc.

Bower, M. (1997): The will to lead. Boston: Harvard Business School Publishing.

Bowonder, B.; Miyake, T. (1993): Japanese Innovations in Advanced Technologies: An Analysis of Functional Integration. International Journal of Technology Management, 8(1/2): 135-156.

Braun, T. (1994): Behördliche Korrektur von Verrechnungspreisen bei multinationalen Unternehmen. St. Gallen: University of St. Gallen.

Brockhof, K. (1998): Internationalization of Research and Development. Berlin, Heidelberg, New York: Springer.

Brockhoff, K. (1990): Stärken und Schwächen industrieller Forschung und Entwicklung: Umfrageergebnisse aus der Bundesrepublik Stuttgart.

Brockhoff, K.; Pearson, A. (1992): Technical and Marketing Aggressiveness and the Effectiveness of Research and Development. IEEE Transactions on Engineering Management, 39(4): 318-324.

Brockhoff, K.; Von Boehmer, A. (1993): Global R&D Activities of German Industrial Firms. Journal of Scientific & Industrial Research, 52(6): 399-406.

Brockhoff, K.; Schmaul, B. (1996): Organization, Autonomy and Success of Internationally Dispersed R&D Facilities. IEEE Transactions on Engineering Management, 43(1): 33-40.

Brockhoff, K. (1997): Industrial Research for Future Competitiveness. Berlin, Heidelberg, New York: Springer.

Brown, J.-S.; Duguid, P. (1991): Organizational Learning and Communities-of-Practice: Toward a Unified View of Working, Learning, and Innovation. Organization Science, 2(1): 40-57.

Buderi, R.; Weber, J.; Hoots, C.; Neff, R. (1991): A Tighter Focus for R&D. Business Week (Dec. 2.): 80-84.

Businessweek (2004): Huawei: More Than A Local Hero. Oct. 11.

Caluori, M.; Schips, B. (1991): Internationalisierung der Forschungs- und Entwicklungsaktivitäten Schweizerischer Unternehmen - Empirische Befunde und volkswirtschaftliche Konsequenzen. Chur, Bern.

Caluori, M. (1993): Internationalisierung der Forschungs- und Entwicklungsaktivitäten: Empirische Analyse möglicher Bestimmungsfaktoren und Konsequenzen für eine schweizerische Forschungs- und Technologiepolitik - dargestellt am Beispiel der schweizerischen chemischen Industrie. St. Gallen: University of St. Gallen.

Cantwell, J. (1992): The Internationalisation of Technological Activity and its Implications for Competitiveness. In Granstrand, O.; Håkanson, L.; Sjölander (Eds.): Technology Management and International Business: Internationalization of R&D and Technology: Chichester, New York, Brisbane: Wiley. 75-95.

Cantwell, J. (1995): The globalisation of technology: what remains of the product cycle model? Cambridge Journal of Economics, 19: 155-174.

Cantwell, J.; Janne, O. (1999): Technological globalisation and innovative centers: the role of corporate technological leadership and locational hierarchy. Research Policy, 28(2-3): 119-144.

Cantwell, J.; Mudambi, R. (2005): MNE competence-creating subsidiary mandates. Strategic Management Journal, 26: 1109-1128.

Carmel, E. (1998): Global Software Teams - Collaborating Across Borders and Time Zones. Upper Saddle River NJ: Prentice-Hall.

Carnegie Bosch Institute (1994): Managing International Research and Development. Working Paper. International Executive Forum. Pittsburgh: Carnegie Bosch Institute: 94-98.

Carnegie Bosch Institute (1997): Managing International for Global Platforms and Local Adaptations. Working Paper. International Executive Forum. Pittsburgh: Carnegie Bosch Institute: 98-91.

Carrincazeaux, C.; Lung, Y.; Rallet, A. (2001): Proximity and localization of corporate R&D activities. Research Policy, 30: 777-789.

Case, T. L.; Pickett, J. R. (1989): R&D Information Systems. Research Technology Management. 32(4): 29-33.

Casson, M. (1990): Global Corporate R&D Strategy: A Systems View. University of Reading Discussion Paper Series B. III(137).

Casson, M.; Pearce, R. D.; Singh (1992): Business Culture and International Technology: Research Managers' Perceptions of Recent Changes in Corporate R&D. In Granstrand, O.; Håkanson, L.; Sjölander (Eds.): Technology Management and International Business: Internationalization of R&D and Technology: Chichester, New York, Brisbane. 117-135.

Casson, M.; Singh (1993): Corporate Research and Development Strategies: The Influence of Firm, Industry and Country Factors on the Decentralization of R&D. R&D Management, 23(2): 91-107.

Caves, R. (1996): Multinational Enterprise and Economic Analysis. Cambridge University Press. Cambridge.

Chen, M.-J. (2001): Inside Chinese Business. Harvard Business School Press.

Chen, C.-H.; Shih, H.-T. (2005): High-Tech Industries in China. Cheltenham, UK: Edgar Elgar.

Cheng, J. L. C. (1991): Toward a Systems Paradigm for MNC Research: An Organizational Approach. Advances in International Comparative Management, 6: 161-179.

Cheng, J. L. C.; Bolon, D. S. (1993): The Management of Multinational R&D: A Neclected Topic in International Busines Research. Journal for International Business Studies, 1:1-18.

Cheng, S.-H. (1997): Decision-making in research and development collaboration. Research Policy, 26: 121-135.

Cheng, D.; Liu, L. (2003): The Truth of Huawei. Contemporary China Press. Beijing.

Chesbrough, H. W.; Teece, D. J. (1996): When is Virtual Virtuous? Organizing for Innovation. Harvard Business Manager, 1: 65-73.

Chester, A. N. (1995): Measurments and incentives for central research. Research Technology Management. Vol. 38. Arlington.

Chiesa, V.; Coughlan, P.; Voss, C. A. (1996): Development of a Technical Innovation Audit. Journal of Product Innovation Management, 13: 105-136.

Chiesa, V. (1996a): Managing the Internationalization of R&D Activities. IEEE Transactions on Engineering Management, 43(1): 7-23.

Chiesa, V. (1996b): Human resource management issues in global R&D organisations: A case study. Journal of Engineering and Technology Management, 13: 189-202.

Chiesa, V.; Manzini, R. (1997): Managing virtual R&D organisations: lessons from the pharmaceutical industry. International Journal of Technology Management, 13(5/6).

China Business Weekly (2005): Huawei on a Roll with 3G. China Business Weekly.

China Policy Institute (2006). The University of Nottingham. Nottingham.

Christensen, C. M. (1997): The Innovator's Dilemma: When New Technologies Cause Great Firms to Fail. Harvard Business School Press. Boston.

Clsa (2006): Reinventing China - In search of an innovative economy. Shanghai: CLSA.

Coase, R. H. (1937): The nature of the firm. Economica, 4: 386-405.

Cohen, W.; Levinthal, D. (1989): Innovation and Learning: The Two Faces of R&D. The Economic Journal, 99: 569-596.

Cohen, W. M.; Levinthal, D. A. (1990): Absorptive Capacity – A New Perspective on Learning and Innovation. Administrative Science Quarterly, 35(1): 128-152.

Comello, V. (1998): Hot High-Tech Locations. R&D Magazine, www.rdmag.com.

Conner, K. R.; Prahalad, C. K. (1996): A resources-based theory of the firm: knowledge versus opportunism. Organization Science, 7(5): 477-501.

Coombs, R.; Richards, A. (1993): Strategic Control of Technology in Diversified Companies with Decentralized R&D. Technology Analysis and Strategic Management, 5(4): 385-396.

Cooper, R. G.; Kleinschmidt, E. J. (1991): New Product Processes at Leading Industrial Firms. Industrial Marketing Management, 20: 137-147.

Cooper, R. G. (1994): Third-Generation New Product Processes. Journal of Product Innovation Management, 11: 3-14.

Cordell, A. (1973): Innovation, the Multinational Corporation: Some Implications for National Science Policy. Long Range Planning: 22-29.

Coriat, B.; Orsi, F. (2002): Establishing a new intellectual property rights regime in the United States: Origins, content and problems. Research Policy, 31(8-9): 1491-1507.

Currie, G.; Kerrin, M. (2004): The limits of a technological fix to knowledge management. Management Learning, 35(1): 9-29.

Cuypers, F. (2003): The path to knowledge is patently clear. Swiss Reinsurance Company. Zürich.

Daenzer, W. (1982): Systems Engineering (3rd ed.). Zurich.

Dalton, D. H.; Serapio, M. G. (1995): Globalizing Industrial Research and Development. U.S. Department of Commerce.

Dalton, D. H.; Serapio, M. G.; Yoshida, G. (1999): Globalizing Industrial Research and Development. Washington, D.C.: U.S. Department of Commerce.

Davenport, S.; Davies, J. (1998): Managers and Researcher Collaboration: Opportunities for Organisational Learning. In Lefebvre, L. A.; Mason, R. M.; Khalil, T. (Eds.): Management of Technology, Sustainable Development and Eco-Efficiency: Amsterdam: Elsevier. 111-120.

Davenport, T. H.; Prusak, L. (1998): Working knowledge. How organizations manage what they know. Boston: Harvard Business School Press.

Davis, S.; Botkin, J. (1994): The Coming of Knowledge-Based Business. Harvard Business Review, 5: 165-170.

De Boer, S.; Gan, W.; Shan, G. (1998): Critical issues facing R&D managers in China. R&D Management, 28(3): 187-197.

De Meyer, A.; Mizushima, A. (1989): Global R&D Management. R&D Management, 19(2): 135-146.

De Meyer, A. (1991): Tech Talk: How Managers Are Stimulating Global R&D Communication. Sloan Management Review, 32(3): 49-58.

De Meyer, A. (1992): Management of International R&D Operations. In Granstrand, O.; Håkanson, L.; Sjölander (Eds.): Technology Management and International Business: Internationalization of R&D and Technology: Chichester, New York, Brisbane. 163-179.

De Meyer, A. (1993a): Internationalizing R&D Improves a Firm's Technical Learning. Research Technology Management, 4: 42-49.

De Meyer, A. (1993b): Management of an International Network of Industrial R&D Laboratories. R&D Management, 23(2): 109-120.

De Pury, D. (1994): 'Innovate or Die' Is the First Rule of International Industrial Competiton. Research Technology Management: 9-11.

De Pury, D.; Hauser, H.; Schmid, B. (1995): Mut zum Aufbruch - eine wirtschaftspolitische Agenda für die Schweiz. Zürich.

Dimanescu, D.; Dwenger, K. (1996): World-Class New Product Development. New York: Amacom.

DIW (1996): Internationalisierung von Forschung und Entwicklung in mutlinationalen Unternehmen. DIW Wochenbericht. 16/96: 258-265.

Dixit, A. (1988): International R&D Competition and Policy. In Spence, A. M.; Hazard, H. A. (Eds.): International Competitiveness. 149-171.

Domsch, M. (1993): Laufbahnentwicklung für Industrieforscher. In Domsch, M.; Sabisch, H.; Siemers, S. H. A. (Eds.): F&E-Management: Stuttgart. 153-178.

Doz, Y.; Wilson, E.; Veldhoen, S.; Goldbrunner, T.; Altmann, G. (2006): Innovation: Is Global the Way Forward?: Fontainebleau, France and Booz Allen Hamilton.

Drews, J. (1989): Research in the pharmaceutical industry. European Management Journal, 7: 23-30.

Drews, J. (1998): Die verspielte Zukunft: Birkhäuser.

Drucker, P. (1992): Managing for the future: Butterworth Heineman.

Duga, J.; Studt, T. (2006): Global R&D Report. Insert to R&D Magazine (September 2006).

Dunning, J. H. (1992): Multinational Enterprises and the Globalization of Innovatory Capacity. In Granstrand, O.; Håkanson, L.; Sjölander (Eds.): Technology Management and International Business: Internationalization of R&D and Technology: Chichester, New York, Brisbane. 19-51.

Dunning, J. H. (1993): Multinational Enterprises and the Global Economy. Wokingham, UK: Eddison Wesley.

Dunning, J. H.; Narula, R. (1994): The R&D Activities of Foreign Firms in the U.S. University of Reading Discussion Paper Series B. VII(189).

Dunning, J.; Narula, R. (2005): The R&D Activities of Foreign FIrms in the United States. International Studies of Management and Organisation, 25(1-2): 39-73.

Dyer, W. G.; Wilkins, A. L. (1991): Better stories, not better constructs to generate better theory: a rejoinder to Eisenhardt. Academy of Management Review, 16(3): 613-619.

Easton, T.; Parbhoo, B. (1998): Clubs Promote R&D Interaction at Dow Corning. Research Technology Management, 41(1): 12-15.

Ebadi, Y. M.; Utterback, J. M. (1984): The Effects of Communication on Technological Innovation. Management Science, 30(5): 572-885.

Edelheit, L. (1998): GE's R&D Strategy: Be Vital. Research Technology Management, 41(2): 21-27.

Edersheim, E. H. (2004): McKinsey's Marvin Bower. Vision, leadership, and the creation of management consulting. Hoboken: John Wiley & Sons.

Eirma (1993): Managing In-House Information, Working Group Reports: European Industrial Research Management Association.

Eirma (1995): Globalisation of R&D. EIRMA Conference Papers XLIV. Paris.

Ensign, P. C.; Verhulst, K. (2000): Innovation in the Multinational Firm with Globally Dispersed R&D: Technological Knowledge Utilization and Accumulation. The Journal of High Technology Management, 10(2): 203-221.

Erens, F. J.; Verhulst, K. (1996): Architectures for Product Families. Eindhoven: Working Paper University of Technology.

Erickson, T. (1990): Worldwide R&D Management: Concepts and Applications. Columbia Journal of World Business, Winter: 8-13.

Espinosa, J. A.; Carmel, E. (1993): Modeling Coordination Costs due to Time

Separation in Global Software Teams. ICSE Workshop: A co-located event at ICSE 2003. Portland, Oregon, USA.

Etzkovitz, H.; Leydesdorff, L. (2000): The dynamics of innovation: from National Systems and "Mode 2" to a Triple Helix of university-industry-government relations. Research Policy, 29: 109-123.

Eversheim, W. (1997): Globales Innovationsmanagement - Produkte und Prozesse. Workshop presentation on international innovation management. Zurich.

Fagerberg, J.; Mowery, D.; Nelson, R. (2005): The Oxford Handbook of Innovation: Oxford University Press.

Faz (2001): Der Nutzen von Softwarepatenten ist umstritten. Frankfurter Allgemeine Zeitung, Vol. 101: 31.

Field, T. (1997): Getting In Touch with Your Inner Web. CIO: The Magazine for Information Executives, Jan 15.

Fischer, W. A.; Behrman, J. N. (1979): The Coordination of Foreign R&D Activities by Transnational Corporations. Columbia Journal of World Business: 28-35.

Fischer, W. (1983): The structure and organization of Chinese industrial R&D activities. R&D Management, 13(2): 63-81.

Fischer, W. A.; von Zedtwitz, M. (2004): Chinese R&D: Naissance, Renaissance, or Mirage? R&D Management, 34(4): 349-365.

Flaherty, M. T. (1986): Coordinating International Manufacturing and Technology. In Porter, M. E. (Ed.): Competition in Global Industries, Vol. 198: Boston, MA. 83-109.

Florida, R. (1997): The globalization of R&D: Results of a survey of foreign-affiliated R&D laboratories in the USA. Research Policy, 26: 85-103.

Foster, R. (1986): Timing Technological Transitions (2nd ed.): HarperBusiness.

Frosch, R. A. (1996): The Customer for R&D is Always Wrong. Research Technology Management, 39(6): 22-27.

Frost, T. S.; Zhou, C. (2005): R&D co-practice and 'reverse' knowledge integration in multinational firms. Journal of International Business Studies, 36: 676-687.

Fusfeld, H. I. (1995): Industrial Research - Where It's Been, Where It's Going. Research Technology Management, 38(4): 52-56.

Galbraith, J. R. (1993): The Business Unit of the Future. In Galbraith, J. R.; Lawler, E. E. (Eds.): Organizing for the Future. The New Logic for Managing Complex Organizations: San Francisco. 43-65.

Galia, F.; Legros, D. (2004): Complementarities between obstacles to innovation: Evidence from France. Research Policy, 33: 1185-1199.

Garten, J. E. (1996): The big emerging markets. Columbia Journal of World Business, 31(2).

Garvin, D. A. (1993): Building a Learning Organization. Harvard Business Review, 71(4): 78-91.

Gassmann, O.; Gaso, B. (2004): Insourcing Creativity with Listening Posts in Decentralized Firms. Creativity and Innovation Management, 13(1): 3-14.

Gassmann, O.; von Zedtwitz, M. (1996): Internationales Innovationsmanagement -

Gestaltung von Innovationsprozessen im globalen Wettbewerb. München.

Gassmann, O.; von Zedtwitz, M. (1996a): Ein Referenzrahmen für das Internationale Innovationsmanagement. In Gassmann, O.; von Zedtwitz, M. (Eds.): Internationales Innovationsmanagement: München. 3-15.

Gassmann, O.; von Zedtwitz, M. (1996b): Marktorientiertes Forschungsmanagement. Wissenschaftsmanagement, 3: 138-144.

Gassmann, O.; von Zedtwitz, M. (1996c): Internationales Innovationsmanagement - ein Referenzrahmen. In Gassmann, O.; von Zedtwitz, M. (Eds.): Internationales Innovationsmanagement: München: Vahlen. 3-15.

Gassmann, O. (1997): Kreativer Freiraum für Entwickler - Eine Zweiteilung des F&E-Prozesses steigert die Innovationsrate. io Management, 07. Aug: 26-33.

Gassmann, O. (1997): F+E: Multikulturelle Teams - Kreativität fördern durch Vielfalt. Technische Rundschau, 23: 26-30.

Gassmann, O.; Boutellier, R. (1997): Informationstechnologien in virtuellen F&E-Teams. Technologie & Management, 46(4): 28-31.

Gassmann, O.; Roux, M. (1997): Einsatz von Informationstechnologien in länderübergreifenden F&E-Prozessen. Wissenschaftsmanagement, 3: 130-136.

Gassmann, O. (1997a): Internationales F&E-Management - Potentiale und Gestaltungskonzepte transnationaler F&E-Projekte. München, Wien: Oldenbourg.

Gassmann, O. (1997b): Organisationsformen der internationalen F&E in technologieintensiven Grossunternehmen. Zeitschrift Führung + Organisation, 6: 332-339.

Gassmann, O. (1997c): F&E-Projektmanagement und Prozesse länderübergreifender Produktentwicklung. In Gerybadze, A.; Reger, G.; Meyer-Krahmer, F. (Eds.): Globales Management von Forschung und Innovation: Stuttgart. 127-168.

Gassmann, O.; Bosshart (1998): Strategische Technologieallianzen. Technische Rundschau, 6: 22-25.

Gassmann, O.; von Zedtwitz, M. (1998): Organization of Industrial R&D on a Global Scale. R&D Management, 28(3): 147-161.

Gassmann, O.; von Zedtwitz, M. (1998): Towards the Integrated R&D Network - New Aspects of Organizing International R&D. In Lefebvre, L. A.; Mason, R. M.; Khalil, T. (Eds.): Management of Technology, Sustainable Development and Eco-Efficiency. Selected papers from IAMOT Conference: New York, Oxford, Tokyo. 85-99.

Gassmann, O. (1999): Parxisnähe mit Fallstudienforschung. Wissenschaftsmanagement, 5(3): 11-16.

Gassmann, O.; von Zedtwitz, M. (1999): New Concepts and Trends in International R&D Organization. Research Policy, 28: 231-250.

Gassmann, O.; von Zedtwitz, M. (2003): Innovation Processes in Transnational Corporations. New York.

Gassmann, O.; von Zedtwitz, M. (2003): Trends and determinants of managing virtual R&D teams. R&D Management, 33(3): 243-262.

Gassmann, O.; Han, Z. (2004): Motivations and Barriers of Foreign R&D Activities in China. R&D Management, 34(4): 423-437.

Gassmann, O.; Reepmeyer, G.; von Zedtwitz, M. (2004): Leading Pharmaceutical

Innovation, Trends and Drivers for Growth in the Pharmaceutical Industry. Berlin, New York, Tokyo: Springer.

Gassmann, O.; Bader, M. A. (2004a): Bodyguards für Ihre Ideen. io new management, 4: 10-14.

Gassmann, O.; Bader, M. A. (2004b): Geschickter Einsatz von Patenten. Mit Schutz- und Störstrategien zu Wettbewerbsvorteilen. Neue Züricher Zeitung, Vol. 128: 29.

Gassmann, O.; Bader, M. A. (2004c): Abschlussbericht des Arbeitskreises Intellectual Property Management. Paper presented at the Indisclosed workshop report. St. Gallen.

Gassmann, O.; Bader, M. A. (2004d): Intellectual Property Management in Internfirm R&D Collaborations. Paper presented at the International Symposium of Knowledge and Intellectual Property. Taichung, Taiwan.

Gassmann, O.; Gaso, B. (2005): Insourcing Creativity with Listening Posts in Cecentralized Firms. Creativity and Innovation Management, 13(1): 3-14.

Gassmann, O.; Gaso, B. (2005): Organizational Frameworks for Listening Post Activities in China. International Journal of Technology Intelligence and Planning, 1(3): 241-265.

Gassmann, O.; Becker, B. (2006): Towards a Resource-based View of Corporate Incubators. International Journal of Innovation Management, 10(1): 19-45.

Gassmann, O.; Sandmeier, P.; Wecht, C. H. (2006): Extreme Customer Innovation in the Frond-End: Learning from a New Software Paradigm. Internationa Journal of Technology Management, 33(1): 46-66.

Gassmann, O.; Bader, M. A. (2006a): Intellectual Property Management in Interfirm R&D Collaborations. Taiwan Academy of Management Journal, 6(2): 217-236.

Gassmann, O.; Bader, M. A. (2006b): Patentmanagement Innovationen nutzen und schützen. Berlin: Springer.

Gassmann, O.; Bader, M. A. (2007): Patentmanagement Innovationen nutzen und schützen (2nd ed.). Berlin: Springer.

Gates, S. (1995): The Changing Global Role of the Research and Development Function. New York: The Conference Board.

Geisler, E. (1995): Industry-University technology Cooperation: A Theory of inter-organizational Relationships. Technology Analysis and Strategic Management, 7(2): 217-229.

Gerpott, T. J. (1990): Globales F&E-Management. Die Unternehmung. 44(4): 226-246.

Gerpott, T. J. (1991): Globales F&E-Management: Bausteine eines Gesamtkonzepts zur Gestaltung eines weltweiten F&E-Standortsystems. In Booz, A.; Hamilton (Eds.): Integriertes Technologie- und Innovationsmanagement: Berlin. 49-73.

Gerpott, T. J. (1995): Successful integration of R&D functions after acquisitions: An exploratory empirical study. R&D Management, 25: 161-178.

Gerybadze, A. (1994): Technology Forecasting as a Process of Organisational Intelligence. R&D Management, 24(2): 131-140.

Gerybadze, A. (1995): Strategic Alliances and Process Redesign. Effective Management and Restructuring of Cooperative Projects and Networks. Berlin, New York.

Gerybadze, A.; Meyer-Krahmer, F.; Reger, G. (1997): Globales Management von Forschung und Innovation: Stuttgart. 11-31.

Gerybadze, A.; Reger, G. (1997a): Globalization of R&D: Recent Changes in the Management of Innovation in Transnational Corporations. Discussion Paper. Vol. 97/1. Stuttgart.

Gerybadze, A.; Reger, G. (1997b): A New Framework for Analyzing Globalisation of R&D and Innovation in Transnational Companies. 7th IFTM Conference. Kyoto (Japan).

Gerybadze, A.; Reger, G. (1999): Globalization of R&D: recent changes in the management of innovation in transnational corporations. Research Policy, 28: 251-274.

Ghoshal, S.; Bartlett, C. A. (1988): Creation, Adoption, and Diffusion of Innovations by Subsidiaries of Multinational Corporations. Journal of International Business Studies, 19: 365-388.

Ghoshal, S.; Westney, D. E. (1992): Organizing competitor analysis system. Strategic Management Journal, 14(5): 371-385.

Glenn, J. C.; Gordon, T. J. (1997): The Millennium Project. Technological Forecasting and Change, 56(3): 203-296.

Goldman, S. L.; Nagel, R. N.; Preiss, K. (1994): Agile Competitors and Virtual Organizations: Strategies for Enriching the Customer. New York: Van Nostrand Reinhold.

Goto, T. (1997): Technology Transfer as a Cornerstone of Globalization and Innovation. In Hirasawa, R. (Ed.): Challenges for the 21st Century. Proceedings of the 7th International Forum on Technology Management: Kyoto (Japan). 475-480.

Graham, R. J.; Englaund, R. L. (1997): Creating an Environment for Successful Projects: The Quest to Manage Project Management. California: Jossey-Bass.

Grandstrand, O.; Bohlin, E.; Oskarsson, C.; Sjoberg, N. (1992): External technology acquisition in large multi-technology corporations. R&D Management, 22(2): 111-133.

Grandstrand, O. (1999): Internationalization of corporate R&D: a study of Japanese and Swedish companies. Research Policy, 28(2-3): 275-302.

Granstrand, O.; Sjölander (1992): Internationalisation and Diversification of Multi-technology Corporations. In Granstrand, O.; Håkanson, L.; Sjölander (Eds.): Technology Management and International Business: Internationalization of R&D and Technology: Chichester, New York, Brisbane. 181-207.

Granstrand, O.; Håkanson, L.; Sjölander (1993): Internationalization of R&D - a Survey of Some Recent Research. Research Policy, 22: 413-430.

Grant, R. M.; Baden-Fuller, C. (1995): A knowledge-based theory of inter-firm collaboration. Academy of Management Journal: 17-21.

Greatwall (2002): R&D Yongboa Zhongguo. Nannin: Guangxi Renmin Publishing Company.

Groenveld, P. (1997): Roadmapping Integrates Business and Technology. Research Technology Management, 40(5): 48-55.

Grove, A. S. (1997): Only the paranoid survive. Boston.

Grupp, H. (1994): The measurement of technical performance of innovations by technometrics and its impact on established technology indicators. Research Policy, 23: 175-193.

Gu, S. L.; Lundvall, B. A. (2006): China's Innovation System and the Move Toward Harmonious Growth and Endogenous Innovation, eContent Management Pty Ltd. Maleny.

Gupta, A. K.; Wilemon, D. (1996): Changing Patterns in Industrial R&D Management. Journal of Product Innovation Management, 13: 497-511.

Haas, M. R.; Hansen, M. T. (2005): When using knowledge can hurt performance: the value of organizational capabilities in a management consulting company. Strategic Management Journal, 26: 1-24.

Haedrich, H. (1996): Marktorientiertes Forschungsmanagement. In Gassmann, O.; von Zedtwitz, M. (Eds.): Internationales Innovationsmanagement: München. 127-142.

Hagström, P.; Hedlund, G. (1994): The Dynamic Firm: A Three-Dimensional Model of Internal Structure. The Prince Bertil Symposium.

Håkanson, L. (1981): Organization and Evolution of Foreign R&D in Swedish Multinationals. Geografiska Annaler. 1(63 B): 47-56.

Håkanson, L.; Zander, U. (1988): International Management of R&D: The Swedish Experience. R&D Management, 18(3): 217-226.

Håkanson, L. (1990): International Decentralization of R&D - the Organizational Challenges. In Bartlett, C. A.; Doz, Y.; Hedlund, G. (Eds.): Managing the Global Firm: London, New York. 256-278.

Håkanson, L. (1992): Locational Determinants of Foreign R&D in Swedish Multinationals. In Granstrand, O.; Håkanson, L.; Sjölander (Eds.): Technology Management and International Business: Internationalization of R&D and Technology: Chichester, New York, Brisbane: Wiley. 97-115.

Håkanson, L.; Nobel, R. (1993a): Foreign Research and Development in Swedish Multinationals. Research Policy, 22: 373-396.

Håkanson, L.; Nobel, R. (1993b): Determinants of Foreign R&D in Swedish Multinationals. Research Policy, 22: 397-411.

Håkansson, H.; Laage-Hellman, J. (1984): Developing a Network R&D Strategy. Journal of Product Innovation Management, 4: 224-237.

Hambrick, D. C. (1982): Environmental scanning and organizational strategy. Strategic Management Journal, 3: 159-173.

Hamel, G. (1991): Competition for competence and inter-partner learning within international strategic alliances. Strategic Management Journal, 12: 83-104.

Handy, C. (1992): Managing the Dream: The Learning Organization. London.

Hansen, M. T.; Nohria, N. (2004): How to build collaborative advantage. MIT Sloan Management Review, Fall 2004: 22-30.

Hanson, W. T.; Van Rumker, R. (1971): Multinational R&D in Practice - Two Case Studies. Research Management, Jan: 47-54.

Haour, G. (1992): Stretching the knowledge base of the enterprise through contract research. R&D Management, 22(2): 177-182.

Harasim, L. M.; Walls, J. (1994): The Global Authoring Network. In Harasim, L.

M. (Ed.): Global Networks: Computer and International Communication: Cambridge (MA), London. 344-355.

Harhoff, D.; Licht, G. (1996): Innovationsaktivitäten kleiner und mittlerer Unternehmen. Ergebnisse des Mannheimer Innovationspanels. Baden-Baden: Schriftenreihe des ZEW.

Harris, P. (1987): The Global Management of R&D Resources. Outlook, 11: 22-30.

Harris, C.; Insinga, R.; Morone, J.; Werle, M. (1996): The Virtual R&D Lab. Research Technology Management, 39: 32-36.

Harryson, S. (1995): Japanese R&D Management: A Holistic Network Approach. University of St. Gallen. St. Gallen.

Harzing, A.-W. (2002): Acquisitions versus Greenfield Investments: International Strategy and Management of Entry Modes. Strategic Management Journal, 23: 211-227.

Hasler, R.; Hess, F. (1996): Management der intellektuellen Ressourcen zur Steigerung der Innovationsfähigkeit. In Gassmann, O.; von Zedtwitz, M. (Eds.): Internationales Innovationsmanagement: München. 157-174.

Hedlund, G. (1986): The Hypermodern MNC - a Heterarchy? Human Resource Management, 25: 9-25.

Hedlund, G.; Rolander, D. (1990): Action in Heterarchies - New Approaches to Managing the MNC. In Bartlett, C. A.; Doz, Y.; Hedlund, G. (Eds.): Managing the Global Firm: London, New York. 15-46.

Hedlund, G., Ridderstråle, J. (1993): Toward the N-Form Corporation: Exploitation and Creation in the MNC. Stockholm Scool of Economics Working Paper. RP, 92/15.

Hedlund, G.; Nonaka, I. (1993): Models of Knowledge Management in the West and Japan. In Lorange, P.; Chakravarthy, B.; Roos, J.; Van De Ven, A. (Eds.): Implementing Strategic Processes, Change, Learning & Co-operation: Oxford. 117-144.

Hedlund, G.; Ridderstråle, J. (1994): International Development Projects - Key to Competitiveness, Impossible, or Mismanaged? International Organizational Studies Conference. Michigan.

Henderson, R. M.; Clark, K. B. (1990): Architectural Innovation: The Rekonfiguration of Existing Product Technologies and the Failure of Established Firms. Administrative Science Quarterly, 35: 9-30.

Herbert, E. (1990): How Japanese Companies Set R&D Directions. Research Technology Management, 33(5): 28-37.

Herzberg, F. (1966): Work and the nature of man. New York.

Hewitt, G. (1980): Research and Development Performed Abroad by U.S. Manufacturing Multinationals. Kyklos, 33(2): 308-327.

Hicks, D.; Ishizuka, T.; Keen, P.; Sweet, S. (1994): Japanese Corporations, Scientific Research and Globalization. Research Policy, 23: 375-384.

Hicks, D. M.; Israd, P. A.; Martin, B. R. (1996): A morphology of Japanese and European corporate research networks. Research Policy, 25: 359-378.

Hipp, C.; Gassmann, O. (1999): Innovation Management and New Forms of Knowledge Creation: The Role of Technical Services as External Sources of

Knowledge. Portland.

Hirano, Y.; Nishigata, C. (1990): Basic Research in Major Companies of Japan. Tokyo: National Institute of Science and Technology Policy (NISTEP).

Hirschey, R. C.; Caves, R. E. (1981): Internationalisation of Research and Development by Multinational Enterprises. Oxford Bulletin of Economics and Statistics, 42(2): 115-130.

Hirshfeld, S.; Schmid, G. (2005): Globalisation of R&D. Technology Review, 184.

Hirst, P.; Thompson, G. (1996): Globalization in Question. Cambridge.

Hofstede, G. (1980): Culture's Consequences: International Differences in Work Related Values. Beverly Hills (CA).

Hofstede, G. (1994): Cultures and Organizations - Intercultural Cooperation and Its Importance for Survival. London.

Hoppe, M. (1993): The Effects of National Culture on the Theory and Practice of Managing R&D Professionals Abroad. R&D Management, 23(4): 313-325.

Howells, J. (1984): The Location of Research and Development: Some Observations and Evidence from Britain. Regional Studies, 18: 13-29.

Howells, J. (1990): The Location and Organisation of Research and Development: New Horizons. Research Policy, 19: 133-146.

Howells, J. (1990): The Internationalization of R&D and the Development of Global Research Networks. Regional Studies, 24(6): 495-512.

Howells, J. (1995): Going Global: the Use of ICT Networks in Research and Development. Research Policy, 24: 169-184.

Huff, T. (2003): The Rise of Early Modern Science: Islam, China, and the West, 2nd ed.: London: Cambridge University Press.

IBM (1993): IBM VSE/Enterprise Systems Architecture. Böblingen.

IDC (2006): Huawei: Vendor Profile IDC #AP204112N. Singapore: IDC.

Ishii, H. (1994): Cross-Cultural Communication and CSCW. In Harasim, L. M. (Ed.): Global Networks: Computer and International Communication: Cambridge (MA), London. 143-151.

Jaikumar, R.; Upton, D. M. (1993): The Coordination of Global Manufacturing. In Bradley, P.; Hausman, J.; Nolan, R. (Eds.): Globalization, Technology, and Competition: Boston (MA).

Jankowski, J. (1998): R&D: Foundation for Innovation. Research Technology Management, 41(2): 14-20.

Jaruzelski, B.; Dehoff, K.; Bordia, R. (2006): Smart Spenders: The Global Innovation 1000. Booz Allen Hamilton's Annual Study. 2006.

Jensen, M. C.; Meckling, W. H. (1996): Specific and General Knowledge, and Organizational Structure. In Myers, P. S. (Ed.): Knowledge Management and Organizational Design: Newton. 17-38.

Johannessen, J. A.; Olsen, B.; Olaisen, J. (1999): Aspects of Innovation THeory Based on Knowledge Management. International Journal of Innovation Management, 19. 121-139.

Johnson-Lenz, P.; Johnson-Lenz, T. (1982): Groupware: The Process and Impacts of Design Choices. In Kerr, E. B.; Hiltz, S. R. (Eds.): Computer-Mediated Communication Systems: Status and Evaluation: New York.

Jolly, V. K. (1997): Commercializing New Technologies. Cambridge.

Jones, G. K.; Davis, H. J. (2000): National Culture and Innovation: Implications for Locating Global R&D Operations. Management International Review, 40(1): 11-39.

Juran, J. M. (1988): Juran on Managing for Quality. Boston.

Kanter, R. M. (1988): When a Thousand Flowers Bloom: Structural, Collective, and Social Conditions for Innovation in Organizations. Research in Organizational Behavior, 10.

Katzenbach, J. R.; Smith, D. K. (1993): The Wisdom of Teams. Boston.

Katzenstein, G.; Mckern, B. (1995): Managing International Research and Development Networks. Working Paper. Pittsburgh: Carnegie Bosch Institute, International Executive Forum.

Kealey, T. (1996): The Economic Laws of Scientific Research. New York.

Kedia, B. L.; Keller, R. T.; Julian, S. D. (1992): Dimensions of National Culture and the Productivity of R&D Units. Journal of High Technology Management Research, 3(1): 1-18.

Keller, W. (1997): Are International R&D Spillovers Trade-Related? Analyzing Spillovers Among Randomly Matched Trade Partners. NBER.

Kenney, M.; Florida, R. (1994): The Organization and Geography of Japanese R&D: Results from a Survey of Japanese Electronics and Biotechnology Firms. Research Policy, 23:305-323.

Khurana, A.; Rosenthal, S. R. (1997): Integrating the Fuzzy Front End of New Product Development. Sloan Management Review (Winter): 103-120.

Kim, L. K. (1997): Imitation to Innovation: The Dynamics of Korea's Technological Learning. Cambridge: Harvard Business School Press.

Kimura, T.; Tezuka, M. (1993): Managing R&D at Nippon Steel. Research Technology Management, 36(2): 21-25.

Kimura, T.; Schulz, M. (2004): Industry in Japan. Structural Change, Productivity, and Chances for Growth. The Japanese Economy, 32(1): 5-44.

Kloth, B. (1996): Technologietransfer im Rahmen schweizerisch-chinesischer Joint Ventures. University of St. Gallen. St. Gallen.

Kluge, J.; Stein, W.; Licht, T.; Kloss, M. (2003): Wissen entscheidet. Wie erfolgreiche Unternehmen ihr Know-how managen - eine internationale Studie von McKinsey, Frankfurt/Wien. Redline Wirtschaft Ueberreuter.

Kodama, F. (1986): Japanese Innovation in Mechatronics Technology. Science and Public Policy, 13(1): 44-51.

Kodama, F. (1992a): Japanese Innovations in Mechatronics Technology. Science and Technology Policy, 17 (Sonderheft): 94-101.

Kodama, F. (1992b): Technology Fusion and the New R&D. Harvard Business Review, 4: 70-78.

Kodama, F. (1995): Emerging Patterns of Innovation: Sources of Japan's Technological Edge. Boston (MA).

Kogut, B.; Zander, U. (1992): Knowledge of the firm, combinative capabilities, and the replication of technology. Organization Science, 3(3): 383-397.

Kogut, B.; Zander, U. (1993): Knowledge of the Firm and the Evolutionary Theory of the Multinational Corporation. Journal of International Business Studies, 24(4): 625-645.

Kogut, B.; Zander, U. (1996): What firms do? Coordination, identity, and learning. Organization Science, 7(5): 502-518.

König, R.; Zoche, P. (1991): Möglichkeiten und Grenzen von 'Cooperative Work'. Neue Perspektiven gruppenorientierter Büroarbeit. In Encarnação, J. (Ed.): Telekommunikation und multimediale Anwendungen der Informatik. Proceedings der GI-Jahrestagung, Oct 14-18: Berlin, Heidelberg. 293-302.

Krogh, L. (1994): Managing R&D Globally: People and Financial Considerations. Research Technology Management, 37(4): 25-28.

Krubasik, E. G., Schrader, J. (1990): Globale Forschungs- und Entwicklungsaktivitäten. In Welge, M. K. (Ed.): Globales Management: Stuttgart. 17-27.

Krugman, P. K.; Obstfeld, M. (1994): International Economics (3rd Edition ed.). New York.

Kuemmerle, W. (1996): Home Base and Foreign Direct Investment in Research and Development. Boston: Harvard University.

Kuemmerle, W. (1997a): Building Effective R&D Capabilities Abroad. Harvard Business Review (March-April): 61-70.

Kuemmerle, W. (1997b): Optimal Scale for Research and Development in Foreign Environments - an Investigation into Size and Performance of R&D Laboratories Abroad. Research Policy, 27: 111-126.

Kuemmerle, W. (1998): Strategic Interaction, Knowledge Sourcing and Knowledge Creation in Foreign Environments - An Analysis of Foreign Direct Investment in R&D by Multinational Companies. Working Paper: HBS.

Kuemmerle, W. (1999): Foreign direct investment in industrial research in the pharmaceutical and electronics industries-results from a survey of multinational firms. Research Policy, 28(2-3): 179-194.

Kusonoki, K.; Nonaka, I.; Nagata, A. (1998): Organizational Capabilities in Product Development of Japanese Firms: A Conceptual Framework and Empirical Findings. Organization Science, 9(6): 699-718.

Kutschker, M. (1989): Akquisition, internationale. In Macharzina, K.; Welge, M. K. (Eds.): Handwörterbuch: Export und internationale Unternehmung, Vol. Col. 2-22. Feb 22.

Kutschker, M. (1995): Re-engineering of Business Processes in Mutlinational Corporations. Working Paper: GSIA Carnegie Bosch Institute.

Kuwahara, Y.; Takeda, Y. (1988): Some experiences with HIVIPS. IEEE/EM Annual Conference: 210-212.

Kuwahara, Y. (1989): Extracting maximum benefits from an international R&D partnership - a case study of a Japanese industrial laboratory. ICEM-2: 278-283.

Kuwahara, Y.; Okada, O.; Horikoshi, H. (1989): Planning Research and Development at Hitachi. Long Range Planning, 22(3): 54-63.

Kuwahara, Y. (1992): Proposing new concepts for global R&D management: NISTEP Third International Conference on Science and Technology Policy Research, Vol. March. 359-365.

Kuwahara, Y. (1994): Creating new concepts and new technologies through global research collaboration. Lecture note for University of Tokyo: Dept. of General

Systems Studies.

Kuwahara, Y. (1995): Generating advanced research concepts. Paper presented at the Gerneral Meeting. Prague.

Kuwahara, Y. (1996): Lecture notes for MBA course of Bristol University.

Kuwahara, Y. (1997): Innovations and Management Practices in Hitachi's European R&D. IFTM-7. Kyoto (Japan).

Lall (1979): The International Allocation of Research Activity by US Multinationals. Oxford Bulletin of Economics and Statistics, 41: 313-331.

Lane, H. W.; Distefano, J. J. (1992): International Management Behaviour: From Policy to Practice (2nd ed.). Boston.

Lasserre, P.; Schütte, H. (1995): Strategies for Asia Pacific. London.

Lautz, A. (1995): Videoconferencing. University of St. Gallen. St. Gallen.

Leifer, R.; Triscari, T. (1987): Research versus Development: Differences and Similarities. IEEE Transactions on Engineering Management, EM-34(2): 71-78.

Leonard-Barton, D. (1995): Wellsprings of Knowledge - Building and Sustaining the Sources of Innovation. Boston, MA.

Lerner, J. (2004): The new financial thing: the sources of innovation before and after state street. NBER.

Les Bas, C.; Sierra, C. (2001): Location versus home country advantages in R&D activites: some further results on multinationals' locational strategies. Research Policy, 31: 589-609.

Les Entretiens De La Technologie (1995): Proceeding of Conference (4th ed.): Association des Centraliens.

Li, H.; Atuahene-Gima, K. (2001): Product Innovation Strategy and the Performance of New Technology Ventures in China. Academy of Management Journal, 44(6): 1123-1134.

Li, J.; Zhong, J. (2003): Explaining the growth of international R&D alliances in China, Managerial and Decision Economics, 24. 2-3: 101-115.

Lichtenthaler, E. (2004): Technology intelligence processes in leading European and North American multinationals. R&D Management, 34(2): 121-135.

Lichtenthaler, E.; Savioz, P.; Birkenmeier, B.; Brodbeck, H. (2004): Organisation of the early phases of the radical innovation process. international Journal of Technology Intelligence and Planning, 1(1): 100-114.

Liebeskind, J. P.; Oliver, A. L.; Zucker, L.; Brewer, M. (1996): Social Networks, Learning, and Flexibility Sourcing Scientific Knowledge in New Biotechnology Firms. Organization Science, 7(4): 428-443.

Liu, X.; White, S. (2001): Comparing innovation systems: a framework and application to China's transitional context. Research Policy, 30: 1091-1114.

Lucas, H. C.; Baroudi, J. (1994): The Role of Information Technology in Organizational Design. Journal of Management Information Systems, 10(4): 9-23.

Lullies, V.; Bolinger, H.; Weltz, F. (1993): Wissenslogistik: Über den betrieblichen Umgang mit Wissen bei Entwicklungsvorhaben. Frankfurt, New York.

Lynn, L. H.; Piehler, H. R.; Kieler, M. (1993): Engineering Careers, Job Rotation, and Gatekeepers in Japan and the United States. Journal of Engineering and Technology Management, 10(1): 53-72.

Lynn, L. (1994): Japan's systems on innovation. International Business and International Relations, 6: 161-187.

Maddisson, A. (2001): The World Economy: A Millennial Perspective. OECD.

Maister, D. H. (1993): Managing the professional service firm. New York: Simon & Schuster.

Malecki, E. J. (1980): Corporate Organization of R and D and the Location of Technological Activities. Regional Studies, 14: 219-234.

Malnight, T. W. (1995): Globalization of an Ethnocentric Firm: An Evolutionary Perspective. Strategic Management Journal, 16: 119-141.

Manheim, M. (1994): Integrating Global Organizations through Task/Team Support Systems. In Harasim, L. M. (Ed.): Global Networks: Computer and International Communication: Cambridge (MA), London. 121-141.

Mansfield, E., Teece, D., Romeo, A. (1979): Overseas Research and Development by U.S. Based Firms. Economica, 46: 187-196.

Mansfield, E. (1984): R&D and innovation: some epirical findings. Chicago: University of Chicago Press.

March, J. G.; Olsen, J. P. (1976): Ambiguity and Choice in Organizations. Bergen.

Marquardt, G.; Herstatt, C.; Dombach, G. (1996): Gestaltung internationaler Innovationsprozesse auf der Basis von Kernkompetenzen. In Gassmann, O.; von Zedtwitz, M. (Eds.): Internationales Innovationsmanagement: München. 175-186.

Martin, X.; Salomon, R. (2003): Knowledge transfer capacity and its implications for the theory of the multination corporation. Journal of International Business Studies, 34: 356-373.

Matson, E.; Patiath, P.; Shavers, T. (2003): Stimulating knowledge sharing: Strenghening your organization's internal knowledge market. Organizational Dynamics, 32(3): 275-285.

Matsuo, H. (2000): Liability of foreignness and the uses of expartriates in Japanese multinational corporations in the United States. Sociological Inquiry 70. 1: 88-106.

McGrath, M. E.; Anthony, M. T.; Shapiro, A. R. (1992): Product Development: Success through Product and Cycle-time Excellence. Boston, London.

McGrath, M. E. (1995): Product Strategy for High-Technology Companies. How to Achieve Growth, Competitive Advantage, and Increased Profits. New York.

Mckern, B. (1994): International Network Corporations in a Global Economy. Working Paper.: GSIA Carnegie Bosch Institute.

Medcof, J. W. (1997): A taxonomy of internationally dispersed technology units and its application to management issues. R&D Management, 27(4): 301-318.

Meyer-Krahmer, F.; Reger, G. (1998): European Technology Policy and Internationalization: An Analysis behind the Background of the Innovation Strategies of Multinational Enterprises. DRUID Summer Conference. Bornholm.

Miller, R. (1994): Global R&D networks and large-scale innovations: The case of the automobile industry. Research Policy, 23: 27-46.

Moenaert, R. K.; Souder, W. E.; De Meyer, A.; Deschoolmeester, D. (1994): R&D-Marketing Integration Mechanisms, Communication Flows, and Innovation Success. Journal of Product Innovation Management, 11: 31-45.

Moore, W. L. (1982): Concept Testing. Journal of Business Research, 10: 279-294.

Moore, J. F. (1994): The Death of Competition: Leadership & Strategy in the Age of Business Ecosystems. New York: HarperCollins.

Morris, C. R.; Ferguson, C. H. (1993): How Architecture Wins. Harvard Business Review (March-April): 86-95.

Moss, R. (1997): Electronic Product Design. In Kimber, R. J.; Grenier, R. W.; Heldt, J. J. (Eds.): Quality Management Handbook, 2nd ed.: New York.

Mowery, D. C. (1992): International Collaborative Ventures and US Firms' Technology Strategies. In Granstrand, O.; Håkanson, L.; Sjölander (Eds.): Technology Management and International Business: Internationalization of R&D and Technology: Chichester, New York, Brisbane. 209-231.

Müller, L. (2004): Kooperationen für Innovationen. Erfolgsfaktoren in der Setup-Phase unter besonderer Berücksichtigung von Intellectual Property. St. Gallen: Institut für Technologiemanagement (ITEM), Universität St. Gallen.

Myers, M.; Smith, K. (1999): Xerox: The Global Market and Technology Innovator. In Boutellier, R.; Gassmann, O.; von Zedtwitz, M. (Eds.): Managing Global Innovation: Berlin, New York, Tokyo: Springer. 299-315.

Naisbitt, J. (1996): Megatrends Asia. New York.

Narula, R.; Zanefi, A. (2005): Globalization of innovation. The role of multinational enterprises. In Fagerberg, J.; Mowery, D.; Nelson, R. (Eds.): The Oxford Handbook of Innovation, Vol. 12: Oxford University Press.

Narula, R.; Criscuolo, P. (2006): Using multi-hub structures for international R&D: Organizational inertia and the challenges of implementation. Management International Review, 46, in press.

National Bureau of Statistics of China (2006): China Monthly Statistics. China Statistics Press. Beijing.

National Science Board (1996): Science & Engineering Indicators 1996. Washington D.C.: U.S. Government Printing Office.

National Science Foundation (various years): R&D in Industry: Washington: www.nsf.gov. 90-313.

National Summit on Competitiveness (2005): Statement of the National Summit on Competitiveness. Investing in U.S. Innovation. Washington, D.C.

Nefiodow, L. A. (1990): Der fünfte Kondratieff. Frankfurt.

Nelson, R.; Winter, S. (1982): An Evolutionary Theory of Economic Change. Cambridge.

Nikias, C. (1998): Integrated Media Systems: Towards Cooperative Immersipresence. Presentation. IAMOT 1998. Orlando, Florida.

Niosi, J. (1997): The Globalization of Canadian R&D. Management International Review, 37(4): 387-404.

Niosi, J. (1999): The Internationalization of Industrial R&D - From technology transfer to the learning organization. Research Policy, 28(2-3): 107-117.

Niosi, J.; Godin, B. (1999): Canadian R&D abroad management practices. Research Policy, 28(2-3): 215-230.

Nippa, M., Reichwald, R. (1990): Theoretische Grundüberlegungen zur Verkürzung der Durchlaufzeit in der industriellen Entwicklung. In Reichwald, R.;

Schmelzer, H. J. (Eds.): Durchlaufzeiten in der Entwicklung: Praxis des industriellen F&E-Managements: München. 65-114.

NIW; DIW; ISI; ZEW (1995): Zur Technologischen Leistungsfähigkeit Deutschlands. Erweiterte Berichterstattung 1995. Endbericht an das Bundesministerium für Bildung, Wissenschaft, Forschung und Technologie (BMBF), Hannover, Berlin.

Nonaka, I. (1988): Creating Organizational Order Out of Chaos: Self-Renewal in Japanese Firms. California Management Review, 30(3): 57-73.

Nonaka, I. (1989): Organizing Innovation as a Knowledge-Creation process: A Suggested Paradigm for Self-Renewing Organizations. Walter. A. Haas School of Business. Vol. Working Paper No. OBIR 41. Berkley: University of California.

Nonaka, I. (1990): Redundant, Overlapping Organization: A Japanese Approach to Managing the Innovation Process. California Management Review, 32(3): 27-38.

Nonaka, I. (1991): The Knowledge-Creating Company. Harvard Business Review, 6: 96-104.

Nonaka, I. (1992): Wie japanische Konzerne Wissen erzeugen. Harvard Manager (2): 95-103.

Nonaka, I. (1994): A Dynamic Theory of Organizational Knowledge Creation. Organization Science, 5(1): 14-37.

Nonaka, I.; Takeuchi, H. (1995): The Knowledge-Creating Company. How Japanese Companies Create the Dynamics of Innovation. New York, Oxford.

Norling, P. (1996): Network or Not Work: Harnessing Technology Networks in DuPont. Research Technology Management, 39(1): 42-48.

Norson (2005): R&D Strom Rising: China's Rush to R&D. Beijing.

Nouvortne, D. (1991): Videokonferenz und Bildübertragung per Standleitung. FAZ, Blick durch die Wirtschaft: 7.

Nystrom, H. E.; Shunk, D. L. (1998): Technology Transfer for Bi-National Economic Development. In Lefebvre, L. A.; Mason, R. M.; Khalil, T. (Eds.): Management of Technology, Sustainable Development and Eco-Efficiency, International Conference on Management of Technology Proceedings: Amsterdam: Elsevier. 861-869.

O'Connor, P. (1994): Implementing a Stage-Gate Process: A Multi-Company Perspective. Journal of Product Innovation Management, 11: 183-200.

Odagiri, H.; Yasuda, H. (1996): The determinants of overseas R&D by Japanese firms: an empirical study at the industry and company levels. Research Policy, 25: 1059-1079.

OECD (1992): Die Messung wissenschaftlicher und technischer Tätigkeiten - Allgemeine Richtlinien für statistische Übersichten in Forschung und experimenteller Entwicklung. Frascati-Handbuch. Bonn.

OECD (1993): Main Science and Technology Indicators 1981-1994. Paris.

OECD (1996): Science, Technology and Industry Outlook 1996. Paris.

OECD (1996): Measuring Globalisation: The Role of Multinationals in OECD Economies. OECD. Paris.

OECD (2003): OECD Science, Technology and Industry Scoreboard 2003.

OECD. Paris.

O'Hara, J. P.; Evans, H. E.; Hayden, T. F. (1993): Developing New Manufacturing Processes: A Case Study and Model. Journal of Engineering and Technology Management, 10(3): 285-306.

O'Hara-Devereaux, M.; Johansen, R. (1994): Globalwork. Bridging Distance, Culture, and Time. San Francisco.

Orr, J. (1990): Sharing Knowledge, Celebrating Identity: War Stories and Community Memory in a Service Culture. In Middleton, D. S.; Edwards, D. (Eds.): Collective Remembering: Memory in Society: Beverly Hills: Sage Publications.

Packard, D. (1995): The HP Way: How Bill Hewlett and I Built Our Company. New York.

Page, A.; Rosenbaum, H. (1987): Redesigning Product Lines with Conjoint Analysis: How Sunbeam Does It. In Tushman, M. L.; Moore, W. L. (Eds.): Readings in the Management of Innovation, 2nd Edition ed.: Cambridge (MA). 379-400.

Papanastassiou, M.; Pearce, R. (1994): The internationalisation of Research and development by Japanese enterprises. R&D Management, 24(2): 155-165.

Papanastassiou, M.; Pearce, R. (1995): Decentralisation of technology and organisational restructuring in the Multinational Enterprise (MNE) group. Discussion Paper: University of Reading.

Papanastassiou, M.; Pearce, R. (1996): Individualism and Interdependence in the Technological Development of MNEs: The Strategic Positioning of R&D Overseas Subsidiaries. Working paper: University of Reading.

Papo, M. (1971): How to Establish and Operate Multinational Labs. Research Management (Jan): 12-19.

Parkes, P. (1997): Marrying R&D to the business. R&D Management Conference. Manchester.

Pascale, R. T. (1990): Managing on the Edge. New York.

Patel, P.; Pavitt, K. (1992): Large Firms in the Production of the World's Technology: an Important Case of Non-Globalisation. In Granstrand, O.; Håkanson, L.; Sjölander (Eds.): Technology Management and International Business: Internationalization of R&D and Technology: Chichester, New York, Brisbane. 53-73.

Patel, P.; Pavitt, K. (1994): Technological Competencies in the World's Largest Firms: Characteristica. Constraints and Scope for Managerial Choice, Working Paper. Stockholm: Prince Bertil Symposium at Stockholm School of Economics.

Patel, P. (1996): Are Large Firms Internationalizing the Generation of Technology? Some New Evidence. IEEE Transactions on Engineering Management, 43(1): 41-47.

Patel, P.; Vega, M. (1999): Patterns of Internationalisation of Corporate Technology: Location vs. Home Country Advantages. Research Policy, 28: 145-155.

Patterson, M. L. (1993): Accelerating Innovation: Van Nostrand.

Pausenberger, E.; Volkmann, B. (1981): Forschung und Entwicklung in internationalen Unternehmungen. In Moll, H. H.; Warnecke, H. J. (Eds.): RKW-

Handbuch Forschung, Entwicklung, Konstruktion (F&E), Stand: Okt. 1990 ed., Vol. 3: Berlin: Kennzahl 8400.

Pavitt, K. (1985): Technology Transfer among the Industrially Advanced Countries: An Overview. In Rosenberg, N.; Frischtak, C. (Eds.): International technology transfer: New York.

Pavitt, K. (1991): The Internationalisation of Technological Innovation. Conference on Technological Innovation and Society, Vol. 1-7. London.

Pavitt, K.; Patel, P. (1991): Technological strategies of the world's largest companies. Science and Public Policy, 18(6): 363-368.

Pavitt, K. (1998): Technologies, Products & Organisation in the Innovating Firm: What Adam Smith Tells Us and Joseph Schumpeter Doesn't. DRUID Summer Conference. Bornholm.

Pearce, R. D. (1989): The Internationalisation of Research and Development by Multinational Enterprises: Basingstroke.

Pearce, R. D.; Singh, S. (1992): Internationalisation of Research and Development Among the World's Leading Enterprises: Survey Analysis of Organisation and Motivation. In Granstrand, O.; Håkanson, L.; Sjölander (Eds.): Technology Management and International Business: Internationalization of R&D and Technology: Chichester, New York, Brisbane. 137-162.

Pearce, R. D.; Singh, S. (1992a): Globalizing Research and Development. St. Martin's Press. New York.

Pearce, R. D.; Singh, S. (1992b): The Internationalisation of Research and Development by Multinational Enterprises: A firm-level Analysis of Determinants. GB-Whiteknights.

Pearce, R.; Papanastassiou, M. (1995): R&D networks and innovation: decentralised product development in multinational enterprises: University of Reading Discussion Paper B.

Pearce, R.; Papanastassiou, M. (1996): Overseas R&D and the Strategic Evolution of MNEs: Evidence from Laboratories in the UK.: University of Reading Working Paper Series B.

Pearce, R.; Poni, G. S. (1996): The Globalisation of R&D in Pharmaceuticals, Chemicals and Biotechnology: Some New Evidence: University of Reading. Discussion Paper B.

Pearce, R. D. (1999): Decentralised R&D and strategic competitiviness: globalised approaches to generation and use of technology in multinational enterprises (MNEs). Research Policy, 28(2-3): 157-178.

Pearson, A.; Brockhoff, K.; Von Boehmer, A. (1993): Decision Parameters in Global R&D Management. R&D Management, 23(3): 249-262.

Pearson, A. W. (1993): Management Development For Scientists And Engineers. Research Technology Management, 36(1): 45-48.

Penner-Hahn, J.; Shaver, J. M. (2005): Does international research and development increase patent output? An analysis of Japanese pharmaceutical firms. Strategic Management Journal, 26: 121-140.

People's Daily (2003): Transnationals Locate More R&D Centers in China. People's Daily.

Perks, H.; Jeffery, R. (2006): Global network configuration for innovation: a study of international fiber innovation. R&D Management, 36(1): 67-83.

Perlmutter, H. V. (1969): The Tortuous Evolution of the Multinational Corporation. Columbia Journal of World Business, 4: 3-18.

Perrino, A. C.; Tipping, J. W. (1989): Global Management of technology. Research Technology Management, 32(3): 12-19.

Perrino, A. C.; Tipping, J. W. (1991): Global Management of Technology: A Study of 16 Multinationals in the USA, Europe and Japan. Technology Analysis and Strategic Management, 3(1): 87-98.

Persaud, A. (2005): Enhancing synergistic innovative capability in multinational corporations: an empirical investigation. Journal of Product Innovation Management, 22: 412-429.

Petrovic, O. (1992): Groupware - Systemkategorien, Anwendungsbeispiele, Problemfelder und Entwicklungsstand. Information Management, 1: 16-22.

Pfiffner, M.; Stadelmann, P. D. (1995): Arbeit und Management in der Wissensgesellschaft. University of St. Gallen. St. Gallen.

Picot, A.; Reichwald, R.; Nippa, M. (1988): Zur Bedeutung der Entwicklungsaufgabe für die Entwicklungszeit - Ansätze für die Entwicklungszeitgestaltung. In Brockhoff, K.; Picot, A.; Urban, C. (Eds.): Zeitmanagement in Forschung und Entwicklung, Sonderheft der Zeitschrift für betriebswirtschaftliche Forschung, Vol. 23. 112-137.

Pitt, M.; Clarke, K. (1999): Competing on Competence: A Knowledge Perspective on the Management of Strategic Innovation. Technology Analysis & Strategic Management, 11(3): 301-313.

Plafker, T. (1997): "Western Companies Go Slow on China R&D Operations; Quality, Intellectual Property Are Concerns". Research Technology Management, 40(3): 2-3.

Polanyi, M. (1962): Personal Knowledge: Toward a Post Critical Philosophy. New York.

Polanyi, M. (1966): The Tacit Dimension. London.

Porter, M. E. (1985): Competitive Advantage: Creating and Sustaining Superior Performance. New York.

Porter, M. E. (1986): Competition in Global Industries: A Conceptual Framework. In Porter, M. E. (Ed.): Competition in Global Industries: Boston (MA). 15-60.

Porter, M. E. (1990): The Competitive Advantage of Nations. The Free Press. New York.

Porter, M. E. (2001): Innovation: Location Matters. Sloan Management Review, 42(4): 28-36.

Prahalad, C. K.; Hamel, G. (1990): The Core Competence of the Corporation. Harvard Business Review, 3: 79-91.

Quinn, J. B. (1985): Managing Innovation: Controlled Chaos. Harvard Business Review, 3: 73-84.

Raymond, S. U. (1997): Global Cooperation in Science, Engineering, and Medicine: An Overview of the Issues. Technology in Society, 19(1): 7-16.

Reger, G.; Kuhlmann (1994): European Technology Policy in Germany, FhG-ISI-Report. Karlsruhe.

Reger, G. (1996): Mechanismen zur Koordination von Forschung und Innovation im internationalen Unternehmen. In Gerybadze, A.; Meyer-Krahmer, F.; Reger, G. (Eds.): Globales Management von Forschung und Innovation, Bericht für das Bundesministerium für Bildung, Wissenschaft, Forschung und Technologie: Bonn: BMBF. 75-126.

Reger, G. (2004): Coordinating globally dispersed research centers of excellence - the case of Phillips Electronics. Journal of International Management, 10: 51-76.

Ridderstråle, J. (1992): Developing Product Development: Holographic Design for Successful Creation in the MNC. EIBA Annual Meeting. Reading.

Roberts, E. B.; Malone, D. E. (1996): Policies and structures for spinning off new companies from research and development organizations. Research Policy, 26(1): 17-48.

Roberts, E. B. (2001): Benchmarking Global Strategic Management of Technology. Research-Technology Management, 44: 25-36.

Robinson, R. D. (1988): The International Transfer of Technology - Theory, Issues, and Practice. Cambridge (MA).

Robock, S.; Simmonds, K. (1989): International Business and Multinational Enterprises. Irwin, Boston.

Ronstadt, R. C. (1977): Research and Development Abroad by U.S. Multinationals. New York: Praeger.

Ronstadt, R. C. (1978): International R&D: The Establishment and Evolution of Research and Development Abroad by Seven U.S. Multinationals. Journal of International Business Studies, 9: 7-24.

Ronstadt, R.; Kramer, R. J. (1983): Internationalizing Industrial Innovation. Journal of Business Strategy, 3(3): 3-15.

Ronstadt, R. C. (1984): R&D Abroad by US Multinationals. Boston: Harvard Business School.

Rose, K.; Sauernheimer, K. (1992): Theorie der Außenwirtschaft (11th ed.). München.

Rosenbloom, R.; Cusumano, M. (1987): Technological Pioneering and Competitive Advantage: The Birth of the VCR Industry. California Management Review, 29(4): 51-76.

Ross, S. A. (1973): The economic theory of agency: The principal's problem. American Economic Review, 63: 134-139.

Roussel, P. A.; Saad, K. N.; Erickson, T. J. (1991): Third Generation R&D: Managing the Link to Corporate Strategy. Boston (MA).

Rubenstein, A. H. (1989): Managing Technology in the Decentralized Firm. New York, Toronto, Singapore: Wiley.

Rugman, A. M.; Verbeke, A. (2003): Extending the theory of the multinational enterprise: internalization and strategic management perspectives. Journal of International Business Studies, 34: 125-137.

Sakakibara, K.; Kosaka, M. (1991): "International Product Development of Japanese Firms; Product Coherence and Internal Isomorphism Matrix". Conference on Competitive Product Development. Fontainebleau: INSEAD Euro-Asia Center.

Sartain, J. R.; Dean, B. V. (1998): International Technology Transfer Sucess Factors in Hewlett-Packard. In Lefebvre, L. A.; Mason, R. M.; Khalil, T. (Eds.): Management of Technology, Sustainable Development and Eco-Efficiency: Amsterdam: Elsevier. 309-318.

Saynisch, M. (1979): Grundlagen des phasenweisen Projektablaufs. In M., S.; Schelle, H.; Schub, A. (Eds.): Projektmanagement: Konzepte, Verfahren, Anwendungen: München, Wien. 33-58.

Saynisch, M. (1989a): Anwendungsbeispiele des phasenweisen Projektablaufs in der Praxis. In Reschke, H.; Schelle, H.; Schnopp, R. (Eds.): Handbuch Projektmanagement, Vol. Bd. 1, 2: Köln. 745-763.

Saynisch, M. (1989b): Phasenmodelle und Ablaufstrategien in der industriellen F&E. In Schelle, H. (Ed.): Symposium phasenorientiertes Projektmanagement: Köln: GPM.

Schlobach, T. (1989): Die wirtschaftliche Bedeutung von Videokonferenzen im Informations- und Kommunikationsprozeß des Industriebetriebs: Stand und Perspektiven. Thun, Frankfurt.

Schoonhoven, C. B.; Jelinek, M. (1990): Dynamic Tension in Innovative, High Technology Firms: Managing Rapid Technological Change Through Organizational Structure. In Von Glinow, M.; Mohram (Eds.): Managing Complexity in High Technology Organizations: Oxford. 90-118.

Schwarz, B. (1994): Prozeßorientiertes Informationsmanagement in multinationalen Unternehmen: Eine empirische Untersuchung in der Pharmaindustrie. Wiesbaden.

Securities Data Company (1998): Worldwide Mergers & Acquisitions - Ein steiniger Weg für junge Biotech-Firmen. Neue Zürcher Zeitung. 9(286): 24.

Senge, P. (1990): The fifth discipline. Doubleday.

Serapio, M. G.; Dalton, D. H. (1997): Foreign-owned Companies Continue to Increase Their Spending on R&D in the United States. Research Technology Management, 40(5): 2-3.

Serapio, M. G.; Dalton, D. H. (1999): Globalization of industrial R&D: an examination of foreign direct investments in R&D in the United States. Research Policy, 28(2-3): 303-316.

Servatius, H.-G. (1987): Internationales Technologie-Management zur Koordination von strategischen Allianzen und F&E-Netzwerken. Strategische Planung, 3: 217-243.

Shane, S. (1993): Cultural Influences on National Rates of Innovation. Journal of Business Venturing, 8: 59-73.

Shapard, J. (1994): Islands in the (Data) Stream: Language, Character Codes, and Electronic Isolation in Japan. In Harasim, L. M. (Ed.): Global Networks: Computer and International Communication: Cambridge (MA), London. 255-270.

Sheen, M. R. (1992): Barriers to scientific and technical knowledge acquisition in industrial R&D. R&D Management, 22(2): 135-145.

Sherman, S.; Tymon (1994): The Unfulfilled Promise of an Envisioned Jewel: An Attempt to Transfer Technology out of the Splintering Soviet Union. Technology Transfer(Fall).

Sihn, W.; Klink, J. (1998): The Added Value Network: Innovative Power and

Productivity through Network Cooperation. In Lefebvre, L. A.; Mason, R. M.; Khalil, T. (Eds.): Management of Technology, Sustainable Development and Eco-Efficiency, International Conference on Management of Technology Proceedings: Amsterdam: Elsevier. 734-743.

Simon, H. A. (1997): Administrative Behaviour, New York.

Sofka, W. (2005): Global Idea Sourcing, at Home. An empirical investigation into the mechanisms behind the usage of foreign business sources for innvovation. Proceedings of the R&D Management Conference 2005. Pisa.

Souder, W.; Nashar, A.; Padmanabhan, V. (1990): A Guide to the Best Technology-Transfer Practices. Technology Transfer(Winter-Spring).

Stahl, M. (2002): New Business Development in der Automobilindustrie. University of St. Gallen. St. Gallen.

State Council of China (2006): National Guideline on Medium - and Long-term Program for Science and Technology Development: Beijing: People's Publishing House. 2006-2020.

Stevens, G.; Burley, J. (1997): 3,000 Raw Ideas = 1 Commercial Success! Research Technology Management, 40(3): 16-27.

Steyaert, C.; Bouwen, R. (1996): Telling Stories of Entrepreneurship. RENT X, Research in Entrepreneurship and Small Businesses. Brussels.

Steyaert, C. (1997): A Qualitative Methodology for Process Studies of Entrepreneurship: Creating Local Knowledge Through Stories. International Studies of Management and Organization, 27(3): 13-33.

Stopford, J. M. (1994): The Impact of the Global Political Economy on Corporate Straegy. Working Paper: GSIA Carnegie Bosch Institute.

STS: R&D in China; http://www.sts.org.cn/REPORT_3/documents/2003/0301.htm.

Subramaniam, M.; Venkatraman, N. (2001): Determinants of Transnational New Product Development Capability: Testing the Influence of Transferring and Deploying Tacit Overseas Knowledge. Strategic Management Journal, 22: 359-378.

Sundbo, J. (2001): The Strategic Management of Innovation: A Sociological and Economic Theory. Cheltenham, U.K.

Sutter, R. (2003): Intellectual Property Management in Cooperative Innovation Processes. Institute of Technology Management (ITEM), University of St. Gallen.

Swiss Re (2004a): Intellectual Property Report 2003. In Bischof, D.; Cuypers, F. (Eds.): Swiss Reinsurance Company: Zürich.

Swiss Re (2004b): Geschäftsbericht 2003. Jahresbericht. Swiss Reinsurance Company. Zürich.

Takeda, Y.; Kuwahara, Y. (1992): R&D Synergy for Innovation. The Journal of Japanese Society for Science Policy and Research Management. 7(2): 129-146.

Takeuchi, H.; Nonaka, I. (1986): Das neue Produktentwicklungsspiel. Harvard Business Manager, 3: 40-47.

Taylor, S.; Napier, N. (1996): Working in Japan: Lessons from Women Expatriates. Sloan Management Review(Spring): 76-84.

Teece, D. (1986): Profiting from technological innovation: Implications for integration, collaborations, licensing, and public policy. Research Policy, 15: 285-305.

Teece, D. J.; Pisano, G.; Shuen, A. (1990): Firm Capabilities, Resources and the Concept of Strategy, Consortium on Competitiveness and Cooperation. Working Paper. Berkley: University of California, Center for Research in Management.

Teece, D. J.; Pisano, G.; Shuen, A. (1997): Dynamic capabilities and strategic management. Strategic Management Journal, 18(7): 509-533.

Terpstra, V. (1977): International Product Policy: The Role of Foreign R&D. Columbia Journal of World Business, 4: 24-32.

The Nation (2007): Huawei plans R&D center in Thailand.

The Register (2003): Cisco halts Huawei piracy suit. The Register.

Thompson, J. D. (1967): Organizations in Action. New York, London, Sidney.

Thurow, L. (1996): The future of capitalism, London.

Torii, H. (1997): The R&D Policy of Japanese Companies. Bi-monthly review of the Swiss-Japanese Chamber (Mrz 97): 66-67.

Trevino, L.; Lengel, R.; Draft, R. (1987): Media Symbolism, Media Richness and Media Choice in Organisations. Communication Research, 14: 553-575.

Tushman, M. L. (1979): Work characteristics and subunit communication structure: A contingency analysis. Administrative Science Quarterly, 24: 82-98.

Tushman, M. L.; Anderson, P. (1986): Technological Discontinuities and Organizational Enviroments. Administrative Science Quarterly, 31: 439-465.

Tushman, M. L.; Rosenkopf, L. (1992): Organizational Determinants of Technological Change: Toward a Sociology of Technological Evolution. In Burgelman, R. A. E. A. (Ed.): Strategic Management of Technology and Innovation, 2nd Edition ed.: Chicago, Boston. 186-207.

UNCTAD (various years): World Investment Report. Geneva: United Nations.

US Department of Commerce (1997): International science and technology: Emerging Trends in Government Policies and Expenditures. Washington, D.C.: U.S. Department of Commerce.

Utterback, J. M. (1994): Mastering the Dynamics of Innovation. How Companies Can Seize Opportunities in the Face of Technological Change. Boston.

Van De Ven, A.; Angle, H.; Poole, M. (1989): Research on the Management of Innovation: The Minnesota Studies. New York.

Varma, R. (1995): Restructuring Corporate R&D: From an Autonomous to a Linkage Model. Technology Analysis and Strategic Management, 7(2): 231-247.

Vincenti, W. G. (1990): What Engineers Know and How They Know It - Analytical Studies from Aeronautical History, Baltimore, London.

Voelker, R.; Stead, R. (1999): New Technologies and International Location Choice for Research and Development Units: Evidence from Europ. Technology Analysis & Strategic Management, 11(2): 199-209.

Völker, R. (1996): F&E-Standortwahl von multinationalen Unternehmen. Die Unternehmung, 1: 51-67.

von Boehmer, A. (1991): Global R&D Activities of US Multinational Corporations: Some Empirical Results. In Kocaoglu, D. F.; Niwa, K. (Eds.): Technology Management, Proceedings of Portland International Conference on Management of Engineering and Technology, Oct 27-31: Portland. 135-140.

von Boehmer, A.; Brockhoff, K.; Pearson, A. W. (1992): The Management of International Research and Development. In Buckley, P. J.; Brooke, M. Z. (Eds.): International Business Studies: Oxford. 495-509.

von Boehmer, A. (1994): Internationalisierung industrieller Forschung und Entwicklung. Wiesbaden.

von Boehmer, A. (1994): Information Systems for Global Technology Management. In Deans, P. C.; Karwan, K. R. (Eds.): Global Information Systems and Technology: Focus on the Organization and Its Functional Areas: Harrisburg, London. 345-360.

von Boehmer, A. (1995): Internationalisierung industrieller Forschung und Entwicklung. Typen, Bestimmungsgründe und Erfolgsbeurteilung. DUV. Wiesbaden.

von Hippel, E. (1986): Lead Users: A Source of a Novel Product Concepts. Management Science, 32(7): 791-805.

von Hippel, E. (1988): The Sources of Innovation. New York, Oxfod.

von Krog, G.; Ichijo, K.; Nonaka, I. (2000): Enabling Knowledge Creation: How to Unlock the Mystery of Tacit Knowledge and Release the Power of Innovation. Oxford University Press. New York and Oxford.

von Krogh, G.; Roos, J.; Yip, G. (1996): A Note on the Epistemology of Globalizing Firms. In Von Krogh, G.; Roos, J. (Eds.): Managing Knowledge: London.

von Remoortere, F.; Boer, F. (1992): Globalization of Technology - What It Means for American Industry. Research Technology Management, 35(4): 8-9.

von Zedtwitz, M.; Schadt, M.; Brauchli, M. (1996): Überwindung nationaler Grenzen dargestellt am Beispiel der Liquid Crystal Display (LCD)-Technologie. In Gassmann, O.; von Zedtwitz, M. (Eds.): Internationales Innovationsmanagement: München. 143-154.

von Zedtwitz, M. (1999): Managing Interfaces in International R&D. Bamberg: Difo-Druck, University of St. Gallen.

von Zedtwitz, M. (2002): Organizational Learning through Post-Project Reviews in R&D. R&D Management, 32(3): 255-268.

von Zedtwitz, M.; Gassmann, O. (2002): Managing Customer Oriented Research. International Journal of Technology Management, 24(2/3): 165-193.

von Zedtwitz, M.; Gassmann, O. (2002): Market versus Technology Drive in R&D Internationalization: Four different patterns of managing research and development. Research Policy, 31(4): 569-588.

von Zedtwitz, M. (2003): Initial Directors of International R&D Laboratories. R&D Management, 33(4): 377-393.

von Zedtwitz, M. (2004): Managing Foreign R&D Labs in China. R&D Management, 34(4): 439-452.

von Zedtwitz, M.; Gassmann, O.; Boutellier, R. (2004): Organizing global R&D: challenges and dilemmas. Journal of International Management, 10: 21-49.

von Zedtwitz, M.; Moitra, D. (2005): MNC R&D in India: Towards a New Understanding of Gloabl R&D R&D Management Conference. Pisa, Italy.

von Zedtwitz, M. (2006): International R&D strategies in companies from developing countries: the case of China. In Unctad (Ed.): Globalization of R&D and Developing Countries: New York & Geneva: United Nations. 117-140.

von Zedtwitz, M.; Ikeda, T.; Gong, L.; Carpenter, R.; Hämäläinen, S. (2007): Managing Foreign R&D in China. Research Technology Management, 50(3): 19-27.

Vorort (1994): Forschung und Entwicklung in der schweizerischen Privatwirtschaft 1992. Zurich: Schweizerischer Handels- und Industrie-Verein.

Walsh, K. (2003): Foreign High-Tech R&D in China. Washington, DC: The Henry L. Stimson Center.

Wang, C. (2004): The impact of FDI on domestic technology improvement: Annual Report of Science and Technology Development of China 2003 Economic Management Press. Beijiing: 18-31.

Wathne, K.; Roos, J.; Von Krog, G. (1996): Towards a Theory of Knowledge Transfer in a Cooperative Context. In Krogh, G.; Roos, J. (Eds.): Managing Knowledge - Perspectives on cooperation and competition: London: Sage Publications.

Weil, T. (2000): Why and How European Companies Reach Out to Silicon Valley. Institut francais des relations internationales.

Welt (2004): Microsoft kommt in Patentstreit ungeschoren davon. Die Welt: 13.

Wernerfelt, B. (1984): A resource based perspective. Strategic Management Journal, 5(2): 171-180.

Werther, W. B. (1998): Creating Strategic Technology Alliances. In Lefebvre, L. A.; Mason, R. M.; Khalil, T. (Eds.): Management of Technology, Sustainable Development and Eco-Efficiency, International Conference on Management of Technology Proceedings: Amsterdam: Elsevier. 793-804.

Westhead, P. (1997): R&D 'inputs' and 'outputs' of technology-based firms located on and off Science Parks. R&D Management, 27(1): 45-62.

Westney, D. E.; Sakakibara, K. (1985): The Role of Japan-Based R&D in Global Technology Strategy. Technology in Society, 7: 315-330.

Westney, D. E. (1992): Organizational Change and the Internationalization of R&D. In Kochau, T. A.; Useem, M. (Eds.): Transforming Organizations. 245-260.

Westney, D. E. (1993): Cross-Pacific Internationalization of R&D by U.S. and Japanese Firms. R&D Management, 23(2): 171-181.

Weyrich, C. (1995): Corporate Research: Spearheading Inovation. Siemens Review, R&D Special(Fall): 1-3.

Weyrich, C. (1996): Zentrale Forschung und Entwicklung als Speerspitze der internationalen Innovationsaktivitäten bei Siemens. In Gassmann, O.; von Zedtwitz, M. (Eds.): Internationales Innovationsmanagement: München. 119-126.

Wheelwright, S. C.; Clark, K. B. (1992): Revolutionizing Product Development - Quantum Leaps in Speed, Efficiency, and Quality. New York.

Whitley, R.; Bean, A.; Russo, M. (1998): Using the IRI/CIMS R&D Database. Research Technology Management, 41(2): 12-13.

Williams, R.; Bertsch, B. (1998): The development of TQM. In Boutellier, R.; Masing, W. (Eds.): Qualitätsmanagement an der Schwelle zum 21. Jahrhundert: München.

Williamson, O. E. (1987): Transaction cost economics: The comparative contracting perspective. Journal of Economic Behaviour and Organization, 8: 617-625.

Wilms, W. W.; Zell, D. M. (1994): Reinventing Organizational Culture Across International Boundaries, GSIA Carnegie Bosch Institute Working Paper.

Wilson, J. Q. (1966): Innovations in Organizations: Notes Toward a Theory. In Thompson, J. D. (Ed.): Approaches to Organizational Design: Boston (MA). 193-218.

Wohlenberg, H. (1994): Gruppenunterstützende Systeme in Forschung und Entwicklung: Anwendungspotentiale aus industrieller Sicht. Wiesbaden.

Wolf, J. (1994): Internationales Personalmanagement: Kontext - Koordination - Erfolg. Wiesbaden.

Worldbank (2007): Worldbank Development Indicators Database: worldbank.org.

Wortmann, M. (1990): Multinationals and the Internationalization of R&D: New Developments in German Companies. Research Policy, 19: 175-183.

Wu, Y. (2000): A survey on foreign-established R&D units in China (in Chinese). China's Soft Science, 1: 64-66.

Xue, L.; Wang, S. (2001): Globalization of R&D by Multinational Corporations in China: an Empirical Analysis. NSF Tokyo.

Yin, R. K. (1988): Case Study Research: Design and Methods. Newbury Park, London, New Delphi.

Yoshihara, H.; Iwata, S. (1997): Results of the Questionnaire on the "Overseas R&D of Japanese Companies".

Yuan, C.; Lu, T. (2005): FDI and Knowledge Spillover: Evidence from China's Private Entrepreneurs (in Chinese). Research Policy, 2: 69-79.

Zander, I. (1997): Technological diversification in the multinational corporation - historical evolution and future prospects. Research Policy, 26: 209-227.

Zander, I. (1999): How do you mean 'global'? An empirical investigation of innovation networks in the multinational corporation. Research Policy, 28(2-3): 195-214.

Zeira, Y.; Banai, M. (1985): Selection of Expatriate Managers in MNCs: The Host-Environment Point of View. international Studies of Management and Organisation, 15(1): 33-51.

Zhang, M. (2006): Huawei's Strategic Review (B). Paper presented at the Case #02-2006/5333.

Zheng, Y. N. (2006): China's Rise: What it Means for the World?

Zhou, P.; Leydesdorff, L. (2006): The emergence of China as a leading nation in science. Research Policy, 35: 83-104.

Index

Index of Companies

Editors

Prof. Dr. Roman Boutellier teaches technology management and innovation management at ETH Zurich and is adjunct professor at the University of St. Gallen, Switzerland. Between 1999 and 2004, he was CEO of SIG, a Swiss industrial company focusing on packaging. He was director of the Institute for Technology Management at HSG, University of St. Gallen. Prior to joining the University in fall 1993, he was member of management at Leica Ltd., Heerbrugg, where he was responsible for the Central Technical Department including quality, production, purchasing and development. From 1981 to 1987 he was head of the optical lens design and fabrication department with Kern Ltd., Aarau. During this period he spent several months at the Optical Sciences Center in Tucson, Arizona; later he finished an additional degree in business administration. After his graduation in 1979 to Dr. sc. math. at the Federal Institute of Technology, Zurich, he spent the following year as a post doctorate at the Imperial College, London. Prof. Boutellier has been publishing in the fields of function theory, optical lens design and business administration. His present research focuses on innovation and technology management. He is member of several boards of directors and committees dealing with technology transfer, logistics and academic education.

Prof. Dr. Oliver Gassmann is professor for technology management at the University of St. Gallen and director at the Institute of Technology Management since 2002. Between 1996 and 2002 he worked for Schindler and lead its Corporate Research as Vice President Technology Management. Today he serves in several academic and managerial boards, e.g., editorial board of R&D Management, co-director of GLORAD Beijing-St. Gallen, member of Economiesuisse, chairman of Project Management Academy, audit committee of Schindler, co-founder and board member of BGW St. Gallen-Vienna, president of HSG Research Committee. He has published 11 books as author, co-author and editor, and over 150 publications on management of innovation. In 1998 he won the RADMA prize for best paper in R&D management. His work has been published in English, German, French, Chinese, and Japanese.

Prof. Dr. Max von Zedtwitz is a Professor of Strategy & Technology Management at Tsinghua University, Beijing, P.R. China, and Director of the Research Center for Global R&D Management with locations in Beijing and St. Gallen, Switzerland. He teaches in MBA, Ph.D., and executive education programs. Before joining Tsinghua in 2003, he worked for Siemens, ATR, the University of St. Gallen, Harvard University and IMD-International. He is also a visiting professor at the University of St. Gallen, Switzerland. He holds M.Sc. and B.Sc. degrees in computer science, and MBA and Ph.D. degrees in business administration. He has published ten books and more than fifty journal articles in English, German, French, Japanese and Chinese, and has been cited in The New York Times, the International Herald Tribune, Der Spiegel, Le Temps, and NZZ. He serves on the editorial boards of R&D Management, Journal of International Management, Technological Analysis & Strategic Management, and three other international journals. He is also President of AsiaCompete Int'l, Ltd., a Hong Kong-based innovation advisory company, with offices in Shanghai and Beijing, and a Senior Advisor to Arthur D. Little China Ltd. He is on the advisory boards of GetAbstract, the Swiss Federal Science Consulate, and the Dutch consulting firm Squarewise.

Case Study Contributors

Dr. Rudolf H. Andreatta was born and raised in Herisau, Switzerland. He obtained his Diploma in chemistry at the Federal Institute of Technology in Zurich in 1960, and his doctorate at the same school in 1963. Subsequently, he was assigned with some of the leading peptide and protein research centers in academia, serving a total of seven years at the universities of Sydney, Australia, Pittsburgh, Pennsylvannia and Cornell, New York. Since joining Ciba-Geigy in Basel in 1970, he served the company in the following capacities: chemistry research, 1987-93 Head, exploratory research and services of the pharmaceutical R&D; 1993-96 Head of research support of Pharma R&D international and 1996-7 Director of International Research Laboratories (IRL) in Takarazuka, Japan. He retired from Novartis in 1998.

Dr. Martin A. Bader is Managing Partner of the innovation and intellectual property management advisory group BGW AG, St.Gallen, Switzerland and Vienna, Austria. He is qualified as European and Swiss Patent Attorney and holds an engineering degree in electronics. Martin Bader started his professional career at Siemens and then joined Infineon Technologies in Munich, Germany, as Vice-President and Chief Intellectual Property Counsel being responsible for patents and trademarks, licensing and transactions as well as for knowledge and idea management. From 2002 to 2005 he followed the PhD program at the Institute of Technology Management at the University of St.Gallen, Switzerland. His research focused on intellectual property management in research and development collaborations with special interest in the service industry sector. He has been key speaker in numerous expert groups and conferences on innovation and intellectual property management and has published two books and several articles so far.

Prof. Dr. Daniel Bellus studied chemistry and obtained his Ph.D. in Bratislava (Czechoslovakia) in 1967. From 1967 to 1969 he carried out postdoctoral research studies at the ETH Zurich. In 1969 he joined Ciba-Geigy in Basel, where he was Head of Corporate Research Units from 1991 to December 1996, thus responsible world-wide for research programs in selected areas of the chemistry of bioactive compounds and materials. He is the author of 90 publications and holds 48 patents. From 1980 he has also lectured at the University of Fribourg (Switzerland) and received the Science Prize of Basel (1982) and honorary doctorates from the Slovak Technical University (1991), Cornelius University in Bratislava (1992), and the Technical University in Prague (1997). Presently, he is president of his own international consulting company for science and innovation in Basel as well as chairman of the Corporate Research Board of Ciba Specialty Chemicals Inc. in Basel.

Marc-Michael H. Bergfeld is Senior Program Manager International Innovation at Giesecke & Devrient and conducts his Ph.D. studies at the Institute of Innovation Research (PREST) of Manchester Business School. He has previously worked as management consultant for numerous German corporations on strategy development and implementation and market-focused and cost-conscious product development in Europe, the Americas and Asia. Further, he served as responsible for Marketing & Communication and assistant to the General Manager in the Latin America office of a German technology corporation.

Mr. Bergfeld graduated in business administration from the Catholic University of Eichstaett – Ingolstadt School of Business including studies in Salamanca, Buenos Aires and Washington D.C. and grew up in Asia. His research interests include corporate innovation in family- / private equity-controlled firms, global innovation networks and social innovation.

Dr. Peter Borgulya was born in 1964 and received his Ph.D. in cellbiology. He joined Roche in 1993 working as a Data Manager in a project aiming at linking all marketing activities worldwide with a computer network. This position provided him with a strong background in informatics and an insight into the details of pharmaceutical marketing. In 1995 he changed to the Pharma Research staff, supporting research management. This also involved scientific input to the investments of the Roche Venture Capital fund and the development and operation of the Pharma Drug Discovery Portfolio system. In 1999 he changed to Scientific Information Services within Pharma Research where he is responsible for the management of the corporate knowledge repository of R&D reports, the collection and analysis of competitive information and the support of Research project teams with online database searches.

Dr. Martin Bratzler was assistant to Roman Boutellier, then CEO of SIG Swiss Industrial Company in Neuhausen, Switzerland. He received a Ph.D. from the University of St. Gallen where he worked as a research assistant at the Institute of Technology Management. Prior to that he studied industrial engineering and business administration at the universities of Karlsruhe (Germany) and UC Berkeley (USA). During that time he developed a systematic approach to technology monitoring for the Porsche development center. Recently, he benchmarked nine international companies in the area of strategic technology management. His current research interests are the role of technological core competencies and the strategic technology management of suppliers.

Prof. Dr. Klaus Broichhausen is Vice-President of Product Design and Engineering at MTU Munich. Between 1974 and 1985 he was a scientific assistant and counselor at the Institute for Jet Propulsion and Turbomachinery, receiving a doctorate in 1981. He joined MTU Munich as an engineer and team leader in the Compressor Aerodynamics department. He hold various senior specialist and management positions with MTU. Since 1986, he has also been lecturing on transsonic compressors and modern methods in compressor development at RWTH Aachen, and was appointed professor in 1992.

Dr. Urs Burckhardt studied chemistry at the University of Basel (Switzerland) to obtain his Ph.D. in 1961 presenting a thesis with Prof. C.A. Grob. Postdoctoral studies followed at the University of Michigan with Prof. R. M. Stuiles and at Stanford University with Prof. W.S. Johnson. In 1965 he joined the pharmaceutical research department of J.R.Geigy AG in Basel, first in animal health research, later to the insect control research, where he became Head of the chemistry section. In 1991 he took the position of the Research Liaison Officer in the Corporate Research Units of Ciba, thus being responsible for coordination with international research centers. He retired from Novartis in 1997.

Prof. Dr. Maurice Campagna received his Ph.D. in Experimental Physics from ETH Zurich in 1972. He was a member of Technical Staff at Bell Laboratories, Murray Hill, NJ, USA until 1977. He became full professor for Applied Physics at the University of Cologne and Director at the Institute for Solid State Physics (IFF) of Kernforschungsanlage (KFA) Jülich, Germany in 1977, which he headed as Managing Director from 1980 - 1986. In 1986, he was appointed full professor of physics at the Federal Institute for Technology (ETH) at Zurich, Switzerland. In 1988, he became Senior Vice-President & Director of ABB Corporate Research, Switzerland. Since 1995, he was the deputy to ABB Senior Technology Officer for Business Area Technology. Prof. Campagna war also a Fellow of the American Physical Society (since 1984), a member of the Swiss Science & Technology Council (since 1988) and in the Research Commission of the Swiss Chamber of Commerce. Since 1997, he was a Board Member of IEEE. As of July 1, 1999 Maurice Campagna joined ABB Alstom Power Ltd. in Brussels in his new function as Chief Technology Officer.

Dr. Frank Cuypers graduated from the Free University of Brussels (ULB) in 1984 as a nuclear engineer. He completed his studies with a M.Sc. in nuclear physics from the Rensselaer Polytechnic Institute (RPI) in 1985 and a PhD in high energy physics from the University of North Carolina, Chapel Hill (UNC) in 1989. He held several research and teaching positions at the Academia Sinica, the University of Durham, the University of Munich, the Max Planck Institute and the Paul Scherrer Institute. His research dealt mainly with theoretical nuclear, particle and mathematical physics.

In 1998 he became an actuary with Zurich Re in Zurich, where he assumed pricing responsibility for the Iberian market and world-wide credit & surety reinsurance. He also developed Zurich Re's cost and capital allocation methodology. In 2000 he became Chief Actuary in Cologne, in charge of pricing, reserving and risk management. He joined Swiss Re in 2001 to build up its Intellectual Property department and was appointed to the Executive Team in 2002. As Head of Intellectual Property, he developed the patenting and technology transfer program for Swiss Re.

Michael P. Edgar is Engineering Manager at the International Engineering Center, Unisys Corporation. During Mike Edgar's eight years with Unisys, he has worked in the areas of software internationalization, asianization, and localization. His roles included internationalization developer, asianization joint-development coordinator, and project manager/business manager. These projects have involved over 20 languages from Asia, Europe, and the Middle East. Mr. Edgar has lived in Asia for four years. He has spent the last four years in Western Europe and currently resides in Belgium. He earned a Bachelor of Science in Commerce from Santa Clara University in 1986. He is fluent in Japanese.

Ah Bee Goh has worked in various multinational companies and held positions as General Manager, Executive Director and Director of Manufacturing. He holds a B.Sc. (Hons) in Production Engineering and Management from the University of Strathclyde, Scotland, MSc in Industrial Engineering from the National University of Singapore and an MBA from the University of Surrey. He is a Chartered Engineer and also a registered Professional Engineer with the Singapore Professional Engineers Board. He participates actively on a national level in Singapore on quality and productivity issues. At present Mr. Goh is the Managing Director of Leica Instruments (S) Pte Ltd. and his company has achieved awards for ISO9001, 14000 and is the first multinational company in Singapore to achieve the Ozone Depleting Substance (ODS) Free Certificate from the Productivity and Standards Board of Singapore.

Dr. Kenji Hara currently is the Director of the Division for Product Safety at Kao Corporation, Professor at the Center for Cooperative Research and Development at Ehime University and the secretary vice-general of the Kao Foundation for the Arts and Sciences. He is the former Director of Research and Development Division at Kao Corporation. He received his Ph.D. from Kyushu University, Japan, in 1973. He joined Kao Corporation as a biochemist in 1977, being engaged in research and development of health care products.

Dr. Richard Hausmann studied physics at Regensburg University and the State University of New York with obtaining his Doctorate in Physics. In 1988, Dr. Hausmann joined the Siemens Medical Engineering Group where he has held various positions in the Magnetic Resonance Division. In 1998, he joined the Computer Tomography Division, where he became Division President and also was responsible for the entire China business of the Siemens Medical Solutions Group. In 2005, Dr. Hausmann assumed his current position as President & CEO of Siemens Ltd, China. He actively helps to shape the country's business environment, and is the Chairman of the Executive Committee of Foreign Invested Companies in China and the Chairman of the Board of the German Chamber of Commerce in China. In addition he serves as an advisor to the governors of Yunnan province and Shaanxi province, and member of the consultant committee of

Wuhan Municipal Government. Dr. Hausmann has published numerous articles on modern applications of Magnetic Resonance and holds various patents related to Magnetic Resonance and Imaging.

Prof. Dr. Lutz Heuser is head of SAP Research and Chief Development Architect at SAP AG. SAP Research encompasses a number of worldwide Research Centers and SAP Inspire. Lutz is responsible for all strategic research programs and the global research transfer into the product portfolio of SAP as well as for internal venture ideas. His main areas of expertise include eLearning, pervasive computing, Internet services, and CRM. Prior to joining SAP, Lutz Heuser was managing director of the European Research Organization of Digital Equipment Corporation and member of the extended board of the German subsidiary of Digital. He was co-founder of the renowned research center CEC Karlsruhe, as well as three joint venture research centers with Universities of Karlsruhe, Darmstadt, and Dresden. Lutz received his doctoral degree in Informatics from the University of Karlsruhe and his diploma in Informatics from the University of Darmstadt. Recently he received a diploma from the National University of Paraguay to become a "Profesor Visitante" of the Faculty of Economics.

Dr. Arding Hsu is a Sr. Vice President of Siemens Limited China and the Head of Siemens Corporate Technology in China. He has the responsibility to build up a world class Siemens research lab in China with 300 top researchers by 2008. Before coming to China in 2004, Arding Hsu was the President & CEO of Siemens Technology-To-Business Center (TTB) in Berkeley, California with the responsibility to bring outside innovations into Siemens by working with universities, research institutes, start-up companies and entrepreneurs. Prior to TTB, Arding Hsu was the department head of Multimedia/Video Technology in Siemens Corporate Research in Princeton, New Jersey. Arding has 22 years industrial R&D experience along with venture investment and business development. Dr. Hsu has published more than 30 papers and holds many patents. He holds a Ph.D. in Computer Science from Rutgers University in New Jersey.

Dr. Yasuo Kozato is Manager of Information Technology Laboratory, Canon Inc. Yasuo Kozato joined Canon Inc. in 1981 and was engaged in R&D on image processing for Bubble Jet color printers. He was a recipient of the Canon Technical Traineeship, with which he spent two years from 1986 as a research student at University College London. From October 1988 to December 1992, he was a software researcher at Canon Research Europe in Guildford, UK. He returned to Japan in 1993 and was in charge of management and coordination of Canon's overseas R&D centers. He has been in the current position since July 1999. He obtained a Ph.D. in computer science from University of London in 1994, and a Master of Engineering from Tokyo Institute of Technology in 1981.

Dr. Yutaka Kuwahara was General Manager, R&D Center, Hitachi Europe Ltd. He joined Hitachi in 1964 and had responsibility for developing collaborative global research initiatives between Hitachi and European research institutes. These initiatives - in the UK, Germany, Italy, Nice, Dallas and Ireland - focus on the-creation of new concepts and technologies for future electronics and optical devices.

Prior to working in the UK, Dr. Kuwahara held a number of positions with Hitachi Central Research Laboratory and the R&D Promotions Division of Hitachi's Head office in Tokyo and was responsible for initiating the globalization of all corporate R&D in Hitachi. During his research period in HCRL, he researched computer architecture and led various projects in computing, such as high speed optical computer links. From 1991-92, he served as a member of the NISTEP of STA (Science and Technology Agency in Japan), and also as a member of Economic Planning Agency's Year 2010 Committee set up to study and predict technologies in the 21st Century. Dr. Kuwahara holds a B.Sc. and Ph.D. from the University of Tokyo and has written widely on technology management for professional journals. He is a regular lecturer at International scientific conferences and academia in Europe.

Karin Löffler works as research associate at Swiss Federal Institute of Technology (ETH Zürich) within the team Technology and Innovation Management of Professor Dr. Roman Boutellier. For a research project on problem solving in Japanese R&D teams she transferred to Tokyo Institute of Technology in Japan.

Dr. Joseph Miller is chief science and technology officer and senior vice-president for Research and Development at E.I. Du Pont de Nemours & Co., Wilmington DE. Previously he held a number of positions in R&D, manufacturing, and marketing. He has a B.S. degree from Virginia Military Institute and a Ph.D. in chemistry from Penn State. He is a member of the Board of the Chemical Heritage Foundation, the National Science & Technology Board International Advisory Panel of Singapore, the National Science Board (US), and a Fellow of the American Association of Science. He most recently led a commission to reform science education in Delaware Public Schools.

Dr. Bernd Müller VMD is a pharmacologist and toxicologist. Present position: Head of Biological Development, Schering AG. Former positions: Research Scientist at Schering AG and Grünenthal GmbH. Head of Cardiovascular Research at Schering AG, Corporate R&D Staff, Schering AG. Professional areas of interest: Cardiovascular Pharmacology and Toxicology; Pharmaceutical R&D organization and management. 70 Publications.

Dr. Mark B. Myers is senior vice-president, Corporate Research and Technology, Xerox Corporation where he has worked since 1964. Dr. Myers' research interests involve digital imaging systems and the creation of new business enterprises involving emerging technology. He serves on several advisory boards with an interest in science and engineering education and government technology and economic policy. Dr. Myers has held visiting professor positions at the University of Rochester and Stanford University.

Parry Norling, Ph.D. is Corporate Technology Advisor for E.I. du Pont de Nemours & Co. Previously he held a number of positions in R&D and manufacturing and was Corporate Director of Health and Safety. He has an A.B. degree from Harvard and a Ph.D. in polymer chemistry from Princeton. He is currently vice-president of the Industrial Research Institute and vice-chairman of the CHEM-RAWN (Chemical Research Applied to World Needs) committee of the International Union of Pure and Applied Chemistry (IUPAC). He also serves on the board of the American Creativity Association.

Manfred Renkel studied physics and mathematics at the University of Marburg, concentrating on research in the fields of non-linear stochastic processes and stability theory. He has worked at MTU Munich for 18 years in turbine design holding various positions. As a program manager, he was responsible for MTU's part in the tri-national ADP/UHB program. In 1996 he was appointed manager of technology coordination, being responsible for technology cooperation with national and international partner companies and research establishments. He focuses on planning and controlling of MTU's technology strategy and processes, and management of technology programs by national and European ministries of research.

Dr. Anton Roeder studied Mechanical Engineering at the TH Darmstadt and at the ETH Zurich. He received Dr.sc.techn. for his dissertation in Experimental and Theoretical Investigation of Turbine Stages in 1969 and then joined BBC Brown Boveri 1969. 1969-79 he held several positions within the steam turbine department, heading it 1980-88. Between 1985-88, he was head of Large Steam Turbine and Turbogenerator Main Department. He was appointed manager of Gas Turbine and Combined Cycle Power Plant Division in 1987. In ABB, after the merger of BBC and ASEA, Dr. Roeder was Business Area Manager Gas Turbines 1988-90, and General Manager of ABB Joint Venture in Karlovac (1990-91). From 1997, he was SVP Technology Planning & Administration Corporate Staff R&D.

Ruedi Rottermann is the director R&D of Leica's Business Unit Stereomicroscopy located in Heerbrugg, Switzerland. He joined Leica (respectively the former Wild Heerbrugg) in 1981 as project manager for the development of new stereomicroscopes. Since then he has been involved in the creation of several generations of stereomicroscopes and their accessories. Prior to his employment at Leica he designed electronic controls and drives for coating machines. He started his career with an apprenticeship as electrician and studied afterwards electrical power engineering at the Technikum Winterthur.

Manfred Roux is director of Software Solution Department at the IBM Development Laboratory in Böblingen, Germany. He joined IBM Development in 1974 as a programmer. Since 1979, he held numerous positions in large-scale system software development and design. In 1995 he assumed responsibility for all S/390-based system software development at the Böblingen laboratory. In October 1997 he took his present position which is focused on leading the development of IBM middleware, specifically in the areas workflow management, text search, and data mining. In addition, he is building up a technical support and services capability around core products and competencies.

Kim Smith was the executive assistant to Dr. Myers, senior vice-president, Corporate Research and Technology, Xerox Corporation where she has worked since 1984. She has held various staff operations and management positions in Manufacturing, Product Design and Development, Business Quality Management, Systems and S/W Assurance and Product Program Delivery. Ms. Smith holds a Bachelor of Science in Electrical Engineering from Boston University, a Master of Science in Manufacturing Systems from Clarkson University and an MBA from the Simon School of Management at the University of Rochester.

Luitpold Schulz graduated in 1963 in Munich in High Precision Engineering and Optics. As an R&D engineer, he started work at Kern Aarau to develop target finders for guns in cooperation with Bofors and 3D Cinetheodolites for Contraves. In 1966, he joined Wild Heerbrugg. In the R&D department Photogrammetrie, he developed products for Photogrammetrical Cameras, like View Finder Telescopes and Overlapping Regulators. In 1969 he became Section Manager at the Microscopy Business Unit, in charge of a team of R&D Engineers for development of Stereomicroscopes and Surgical Microscopes, since 1983 as the department head. He transferred in 1993 as R&D Manager to LEICA Instruments Singapore to build up a local R&D department. Acting since 1996 in Heerbrugg as Manager customized products and applications for the Business Unit Stereomicroscopy.

Dr. Martin Stahl obtained a degree in industrial engineering from the University of Siegen, Germany, in 1999, with majors in marketing and combustion engines. He gained initial professional experience in several projects at the BMW Group in Munich and Pretoria, South Africa. Dr. Stahl started his Ph.D. thesis at the BMW Group R&D center in Munich, Germany, in 1999, focusing on collaboration processes (Cross-Industry-Innovation Process) between innovative high-tech start-ups and large automotive manufacturers. During this time he consulted small high-tech companies on product strategy and business planning. He received his Ph.D. in technology management from the University of St. Gallen, Switzerland, in 2002. He worked for the BMW Group in R&D strategy from 2002 to 2005. In this position he dealt with topics like new car concepts, lightweight construction, and future trends in the automotive industry and was responsible for the strategy cluster design/craftsmanship for all brands of the BMW Group. Since 2005 he is working in the BMW Group's central marketing department, responsible for the BMW Group product portfolio.

Arnold Winkler is with Advanced Technologies, Standards Management, Unisys Corporation. Arnold Winkler came to the U.S. from Austria where he held various positions in support and education for Sperry Univac Austria and the countries behind the Iron Curtain. Intimately familiar with the requirements of the global market, he deals with internationalization issues in the Advanced Technologies' Standards Management group and is today convenor of an ISO working group on internationalization, chair of the U.S. group for character sets, and vice chair of the Unicode Consortium's Technical Committee.

Clement Woon is Business Director at Leica Geosystem AG, Heerbrugg. Prior to joining the company in 1997, he was the Operations and Business Development Manager at Leica Instruments in Singapore. He was responsible to lead the operations department for Optics and Mechanics production. He directed the re-engineering of the production process to achieve productivity gains. He actively participated in the transfer of microscopy products from Heerbrugg to Singapore for production. Prior to the responsibility in the Operations Department, Clement had already more than ten years of experience in quality management, including the implementation of participative teams that focus on engineering and production. He holds a Bachelor degree in Electrical & Electronics Engineering, and a Master of Science degree in Industrial Engineering from the National University of Singapore. In addition, he has also obtained a degree of Master in Business Administration from the Nanyang Technological University.

Rosanne Wyleczuk has worked at HP for 17 years within many marketing, R&D and field departments as an individual contributor, first level and second level manager. Her product experiences, mostly within HP's computer organization, include real-time computing, measurement systems, engineering workstations, software applications, computer aided design software, customer education, and professional services (including consulting and systems integration). With HP she worked for almost two years in Boeblingen, Germany. Within HP Labs, she is challenged to identify new HP business opportunities that will grow to greater than US$ 1 billion, and that capitalize on HP Labs technologies. Rosanne's educational background includes Bachelor and Masters degrees in Electrical Engineering and Computer Science from the Massachusetts Institute of Technology, and an MBA from the Wharton School at the University of Pennsylvania.